The South Goes North

Books by ROBERT COLES

CHILDREN OF CRISIS: A STUDY OF COURAGE AND FEAR
STILL HUNGRY IN AMERICA
THE IMAGE IS YOU
UPROOTED CHILDREN
WAGES OF NEGLECT
(with Maria Piers)
DRUGS AND YOUTH
(with Joseph Brenner and Dermot Meagher)
ERIK H. ERIKSON:
THE GROWTH OF HIS WORK
THE MIDDLE AMERICANS
(with Jon Erikson)
THE GEOGRAPHY OF FAITH
(with Daniel Berrigan)
MIGRANTS, SHARECROPPERS, MOUNTAINEERS
(Volume II of *Children of Crisis*)
THE SOUTH GOES NORTH
(Volume III of *Children of Crisis*)

For Children

DEAD END SCHOOL
THE GRASS PIPE

The South Goes North

VOLUME III OF CHILDREN OF CRISIS

ROBERT COLES, M.D.

An Atlantic Monthly Press Book

LITTLE, BROWN AND COMPANY • BOSTON • TORONTO

LIBRARY OF CONGRESS CATALOG CARD NO. 70-162332

C

"Those Places They Call Schools" appeared in *Harvard Educational Review*, 39, Fall 1969, 46–57. Copyright © 1969 by the
President and Fellows of Harvard College.

ATLANTIC—LITTLE, BROWN BOOKS
ARE PUBLISHED BY
LITTLE, BROWN AND COMPANY
IN ASSOCIATION WITH
THE ATLANTIC MONTHLY PRESS

*Published simultaneously in Canada
by Little, Brown & Company (Canada) Limited*
PRINTED IN THE UNITED STATES OF AMERICA

To the black and white children mentioned in this book, and to millions of others like them, newcomers to America's cities in the second half of the twentieth century.

Proverbs 8: 1–4

Doth not wisdom cry? and understanding put forth her voice? She standeth in the top of high places, by the way in the places of the paths. She crieth at the gates, at the entry of the city, at the coming in at the doors. Unto you, O men, I call; and my voice is to the sons of man.

FOREWORD

I N *The South Goes North,* this third volume of *Children of
Crisis,* I both continue my work and bring one extended phase
of it to completion. In the foreword to the previous volume,
Migrants, Sharecroppers, Mountaineers, I recounted the nature
of my involvement with migrant farm workers who work in the
eastern United States, with sharecroppers or tenant farmers of the
rural South, and with Appalachia's mountain people. I also mentioned what is certainly no secret, that in this century millions of
black and white people have steadily, year by year, abandoned
Alabama's "Black Belt" and Mississippi's Delta country, deserted
the hills and mountains and hollows and creeks of eastern
Kentucky and West Virginia for cities "up North," for border
cities like Cincinnati, for cities like Chicago, Cleveland, Detroit,
New York, Philadelphia, and Boston. If one wants to learn some
of the reasons America's cities are now struggling so hard with
certain problems, one place to find out is "back there," back on
the American earth, the farmland and hill territory from which
came so many of our nation's present-day urban poor. Men and
women and children come North in pursuit of bread and work
and freedom and dignity; but they arrive with more than their
needs and hopes. They arrive as particular individuals with
ways of seeing things and doing things, with their own ideas
about the world and God and man, with their beliefs and values,
their rhythms of speech and habits of cooking and preferences in
music. These people carry with them a history: memories of the
past, diseases and lacks and wants that linger in the form of
scars and wounds and hurts and injuries, but also recollections of

good times — real triumphs, or simply remembered moments of
delight and contentment.

About half the black people of America still live in the eleven
states of the old Confederacy. Some seven million people live in
the states or parts of states known as Appalachia. If many have
left, many have stayed. Nor are they two separate worlds, the
rural South on the one hand and Harlem, say, on the other.
Or Harlan and Hazard, Kentucky, and McDowell and Logan
Counties, West Virginia, on the one hand; and Dayton or Cleveland or Detroit on the other. Unquestionably there are distinctions between the urban North and the rural way of life; yet for
thousands and thousands of families, the North and the South
are intimately tied together. Few black families in Alabama and
few white families in Kentucky's eastern counties don't know
about those northern cities: sons, daughters, uncles, cousins,
friends, neighbors have gone to live in places like Chicago or
New York, and in some instances have come back to visit and
talk and exchange news — sometimes to stay, but not often. "We
know about New York City," I have heard from people in
Marengo County, Alabama — and they are people who have
never, ever left the county, let alone the state or the region. They
do know, too; they have received notes and letters; some have
heard things on the radio; and some have been lucky enough to
watch television and see what goes on "far away in other places."

Meanwhile, up North, I hear every day a remark or two of this
kind: "I heard from my sister in Georgia today. She's fine. She
says they're having their spring there. Oh, I'll bet they are. It's
March." Or this kind: "The hills are buried in snow. My daddy
says don't try to come home this weekend. 'Stay in Dayton,' he
says. 'They can move the snow in a city,' he wrote in his letter."
So, to understand that man's "daddy" requires an understanding
of the city, the very city that proud, old man denounces and
refuses to visit, yet encourages as a place of residence for his
sons.

The second and third volumes of *Children of Crisis* have been
prepared both in progression and (in recent years) more or less
simultaneously, but at all times as part of one study — a study of

individual lives, but also of lives that are part of a nation's history and lives whose complexity often enough defies the willful approximations of any one "discipline" or profession. As I indicated in earlier volumes of this series, it was in 1958, in Mississippi, that I began what has turned into a life's work. For a number of years I lived and studied in the South and in Appalachia, until finally I came home to the North, where I was born and grew up. In a sense, my work has in its sequence followed a certain line of American history: from south to north, from rural living to city living, from isolated hills to more populous flatlands. As I have mentioned in earlier volumes, I did this work as a physician, as a child psychiatrist, but out in "the field," at times far out. There is a dimension of social anthropology and sociology and political science to all of this — and yet, I add quickly, in visiting homes and schools in our black ghettos or our white working-class neighborhoods, and in talking with children and listening to them, I have never felt myself too far away from the essential spirit of medicine I once heard advocated by some fine teachers in medical school: a clinician must try to see what is strong as well as what is weak, what is sound as well as what ails, what might be struggling for expression in a person's life as well as what is lacking.

Perhaps I should say, in explanation, why this phase of the series is divided as it is. It seemed to me that no single volume that concerned itself with both rural problems and urban problems, however intimately connected they may be, could help being both too long and too much for the reader. As it is, each of the volumes is quite long enough! If rural and urban problems have a continuity to them, the lives of the people do not. Even within the range of rural life, migrants and sharecroppers and mountaineers live in thoroughly different ways, although they also share certain experiences and assumptions. An Appalachian family newly come to Chicago is hardly like a black family just arrived in that city — though, again, there are things they do indeed have in common: struggles, needs, dreams, and memories. It seemed to me that the most sensible thing to do was pay respect to the dramatic change embodied in a move to the city from a mountain hollow or plantation. I have therefore divided what in history and in individual lives has been very much part of the flow of events, both in a large nation and in thousands of smaller communities, into two separate if related books for the sake of convenience and coherence. I believe there is a natural and obvious reason for the separations I have made in these two books, even though some of the families I have worked with have lived, for example, in *both* West Virginia and Chicago, *both* Alabama and Boston; indeed, I have followed them in their migration, in some cases traveled with them, *been* with them.

I have not used the real names of the people I have interviewed, and I have done as much as possible to conceal their real homes and identities. If I have unwittingly used the name of any living person in this book, I offer my apology here. It has been my wish to protect at all costs the privacy of those people, many of them friends, whom I have interviewed over the years.

I want here to repeat briefly some loyalties and obligations, as well as give the reader an idea of how all this work will, I hope, continue. I wrote much of this book in 1970, which as mentioned, is twelve years after I began taking notes about certain people I had met in rural Mississippi, where I once lived. I am now, in 1971, beginning to talk with Mexican-American and Indian children in the Southwest and will eventually extend those observations to the Eskimos of Alaska. In the West — the Southwest and the Northwest and indeed the far North — live still more "children of crisis," others whose lives are every day fraught with severe hardships: not enough or inadequate food, poor schools, the scorn of a dominant majority, or indeed, in some places, a dominant minority, threats and violence, open or thinly disguised, and so on. I suppose, then, that there will one day be a fourth and last volume in this series, entitled *Chicanos, Eskimos and Indians.*

I again mention the names Erik H. Erikson and Anna Freud. When I look at children and talk with them and play with them and watch them draw I hear the words of those two first-rate clinicians and try to be equal to their sense and sensibility; and I have had the good fortune to know both individuals not only by reading their books but through personal conversation. And again I acknowledge the constant and enormous help given me by the New World Foundation, the Field Foundation and the Ford Foundation. I never could have done this work without the assistance they have given me; and I certainly never could have done this work in this way had not they let me and encouraged me to do so — and enabled me to work full time at the job. So, thanks to Vernon Eagle and Leslie Dunbar and Edward Meade and Marjorie Martus. And thanks to Dana Farnsworth for the home base he has given me "up North" at Harvard, and the freedom to roam about as necessity demanded. Thanks, also, to Martha Stearns and Elizabeth Garber, who have worked long and hard on this manuscript and, as always, I owe much to Peter Davison, whose editorial help and friendship I value very much.

Parts of this book in different form have appeared elsewhere. The section of Chapter III entitled "I Am a Maid, and What Do I Know?" was published in *The Atlantic Monthly*. Most of Chapter VII was included in a special issue (on "Architecture and Education") of the *Harvard Educational Review*. Part of Chapter VIII originally appeared in *The New Yorker,* and most of the balance of Chapter VIII, in different form, was published as a monograph by the Potomac Institute. Sections from Chapter IX first appeared in *Daedalus;* parts of Chapter X first appeared in *Harper's, The American Scholar, Children* and *Federal Probation;* finally, part of Chapter XI was published in late 1970 by *Commonweal.* And the poem in Chapter X was originally published in *The Massachusetts Review.*

I have, in addition, two more acknowledgments: to the children described in this book and their mothers and fathers and teachers — but especially to the children, whose lives I have encountered and tried to comprehend and, within the limits of my ability, bring to expression; and to my wife Jane and my three children for all that their presence has meant. A few of the many families I work with have met and come to know my wife, and certainly they have heard of my children. "Give her our best," I have heard, and, "Give them our best." I believe those words were meant, really meant; and I can only repeat them here.

CONTENTS

PART ONE

THE SETTING

I

THE STREETS

THEY come to the city streets. They come by car and by truck and by bus and by train. Rarely do they come by plane. They have said good-bye to a little town in the Delta, good-bye to Alabama's "Black Belt" or those towns in south Georgia just north of the Okefenokee Swamp or the lowlands of South Carolina or the eastern shore of North Carolina. Perhaps they have left one of Louisiana's parishes. Perhaps they once lived in Arkansas, near Little Rock or near Pine Bluff. Maybe they are not from the deep South. Maybe they are from Appalachia, from eastern Kentucky or western North Carolina or north central Tennessee or indeed just about all of West Virginia. Maybe they are from no single place; that is, maybe they have been migrant farm workers, who wander and wander, who may once have lived here or there, but now consider no town, no county, no state or even region their "home."

They come to the streets, all of them, from cabins and shacks, flat and rich farmlands or hills that somehow have been made to produce at least something. They come to the streets familiar with a way of life. They have, many of them (though by no means all of them), known the advantages of electricity, of a naked bulb to provide light, of an old refrigerator to keep food from rotting too fast. Good plumbing and heating are rather less familiar to those whom we call sharecroppers or tenant farmers from the rural South, whom we call migrant farm workers, whom we call mountaineers, Appalachia's yeomen from up the hollows. Other things are not familiar at all to such people: well-paid jobs, a sense of political power, a feeling of acceptance from school-teachers or businessmen or sheriffs or county officials, and in addition, the experience of having a paved road near one's home, or sewer pipes leading to it, or good drinking water nearby.

They have said their good-byes, made their peace with their past, walked away, been driven away, slipped away, been picked up, been sent for. Some may have seen or been in a city before: Greenwood and Greenville in Mississippi, or Selma and Mont-gomery in Alabama, or Lexington in Kentucky or Charleston in West Virginia or Atlanta and New Orleans, those big, big cities. For many, though, the cities up North are the first cities they have looked at and lived in.

"Lord, I never knew there were so many buildings. Lord, I never knew what a street was, not really, not streets like we have up here, not miles and miles of them." In Tunica County, Missis-sippi, he had not been totally confined to a plantation, to a share-cropper's cabin and the land nearby that needed his care. He had gone into a town or two, walked down muddy paths along which one home after another stood. And he had even caught a glimpse of Memphis; on his way north he had seen the city he used to hear the Mister talk about, and the Missus, and those laughing, romping children not yet old enough to keep their distance — yes, he'd heard them, too, the little white boys and little white girls, talk on and on about Memphis. But now he is in a city, up North in one. Now he lives there. Now, every single day, there are those streets. And now he is "used to things." What things, though? What up North has he day by day come to accept as the ordinary, the expected? "It started with the sidewalks and the sewers," he will say. He is trying to convey what took him by surprise when he "hit" Chicago, when he entered the city and saw one street and then another. They were beautifully paved. There were sewers. And black people lived all around. He had never before seen so many sewers. He had never before seen so many people, so many black people, and so many sidewalks and paved streets and sewers "that belong to them, the colored man."

So it was that a "colored man" like him could at one point talk about "them." So it has been that mountaineers from eastern Kentucky and West Virginia can also feel a sense of detached surprise and wonder when they come to a city like Chicago and see those streets: "Who would ever believe it? Who would ever believe people live like this?" Then one asks what it is that he finds so unbelievable, and one hears again about sidewalks and sewers and firmly paved *roads*. It takes time for a man from a mountain hollow to talk about *streets*.

Yet, eventually they do; those former coal miners or subsistence farmers from Appalachia begin to say a lot about those streets. Friends or relatives come to visit or stay, and they must be shown things. There are lamps for instance, "outdoor lamps." Who would ever have thought that man could so firmly take command of night? A little girl from a place in Kentucky she is rapidly forgetting, but still just about remembers as "Winding Hollow," wants very much to remark upon that light, the light of streetlights: "I wonder how the moon feels? If I was the moon, I'd make a face at all the lamps on all the streets." She used to love the moon, her mother observes. The world seemed safer for the moon's night-light. But now the moon is almost unnecessary, one more faded miracle, one more outworn imperative. The city's streets conquer everything.

A black child in another city uses such military imagery, talks of conquests; he also hasn't been "up North" so long that he can't recall what it was like "back South," but he wants a visitor to know "there isn't any trouble around here you can't conquer, lick it and beat it flat, so long as you know the right person." He has heard that from others on the street, from others his age and older; "street talk" his mother calls the boy's statements and those streets do indeed define one's sense of space, determine a good deal of how children speak and what they learn. Nor does the child's mother fail to comment on all that and more. The street she lives on is her backyard and front yard; it is the woods and the plantation and the county seat and the long road that leads to it. The street is flat, has no hills and no stream nearby, has no bank to sit on and lie down upon and use to "collect" one's strength. The street is lined with houses; it is "thick with them" — to the point that she and her neighbors sometimes take to wondering. Who in God's world ever had the gall to build so many houses? Where did they come from, all the people who live in those houses now and once lived in them over the years?

Other things inspire comment, too. As a matter of fact, these newcomers to our cities, these émigrés who have never left our own borders, these long-standing American citizens who have fled in desperation from the South to the North, from the quiet and isolated mountains to the crowded flatlands, be they white men or black men, young women or old women, they talk about flights of stairs or door locks or street numbers or mailboxes or light switches. For a while one thinks the problem is that of language; "they" have their words, their dialect, their way of putting things, and it is a matter of time before an outsider will be able to get the point, to understand why those simple, everyday words get mentioned so often — as if they are the keys to some mystery: "I've been here since the war, the Korean War. I came here from South Carolina. My husband was stationed up here, and he sent me a bus ticket. I never went back. I had my first baby inside me. The first surprise I had was the apartment building — I mean all the steps in it, the stairs and more stairs, until you think after climbing so many you'll be seeing the Lord himself." She goes on to remind her listener that in South Carolina there was exactly one step from the ground to the cabin in which she and her parents and her grandparents ("and the others before them") were born. That step was actually a stump of a tree half buried in the ground. The church she went to had "proper steps," two of them. And then suddenly she came to Boston, and encountered steps and steps and steps until she wondered in the beginning whether she could ever survive it all — lifting herself up and taking herself down again, and with no sunlight to help either. As for the hall lights in her "building," as she calls it, "they never have worked, not once."

More than the steps get to her, though. The locks do, the endless numbers of door locks. She was poor in South Carolina and she is poor now. But back South one doesn't have to fasten down one's poverty, defend it fearfully, worry about its vulnerability. Up North it seems nothing can go unguarded, and indeed, "the nothing we have is all locked up." She does, however, lose her keys sometimes — yes, the three keys, to the front door of her apartment and the back door and the street door downstairs. Then she becomes irritated and half amused. She also becomes nostalgic for a minute: "I think to myself that before I came to the city I'd never seen a lock in my life. That was the first thing I told my mother when I went back to see her. I told her they're lock crazy up North. And it isn't as if they're millionaires, our people up there."

She speaks about other matters to her mother. There are, again, those flights of stairs that go round and round and lead from one story to another. In one building she lived on the second story; in another on the fifth, the *fifth* — which means she was so high up she could imagine herself looking down on that small rural church she recalls being so tall. She wonders to this day whether the water tower she used to believe to be the tallest thing in the whole wide world is as tall as her apartment house, which she now certainly knows is far indeed from being the tallest building on her street, let alone other streets. And since she tries to keep in touch with her mother, even though neither of them is very good at writing, there are those numbers to keep in mind. Whoever got *that* idea anyway — of putting numbers on houses? Where do the numbers on her street start? Where does the street start, for that matter? In Dorchester County, South Carolina, so far as she knows, "there's not a number there on any home." She never had a post office box number, nor does her mother even today: "I write her name; I write the town; I write South Carolina — and it gets there faster than letters from her get to me."

Of course she gets her mail put into a mailbox, another one of those newfangled devices that go with city living. Since letter boxes in her building are private but commonly trespassed, she has to have a "mail key," too. For a long while the boxes in her apartment house were hopelessly inadequate — bent and punctured and covered with grime and scrawled words. Finally the

postman complained, or higher officials in the post office did, or
maybe it was the welfare department, which mails out checks.
Someone did, she knows that, because the landlord was compelled to put in new boxes, and a policeman stood there watching
while the job was done. It was a mixed blessing, needless to say:
"I love the box, but the keys, all the keys you need — just to stay
alive up here in the city." She told her mother about her new
mailbox. Her mother told the news to the lady who runs the
grocery store and gasoline station and post office down in Dorchester County, South Carolina. She is a white woman, and her
name is Mrs. Chalmers, and she had a laugh over that. She told
her informant to write back to "the poor girl" in Boston and ask
how the mailman ever makes sense of them all, the hundreds of
boxes he must have to fill up every morning.

People manage to make their adjustments. There are spurts
and lags, naturally. Some habits and customs are mastered more
quickly than others. Some undreamed-of luxuries try the mind
and soul more than others do. In Cleveland a man from "near
Beckley," West Virginia, laughs about a few of his recent tribulations and compares them to what his ancestors had to go
through — for they were also Americans who moved on (from
the East Coast westward) when they had to: "I can't keep up
with the light switches in this city. I think it's harder for me to
figure out these lights than it was for my kin way back to cut a
path through the hills and settle there. Everywhere you go here
there's a switch. On and off, that's what you have to think about
when you go into a room. Now who's supposed to know every
minute of his life where the switch is? I've been up in this place
over a year and I forget, and I have my wife on my back, saying,
'The switch is here, don't get dressed in darkness.' Well, what's so
damned wrong about darkness when it's early in the morning!"

In the cities late in the afternoon the lights appear, whether he
or any other particular person likes it or not, and does or does not
join in the act by turning a switch to ON. In the cities people seem
to insist that darkness somehow be pushed into corners. There
are plenty of those corners, especially in his neighborhood, but
never in Ohio has he lived with the kind of darkness he everyday

took for granted in West Virginia. He is the first one to point out that almost every street corner has lights, lights of all colors. There are streetlights — and the stores with their lights, and the gas stations with theirs, and the police cars with lights on their roofs, whirling around and around. And there are those signs, signs full of bulbs, signs that wait on the sun to leave so they can take over and say: look over here, look and remember and buy, and if you do, we'll stay around and get called a success, catchy and clever and able to do our job, which is to light up your mind with desire.

He wants people to know he didn't live so far up a hollow that "this whole electric-light world up here in the city" is in and of itself strange to him. He had sockets with bulbs in them "back home" in his house, and he had television, also — so he really didn't expect to be as surprised as he was when he first came into Cleveland. He used to tighten the bulb in the evening, when he'd sit and smoke his pipe and get drowsy and half watch television. It was his children who often would pay full attention to it, "that picture box." And as a matter of fact, they were the ones who wanted him to loosen that bulb, so they could have the picture and nothing else all to themselves. But he liked to whittle, sometimes. And even if he didn't, the evening is the right time to have a little light around. Mind, he says a *little* light, not so much light that one feels in China during the night — which is where he sometimes thinks he might be as he sits in his Cleveland apartment. China, he learned from a teacher a long time ago, is where the day goes when we have night.

In any event, now his children can't understand why he doesn't switch on all the lights, come dusk. Nor would they think of sitting and watching television in complete darkness. Why do his boys and girls require what they once would have abhorred, glowing lamps? He is quick to note the change and explain it: "It must be they used to want to have our cabin so pitch-black because that way they could lose themselves watching the programs and forget where they were. Now they're gone from there and up here. Now they're in the city, and the television programs are about the city. They don't have to imagine they're someplace else. They don't need it dark, so their minds can wander. *We've* wandered."

For people who come to the city from rural America, there is another irony awaiting them, in the form of cellars. How can it be that these city people — who live so curiously high up in the air, so removed from farms, so oblivious of all that goes into growing food and fetching water and hunting and fishing — how can it be that they have dug themselves so far into the ground? And anyway, what does go on in those cellars? They can be frightening places — dark as can be, low and dank and just plain underneath everything. Heat is made in them, in things called boilers. Pipes and wires go in and out of cellars, or basements, as some call them. And the rats, the rats that are so common, the rats that seem to a mother an inevitable part of her child's life, they also are supposed to come from those cellars: "I'd sooner die than go down into that cellar. I've heard about it. I've heard stories; I've heard there are so many rats down there you can't see anything but them, running all over, faster than squirrels and raccoons and rabbits, much faster. They tell me a city rat is like no other animal. They're in the biggest hurry. They're mean. They don't care about each other and they run and run, on the hunt for scraps of food. They don't know the sun. I do believe rats come into the cellars up from Hell. Hell can't be too far from here, anyway."

She has learned from her neighbor that down in the cellar of her building is a huge boiler, a furnace, "a hot, hot oven." Again she thinks of Hell — and expresses the mixed awe and astonishment and dread she feels, perhaps about a wider range of subjects than the one she mentions: "I never would have believed it until I saw for myself — the heat you can get in this building. You need no fireplaces and no stoves. All you do is turn them on and those radiators start click-clacking, knocking and knocking, *dancing*, my little girl says. Not always, of course; sometimes we don't get any heat — and then the city has to come and scare the landlord. But I still can't get too mad, because back home we'd sit around the stove, and if we went too far away, we'd just have to be cold. It was hard on the children; they didn't have the winter clothes they needed. In the city we get more heat than we ever dreamed we'd have, but my neighbor says they can explode, the boilers. I told her Hell will open up one day, and we'll all sink in — and maybe the boilers are owned by the devil. She thought I was fooling. I was — but maybe it's true. Maybe up here that can happen."

She believes that anything can happen "up here," in the noisy, crowded world of her building, her block, her street. In many northern cities a street contains thousands of people — as many, for instance, as everyone in a whole county of the rural South or Appalachia. And, of course, a street can be a center of commerce, a place where people buy and sell and eat and entertain and are entertained. I have walked a mile on her street with her two sons and seen the stores: the regular grocery stores; the Dignity Grocery, whose owners emphasize their Afro-American spirit; the large drugstore that sells just about anything; the hairdressers, some of whom sell wigs, straighten hair, have white women's faces and hairstyles in the store window, and some of whom say no, no, no — Afros, and nothing else. And there are the funeral parlors and insurance agencies, not unlike those one sees in southern towns. The two boys told me that when their mother came North she went to an undertaker to register with him. I asked them why she would do that, and one of them replied: "My grandma told her to do it, otherwise we could die, one of us, and there'd be no one to bury us, and no place to rest in." They worry about rest, such families do, worry a great deal about what will happen to them, finally, and where they will go next and, most of all, whether always and always they will be tired and unsatisfied and fearful — destined, that is, for "no place to rest in."

On that street there are, in fact, people and places which offer a haven of sorts, if ever so temporary. There are women, mostly, who advertise themselves and their abilities with signs like "Reader-Adviser." There are bars and lounges and coffee shops. There are places that say "Keys Made," but specialize also in taking bets, which means one can sit down, make a telephone call, and have a friendly and informative talk with a broker of sorts, a man familiar with the odds, aware of hot tips, and not always on "the company's side." And there are those pawnbrokers, who are still around, still mostly white, still ready to cash checks and offer money (no questions asked) in return for "goods." But the two boys like most of all a Soul on Wax store. "How Much Can U Stand?" the sign asks, and the boys say there is no limit. Soul pours out of the store. Soul is turned up high inside and demands to be heard outside. "Soul Unlimited," another sign on the window says, and one's ears are inclined to offer no argument to the claim. The boys' mother finds the store an outrage. What right have they to make all that sound, assault one with all that "crazy music"? She loves hymns, passionate hymns. Her sons, though, are really turned on, have a lot of soul in them, and can stop and listen and snap their fingers and move their feet and knees and hips and torso and arms and neck and head in ways I can only marvel at, envy, and (in self-defense) dismiss as "foreign" or "alien" or a touch "wild" and "hysterical."

Among Appalachian whites newly settled in midwestern cities, mothers and children can take me on similar walks. Absent are the many hairdressers and funeral directors. Soul is not there, but God is; and so are country music, hillbilly music, and a gospel music not unlike the kind many blacks find congenial, important and necessary. Missions are often present, their doors open, their signs prominently displayed and full of urgency. The mountaineer must know that he is not forsaken, that Christ follows His children into the cities, that prayer helps, works, makes a difference, saves. And the mountaineer will need to be saved, too, because those streets of his have stores that are labor agencies of sorts, stores where an earnest, tough, willing, hardworking mountaineer can be guaranteed work all right — hours and hours of it, with very little reward: "They say they'll pay you a couple of dollars an hour, but they take half *and more* out as their fee. I'm left with so little, and it costs so much here, the rent and the food, that I can't keep up with it." So, he goes to the loan company. There are plenty of those, in all the cities, ready with money for the black man, money for the white man, money for anyone prepared to assume undreamed-of debts in the course of paying off other debts.

Once up North, once on those streets and in those buildings, more forms of escape can be sought. Mountaineers like beer and whiskey; so do black men. So, they drink. Do they! One has to add quickly that only some mountaineers get excessively taken up with liquor. One has to add quickly and with particular emphasis (because so many of us are ready to believe otherwise) that only some black men get similarly dependent on liquor — or hooked on God knows what drug. Nevertheless, the streets have their fair share of them, the alcoholics and addicts, as a doctor calls them; the "lost people" one child I know calls them — and then he makes his emphasis: "the *real* lost people."

Does he distinguish "them" in that way from himself and his parents — who presumably are also lost, but by no means *real* lost? "In life some people lose more than others," his mother often says, so perhaps that is just what the boy of nine had in mind. He and his parents are losers, but not driven mad by cravings for shots, shots of whiskey and shots of heroin, which others call "smack" but the child calls "the silent smack." He will tell a listener why he uses that expression, and by the time he has finished he has revealed a lot about a particular child's sensibility and a lot, also, about the streets of a great American city: "I've only been here a year. I'm used to the streets now. You get used to them. I used to wonder if I ever would. I once thought I never would. It hurt my feet to walk on so much sidewalk. Before I came here I never wore shoes. Now I have to wear them all the time, and they hurt. You can't walk on the sidewalk barefoot; glass is everywhere and your feet get cut and bleed. I used to think I might dig up some sidewalk so I could have some earth to rest my feet on, soft earth. My mother says the earth up here must be hard. I asked her how she knew — since we never see any earth here. She said I should stop being smart with her. She says up here if you get too smart, you can get into trouble. I don't want any trouble, not the kind I see hereabouts. Look at those lost people out there; I mean they are *real* lost. I mean, they are gone. They'll never come back. They're on smack. Smack is the

end of the road — the last trip, they say. You've arrived when
you take it, they say; you can't go any further, they say. They
take it and you can see them — going up, up, up. They don't
make a sound when they take smack. That's why I say smack is
silent — it's the silent smack. You know what? My granddaddy
used to say to me: watch out there, you boy, or I'll give you a
smack. My mother thought we were trying to be funny when we
told her what a smack was up here. Granddaddy would hit us
and *his* smack you could hear all over, into the middle of the
field. Here I see them taking smack right out in the street,
almost; maybe in the hall or in an alley. They don't make any
noise, not a sound. When my mother gets mad and shouts about
how wild it is here, crazy, she says, and noisy as can be, I'll
sometimes argue with her. Some people here never talk, and
they're not wild. They're as silent and still as if they're already
dead. I do believe if my granddaddy gave them a smack they
wouldn't make a sound or a move. I'd wriggle and cry when he
hit me, and he'd say, 'Good, it shows you're alive and kicking.'
Like I say: on smack, you're dead and gone."

Children like him, black children, or white mountain children
newly settled in a northern city, notice all sorts of voices, all sorts
of clatter and cries; they are sensitive to noises and curious about
where they come from. The streets never seem to quiet down.
Even in the middle of the night there are cars moving, people
walking, things going on. Why is that? Why is the whole rhythm
of life so different in New York or Philadelphia or Boston or
Chicago? Why don't people live the same way they did "back
South" or "back home" in the mountains? That is to say, why
don't they move the way they used to move, and divide up their
time in the old ways? What is it about those streets that "gets
into you so," to call upon the words I heard one mother use? She
was always asking questions like the ones I have just asked. She
is utterly convinced that the streets really do change the bodies
of those who move into them from the countryside. She would
list her reasons rather like a good scientist does, briefly and to the
point: "The sun, it's never around. The sky, who sees it? The
clouds, they're always over you. The moon, poor thing, fights like

Hell to get out from under those clouds; it probably thinks the clouds will get tired, after being there all day. But that's not the way it goes, no sir. They're tricky, those clouds. They let the moon through, then quick as can be, they shut it out again. There are no birds around, except a few pigeons, and they're in a bad state, you can see. They're always at each other. They're not relaxed and easygoing like the birds we had back home in the hills. A day doesn't go by that you're not trying to get something out of your eye. A day doesn't go by that you don't hear the cars hitting into each other, or the fire trucks racing by, or the police and their sirens. Will it be my building next, you wonder? Will it catch on fire or lose its heat? No wonder your body shakes all the time and begins to fall apart. There's just so much a body can take."

Those complaints are by no means the whole story, so far as she is concerned. She simply is not used to the "clock life" of the city. In the country everyone got up when the sun came up, and prepared to go to sleep when the sun left for other places. She and her family lingered, of course. They talked, and after they shared a secondhand television set, they listened to it for a while "into the night." But "come sundown" they withdrew from the outside world into their own world, the world of their cabin — ever so frail, likely as not perched on those cinder blocks, the floors full of holes and cracks, the roof made of rusted tin equally full of leaks. Nor does she fail to notice a bit of a paradox in her current situation: "I used to think to myself that one day I'd go into a city and I'd live better. I'd have a house where I'd be able to close my door and not worry that it's cold outside or raining. Now we have bricks in this building, and it sure is stronger than the cabin we had back there. The cold stays out, and the wind and the rain, but everything else comes in here from outside: the whole street, with its sirens, and the rats, they're always eating their way in, and the bugs and more bugs, and the roaches, huge they are. We had some roaches back home. I'm not denying it. But I kept on top of them. I cleared them out. I kept the mice out, too — field mice, and you'll always have them. But there weren't rats trying to *eat* you, and bugs that *bite* you, and the walls didn't have the lead poison in them that nearly *killed* my girl last year. I used to be afraid of coal. My father was killed down in a mine. Now it's lead you have to fear, around here it's lead."

She is afraid that she and her children will never really accommodate themselves to the "schedule of this place," or as mentioned above, the "clock life." In the city she is supposed to sleep, even though it is light outside early in the morning. In the city she is supposed to ignore dusk, the evening, the night. In the city her husband comes home tired but fretful — when he is lucky enough to have left home and stayed away doing a good day's work. He doesn't carve wood, make things anymore. Where indeed would he get the wood? He doesn't go walking — all the while talking with his dog. ("You'd have to be a murderer to keep a dog up here. Some do, but I can't. I just couldn't.") He doesn't try to fix things, or stand there outside his cabin, lost in his thoughts, alone with his memories, or maybe just still and unbothered and without anything at all on his mind. What he often *does* do is describe those times that are gone and compare them with the "better life" he now has: "I'd get myself in a nice place, where I might hear some birds and listen to some animals sounding off, really sounding off, or where I could look out — no, not at anything special, just at everything, you might say. I'd rest myself standing there. It's hard to explain to you, it is; after being up here a while, it's hard to explain to myself! But we have a better life up here. I don't say it's a happier one. I don't. But it's better, the way we live. Hell, maybe it's happier, too! I always was one to forget the troubles I had and remember only the good. We had more troubles back in those hills than we do here in this city, living on this street."

And I had better remember those words. More than once he has brought himself up short and let me know how misleading he could be about his own life, about the advantages and disadvantages of one or another part of that life. More than once he and others like him have let me know that I ought be as wary of their words and sentiments, and above all their nostalgia, as they themselves from time to time become — wary and self-mocking

and delightfully clever and shrewdly philosophical: "I'm the kind
of man who turns his miseries into a good time — once he's
feeling fine. That's when you should turn sweet on the sourness
you've been through, when you're through with it, the bad time.
When I first came here to the city I used to miss it back there,
real bad I did. I'd go to bed thinking of our little house and the
hollow and the creek and the trees I'd carved my initials on when
I was a boy, and the ones my own boys were starting to carve.
Well, I had to stop that. But you know, the thing that made me
stop was the minister up here I talked with. He said to me one
day: would you go back? Would you really go back? And I came
home and I thought, and by God if I didn't decide that a lot of
my bellyaches are now gone, and even the worst of what I don't
like isn't as bad as some of the troubles we had back there."

He meant "bellyaches" quite specifically and concretely,
though he also was speaking symbolically. He and his family are
no longer as hungry as they used to be during those long winters,
when no money came in, when no work was to be had, when
they were denied welfare, when bottled and canned food, grown
outside, "up the mountain," and put away for January and
February, began to run out, while at the same time the weather
remained bitter cold and snow simply would not stop falling. But
he used to have other bellyaches, too. Not only could he find no
job, not only did he get no help at all from county officials, there
was, additionally, the sight of his children. Before his very eyes
they were "growing into his shoes," which ironically means
growing up to have no shoes, to walk barefoot, to miss school on
that account as well as for other reasons, all of them "part of a
bundle" he would say: sickness with its attendant weakness;
gloominess and self-doubt; and indifference, a child's realization
that books don't matter in a neighborhood where very few
people, literate or not, can find work.

The streets, then, offer hope. The streets have received, continue to receive, men and women and children who have had to
leave their homes elsewhere; they are people driven and forsaken, compelled by fate to seek not merely a new life, but the
conditions under which survival is possible. Hard pressed and

afraid and tired, they arrive determined to live, anxious to find shelter and food and "something to do, anything that will fill up the hours." Bitter and fatalistic and bewildered, they are also resourceful and canny and inventive. There is the address of a brother to find or the address of kin, not close kin, but above all kin. There is a piece of paper to keep, to show, to look at and use; on it is a telephone number, a contact, the name of a person or an organization. The hand holds on to that paper. The arms lift that paper up again and again so that people of the city can see it. The lips say the word or words one time, two times, ten times. They are tentative hands and arms, and God knows, the voices let out by those lips tremble, falter, are often barely audible. Still, the hands and arms and voices belong to men and women who have picked themselves up and done the moving, the traveling, "the carrying of ourselves"; and once arrived, those men and women persist. Only later will they recall the first moments up North, and reveal why they very much want to stay where they are (even if they at times talk like prisoners condemned). But as they talk they also reveal what it meant to decide upon a departure, to pack up and go off, to get someplace, however far away it may be, however strange and forbidding it may appear to be when reached.

"We got here, we did," a man from Kentucky's mountains could say, three years after he arrived. And then comes, with a shudder one moment, a look of fierce pride the next, an account of what it was like to get there, to see those streets and try to fathom them out, master them: "I near turned back — so near I almost shake thinking about it. I saw the city from a distance, you know, and I thought I was having myself a dream. I said to my wife, it's not true. She said that it is, and we've seen pictures on television to prove it. I said I never believed those pictures. She said it was true, what we'd seen, and there's the proof over yonder. Well, we got closer and closer, and all I could think was that we were going to die, once we got right in the middle of the city, and probably God Himself would be there, waiting to judge us, like He does. So, I said to myself we'd better just keep right on going, and let what happens happen. And we did. I had a piece of paper with an address written down; it was given to me by our minister. And I had another piece of paper with another address, kin of my wife's. I kept stopping and asking. I asked the police. I asked the people in gas stations. I asked someone walking down the street, and then someone else, and finally we got there. We got to our kin, and we got to the mission, where they helped us find a place to stay and some work for me."

He goes on. He tells about the sad times he had, the low times, and later on the better moments. At one point he thought he might have to move yet again: "I was stalled. I couldn't go back to the mountains, I knew that, and I couldn't stay here and sit around and sit around. Hell, I hate that. I'd die if that's all there was for me, the rest of my life. Maybe there's another city, I thought — where I could work." He found work, though. He didn't have to move. But the point is that he was prepared to do so. At times an observer can find him sullen, morose, resentful. At times he gets irritated, indignant, flushed with anger. He snaps. He looks daggers at people — including his own wife and children. He grinds his teeth. He quivers with rage, and his wife fears he will explode, pack them all up, make for the hills, the hills he loves and talks about and dreams about, the hills whose beauty he cannot get out of his mind, the hills whose praise he sings all the time, it seems — to the point that his younger children get cross and a little contemptuous. "That's silly," says his seven-year-old son, and then he tells why: "We're here. We're living here, and look how we have the food to eat, every day. I have good friends here. I like it. I'd like to go back, but I'd like to stay here until we know if there'll be anything for us back there." And the father nods his head, agrees, even manages a smile for himself and a pat on the head for his seven-year-old son, who is now a Chicagoan.

He has stayed because, as his son points out, there wasn't "anything" back home for his family and many thousands of other families. For all his bitter moments he is a man of moral courage. As he describes himself holding those two pieces of paper and asking, asking again, continuing, following directions, getting more directions, one can sense in him the self-possession, the self-reliance, the self-command he has always had, however petulant and brooding he sometimes is. People like him somehow got to the cities in which they now live. It is less apparent to us that their arrival was preceded by an act of will, by intention become a deed — *and* that to stay meant to resolve something, to settle something in one's mind as well as to settle down in an apartment house. A black man in Harlem describes what he, like the white mountaineer just quoted, went through as he arrived in New York City: "I came by bus. All I had when I got on the bus was a box, a box made of cardboard, and it had a rope around it to hold my things together. I had some socks and underwear, two pairs of each, and a picture of my wife and my kids that we took in a five-and-ten store in Macon, Georgia. I'd only been in Macon two or three times in my life, so New York was more than I could believe. I just couldn't believe it. How could there be a place like that? Of course, I've been here five years, so it's hard to tell you what was on my mind back then, but so far as New York is concerned — how I felt when I saw it for the first time — I *can* tell you, because there are some things in your life that you just don't forget, never. How could you?"

He works himself up to the description of his first thoughts and feelings in New York by doing what a good novelist or historian would do. That is to say, he goes back and makes sure that his listener is thoroughly aware of, reminded of, what preceded that arrival: "Now, you have to picture our place back there in Georgia. Oh, it was something! Today I can't figure out how we did it, live there. It's no paradise up here, but like my wife tells me when I get down in the dumps, a day doesn't go by that we don't take something for granted up here that back there we believed we'd never, never live to have. That's the truth. It was bad for us down South, and getting worse all the time. Some of my family, they went into Atlanta; and even there they couldn't find work. They stood around and sat around. They tried to find jobs. Then they gave up. They came back here and they told me that if I wanted to get out, I'd better go all the way and leave the whole state of Georgia. So, I did. I went to New York because we had an uncle here. Then I sent for my wife and kids, and after a while we sent for my cousins, too. They said they'd been in Atlanta, but compared to New York, the whole state of Georgia was just a little town, that's all it is."

How did he manage, though, during those first minutes and hours of his arrival North? How did he come to terms with Harlem? Where did he go? Whom did he initially see, talk with, ask for help? No world-shaking psychological and sociological conclusions will come out of whatever answers and thoughts and memories he manages to give to someone like me. Nevertheless, he himself says that he lives to this day with, will always live with "a little bit of that first day in me." Now what does *that* mean? What unforgettable drama unfolded then? The answer is that nothing terribly shocking or melodramatic took place. He simply wants it known that "you don't just move up here and find a room in Harlem and send for your family, no sir." If not that, then what? Oh, a lot, he will say, tossing the ball right back. It is hard for him to put some things into words, and he isn't really interested in doing so. But he has memories, a number of them, and as he keeps on saying, something seems to come up all the time that makes one or another of those memories assert itself in his mind: "I'll be walking down the street and my eye will catch a junkie, and I'll say to myself: Louis, remember the time you saw your first junkie? And then I'll say to myself: Louis, you are here; you're no longer down South; you're here."

With such a remark he can be through with talk, or on his way to a long marathon of it. The fact is that he has become a taxi driver, and so he knows his Harlem. He can take a visitor on a street-by-street tour. He knows that city within a city well enough (if not inside out, which is what he only sometimes claims) to qualify as a guide: "Some people said they wanted a few of us to take the whites on a tour and show them a lot of places. I said sure, sure I would. Maybe it was a mistake, but their white eyes were opened, they were; and you know, that's the same thing that happened to me. My eyes got opened when I came up here."

When he first saw New York he had one thought: how could he get together the money necessary for a return ticket? For one whole week his mind was almost obsessed with that question. He got off the bus and asked the driver if it cost the same fare to go back South. When he got to his uncle's house he asked his uncle if he could loan him the money for the trip back. Yes, but stay, the uncle said repeatedly. No, he would not stay. The city hurt him. His eyes watered when he walked the streets of Harlem — and no, it wasn't because he was crying. Well, maybe "on the inside" he was, but he was *also* crying because things would unaccountably get in his eyes. Things don't get in his eyes now — and that, he says, is because "you learn to close your eyes a little up here, you learn to protect yourself." Nor were his eyes the only problem he had. His ears had never heard so much, so many different kinds of noises. He felt like the squirrels he used to shoot: "They'd always be sitting and trying to figure out where to go, which tree to climb, which way to turn. The same with me. I'd leave my uncle's place and I'd have my eyes watching all over, and my ears as open as they could be — and the result was I didn't know what to do. It seemed that every direction I would go would only mean trouble, trouble."

He goes on. He describes all the "trouble" he met up with and came to understand — and not to fear quite so much. He describes the things he gradually took for granted: those junkies, the soot in the air, the roar of buses and garbage trucks and freight trucks and the elevated railroad and the machines being used to build or tear down or repair buildings. He describes gutters and hydrants and lampposts and automobile meters; they are all part of the city, part of the streets of Harlem — and it was only when his family did at last come up, and when he saw *them* noticing all those things, and complaining about any number of other things, it was only then that he realized what *he* had gone through: "My boy asked me about the hydrant. After I told him, he wasn't satisfied; he wanted to know where the water comes from. You see, back home we used to walk three or four miles every day to get water and bring it back to the house. We went to a little pond, it was. Don't ask me if the water was clean! I don't want to think about the germs I got into me over all those years. My little girl comes home and talks about vitamins and minerals in her food, how she needs vitamin ABC and XYZ. I tell her: look, Sally Mae, your daddy lived on grits and the water in that pond, back in Peach County, Georgia. He didn't die. He *lived* on it, you hear!"

The little girl is, of course, surprised, and she doesn't really know what to say in reply. All right, *all right,* so he did manage to live on grits and that dirty water. What is *she* supposed to do? She was two when she came to Harlem. She is a New Yorker. Her daddy is no desperate, dispossessed sharecropper. Her daddy is a taxi driver. Her daddy knows a lot; in fact, he knows most everything there is to know about New York City, or at least the only New York City she, Sally Mae knows about — so why does he every once in a while bring up "all that South business"?

Sally Mae's father agrees with her. Why go back to what is over and done with? Yet he does. He recalls things nostalgically, bitterly, and with a touch of envy directed at others who lack his kind of memories. Most of all he recalls things with decreasing frequency and increasing self-consciousness. And almost invariably he finds that when he lets his mind go back, when he dwells upon the past, he ends up remembering not the South but himself as new to the North, new to New York City and Harlem and those streets he now drives over, all over — to the extent that sometimes his wife will wake up in the middle of the night and hear him reciting them, their numbers, their names, their origins, their endings. During the day he also says a lot of things out loud. Doesn't he have to make himself heard above all those sounds? Doesn't he have to remind himself by talking at the top of his voice that with so many people on those streets, he is himself, a person, Mr. James Tilley and no one else? The time was that he could walk miles and hear no one's voice, see no one's face. He walked on red earth, grew tired, and sat down on that earth, maybe under a tree or beside some bushes or on some grass. The time was that he'd come home and do some more sitting: there was the sun to watch as it slowly seemed to settle itself down from the sky — and then all of a sudden disappear; there were the sunflowers to look at and shower with a little water; there were the dogs to play with, throw sticks toward and away from. Now he never looks at the sky. He just doesn't. He knows about the weather by the feel of things. Is he cold? Is he sweating? Is he getting wet? Does he see whiteness slowly growing and growing, covering up Harlem's streets, making them look different, making them harder to navigate, making his driving more difficult — and more in demand? And now the trees are practically nowhere, sunflowers are unheard-of, and as for dogs, they are around, yes, they are, but he thinks that is rather a shame: "I wouldn't bring a dog into the city, not here anyway. It's unfair to them. We left our dog home. We left her with my sister. The dog is still alive. My sister writes and tells us that Rosemary misses us. I'm sure she does. I miss her. We named her after my younger sister. She got sick and died all of a sudden. She coughed up blood and the next thing she was gone. I wouldn't have named the dog Rosemary, but my mother asked me to. She said she liked hearing the name Rosemary called again. She said she was sure Rosemary was near us and listening and waiting for us to come and join her."

As for his mother, she won't leave Georgia. She wouldn't think of coming to New York. She was born in Peach County and she will die there. Why is that? Why doesn't she follow her brother, follow her son? The son Louis has an answer: "She'd be leaving her child Rosemary, and not only Rosemary. She's lost other children, you know. There's no Harlem Hospital for us in Peach County. There's nothing for us there, the fact is, when you stop and think about it. It was awful for her to see Rosemary die like that. It was awful for her to give us children roots to chew on so we wouldn't get too hungry. But even so, my mother can't leave. She's got to stay. She's got to stay and 'lock up the store.' I hear my customers say, 'I'm glad you came by; I need a taxi; I'm tired.' They've just 'locked up the store' after a long day. I guess the good Lord will send a taxi for my mother one of these days, and when He does she'll get in and be glad. Yes, she will. And you want to know something? She won't turn around, no she won't. There will be no regrets. She'll get in that cab and say, 'My good Lord, how I've been waiting on you! Oh have I!' and then she'll be driven to some city, I guess!"

It is precisely a place like Harlem Hospital that lifts this man's spirit and makes him proud to be living where he is. It isn't that he is completely satisfied with the care his wife and children have received there for a variety of complaints. It isn't that he himself has been showered with love and affection and prompt service there. Still, Harlem Hospital has black doctors and nurses. Once, in an emergency, his girl was treated very well, so well that he could only think, again, of Rosemary — and of what it means to be up North and in a big, modern city, for all its drawbacks and troubles: "I took her there, Sally Mae, and she was coughing bad and wheezing, that's what the doctor told me it was, wheezing. He said her lungs were sick, she had trouble in them, but they had drugs and they'd get her well, they were sure of it. I was reminded of Rosemary, my sister. I thought of her, coughing and coughing, and finally the blood came up, and all of a sudden she was gone. Do you think a poor man down there in Peach County, Georgia, can go to Harlem Hospital and have his daughter fixed up? Do you think even if you're white a doctor down there will see you if you're poor? They wouldn't see a white man's kid, either! I knew a white kid who was sick; I knew his daddy too, because he worked in the gas station near the bossman's house. The doctor saw the white kid once and said he was in *private practice,* that's what the doctor said. He told the man to take his kid up to Atlanta, someplace like that, where they have money and they have 'free hospitals,' something like that. Well, then I could only shrug my shoulders. I thought he was a lucky man, come to think of it! I said to my wife, 'If he was colored, he never would have gotten to that doctor's office in the first place. At least this way he knew where he stood.' "

The long and short of it is that *he* now knows just about where he stands. He lives up North, in America's most populous and richest city, its first city in many respects. Every day he stands there at a corner, waiting for a fare, talking and joking with other cabdrivers. He leans against lampposts. He leans against the walls of buildings. He leans on parked cars. He has his coffee standing up. He can look out at the street that way. For one thing, he can see anyone who might be tempted to get into his cab and drive off, but just as important, he likes to look outside, look at passersby, take in the scene, "watch the world go by," he puts it — by no means with a unique turn of phrase, but with obvious conviction and even a trace of excitement. The streets of that city have caught hold of him, as they have so many others from various classes and races and backgrounds. He is not uncritical of those streets; he sees "a lot of misery every day," and he wants that known. At times he is so critical that if his mind does not seriously take him and his family back to the rural South, it does indeed prompt him to think of other streets, perhaps in smaller towns. But no, that is not for him; maybe for his children but not for him. Nor is the problem only one of race, though God knows "a black man can't just decide to move and expect a big reception out there in the big, fat white suburbs." The fact is that he spends only the very briefest time in the suburbs and he does not know how he would ever get to live in one of them: "Should I take my cab one day and drive out there, over one of the bridges, and go talk to someone about a home? I take fares all over, but I can just imagine what would happen if I tried moving in some of the places I drive through. My kids, they are learning more than I ever dreamed there was to learn in school; so maybe they'll learn how you get to live someplace else. Black people get out of here, I guess, just like I got out of Georgia."

He is optimistic at that moment. Sometimes he sees things far less hopefully. At other times he becomes afraid. He hears talk of violence, of revolution. He sees buildings condemned. He sees fires consume buildings that ought never have been left standing. He sees everything as he drives and stops, picks up people and takes them where they want to go: "I'll hear people talking and I think to myself there won't be a Harlem left. The white man doesn't care about these streets here; some black people do, but some have reached the point that they don't care either." But he does, he very much cares: "I'm not tired of these streets, not yet. If you asked me what I think of my being here, I'd say I'm glad I came. That poor white guy I told you about, the guy who worked in the gas station — well, you know what? He went to the city, too. My mother told us that. She said he up and left. Maybe he went to Atlanta, or maybe he went some other place — up North, maybe. I understand the whites in the South have been going the same way we have. If the land won't take care of but a few rich farmers, and the poor people have got nothing to fall back on, except to sit and starve to death, then they're not going to do that. They're going to leave. They'll come up here."

And so people of both races have; they have left for reasons he knows about, and settled on the streets he virtually hunts along, so agile and forceful a driver is he. In a city people want to get someplace, he reminds his passenger. In a city there's no point lingering and waiting. The streets are there to live on, play on and ride on. He lives on the streets at night, and his kids play on the streets in the late afternoon, but in those morning hours he's got to ride, ride, ride those streets. The streets will give him money, will take him and his family someplace. He doesn't know exactly where. But who really does? He knows enough to know *that*, though — and so unbothered, unexhausted by large questions, he guns the engine, spots the customer, asks where, and shows what he knows, what he can do: go right to the desired address the fastest way allowed by the city's streets.

II

THE METHOD

IN 1970 as I looked back at the work I had done in northern cities, in Boston and Cleveland and Chicago and New York, I realized that there were two moments that decisively influenced that work. In 1960 I was told this by a black mother in Louisiana: "If you're going to know our family, you'll have to go up North, besides being here. My sister is up there, she's in Chicago, and my brother, he's in Chicago, too. My mother won't leave Holmes County, Mississippi, and my husband's mother and daddy, they won't either. But we've been leaving, the younger ones. I don't know if I want to go North, no I don't. That's why we thought we'd try New Orleans. But we may have to. We may have to. A lot of us, a lot of our people have gone up there."

Of course I knew what has happened in this century — a northward flow of out-of-work sharecroppers and tenant farmers, loyal to a land no longer in need of their hands, hungry, ailing, fearful, quietly desperate; often enough sad at leaving, if at the same time glad to depart and eager to arrive.[1] The destination might be called "freedomland" by some hopeful and trusting souls, or more guardedly, "the cities up there." Once I heard the destination described in a grimly realistic way as "a little better place, only a little better place." And if many have become bitterly disappointed up North, by no means have all the South's exiles come to feel unhappy where they are, far away from an ancestral homeland — "the slavery states." A fourth-grade black child let me know that he considered the term "Confederate States" misleading or not quite to the point, the brutal point, of his people's utterly essential role: "The Confederate States were states that wanted to keep us, the black people, as slaves; so they were slavery states." Yet, his black grandmother still lives just north of Mobile, Alabama.

So I was told, even warned: I would at some point have to go North if I was going to study the way a black family survives — survives the hazards and threats of school desegregation or the extreme hardship that goes with continued living in, say, Tunica County, Mississippi, where less than a thousand dollars a year, considerably less, is "what you expect here, what you get here."[2] By the same token, in 1963 I heard similar advice from mountain people in western North Carolina. I was in Burnsville, in Yancey County, studying school desegregation, and doing so by getting to know a few families of both races.[3] I was at the same time, unwittingly in the beginning, learning about kith and kin, learning what that word "family" means to others, not me. When I asked a white father how he felt about the entrance of a handful of black children into his child's school he replied this way: "I don't much care. We only have a few of them here in the county; and we've never had trouble with them, the colored. They don't bother us and we don't bother them. My two older boys could tell you some stories, though." Well, what were they? "The boys aren't around to say," he announced — and I could see that he wasn't going to volunteer to a stranger one more thing than he thought both polite and necessary. Eventually I did find out where they were, and eventually I went to see them — in Chicago, where they lived "for a while," as they kept on reminding both me and themselves. Someday they will be back where they belong, they almost passionately feel. Yet they remain there, in Chicago, Illinois, as they sometimes put it, as if by saying both the city and the state they confirm to themselves the fact that they really are there (where they can make some money and send part of it to their parents) and not home near their kin and near those mountains they never for a day stop thinking about — so they say, though they also say that they do indeed forget,

sometimes to their surprise and sometimes simply because there
is work to be done.

I suppose that because I had heard from those two parents, a
mother in Louisiana, a father in North Carolina, about brothers
"up there" and sons "gone North to the city," and because I was
by 1963 and 1964 also working with migrant farm workers, who
certainly know what it is to travel from Florida to New England,
I would eventually have found some way to study more closely
what happens to farmhands become ghetto residents, mountaineers become "city folks" — as some Appalachian people refer
to themselves, mockingly, derisively, and underneath with a good
deal of sadness. But it took an event in my native Boston to get
me going. I had myself "gone North," so to speak, at the end of
1964 — the year of the Mississippi Summer Project, the year
when many in the South who were involved in one way or
another with that region's social and political struggles had
decided that only outside help, be it from northern college students or lawyers or from Congress itself, could achieve for millions of blacks in states like Alabama and Mississippi the right to
vote, the right to attend the public schools that all other children
go to, the right to stop here and get a milk shake, stop there and
see a movie. In the autumn of 1964, after six solid years of living
in Mississippi and Louisiana and Georgia, I was working with
migrant families who were finishing up the odds and ends of the
harvest season by picking apples in Massachusetts. It was September, in fact, and the schools of the nation were once again
opening their doors. Suddenly the Boston newspapers were filled
with news then rather unusual for that city, with its abolitionist
history. A group of black parents were insisting that under no
circumstances would they send their children to the overcrowded, ancient and broken-down school they were supposed to
attend. The school belonged to another century. Now, to add one
more insult to a pile of injuries, the streets nearby were particularly dangerous because houses were being razed. Mothers and
fathers feared that their children would be walking through and
around broken glass and nails and pieces of sharp metal — all in
order to squeeze themselves among far more children than "a

building twice bigger ought to have in it." The result was that some mothers like the one who spoke those words insisted that they would send their children elsewhere; indeed, if necessary they vowed to go all over Boston until they found "a school better than a prison, a school where the kids aren't without desks and sitting all over the place and being told to shut up, shut up all day long."

Thus did a bussing program in Boston begin.[4] No courts ordered those parents to bus their children. No civil rights activists "organized" the neighborhood, or decided on a particular strategy with respect to a particular school. Here were parents from a ghetto who felt they had had quite enough and were willing to do something about their complaints — like staging a sit-in on the steps of another school, and appealing for funds to hire a bus that would transport their children to other parts of Boston.

I read about all that and decided to find out more. The only way to do so was to go to Roxbury (Boston's ghetto district), meet the parents and the children, observe their deeds, get some sense of their purposes, their wishes, their fears and resentments. For me personally, this was coming full circle. In 1957 as a child psychiatrist in a Boston hospital I had treated an eight-year-old boy from Roxbury. He told me in the course of one session that I should come and see where he lived. I asked him why. He had no answer, not at least one he was willing to give me in words. As for me, I had my own ideas why he had made the suggestion. Did he not need a father? Was he not lonely and troubled, with a variety of fears, awakened constantly by nightmares? Was he not, in treatment with me, week by week becoming more "involved," more "dependent," more in the middle of a "transference relationship"? I believe today, as I did then, that in his case, at that juncture in his therapy I did well to stay in my office and try to understand what was happening in his mind, rather than in his neighborhood — not that the two can always be conveniently separated. The boy had fairly specific psychological troubles, and I believe that the two of us did manage to weaken the hold those troubles had on his mind. Yet I also believe today that at some point, perhaps toward the end of our meetings, when he again asked me to go see Roxbury, I should have said yes. Instead I again said no — politely and gently and tactfully, of course (so we say to ourselves afterwards, so we congratulate ourselves, so we get ourselves off the hook). I said no because I did not want to get "overinvolved," because I felt it "improper" to say anything but no; because, really, I was compliant and timid and intimidated, like all too many young psychiatrists in training, and other "good students."

I was born in Boston and grew up there, but not near black people. I have in the first volume of *Children of Crisis* explained the way I became involved in the work I have been doing this past decade in the South. So let me skip that and reiterate a remark made to me by a strong segregationist whom I have elsewhere described: "You'll go back to your North, one day, and you'll see the same things up there. You'll see that your backyard has problems in it, and they are as big as ours, bigger I'd say, growing bigger all the time."[5] He was right then, and I knew it then, but knew it in the abstract way people like me tend to know things. I think it fair to admit that this book tells what I eventually did see — the very things that segregationist from Louisiana told me I would. And my "method" has to do with how I went about confirming that statement by a onetime member of the Ku Klux Klan to be absolutely correct.

By October of 1964, I was visiting certain homes in Roxbury, homes in which black children lived, homes which black children left in order to board a bus and go "across town," as they would put it, to schools full of white children. I was also meeting regularly with the mothers of those black children in the basement of a church; they came together because they wanted to discuss what was happening to their children, exchange news and talk about the inevitable problem of raising money to keep the buses going. They had started more than they themselves realized when they decided in late September, after a series of arguments with officials of the Boston school system, to shun all the old, crowded "neighborhood" schools in Roxbury and instead seek places for their children in other sections of the city. This meant arranging for the transportation of about thirty young boys and girls, aged six to eleven — since Boston's "open enrollment" plan, on the books for year and years, allowed any parent who didn't like what his child got at a nearby school, to take the child anywhere in the city, but the parent had to pay for the privilege and make sure the child got there on time and somehow got home.

In early 1965 I decided to do what I had done in the South, try to find out not only how black children managed a certain kind of school desegregation — self-initiated rather than court-ordered — but also how white children responded to what was in Boston, as in Louisiana or Georgia, an educational and social crisis. Once again I began to talk with teachers, visit classrooms, select among children and their parents the widest possible range of social and economic backgrounds, so that I would be sure to know not only white children who were by and large ready to welcome black children in their midst, but also white children who would be at the very least quite willing to repeat for me a question one of them asked her teacher: "Why don't they stay where they live, instead of coming all the way over here?"

Over the years I believe the purpose of my work in Boston has changed somewhat. I did indeed learn something about how black and white schoolchildren get along when newly placed together in a school setting. I did indeed study the effect of bussing itself on black children from a ghetto. I rode on a school bus myself for a whole school year, and in so doing saw what the children saw as they moved out of the ghetto and into other streets, other neighborhoods. I could watch them for evidence of fatigue, boredom, exhaustion — or indeed, excitement, curiosity, exhilaration. But in time I began to study a little more than that; I began to look at family life in the ghetto, at the way ghetto children, be they bussed to white schools or not, get along and play and talk and dream and question things and grow and think about themselves and their future. And on the white side of town I began to have similar interests. How do so-called working-class or lower-middle-class white families live and view the world and plan ahead? What do the children in such families believe their future to be? How do those children feel about black children when all of a sudden they have them as classmates; and how do the children of both races manage together in the classroom, in the school yard, and outside the school — say, near the street corner where the bus stops to let off or pick up black boys and girls? Are there certain concerns and habits and values that characterize people whose skins are white and incomes range from, say, about seven or eight thousand dollars to ten or twelve or thirteen thousand a year? How do those families (white collar, blue collar, all the sociological labels) differ from poor black families or better-off white ones — differ in ideas preached, customs practiced, beliefs affirmed and taught to children?[6]

More specifically, for the last five years before I sat down to write these words I had been visiting ten black and ten white families in Boston. Sometimes once a week, sometimes twice a week I would go to homes, sit and talk with parents, talk with children, play with them, ask them to draw and often draw or paint myself as they draw or paint. At times I would meet with several sets of parents for a talk about their children, their neighborhood problems. At times I would meet with schoolteachers, who have their own views not only about the children they teach, but the families those children belong to. And, needless to say, when one keeps coming to a home or an apartment house, one gets to know others: neighbors and friends and relatives. One also gets to know the spirit of a street, a block, a section of a city. One is taken to stores, introduced to passersby — people of significance, people respected, people feared, people admired, people hated, people deferred-to but behind their backs scorned.

A year after some thirty children were bussed out of Roxbury to one school well across the city of Boston, hundreds of other children were bussed to various Boston schools ("white schools," the black children sometimes called them), and two years later a number of suburban towns and villages became involved in a fairly large-scale bussing program which affected additional hundreds of black children and white children by the thousands who for the first time found themselves at school with children unlike themselves not only with respect to skin color but "socioeconomic background" — a phrase I kept on hearing a number of proudly "progressive" or "liberal" parents use. If those parents were glad to have their children at school with black children, and indeed, rather quickly welcomed black children to their fine suburban homes, then how did the black children who visited such homes, often with their parents, come to feel about themselves as guests, or come to feel about all they saw and heard for the first time in the different world — "the new, unexplored continent" a twelve-year-old black girl put it with a wry mixture of appreciation and scorn? In return, how did suburban white children, in contrast to white children from more modest homes located within the city's limits, find themselves getting on with their new classmates?

To find out the answers, some of them at least, to those questions, I extended my observations. As more and more buses were put into operation, I rode them. I talked with more children of both races, and I did so in a range of neighborhoods that extended from the very heart of the ghetto to some upper-middle-class towns many miles away. Those latter observations and interviews, those conversations with parents and teachers as well as children, have continued through 1970, when I wrote these words, and will continue, I hope — because the kind of work I do has to make up "in depth" for its obvious shortcomings, some of which had better be stated right now just as they have been set forth in the preceding two volumes of this series: no statistics are offered here, no graphs or charts, no surveys of attitudes or beliefs, nor is a "representative sample" with respect to this or that "variable" to be presented and analyzed. I have not used questionnaires. I have no percentages of anything to give anyone. I have no idea how accurately the children discussed here, and indeed the children who speak in this book, reflect the way various other children, millions and millions of them, think and feel and talk. I have no "conclusions" or "findings" to offer, either. I have simply tried to know as best I can twenty families, ten white and ten black; and at the same time I have talked with other children, rich ones and poor ones, black and white ones, twice a month rather than every week. And I have tried to continue with a small number of families (and teachers and principals and neighbors) the same long period of time, though after five years the visits have become less frequent, and now that I am beginning to work in the Southwest I shall "drop by" only occasionally, as indeed I have been doing with the southern families I know since I moved North.

All of this work can be called an application of the clinical method — which assumes that an intensive study of a relatively small number of individuals can shed some light, a little light, on matters that many of us are concerned with in one way or another: the emotions and purposes and beliefs that make us human beings. All of this work can also be called an example of what Anna Freud keeps on urging upon us child psychiatrists: "direct observation."[7] If we would only truly watch and hear children, be alert to what they want to do, the playing they do, the drawing and painting they do, we could learn not only about their daydreams, their fantasies, their obscure or at least unstated strivings or doubts, but also about their more outward attitudes and feelings, which so often are explicitly there, waiting to be recognized by the rest of us, who are so convinced of what is right or best or possible for "them," the children. "I wish every once in a while the teachers would stop trying to get us to say what they want us to say, and let us just say what we think is important." The child who said that is no social or educational critic, no advocate of "black power" or the "white backlash." She is nine years old; she gets C's in most of her subjects, and is quiet and unassuming. To be honest, for two years I privately rated her "average," or maybe a little less than that. Yet slowly I was privileged enough to notice things about her, things she did and said and asked. I am not about to call her a hidden genius whom the world will someday have to stop and take notice of. I must insist, however, that I have unfairly judged her. I have denied her a range of possibilities, a range of sensibility, that she has possessed right along. I have failed to recognize how alert she is to the duplicities and evasions of those who question her, how shrewd and resourceful she is in spite of her apparently bland and conventional exterior. Once she told me this: "I think a lot of teachers decide about you by the first week. Then you're lucky or you're unlucky."

She spoke like a tough, tired, fatalistic philosopher, who knows life's ironies and disappointments and wants only to "get along" as best she can. But her mind has dozens of surprises for such as me, with my notions of "average" or "ordinary." I will talk some more about Laura in another section of this book. Without prejudice to other modes of inquiry, which have their own purposes and value, if we are to know certain things about Laura as a girl, a white student at a school with black students, an American citizen who with others is caught up in a social and political struggle, then we had better at least try to earn her confidence, and somehow get beyond a few of the masks she uses both knowingly and unwittingly.

So, in the cities as in the rural South and in Appalachia, it has been a matter of going to homes and schools and seeing people who are not patients, who have no reason or interest or inclination (and often enough lack the money and the time needed) to visit a doctor in his office, a child psychiatrist in a clinic or a hospital setting. They are not to be called "sick" people, or people in need of "help." They are to be considered, above all, citizens — not "neurotics" or "antisocial" or "conformist" or "authoritarian" or "delinquent" or "aggressive," but American citizens who are taking part in a social crisis which, for their nation, is a historical crisis.[8]

Needless to say, I have disguised names and a host of other facts that might make it possible to identify particular children or particular adults. I have, as always, edited taped interviews, interrupted them for my own comments, and tried to give a degree of intactness and concreteness and structure to the remarks made, the attitudes proclaimed, the experiences described by various individuals. I have in previous books described the problems that have to be weighed as one goes about doing or giving such an account or narrative. What words, what sentences, what idiomatic constructions are to be used? Who will read the book? What knowledge can be assumed on the part of those readers? And anyway, what is the purpose of a book like this one? I suppose in the end the writer has to make his own decision, then try to justify what he has done. Certainly he owes it to the reader at least to clarify the nature of the effort, so that if there are disappointments and omissions ahead, there is at least given at the outset some reason why. I am in my everyday work a social anthropologist, a pediatrician, a child psychiatrist, a teacher and a friend, a visitor and a welcome guest, a busybody and a nuisance somehow to be tolerated and endured and (at last!) sent off with a sigh of relief or worse; but in this book I am only an observer who is trying to make both himself and the people he has spent time with as intelligible as possible. My main hope is to convey directly and simply what I have heard and seen, and I hope the reader will be able to understand what I am getting at — perhaps an obvious wish for any writer.[9]

Wishes, however, often go unfulfilled, and so it has seemed to me wise to avoid turning this book into a word-for-word tapescript, or even a slightly or heavily edited version of the same thing. If I am to bring alive as best I can the presence of certain people, the things they *don't* say, and the things they do say but in their own time and in ways I have only to some extent comprehended over many years, then I myself had best assume the responsibility of speaking. I therefore do not speak for particular people, nor do I speak as a translator; essentially I am speaking to the reader as an observer and writer. All of which is, anyway, what I was told to do by a young black man who doesn't see the reason I get into this kind of a "fix," and by that he means a muddled, wavering, uncertain, worried, long, talking spell: "You tell it. You tell it. I'm not going to speak to anyone out there. That's not my business. To Hell with them. You've been coming out here — and Christ knows why! I mean it's all right, man, it's all right. We know you. But don't go giving my voice to them over there, to listen to. Because if I'd known I was going to have a crack at them, I'd have told them off, man would I! If you're going to get their ear, though, don't use me. They turn away from us. Isn't that the truth? Don't they always? Who listens to the poor man? Who listens to the black man?"

When I told him that some people do, some people want to,

ought to have the chance to listen, he didn't hesitate long before he had a reply: "Sure, sure they do. We've always entertained them. Sure they listen. They smile. They'll even cry for us. They like having us around to think about every once in a while — so they can shake their heads and say isn't it too bad, the way they look and how they dress and the way they talk. That's what I heard a teacher say once. She said she was all in favor of us, and it was too bad that we make such a bad impression, because we say the words wrong and we use all these terrible, terrible words, and we don't *speak up,* that's what she said real loud, that we mumble all the time. I was going to scream at her. I was going to say, 'You said it, sister, but one day you'll hear us shouting, oh boy will you, and it won't be the old Uncle Tom words we've been whispering in your goddam ears all the time.' But I pretended I didn't hear what I heard."

We shall hear more from him later on — in a section called "I am Black and Nothing Else." What he warned me about, a white youth also warned me about — if not in the same way, at least with the same idea in mind: "I've been talking with you, but I don't recollect what I've been saying all this time, and I'd hate to think someone isn't keeping track — I mean you. The trouble is that up here in the city there's no one paying us any attention, none at all. We should try to talk to the teachers, but they won't listen; I don't believe they will. If I thought they'd listen, maybe I'd try. But I know they won't, I do. That's why I wish you'd go try and tell people what you've heard and what you believe the story is. You go talk with all the people you can find. Then you let me know what you hear. But be honest; if they're not speaking sense, don't go telling yourself they were."

I believe those two youths, one black and born in rural Louisiana, one white and born among the mountains of West Virginia, both now living in northern cities, were telling me essentially the same thing. Although I had sought them out and heard them speak, still, I had left my world to enter their world. Even when I was with them for hours, having been with them many times before, we each of us had to fumble and stumble with words and silences, because it is not easy to come and go from one world to another. Nor is the issue always one of suspicion, fear, distrust, racial hate, middle-class arrogance, or that sacred cow of a word, "communication" — which is supposed to be, like almost everything else, a "problem." No, it wasn't that we didn't "communicate," or that we had a poor "relationship." Nor was the issue words, my choice of words in contrast to a child's, a youth's, a parent's, a teacher's, a bus driver's. In a sense, the issue is the purpose of these words rather than their accuracy. I think that both as a writer and a clinician my purpose has been to distill here, emphasize and expand there, and present what seems to be, so far as I can humanly tell, *some* truths about *some* lives I have been able to watch unfold.

I hope the reader will pick up certain nuances of language, a certain tone that comes across in a speaker, at once individual and the result of his or her particular kind of upbringing. I could easily have kept a number of dramatic or idiomatic expressions in the narrative and gone on to make a great deal out of them, to "explain" their meaning. But again, I believe that the people who speak in this book have wanted, when all is said and done, to give me, as one mother put it, "something to go home and think about," to mull over in my own words. In any event, much of the narrative in this book and in the previous two volumes of *Children of Crisis* comes across as a mixture of what I heard others declare and what I hear my own mind speak. That is to say (and I find it hard to be exact here, as hard as it is to write down how one goes about writing) I have inevitably had to choose from interviews, choose among sentences and paragraphs, choose from a host of experiences. How can I capture on paper the blues I have heard sung, the spirituals, the jazz talk, the silence that more than words is part of the drug scene, the guitar music, the hillbilly songs, the spirit with which an ever-so-proper teacher says what is unexceptional in print but to a child is devastating? Conversely, how can I arrest the marvelous gestures or looks and glances or uses of emphasis in a sentence that in sum can mean reassurance and so much more to a child? The answer, naturally, is that one tries; and ultimately, as I was warned by those two youths, one is left with their words and thoughts, their voices, the drawings and paintings of their younger brothers and sisters, the views their parents or teachers or friends or enemies may have to offer — but all of that filtered through my own head, my own life, my own background and standards and beliefs and purposes. Much of this may be thoroughly obvious, but it still has to be stated and discussed, because words like "research" or "tape-recorded interviews" or "participant-observer" or "clinical investigation" or "the methodology of psychoanalytic inquiry" can not only intoxicate a writer, but more insidiously, those words can also affect the reader and cause him to expect either too much or too little — too much in the way of "conclusions" and too little in the way of acknowledgment by the writer of his mistakes or handicaps or professional limitations. I believe that books like this one can only be as successful as the questions they provoke, the second thoughts they encourage, the doubts they stir up, the firmly made-up minds they undo, jolt a little.

I hope I can convince a few readers that our cities contain poor people who are not fools and are not to be fooled with, people who submit but don't acquiesce, who surrender completely but can catch fire with pride and indignation and an eloquence all too many of us would recognize only with raised eyebrows or a bitter look in another direction. I hope that the reader will make no easy allowances for me because I happen to be writing a book that has been prompted by a "long-term study"; but rather will ask himself, with respect to every single page of this book, what do I share with this writer, this doctor, and *therefore,* what are we both most likely never to know, never really to feel and experience in the living, breathing everyday way "those people" do? What was he after, and what did he learn? And maybe more important, of the assumptions, the conclusions that he no doubt had in his mind before he ever started his "research" what did he unlearn? What will he *not* be able to tell us about the people he claims to know, the people he has brought to our notice? What must those people have in their minds that they *cannot* say, maybe even to themselves?

There are other questions, too, for us to ask ourselves. Do we dare wonder whether our "enlightened" interest in "the poor" and our earnest curiosity about "them" matter very much — except, of course, to our own consciences? That is, what, if anything, will bring about a more equitable distribution of economic and political power in this nation? And do we dare face some of the more uncomfortable accusations that are also to be heard in the cities, along with the messages to be spoken in the pages ahead by various individuals? For example: "I have nothing against you, man. You can come here if he says he wants you to come and visit his brother. But he's stupid, and so is his mother, and we're all dumb, we're all *Negroes,* that's what — until we tell people like you to get the Hell out of here and leave us alone. To Hell with your studies! To Hell with the 'support' you people want to give us! To Hell with your alliances! To Hell with that goddam world of yours! You come here. You learn off of us. You get your audience, your white audience to listen. You become someone to them, the someone who knows about us — *us!* You tell people only what you know will get you ahead, make money for you. You don't tell them the truth. You tell them the white man's truth. And you get paid for doing it. You live off of us. And us, we're lucky if we live at all, if we stay alive."

To be sure he was being somewhat unfair and abusive, I can honestly say to myself, and by God mean it. Yet, it is interesting how social scientists will discuss and discuss, indeed virtually haggle over obscure if not insignificant issues, and then brush aside haughtily or with annoyed incredulity the accusations of a man like that — at the age of fourteen quite a man: on his own and sure of himself and able to take care of himself. Some of us will not dismiss him, not openly or directly; but we have our own ways of showing ourselves hurt, aggrieved, embarrassed — and underneath, just as bothered as more outspoken observers by the "irrationality" we have heard, the malevolence, the misdirected anger. James Lewis, at fourteen (I have to keep reminding myself), is poorly educated, and is badly in trouble with the law, and is a threat to black as well as white people, but he is also fiercely outspoken and "fast and clever as a jungle cat," as he has declared and proven himself to be. He makes me uncomfortable, which is just what he wants to do. I doubt whether the only explanation I find for my discomfort ought to do with *his* prob-lems, *his* arrogance and exploitative belligerence, *his* thoughtless-ness and presumptuousness and self-serving rhetoric. Discussions of "methodology" can so often become exercises in self-justifica-tion. And if one examines one's motives, and worries out loud about some of the accusations a youth like James Lewis makes, one can then be called things like arrogant in a self-deprecating way or "masochistic" or God knows what. The fact is that we in the universities or medical schools or psychiatric training centers can be as ruthlessly ideological as James Lewis is — all under the veneer of our stated willingness to examine issues fully and speak with candor and self-scrutiny. As psychiatrists and psychoana-lysts, we even take pains to insist upon the latter, the obligation for constant and persistent self-analysis. Yet how automatically we fall into the habit of dismissing any really trenchant or pro-vocative attack upon our work and its underpinnings as a measure of the critic's state of mind — his "problems," his "resist-ances." Surely in the James Lewises of this world I can identify political hysteria, vengefulness, a capacity for distortion, and an ability to use dozens of irrational and sometimes even bizarre turns of phrase. But such qualities of mind and such polemical postures are also to be found in other worlds, including the edu-cated, white, middle-class world to which I happen to belong. What really matters is whether underneath it all, the noise and rancor and braggadocio, James Lewis doesn't have something to say, something that investigators like me simply cannot ignore.

"You can't know us. You're white and you can't know us." James Lewis also said that. I have told him I don't pretend to "know" him or indeed the many black children I work with. I have told him that I try to understand some, it can only be some, of the things on their minds, and that I believe I can manage to do that much, provided only I try to be honest and diligent, respect-ful and thoughtful and patient — admittedly not so easy for anyone, day in and day out. But no, he will not go along; for him the important thing about me is not the work I try to do, but the following facts of my life: I am white and my mother came to Boston from someplace called Sioux City, Iowa, and my father came to Boston from someplace called Leeds, Yorkshire, England, and they never have lived in ghettos and I never have and I grew up to expect things, to believe that what I wanted to happen to me in life would indeed happen, given my willingness to work — and the money my parents had which enabled them to pay my bills at college and at medical school. I need not go on at any more length; the thrust of the discussions and arguments I have had with James Lewis are not unfamiliar to many of us these days. The question remains, however — and has to be mentioned: what is invisible to me while I am sitting and talking with a child in a ghetto tenement in, say, Chicago? Often I am confident that such a question really means very little, that a child is, after all, a *child*, in addition to being a black child or a white child or a child of this or that parentage or background.[10] Moreover, I reassure myself, I am always keeping those "factors" (of race, class, nationality) in mind. Indeed, haven't I spent over a decade trying to do just such studies, ones that help us to know what growing up is like for children in social circumstances other than those a child psychiatrist like me usually sees?

Nevertheless, after the legitimate self-explanations are over and the rational affirmations have been made, one still wonders. How free can an observer like me be, free of dozens of obligations and assumptions that indeed deeply affect the way I put together what I see, interpret it, write about it? I will never quite be able to answer a question like that; we can never avoid being bound by the implications and continuity of the particular lives we have come to live. By "bound" I mean limited and to some extent denied vision — though also, naturally, allowed vision, too. I cannot myself know what it is I don't see, ignore, pass over, or else wretchedly misinterpret. That is for others to point out, and I would include among those others men like James Lewis. The reader should know before he comes to the remarks of Mr. Lewis that for obvious reasons I have shown him what I have done and obtained his explicit approval, so that at least I know I am offering in this book a thoroughly representative presentation of his ideas and sentiments. I think it fair to say that I am no personal enemy of his. He has insisted that I am a friend of sorts.

As a matter of fact, he can be as coolly abstract and impersonal as any ideologue or theoretician: I may be all right personally, but I am a self-centered and self-serving person who learns things, then profits enormously from what he learns, and satisfies whatever remorse or guilt he feels about his position in society, further enhanced as that position is by books like this, with the notion that he does "good," he educates the public, he brings things to light, he calls attention to awful circumstances that badly need correction and that perhaps will indeed get changed if only more and more gets written up, hence made available to people — because an informed and aroused public, so it is assumed, will somehow do something, will clamor for change, will insist that things be different in America. For James Lewis, though, such ideas are fantasies, pure and simple; or better, illusions necessarily held by me and my kind. For one thing, he says, books like this do precious little to change anything: "The only thing that will change my people's condition is their *acts*. We must act."

Nor does he merely pause after a remark like that. He stops and stays quiet long enough for me to get uncomfortable, to get his point: words and more words, from me or even from him, are empty substitutes for deeds. He will talk, though. He will argue. He is a self-taught, voracious reader. He never goes to school, but he reads. Some of what he reads I find to be full of black racism, full of reckless and apocalyptic talk. He himself has upon occasion smiled as I mention in my history-minded and factual way how incorrect this is and utterly wrong that is. But all of a sudden he will correct himself and tell me that what I call crazy and wrong makes a great deal of sense to him and others like him. His claim, I believe, at least deserves mention here, and has to be systematically confronted, as I will try to do later in the book. But the charges some people make, charges which characterize observers from "outside" as hopelessly blind and biased, self-aggrandizing and exploitative, must be respected from the outset and not self-righteously dismissed but kept in mind at every turn of one's work, on every page of one's notes.[11] I can only hope and try to prove that something other than what James Lewis says is true so far as this book goes.

In any event, this is the third volume to come out in the series called *Children of Crisis,* and I had better say that I do not stick to that title out of laziness or without a definite purpose. For James Lewis, as for his sharecropper grandparents and chronically unemployed and grievously disturbed parents (his father is an alcoholic and at this writing is dying of tuberculosis, and his mother has twice been in a mental hospital with a diagnosis of "schizophrenia, paranoid type") life is a constant crisis, which may mean that the word "crisis" is not literally appropriate. Still, he once said to me: "I go from trouble to trouble, but I try to keep my cool, and I do, let me tell you, I do. If there's something in your way, you get around it. You plan. You keep on your toes. You don't let the latest bad thing get you down, because sure enough it won't be but a minute before you've got a new thing, a new thing on your back to shake off." So he gets his next meal, and fights his way through the street scene, and covers himself with blankets on a cold night in a building that for some reason doesn't get heated. I believe he knows, if he doesn't ever use it, what the word "crisis" means, knows it in ways I cannot know, which is, I recognize, one of his points, and a substantial one it is.

Who, then are the "children of crisis" in this book? They are, as already indicated, black children from ten families in Boston and white children from ten families in Boston, all of whom I have been visiting at home or riding to school with on buses or observing in school — for six years it is as I write these words. They also include other children: boys and girls I knew in Appalachia and boys and girls I knew in the rural South. When their parents took them North, I went along. Three times I have been with a family as it packs up and leaves West Virginia, drives to Chicago, finds a place to live there, and tries to settle down, or "settle in," as they put it. And over the years I have come back, tried to see how things have gone, or at least see how the children and the parents feel things have gone. Four times I have gone through the same experience in the South, once in Alabama and three times in Mississippi: watched the family slip away from the plantation or the cabin in the woods or on the dusty road near town — and drive off, or get on the bus and take a seat and look out and say good-bye, not with words usually, but a look of relief and bitter joy and regret and sadness and triumph. (Who can dare single out any one of those emotions for exclusive mention?) When they get "up there," when *we* have done so, I could watch the effort to find a place, to "get located," and maybe upon occasion help. Meanwhile, for the children, be they black or white, their memories of what is gone soon begin to mingle with their everyday realization of what "city living" is like. For a while they are self-conscious enough to use expressions like that one, but eventually "city living" ceases to be called anything, because life simply *is* — except for those who have to sort things out and apply all kinds of words and names and labels to what goes along, moves along, happens, or again, *is*.

So, I am writing here about families just arrived in our northern cities from the rural South and Appalachia and families long settled in those cities. I am writing about some of the same families in Volume II of this series, families that stopped living as "migrants, sharecroppers, mountaineers" and instead took themselves to the distant shores of New York's streets, or Chicago's or Boston's — hence *The South Goes North*. And I suppose in a way I am writing about the rest of us, still in the cities or nearby in suburbs, but apprehensive and angry and confused and sympathetic and earnestly trying to be of help. I have decided to leave intact yet another discussion of "method," which the reader will encounter in Chapter VIII, because this book offers, in addition to a write-up of the day-to-day kind of research just described, a report upon a separate study I did during 1967 and 1968 which, as mentioned in the preface, was published by the Potomac Institute as *Teachers and the Children of Poverty*. I made that study, as I did some of the work in Tennessee and North Carolina which was mentioned in Volume I of *Children of Crisis*, because I felt it was important for me to go all over the country and talk with children other than the relatively small number I see so frequently, so intensively. By going to urban school systems in every region of America I could more briefly test on children and their teachers some of the impressions and opinions and ideas I have been gradually coming to. Likewise, I went to Cleveland in 1966 to do a study for the United States Commission on Civil Rights.[12] There I talked with black and white children and their teachers and their parents — again, in hopes of learning whether school desegregation was working, but also in order to see how black children in the city's Hough region and white children "across the way" (as one black girl kept putting it) looked at a whole range of things: their schools, their neighborhoods, their very future as American citizens. At a public hearing I presented to the commission the words of those children and also their drawings.

This book, then, comes from those two studies, for the Potomac Institute and the Civil Rights commission, from my work with rural people who have gone North, from my continuing work in Boston's Roxbury section with black families, from my continuing work in Boston's Hyde Park and Roslindale section with white "working-class" families, and from the interviews I have done in several suburban towns — which both depend upon Boston and keep their distance from the city, however near to it they are. I have tried, as I have in this volume's two predecessors, to present a wide range of children, and indeed to indicate that part of every child's world is made up of people the child himself may mention rarely if at all: a school principal or a fireman or a real estate owner or a druggist. Needless to say, the adults in a boy's or girl's life — the parents and relatives and teachers — have to be part of any book that tries to comprehend what those "crises" are that particular children face and struggle to surmount.

One more thing about "method" before the book itself can be allowed to develop: in each volume of this series (and one more is to come) I have gone through a discussion somewhat similar to this — that is, told about the work done, its manner or style or nature; and each time I did so the issue of my "objectivity" or "subjectivity" came up, as did the question of my own position, my own values and beliefs, the degree to which I am, as some put it, a "participant observer." I have discussed all of this before and elsewhere.[13] I have tried to see all that I can see; I know I can do no more, and I hope I have done no less. In 1967 the girl Laura, whom I have already mentioned in this chapter, asked me two questions I often hear from the children I work with: "Why are you coming here and visiting us? Is it your job?" She listened gravely to my reply. Then she spoke up: "You mean you want to learn about us, so then you can be our friend, and then you'll go and try to tell other people to be our friend, because you'll tell them they *should* be."

Alas, it is not quite possible for me to do what she surmised I have in mind as a purpose. One cannot so easily win friends for people, nor at times persuade oneself that everyone being visited is a friend, wants to be a friend or indeed is to be desired as a friend. But one can try to learn, and that way try to come as close as possible to the people who are one's teachers; and then, as Laura said, one can try to "tell other people," tell them as much as is possible, and perhaps let them decide about matters of friendship or advocacy or partisanship. At times I have indeed felt myself close to some of the people I write about in this volume. Yes, I have become "involved" with them; maybe even "participated" with them as they met and talked and took action on behalf of their children's education, their children's right to decent medical and dental care, their children's right, actually, to live and grow. But mostly it's been the first thing Laura mentioned, learning from her and many other teachers of all ages. I only hope that work has measured up, in breadth and subtlety, to the day-by-day growth the children in this book have demonstrated, the awareness and discretion and humor and seriousness and common sense they continue to possess, and learn to exercise, often enough against great odds indeed.

PART TWO

THE PEOPLE

III

BLACKS IN THE CITY

1. *I Am Black and Nothing Else*

H E is tall and very thin, so thin that at times I would remember the anatomy I studied in medical school and try to figure out how his lanky, almost threadlike body could possibly hold all those bones and muscles and vital organs I knew must be somewhere under his skin, all inside him. He is fast-moving, too. Long-limbed and lithe, he declares himself able to disappear from anyone's sight "faster than it takes to pronounce my name or where I was born." He laughs when he says that, because he knows he has three names as well as a last name: Thomas James Edward Robinson. His father had three brothers by those names, and they all died before they ever grew up; so, when he was born after four girls, his father decided not to take any chances at all: "He gave me all his brothers' names, and used to tell me that I'd better stay alive, and he meant it." As for Tom's birthplace, it was in Opelousas, in St. Landry Parish, Louisiana, that he was born in 1955. Let people try to say his full name or pronounce "that place" in Louisiana; Tom is sure he can "clear away" before they finish.

Is he a runner? Is he on some track team — perhaps at high school? Is he trying to keep himself in good condition? Three no's and a yes: he doesn't go to school; he would never call himself a runner; and he has never been on any "team," but he very much wants to be in shape. He doesn't exercise formally or methodically. He simply races down the street, "flies down," as the younger children on the block say. He is a hero to them, the seven- and eight- and nine-year-old boys who live in the tenement house he lives in. They are all bunched together, those tenement buildings. They don't stand near one another or lean on one another; they are in fact one thick continuous stretch of brick, and only the end of the block puts an end to them. But as soon as the next block starts one is back with the same problem: which entrance is what number of what street. Minds like mine for a while cannot stop doing things like that, trying forever to figure out what Tom's *address* is, what number it is — or was, before some "vandal" ripped off all the numbers on the entrances. Finally I did learn to relax. Tom told me to relax. He told me to feel my way down the block. He told me to stop looking lost when I saw each time that there were no numbers to be found. He told me to stop counting the entrances from the corner until I came to his, near the middle. How did he know I was doing that, counting and counting? I wasn't talking out loud, I knew that, and I wasn't moving my lips. Of course I wasn't; *he* knew that, too. The giveaway was my face; he could tell by the frown on my face: "Your face was just working too hard, man, concentrating too much. That's all." I suppose it is a curse of mine that I couldn't relax then and there and smile and tell him: right, right. Nervous and cerebral, and in a way silently rude, I had to take note of his "intuitive" nature, his dislike of details like street numbers, his ability to do things without seeming to try.

I did learn eventually to walk down that block somewhat casually and knowingly. I was taught to do so by the boys and girls I came to visit. Another thing I learned from the younger children on that block had to do with Thomas James Edward Robinson, formerly of Opelousas, St. Landry Parish, Louisiana, and now of Roxbury, Suffolk, Massachusetts. The children call him T.R., sometimes Tom, but never Tommy. He bristles when he hears himself called Tommy, though the teachers used to do it all the time and he never used to mind until he was thirteen or so; until he began to awaken, began to realize what the world is like and what his people are struggling for and what "that name Tom means." He is not, however, without humor when he talks about such matters. He doesn't dislike the name Tom or Tommy in and of itself. He simply feels sensitive about the meaning the name has come to have, especially these days. Actually, he feels sensitive about a lot of things. He doesn't at fifteen know exactly what to do with his feelings.

"I know some of the little kids look up to me," he says, but then he makes a dramatic turn, a reversal in his line of reasoning: "It's not me they turn to, though. It's not. They're no longer Negroes, who find a boss and obey and *obey*. You see that? When you live up here and you're my age, you've been doing some learning, and not in school, and you've been doing some figuring out, and not with the help of any white teacher, or Negro teacher. You've discovered something. You've discovered that either you stand up and think for yourself and be free, or you're a slave, just like we were before, down there in the South. You're either black or you're nothing at all. I am black and nothing else; if I'm not black I'm nothing. You can't be a Negro and be anything but a tool of the white man's. That's what we're learning. That's what we've got to learn, or else it'll be no good, *no good*. They'll just keep on walking all over us. They always have. They still do. Why should they stop, unless we make them stop, *make them stop?*"

He does that often; he says something emphatic, then repeats himself, word for word, even more emphatically, and I am then half ready for a third repetition, but it never comes. He wants me to know that he has his convictions. He wants to know himself that there are convictions he has and will keep and not lose, no matter what the temptation, no matter how sad or lost or grim he might someday feel. And he has seen that in others, in older men — "the defeat in them." He talks about that defeat a lot: "You've got to know that you may never win, not with us outnumbered. If you fight, though, you're winning right there. The only way you can lose is to be an Uncle Tom. That's the way they get you; the way they always have. I used to sit there in school and the teacher would ignore us and be ready to insult us no matter what we said, and I'd take it, man, *I'd take it*. They had me believing I was no good, *no good*. They had me ready to go scrubbing their floors, and opening their doors, and washing their cars. That's what they want us for. They've always needed us to do their dishes and carry their trash away.

"The black man is waking up. I hear my brothers talking all the time. We're brothers and sisters, all black men and all black women. The kids on this block, they've got to be black, *black*. I laugh with them. I kid them. I say, 'Oh, I think I see a big patch of white on you.' Then they'll laugh back. They'll say they see a little speck of white on me, too — a speck over here, and a spot over there. So, I've got to watch out, too. They're right. You can't just shake off your people's past and start fresh. I heard a man, he knew Malcolm X, say that the other day. He said, 'Brothers, it takes time to get yourself free.' He said, 'You can't free yourself of the white man until you free yourself of the Negro you carry around inside yourself.' Now there's something to remember. I told some kids that; they were playing on the street, and I called them and they came running over. I told them what I'd heard. I told them Malcolm X, he lived right here in Roxbury, and he knew; he knew like no one else has. They all said I was right, but they wanted to get back playing. I can't blame them. I like pool better than anything. I like motorcycles. If I had the money, I'd get on one and I'd never stop. I'd drive until there was no more land left for me to drive on. I'd drive up every road in the world. Do you think anyone has tried it? I'd grab me a sandwich and eat on the bike. I'd sleep by it and keep moving. But you have to have a fortune to own a motorcycle. You have to get rich. And like that man said, the friend of Malcolm X, when you try to get rich you either find you can't, or you start climbing all over your own people and kicking them and shoving them and knocking them down and pushing, *pushing*."

He uses those last two words, that word "pushing," both literally and figuratively. He is speaking of the elbowing that a man on the make, on the rise, can demonstrate. But, of course, he is also talking about drugs, about the pushers he knows and every day watches, sees at work. They do well, make a great deal of money, and tempt him. Nor does he need anyone to point out that last fact, that psychological fact. He knows the facts of envy, rivalry, greed. He knows that people have to deny what at the same time they are drawn to do. He knows the mind's struggles, and in a straightforward and unpretentious manner he can talk about them, even explain the particular ways he has come to deal with such difficulties: "Who can say no to them? The dealers here, the pushers, they've told me I'm a smart boy. That's what they call me, a boy. They say I'm a natural born leader, and there's a place for me in that setup. They say I can be the closest thing to a millionaire I'll ever see. They say I can carry around as much cash as my pockets will hold. They say I should just say yes, and they'll start me out. I can get pants with pockets that stretch down to my shoes, and they can guarantee they'll be filled up with dollar bills, those pockets, before I'm a year older. They're fooling. I know they are. But they make plenty. I would have cash, a lot of cash. We could move to a better building. I could get the bike I want. I could drive up and down this street on the biggest motorcycle you'll ever see.

"I told my dad, and he said he'd kill me first, rather than let me do that. I told him he was a real square guy. He got mad. Then I told him to cool it, *cool it*. I told him I was fooling him, trying to trick him. I just wanted to get his reaction, that's all. I wanted to see what he'd have to say. He didn't believe me at first, though. He thought I was just backing down because he was so mad, and I was scared. He thought I was really trying to con him. But I wasn't, and finally I made him believe me, I made him. I shouted. That's the way he knew I was serious. I told him what I believe. He didn't like what I told him, but he said so long as I don't become a pusher, he won't care what I believe — about being black, you know. I told him he should care, he had to care. I told him the reason I wasn't becoming a pusher. I said if I didn't think it was better to be black, to be a black man, than to be a pusher — well, then I'd go and be a pusher. He couldn't follow me. He kept telling me he couldn't follow me. I didn't know what I could say to him. I thought to myself: it's Louisiana, it's the state of Louisiana that's in his head, and he can't get it out. He'll see a white man and he begins to move out of his way,

the Man's way, but he doesn't. He's learned. He's stopped doing
what he did down there. But it's in him; I can tell. My grandmother, she says I'm wrong. She says you can't do it, fight the
bossman. She still calls them that. I said we have to, or else we'll
be slaves. She said she was never a slave. Then I decided I'd
better shut up. But she wouldn't stop. She said all I was trying to
do was see the bad side, *the bad side.* I said no, that wasn't true.
She said I had no faith. I said how could I, looking around and
seeing what I did. Then she recited her Bible.

"But my father is glad I'm no pusher, and so is my mother and
my grandmother. They don't care whether they're called black or
Negro or anything. My father told me I could call him white if I
wanted to. He said I could even call him an Uncle Tom. He was
setting us up for a fight. He was kidding. He works in a car wash.
He hates the white man. Usually he says he doesn't, but once in a
while he'll come home dead tired; and then he admits it — that
they bleed us, *they bleed us white.* He's bled white, for sure he
is, by the time he's ready to go home. All day he's heard his boss
tell him to hurry up, move fast, keep on it, stop delaying — and
work, work, work. He's the hardest-working man that ever lived.
You should see his muscles. When I was a little kid he used to
tell me that the colored child, that's what he'd say, the colored
child is born with big, big muscles, because there's the cotton to
pick and everything else the white man needs doing. You think
he was fooling? No sir, he sure wasn't fooling. He'd be serious.
He'd be trying to clue me in. He'd be telling me so I wouldn't be
surprised later on. I recall asking him about why it is that the
white people on television seem to be the big shots, and we have
nothing. I asked him if there are a lot of black people with big
money, and if there are, why don't we see them on the television.
I don't know how old I was then; I know I asked him, I know.
And I can tell you what he said. He said white is white and
colored is colored, and the whites own the world, most of it, and
the colored don't and that's the way it is, and no one can go and
do anything about it, and maybe the second time around, in the
next world, it'll be the opposite, and won't that be good — a
relief, a big relief. My poor dad, and all the poor Negroes, waiting for the second time around, *the second time around!*"

He has gone to work with his father upon occasion, but finds it
an impossible job. The whites come in, one after the other in one
big new sporty car after the other, and his father washes, washes,
washes. He wonders at his father. Where's the man's anger? How
can he take it, all day long take it? How can he let himself be
ordered around so, treated so abruptly and imperiously? How
can he *not* think of becoming a pusher himself? The man must
have his secret thoughts, his dreams of triumph and glory. He
must — yet he apparently doesn't; or so T.R. believes. And he
has indeed tried to find out: "I've asked him, I've said tell me, tell
me why you and I and every other black man doesn't go after
them, jump them, get them out of our lives for good. He told me
to shut my mouth up and not open it again until I got some sense
in my head. So, I didn't say anything the rest of the day. Then
after we finished supper you know what he said? He asked me if
I didn't like what my mother had gone and cooked for us. I said
yes I did, I always did. Then he said *that* was why he keeps his
cool: if he got wise and started fighting with the white man, he'd
soon be out of a job, and we'd have no money, and no food, and
we'd starve to death. 'Someday you'll have a family, son. You'll
know then; you'll know the difference between a lot of big talk
and what you've got to do if you want your wife and kids to eat.'
That's what he said, and I didn't even try to answer him. My
grandmother was nodding her head off, and I near got sick to my
stomach. I wanted to throw up that meal. I really did!"

For money he works in a grocery store, stocks the counters and
sweeps the floor. At least his immediate superiors are not white,
though the store is owned by whites, he knows that. He is
tempted to steal from the store. He is tempted to tell his boss —
the manager, "the front man," the Negro — to stop it, to stop
fooling himself and everyone else. But he is a young man, and
jobs for people like him are quite scarce, he knows that. And he is
afraid. If he were idle all day and penniless; if he had nothing to
do but sit around and stand around and have his dreams of
driving around in a motorcycle or a car; if he had to go wash cars
and be bossed by a white man and told he was lucky even to
have that job; or if he had to go back to school, in the unlikely
event a truant officer tracked him down and hauled him into

court for being under sixteen and so illegally out of school — if any of those things were to happen he might take to stealing regularly and maybe even pushing, yes maybe even that.

Indeed, he doesn't understand the patience other young men his age show. How can they be so indifferent to the world's injustices? How can they shrug their shoulders and laugh or shake their heads and then forget, all the time forget? Forget it, they tell him. Forget this and forget that he is urged. Why worry, they ask. What's the point, they declare rather than inquire. Why sweat it? Why lose your cool? Why get all hot and bothered and worked up and talkative, "full of speech," his friends will some-times put it. And more to the point, what can he actually do — that is, besides say all he does, and then repeat himself over and over again? The last question does indeed bother him. He knows that he can right now do very little. He is no Black Muslim, no Black Panther — not yet, anyway. He belongs to no organization, no club, no group or party. He isn't in his own mind agreed upon a course of action, a plan, a way of doing something, anything. He doesn't read much. He hears the radio. He watches television. He listens to records. He listens to older people talk. Then it all goes through his mind, the words and sights; and out of the experiences, the listening and seeing, come *his* idea, *his* view-point, *his* words: "I speak for myself and no one else. Can't a black man do that? Can't they let us be different, each one of us? I hear on the television that the black man thinks this way, and he says this, and here's what he believes on that score. I say that's not right; that's not *me* and that's not what I think. They're always trying to corner us, the white man is. But I do believe that today he's worried over us, he surely is.

"I think it was the last day I went to school that I heard my teacher lose his temper and say he was sick of us, sick as he could be and fed up, because he couldn't figure out what it was that we wanted; and we were driving him crazy, he said. I'm mixed up myself. I mean, I don't know how we can beat him or drive him crazy, Mr. White Man. He's holding all the strings, Whitey is. And he's got a lot of us scared. A Negro is a scared black man. I'm scared but I'm not a Negro. You want to know why? It's

because I'm saying it, right here and now: I'm scared, but I'm
not going to turn into a Negro over it. I'm going to be black. I'm
going to look for ways to outfox Whitey and I'm going to go fight
him when I can win. 1 tell the kids — I say look: don't go fight
with those white teachers. They'll come down hard on you.
They'll have you over at the police station in five minutes. They
have cops right inside the schools now; and those cops are just
waiting for the teachers to say go ahead, go ahead and get them.
That's why you have to be careful. I agree with my dad on that;
you've got to watch your step."

He does watch his step. He keeps an eye out for the police.
They make their rounds, drive up and down the street; and all
the while he looks at them and mutters or swaggers and smiles in
an angry, mocking way. Or he may simply turn his back on them,
go inside, get out of their sight. He loves to run and pretend he's
on a motorcycle and watch the buildings go by and the street
lamps and the people and the stores and buses. But when the
police are around he never runs. He stands still, or he quietly and
unostentatiously retires into the background. He is convinced
that if he were seen running by the police he would be arrested
immediately on suspicion of stealing something, doing something
wrong. He is convinced that they would not stop him and talk
with him and ask him questions. They would grab him and
maybe beat him but certainly take him away and hold him and
not easily let go of him: "They see a guy like me running, and
they go click, click, click in their heads, and I come out a crook, a
robber. Where's your knife, they ask. Where's your razor blade,
they ask. I see the manager of the store punching that cash
register and I think to myself that the police have a cash register
in their heads, and there's a button called 'nigger' on it, and every
time they see a black man, they push the button and the same
answer comes out — go get him, fast. If I had a motorcycle, I'd
like to see them go get me. I'd give them a chase."

Until that day comes, he gives others a chase. He runs against
anyone who wants to challenge him; and so far no one around
has done so successfully. He has speed. He has staying power.
He runs effortlessly, too. He seems to be enjoying himself as he

moves along, not trying hard, not running out of breath, not running down minute by minute, just running. The children watch, and they run, too. They run to catch him, to be near him when he does stop, so that they can listen to him panting, and no doubt thereby prove to themselves that he is, after all, human and he does tire and he does have to stop and he does need rest. So, they hover close and he laughs and jokes with them and they ask him where his motor is (where *is* it?) and he says he'll be damned if he'll let them in on the secret, no sir. Then they fall to talking about other things: what they did and did not do in school, and what they would like to do "later on" when they get big, and what they think *he* should be doing and what *he* thinks he should be doing.

They are bittersweet conversations, the ones he and his young admirers have. He is struck by the innocence of younger children, the still undampened hopes they have — for him as well as for themselves. He tries to recall whether he was like that, so buoyant and optimistic, so full of gall almost. Yes, he decided, he probably was. He is too young to remember the trip north from Louisiana, but he does have in mind a time when he told his father he wanted to fly airplanes and even make them — have his own factory, so to speak. His father laughed, and he didn't like the way his father laughed. He felt both annoyed and curious. *Couldn't* he someday own an aircraft company? No, he was told, and don't get such silly, crazy ideas any more.

Soon he stopped having those ideas. Now he tells young boys and girls not to waste their time with idle dreams. They've got to build themselves up, he says. They've got to know how to run, run as fast as they can. They've got to be quick of mind, too. True, he himself falters upon occasion, lapses into reveries: he is a junkie; he has a million dollars; he can run for miles, run until he drops into a pool of his own sweat, and by God, the pool is still on his land, on land he owns outright, on land that stretches as far as the eye can see, as far as his body will go. He will go on further, think of the motorcycles, the cars, the Mustangs and Cougars, and think of the suits and shirts and shoes and coats, think of everything a young *American* thinks of.

I have said so, told him I thought he was more a citizen of this nation than he believed, and in reply he has said I am hopelessly white and he is thoroughly black and that is that. Then I mention television and the radio and how they cultivate common desires in millions of people; I mention the appetites and hopes I feel he shares with many others of his age, not just his race, in this big and rich country. Then he in turn has his say: "Sure I live in this country. They get to me when I see them driving in a car, the junkies do. So do the people on television; they say, go to your nearest dealer and get yourself a big new Buick, and I want to go. Only the trouble is I don't know that kind of dealer. I know the dealers we have around here: smack, smack, smack — heroin they call it on the TV news. I could be making two hundred a week or more, right now I could. I'm not religious like my grandmother, and I'm not scared like my parents are. I don't know why I hold back. I do, though; *I do.* I don't want to see us killed. You take drugs and you die. I see people sitting around; they're staring off into space and they aren't really alive at all. If I push drugs, I'll be killing them. That's how I see it. I wouldn't be able to run away from that — no matter how fast I run I couldn't.

"You have to believe in yourself. You can't be a pusher and believe in yourself. They have the cars, but they're no good. They're bad people. They're like a lot of your whites. They make a lot of money, and they don't care how, and they don't ask questions. They just go ahead and sell and sell and sell, and spend all they make to live it up. I couldn't do that. If I was arrested by a cop for selling smack, I'd say I should be, and I'd go along and take the prison sentence. A dealer once asked me what I'd do if I was hungry and didn't have a cent to my name. I told him I'd die, I'd sooner die than take his smack. I'd sooner die than sell it. A lot of my friends think the same way. You don't see them all taking drugs, do you? Some do, but a lot don't. It's not fair, the way they say we're all going to go on drugs when we grow up. That's what a teacher told us. That's right; that's what she said. I wanted to shout at her and tell her that I'm a black man, and I'm not going to take drugs, because that's the way we become weaker and weaker, and then the white man can just keep on doing anything he wants to us, anything."

Always the runner, also a fast talker once he gets going, bristling with anger at times, uncertain about his "future," unsure of himself despite all his pointed remarks and cutting observations, he is above all a deeply ethical youth. He is ethical in ways that defy words, his or anyone else's. As he once said: "I do what I do, and I believe my body pulls on me to stay clean and do the right thing. I don't know sometimes which is the right thing and which is the wrong thing, but all of a sudden I find out, and it's because there's something inside me that lets me know. I think it's in my chest, my heart maybe." *What* is in his heart? Why, the voice of his heart is in his heart, he says impatiently — as if an inheritance like that need be mentioned or discussed or asked after or pinned down by someone! And of course his impatience reveals his ignorance; for the fact is these questioners are indeed people who need to ask all sorts of questions and hear all sorts of wordy explanations before they can, finally, catch sight of the most obvious thing in the world, an ethical young man's effort to remain precisely that — no matter what and against all the odds.

2.   *To Hell with All of You*

Curses, threats, diatribes, oaths, warnings, one indecent or coarse word after another, they all come easily to James Lewis, who is *only* fourteen, someone like me cannot stop thinking to himself. He talks and talks, and if a listener hears him but does not look at the young man's extraordinarily expressive face, the temptation is to surrender or flee immediately to whatever sanctuary can be found. Nor is James (he will not be called Jim) unaware of all that: "I'm a big guy with words, I know. The black man has been listening to the white man's words all his time in this country, so it's good we're finally coming up with our own words. We've got to be rid of Whitey; everything's he's done to us has to be washed away, with the strongest soap we can find. It's the white man who has dirtied up everything: he's ruined the air and the water; he's exploded atomic bombs; he's killed the

Indians and made us slaves. He's been murdering and stealing for hundreds of years — and then when we try to stand up for our rights, he calls us thieves and hoodlums and everything else. The white man lives off the black man and the brown man and the red man. That's the truth. I don't hold it against any *one* white man; it's all of them — all of you."

I have to say it again: James Lewis is only fourteen years old, and he goes to school only fitfully. His father is dead. His mother is dead. He has no grandparents alive. He lives with an aunt, his mother's sister. His aunt tells the story directly and to the point: "James was born and a year later his mother died. She had an infection and it hurt her heart, the doctors said. There wasn't anything we could do to save her. They said if we'd brought her to the hospital right away she would have lived, but we had no way of getting her there, and I didn't know then that up here they'll take you even if you don't have any money. In Alabama it sure wasn't like that. They didn't have a 'city hospital' where we lived. James lost his father a year later. He was a young man, but they said he had high blood pressure. He fell dead, yes sir; it happened right in front of the little boy. He was two, yes sir. I lived across the street and the older children came over and told me their father was on the floor asleep, and they couldn't wake him. So, I took them all in: James and Henry and Lois and Florence. It's only James I have left of my sister's children. Henry is married. He can't find a good job. He didn't stay in school, like he should have. He was the only one born in Alabama. I told him once that he had that lazy South in him and he'd never amount to anything. Lois and Florence, they're working. I'm proud of them. Lois works downtown. She works an elevator. Florence works in a candy factory, yes she does. She makes candy all day! Can you imagine that? And she hasn't put on a pound so far as I can see, not one!"

As for James she worries about him. He is exceptionally smart, she knows that, and in fact he has always been a talkative person, a tough fighter of sorts, a child whom no teacher could ever quite bend to his or her ways: "They tried to tame him in school, oh did they! They smacked him and hit him, I know it. I did too; I had to, I just had to. The teachers called me in, and I did what I could. I tried to explain that I had my own children and my sister's, and it's been hard on me. Back South we were close, all of us brothers and sisters, but up here we've lost touch. My older sister won't take any part in helping out. She has no children, mind you. She's been married, I think, four or five times. I've lost track of the men, and I couldn't swear it was ever legal, the way she lives with those men. I'll get to know the guy, and then the next thing I'll hear there's a new one. James used to like her when he was very little. Now he hates her; he hates her so strong that I pray to God he never sees her. She lives away over from here, and I only see her when I go to see my brother, who's down the street from her. I never take James with me. He calls her the worst names. He says she sleeps with white men all the time — and he's right, I know it. But she's my sister. We were both born of the same mother and the same father, and we can remember where we grew up — Beatrice, Alabama; yes sir, that was the town, and we lived a mile or so down the road outside.

"I try to tell James about Beatrice and he won't listen. He only listens to the speakers, the people who want to build an army or something. I don't know — black, black, that's all those speakers say. I told James that in Alabama black was a bad, bad word to us; but it doesn't register on him, what I say. He likes to talk so much himself that he hasn't got the time for anyone else. I told my minister we'd better pray for that boy. He said yes; he said that the Panthers have got him, or some other people I've never heard of. I asked, what can we do? He said there wasn't anything we can do, except pray, and the harder the better, because there's a devil around up here, and he's getting his hands on our children, and turning them into mean, mean ones. So, every morning I hold up my hands and pray. I even tell James what I'm praying for. He laughs, of course."

James can indeed laugh. For all the strident, stern, unforgiving side to him, the young man also has a light and humorous touch, and it comes across his face rather than out of his mouth. That is to say, he can tell me things I will later think about with a great deal of sadness or apprehension or anger or whatever — while at the time his quick eyes and the sardonic tone of his voice and the smile, at once charming and challenging, all seem to soften somewhat remarks spoken in utter seriousness. "My aunt, she was good to me," he declares with a broad grin of approval. One begins to relax: today will be an easier day; he will be talking about his aunt, and if we can hold to that, have a more personal and warm-hearted conversation, we will not once again end up talking about racist America, racist America — to the point that he himself is exhausted and at a loss to know what can be done, after all his self-described "speeches" have been made. "She was the one who saved my life, I know that." Now the grin leaves his face, but he continues with affection and nostalgia: "She's the nicest woman you could ever want to know. She's my mother, you know. My mother died when I was a baby, and all I remember is my aunt. My father died, too; my aunt tells me I should remember him, because I was two when he passed, but I don't. I've had dreams: I've dreamed I was walking down this street, I don't remember what its name is, and all of a sudden a man comes up to me, he must be ten feet tall, as big as a building, and he says, 'James, I'm your father.' But I tell him I don't have a father. He picks me up, but I fight him off. I get down and run away. I hide, and he's looking for me, but he never finds me. He goes away and I'm glad. Then I wake up. Sometimes in the dream I try to get him arrested. I guess I think he's a crook, some kind of crook. But I don't want to turn him in to the police because they're even worse than any crook. I guess that's why he never gets caught or arrested. I always wake up first."

Then comes the beginning of a switch: "The trouble with my aunt is that she doesn't stop and question herself. She takes everything; she accepts all the troubles she's had, and she never wants to fight back. I've tried to talk to her. I love her. She's my mother, she's my mother. But she'll not listen to you, she really won't. She starts in with her mumbo-jumbo talk, about God and Jesus Christ and being saved, and the next world, and all that. She's drugged up, drugged with religion, don't you see. She's on drugs, just like all the other *Negroes*."

The word gets him going. Like Thomas James Edward Robinson, whose views have just been presented, James Lewis hates the word "Negro." But unlike T.R., who is slightly older, James Lewis has already committed himself to a life of intensely political activity. He does not know T.R.; he lives several miles away. He does know the difference between them, though: "There are a lot of cats around talking black these days. I'm not against them. It's good that we're all waking up. But it's one thing to talk black, and it's another thing to *be* black, and I'll tell you something: I'm not black yet. It'll take me all my life to get black. Do you see?"

I tell him that the answer is no, I don't quite see. All right; he is not in the least set back. Patiently and generously he will try to show me: "I can understand. You're you. I'm me. You try to know the black man, but you're lost before you ever start. You're looking through a white man's eyes. Here in America the black man is just being born. We're all Negroes; we've been Negroes ever since they brought us here. But a lot of us are through being Negroes. No more, no more, we say! And you'll see how we mean it. It takes a lot of time, though, if you're going to walk with your head up. Look at most black people; they walk with their heads down. I never noticed it myself until I heard a man speak and he told us that after we left the place, we should keep our eyes open and see how our people walk. So, I came home and nearly broke into tears right in front of her, my aunt. She goes and cleans up a white woman's house, that's the job she has. She washes the dishes and scrubs the floor and cleans the bathroom and she even has to help her, the bitch, get food ready for supper. What does the white woman do all day, I ask my aunt. Well, she has 'activities,' that's what my aunt says. She doesn't know which 'activities' they are, but she saw some letter and it was about the NAACP, and the woman was giving twenty-five dollars, twenty-five bills. I told my aunt to go and tell her to keep the goddam money. I told her to sit the woman down and say to her, 'To Hell with all of you, to Hell.' My aunt told me to shut up.

"But that's my aunt. She's been brainwashed. You can't change her. She's too old. Like I said, I came home and saw her, all stooped over, and I realized how right that man was: my aunt has been saying, 'Yes, yes' to the white man so long that her

whole body now does it, says, 'Yes sir, yes sir.' It hurts me more
to see her bending than to hear her talking about 'the good white
people.' *Which* good white people!"

He wants to fight a battle someday, take on all those 'good
white people' and beat them, beat them decisively, beat them for
good. He knows how to fight. He can use a knife, a razor blade,
and yes, a gun. The black man has to be armed; he tells me that
an unarmed black man is not a black man at all. The white world
spends billions of dollars arming itself, but when a black man
carries a pistol, everyone shudders, Negro and white alike. So it
goes — but so it must no longer be: "We can't always take it; we
can't always be on the weak side. We've got to be as strong as the
white man — stronger. I can't let the pigs scare me. They're
working for whites, every cop is. Sure there are Negro pigs. Who
said there aren't? You drive by the police station and you see
them, the white pigs and the Negro ones, they're buddies. Do
you think that fools us? A man has to be stupid to be taken in by
that trick. They hire a few Uncle Toms and march them up and
down our streets; then we're supposed to bow down and be
good, be real good. All the time my aunt used to say that: be
good, be real good. You know what she meant? She meant to do
whatever they tell you, the white teachers and the white police
and the white landlord and the white store people. Black people
live here, but it's the whites who own us. They'll always own us
until we stop them — and that means it'll come to a fight. It has
to be a fight. I've been fighting for a long time, but that was
wasting my time. The whites like it when we have our gangs and
beat up on each other: the more we hurt each other the weaker
we are, and the stronger they are, and the safer they feel. It's
easy to figure that one out!"

He constantly tries to figure things out, and when he does he
doesn't hesitate to speak out. If I try to tell him that he sees
things in too conspiratorial a fashion, he replies that I can afford
not to look underneath and see all the ugliness and meanness and
treachery which really do exist in this world. He doesn't quite say
it that way; indeed, he speaks eloquently and sharply: "If you
have an easy time; if you're rich; if you're on top; if the world is

always waiting on you — then sure you can look around and say everything is going fine, and what's the matter with all these people who keep on digging up trouble all the time. But if you're down, way down on the bottom, then you either learn the score or you're a slave. If you want to be a black man, a free man, you have to keep awake, wide awake. You can't miss the tricks. The white man has his tricks, and you can't fall for them."

I do not know how a young man of fourteen whom teachers have described to me as silent, sullen, disobedient, moody, a truant, "up to no good," of "limited intelligence," and yes, "possibly retarded" manages to be so alert, aware and articulate. He is a very shrewd youth, I can say — and yet somehow those words fail to do justice to him. Perhaps the point is that he has a highly developed political sensibility. He also has a sense of history, a sense of his own personal history and of his people's history. At fourteen many of us are thoroughly self-absorbed, hence indifferent to a host of political and economic "forces" or "pressures" that do indeed exert enormous influence upon everyone. In contrast, James Lewis is jolted out of himself every time he leaves school, leaves his aunt's house, leaves the particular neighborhood in which he grew up — and goes to a store, a clubhouse, a meeting place, where he listens to what most Americans would consider to be revolutionary talk. Yet, even before he became "politicized" (as some would put it, though he doesn't) there were those moments of awareness — and he can remember them and talk about them: "I'd be a kid, a little kid, and I'd look at myself in that old mirror. My aunt, she said she brought it up here from that town of hers in Alabama. I try to forget the name. I don't want to know all about her 'nice times' down there. She'll tell me about them and then she'll tell me that if they hadn't come up here, they all would have 'perished' — that's her talking and not me. So they came up here! A lot it did for them! She has that mirror, but she would often tell me she didn't want to look in it, because she was afraid she'd see her mother, because it was hers, the mirror was, and she used to look into it. You know who gave it to her mother, don't you? A white woman did. I told my aunt it was hers and not her mother's or that white woman's. She said yes, she knew. But she's tired, all the time she is, and she says that she wants to remember herself like she was a long while back and not like she looks now, all old. I'd go and stare at myself and I'd say to myself that no mirror is going to scare me, and I'll never be afraid to look into one, no matter if I live to be one hundred years old.

"I'd look at my skin. I'd look at my nose and my lips and my hair. I'm not ashamed to talk about it; no, I'm glad I can talk about it. Over at the office we make each other talk about how we look. We tell each other how we used to talk and what we used to say to ourselves in front of the mirror and what we say now. I used to think that if I could just hold my nose in, it would look different, thinner. I'd practice, tightening my lips up. My aunt said a lot of women get their hair straightened. She's never done it, but my other aunt, you can bet she does — for the white man! Today I can admit it! I used to think I'd look great if I had straight hair and if I could change my face. I wanted to be white. I didn't dare admit it then, even to myself. Once, though, I did. My friends here really make me admit it every day; but before I joined up, I admitted it to myself for a few minutes. I was in her room, my aunt's. I looked in her mirror. It's the only one we have. She keeps it beside her bed in a drawer. She's even got part of her ticket from Mobile, Alabama, to Boston in that drawer. Can you imagine that? She has a bus ticket from that far back! I looked in the mirror and I saw the same old face, and all of a sudden I thought it would be great if I looked like the kid my aunt talks about — he's in the place she works, the white woman's house. He's the white woman's son, and he's my age. I've never seen him. I've never seen a picture of him. All I know is that she says he's blond; so, when I looked in the mirror I dreamed I was him. I was a white boy with blond hair! I didn't really believe I was, but for a few seconds I almost did convince myself. I tried walking like I thought he would — fancy-like. I swung my hands. I tried to make myself bigger. I tried to talk white. Then I heard my aunt. I put the mirror away. She asked me where I was. I told her I'd been tired and I had gone to sleep on her bed. She said that was OK. She said she was sorry that she had a softer bed than us kids, but she guessed she needed her sleep, because with her husband dead and us to feed, she had to work, and when she came home she was almost as dead as him — but she had to care for us, and cook and all, that's why she needed the best sleep she could get. I told her yes, I was glad she had the soft bed she did, and I left because I wanted to go out and be with my friends. I was glad to see them. I was glad I was right in front of our building and not over in some lousy, rotten white neighborhood; I was glad I was not that white lady's kid and not a damned white cowboy like you see in the movies. The white cowboys almost killed every Indian in America. Didn't they?"

One answers questions like that as faithfully and honestly as one can, but they are, I believe, unanswerable questions. James Lewis knows what he knows, and sees what he sees. I come to hear him, and when we talk I try to tell him what I know, what I see. And he listens as intently as I do. But he continues to say what he believes he ought to say, what he must say, what he wants with all his might to say and to have heard. And I answer back and he looks directly at me and tells me how sorry he is that I am deceived, but how he understands, he understands. And sometimes as I listen to him I remember those moments when I as a doctor, a psychiatrist, have told a troubled, confused patient that yes, I understand, I understand.

3.   *What but a Negro?*

"Schoolteachers are schoolteachers." Isn't that the most obvious thing in the world? Mrs. Jones says so. She also says that her name is a common one; and she says that her common name is matched by her common sense. She says that life is made far too complex these days — by people who want to take perfectly apparent and clear-cut matters and mix them up, turn them around, and make them come out involved and entangled and messy and sloppy. The only thing for others to do, "the rest of us," is stand up and speak out and not be intimidated, not be pushed headlong into silliness and spitefulness and vulgarity and brutality. Otherwise, she concludes, "we will have a second Civil War on our hands." How does a worried, dedicated teacher like her respond to all the changes she has seen of late? She has no answer to such a question. All she can do is talk about her life, and hope its continuity provides an answer. She was born in 1935, not far from Warm Springs, Georgia, where President Franklin D. Roosevelt used to go for a rest. She is a second-generation teacher. Her mother taught school in Georgia. During the war an older brother went overseas to fight and came back wounded. He received treatment in a northern hospital. His mother and two sisters visited him and decided to stay North. The father died long ago, in 1939. Of what, one asks? It was an automobile accident, a bad one. He was instantly killed. So Mrs. Jones tells it at first. A year later she adds a detail or two: "I believe I told you my father died in an automobile accident. That is the story my mother told me. I was only four years old, you know. Later I found out the rest. He was called an 'uppity nigger' by the white people. He was a minister. He was a member of the NAACP — yes, way back then. They called him a 'Communist.' They called him a 'red darkie.' He was fearless, my mother told us. She said she would be so scared for him that she would cry and cry, but he never once showed any fear. He had a friend in the superintendent of the schools. He was a fine white man, and he would come visit us. He said Mr. Roosevelt was fighting to make it a better country for all people, the white and the colored both. I guess he was the one who told my mother what he thought happened. He would have denied it if he'd been with my grandmother, my father's mother. My father was on his way to his church, and he was kidnapped, I guess. They pushed his car off the road and into a swamp. They killed him first. They shot him. No one was ever caught. So far as we know the sheriff didn't even investigate. It wasn't mentioned in the paper. They never found his body. My mother says one of the men who was there got to feeling guilty and he told the school superintendent what he thought happened. He would have denied it if he'd been brought before the sheriff — and anyway, no sheriff then would have brought white men before a judge and demanded they go

to jail for murdering a Negro, and especially my father. He provoked the white people. He was too proud, I guess. I think from
then on my mother wanted to leave Georgia."

Yet, she now finds the pride of avowedly black men and
women difficult to accept. They protest their blackness too much.
They have allowed the contempt white people have shown for
the word "Negro" to affect *their* feelings toward the word — and
"that's what we *are*, Negroes." She sees no reason to rush about
and try to accommodate herself to every fad, every "passing fad"
at that. "I am a Negro," she declares. The Negro is the one whom
whites could not bear to recognize, because he would not bow or
bend or scrape or beg. The white people called him "nigger" and
"the colored man" and "nigra" when they wanted to be nice.
They called him "darkie" and "coon." They called him "black
man." All the while he was a Negro — her father and many like
him throughout the South, even the rural South. Up North it is
the same thing: "White people, I believe, enjoy seeing us lose our
dignity. They have wanted to call us 'black' for the longest time.
Now they don't have to do it. We do it for them. Mind you, I
have no great objection to the word 'black.' What I resent is the
way we always run scared. We decide that we're not winning our
struggle fast enough. Then someone uses the word 'black' — and
the next thing you know we're off on that tangent. Suddenly the
NAACP is called an 'Uncle Tom' organization. Suddenly the
word 'Negro' becomes virtually a swearword. Suddenly we must
be African, or Muslims, or 'black nationalists.' Suddenly we must
look Afro, be Afro, dress Afro, learn to talk Afro — Swahili or
some other language.

"I am an American citizen. It may sound corny and old-
fashioned these days, and I may be Uncle Tom's daughter, that's
who, but I haven't the slightest intention of trying on any new
mask or wig or costume or anything else that would conceal
what I am, what my life has been all about. What are my earliest
memories? I recall President Roosevelt riding in an open car and
lifting his hat and waving with it to us as we stood along the
road. I recall those dirt roads in Georgia. I hate the white men
who killed my father, but I don't hate the whole state of Georgia.

I had a happy time there as a child — and we were by no means rich. Nor were we 'exploited' by anyone. My, how I'm tired of hearing that word! Of course we have been 'exploited' as a people; but that is not the whole story of our experience here in the United States. No, it certainly is not the whole story! There are moments when I believe that some of our so-called militants are members of the Ku Klux Klan in disguise. They talk about several centuries of Negro history as if we were nothing at all but the animals the Klan people always said we were.

"I am interested in the response of white liberals to our militant fringe. There is something disgusting — I'd say something terribly racist — about the easy acceptance any crazy Negro gets in certain white quarters. It is almost as if our so-called friends and supporters were looking for justification of their notion that Negroes are all wild, hysterical, thoughtless people — animals really, ready to go on a rampage given any leeway at all. It's a terrible alliance in my opinion: white so-called radicals who egg on Negroes consumed with rage and scared half out of their wits. Have you read Robert Penn Warren's *Who Speaks for the Negro?* He understands us. He knows that we are human beings and capable of being a wide, wide variety of people — which means we can produce sensible, strong people who will outlast every mean person in the world, and we can produce our own bigots: loudmouthed and nasty and unworthy of the attention they are receiving today, I'll say that!

"I find the attention given to a very small number of us by television and the newspapers and magazines an outrage. We are millions. Most of us go to work, or want to go to work. We have fought in this country's wars, and we consider ourselves Americans. Our music is part of America's music. We are Christians — and I wish some of those white radicals, atheists as they are, would get that through their heads. I wish they'd come and see us at church. I wish they'd realize that the great majority of Negro people in this country are churchgoers and believers. I know what they say, that the churches weaken people, undermine their determination to fight the white man, the oppressor. Do those people — intellectuals, they call themselves — have any idea of how we have lived in the South and now up here? Do they know what Negro ministers have done for their people over the centuries? It is easy to get angry and swear and curse and call names. The people who do so, certainly the white people, have no idea at all what it was like living in Georgia and what frightened, extremely poor people — the sheriff and his deputies are never very far away — need to hear and believe in their minds and hearts if they are going to survive at all. I never knew my father. But he wrote a letter once to my mother, maybe twenty years ago, and it means more to me today than ever before. He had gone to a meeting in Atlanta, a typical minister's meeting, I guess. Something must have got to him. I gather from the letter that he had walked through the Negro section of the city, and somehow everything seemed more hopeless — in view of the slums there, with so many people cramped into so little space, and more coming, he knew that, many more coming."

She showed me that letter. It was not a long one, and it had no "solutions" to offer. The man who wrote it had what in other times was called a strong and clear head; he wrote a little formally, but with passion, and above all he wrote openly about himself, his ideas and struggles. The letter was written to his family, his wife and his boy and his girls:

Dear Mother and Dear Children,

I am here in Atlanta, and I wish I were back home. It seems harder here in the city. It seems harder for our people. They live on crowded streets, and my minister friends at the meeting tell me that their people weep for the land they once knew — break down and cry in church on Sundays. I asked several ministers what our people can do. Of course they said there isn't much our people can do, except to be grateful that God has given us our churches, so that the Negro people of Atlanta, and the Negro people all over the nation have somewhere to go, a place where they can cry if they have to cry. I was walking down one street and I saw some sad children, and I myself wanted to cry. We have sad children where we live, too. I realize that. Perhaps you have to go away from home to see what is right in front of your eyes all the time.

All I know is that God Himself was sad for much of his life, and He knew at the end He was going to be betrayed. That is why the Negro people are close to God. That is why I told the ministers that if our people cry in their churches, the Lord Who must have wept on the Cross will hear, and someday His justice will be done. That is not completely a consolation, I know, to our people right now, today. But nothing in the big city consoles them, and they need what help they can find if they are to live at all — so that someday, when the country becomes a better country, we will be here to rejoice. I want the Negro people to rejoice on earth as well as in Heaven. I must say that. I do not know when a better time will come. Our President wants it to come. But during the long night we need to look up and keep some hope alive, and that is what the church can do, the good church. Here at the meeting I've met some poor ministers, very poor ones. But Christ Himself was poorly served by at least one of His disciples! I must go now. I send my love to each one of you.

Father

What Mrs. Jones likes about that letter has to do with more than its personal value as something written long ago by her father. She sees in those words a mixture of social consciousness and historical awareness that is impressive and sorely lacking today. She teaches history, and she tries to offer the very same things she believes her father offered in his letter: "He was giving of himself in that letter, I can see that in every sentence. And he was saying something I think he hoped we'd never forget. He was saying that we are not alone, not outcasts of the human race. We have a history as sufferers that goes back to Jesus of Nazareth. Our experience was His. We must not sit back and pray — in such a way that we never do anything here on this earth and die believing Heaven is ours. Heaven is for those who work to be worthy of it, and I mean work right here and now. My father used to say that — my mother has told us. But on the other hand, people need to hold on to something; they can't be treated as if they all were brilliant philosophers. They don't sit down and study logic every morning. And they can't be asked to turn against their own history — so that they have nothing but a lot of new slogans.

"I've gone to meetings and heard our more radical people talk. The church, they say, oppressed 'the black masses.' Not the white man but *the church!* Then I hear that my father and people like him were 'lackeys of the capitalists' or they were 'exploiters.' The minister and the undertaker, *they* were the ones who ruined the black man! I'm sure — my father says so in his letter — there have been corrupt and stupid and selfish Negro ministers and undertakers, just as political leaders or radicals or 'organizers' can also be dishonest and cruel and as egotistical as anyone else. My father made practically no money. You know how we got by? Our food was brought to us by the people. My father took an old cabin and with his own hands made it into a halfway livable house. The people built our church with their own hands — and all over the rural South Negroes have done that, millions of them have for generations. It was a 'labor of love,' my mother used to tell me. Is that so awfully bad for people, that they come together and try to build a house of worship?

"My father's people had no money to give. How could he exploit people who didn't have anything in the first place? I've never quite understood that. He was the one who would write letters for his people, letters to public officials and religious organizations all over the country. He was a spokesman. If someone was in an especially desperate situation — I guess they all were, in one way or another — he tried to get what help he could for them. He wrote to Georgia's senators. He even wrote to the White House. I have a letter sent to him by one of Mr. Roosevelt's aides, I believe his name was Marvin MacIntyre, something close to that. He said he was answering for the President, and he was sending my father's letter to Senator George. Remember him?"

She lives in the ghetto, a relatively well-to-do section of it, but within a block of her home are extremely poor, black families, some on welfare, some with men at home and barely self-sustaining without welfare. Once, when she went to a "community meeting," she heard one person after another stand up and call America a host of angry, contemptuous names. She heard whites denounced en masse — and Negroes, too. She became agitated. Finally she spoke out: "I told them that they were laughable, all of them. I told them that they were only a handful there. Thousands and thousands of Negroes live nearby, but about fifty came to that meeting. And *some* fifty they were! You should have heard those slogans. The people want this! The people want that! I speak for the black people! The black people are on the march! Down with the high-yellow types! Down with the black bourgeoisie! Negroes are our enemy!

"I became sick. And I got sicker trying to follow their line of reasoning. I heard not a flicker of understanding and compassion for their people. I heard only arrogance. *We're not, we're not* — that's all they could say about themselves. How can you only be a series of *not's?* And when they weren't saying what they were *not*, they were attacking everyone who has ever tried to do anything for the Negro people, be the person Negro or white. I wasn't surprised when they insulted Ralph Bunche, but they mocked Dr. King, too. He was for nonviolence — and that is the silliest idea around, one of them said. Nonviolence is what the white man has invented to keep the black man in his place. Now how about that! I lost my temper at that. I simply couldn't let them go on and on with their attacks on Dr. King. They were so cheap and insolent, too. They were like little children — the worst kind, fresh and spoiled little children. I realized that later, though. If I had thought about it like that when I was there, I would have simply walked right out and not wasted my time. What can you do when a room full of children like that — hoodlums really — is determined to destroy the reputation and memory of a man like Dr. King? Nothing.

"But I did get up and tell them off! I can't repeat what I said. I don't even remember a lot of it, I was so mad. But I know I told them off; and I know they didn't succeed in silencing me, even though they tried. 'Let her speak,' one of them said to another, 'because she's the enemy and we have to hear her.' That gave me the clue. I think up until then I was just trying to register my sense of disbelief — that they could really think they represented over twenty million people, and that their white friends could actually think so. I know white people have always had crazy ideas about who we are and what we want, but we used to call *those* white people our enemies, not our friends — or as one man put it, our 'corevolutionaries.' I'm the enemy, I told them. I'm the enemy of anyone who wants to turn a single human being into a machine or a number. I'm the enemy of clever politicians, and not all of them are in Washington or in our state capitals. I'm the enemy of ranting, raving demagogues. I don't care if their skin is white, yellow, brown, black or red. What difference does it make if we have white dictators or black ones, white crooks or black ones, white liars and cheats or black ones? But most of all I'm the enemy of those who deny the Negro people, the *Negro* people, enough intelligence and wisdom to know their real enemies when they see them and hear them. And the real enemies of the Negro are not only the George Wallaces; they are also other Negroes — or black men, or whatever they call them-selves. The enemy of the Negro people is any person who slanders *groups* of people, who calls others he doesn't even know all kinds of bad names, and speaks ill of a person because he doesn't agree with some 'program.'

"Oh, I talked and talked. I carried on, as my mother would say. I guess they thought they'd either have to go and silence me with adhesive tape over my mouth, or beat me unconscious, or let me speak. I told them that, too; I mean, I told them that I wasn't afraid of their names, or their muscles either. I told them my father had been killed by racists, and I would just as soon die that way myself. I told them a racist is a racist, no matter what he looks like. I told them I was proud to be a citizen of this country and teach my country's history. I don't like what a lot of history books say — but that is all the more reason for me to find out the truth and to teach the truth. Why should our children have one set of lies replaced by another in their minds? Why should they hear *any* exaggerations, if we can help it?"

She "carried on" in retrospect, too. While talking with me she

made another speech; and when she was finished she called her
considerable statement just that, a long speech. She wonders all
the time what else she possibly can do, except speak out as often
as she can. She talks to her fellow teachers, white as well as
black. She talks to friends and neighbors. Most of all she talks to
her children, who are in the seventh grade, the first year of junior
high school, and "well able to understand all these problems."
She says she would be depressed were it not for the children she
teaches. They listen. They learn. They are not the children she
sometimes reads about when she comes across an article about
the ghetto. They are not beaten down or indifferent or wild.
Certainly she sees her fair share of troubled children from broken
homes, from homes as needy and wanting and hard pressed as
any in America. But once again she worries that not only the
"militants" she talks about will distort "the nature of things," as
she occasionally puts it. A lot of very well-meaning and kind and
sensible people in her opinion get the wrong impression: "Those
people talk about our children as if they're all retarded, or in
rags, or unable to read and write. Those people picture them as
troublemakers, as noisy and disrespectful and poorly behaved all
around. I wish they would come to my school. I wish they could
meet some of the children I teach — and they are from poor
homes as well as solid backgrounds. I used to teach in an all-
white school, located in a well-to-do section of this city. I had
problems there, plenty of them.

"I requested this assignment, and I'm glad I did. I expected
things to be much worse than they are — and if I thought as I
did, you can imagine how others think! The other day a twelve-
year-old girl asked me why it is that people always say such bad
things about our schools. I told her I didn't know. I wanted to
hear what *she* thought. I asked her that, what she felt the reason
was. She said she thought a lot of people just won't give us credit
for anything. They'd rather feel sorry for us and show us pity all
the time. I said yes. Then she added another thought. She said
that goes for our own people as well as others. I asked who
'others' were, and she said 'whites.' I asked her how we could
change all that. She said she didn't honestly know. Then she

came up with something: 'We can, by proving ourselves to be as good as anyone else.' I certainly agree with her. In the last analysis, who but a Negro teacher like me can show children like her that they have a fine heritage — and that they have to make an even finer one in the coming years?"

To her, Negroes are Americans who are not white, who have been here for several centuries, who have helped build the country, who have developed out of hard circumstances indeed a culture both distinctively theirs *and* to some extent everyone else's too — in the sense that Negro words and songs and rhythms and styles of seeing the world, responding to it, have become more embedded in American life than perhaps most people ever manage to know.[1] To her, there is no place to go, nothing to be but "what we've always been, human beings — only human beings who are more free, more in control of our lives, and so *able* to be better." Why does she emphasize that word "able"? She does so "because no matter what we get in the way of 'money and power' — I hear that those ought to be our aims — we will still have to prove ourselves as individuals." She feels that she is trying to do just that. Her husband died two years after they were married of a massive cerebral hemorrhage. She has no children. She teaches all year around. She wouldn't know what to do in the summer, but thankfully there is teaching to be done then, too. She admits she may be wrong. She acknowledges she may be blind. She does insist, though, that she is trying "to walk the long distance that God sets before each of us." Once she told me her legs ache, and so she wonders whether she doesn't need better shoes, and maybe a good checkup from a doctor. But I have yet to see her walk in a manner that is not steady, confident, determined. "I guess I am tough," she will say. She means she will continue to take the long walk every day to school, and get there.

4. Orin

Orin is his name, a name out of Scotland or someplace like that, his father has told him. There were some big, important tobacco people in eastern North Carolina who carried that name, Orin. And as things go in the South, the black man learns from the white man and gets his names from him. So, Orin is eight and black and called Orrie and his father's name is Orin, and he is thirty-three and called Daddy, even by his wife. Orin was born in Old Dock, North Carolina, which is not far from Whiteville, the seat of Columbus County. Orin's daddy once was a field hand, and used to drive a pickup truck; he would also do odd jobs and errands and "everything, you know." At the age of four Orin was brought north to Hartford, and then to Boston. All of which means that he is half a Southerner, half a Northerner — and no kidding: "I'm from North Carolina and I'm from Massachusetts. Four and four make eight, and we've been up here four years and before that I lived four years in Columbus County, North Carolina, my daddy says. No kidding, I'm half-and-half from here and from back home."

He has heard "back home" mentioned and recalled many times. His daddy one day says they'll be going back there soon, and the next day says he won't ever go back. The fact is, though, that every summer for four years in a row Orin has heard his parents debate this question: will we go there to see them or will they come up here — Orin's grandfather and grandmother. Orin's mother has no parents. She was reared by her uncle and aunt. She lost both her parents to pneumonia, she believes. She doesn't know, because no doctor ever got to them. But Orin's father has both parents alive and well. They will live to be a hundred, he hopes and believes, and they are proud and good people, one gathers from listening to their proud and good son. There is only one problem with them; they won't leave that county in North Carolina. They won't go to live in Wilmington or any other city in the state; and they won't go to live in Washington, D.C. — where one of their sons now lives. Nor will they go up to stay in Hartford, Connecticut, where another son lives, or Boston, where their son Orin lives, and where two aunts of Orin's, sisters of his mother's, also live. They will go to those cities to visit, to look around and marvel at what a city can be, but they always want to leave after a week or two; and it seems that if they go North one year, they expect their children to come back South the next year. Young Orin, therefore, has been back to North Carolina twice since he came North to live.

Orin wishes he could live like his grandparents do; but he also is glad to live up North and be with his parents and live the way they do. In Old Dock, Orin loves to go near the mules and the horses and the chickens and the pigs he sees there. He loves to look at fields of tobacco and at the flowers his grandmother grows. He loves to "go exploring": "When I'm in North Carolina I tell my grandfather all about Roxbury. He's been up here, but he says I know a lot more about Roxbury than he does. He says he never hopes to know too much about any city. I told him he was wrong, and he was making a big mistake. He said I should go right ahead and tell him he's wrong; it won't make any difference. He says he's happy where he is and I should be happy where I am."

Orin gets bored with North Carolina after a while. Each time, he has been given a chance to stay longer and return with an older cousin. Each time, he has said no, he will go back with his parents. But it isn't a shy and fearful child, afraid to leave his parents, who refuses to stay longer in Old Dock: "I'd miss my friends. I'd miss the playground. We have a new playground, and all the kids show up there right after breakfast in the summer. We play ball. If I'm going to be a baseball player, I have to practice."

He finds certain things in Old Dock rather hard to accept: the extreme quietness, the flies and mosquitoes that go undeterred by effective window screens or screen doors, the road dust that a car can stir up, the eerie sound of crickets in the early evening, the heat that doesn't come and go but stays and sticks to the body's surfaces and nearly smothers those exposed to it. It can be hot and muggy up in Boston, he knows; and up there one meets plenty of flies and mosquitoes, not to mention mice and rats and cockroaches. Still, there is something nice about a thunderstorm that signals several following days of real cool weather; and most of all, there is something reassuring about all those cars and trucks and buses which ride over smooth, well-paved roads:

"When I'm down there I get to wondering if there are more than ten or twenty people anywhere around. That's scary. What if you want to play a good game of baseball? Where would you get the teams from, and would there be anyone to look at the game and be in favor of your side or the other side? I'll go for a walk with my granddaddy and he'll be talking sometimes, but then he stops, and I can't think of anything to say, and there's no one around. He has a dog, but the dog only stays with us in the beginning of the walk. The dog runs and runs, and I'm sure that he's lost, but he shows up at suppertime, and Granddaddy says to me each time that I'm sure from the city, because anyone knows that a dog will find his way back to supper. He's right, I know. It's in the city that you lose your dog. We brought one up here — Beauty. I remember her. She got killed, you know — Dad says it took only two days. I remember my mother crying. She said, 'Now we really are up here, now that Beauty's gone.' My daddy said he'd try to get another dog. But the city is no place for a dog, Momma said, and so we've never had one since."

He doesn't talk about that dog Beauty very much, but over the years he has drawn pictures of her several times — and then gone on to tell me that he can remember Beauty running across a field in North Carolina, and remember Beauty in the car, resting beside him, on the way up North; and he can remember his mother's scream when she heard that Beauty was dead. Beauty was only six when she got killed, two years older than Orin was. A year after Beauty had died, and several months after I first met Orin, he drew Beauty for me and explained to me that the dog was happy, because she was back in North Carolina. About a year after that, Orin was again going to draw Beauty — but suddenly, halfway through, he stopped. He crossed out the picture and nearby started another one: "I want you to see the new swings they put in the playground," he told me, and then he set to work showing me them. I decided to ask him whether he ever saw any dogs in the playground. "Yes, sometimes. But it's not a place for a dog — unless it's a real smart one who knows how to stay clear of the cars." That was all he had to say for a while. He went back to his picture. He had a few finishing touches to do. There was the fence that was being built. There was a streetlamp. Finally he handed me the picture and said, "Now, that's it."

I was looking at what he had done, and he was looking at a drawing I did — it was a bargain we had made: if he drew, so did I. Suddenly I heard Orin's words: "I'm just as glad." I didn't know what he meant, and I told him so. He let me know exactly what he meant: "My grandmother told me that Beauty went back to North Carolina. That's silly. She died. But it's just as well she did die. She wouldn't even like our new playground if she was here now. Daddy says a dog born in the city doesn't know any better. But Beauty knew better." And he, does he know better? Would he like to go back there, back to Old Dock — that is, if his parents decided to move back? And if they were undecided, what would he advise them? What is his preference? One wonders about such matters, and stumbles forth with a question like, "Orrie, if you had to choose where you and your whole family would live, where would it be?"

Not for a second does he hesitate: "I like to go visit my grandparents in North Carolina, but like my daddy says, we can't live there anymore. The white people there don't like us, and they want us to get out fast. Here you never see much of the white people. Daddy says they're no better up here than in Old Dock, but they'll leave you alone more, so long as you leave them alone. They don't want any part of us. I'm glad we're up here. Daddy said if we'd have stayed there we might all be dead. No work means no money and no money means no food — and then you die. Daddy says the rich white people have been feeding a lot of the black people, even if they don't work because of the machines that do the harvesting. I asked him what would happen when the rich white people died. Would all the black people die right after them? My daddy said the rich white people will never die, but he thinks that soon there won't be any black people left in the county down there."

At eight what does Orin see ahead of him? His father was in the Army, and Orin thinks he might also like a few years in the military, "only maybe the Marines." His father learned "about electronics" in the Army, and Orin thinks that kind of work intriguing. In fact, the more one talks to Orin and his parents, the more one sees that the first departure for Orin's father was ordered by the government, and only upon the soldier's return did the second and final departure from North Carolina take place. Orin has heard his father and mother talk about the sequence, and so understands rather a lot about various social and economic and educational issues: "If my daddy hadn't gone into the Army, he thinks he might still be back home, and we'd all be in bad trouble. He doesn't have the kind of job he wants, but he's on the way to getting one. He works in a factory; they make electrical equipment in it. They've promised that they'll keep on teaching him, and that he can be moved up and be over some of the other men one of these days. We're not rich, but we're not poor. My mother says that she'd like to get us out of here, into a better street. I like it here, but she says there are nicer places to live. The white people don't like us moving out to where they live, though; so we may be here for a long time. My dad says that even if he'd gone to school a long time and had the best job he could ever want, we might not be able to live where we'd like. My mother says she can buy us the food we need, and the clothes; and that's more than she ever dreamed she'd be able to do when she was little. She says she likes to look at some of those dollar bills she has and smile and smile. She says when she was my age she'd never seen a dollar bill, never mind anything bigger. Dad gives her five ten-dollar bills every week to spend, and they have more; they're saving some money and they put away some for the rent. Dad says if he could only get some land he could build a house himself. But you can't just go and get land. Back in North Carolina there was plenty of land. The white people would have let us stay on theirs. They even offered to help fix up the place where my dad was born. But they didn't have money to give us, and that's why we're here. My dad says that when you weigh everything, we come out best right where we are — even if the building we live in is falling apart and you pay a fortune to stay in it."

Orin's dad has fixed up his apartment and has even thought of doing repairs in the halls. The trouble is, how far does one go?

He laughs when he asks a question like that. He'd like to fix up the entire block, the whole neighborhood, all of the streets his people walk and play on and call theirs. He'd like to help turn what others call a "ghetto" into what he calls "a nice-looking place, where nice-looking houses are." He knows those nice places, those nice houses, exist all over; and he feels that with his job and future he ought to be able to live in such a place, such a house. A day doesn't go by when he fails to mention that hope. The television set brings up close the neighborhood he has in mind, and within seconds he has made his remark. The boy Orin describes what happens: "I can tell when my dad is going to speak. He'll see a program and there's a nice house, and I look over and I see him just staring with all his might. Then he says something. He says he wishes we could live there, in a place like that. He says we could, if we weren't black. My mother always interrupts and says we should be thankful that he's got a good job, and it'll be an even better one soon. She says we've come a long way to be where we are, and you can't have everything. She says when I grow up I'll have it better, and I might even go all the way through school, and I could be high up in a company like the one my dad works for. Dad laughs at that. He says you can't be so sure. True, you have to be thankful for what you have. But who knows if we'll keep on being so lucky? And then he'll say he still wishes we lived in some nice house somewhere."

Once again Orin told me where that somewhere might be: "It would be way out where there are trees and plenty of grass and there would only be black people there — no white people. We would have our own police, and if anyone tried to come and bother us, they'd protect us." He had no more to say on that particular subject. I asked him a question or two, hoping he might go on; but no, at the present time he is content to let the matter drop right there. But not far from his home I have stood with him and other children like him and listened to men talking, men saying more emphatically what Orin said — that the black man has to build his own place, his own home, and by God defend it with drawn guns. Orin's father thinks such talk about guns is "foolish." At eight Orin is not so sure.

5. Billy's Bus

"I was the first one to get on the bus. Paul shoved and tried to be first, but he was only second. There are a lot of buses going out every day now; but a couple of years ago we were the first, and they had reporters — remember them? — and they had us on television —remember that? — and I was putting on my best clothes, like it was Sunday and time to go to church, only it was time to go to school. After a while I told my mom to stop worrying and let me go to school regular-like, not all dressed up. I told her how the white kids look, and she said I was trying to fool her. So, she went one day to see for herself. She went on the bus with me to school, and she saw, and then she changed her mind.

"The bus, that's the best part of the day for me. I look out the window and see those kids walking to school — and we go right by them. Pretty soon they're way out of sight; there's not a black person you can see anywhere. It's all white, everyone is white. I knew there were more of the white than the black in America, but I used to tell my grandma, when she told me so, that it didn't look that way to me. Now I forget to look; I mean I don't all the time say he's white and he's white and that lady there, she's white. Twice a day I do look though: when we move into the white part of the city, and when we come back home to our own part of the city. But there will be days when I forget, I completely forget. I'll forget the teacher is white, or a lot of the kids, and I'll forget to notice whether we're driving down a white or a black street. Last week it was funny: a kid got sunburned during the vacation, and he was tan, real tan. He came up to me during recess and said now he looked more like me. I thought he was getting wise, and I said to myself if he wants a fight, he'll get it. But he smiled and pulled me by the arms to a ball game they were starting. The white kids, they're not bad, not really bad, if you put in the time and get to know them."

He has certainly done that, put in time getting to know white children of his age. At seven he had scarcely seen any whites, and at ten, when he spoke the words just quoted, he had not only been to school with them "going on three years" but even stayed in a white home for several weeks one summer. He feels he knows "them" — and he always uses "them" in connection with white people. He also feels that, if anything, he has become "more black," by which he means more aware of his blackness and prouder of his skin color, his background, his race: "I'm not white-hungry, like some kids say. I told one kid who says they're the enemy that all right, you have to know your enemy. Don't you? They're not our enemy. Some of them are, I know that; but a lot of them are no different than a lot of us are. Once the bus driver said he'd let my friend come over with us, and then take him back. He skips school a lot. My friend came and he said our bus was great, and he liked the ride. He said we should take pictures, like they do in a war, so we'd know all about their places — stores and gas stations and like that. He was only kidding! But the bus driver heard him, and the next day he told me it wasn't so funny, because there are black people who really think that way. I asked my friend, and he said no, he was joking — but his big brother knows where some guns are, and he says he'll use them, if he has to, against the white people."

Billy has little interest in waging a war to the finish with white people. He is doing well in an overwhelmingly white suburban school, and he sees ahead of him a life different from any his parents expected for themselves. He would like to finish high school and go to college and then to law school. He would like to fight for his people in the courts, before judges and juries. He once thought he might be lucky if he could do as his father does, work in the post office, but he now is certain that he can do more, be more, get further, go higher, climb up there — and he uses all those familiarly American ways of speaking. "It all started with the bus," he says. What started with the bus? "My big ideas!" He can do that, laugh at himself. He likes to wiggle his feet while talking, or tap the floor with the leather-sole shoes he wears, or twirl his keys around and around — until he himself will remark that one day the chain will have to give, and then they will go scattering, his four keys.

They stand for something, those keys, and he knows it: "We

have locks all over the place, to keep us from losing everything we have. Out where I go to school a lot of people don't even lock their doors at all! Until I started riding that bus I didn't know how other people lived. I agree, you see a lot on television that tells you; but that's not the same as sitting in the bus and looking out of the window and seeing for yourself. The bus driver will say we're getting an education for ourselves, just riding back and forth like we do. I used to think he was crazy with talk like that, but I know what he means. I do. The strangest thing is that some white kids tell me they'd like to ride on our bus. They say they'd like to see where we live, and they think we have a lot of fun riding, because when we get off we're joking around. A lot of them are driven to school by their mothers. A lot of them come by bus, too. The bus driver says that from what he sees on their buses everyone is quiet. He says our bus is too noisy, but he doesn't mind. He's a good driver. He's a good man. He's become our friend."

Billy is outgoing and has many friends. He is a quiet child who can become talkative all of a sudden, then revert to being once again thoughtful, dreamy almost, and more observant than he seems to be. He does not make a point of staring at things; he does not look in a way that calls attention to the act. "He sneaks in what he sees," I heard his mother say. She went on to describe what she meant: "Billy will surprise you. He'll seem to be lost in his thoughts, or he'll seem to be up to no good, but all the time he's watching everything that's going on — and I've never heard anyone who can tell you better what he's seen. He's like my father was. He's a talker, and that's because he has good eyes. Before I ever went on that bus I'd heard everything about the whole city, because he'd come home and tell me. So, I asked the bus driver if my son sits there all the time, scribbling notes to himself or something. The bus driver said no, Billy doesn't; he just fools around, like all the kids do. The driver says those kids see a lot more than he thought they did; he can tell by the questions they ask him."

Billy has a lot of questions; indeed, at ten he can sound like a sociologist or like a political philosopher who doesn't quite know what he believes, and justifiably so because he sees so many sides of so many issues. I suppose he can be called an open-minded observer — though not without definite values and a point of view which enables him to fit things together, then come up with something more than a series of contradictory comments. In a way the bus provides him a means of dealing with a lot of problems: "Why do we go on the bus, I often ask myself. I don't know. I go on the bus to get out of here, where there's a lot of trouble, and go over there, where you can sit and learn in class, and no one laughs at you for trying. In the school I went to over here, even the teachers are always making fun of you when you try to ask them a question and the question doesn't suit them. Over there I can ask anything, anything I want to ask.

"This is a crazy world. I have a white friend, and he says it's a crazy world, and I told him he's one hundred and fifty percent right. The kids who need the good schools are the kids who live where I do. A teacher said that to me; he was trying to be nice. I told him I already knew what he said. I didn't mean to sound fresh. But I have to laugh at the way people out there say things about us. They think they're so smart! The white kids say more things against their parents than we do. Maybe they should bus them over to our side of town. I think if you're black, you're brought up to be more respectful to your minister and your parents and your grandparents. I love my grandma; she's smart and she's been through everything, she says — and I believe her. *Her* grandma was a slave, I think. My grandma was born in South Carolina, but she's lived up here most of her life. She says we got up here before most Negroes did. I can't get her to say 'black.' She hates the word. I think of her when I hear the white kids out there talking about their dumb parents and their dumb grandparents and all that. They think they're so smart, a lot of them. I hope when I'm my grandmother's age I know half of what she knows! I hope when I'm a father, my kids don't knock me, laugh at me, the way I hear white kids doing it now at school. And those kids aren't any older than I am. They're ten, like I am.

"The worst time is when we go to lunch. They're always belly-

aching, a lot of them. 'Look what the maid gave me for a sandwich,' they say. Or: 'That girl, she can't put two pieces of bread
and jam together right!' You know who the 'girl' is, and the 'maid,'
don't you! I listen. I eat *my* sandwiches and they taste good, real
good! I offered half of one to a kid, and he gave me half of his.
Mine was a strawberry-jam sandwich and so was his. He said
mine was a lot better, because it was thick with butter. I said his
was good and mine was good. I told my mother later what the
kid said. She laughed. She reminded me that we never have had
butter, ever. It's too expensive. She told me to go and tell that
boy how he ate oleo — probably for the first time in his life. I
didn't say anything to the kid, though. A little while later in the
English class the teacher was talking about the grass always
being greener someplace else. I thought to myself that if I had
grass near my house, I'd sit on it and like it, and not always be
comparing my lawn with someone else's. Then all of a sudden I
thought of our strawberry-jam sandwiches, that kid's and mine.
Like I say, it's a crazy world!

"Why don't people try to give the next guy the benefit of the
doubt? My dad has been asking that all his life, I think, and now
I know what he means. It took the bus to bring us into the world,
the white man's world — and that's *the* world if you live in
America, I don't care what anyone says. We'd be sitting on the
bus and we'd say: look at this, look at that, look at everything.
Each time there'd be a bigger surprise, you know. They have it
good. Do they! But a lot of them, they don't know, they just don't
know how good they've got it. They have all my mother and my
dad dream about, and it doesn't do anything good for them. I
feel sorry for them, I really do. I asked my dad if that would ever
happen to us — if we'd be like a lot of rich white people if we
had a lot of money. He said yes, probably. I said no, never. He
said money goes to your head. But I think you can keep your cool
with all those one-hundred-dollar bills. A kid that sits near me
says he gets them, one-hundred-dollar bills, for his birthday. I told
him I'd never seen anything bigger than a ten. He said they're all
the same, just pieces of paper with numbers on them. I said that
some paper had more numbers than the others did. He didn't

even laugh. He said, 'Yes, you're right.' I looked at him, and I said to myself that this guy, he's not being cool at all; he's just a big shot who doesn't know about anything except his father's supermarkets. His father owns ten of them. The kid says he'll own them himself one day, and he'll just sign all the checks or something to pay people. I wouldn't mind owning a few supermarkets myself. I'll bet that if he owned his and I owned mine, then I'd beat him. I'd work harder and figure out a good way to make people buy from my stores!"

So it goes with Billy. He is, as his father puts it, "sharp." He is, as his younger brother puts it, "cool." He is, as a friend of his in a black neighborhood puts it, "a fast guy, on the make." He is, as a white boy in a middle-class suburb puts it, "the best kind of Negro kid you'd want to meet." He is, as the bus driver puts it, "always with his eyes open." I asked Billy whether any of those descriptions fitted him. He had been talking with me about the ways he sizes people up and comes to conclusions about them, and I thought we might talk about the ways others have sized him up, the impressive things they have said. He never has been averse to self-criticism, nor did I think he would mind some justifiable praise. There is nothing coy about him; he is, rather, an outspoken and disarmingly open and unaffected child, or *man,* I sometimes find myself thinking — at "only" ten, a man. "I think the driver is right," Billy said; and with a look he let me know that he wasn't going to call the others wrong, simply emphasize the virtue he sought after most. Then he spelled things out a little: "If you're blind you'll be pushed around. The white people, they have eyes all over their heads, not just the two in front. I mean, you can't fool them. They know what they want and they get it. Like the Black Panthers say, the white people wanted to win the whole world, and they've almost done it. But we're going to change that. You know how? I think if we keep our eyes on the white people, we can learn some of their tricks, and then once we've learned them so that we really can use them, then they'll have a fight on their hands.

"I was in this white boy's house for a couple of weeks last summer. His father owns some business; I think it's insurance or

something. All I heard his father talk about was competition, and
how America was made by it, and there's nothing like it, and how
he loves to beat others and get away their customers, that kind of
thing. I didn't say much; I listened and tried to picture him doing
his work. When we went back to school I told the bus driver
about the guy. The reason was that one day he showed up and
was parked right in front of our bus. He was driving his big
Lincoln, dark green. He was waiting for his son. That car has a
telephone in it! I rode in it and listened on the phone, I told the
driver. He smiled. He said that some people sure have it made. I
said yes, they do. Then I told him we could do the same thing, if
we had a chance. Well, he wasn't going to agree with me. I said
the trouble is we've been kept locked up, like you are in jail.
They had us slaves, and we couldn't do anything, except what
they told us to do. Then when they let us free, we had nothing,
and besides, they still had their guns on us. My grandma will tell
you that. But now we can take that bus and go out and see
what's going on. The driver agreed with me there. He admitted I
had a point. I told him I was going to remember everything I
heard, and the time might come that I could try and beat out a
whole team of white guys. I don't know if I really would win, but
I could try. I've been looking over white people since we started
riding the bus, and they don't come over to check us out. That
kid's father, he said he always tries to spy on his competition
and see what they're like. Maybe he should send his kids over to
our street on a bus. But he won't, and I don't blame him. But I'm
glad I'm looking over their setup. The first day we drove near the
school out there, the bus driver said, 'What a setup!' That's what
I say. I told my dad about it, and he said I should get all I can
out of that school and I should learn how the white kids think,
because they're the bosses. I watch them all the time from the
window of the bus. I think I could drive that bus myself to
school blindfolded."

Billy will never do anything blindfolded. He is becoming an
increasingly able student, and it begins to look as if in the
seventies he may well do everything he says he wants to do: go
to school and go to school. He is the first one to admit that

education is like that: an endless time of going — and often enough being bored stiff. But the diplomas are necessary, he knows. And then he says, yet again, that since he started riding the bus he has learned this: he and others of his race are in a white man's world and always will be, and the only thing to do is follow them, stick close to them, uncover their methods and tricks, absorb those methods, make use of those tricks — and win, which means win out over someone, which means win out over *them*.

6.   *Billy's Bus Driver*

Billy's bus driver is a leader of sorts, a hero to Billy and the many other children who ride that bus; but the man is also a follower, a self-declared admirer of the children he drives to school — which means one who looks up to them and mixes generously his admiration with any envy he feels and from time to time puts into words. He does envy them. He wishes he had the "chances" they have. What are those chances? Oh, they defy mention and enumeration. They are so obvious. Why even ask about the most evident of things — the splendid school building, the gym the boys talk about, the "beautiful cafeteria" the girls mention, and on and on? Most of all, he insists, there are all those rich, well-born and lucky white children, who have quite a future ahead of them. He is sure they will inspire the black children now in the same school; he is sure that in the long run the inconvenience of bus travel "will more than pay off."

He never used to be much for "integration of education," or even for any kind of education as a way out for black children: "I was born right here in this city, and I've lived here all my life. No one has anything to teach me about white people. I know them. For years I worked in buildings where they live. I took care of their garbage and I went on errands for them and I listened in on their goddam fights. I learned what they're all about. They're a bunch of fakers and frauds, like I guess a lot of my own people are! I'd come home and I'd go have a beer, and my buddies would ask me about the white man, the white man. I'd say who the Hell do you think the white man is? I'd tell them all I'd pick up there in those swank, luxury apartments: the women playing around with other men, the men cheating on their wives, the bottles of liquor I'd have to get rid of, and one guy, he went to prison for cheating the government out of taxes, and I heard there was a total of a million dollars he'd never even put down. But they caught him. You know what I heard his wife say? I was cleaning out her damn sink. She'd blocked it up. She was on the phone and she said her husband would do it again, because he still came out ahead. That's what she said. I heard that he went to some prison for 'nice people.' I would come home and tell my wife: it's not whether you go and break the law that counts, but who you are when you break the law. I took a few things myself when I worked in one of those buildings. I'll admit it. I'm not ashamed of it: a bottle of booze now and then, and a pair of shoes for the wife. What are you supposed to do when you're in an apartment and the lady has so many shoes you think you're in a shoe store? They never miss stuff like that — so long as you don't take too much at once. But I got sick, and I had to quit being a janitor. The doctor said I was working too hard, and my heart couldn't take it. So, this job has been perfect for me. Besides driving the bus I drive a cab for a few hours, too. I'm on wheels most all the time now, it seems. I get up and I'm driving the bus. Then I drive the cab for a few hours. Then I get the bus and go pick up the kids. I see the white man's world and I see the black man's; and let me tell you, they're not the same."

He is in his fifties, a man scarred by a difficult life. His heart has never been quite right; years of troubles as a result of the damage rheumatic fever did to the organ's valves have now been followed by coronary insufficiency. His wife has had cancer of the breast and also has a cardiac problem. His one daughter died from pneumonia at the age of five. He has a son who is somewhat retarded and lives with his parents. Nevertheless, the man is a friendly, optimistic person who swears much more often than I will reveal here, who provides for his family, who is gentle and tender with his son and nostalgic about the joys of fatherhood he experienced for the few years his daughter lived, who loves his wife very much, who can be brusque and even rude with a visitor, only to turn around and shower him with advice, counsel, information, opinions, and the "common sense" he particularly tries to find for himself and have available for others. Moreover, he is a flexible man, unconcerned with useless conventions, interested in the changes taking place around him, willing to acknowledge his own errors and limitations, anxious to have others take up where he feels he and his generation failed: "When a guy gets to be my age, he looks at a boy like that Billy you go and see — and he's glad. He's glad the world won't stop with him and all he's failed to do. Mind you, I'm no failure, not in my eyes. It's just that I could have been a lot more than I've ever turned out to be. I may sound conceited to you, saying that, but it's true.

"After all, I was born in this city, and so were my parents. We're not the kind of Negroes that have come up here from the South in the last few years. There's nothing wrong with them. I'm not saying a word against them. It's just that they have one Hell of a time getting used to the city, whereas I'm onto things here. Why, I almost graduated from high school. If it hadn't been for the goddam depression I would have graduated. Poverty they call it today; well, in the thirties no one talked about poverty. We were just plain poor, every one of us was. But even though I was poor, I never lost my self-respect. I went to the library and I read. I'd sit there on a Saturday afternoon and it would be a Hell of a lot warmer than in my house, and I'd read the magazines and look into a book or two. I won't say I read them from cover to cover, but I got a lot of the messages in them, I know I did."

In fact he speaks like a Bostonian; on tape he would not impress most listeners as a black man. His ancestors lived in Pennsylvania before they came to Massachusetts — and when he talks about the Georgia from which his family "originally came," he is like the American of English or German stock who is going back, way back to a past that is unreal for him and is more a part of the nation's history than his particular family's. He has his own version of the old-timer's pride — again, it is not purchased at anyone else's expense. He can describe Boston "before a lot of Negroes lived here." He can talk about the Negro families that used to live way out in the country, had small farms, were independent and

"all but white." He can talk about the Negroes who have lived on
Cape Cod for a long time, or up in New Hampshire and Maine.
They were pioneers, willing and able to go places their racial
brothers had not gone, would not make a habit of seeking out.
But maybe such boldness and industry and ingenuity and self-
sufficiency is not enough, not if millions of black children like
Billy are to find *their* destiny: "You see, Billy lives right here in
the city, and even if his family has been around a little longer
than most, they're not going to be able to find a quiet little place
somewhere out in the country, because they're city people. I am,
too. There are some from my background who are pretty well-off,
you know. They became doctors and lawyers and all that. A few
of them have even gone out to the suburbs. They can usually find
a good home where the Jews live. The Jews will take a few
Negroes, provided there aren't too many of them ready to follow.
The Jews pride themselves on being progressive. But most of us
have to stay right here — and that's why I say it's fellows like
that little Billy who are going to be pointing the way for us. He'll
never be a crazy type; they're full of noise, a lot of talk and
nothing else. I guess they'd call me an Uncle Tom, but who
cares!

"No, Billy will go right through school and learn all he can;
then he'll be a credit to his people, his race. And Billy won't have
to move into some white neighborhood just to prove he's as good
as the whites. He'll have them wishing they were living near him!
You know why I say that? Let me tell you. A few years ago I
never would have believed I'd be talking like this. I watch that
boy get off the bus, and sure enough, it doesn't take but a minute
before there are some white kids coming up to him and they
practically fight each other to get a word with him. I know he
won't tell you that. He won't tell his parents, either. Don't you
see, a boy like that has pride. That's *real* 'black pride,' the kind he
has. He isn't going to go bragging that he's popular with the
white ones. No sir, he doesn't even see it that way, because as a
matter of fact he's not trying to be popular with anyone. He's just
Billy, a damn smart kid who knows the score and isn't going to
be tricked by the white man.

"I don't believe those white ones even think of him as a colored kid, a Negro. I've about stopped thinking of all the kids as Negro kids. When they get off my bus, they're just kids. Oh, I don't really mean that, I guess. Can you ever forget? I think Billy probably comes nearer to forgetting than any of us — even if it's always there in the back of his mind, the idea that he's a Negro. You can never quite trust a white man to be above prejudice, even when he swears up and down on every Bible he can get his pale little hands on that he's not prejudiced, he's not, he's not. I remember one man whose apartment was on the top floor of the apartment house where I worked as a janitor. He kept on telling me that he treated Negroes like other people, and he liked them, and everyone is equal and all that. Once I heard him in the hall talking about 'jazz-bos.' I didn't even know what he meant at first. I swear it. Then I figured it out, what he was getting at. He thought he was being funny and smart: 'The jazz-bos are trying, but there's just so far they can push themselves with the raw material they've got.' That's what he was saying — my friend! I'll bet there are other whites who wouldn't ever talk like that — but they're still as prejudiced when you get down to it as he is.

"Now Billy, he's onto all that. He'll never go around trusting white people; but he'll have them trusting him. And like I keep on saying, he'll be a credit to us. We need our leaders, you know. Up here in the North we need the kind of man Dr. King was, only a northern kind of Dr. King — and that means not a minister, probably, but a lawyer or a businessman, something like that. We're still a pretty religious people, I'd say, but not the way the southern Negro is, from what I can tell. I've never been farther south than Washington, D.C., and that was plenty south for me! We're probably the most religious group of people in America, the most Christian. I have a sister and she once said something to me I'll never forget as long as I live. She said it must be real strange for Jesus up there in Heaven. He had all those white people on His side a long time ago, and they were trying to conquer the world for Him. They brought us here, and they told us to worship Him, and we did. Now they've left Him, most of them, and we're sticking closer to Him than they are. When she told me that I thought to myself that this country is a strange, strange place."

He goes on to remind me that the churches are full every Sunday with black families — even though Jesus is still represented as white in many of those churches. He insists that prayer and churchgoing are quite necessary for black people in Roxbury, in Harlem, in Cleveland's Hough section and Chicago's South Side and West Side. "We haven't too much to lean on, or too many friends we can trust," he says. Then, sarcastically but also with real sincerity, he calls Jesus Christ a friend, one of the few the black people have — though he for one catches himself thinking this as he drives the bus past one black church after another: "Where is He? Why does He allow all of this? He must be disgusted with the way things are, but He doesn't do anything. And meanwhile my people go all the time to those churches and they carry on — do they! — and they come out believing, really believing. I wonder. I really wonder!"

In contrast, he has no doubts about the value of the bus. He has seen the children get accustomed to a first-rate school. He has seen them become involved in learning as never before. He has seen his own contribution: he is a strong, well-spoken, active man whom the children admire and talk to all the time, and find it a real pleasure to know. I have often thought as I rode with him that he runs a kind of school on that bus of his. He points things out to the children. He asks them questions. They huddle close to his seat and listen to his stories, his jokes, his clever remarks, full of irony and vigorous social satire. They are allowed to move about, change seats, even scrap a little — and here is why a man with no degrees to his name and no experience as a teacher justifies such an approach: "I don't want to sit hard on these kids and teach them that the only thing they can do is sit, sit, sit, and stay in their place and move nowhere. Hell, I like them to move around and show some fight in them. I tell them they can scrap, but no one is to get hurt, and if a kid says, 'Enough,' the kid he's fighting with has to stop — or else. That way, they get the mischief out of their system here on the bus. That way, they're quieted down and ready for school when we get there. 'Give 'em Hell,' I call to them when they get off. And I believe they listen to me."

He next asks me what I think, and I tell him that I think he is right. I tell him that to those children he is an intelligent man, a wise man, a man they can really feel close to and fall back upon twice a day. He is surprised, or seems to be surprised. Actually, he is not surprised at all. Yes, he eventually admits, he knows that; and yes, he is glad he can do a little for those children. What else better, he asks me, can anyone do in the few years we are given here on this earth?

7. I Am a Maid, and What Do I Know?

There is no light when I get up. It is dark out, black as can be out. The worst thing in the day for me is my feet touching the floor. I hate it, I dread it, that moment. I get shivers up and down my body, way to my head, I tell you. Maybe it's the day ahead; maybe I'm shivering on that account.

But I get over my shivers. You have to get over your troubles. I have never been one to feel sorry for myself. What's the use? You feel sorry for yourself and start weeping for yourself and the next thing you know you're down and out. My daddy used to tell us: be a fighter, be like Joe Louis — hit back, hit back. Well, I've never hit anyone back in my whole life, but I can tell you, I try to hit back by getting up and doing my work and not sitting back and saying Oh, my gosh, and Oh, my gosh, until I'm just so low in my spirits that I'm no good to anyone and no good to myself, either.

I was telling you. I was saying. I get up. I'm over the shivers. I'm standing. I hear the creaks. Sometimes I hear the small creaks in the night when I'm lying there, and I've just been visited by a dream and I'm awake: the rats, they won't let the floor rest. When I start moving, though, the creaks are big ones; I guess the floor is saying ouch, ouch, Mrs. Harold, go easy on me. Well, it's true: I weigh too much; I'm over two hundred, but I don't know how much over. When I went over two hundred I said to myself, Dorrie Harold, you're big, you're tall, you work hard, and you have large bones, your daddy used to say, but there's a limit and you've passed over the limit, and now it's time to stop adding on the weight — or else stop looking at the scale, even if she tells you to, that lady with scales all over her house. So, finally I told her, I said, Mrs. Albert, you're my boss. I clean your house good. Don't I? I do everything I can to be of help. And I have this one thing I'd like to ask. You see, you can't have me weighing myself anymore. You just can't! And she said to me, Dorrie, I'll do anything, anything you want. So she stopped telling me I was free to use her scales. Of course all along, when she was telling me to cut down, cut down, she'd tell me in the next breath to go eat the cake that was left over. If you don't Dorrie, I will, she'd tell me. So I'd eat the cake and I'd eat the leftovers from the night before and I'd eat the ice cream she had — for her kids, she always told me, as though I was checking up on her! — and the rolls, her big weakness, she keeps on saying, I'd eat them, too.

Meanwhile, she'd be riding on that bike she has in her room or doing her exercises — Canadian exercises or something, she calls them. God, she gets into positions. She plays the music and giggles to herself and throws herself all over and I hear bang, bang, bang on the floor. Once I came into her room and she was staring into the mirror and she was doing something awful, sinful it was, to her face. I thought to myself: Jesus Christ, Almighty God, what in Hell is going on. I thought to myself, Dorrie Harold, she's gone and lost her mind, that Mrs. Albert has, and you'd better be careful, because there's no telling what she's liable to do. She looked like a lion, maybe a tiger. I don't know. I've never seen any of those wild animals. I've never been to a zoo in my entire life. But I said to myself, there she is, gone wild like in a zoo, my own Mrs. Albert. Well, you know, it was her exercises, I found out. I guess I just stood there, unable to move; and she caught sight of me and she turned around and said, Dorrie, is there something the matter, and I said no, no, no. I guess she didn't believe me, because she told me she was doing some face exercises. I recovered myself and I said oh, is that it, and then she said yes, that's it, and she turned back to the mirror and there it was again: her face. And I'll let you in on a secret: a month or so later she stopped them, the face exercises. She pulled a muscle under her chin, and Lord, she screamed and came running out of that room crying until I thought she might be getting ready to let go — I mean *really* let go. I had to get the doctor over. And I had to look at her. Oh my God, I thought, what would You say if she left us, and she came up to see You in Heaven looking like that, with a scary face on her and all that noise she can make! Dorrie, help me! Dorrie, call the doctor *again!* Dorrie, why isn't he here by now? Oh, Dorrie, why do I do all this? Why don't I just relax and eat, the way you do?

Finally the doctor came; it was only five or ten minutes, I believe, after we called. And he told her to relax and she'd be OK. He gave her a shot of something and she went and fell asleep and lo and behold, when she woke up she was all cured. She came running downstairs and told me I had to swear not to tell anyone, not her husband and not her daughter and not her son. I said I'd never say a word, of course. Then she said we had to celebrate. So, she made us each a sundae: chocolate ice cream and chocolate sauce and nuts all over and marshmallow. I didn't fancy one, but I knew I'd better join her, so I ate mine up and I saw out of the corner of my eye that she was up to her old tricks again, mixing that sundae up until she ruined it, poking at it, taking some to eat and then returning it instead of having it, cutting into the sauce with her spoon and lifting up a big helping, and then — dear God! — just sticking the whole thing back into her bowl with all her might, so that I thought for sure she was going to break the bowl and hurt herself real bad. I tried not to take notice. I tried not to look even a little at her. But I did, and she caught me. Then she said it: oh, Dorrie, I'm not really hungry at all. Why don't you finish this? It's a shame to waste it, you know. And up she was, and out of sight. I thought to myself like I always do: better to be sitting out in that house having a second helping than to be near death for lack of food, like once we all were when I was a kid. So I ate up everything in her bowl; I cleaned it up real good. When I got up to wash the dishes and wipe out all the 'evidence,' like she'll say sometimes, I heard her on the phone: it was a tennis game she was wanting to go play with someone.

That's a long way around, I know, to tell you about my weight, but like my momma would say to us when we were little: it's true, it's true. Early in the morning I hear the creaks on the floor and I think of her, Mrs. Albert. Come to think of it, I guess I never stop thinking about her. There I'll be, standing beside my bed and trying to pull myself into one piece so I can get dressed and have my coffee and take a look at my children, even if they're asleep, and say good-bye to them without the creaks waking them. They never wake up on time, even with the alarm clock. And do you know what's crossing my mind? One minute it'll be that I've got to stop standing there near the bed and go get dressed; but the next thing I'll think is that she will want some job done today, and she will want some other job done, and she has her club over, and she has her car pool all week, and there's the course she takes, in a college. I never can keep track of her schedule. That's what she calls it, her schedule. She has a big calendar, and she's always writing things on it, her appointments she calls them, and telling me not to let her forget: Dorrie, keep it in mind, won't you. She tries to be so nice to me — and I guess that's why I'm trying when I stand beside that bed of mine, trying to figure out what in Hell it is she's going to do today, and me, what I'll be doing.

But I have no long time for standing there. I go to the closet and I put on my dress. I put on my stockings. And the worst of it is that I put on my shoes. That *is* the worst, worse than waking up — I don't use an alarm, I don't have to — and worse than the shivers I get when I stand up. My feet hurt. They hurt when I take the shoes off and they hurt when I put the shoes on again. When I take the shoes off I can hear my toes saying they'd like to stretch themselves good, but they're all doubled up. Then when I put the shoes on, my toes are aching and crying and saying, Listen Dorrie, doesn't a day go by that you're not pushing on us to get into that little dark corner and stay there, all bent and hurting so bad. Well, every once in a while I give my feet a good talking-to, just like I used to hear my mother do. I say they could know worse, and they already have. What would it be like if I didn't have any shoes, and if we didn't have heat in the building here, and if I was walking all over and they'd be cut up, cut up real bad? This way they're sore, I know, but on Sunday I don't wear shoes for a minute, except when I go to church, and then I have my good shoes, special they are. Of course, *they* hurt even worse, because they're meant to keep your feet looking as thin as possible. I was sitting in church a Sunday back, and all of a sudden my feet were going to explode, I thought; and I said to myself I should go and ask Mrs. Albert if she knows any way I could exercise my feet. But I'd never speak up. I say a lot of things to her in my mind, but I never go any further. It's a long way from your thoughts to your words, my daddy told every one of us, and he knew what he was saying.

I'm out of my building by six o'clock at the latest. In the winter it's the middle of the night. It's light in the summer, I know, but I still feel like it's dark outside. I swear, it takes me half the morning to see the light of the day. I say good-bye in a whisper to each of my three girls and to my boy, and I close the door as real quiet-like as I can, and I test it, to see if it'll open — and then I'm gone. I've got a cup of coffee in me, and that's what I need to find my way down the stairs and into the street. Even if it's noon, it's dark as can be in our building's hall. Then I walk. I walk five blocks. I know the walk by heart. I guess I half sleep sometimes as I walk, because you know what: I'll catch myself sitting in the bus and I have no memory of walking to the bus or getting on the bus or sitting down in my seat. Can you believe it? I get scared when that happens. I asked her, Mrs. Albert, about it one day, and she said that she could understand how I feel, because she'll be in her art class, and the man says something and she doesn't hear him. She says it's "tuning out." She says your mind isn't happy where it is, so it goes someplace else. I believe that's what she said. It's hard keeping track of her meaning sometimes.

She's a fast one, that Mrs. Albert. It takes me over an hour to get to her house, an hour and a half a lot of the time. She has me come early so I can help her with the breakfast. She says she hates to make breakfast, because it's boring and it's no challenge, she says. So I'll be cooking their breakfast and getting them off to school, her girl and her boy. Her husband eats his breakfast later in the day at his office. I'm not sure, but I think he does. He has one cup of coffee, just like I do, then he leaves. He takes the paper with him. They get two copies of the same paper, one for her and one for him to take and read in his office. He's got a factory, I think. He makes dresses maybe, or shirts, or something like that. And his brother is a lawyer, and they're always talking about making money and losing money and borrowing money and loaning it and everything. Everyone has to think about money, even them!

I told you she is fast and smart. I'll get there, and it's a little after seven, sometimes half past. She is supposed to be asleep. I have my key. I come in and I try to be quiet, even though I know the two kids are up, waiting for me to give them a couple of pushes. They just won't come down to breakfast until I go to get them. How do you like that? So, I go. I guess she's trained them to wait and be called, and it's up to me. She's pretending to sleep, I'll be thinking. I'll get them down and I'm giving their father his black coffee, and them their juice and their eggs and cereal and milk and toast. I'm doing the best I can to keep them all happy. Some marmalade, Dorrie. More toast, Dorrie! Can I have another glass of milk? They ask and I go get for them. Their father is a gentleman, though; he'd pour his own coffee if I let him. But so long as I'm in the kitchen neither of those children would go do a thing for themselves. Mrs. Albert says it's like with me, they get distracted, and they forget to do things, so they have to be reminded. But, thank God, they're all gone by eight. He drives off and they get picked up by someone else — except when it's their mother's turn to take them all to school, and then don't even ask me what goes on. It's a bad week, and it's the week I have to get up at five o'clock, at least half an hour or more earlier than usual.

But most weeks I'm the one who sees them leave the house; then I'm supposed to clean up after them and start cleaning up in the other rooms and, of course, wait for her. She's asleep, you might think. There hasn't been a sound out of her while the others are up and washing and dressing and down here eating their breakfast. But no, as soon as his car leaves and the kids have closed the front door and are waiting outside to be picked up — then, quick as lightning she rings for me. I'm always right there, because by now I know her real good. Dorrie, she'll be saying to me, I'm so tired, but I musn't waste the whole day. Would you please bring me the paper and some coffee? I need my coffee. Then, while I'm getting her the coffee, she's quick to sit up, and she puts on the television and she's waiting for the tray. We do the same thing every day, but she just won't let me bring her the coffee until she rings and I hear her little speech: good morning, good morning, and how are *you*, Dorrie, and isn't it a lovely day, except she's still tired, or isn't it a terrible day, and on top of that she's tired.

I help her get over being tired. She wakes up after her coffee, and then she's on the go. She tries to decide what she's going to wear. Sometimes the weather outside isn't the weather the paper says we're going to have, so she asks me what I think. I tell her there's nothing like opening the window or the door and finding out for yourself. After she's got herself all washed and she's done her exercising, she's ready to come down and do her telephoning. She has her friends and she has to speak with them. She wants more coffee. She tells me to get something started for supper, if it's going to take a long time to cook, and to do the cleaning and all that. She's one that likes to tell you what to do, even if you know yourself. Sometimes she'll have her free time, she calls it. She reads books and magazines. She'll be reading something and you hear her saying things: I agree; I disagree; oh no! and oh, that's right! She says she's a great friend of ours, the Negro people. She'll write out a check to someone, and she'll tell me the money is going to help my people. I always thank her.

If she's going to stay at home for lunch, I have to give her the cottage cheese and all that. Lord, I don't know how she does it. She's got a little thing in her study, and she clicks it and clicks it, and it tells her how many of those calories she's had and how many she'll be having — for her supper, you know. Then she'll tell me she can't fit into something, and I'll look and see she's put on some weight around her middle. Once I was cleaning her bureau and I opened the drawer, and there they were under a sweater, M and M chocolate candy, just like my girls like to pop down. You start with them and you can't stop.

I have to answer the phone. She likes for me to say: Albert residence. Then I'm to say that I'll go and see if she's at home, even if I know she is, and even if she's standing but a little bit away from me. Sometimes her husband calls her, and I hear her saying that she's got a busy day, and she's trying to get everything straightened out, and she'll survive, so don't worry. Then she'll hang up and go back to her coffee. And she'll be yawning. And she'll be singing — "Hello Dolly" is her favorite. She says when she's one hundred she'll be singing that song. She sings when she gets dressed and she sings when she changes — from the pants she wears in the morning to her luncheon dress, she'll call it. She has special clothes for painting; they're supposed to be OK if you get the paint on, but she tries to be careful. Don't ask me what it is she paints. It's a big mess, I'll tell you that. I've tried to figure out what she's doing, but I can't. I just can't.

The worst time is when the kids come home. I'm the only one here. She's out doing something. Her husband, he certainly isn't going to be home until much later. Those kids are grumpy. They want attention. Dorrie, where is this? Dorrie, tell me where to go find that. Dorrie, Dorrie, Dorrie — until I could take both of them over my knee and spank them hard. Then their mother comes home and she asks them if everything is OK, and they say yes, and she asks me, and I say yes, and to myself I shake my head.

I wonder sometimes about white children. I'll be honest and say it to you: I worry. There's that girl of hers, Carolyn, and the boy, Peter. I feel sorry for them. They're lost little children; I mean it. You know, before they got me they brought over people from foreign countries, their mother told me. Lord, I've heard her list the countries but I forget — I think there was Scotland and Norway. The girls, she calls them, came and lived for a year. I guess they took care of the little kids while she and her husband went away and traveled all over the world. They were good girls, she'll tell you. They did right by her children, she'll tell you. But I don't think she's half as sure of herself as she sounds. It's funny; sometimes she'll tell me she wished that maybe she'd only had one person with them, and not four or five, and she wished it was me. But I tell her I couldn't ever go and leave my children to stay all night someplace else. Then she says yes, she knows; and then she'll ask me how I treat them, my children. I tell her I treat them real good, like a mother. On my tongue I'll be ready to say that I'd be a lot better mother if I could stay home and give my kids breakfast and be with them when they get home from school, but you know if I said that I'd be asking her to discharge me, and that would be bad, because I'd have no money. My husband is sick in the hospital with bad lungs, tuberculosis. How could I live if I didn't work? How could my children eat? How could I pay the rent? How could I get us clothes? And I'll tell you something else: if Mr. Harold was to die tomorrow — he might go any day the doctors keep warning me — and if I could go and get relief money from someone in the city, I'd still be right here working. I've never taken a cent of money from anyone that I didn't work for, nor has my husband all during his life — no sir, not a cent. I never will.

I can't put my finger on what's the trouble with Carolyn and Peter. The girl is twelve; the boy is eight. I like them. They want me to wait on them, and that's what I'm there to do, I guess. They seem as if they don't know what to do next, because there's so much they have to do. Carolyn has her ballet lessons. She'll tell me one day she wants to be dancing all her life, the ballet. I see her moving all over the place on her tiptoes, and it's not exercising she's doing, like her mother does. The girl wants to paint, like her mother. She says she'd like her mother to build them a huge place, and they could go and paint and paint. She asked me what I thought. I said that I hoped she got what she wanted, and I hoped she learned how to draw good pictures. Well, she got all high and mighty on me and told me that she wasn't going to do anything like that, because today a good artist doesn't bother with pictures. They do *designs*, she called them. I don't know what she's talking about. I've seen her, helping her mother in the basement. They walk all over the place, putting paint here and there and when they're through I catch a look and I say Jesus Christ, our Savior. I asked my minister if it's true that something can go to your head and mix you up and make you do that; because, you know, it's not like Mrs. Albert to be pushing paint all over and end up with no picture. Her husband told his friend that he has to live with those pictures, but if he had his way he'd have them hanging in the garage. I heard him on the phone.

The girl isn't too nice to the boy. Peter is a sorry child; that's what my mother would be calling him if she was alive and if she could look at him. He's been passed from woman to woman to take care of him, and he's scared I'll leave; he told me so. His mother told me a long time ago, a year ago, that she has some kind of *problem* with him. I have a problem with the boy, she announced to me one morning and I started to shake. I thought oh my God, what has happened to the poor little one. But she told me it was in her mind, and it's got to his mind, too; so she goes to a doctor and he tells her what is right and wrong, you know. She was trying to tell me some more, and I was trying to be as good at understanding as I could, but then she told me there was no use, and she wasn't even sure she knew what was the trouble herself, except that the poor boy used to go and hit other kids, and the teacher said he was fresh as could be, mean even. I've never seen him like that, not once. I told Mrs. Albert that. She said she knew he wouldn't be mean to me; it's just the other kids, and I guess his teacher, that he's mean to. I guess he was even mean to his mother. I told Mrs. Albert again: he is good with me, and he used to hold my hand real tight when I took him out for a walk, and even now he asks me if I'm coming back after my day off and if I'll stay next year. And when she and her husband go away on a trip and the grandmother comes to stay with them at night, the kids are especially good to me, and that little Peter, he'll come up to me, no kidding, and tell me I'm a real good cook, and he's sure glad to have me here. Well, I just take that boy around and give him a big kiss, and he'll be beaming right into my eyes.

Once Mr. and Mrs. Albert asked me if there was something they could both do for the colored people. They said they wanted to do more than give money. She said she'd like to give an afternoon of her time. He said he's too busy and he doesn't get home until seven o'clock at night, but he'd be happy if his wife could do something good, and maybe on Saturday afternoon he could come over and help out. I didn't know what to say. I didn't even know what they were talking about. I kept on saying, yes, yes, and yes ma'am, and yes sir. I told them please to give me a few days and I would have an answer if I could find one. You know what I was thinking? I was thinking to myself: God bless our reverend minister, Mr. Lawson. He'll help me out. So, after church on Sunday I asked him if I could please talk with him, just for a minute. He said yes, and he took me to the back of the church, and I told him. He didn't say anything for the longest time, and I thought he was plain stumped — and of all people, Mr. Lawson! Then he told me something. He said, you go tell your people out in the big house that there *is* a way they can help us. They can keep on doing all they're doing, donating money, but as far as coming here on Saturday afternoon is concerned, we don't need them. You can tell them that the best way they can help us is to stay home on Saturday afternoon and be with their kids, so they'll bring up better kids.

I was surprised. I didn't see what he meant. I said to him, Reverend Mr. Lawson, I know that you're right, I just know you are. But if the Alberts help their kids to be better, I'm not sure how that will help us over here. Well, he told me right away. He said there are too many white people coming around here and trying to help us and telling us how to do everything and saying we're in a bad way; and meanwhile, just take a look at *them.* *They're* in a bad way. They're all messed up. They go around feeling sorry for us, but with all their money and everything, they have kids who are crying all the time and mean as can be and getting into trouble, and all that. Mr. Lawson said if they'd bring up better kids, the country would be better, and then we'd have it better over here where we live.

I told him I didn't know how I was going to tell the Alberts, tell them his message. He said just to go tell them. I said no. And I didn't. I'd be fired. I'm no fool. Mr. Lawson, he's a preacher. He can go and say those things, but not me. I told Mr. and Mrs. Albert that I'd been thinking, and I couldn't come up with something for them to do, but I was sure there was something, and as soon as I find it out, I'll tell them. They didn't seem to mind that

I'd failed them. Mrs. Albert thanked me just the same for trying, and she told me later that she was just as glad that Mr. Albert was going to have his Saturday afternoons free from now on through the summer, because he needed to exercise, just like she needs to, and maybe now he'd go and play golf for three or four hours and he'd lose that little rubber tire he's getting, she calls it, around his stomach. Then he would look ten years younger, and that would be good for his mind, and it would help him in his business, too, she said. Isn't that right, Dorrie, she asked me, like always, and I said I'm a maid and what do I know, but she's right, I do know that. And she said I was real good to say so.

8. Vanessa

The girl is thin, small for her seven years, slow-moving. She is shy, but can suddenly gain confidence in herself and lose her fear of a particular stranger. She shows her new-found assurance by blurting out a brief comment or two, then settling into a more relaxed and informal posture. No longer is she sitting at the edge of a chair. No longer does she hold on to that chair for dear life with her small but tenacious fingers. No longer does she fix her eyes upon the intruder — as if, were she to let go of him, God knows what might happen, God knows where she might go. She and her mother both use "God knows" rather often. The mother is a devout, churchgoing lady, but complains that she cannot stop herself from swearing. She has been told since she was a child, growing up in Strawberry, South Carolina, that God deserves better than being shouted out all the time as an expression of one's state of mind — but still she does it, says "for God's sake" and "oh, my God" and "good God," and especially, "God knows." And the reason why is very simple: her mother, little Vanessa's grandmother, did the very same thing — for which she was constantly chastised by Berkeley County's best preacher, maybe the best one in all the state of South Carolina, and maybe even the best one in all of America, Mr. Minister Arthur Henry Redfield, whose qualities Vanessa's mother describes quite briefly and to the point: "He spoke so loud you could hear him across an ocean, and he made your heart beat faster and your back get the prickles, because he had the word of God in him, you could tell, you always could."

Vanessa was born in Strawberry, but just barely. At the age of six months she was literally carried North. Her mother and her grandmother took her out of the cabin in which she was born and walked about five miles, they estimate, until they came to an intersection where buses pick up and discharge passengers. After an hour's wait the bus arrived, the baby was carried aboard, and then held in her mother's or her grandmother's arms for the two days the trip North took. Needless to say, Vanessa now remembers none of that. She finds it strange that she has to tell a friend or a schoolteacher that she was born in Strawberry, South Carolina, and she even finds it strange that others don't necessarily find that fact very strange. To Vanessa it seems only logical that she should have been born in Roxbury, Massachusetts, where she feels she has always been, and where to her eye all her friends and all their parents and grandparents have also always been. That is why Vanessa gets annoyed when she hears a woman from the welfare department saying "of course" in response to the answer "Strawberry, South Carolina" as "the little girl's place of birth."

Nor does Vanessa quite like that expression "little girl." She knows all too well that she is small for her age, but she feels big and important, the apple of her grandmother's eye she is often called by that old, tired, also small lady — who considers herself a lay preacher, and every bit as good as Mr. Arthur Henry Redfield ever was. And so Vanessa, like her grandmother, is given to making comparisons, measuring herself against others and, in her opinion, measuring up to those others: "I'll be as big up as her one day, as big as the welfare lady. I could go around like her right now, if my momma let me, and I could ask the questions she does, and I'd get as good answers as she does. And I wouldn't go around saying, 'You sweet little thing,' and 'Aren't you a nice little girl, a little darling.' She's trying to be *somebody*, somebody big, that's all."

Why is the "welfare lady" acting like that, one wants to ask

Vanessa. But Vanessa doesn't take to those kinds of questions. When she has decided to unbend, when she has decided that she can talk freely and speak out on the things she thinks about and worries over, she becomes forthright and almost truculent in manner, and she does not suffer fools easily. All right, *all right* — she seems to say with her face and breathing but not in words: if you simply have to have the answer to the most obvious and unnecessary question in the world, then I will go ahead and give one to you, as lengthy an answer as I have the patience to offer, hence a very brief one: "Because her supervisor tells her to act like that."

Vanessa has heard the welfare worker mention her supervisor, mention what the supervisor will and will not approve. Vanessa hears everything, it seems, and forgets nothing — or so her mother and grandmother say. The child is bright, they know, and will herself one day be *somebody* — and by that they do not mean a welfare worker or a woman who supervises welfare workers. They would like Vanessa to be a singer, or a lawyer, or a teacher in a good school, or be "in the government," like a black woman they know. The woman's name escapes them, though. Unlike Vanessa they do forget things. In fact, often they ask the girl to remind them to do something, and sure enough they are not disappointed: the "little girl" comes through true to form, and they once again tell her how glad they are that God has sent her down for a time — to be with them on this earth and help them out and give them something they can feel good about.

Vanessa doesn't like that kind of talk, with its implicit pessimism. She is a hopeful, alert child who for a year or so has dreamed of going on a trip to South Carolina so that she might see where she was born. Afterwards she would like to visit Mexico. In school she was shown pictures of Mexican children, gaily dressed and laughing, and she decided that she would like to visit their country. Besides, Mexico is south, too: "I hear it's not in America, though." Well, it actually is, she is told. It is not in *the United States.* "Well, isn't the United States the same as America?" No, comes the answer. "Well, aren't we the biggest, and don't they all want to be part of us?" No, comes the answer.

"Well, a boy told me we can own as many countries as we want. Isn't that true?" Now no answer comes. Instead, I tried to find out about those talks she was having with her friends — about Mexico and the United States and the nature of political power. "I talk with Sidney, and his father tells him about everything the teacher mentions." But that is only the beginning. Vanessa's sources of information are various and complicated — and she wants me to know that. Naturally, her preoccupations are set in motion by what happens in school, but for the most part the schools only prompt new directions for forces that are already at work: "We'll hear the teacher say something, then later, on the way home, Sidney says he'll ask his father. I joke with Sidney. I say, 'Sidney, why should I believe your father knows any more than our teacher?' Sidney says his father never finished high school, but he's been looking into books all his life and he's forty years old, and that's old. I say to Sidney that my mother never looks into books at all, but she's smarter than the teacher, and she could be just as smart as Sidney's father. I don't really know, because I haven't even met him.

"Sidney is always talking about the black man. He says he's going to be a big black man; he'll lead all the colored people. He gets mad. He gets especially mad when I say that — when I say 'the colored people.' 'You stupid Vanessa,' he'll say. 'You Uncle Tom's girl. You're talking like you're an old grandmother.' 'Sidney, *you're* stupid,' I tell him. And he *is*. He thinks he's smart; he thinks he's *so, so* smart. I told him this; I said, 'Sidney, if you're so smart, you won't go around talking about black, black, black, and about the Mexican people being better than we are.' I told him that in South Carolina the colored people hate being called black, because it is a swearword. And who's ever seen a person from Mexico? Sidney hasn't and I haven't. That's silly, to go and say all the people who live in Mexico are better than us, when you haven't even seen them.

"I have another friend, Betty. Betty says Sidney is right, because we should say black and not colored. I guess they're both of them right, though I don't agree with them. They were born here, and my mother tells me that even though I'm up here, I wasn't born up here. But it's stupid to say to me that I wasn't born here; it really is. My mother tells me to hush my mouth and not use the word 'stupid,' but I don't care. If you say something stupid, it's stupid. There's no difference between colored and black — and it's stupid to say there is. They both mean the same thing; that's what I think. But I'd like to go to Mexico. From the pictures I can tell that they're different from us in Mexico, the people are. I think they can dance and they can laugh and they have real nice clothes. They know how to sing. They look real happy."

It is natural to want to reassure her, or even argue with her — by insisting that one needn't go to Mexico to meet a child who can sing and dance well and who by her own accounts is happy. As for nice clothes, Vanessa has two quite lovely dresses (presents to her from her mother) which she wears on Sundays and holidays. They are exactly what the young lady wanted, and she will declare herself as happy as she can possibly be after she has shown them off. The trouble is that although she argues angrily with Sidney and Betty, later, when they are gone, Vanessa comes around to their way of thinking. It is as if she battles her friends as long as she can, insists on winning (to her belief and satisfaction, at least) every argument she becomes involved in — only to surrender quietly to some inner stirrings and voices that get no explicit recognition from her, only the fierce acceptance of her strong-minded manner of putting things: "You hear that sticks and stones will break your bones, but names will never harm you. That's not so. In Mexico the kids probably aren't called 'nigger.' Here, if you go outside this part of the city, you're in real bad trouble. I'm glad no bus is taking me across town to those white people, to their schools. I'm real glad of that! They call you names. Betty says her cousin is going on the bus, and she says it's all right there, but Betty doesn't believe her. Maybe it *is* all right; I don't know. Sidney says no. Betty says no. I told them they were wrong, but afterwards I remembered what my grandmother always says: 'Tell the white people to their face they're wonderful, if you ever have to talk with them, but don't you believe it.' She said there are some nice ones — white people —

but there are so many bad ones that she used to ask her mother the same thing Betty says she's always asking her older brother: why don't we go someplace else — I mean to another country?

"I've never asked my mother why we don't go live in another country, because it's all right here; it's all right. But it probably *is* pretty good in the country of Mexico, and I'd like to go there sometime — just to look around. Sidney and Betty and I could go there, and we could keep on calling Sidney's mother up. She has a phone. Betty doesn't, and I don't. I'll bet no one would call us nigger there, like they do up here. Sidney was right when he said that. I just don't like him always *telling* me things. I told him, 'Look here, Sidney, and that goes for Betty, I know about the whole world, just like you do.' And I really do. My momma tells me things, from what she sees on TV, and I remember. Then I make sure I tell Sidney and Betty and they're surprised sometimes, because they don't know what I've told them until they hear it from me."

So, she gets all taken up with a country like Mexico. She wants to know precisely where it is, that strange and wonderful country of smiling, singing, cheerful girls, whose hair is black, whose complexion is dark, whose rulers are not her rulers, whose customs she has been led to believe, she is firmly convinced, offer a respite of sorts — to whom? The answer is to her — a seven-year-old girl, a New Englander born a Southerner, a "good and tidy" girl, her teacher says, a "smart girl," her minister says, "a domineering little girl" says the lady whom Vanessa herself calls "the nosy welfare lady." And no doubt about it, Vanessa does have a forceful presence, though she seems to push neither her mother nor her grandmother around. They are also "domineering" to my eye; or at least they speak out, speak up, indeed hold forth at great length when asked to, or when given any reasonable chance at all to do so. "Someday," Vanessa once told me around Christmastime, "I might even try to go visit the North Pole. I know there's no Santa Claus. But I'll bet you could have a good time up there. No one lives there, practically, so you could run as fast as you want and never be afraid of falling down and getting hurt. They tell me that in Strawberry, South Carolina, there were fields and I could be running all over if that's where I lived; the only trouble is soon you'll bump into a fence or trees, my grandma says. Around here you can't run at all. I fell down the other day from running, and some glass cut up my knee real bad, and some of it got inside, and I had to go to the hospital and the doctor took it out and took it out, until I thought he'd never stop, and then he told me I shouldn't be running where there's a lot of glass, and I should first clean up the street, and then do my running. I didn't say a word back to him. I was afraid to say anything because he was hurting me, and he could have hurt me more. I told my momma afterwards what he said. It's not my fault that there's so much glass on the sidewalk. I didn't put the glass there."

Then she paused for a long time. She had lost her train of thought. She struggled and struggled with herself and finally saw it, reached for it, got it — her line of reasoning: "I'll bet there's no glass up there in the North Pole, not one piece." Was that true, she asked. I said yes, so far as I knew, quite true. And then her mother, hearing us and a little ill at ease, joined in from the next room: "I'll bet there are no doctors up there, either. Right?" I said, "Right," but Vanessa only shrugged her shoulders. Later on she pointed out to me that one scarcely needs a doctor if one is not going to be hurt; and I didn't think it "appropriate" at that moment, in that rather cold tenement flat, to press facts and a certain kind of logic upon her by reminding her what the weather of the Arctic can sometimes do to a person's health.

9. Vanessa's Mother

"My Vanessa," the mother often says rather possessively. And by no means would that description of her manner of speaking be resented; for Vanessa's mother is quite willing to be candid: "I guess you could say that for my mother and for me Vanessa is all we have. The only thing she has to do is catch a cold, and we're both of us having trouble sleeping, we worry over her so. I have my brother up here, you know, but we don't see much of him. We came here because he was here, he and his family. He says we

treat Vanessa too good for her own good, but that's not so. I'll
whip her sometimes. I have to do it. But I'll admit: I don't like
whipping the most important thing that I have in the whole wide
world."

Is she, perhaps, *too* possessive of that one child of hers? Is *that*
why Vanessa wants to go to Mexico and the North Pole and God
knows where? I very much doubt so. Vanessa's mother, in fact,
has rather a light touch with her daughter. She gives her considerable leeway, lets her have her say, allows her more or less to
do as she pleases — but always within firm limits that have been
thoroughly declared and discussed. She is a talker, the mother;
she likes to say what is on her mind. She is also a tough and
honest woman, who has been ailing for many years with a serious
bone disorder that makes it hard for her to walk and impossible
for her to work: "I have tuberculosis of the bone, the doctors told
me when I got up here, and it means both my knees are in real
bad shape. The best job a woman like me can get is housework,
or scrubbing floors in a business place, and I can't even scrub
floors in my own little place right here in this building. I'm supposed to rest. I have worked all my life, but the doctors say I was
getting sick all the while I was working. Just after we came up
here I couldn't walk far without stopping, because my right knee
hurt so bad. They asked me in the hospital if I'd ever worked on
my knees. Oh God, have I! I told them I'd been in the fields since
I was little, picking and picking, and that's why I have pain down
there now. But they said there might be another reason and
they'd have to check closer. And Lord Almighty if they didn't
come up with something bad — this tuberculosis they say I've
got. My lungs are good, they say. They watch over my lungs.
They're always snapping pictures of my chest. The welfare pays
for me to go there in a cab, because they say I'm too sick to get
there any other way. I take Vanessa and good God, I feel better
having her there with me to hold on to. She's a great comfort to
us, you know, to me and her grandma.

"I've asked myself a lot of the time what would have happened
if I'd stayed there in Strawberry, South Carolina. I can tell you
the answer. I'd be dead now. The doctors up here told me so;

and I believe them. Even if they didn't decide to tell me, I would have thought so to myself. There will be a moment every day or two when I think I'd just as soon be back in Strawberry, but it's only a moment and no more. All I have to do is bend my legs — to get up or to sit down — and I'm in bad trouble, in pain; then I look at the pills they've given me and I'm glad I'm right here. One pill fights the germs. One pill fights the pain. And I'm fighting on my own, you know. My husband walked out on me just before we left South Carolina. I don't for the life of me know what happened. He was tired, and we didn't have a single penny to our name, and if it wasn't for my brother up here, sending us ten dollars every week — yes sir, every week — then I think we all would have starved to death, and no fooling. On Tuesdays, I think it was, we walked to the post office, and the lady gave us the letter and there would always be the ten-dollar bill right inside. Do you know I kissed the money, each time I did. The first time, I started to cry when I saw the bill before my eyes and the number ten on it. I was heavy with Vanessa and I talked to her. I told her: Vanessa honey, this here ten-dollar bill that your uncle Charles has sent us from Roxbury, Massachusetts, way up there, is going to feed you, honey, and you'll be strong that way, and when you come out into the world, you'll be here to stay. You won't die. I think I felt her kicking in me afterwards. She must have been listening real good. And she still does. She hears every word I say, by God.

"I was telling you about her daddy, Vanessa's. I believe it hurt him that my brother had to keep us going. He tried to find work, but there was no use in his trying because there weren't any jobs. Once I saw him with his head into his hands, and I was afraid he might be crying. I'd never seen him cry. A man isn't supposed to cry. I don't even think we should, the women. If you pray to God, He'll help you, and there's no reason to feel so sorry for yourself, because if He's going to call you to Him, He's just going to do it, and tears in your eyes won't change a single thing. My husband wasn't crying. Maybe he was deciding to leave. I don't know. Two days later he was gone. I didn't know what to say. I didn't know what to do. I didn't go to the police, no. They wouldn't do anything, anyhow. They'd laugh at me. They'd tell me to get away, fast. They'd maybe arrest me and throw me in jail. When a colored person is in trouble because of another colored person, the police in Berkeley County, South Carolina, just laugh and laugh and clap their hands. The Reverend Redfield, Mr. Arthur Henry Redfield, he'd been telling us that for a long time, and when I went to see him and told him he's gone, that's what Mr. Redfield said as soon as the word 'police' came out of my mouth.

"I looked all over for him. Mr. Redfield married us on February 1, 1962, and he told us the day and I've never forgotten. Mr. Redfield looked all over, too. He has a car and he said he covered every road he knew in the county. I went to his church one day, while he was looking for my husband, trying to find him, and I prayed all day long. I asked God please to whisper something in my husband's ear so that he'll turn around and come back. I prayed to God that something bad didn't happen to him. I was scared. I'd never prayed so long and so hard in my whole life. I didn't know what He'd think, God, because there I was, calling on Him so much, and I know He always has a lot on His mind. It was getting dark and I was tired. Vanessa, she wasn't far away from being born. I thought I'd better go home. I was getting ready to leave the church. I was saying one last prayer to myself. I was saying good-bye to God and thanking Him for listening to me. All of a sudden I heard a noise in the back of the church, and oh my God, I thought it was him; I thought it was my husband. I thought God had brought him back to me. I screamed out to God. I said, 'Thank you, dear God,' and I ran toward the back of the church and it was dark and I almost tripped and fell — my knees! — and then I saw, I saw him. It was him, the reverend. He told me it was no use. He told me I shouldn't worry too much. He told me I had to think of myself and my little child inside of me. He said he thought my husband had left and was someplace we'd never find him, maybe in Charleston or Savannah, a city. I told him I didn't think so. I told him I feared he was sick someplace, and in bad pain. But I knew he'd gone. I just knew it in my heart. I think I knew he was leaving even before he left. Don't ask me how. I don't know, but I knew.

"Then Vanessa came. She came all of a sudden in the middle of the night. My mother was the one, she was; my mother took the baby from me. My mother has done it before. I was sick afterwards. I blame it on him going. He'd only been gone a week or so when Vanessa was born. I still was missing him awful bad. Why does a man leave before his baby is born? Vanessa will never see her daddy. I'll never get married again. I have a boyfriend up here. I see him once in a while. But he's not the man my husband was. I tell Vanessa the man is a little like her daddy, and then she asks if he's as good — she's always comparing, isn't she? — and I say no, not nearly as good.

"I got better and then my mother said we had to go, all three of us. We had to go up to Massachusetts. My brother Charles said it was hard on him, making only sixty-five dollars a week, to send us ten dollars, and if we came up then we could go on welfare. In Berkeley County, South Carolina, we couldn't get anything. Mr. Redfield asked. He went over and talked with a man, a white man, and the white man said no; he said how did he know my husband went and left for real. Maybe he was pretending. Mr. Redfield said he was a minister of God, and he was ready to take an oath before the man, the white man; but the welfare man told the reverend to get out of his office in a hurry if he didn't want to be in a serious fix. We told Mr. Redfield not to stick his neck out any more. We told him we'd be out of Strawberry as fast as we could. And we left the next day. I'm glad we left. I only wish my husband was here. The last words of the reverend were: be grateful to God that you have that nice, healthy girl to take with you. And I said I surely was. He asked me what I was going to call her, and I said Vanessa, after her daddy's mother, that was her name. He said that was good and it showed I was forgiving him. But I never did blame him! I really didn't. He loved me and he always took good care of my momma, and he wanted that child so bad. I think he was feeling low because he couldn't bring us any money. He didn't see a future for himself, none. He probably decided to go wandering. I guess he thought maybe he'd find some good luck someplace. I don't know why he didn't tell us to go North — or just *take* us there. I don't know the answer to what happened to him. Bad as it was for us, he was making sure I was getting something to eat. To tell you the truth, he wasn't eating much himself. He was pushing all the food into me 'for the baby,' he said — and he must have been so hungry it might have made him weak and gone to his head, and because of that he didn't know what he was doing. We used to see that happen in Strawberry. People would get dizzy from hunger and soon they'd die.

"Up here there's the welfare. Vanessa doesn't like it here, but I'll take the welfare lady to the sheriff back there. Vanessa talks about Mexico, but that's a child's mind imagining things. We've got to stay here. I try to tell Vanessa about how it was back South, but then I have a change of mind and I decide it's better to spare her. And she might start asking too many questions. That would be no good. I wouldn't want to answer her."

Vanessa, to be sure, doesn't now ask her mother those dreaded questions. Instead, she listens attentively to teachers and friends, and wonders about all sorts of things, and is curious about what is going on everywhere. What is more, to the confusion of her mother, the child (at the age of seven) has a way of getting thoroughly political. Perhaps it is the influence upon her of a boy like Sidney. Perhaps she picks up in her school the tensions between teachers and children, and indeed between an entire black community and a particular school system. Perhaps she is simply a sensitive human being, able to respond like many others to obvious, concrete situations which are themselves ultimately political: the welfare lady's remarks she hears; the policeman's constant surveillance she sees; the foul and dank air she smells in one hallway after another; the rats she has felt jumping on her bed. Like so many children Vanessa knows enough to be gentle with a parent she very much loves. Why should she press her mother too hard, her mother who has seen so very much herself, and is tired and in pain and in a new land of sorts? Why should she try to unravel and fathom the bitter private world of her own family, whose mysteries she may sense more deeply than she understands?

Vanessa once told her mother that she knew her father had died in some war. No, the mother replied, that wasn't the case.

But it was, it was, the child insisted. As she became more petulant, the mother became more open to metaphorical answers: "I
told her that her daddy had always been a fighter, and he'd never
given up in any fight. I told her he was a brave man, and he went
to church every Sunday, and with my own ears I'd hear him
asking God for strength to keep up the fight, just the way Mr.
Redfield, the reverend, said we all should do, keep up the fight."
Vanessa apparently listened with approval but was not completely satisfied; she wanted more than generalities, however
clothed in religious sanction. She wanted more drama. She
wanted more details. She wanted Strawberry's fights somehow
connected to Roxbury's; she wanted her past connected to her
present — and indeed to her future. Now, how does one know all
that? Vanessa's mother knows all that because she heard the
child ask this: "Daddy must have been in a big fight, in a war.
Sidney says the Civil War is still going on, and they haven't freed
the slaves yet. Is that the fight Daddy was in?" The answer, of
course, was no. The Civil War is over, Vanessa's mother said. The
Civil War happened a long, long time ago, way before even
Grandmother was born — or so Vanessa heard her mother say,
while her grandmother nodded in emphatic agreement. But later
Vanessa's mother admitted that on especially bad days she does
have her "terrible moods" — when she doubts almost everything,
including "that the Civil War ever *did* end." And Vanessa no
doubt has a fine sense of those moods.

10. *Vanessa's Grandmother*

"I am an old, old woman. I have seen many people die. I don't
understand how I have stayed alive myself. But when I was a
little girl, maybe a few years older than Vanessa, my mother told
me that no matter how bad it is for the colored people, God
keeps a few of us alive for years and years, until we're real old.
The reason is He wants us to know that some of us can outlast all
the troubles we have to carry. I don't know if many of my people
really do want to get older and older, though. A lot of colored

people will tell you after church that they're ready to go right away. I've felt ready for years and years; but He isn't ready, and He's the One who does the deciding. So, I'm here, and at least I can spend some time with Vanessa and my daughter and my son."

She is not just waiting to be called by her Lord. She takes good care of the apartment she shares with her daughter and her granddaughter. She is a spry, lively, efficient woman who tries to keep things neat, and will empty an ashtray quietly but predictably after a visitor has had one cigarette and before another one is begun. As for the rats that plague the building, she goes after them with a broom and finds them not at all unnerving or disgusting: "I grew up with animals," she reminds her urbane and frightened and queasy guests, "and there's no reason to let them get you scared. You *do* know they're scared of you, don't you? I hear talk that the rats up here aren't like that, and instead will come into a room even if you're there and ready to chase after them. I've not met such a rat. I pick up that broom and they run away so fast I can't keep up with them; I can't get to them. And I'm not slow, no matter how many years I'm carrying around with me."

Indeed, she is not slow. She is agile and circumspect and ready in a second to do what has to be done: go on an errand, fetch Vanessa, prepare a meal, or dispatch the vermin that she almost seems to enjoy hunting down, as if through them she can in a way relive the decades she spent in rural South Carolina. I note the pride she has — a pride that defies efforts of sympathizers to pity her, to feel aghast at the circumstances of her life, to remark upon her advanced age and her declining vigor and her marginal, vulnerable "position" in our society. Maybe if she were as "educated" as some of her earnest, sometimes well-intentioned supporters, she would be less quick to justify the status quo, less prone to explain away decades of hardship with a kind of lighthearted resignation — as if what God meant to be must be, and that is that.

In any event, after hearing someone on television express dismay at what her people have experienced in America, and right now continue to experience, the old lady who would rather be called Vanessa's grandmother than anything else in the world responded rather ungratefully: "I guess they want us all to thank them; they'd like us to say thank you, thank you, Mr. White Man, for being so worried over us colored folks. All my life I've hated one thing: to feel sorry for yourself. My daddy, he wasn't so far from slavery. He grew up with old slaves around him, and that's what they used to tell him: son, when you start feeling sorry for yourself, that's the worst kind of slavery. It's worse than chains, moaning over your troubles. I tell Vanessa that she's a good girl, a strong girl, and a child of God's. I tell her not to go around saying, 'Oh, we've got it bad, and oh, if only some nice white people would come and help us out.' They went hounding after Jesus Christ, and he didn't ask them to be kind to Him. He said, 'I am the Way.' He said, 'I am the Lord, so you'd better change — for your own sake, you'd better!' Now, He knew. Like the Reverend Redfield would tell us in Strawberry, Jesus knew and He expected us to follow His example. And that's why I can't have any use, no use at all, for all those nice white folks who say: the poor, poor colored people, they're just in terrible shape, and if something doesn't happen fast to make their life easier, then they're all going to disappear, or they're going to start running crazy all over the place, killing each other off. I think if my daddy heard that, he'd go and fight with the one who said it and knock him out. My daddy was a big man."

I have to conclude, then, that she is a stubborn, proud, unrelenting woman; she asks for no special advantages, and indeed shuns offers of help as patronizing and condescending and demeaning. Or does she "really" want help — "underneath," in the recesses of her thoughts, in the back of her mind? Is she, therefore, combative and suspicious and doubtful because she "masks" that way her unstated and maybe unconscious "attitudes" or "demands"? Who wants to make such clear-cut distinctions? I suppose the answer is: social scientists like me. For Vanessa's grandmother, life simply will not permit psychological categorizations and approximations — unless they are thoroughly full of hesitations and qualifications: "I guess there will be an

afternoon when I wish the whole country would be turned
upside down, and it would come about that the colored people
weren't so poor any more, and we had all we deserve, after these
bad times we've had. If I ever live to see something like that
happen, I'll sure be surprised. I'm glad to hear that a lot of white
people are coming over to our side. I'm glad to see we're moving
along — up the ladder, up and up. But I hate to drop in on
Vanessa and her friends talking; to hear them, it's only in the
coming years that there will be any change, and it's only because
of *them* that the colored folks will be better off. I told her, I told
my grandchild, what I've seen happen in *my* lifetime. She doesn't
know what it was like — the things we got done as well as the
pain we had. And in school, the teachers don't tell children that;
they don't tell children what their own grandmothers and grandfathers accomplished during their lives. Vanessa should understand how others struggled, and how they didn't *only* lose.
Vanessa shouldn't think it's going to be up to her and her friends
and no one else but them. It's like I heard a man say once, a
white man, in Strawberry: we're going to get there in the end,
but it'll take us longer than any of us ever lives. I believe he was
talking about the day everything would be straightened out.

"I want Vanessa to know what good work we all did in
Strawberry: we made that land grow and grow! I wish someday
I could take her back and let her see that it's no deep dark prison
down there. I can't say I was sorry to leave, and I'm as happy as
I can be that Vanessa is growing up here. But up here children
have funny ideas about the state of South Carolina. And it's not
right that they should. I'd like them to grow up to feel they're as
good as anyone else — and that *we always have been* as good.
I'd like them, Vanessa and Sidney and all those wonderful children of God's, to know that He's been smiling on us ever since
He made us, the colored people. I'd like us to be on top, yes I
would. I'd like us to have more of everything, yes I would. I
agree with the young folks: we have to fight for our rights. But I
don't like it when I hear a man say — be he colored or white —
that we've never had anything, and we've always been so low.
We've been without things, and we've been at the bottom; I

agree. But we've been God-fearing. We've had God; and He's something to have — Someone. And I'll tell you: we've had each other to turn to. I'd go down the road in Strawberry and sit with a friend and we'd feel a lot better by the time we'd had a cup of coffee. Bad as it was, we had some coffee. It might not be the good coffee you buy up here. We had to make it weak so it would last longer. But we could heat it up and it felt good going down you."

What she does *not* talk about, what her modesty will not allow her to mention, may well be more significant than anything else: the trust her granddaughter has in her, the questions the child asks of her, the information Vanessa knows that her grandmother possesses, however old and tired she may appear to be. Of course, one can detect a "gap" between the grandmother and the grandchild. Of course, they don't see eye to eye on all sorts of subjects. Yet, every day Vanessa comes to the old woman and inquires about something, asks for an opinion, a statement, a comment. Neither of them is self-conscious. Neither feels awkward or brazen about asking and replying, showing curiosity and demonstrating knowledge. Vanessa puts a question to her grandmother because she knows a sensible and valuable answer will be forthcoming. Her grandmother feels free to do the same, request information as well as supply it. Vanessa tells her grandmother how things are done in Roxbury and is in turn told how once they were done elsewhere. They are natural friends and canny allies. Each of them knows she has a lot to offer, and each of them knows that the point of life is to proceed ahead rather than stop and feel down and out and forsaken and endangered and embittered: "I tell Vanessa, and then she tells me back, that you can't stand around and waste your life. There's every day to get through. She'll be through with her breakfast and there's school and she doesn't want to go. She'd rather be here with her mother and me. I say, 'Come on now, Vanessa.' Then she says, 'I know, I know. I can't sit here, because two of you doing that is enough.' She'll recite back my words, every single one of them. But another time I'll feel low myself, and I can just hear that girl saying,

'Come on, come on, you can't just sit there. The sun doesn't get tired, nor the moon, and you can't either.'

"Lord, when I hear her talking like that I know there's a reason for me to be here. I used to hear the same thing when I was a little girl. I used to hear my momma talk like that. And now my granddaughter, she's heard me, and she won't forget, and she won't let *me* forget, either. I swear to you, she talks as if she's made up her own mind about the sun and the moon, and I'm supposed to hear what she says and forget I've said the same thing myself. I used to tell her mother when she was a little girl that the only thing you can do when you get tired is remember that the world doesn't depend on only you, but on your children and the children they'll have, and on and on it will go. So, when you're as old as me and you hear your words from a child like Vanessa — then you know you can't be discouraged, because there's always help coming. Vanessa will be there to look at, I say to myself sometimes when I can't seem to get myself out of bed. Then she'll get up and the first thing I'll hear her do is call for her mother and call for me. So I figure we're all doing all right by each other around here."

The old woman does have her bad spells, however. It is not nostalgia that seizes her so much as moments of anger and sadness — and those moments both surprise and overwhelm her. She is convinced that had she never left Strawberry, South Carolina, she would not today feel so bitter about some of the things that happened "down there." Instead, she would be living out her life, and if not fully at peace with herself and her condition, at least there would not be for her the "agitation" she now knows — and attributes to the workings of a detached, somewhat liberated mind: "I guess after you come up here you're free of the bossman and the sheriff, and you start getting back at them in your thinking. There's one big difference between Vanessa and me that I can tell you about: when Vanessa doesn't like someone, when she's being put upon by someone, she'll just speak out — and my God it scares me to hear her talk. But that's not how I was reared to be. I was reared to be quiet and say nothing, not if any white man was within five miles, my daddy would say. I was reared to do my best, but not talk back if I wasn't getting the right treatment. We went to a school for a while, and those teachers, they could be mean on a child. I tell Vanessa that to this day I remember a teacher hitting on me and calling me bad names. And Vanessa right away told me that she must have been a bad white woman. 'Oh, Vanessa,' I said. 'You don't know the half of it!' I explained to her that I never saw a white teacher in my life. You don't have to be white to be a mean one, no sir, you don't. If Vanessa only could see that school, she wouldn't be so unhappy about her school.

"But I hear her talk, and I'm sure she's right in what she says. I guess there's no point in her resting on what she's got, any more than I rested on what I had back there. After all, I was the one who told Vanessa's mother that the time had come for us to go, and before that, I told my son to go and never come back, *never!* So Vanessa has to decide on things, too. I don't think she'll be walking to a bus, like I did when I left Strawberry; I don't think she'll move to another part of the country to escape the white man. I think she'll just dig her feet in where she is, and say, 'Look now, I'm staying, and I'm going to have some changes take place right here before my eyes, because there's no place to go to, because this is my home, and you don't leave a home if you can help it.' "

11. *The Wanderers*

They had almost invariably lived in one place all their lives when they came to the city. They were born where they once lived, and their parents or grandparents or great-grandparents had most likely died there and no place else: a cabin, a shack, a place or a "spot" on the bossman's property. Suddenly they are no more there. Suddenly they live in a building in a city, far away from "home." And suddenly they are adrift. They do not settle into one building and stay there and stay there, as their sharecropper ancestors did. They move from one address to another. First there is this building, where a brother or sister or

cousin or uncle or aunt are staying. Then there is the next building, and the next one, and the next one. Sometimes the buildings
are relatively nearby; but a family can just as well hop, skip, and
jump all over a city, within the confines of the so-called ghetto, of
course. A family can even move from city to city: from Boston to
Hartford, or from Harlem to Bedford-Stuyvesant to Newark.

Such families elude creditors, city officials and, significantly,
statisticians who like to know who lives where. Such families can
be called all sorts of things: unstable, shiftless, rootless, disor-
ganized. Such families are, to other families in the ghetto, a
source of apprehension and surprise and speculation and sadness. For a long time I hesitated to talk about "such families."
How did I know that these were in fact a recognizable "group" of
people whose "adjustment" to northern cities has been one of
continual movement — to the point that within a year or so, four
or five apartments are obtained, lived in, then hastily abandoned
for the next one. What distinguishes "such families" from other
people, who find one building too expensive, a second impossibly
infested with rats or cockroaches, a third with no heat, a fourth
so full of addicts that "the children stumble all over them, and
I'm afraid one day a little child of mine will come here with a
needle mark in his arm"?

Over the years I have simply learned to expect that from time
to time a family will be pointed out to me as "movers," as people
whom others quickly come to know as "moving, moving, always
moving." Nor is there any one "explanation" for such behavior.
Some people may be fleeing the police, others have no money to
pay bills and find a midnight departure the best way to wipe
clean the slate, still others have less obvious reasons, reasons of
the mind and heart, I suppose it can be said. For example, they
can't "take" the city but can't go back South, either — and so they
hope that a new building, a different street, will perhaps "quiet
their nerves down," give them a feeling, at long last, of the
"peace" they openly say they are seeking. Words like crime,
poverty, indebtedness begin to explain something; but again, for
certain people there are ghosts that are to be fled, shadows that
make inexplicable visits, noises that unaccountably are taken to
mean danger, mean the presence of the devil himself.

Here is a woman talking about her own sister: "I can't figure out what has happened to her and her husband. They're always in trouble. He's had a few jobs, but in one they closed up the store, and then he was let off the second time because business is slow and they didn't even want a man around to clean up. My sister said she had no money, so I told her to stay with us while she goes on welfare, and then her husband could come and be with her except for when the welfare lady shows up. But he wouldn't listen to me, nor she; I couldn't talk with her, my own sister. They kept on telling us that they were going home, and they'd rather be in Georgia than up here. Now, can you imagine that! I reminded them that they shot and killed our brother because he stared back at a white man and wouldn't apologize to him for saying something bad under his breath. I reminded them of *everything*. But they said we had to be real fools to stay in this city. Then, the next thing I knew they left the building where they'd been a year, and I thought they'd gone back to Georgia. I was beside myself. One afternoon I'd seen my sister and the next afternoon I went over there and there was no answer and I thought something was funny, but I went back to my place and my sewing, and I went over again around suppertime and still there was no answer. Well, I was scared. I scratched my head and tried to figure out what could have happened. Then I guess I must have leaned on the door, because it opened — and it was empty. They never did have much furniture in there. But what there was, it was all gone. I ran back so fast to my place that I fell. What's the matter, a kid asked me? I wish I knew, I told her. I got upstairs and I told my husband and he said we should go to the police. But he thought better, and he decided no, that was the wrong thing to do. We figured that they must have gone someplace, and we'd hear from them after they'd settled into their new place. I went over and asked their neighbors, and they said it must have been in the middle of the night that my sister moved, because they don't recall hearing any special noise in the hallway during the day.

"Well, about a week went by and all of a sudden my sister showed up one morning. I pinched myself, and I went over and kissed her, and I wanted to pinch her, too. I asked what happened, and she said nothing, and then I started crying, and then she did. She told me everything. She said they didn't have any money and he didn't know where he could get a job, her husband, and they owed on the rent, three months of it, and the landlord was threatening to kick them out, and they owed other people, and they didn't know what to do. Her husband has a friend who has a car and he said he could come and get them out in an hour, and they could go someplace else, and that way they wouldn't owe anyone a penny anymore, because when you're gone, you're gone, and who's going to go find you out? So, the friend came, and they went to a building way away from here, about two or three miles, my sister figured. Her husband's friend knew a building where they could stay for nothing, because it was closed up by the city, and no one was supposed to be there, but some people were there anyway."

She has a lot more to tell. That move was a mere beginning. The husband got another job, and they moved nearer to their original apartment. He lost the job and they moved to another abandoned building. They have a cousin in a city about one hundred miles away. He thought there was a better chance for both families in his city, so the already wandering family went there. The woman quoted above refused to budge, even though her husband was barely holding on to a low-paying job, and their bills were also mounting. Within six months the sister was back and installed in an apartment not far from the very first one she had upon arrival from Georgia. And there have been three other abrupt moves since that last one just mentioned.

If anyone asks why, why all those moves, there are always thoroughly "objective" reasons. Yet the woman who has not moved once can say this about all those expeditions of her sister's family, which includes three children below the age of five: "I think it's gone to their head, living up here. I've decided that they *should* go back to Georgia, but I know they can't go. They won't go. They'd die down there. They'd starve to death. They might be killed by the sheriff for coming back. He told both of us to 'get the hell out.' But up here, my poor little sister, I don't see how she'll survive this going here and going there. As soon as they run into any trouble they up and go. They don't seem able to sit back and try to get used to a place, and they can't find help for themselves from their neighbors. My sister was always shy, but now she can't talk to anyone but her husband and her children and me. She says that she'll go to a store and she starts trembling and she can't speak. She's afraid the police will come in and arrest her. She's afraid she'll just start crying and then fall down in a faint. And her husband, when any trouble comes he just stares, and then he starts whispering to her: let's go, let's go, let's move. She says she's glad when they *do* go. She says she feels each time that they may hit upon luck and start a new life and have none of the old trouble. But of course it doesn't take her long to see that it's the same old life, and nothing more."

I realize that the sister and the brother-in-law sound "disturbed," perhaps a little too suspicious, a little too fearful. No doubt they feel sad and bitter also. No doubt they are subject to confusion and spells of disoriented apathy. And I could escalate the language here; I could call them all sorts of psychiatric names. However, I have only met them intermittently; never have they sat down with me and talked about their innermost worries and fears. Their talk has had to do with their struggle for work and a place to stay and a means of obtaining the money they need for themselves and their young children. And it is significant that a sister looks upon them as "different," as badly "upset," as "in trouble" — by which she means psychological trouble. Yet, I have come to know dozens of families whose mode of survival in the city is not unlike the kind just described by this black woman, and I am assured by the people I work with that thousands of families live similarly nomadic and clandestine and hunted and wayward lives. I hesitate to draw upon my clinical vocabulary to describe such people. Their actions obtain from others a degree of social acceptance. There is almost a tradition among some people in our ghettos that under certain circumstances one "picks up and leaves."

Put differently, when a black family comes North and runs into trouble, the husband and wife soon learn that there are indeed dozens of "outs." There is a building here, another one there;

they are buildings condemned, abandoned, half torn down, but, most important, rent free. And in those buildings live others — families also on the run, also up against it, also not able to deal with the world as "the rest of people" do. Such troubled, hunted, apprehensive people leave quickly, under cover of night, with a minimum of belongings (not that there is usually an alternative), leave for a friend's house or for a different city, where a relative lives, and perhaps then scatter — a boy here, a girl there, the father in one section of the city and the mother, perhaps with an infant child, way across town. I am trying to emphasize that such practices are not as surprising and shocking as they may seem to outsiders. I am *not* saying that the woman I have already quoted was undismayed at the turn of events in her sister's life. Nor am I denying the obvious torment such nomadic individuals carry around inside themselves, and manage to express by constant change. However, those of us who want to comprehend this way of living must face something that can almost be described as a social custom, an established, widespread manner of attempting to diminish personal fears and anxieties on the one hand and severe social stresses on the other — and surely what is "personal" and what is "social" ought to be categorically distinguished.

I did eventually get to know two such wandering families, and in a sense my efforts to follow them from place to place reminded me of my work among migrant farm workers — which is described in *Migrants, Sharecroppers, Mountaineers* (the second volume of this series). I had to attach myself to the children and their parents, and I had to ask them to promise me that when they moved, I would be allowed to follow. They would leave word for me through a mutual friend, however suddenly they decided to depart. And so, we kept up our meetings over three years of time, and I had a chance to get some sense of why it is and how it is that particular families persist in so extraordinarily mobile a life — in the very shadow of slums which can appear to be so solid and impenetrable and unyielding, so static, so unchanging, so *there*. Perhaps I should claim only that I learned what such people *say* about their urban moves, their inner-city travels. For the fact is, a man like James Hudson and his wife

Josie Hudson ask the same questions I do, and maybe those
questions tell as much as any explanations I can come up with.

"I get to wondering," says Mr. Hudson. Then he stops; indeed,
he stops for such a long time that I think to myself that he is
confused or troubled. Is he in a daze, in a "state" of some kind?
Is he suffering from some injury to his head, some degree of
"retardation," some "psychotic process"? Then he brings me up
short, and perhaps reveals to me how impatient and how slyly,
brazenly condescending one like me can get when he is faced
with a person who is different from himself and simply being
himself: "I wonder why I brought myself and my wife and my
little ones all the way up here. I wonder if there will ever be an
end to it, the jobs that don't last. I got a job; they said I should
come there at seven in the morning and I'd be washing dishes in
the back of the restaurant. They said that in between I could
mop the floor. They said I looked strong, and they would pay me
fifty-five dollars a week, and I'd go up to sixty if I could prove
myself. They said I'd have to come in every day but one, and
they'd tell me which day to stay home, and each week it would
be different, because they're open all the time. I said good, and I
started working. I had to leave way before sunlight to be there at
seven. The place is all the way on the other side of the city. If I
miss one bus, I'm late. But I never did miss the bus. The bus kept
coming late; it was the fault of the bus company. The man who
runs the place, he told me I was late three times in a row and I
was through, fired. I'd been there on time for two weeks. I was
trying to do the best I could. I near cried. I said to him *please*.
He said to get out. I tried to tell him about the bus, and he said
that everyone always has an excuse, and he wasn't one to be
fooled by me or anyone else. Then I came home and I did cry,
and so did Josie. My boy asked me why, and I told him not to
ask, and soon enough he'd find out.

"I didn't know what to do. I got to wondering. I had the rent
to pay, and it's eighty dollars a month, and that's so much money.
They collect it, too. They're after you the first day of the month.
A man comes and says you've got to pay. If you tell him you can't
get heat from the pipes and the rats are all over, he tells you to

go find some other place. Well, that's why we moved the first time. I couldn't have two people talk like that to me, not on the same day: the man in the eating place and then the man who works for the landlord, collects his rent. I told the people who live next door that I wish I had a one-way bus ticket back to Echo, Alabama; it's bad there, but it's bad here, and maybe worse if you're me and you grew up down there and not up here. But Josie said she wouldn't go back, even if she had to die up here. She said she missed being down there, but we had nothing down there, *nothing*, and if he hadn't given us some food, the bossman, we would have starved to death every winter.

"I guess you only starve to death once. I guess somehow we made it from year to year back South. But Josie said that the bossman could take a disliking to us, because he has bad digestion one day, and that would be the end of our eating, and we'd all perish. Yes sir, we'd perish, and that's the story. That's why we're here, up here. I had an uncle who said he'd never go North, no matter what. He left Echo a long time ago and went to Birmingham. He said it's better to be in the South, if you have to live in a city. Now he wishes he'd never left Echo. It's worse in Birmingham than here, though. It can't be *too* much worse, I guess. If I took off, my family could get some help from the city. In Birmingham they'd get a lot less than up here. I'm staying here. Why should we move back there? We'll keep moving up here, if we have to, until I find a job that's going to last. You see, Josie has won, and I believe everything she says. We'll never go back, not with things as they are down there.

"I was telling you something. I know: I was telling you how we moved. We just did. I told the people down the hall I was thinking of going back South, and they said I was as crazy as I could be. I told them, just like I did you, about my uncle in Birmingham, and they said they could suggest something a lot better than going to Birmingham and that way I wouldn't end up in Alabama all over again. And the next thing I knew they were showing us a building where we'd be living more or less like we already were; only there'd be no rent, and no one would know where we were, so they couldn't come and collect on us. So when night came we just slipped out, real fast. It was the same when we left Echo and headed up North to Birmingham and then further up North until we came here, and I guess we can't be any further North than Roxbury.

"We have tried going to other cities. We tried Springfield, Massachusetts, because someone knew people there, and they said you might get a job if you looked real hard. We tried Hartford. I knew enough not to go to Harlem — no sir! I got a job in Springfield, waxing floors. The only thing was, the place closed down. All of a sudden they said we were fired, each one of us. They gave me the cash and said good-bye. I went to three or four eating places and tried to sign up, but they had all they needed; one man said, 'There are plenty of you guys around, and we only need one at a time.' Then he said, 'They come and go, so try again in a few weeks.' I told Josie I was going to ask him if he'd feed us while we waited, but I couldn't say what was on my mind. It's not easy to find yourself work, no sir. Anyway, we left Springfield and came back to Boston. There was nothing else to do. We knew a place to stay — with people, and they were the ones who told us to try Hartford. So, we did. And that was real bad there. I stood in some lines and each time they stopped picking men just a little ahead of me. It was worse on Josie than me. She'd be hoping; then I'd come back and I wouldn't have to say a word, because she could tell on my face what happened. It was good we knew people, and they helped us out. People will do that, you know. It was the same way back in Echo, Alabama."

Eventually he got and held on to a job. He works in a warehouse. He packs boxes of greeting cards and takes what he has done to the post office. He likes his work and likes the money — though it is no great sum in view of the rent he must pay and the price of food and clothing. Still, he has been able to stop wandering, to settle down and stay put. He can now talk about that year of movement, constant movement, as if it were thoroughly a thing of the past. He is a steady worker, and he will stay right where he is and never leave if he can help it. Indeed, one senses again and again the man's strong wish to avoid the unstable, migrant life he lived for those months before he was fortunate

enough to find his present job. Yet, one also senses in him a
conviction that nothing is to be taken for granted, that anything
might happen — which means at some point in the future he and
his family may again have to disappear from view: "You lose
your job, and they still want your money, and you don't have it,
and they say they're going to throw you out of your place anyway, and you owe at the store, and they won't sell to you, so you
go away. You find a place where there's no one always trying to
collect, collect. When you're living like that — I guess it's hiding — you meet some good people. I never knew that there could
be so many real good, nice people. They'll go and take some food
from a store, and they'll divide what they got with you. They'll go
and take shoes for your kid, not only theirs. I've never done that;
I just couldn't get myself to. I'm sure if I had to, I would. I was
lucky to know people who would, and then I got myself this job.
But if a man sees his kids needing food, is it wrong to steal? I
don't believe those store people starve. They drive up in their big
cars, I notice. I don't know how we would have eaten if a few of
the guys over in those buildings didn't go and get the food —
take it. And when I hear they're going to condemn some building, it always makes me feel good, because I say to myself: some
people will go and find a rest for themselves in that building, and
it won't be the best place in the world, but they'll be able to come
there and stay there for a while. Of course, you always hope
they'll get a good break and find a place to remain in, and not
leave. It's a bad life, always packing up and unpacking, don't you
think?"

I told him yes. I also told him how impressed I was with the
informal network of friends and relatives and comrades-in-
distress he had found all over New England. He said yes, it is
true that black men will help other black men, that people in
trouble will help other people in trouble. Then he added another
"don't you think" — a characteristic flourish of his meant to make
his point stronger rather than get a reaction from me. I told him
yes again; but I found myself wondering, too, how the kind of
"helping" spirit he described might become more widely present

in those "better" communities he unquestionably envies and no doubt wishes his children would one day be able to join.

12. *Taking It*

"Well, I take it all the time. I take smack. I've taken everything. Why not? I slip in the needle and I'm off, man. What else is there to do? I ask you. You go and tell me, and I'll listen, I promise." I never know what to say when he throws that kind of vague, hard-to-answer question at me. I suppose I could tell him to start all over again and live life differently. I suppose I could tell him to go get "help," though he has in the past made an effort to do so — when he nearly died because he took an overdose and collapsed and was spotted by a policeman and taken to a hospital: "I told them to get me off the habit and keep me off. I meant it. I was scared, man, plenty scared. They nearly killed me, though. They took me down cold turkey. They said they didn't. They said they gave me those pills. Those pills! They did nothing for me; nothing at all. I swallowed them and waited for the help, but none came. If they'd have helped me in the hospital, maybe I'd have kicked the habit for good. But I'm just as glad, to tell you the truth. I'm not doing so bad. I have good friends. And I manage to keep myself going. I do fine, come to think of it. I'll say that to you: I'm doing fine."

He doesn't always say that, or feel like saying that. He can feel low, dispirited, sullen, and if he is to be believed, on the verge of suicide. I qualify the assertion and seem to impugn his credibility only because he does so himself. He will openly tell me that he says things he doesn't mean and only means what he says "sometimes." It is his way of indicating that he has many different things going on inside his mind at the same time, that he is a man of many moods, that he never quite knows what he will be feeling or doing a few minutes later, let alone a day or two into the future: "I live for now, and not tomorrow." He is speaking quite literally.

How about yesterday, how did it go then? I ask him that. I try to turn his concrete preoccupations into something symbolic. I try to tell him that he has a history, that things happened and happened until, finally, he became the addict he is, the man who begs, borrows and steals to keep himself on the habit, the man who does some pushing but is not "a big-time guy, smack-rich." He gets the point, but is at a loss to oblige my chronological mind, hungry for details about one thing or another: "Relax, man," he tells me. "Don't go jumping all over the place like a frog." I smile, and for a while I actually do relax. I begin to wonder why in Hell I *am* pushing him so much. Oh, I'm not being too forceful or arrogant or inconsiderate. Or at least people like me usually don't know when we are behaving like that. We try very hard to be tactful, to pace ourselves, to ask the "right" questions at the "right" time — "right" for the other person, "right" for the "relationship," "right" because we feel "right" in asking what we do. But he is no fool. He senses me pressing him. He senses a lot, actually. I won't claim that drug addicts are especially intuitive and canny about human nature and the mind, but for a young man like him survival depends on sizing up people, learning what others are like and what they are probably going to do, and in general keeping in close touch with certain individuals. Moreover, when high on heroin, or better, when just over the highest point of the high but not at all near withdrawal, he claims he feels very "sharp" about what is happening around him. It goes something like this: "When I'm way up, I'm out. I don't see anybody. I'm lost. I'm gone. I've left this world for a better one; and it sure *is* better. But when I start coming back, I see everything. You know why? It's like with those guys who go all the way up to the moon. Man, when they're on their way down again, they sure catch a look at this setup we've got here on this planet. I saw on television that old mother earth looks like the moon to them up there on the moon. Wow, isn't that the truth!

"I'll be floating *my* way down to the earth, and if someone is around I can read him, read everything that's going on behind those eyes. Did you know that the eyes give all the clues? My old lady, she was something. I'd be getting one beating after another from her. And you know what? Each time she'd tell me: Johnnie, I know you. I can see right through to your bad, bad head. I'd tell her no, no. She'd say oh yes, she could tell. Someone taught her some card tricks, you know. She'd read cards and get some money for it. I'd listen in the next room and I'd say to myself: isn't that something, making up all those fool stories. But she said she was getting *messages*, and that's what told her I was a no-good boy, the *messages*. So she'd beat on me and tell me to shut up. She said my eyes sent them out to her, the messages. That's why I'd close my eyes every time she tried to look at me. She'd tell me to open them, and I wouldn't. So I'd get beat up. If I did open my eyes up, I'd get beat anyway! But I guess she taught me how to read people. I go for their eyes right away. When I'm in a store and I'm ready to take something, I first look at the clerk. Is she off with herself someplace? I mean, is she really paying attention? Some of them, they'll be staring at you, and you could lift everything away and they'd not catch on. Some of them are following you with their eyes, but they're pretending not to. I know eyes like that kind! I've been caught a few times!

"If I'm going to be cheated, I know it. I can tell if a dealer is in trouble, and he's watered his stuff down real bad. I'll be taking it, and I'll say to myself: Johnnie, you knew this wasn't good stuff. You knew this would hold you, but it wouldn't send you any-place. You knew you wouldn't even go up to the roof of this goddam building. See what I mean? The dealer, he'll give me one shift of his eyes, and I'm thinking to myself: better go get some more from somebody else, because you'll be in trouble sooner than you think. And I try to stay out of trouble, stay out of hospitals. The next time I go to a hospital, I hope I'm dead. I hate to walk near them. If I see one, I speed up and get away fast."

It is hard to gauge what might have been done for him when he was in the hospital years ago — in the unlikely event that the hospital, in fact, possessed a medical and psychiatric ward whose purpose was to do any more than hold addicts until they had gone through the hell of withdrawal. He himself constantly insists that he has been an addict for years, that he doesn't remember when he first took heroin, that he has tried marijuana and speed and alcohol, but they are "nothing" compared to heroin, that his whole life is now tied to getting the drug and taking it and getting it again. And though he is a hurt man, upon occasion exquisitely aware of the brutish childhood he had, he is also at other times affable and humorous, which means he enjoys his friends — and all of them use heroin. Under such circumstances, how might he be "rehabilitated"? I have asked him that. I have asked him whether he wants to shake off the habit, and if so, what he would like to be doing, given that he could indeed somehow be rid of his need for heroin. He laughs. He thinks my hypothetical way of putting things is rather amusing and thoroughly revealing. He becomes ironic and sardonic. He glares at me, then looks off and seems to be collecting himself for a reply. He sighs, as if weary already of the speech he is about to make: "I'm feeling good now. Why should I toss it off? Why should I walk around with my head down and feel as bad as can be? The people I like take smack. My wife, she used to get high. She's gone — don't ask me where. She up and walked out. She said she was going to sign in someplace, some hospital, and get herself all cleaned out. She was always bragging to me about herself! *I* can do this; *I* can do that. Sure, honey, I'd say, go ahead and come back and show me. She's never come back.

"Sometimes I miss her. I even ask around if anyone has seen her. She can't be too far away from here. Then I forget about her. I've got something else to do! I'm not by myself though. Don't worry! I have my women. I have my friends. My sister comes and tells me to kick the habit. She says it's killing me. You ought to see *her!* She waits on tables near here, and she's thirty and looks as if she's ready to be seventy, *that old!* I tell her she should quit fooling herself. What's so good about her life? What was so good about my old lady's life? She'd tell those stories to pick up a few pennies. She'd try to find a job, then she'd get sick and lose the job. My old man, he was no good. He drank all the time. You can have it; I like beer, but I don't drink the way he did. They found him dead in some alley. He was frozen to death, buried in snow. Can you beat that! And when they told her, my old lady, she didn't say anything. She didn't cry. She said she didn't even care. She told me my father really had been dead for five years, and the Lord was just too busy to notice and call for him. I thought she was fooling me, but she wasn't. My old lady, anything she says, she means. By then I was thirteen and she wouldn't dare touch me, beat on me. I'd already told her that the next time she touched me I'd kill her. She *did* come toward me once. She'd forgotten, I figured. I reminded her. I told her: another move, and you'll be as dead as your old man. She looked right into my eyes — and she saw I was serious, *man, was I*. She just turned right around and left the room. I said to myself: Johnnie, you've got her right where you want her. After that I took money from her if I needed it. She knew how to get money, and I knew where she hid it. She had to start carrying it on her. Don't get the wrong idea, though: she was no rich lady. She never sold herself, and she could have. She was a good-looker once, *tough,* the men would call her. Yes, that meant they liked her.

"My mother, she had slippery fingers. She'd go into a store, and she was fast as lightning. You know what I heard her tell a friend of hers? I was a little kid, maybe six or seven. I'd just started school, I know that. I heard her in the kitchen talking, and she was saying that she had a trick. She was full of tricks! The trick was: stare at the girl behind the counter, stare at her so hard she's scared of you — and then pick up what you want and walk out. I thought she was fooling. I thought: now how can anyone do that? But later on — I don't know, a year or two years later on — I saw her do it. I saw her go up to a counter and look at a clock. Then she moved right to the clock as if she was going to pick it up. Instead, she called the girl over and the next thing I knew, the girl was turning her face away, I guess because the old lady was tricking her, staring into her eyes. Then my mother picked up the clock and walked away with it. No one stopped her. I thought that girl was blind. I was watching from outside the window. I came up to my old lady and before I could say a word she hit me one across my face. I guess she saw in my eyes what I was going to say. I was going to tell her that she was good, real good. You see, she never once admitted to me that she took anything from a store. Even when I was too big for her, and she was real scared of me, I couldn't get her to tell the truth. I called her a liar once, and she said I was the liar. I told her I saw her stealing. She said I was like my father: no good. I told her she was like herself: no good. We never got along with each other. She's still around, but I never see her. Why should I?"

Who *are* the people he sees? What does he do with his time? Where does he get the money to buy heroin? He will hear questions like that and smile. He will point out to me that he can't answer such questions as flatly and unequivocally as I might like. He will turn the questions around, and in so doing tell me as much about myself as about himself. He will let me know that my concerns are not necessarily his, that he doesn't look at "time" as I do, at a day as a stretch of hours in which people are seen, things done. Nor does he look at money as something one goes and "gets." Instead, it is like this: "One day I see people. One day I don't. Sometimes I push a little. In return, I don't ask the dealer for money. He gives me what he knows I want. I trust him. He trusts me. I'd as soon never have to think about money. I don't keep track of the days. What does it mean, calling today Sunday or Monday or Tuesday? Who wants to get into that? My sister, that's her style. She can have it! If I see someone I like, a woman, I don't say to myself: Johnnie, do you know her? I'll just go up to her and either we make it or we don't. That's the way. The same with smack: I want it, I need it, I get it. There's always something to do. There's always someone to see. There's always a place to go."

He is both vague and precise. He doesn't want to get into the details of his life — but not out of shame, or because he will incriminate someone, or because he feels that I won't understand what I hear. The plain fact is that he doesn't feel tied to a specific pattern of things. He doesn't, that is, have a regular schedule, a predictable series of appointments or a definable set of obligations — except for one: "With me it's the habit; when I hear my blood telling me to go get some smack, I go get it, I take it, and then I say: Johnnie, you're all set for a while. Cool it. See what comes along. See who you meet. Meanwhile, talk to yourself, because you're not bad company! I have my records. I put them on and I make sure I can hear them. None of that low, soft stuff for me. I like to *hear* my music! I take care of myself. I'm not going to get buried in any snowstorm. I'm not like my old man was.

"I see people running to get on a bus so they can get downtown and do the white man's dirty work, and I say to myself: Johnnie, you're doing all right man, yes, you are. You're sitting here, and you'll be here when they get *off* those buses, and poor souls, poor souls, they'll be tired, real tired. You talk about keeping time: if you don't watch out people will push their revolving-door life on you. Who needs a watch? People force other people to look at watches. That's how it goes; but not for me. I've got that clock in me, I told you. If I can just keep that one clock going, I'm doing fine. And so far I have; I get the smack I need. I don't need too much more, if you'd like to know. The old lady, she helped me in a way. She knocked a lot of ideas out of my head. I'd tell her I want to be someone big, someone important, and all like that, and she would tell me shut up or else. And I guess I took her advice. I'm no one. I know that. I've been picked up by the police a few times, but they tell me I'm no one, and they're not after me. They're after the big-time dealer. You know what they want from them? Money! A cut! They pull in guys like me every year or so to make the judges happy; and the people, they like to read that the cops have pulled in a few people. But they never have sent me to jail for very long. They come and tell me to get out and they're not going to press charges on me. And we go, twenty-five or fifty of us. They've put on their show for the people!"

Full of such wry resignation, able to laugh one minute and be scornful the next, he is most of all concerned: concerned with heroin; concerned with a world he sits and thinks about but will not describe in words; concerned with keeping about him now a woman, now a record player, now a very modest supply of beer and bread and sausages and chocolate cupcakes, which he especially likes to eat; concerned with not freezing to death as his father did. He loves to be warm, loves to feel warm inside (as he does after taking heroin) and feel the outside warmth of a room. In winter he keeps the radiators full blast; he makes sure he lives in a well-heated if not expensive apartment. He told me one day that if he had another life he would live in Africa — not because he believes the continent to be the homeland of black people, but because it is warm there. He speculated that maybe then he would not even be an addict, because he'd be so warm. And I said maybe; and he said maybe; and he reached for a beer and shifted to talking about the brands of beer; and he told me he liked his beer very, very cold.

13. My Room

At least there I have a little home, you know. I have my room. I just stay there. I don't have to do anything else but be in that room. I hate the street. I used to be on the street. I'd stand there and wait. I'd give the man a look. If he looked like he had money and he was shy a little, I'd even follow him a block or so. I'd never do that again. I can't explain to myself how I lasted. I'd rather stand around, but I wanted to run. Once I did. I started running and I didn't stop until I was out of breath. Then I went home. But I didn't have any money the next day, and I said: sister, is it better to eat or to starve? Is it better to have good clothes or be dressed in rags? Do you want to be a washwoman like your mother? She had no hands left after her bosses got through with her. She had no money, either. I put away money. I go to the savings bank every week, and I put in the cash there, and they give me the book with the numbers in it. I have it with me, and it reminds me when I look at it that I'm somebody — because money talks.

I feel sorry for my sisters. There are three of them, and they're all poor as can be. I give them some money every once in a while. They come to me and they say, Jeanne, you've got to help me out. I say, sure I will. Blood is blood. Then they kiss me. They say I'm wonderful. My sister Ann told me once I was a gift from Heaven. Me! I say yes, Ann. I told her I hoped she was right, but I wasn't sure. But *she* was.

I try to live a quiet life. I don't drink. I never have liked the taste of liquor. I smoke, but I could stop if I wanted. It's a habit. My favorite way to spend a day is go looking for a new dress. I love my clothes. I love to buy shoes. I love to buy a pocketbook that goes with a pair of shoes. I have my shoes in the closet, and they're all there when I open it up. I look at them and say, it's a good life if you have the money to own what you like. I counted up fifteen pair. Maybe the day will come when I have a hundred pair. And I could have a different pocketbook to go with each of the shoes.

It used to be I'd take a pocketbook. I'd go into a store and lift one. But I've stopped. Why should you steal if you can afford to pay? I could get caught. I don't want to go to jail. What can you do in jail but sit there? You can't dress up. They push you around. You don't have a penny to your name. It's as bad as the grave, jail is.

My mother is dead. I never saw much of my father. He left when I was little. I remember some men, all right, but none of them was my father. I'm twenty-four. I hope I'll live longer than my mother. She dropped dead right before my eyes. What do you think of that! I was standing in the kitchen and doing the cooking for her because she said she had a headache, a real bad one. I said, Momma, sit down. She did, but the headache didn't go away, so I said, Momma go lie down. She got up to lie down and she fell down, and I heard a big sigh come from her, and her eyes went moving all over the place, and that was the end. She was gone. I didn't know, not then. I ran and got the woman across the hall. She ran and got a policeman, and he came and he was the one who said she wasn't unconscious, she was dead. You know what he asked me, the first thing? Was I fighting with her? He checked her over to see if I cut her up, and he checked me over, and he looked all through the apartment. That's the police for you.

I could tell you a lot about the police. I know them. I know more about the police than anyone does. They collect, you know.

They take a cut of everything. The lady I work for, they get money from her. My friend Bill, he always pays the police. Then they get on their high horse and play minister. They preach to you with one hand and take your money with the other. That's the way it is. I know my way around. I know how you go and do your business and how you get in trouble. The secret is money. If you have money, you're doing fine. If you don't, brother, you're in trouble, no matter if you did anything or not, no matter if you're in the right or in the wrong. When I was a little kid my mother would shout at us to be good, be good. A lot of good it does you to be good. And our minister, he'd be shouting at my mother and all the mothers, to make sure we were God-fearing. That's all he ever told us: fear God, fear Him plenty, or you'll sure enough be in a lot of trouble. And he said we should never do anything bad, and we should always obey the Commandments. Well, you know what I found out about him? It took me until I was about twenty years old to do it, but I did. I saw him. I saw where he goes. He's no different than me. He's full of talk about God, but he's a man, and he's the same kind of animal he used to tell us we never, never should be. And my poor old momma, she'd listen to him and nod her head and say yes, yes, and believe every word that came out of him, the minister.

I never knew what I wanted to be when I grew up. A teacher once asked me what I'd be doing later, and I felt like sticking my tongue out at her, but I didn't. I had on the tip of my tongue the words: I won't end up being like you, sister. I didn't do that, though — tell her off. I used to dream that maybe one day I'd be rich and I'd have a big house and servants and all the clothes and shoes I wanted, closets full of them. I'd even picture the maid being white, and I'd be good to her, real good. I'd give her days off, and I'd slip her money, and I'd buy her things, a convertible and some nice clothes. No white woman ever did that for my mother, or my grandmother. White people are stingy. The white men that come here to my room, I'll tell you I've had to pull a knife on some of them. They tell me they don't have the money, after they've already agreed to pay it. They want to give less, and I tell them they won't get out of the building alive if they don't give me the money, *all* of it we agreed was the price. Then I reach for my knife. And then every time they come up with the money, every time. What does that show you about white men?

Look, the black man is no angel, either. I'm not standing up for black men. I know them. I know them better than anyone else in the world. *Do* I know them! They're lazy, a lot of them are. It's their wives and their sisters and their mothers and their grandmothers and their aunts, it's the black women who keep the men going. Our men are no good. They've never been any good. But no men are good; that's what I believe. I know them all. I see them, and I can tell you: they're all out for themselves and no one else. A man, he's full of himself. He wants to be satisfied, but he doesn't really care about a woman. They'll say they do, some of them. But I give them a look-over, and I can tell. One guy, he was white, and he was crazy; he talked all the time, and he said he wanted to make me happy, that's all he wanted. I told him, finally, to go ahead, go and see what he could do. Well, he couldn't do a thing, not a goddam thing. I said to him — since he was talking so much, I thought I'd join in and talk — that he had the white skin and his hair was so yellow and his eyes were so blue, so why in Hell couldn't he do *anything* he wanted to do. I wasn't kidding. They think they're so wonderful. They're little babies, spoiled children. They don't know what's going on in the world. They don't know so much that it would take a year for me to tell what they don't know.

I feel sorry for them, though, the white men. They're scared, and they're no good, most of them. They'll tell you how excited they get, on account of my skin being black, and then they don't get excited at all. It's all talk, a lot of talk. That's the white people: talk and more talk, until they put you to sleep with their talk. The black men don't talk much, but some of them are as mean as can be. They're like a German police dog: their teeth and their noises. I heard a white woman say that black people are like animals; I was in a shoe store and she didn't know I was behind her, and I heard her say it to her friend. I had to think to myself: maybe she's right. Those niggers, I call them, that come knocking on my door, I hate to let them into the room. But a man's money is a man's money; and they don't stay too long. I know how to get rid of them. I give them a look and they leave. I can stare them down. I can get them so worried that they will go fast, rather than keep on trying to bother me. Sometimes I will say: mister, you have had it, and it's time to go — hear! They leave.

I'd like to leave myself one day — and never come back. I'm saving up. I'm putting some cash away, every week I am. I don't put everything away. I have to live. I like to look nice. And I like to have flowers near me. They're enough to get me through a night. I go into town and I buy them, then I bring them back to the room. They're all I have to look at. I need them so bad! In between customers I look at the flowers — roses, red roses — and I picture where they were before someone cut them. They were in a field, don't you know. There must have been a fence, so the rosebush could lean on it. Sometimes in my mind I see the sun shining on the roses, and sometimes it's cloudy, and it's raining, and there's a wind blowing. I take the roses home with me in the morning and I give them to the kids on the street the next day.

They think I'm a millionaire, the little kids do. They ask me how I make the money to buy so many flowers, and I tell them I know a man who sells them, and he gives them to me, gives them away. They believe me. They say they wished they knew some-one, too. I tell them they will, they will, later on. They're so good, the little kids. It's when they get to be eight or nine that they turn sour. Oh, they get awful right before your eyes, and I'm not their mother. I'm glad I'll never be a mother. I don't want to be. I don't want the heartache. I'd die as soon as I started seeing my children going bad. What's the use of bringing them into the world and trying to do everything you can for them? What's the use if all your work goes down the drain? There's no kid on my block who's not going to be bad. I just know it. Even the people who *look* to be good, they're bad underneath. I see them. Every night I see them. I should know. If anyone knows, it's me. They wear their nice suits. They have a tie on, a lot of them. They're dressed as if they're going to church. A lot of the black men, I'll bet they get all dressed up like that for only two things: the church and me. It's like I always say: it's a funny world, mister.

Sometimes the man, especially if he's white, starts trying to tell me a story. He wants me to know all about his life, and I keep on telling him to forget it, just forget it. To get them out, I say to them: it's a funny world, mister, it sure is, and they usually leave right away. If they don't, I go to the door and hold it open. I can't stand the sight of them for longer than I have to.

When I'm not looking at my roses, I close my eyes. I don't like the light on. I like to keep my eyes closed. Then I can picture things. I can go anyplace I want, in my mind. You don't have to travel to get away. You can shut your eyes and use your head! My mother used to tell me when I was real little that the best thing to do when you have a few minutes is to dream, and then the time goes faster. Just close your eyes, she'd tell me, and think of someplace real good and nice. When I've got a lot saved up, five thousand dollars, I'll stop working and go around the world. I'll visit California and Mexico and Africa and Trinidad, those are my favorite places to go visit. I've heard about them.

The only time I talk with a man is if he mentions a foreign country. Then I'll sit down on the bed and ask him all about it. I'll stay a long time with them if they'll tell me something interesting about a place like Mexico. It's when they want to talk about *themselves* that I can't stand them. Why should I listen? They give you a big headache. They don't know there are other people in the world besides them. If you remind them, they look as if you just gave them a spanking, and you were wrong, because they're the nicest one who ever lived. Well, I don't let them get me feeling sorry for them. Their pockets are full of money, aren't they? I should be feeling sorry for the people they got the money from. In this world, if you can make a lot of money, that means someone has lost a lot of money so you can have it. That's my philosophy. Nothing comes easy in this world, nothing.

Let the ministers and teachers preach and tell you to be good; meanwhile, the landlord is squeezing you hard, and so is the grocery man, and so is everyone. I always watch the store people at work in the stores near where I live. They try to get everything they can from their customers. The same goes with the fancy stores downtown. They're just smoother. They put on airs. They try to be so polite with you. White people seem to think that if they can just talk pretty words to each other, and have a big smile, then they can stick the knife in and no one will notice. I hate our black men and their loud mouths; but I hate worse the whispers and the sweet smiles of those white men. And that goes for the women, too — the white women. Black women are mostly too much in pain to be bad; that's what I believe. They're aching and aching all through their lives, they are. I'll be going to my room or coming back home, it doesn't matter which, and I'll see a black woman, a mother, walking down the street, and I'll feel like crying. I admit it. I have to fight back the tears, and sometimes I don't win. I think of my mother. I think of her mother. I think of an old aunt of mine who's still alive, and she's so tired and she thinks she's going to Heaven, so she's so happy. I go visit her once a week. I bring her roses. I bring her money. I give her enough to keep her happy. She thanks me, and she tells me that God is smiling on her through me. I asked her once how she ever got *that* idea. She said she was in church and doing her praying — she prays hard, real hard — and she was answered by the Lord, and He told her yes, I was coming as a favor to Him. *Then* you know what? She went to that minister and told him what she'd heard. She told him I was coming for Him, so as to do His bidding. And he's the one I've seen — he's the minister I mentioned. They almost sent him up to my room by mistake. It's a good thing I told them no in time. But he saw me anyway. And to think: that's what my aunt told him. I asked her what he said back to her. She said he didn't say anything. She said he just nodded his head, and she knew how busy he is, because everybody likes to come and have a word with him, so she just moved away. I told her I was sorry I wasn't there with her. I told her that one of these days I'd like to go there and talk to him myself, that wonderful minister she keeps on mentioning to me.

Yes, I'm sure it would be good for that "man of God" to see my old aunt and me together. He's so convinced he can separate everyone into the saved and the damned, and the good and the bad, that I'd like for him to separate my aunt from me — and himself from me. That's what I'd like. And he could separate some of his deacons from me, too; while he's at it. They own buildings, but they go and visit the building my room is in. The other day a man told me how he liked to travel a lot. I thought to myself that he sure does. People just don't stay at home, like they should. Then they go and call the people they visit bad names. But names don't hurt me. Not while I have a big leather pocketbook and cash inside it and my bankbook. I figure that way I'm as honest as anyone around, as honest as any businessman, as honest as those politicians. You start being a crook and a bum when you don't have money and your clothes are no good. That's what I've learned in my life, and I'm glad I've learned it, let me tell you.

14. Black Fathers

We have heard so much, and properly so, about the difficulty that black men have obtaining work, hence becoming good providers for their families. Needless to say, a man who cannot bring home money gets discouraged and bitter. Nor can we forget that, until recently, in many cities and counties families became eligible for welfare only when the father was dead or disabled or no longer at home. In thousands of instances, men have left their families for just that purpose. They sneak away when the welfare worker is expected, and return in-between her visits. Or go away and stay away. In Roxbury and Harlem and the Hough section of Cleveland and Chicago's West Side I have over and over again encountered families headed by mothers; and often the various children have different fathers. I have met up also, however, with sturdy, tough, outspoken black fathers, men of astonishing independence and vitality and resourcefulness, for all the burdens they bear, the doubts they have, the fears they fight every day. Somehow, those fathers are less apparent to the outsider than fatherless families, however careful and curious the observer may be. For one thing, they are working, or trying to find work, or off in some corner talking with a friend or two about how hard it is to get a good job and keep it. For another, they frequently are quiet, unassuming, quick to retreat when the children burst forth with remarks or the wife speaks out. But that is not to say a modest and reticent black man (worker, husband, father) needs to be labeled "weak" or "submissive" or "passive" or "dominated" by some "matriarch," some black virago who need only raise her eyebrow to have her way.

During the years that have gone into the work I am trying to report upon here, no individuals have confounded me so persistently as the "black fathers" I have met and spoken with and listened to and for long stretches of time, I believe, sorely misunderstood. Not that I understand black women all that clearly, but I have often found that black mothers can somehow find words for a passionate voice, a cry of mixed despair and hope. I once asked a black mother in Roxbury where, just where, she learned how to give forth so, assert herself, make her wishes and fears so vividly, compellingly known. She had a little trouble putting into words that particular answer, but soon one was forthcoming: "I'm not talking for myself. I'm speaking for Joseph and Sally and Harry and Stevie and Benjie and Mary. I'm speaking for them, and they push on me until I get the words out, that's what I believe. Because if ever I have trouble saying something, I look at my boys and my girls and the words come to my mouth."

One has to ask how black fathers can talk the way so many of them do, with their own kind of cleverness, guile, humor, sarcasm, exuberance, and often, in spite of everything, a certain guarded confidence. For instance, Henry R. Rollins speaks like this: "I'm poor, and I'll never be anything else. I don't care, because I'm rich, too. I have five children, four sons and a daughter, and they're the most wonderful people in the whole, big, wide world. I don't do right by them, I know. I don't bring home the money they all need. All the work I can get I do. I'm a janitor, and I keep on trying to take care of more buildings and more. I wouldn't mind taking care of every building in Roxbury, I'll tell you that, if it meant that my children had a little more. I'm their father and I owe them three meals, the best we can afford, and a good place to live. I'd like them to have more clothes. I wish I could get them a lot of toys. My oldest boy wants a baseball bat so bad that it hurts me to think about it, and he wants a glove, too. But there's no money for that. I took him aside and I told him. I said, 'Look here, son. I know, I know how bad you want it, the bat and glove, but we can't, we just can't go and get them.' Well, he said that he understood, and he won't tell me he doesn't still want them, but he was all the way with me, and he wished he was old enough to be working like I do, so there'd be a little more money for all of us."

Mr. Rollins's oldest son is nine, and if he is obviously close to his mother, and after a fashion a father to his younger brothers and sister, he is also close to Henry R. Rollins, though in more subtle ways. He does not stand next to his father, as he does with his mother, when a visitor comes. He does not give his father the intense and serious glances he casts toward his mother. He does not ask his father the questions he asks his mother: what to do and when and how. His mother affects him more, moves him and the other children emotionally, generates in them joy or disenchantment, the anticipation of pleasure or the expectation of those seemingly inevitable disappointments that come and come and come. But his father has his own kind of influence on the eldest son, and all the other children as well. The boys imitate him without being aware that they do: the way he puts his hands in his dungarees; the way he walks; the way he sighs about once every sentence spoken; the way he gazes off sometimes and seems utterly inaccessible, even though he is there, right there, and ready to respond, given a raised voice, a repeated request, a tap on his shoulder, or merely an impatient but persistent spell of silence which will cause him suddenly to come out of his thoughts and look sheepish and apologetic and faintly amused, as if to say: I just have to do that every once in a while, and I am grateful to you for being courteous enough not to hurry me along with remarks and shouts and a push or two.

All day long the man cleans out buildings, chases rats and mice, tries to keep hallways clear and reasonably well lighted, and responds to urgent pleas for help with a cautious and sincere interest, but by no means with promises of immediate action. He has so many buildings to oversee, and his employers, members of a large real estate company, have no great desire to keep the property in the very best of condition. Mr. Rollins is loyal to them, however — if that is the word. He has heard "the bosses" complain about their problems so often that he at least can make a pretense of sympathizing with them, and certainly he can imitate them. He can insist upon the rising cost of taxes, and the pressures upon owners of property not to raise rents, and the high price of all repair work. He can even talk this way about "the people," the families in those buildings: "It's hard keeping a place clean when you have everyone making a mess. They throw garbage right out the windows, a few of them do. The kids kick at the walls and write things and throw rocks at the light bulbs. What can you do? The owners say that they could go broke keeping up with the kids, and maybe it would take away from their profits."

That last phrase is very much Mr. Rollins's style: he can be truthful, ironic, sarcastic and utterly sincere and polite, all in a few words. He knows how to understate things. He has a smoldering sense of humor; even when he is sad and downcast he can find something to smile about, if not laugh at. He is tentative and almost self-effacing, yet he manages to say something that catches his listener's ear and isn't easily forgotten. He is an undramatic person, but he can readily summon the attention of his wife, his children, his neighbors. He can speak up, or simply move nearer and nearer without saying a word, all the while looking right into one's eyes. Here, for example, is what the man can say when he wants to say something: "I don't like to talk very much. I find that the more I get talking with the tenants, the less I can do, and the more fights I have. They want to blame someone, and I don't blame them for that; and I'm right here, around every day, so they blame me. They shout at me, and I nod to them and tell them that they're right. I promise I'll go tell the bosses, and maybe they'll come around and see for themselves. A tenant doesn't like to hear that, though. They want their satisfaction. They want something done. I'll be telling them that maybe something will happen in a few weeks or a few months, and they'll be registering in their minds that I'm *really* telling them I can't do a single thing. Then they get real mad at *me*. They want to know how I can work in a job like I have. They say I'm as bad as the white man, the owners of the buildings, and I'm an Uncle Tom and I'm a slave and — well, there isn't much I'm not called by the time the week has run out, I'll tell you.

"One woman keeps on telling me I should be shining the shoes of the owners. She says I'm the errand boy. I smile when she tells me that. What else can you do? Then she tells me to go look at my smile in the mirror, and I'll see what a nice yes-man I am, the worst Uncle Tom she's ever seen. I asked her what her husband did to earn a living. She shut the door in my face without telling me; she just pushed me out and slammed that door — and the next thing I knew she was complaining that the lock was broken and thieves will be opening up the door and stealing her property. Well, I fixed her door, and I found out from her neighbor about the husband. He doesn't have a job, no job at all. He shoots horse. She's telling me I'm no good and an Uncle Tom, and meanwhile her husband is an addict and he doesn't bring in a cent and he's never around! I went home and told my kids the story. I want them to know what's going on in the world. That's what a father can do for his kids. He's out in the world, and he finds out what is happening, and he can go back and make sure the wife and kids get to know."

He does more than that. He lifts his children up in the air and holds them there and tells them that one of these days — years from now, true, but *one of these days* — things will be different and they as grown-ups will be better off and higher up in the world, way higher up. Then, to make certain they get his point, feel its thrust, he gently bumps the child's head on the ceiling of the room. He also watches television with them. He doesn't say much, but he will smile, and upon occasion say "hah!" when he wants to underscore a particular thing said or shown. The children of course hear him when he shouts or mumbles his "hah!" or murmurs some indefinable phrase, but they also uncannily know when he is smiling, but making no sound at all. They look at him, immediately smile in response to his smile, then try to figure out what it was that occasioned his amusement in the first place.

And one more thing he does: he says good-night to his children. No matter how busy he is, and unless there is an emergency in one of the buildings he has to oversee, at bedtime he is there to kiss his children and tell them "good-bye, spend a good night sleeping, and come back to us all fresh and good in the morning." He is, again, not passionate and outspoken like his wife can be, or their minister, but he does have his stories to tell. Often those stories are about the South. Whereas Mrs. Rollins talks about the South moodily, nostalgically, bitterly, wistfully, Mr. Rollins has concrete stories to tell: "I like my kids to know that there once was a place where the black man lived different than up here. When I was their age I was down there, living in that cabin we had in Tunica County. Mississippi is a bad state for the black man; but my brother and I, we managed to squeeze some laughing out of our life down there. We had to go help our daddy, and we had to wash the bossman's cars. He had three of them, one for himself and one for his wife and one for his daughter. That was a lot of cars for someone to have in those days. We don't have a car even now, but today people who have money, I mean ordinary people making a good salary, they have two cars, I believe. Well, back in Tunica County the bossman's wife, she never wanted those cars to get dust on them. She'd go out for a drive after we worked on her car, and then she'd come home and we had to hose the car down again and polish it again. She was the neatest woman you'll ever meet. She was always complaining that her furniture got so dirty. She said the best colors are green and brown and black, because they don't show dirt and the worst are white and yellow and pink. My daddy used to say she should have been born black, and then her skin could hide dirt better, and she'd be happier.

"But I'll tell you, we kept those cars clean. As fast as anyone brought them back from a drive, we'd be at the garage, and we had the hose and the soap and we worked. Then she would come out and give my brother and me a lollipop. Sometimes she'd run out and she'd give us some sugar instead. I used to love sugar then. Now I can't bear to look at it, I mean the kind that's in those squares. 'Here's a cube of sugar for you, Henry,' she'd say, and I'd come running fast. The other day I saw a woman in one

of the buildings lift one of those cubes out of a cup and put it in
her mouth, and I thought I was going to pass right out. She
asked me what was wrong, and I said, 'I don't know.' She said I
didn't look too good. I didn't say anything, and I was just about
recovered, when all of a sudden I heard her chewing on the
sugar, and cutting it up with her teeth, the way I used to do, and
I had to excuse myself real fast. I got out into the hall, and it was
like I was back in Tunica County and I was eating the sugar,
except my stomach was hurting. That used to happen sometimes.
My daddy would say it was from eating the sugar too fast, and
once I told the bossman's wife, and she said, 'Poor child, sugar
probably brings on worms.' I told my daddy that, and he said not
to believe her, but say yes to everything she says, no matter what
it is. In the hall of the building I thought of the bossman and his
wife and my daddy and those worms she told me I could get. I
used to see a worm in the ground, wriggling and moving along,
and I'd think to myself: is one of them inside me? In the hall I
thought I should go and tell the woman not to take sugar that
way, not to *eat* it, not to *chew* on it. But I caught myself and I
said, Henry, you're thinking the wrong thing, and stop. Instead I
went back and knocked on the door and told her that I'd go and
find a bulb, if I could, and put it in the hall so she wouldn't be
stumbling all over the place. Being old, it's dangerous for her to
fall, and if she can live to be as old as she has and eat those cubes
then I thought: how could they be so bad for you? She doesn't
look as if the worms have gotten much to eat from her. She's fat
and she likes her food and, like I said, she's over seventy, she told
me. That's not a bad age to pile up."

Not everyone can get to be seventy, he says rather more often
than one might expect from a man in his early thirties. He has
one ambition in life, and if he can realize it he will die happy. He
wants his children to live elsewhere, to have jobs, to be better off
than he is — which means he wants them, first, to stay in school
and graduate from high school, and, second, to keep a safe distance from some of the things that go on near at hand: gambling,
drinking, the use of drugs, prostitution and gang warfare. It is
easy, all too easy, for someone like me to highlight those elements

of Roxbury's life, or Harlem's. Again and again one hears about how awful it is in our ghettos, how mean and vicious and degrading life is there; and there's no doubt it is for some children and some grown men and women. Yet, a lot more goes on than often gets told, reported, described; and I fear that these days it is more than likely that observers like me will fail to take note of what is strong and balanced and growing and settled and utterly impressive about many, many so-called "ghetto families." And if we do so, if we try to convey the self-confidence and dignity and adroitness and moral sensibility and thoughtfulness of a Henry R. Rollins — poor and uneducated, upon occasion worried and fearful and at a loss to know what his future and his children's future will be — if we try to indicate the dimensions of Mr. Rollins's character, the range of his experience, the spread of attitudes and loyalties and commitments to be found in him, the possibilities he himself takes note of, the ambiguities he every day struggles to comprehend and contend with; if we attempt to do all that — even so we will have to remind ourselves that no life can ever be fully approximated by any observer, however bent he is on suggesting nuances and highlighting a person's vitality as well as his or her shortcomings.

We "observers" often fail to insist upon a complexity that gets more intricate the longer we look. I suppose we want to simplify and take a firm, clear-cut "stand" on some side, any side — and in so doing I fear we cannot do justice to the life of a man like Henry R. Rollins in our written descriptions. Ironically, I believe Mr. Rollins himself knows that people like to come upon conclusions and findings and discoveries that fit their own preconceptions. He knows that to be poor and black can often enough mean, among other things, to be misheard, misinterpreted, misunderstood — sometimes by people who loudly proclaim their good faith, their compassion, their benevolence: "I keep quiet a lot. I let the landlord have his say; then he goes away and I do what I do. You don't argue when it won't do any good. I come home and I'm tired. I'm glad to be able to sit down and listen to the kids make noise. My wife doesn't ask me to do things for her. She says there has to be *one* tenant who doesn't complain all the

time to me! I hear white people talking, and black people. I have
to take care of some stores as well as apartment buildings. I hear
the police talking, and the real estate people, all kinds of people.
Then I come home and I'll see my kids, and they'll go to bed, and
next thing there's someone on television talking about the poor
black man and all his troubles — you know, on the news and late
at night on those programs. I fall asleep in my clothes early, then
my wife wakes me up and I have some cookies and we watch
television a little and we go to sleep. That's like having two
nights of sleep in one!

"Why does everyone want to feel so sorry for us? Why do they
all talk about us as though we're the worst-off people in the
world? I'm a poor man, I know it; and I'm black, or a Negro, I
don't care which it is they go and call me. But to Hell with being
called everything under the sun! I'm Henry Rollins, that's my
name and that's who I am. 'You black people,' I heard a cop
shout at a friend of mine the other day, and my friend didn't say
anything. Maybe I'd have been scared, too. But I'd *like* to say
this to a cop: mister, what is your name? Then, if he told me, I'd
say thank you, thank you very much, and *my* name is Henry R.
Rollins and that's who I am. See what I mean? I bet he'd understand me. If you keep reminding people, they'll remember after a
while. I told my boss that I'll take care of his buildings, and I'll
never do a thing wrong if I can help it. I told him I'd like to
prove I can be my own boss. He said that was fine, but he hoped
I'd be true to my word. I said I would be. If he heard some of
the people talking about us on television, I can see why he'd
think I'm no good. I could see why he wouldn't trust me. I don't
think a lot of white people know us; that's what I believe. I don't
even think one black man knows another. I hear people talking. I
hear my own neighbors talking. Everyone has *ideas* about us,
opinions about us. Who is 'us'? I'm me! I think they ought to
leave the black man alone; I mean, I'm just trying to be myself,
and it's like I'd tell the cop if I didn't think he'd pull a gun on
me: I'm Henry Rollins, and that's all I can say.

"My kids tell me they're glad I'm their dad. To my kids I'm a
father, not a black man. Yesterday I was telling their mother

about the big signs that say YOU ARE BLACK: ACT IT! I can't even figure out what those signs mean. I read them and then I read them again, and then I say to myself: that's just no good, that message. What am I supposed to do? I can only act myself. I can't go acting the color of my skin. The color of my skin is me; yes, sure it is. But I'll be truthful: I don't have the time to be thinking of all that. When I come home I want to be my kids' daddy. How can I "act black," when I'm trying to be their *daddy?* It's a lot of talk, if you ask me."

We get further into the issue, though. I once tried to paraphrase as fairly as I know how the reply he would hear from the man who made up the slogan he happened to read, posted as it was in the window of a store he takes care of. He listened and he said yes, and he added some comments of his own, and he insisted that he quite understood what the man was getting at. Nevertheless, he had to make clear his amusement and surprise and mild annoyance, and he had to make clear that he was not to be confused in anyone's mind with any particular notion of how a person acts or should act or might someday come to act: "Like I said, I'm me — period. I don't know how to act, except to act like I do. I may be wrong about a lot of things, but I try to keep my head, I try to do my work. I try to tell my kids that they should respect their mother and respect me, and they should think for themselves and not let everyone they meet and play with tell them what is right and wrong. I want my kids to be as good as my grandfather was. That's right! He was called a 'big black buck' by some of the white people back in Mississippi. Yes, that's what my daddy told me. My grandfather was tall and heavy, and he was as strong as a man could be. There was a doctor there in Tunica County, and he told the bossman that my granddaddy was 'superior': he could lift things and break things and do anything, it seemed. They called him a 'smart nigger,' too. That's what my daddy told me. He had a big, deep voice, and you could hear him all the way across the field. He sang songs. He shouted. He marched down the road and the white people would go by and turn around and stare, and the black folks just said: that's our Robbie. That's what he was called, Robbie.

"I was saying I'd like my kids to be like my grandfather. I mean, I'd like them to feel as big as he was and be as smart as he was. I don't care how they act, so long as it's like him. I try to think how he'd act if he'd have come up North, but there's no telling. He might have been pretty low. He might have decided to go back as fast as he could to Mississippi. He got the white people down there to be a little careful about him, and he got our own people to look up to him, and that's all anyone in Tunica County could have done, anyone who picked cotton! So, I'm not ashamed of him. He couldn't read and he couldn't write, but I'm glad he was my grandfather. I can recall him a little. He took me on his knee and said to me that I should never forget that God gave me good strong arms and legs, and He gave me ears and eyes and my head to use. He said if I learned to use my arms and legs as best I could, and if I used my head all the time and didn't get tricked and fooled, then I'd be a real big success in my life. He told me I was going to have a better life than he did, he believed that, but he wanted me to know something very important, in case he should die: never forget that he was glad he'd been born and he was proud of what he'd done in his life and he didn't feel he'd done a bad job, no. He kept on repeating himself. He said he was doing it because later on a lot of people were going to try to convince me that I was no good and he was no good and my daddy was no good, and if only we were different — if only we were white! — *then* we'd be good. Don't you believe that, he told me. Believe in yourself, he told me. I told him my daddy would say the same thing, and then he said *good*, *real good* and he put me down from his knee and gave me some gum.

"I'm sure my grandfather had a lot to learn. I'm sure he was wrong a lot of the time. But I'm proud of him when I think about him. He was a real good man, a mighty good one. It's too bad my kids never will see him. All I can do is talk about him to them — and I can try to be like him. I know it's different up here, and I can't be the cotton picker he was, or go do all those jobs they had him do in Tunica County. But I can show my kids, like he did, that they've got me here as their daddy, and I put in my time on the job, and I can honestly say: I got this far; now you go and do the same, and do more, and go even further. That was something else my granddaddy used to say. He'd say: I'm walking down the road as far as I can, and your daddy, he's walking along, and he'll get farther along than me, and you, I'll be hoping you go farther along than both of us. I tell that to my kids. I tell them they've got to keep walking and it won't be long before they're way out ahead of me; and their mother and I, we'll be pleased to be looking at them, out there in front of us."

When black families are discussed, such a father has to be thought about; he also is part of a particular race, and he also has behind him a particular cultural tradition. He cannot be dismissed as rare or unusual, or for that matter "atypical" and "unrepresentative." Once he made me smile by laughing out loud and saying this: "You'll probably find what you're looking for. I believe that." He was answering two questions I put to him: "Do you think there are many others who think like you? Do you think I'll find other fathers who are like you?" After he had been laconic and cryptic and a touch sarcastic, he decided to expand his remarks. He mentioned one man's name after another. He insisted that of course he was no rare bird. He let me know that nothing was more appalling to him than the misconceptions he in his own way has noted that millions of people like me have about people like him. He told me that a "plain, ordinary guy" like himself is to be found in apartment after apartment, in one street after another. Yes, there are all sorts of hurt, wretched, tormented people nearby — and far away, too: across town, across the tracks, among white people. But why is it, he both pleaded and asked, *why, oh why,* is it that a man like him, and all the other men he knows to be basically and at heart and in essence and fundamentally like him, never seem to catch the eye of people who talk about the black man and say "all those things about us?"

He is sure, he is very sure, that the various commentators and critics and scholars and writers are right and well intentioned and careful; and certainly they know much more than he ever will. Still, there is this to say: "I hear a man talking on television.

He says he knows what we want, the black people. He says he knows us. He says he's black. Or if he's white he says he's looked into us. Then he says what the 'truth' is, and I've got my ears wide wide, open, and I'm listening, I'm really tuned in. But a lot of the time, I say: Hell, he's not talking about me; I'm Henry Rollins, and he hasn't told what goes through my mind. And a lot of other men I don't know, I'll bet he hasn't told what they're like, either."

Indeed there are men he does not know, men he might actually want to know, men both like him and unlike him, men whose roots are in, say, North Carolina and not Mississippi, who live in, perhaps, Cleveland and not Boston. One such man is Ray Phillips, a cabdriver, a black cabdriver. He says that, calls himself "a black cabdriver." He still remembers when many white people wouldn't take a cab driven by a black man, and when blacks took cabs far less frequently than they do today, and when white cabdrivers bumped him with their cabs and swore at him, and when the police were constantly asking him to identify himself and show cause why he should not be called a liar, a crook, a pretender, a public nuisance or menace. Now, at forty-eight, he is a father, a grandfather, a fairly good wage earner and, most important, he emphasizes, a husband: "I love my children, but most of all I love my wife. We've been married for thirty years. Yes, that's right: I was eighteen and so was she when we got married. The minister told us no, because our parents told us no, but then I got my dad to say yes, and pretty soon we were in the church there, swearing we'd stand by each other until the end of our lives. Thank God we *did* get married; a year or so later I was in the Army, the Second World War. My son was born when I was out in California and then I was sent to the Pacific and I didn't see him until he was five, I think it was. I'm getting hazy about all that. He's got two of his own children now. After the war we had a girl, then another girl, and then I said the time has come to stop. I'm no millionaire, and three kids is enough. Sometimes I think: I grew up and there were six of us, and maybe it would have been better with more children. But I'm glad we stayed at three. My wife would look a lot older than she does if she'd have had three or four more kids pulling on her and taking it out of her. A man doesn't know what his wife goes through all day. All he knows is his own troubles. He forgets what it means to bring up kids — and I mean *bring* them up, not drag them up.

"I'll be driving a customer someplace in the city, and if he's a nice, friendly guy he'll start telling me about all his troubles. He'll tell me his business is good, but it could be better, then he'll tell me some other worry he has. Then I'll try to change the subject. I ask if he's married. Yes, he says. Children? Yes, he says. How's the wife find *her* work, I say. Oh, fine, fine — that's what they'll say, unless they come at you with: *what* work? A lot of husbands just don't know what their wives do all day. I'm the kind of husband who does. I've tried to pitch in and help my wife every way I can. I've tried to be around my kids, too. I was a real father to them, not a man they called father. And I'm a good grandfather, I believe, a very good one. That means I spoil them the way someone should!"

The more he talks the more one forgets that he is anything but an American taxi driver who doesn't make a huge amount of money, who hustles (he puts it) for what he does make, who happens to know just about every street, or so it seems, in Cleveland, Ohio, and who happens also to be close to his wife, devoted to his children, and anxious to be a grandfather about nine or ten times, he says. He never finished high school. He was born in eastern North Carolina, but was brought to Cleveland at age three. His parents were not members of the "black bourgeoisie." His father left North Carolina because he told a white man to go to Hell and was promptly arrested. He escaped from jail, though Ray Phillips was told that the escape was permitted by a deputy sheriff who disliked the man who was insulted and who caused the black man's arrest. How, then, did Ray Phillips manage to do so well, become a successful cabdriver, be so good a husband and father?

Perhaps he has a right to ask me why I have to ask such a question, though God knows even more insulting and patronizing questions are asked these days. However, because Mr. Phillips has a radio in his car and hears a lot of "talk shows" and "call-in" programs, and because he also reads the papers regularly, and because he watches television documentaries, he is prepared for the likes of such questions: "Everyone is looking at the black man today and saying: who is he, and what's on his mind? I know. I flip from one station to another, or I'll meet a real honest fare and he'll say to me: come on, level with me and tell me what you think of all our race problems. Well, I do tell him, even if he's a big, fat white businessman. I say: mister, I'm a citizen of this country, just like you. I was over in the Pacific, fighting to beat Japan and win. I was under MacArthur. I've seen other parts of the world, and I'm glad to be living right here. If the white people would only get off our backs and leave us alone, we'd be the best citizens this country has, and everyone could relax and stop being so damn nervous. That's what I tell people. Sometimes they listen, and sometimes they don't. I can tell. If they want to hear more, I've got through to them. If they shut up and don't say another word, I know I haven't; and I know I'll be getting a real small tip — if I get *any* tip."

The more he talks the more he decides to call himself a teacher. He is only being half humorous. He sees a lot of people in the course of a day, a week, a year; and he tries to get the word across, spell out a certain message that he believes, that he considers just and sensible, and that he wants others to hear. He doesn't have the same words for each person. He realizes that many hear nothing, that many are hopeless causes, are unapproachable. He is an observant and intuitive man, a person who can sense what other people are like, can quietly and without a lot of trial-and-error exchanges decide who might and who might not want to hear some of his ideas. And as he gives expression to those ideas, he rather often hears in the casual atmosphere of his cab much the same kind of question I more formally have had in mind over the years, and indeed have just set down above: how is it that this man has become — well, "just like anyone else"? That is the way he finds a lot of white men putting it — tactfully, they believe. He does not get excited or angry with them. He smiles and brings out into the open what they "really" want to say, and thus helps them along, shows them how categorical and indiscriminate they have been: "I say, look: you've met me. Think of the thousands and thousands of guys you haven't met who would talk to you like me, if they had the chance. I happen to like to talk. I've been a cabdriver all these years, and it's an education, and you get to feel comfortable with people, so I can speak up. But I'm just one of about twenty million Negroes. Call me black, call me colored, call me a Negro. I don't care, so long as you see that I'm Ray Phillips — you hear? — and I have my wife and my kids and my grandchildren and I watch the same television shows everyone else does, and when the President said we've got to protect the country from Hitler and the emperor of Japan, he got me to go fight along with everyone else.

"They begin to think by then — the customers who have some sense in them to start with, I guess. You're right, you're right they'll say. Then I look at them through my mirror and I can tell by the look on their face that they *still* think I'm someone special. He's different, their face says. He's a real smart one, they seem to be saying. That's why I can't let it drop there. I have to work. I even have to knock myself a few pegs down. I have to convince them that for every me, there's another me — a million other me's. I have to tell them that my dad was a guy on the run, a 'fugitive from justice,' they called him. I have to let them know that I was born poor and if I'm not poor now, I'm sure a lot poorer than *they* are. Otherwise I keep hearing: you're exceptional, you're an unusual guy. When you hear that you know what that means: he thinks everyone else black is no goddam good. I'm supposed to feel big when someone says to me I'm the greatest person he's met, but I could take the guy to the building we live in and the one next door, and all up and down the street, and there would be men just like me: they're not rich; they work hard and they get by, they *just* get by, and sometimes they *don't*, I'll tell you, with prices going up, up; but most of all, they're like other people in this country. I mean, they try to do the best they can by their wives and their kids, and if they can only come home and be with them, they're willing to work hard, plenty hard, and be glad to have the work. If they don't find work, then that's another story. But so long as a man can get a job, and if he's honest and he's not crazy because of drugs or liquor, then he'll be fine, and if his wife is a good woman, he'll stand by her, I believe, and he'll stand by his children."

Of course, there are exceptions, he reminds himself and me. White fathers betray their children, and so do black fathers. Individual men can be fickle, unreliable, devious, awful examples to their children and harsh and callous men to their wives. Moreover, he repeatedly takes pains to remind me that it is "another story" when a man has no job, or has one but then is laid off and cannot find another one, or finds one but gets little pay and works under demeaning circumstances — all of which causes in husbands and fathers a kind of fearfulness and resentment which wives and children do indeed come to experience. I suppose, in sum, Ray Phillips has this to say: There are plenty of aimless, wandering dazed and ruined black men, even as in America white men by the thousands are alcoholics or philanderers or crooks or loafers or clock-watchers or slowpokes or sleepyheads. Yet, there are among black America's people many millions of men who are faithful husbands, devoted fathers and hard workers. By and large those men are not as well off as their white counterparts, do not have access to jobs many whites can either take for granted or obtain with relative ease if they so desire. Yet, despite such "facts of life," black men in street after street of our northern cities struggle to find what work they can, and struggle also to maintain intact homes in which children grow up with a sense of continuity and stability in their lives.

None of what I have just written is extraordinary or surprising, but I fear it is quite necessary to bring before the reader men like Henry Rollins and Ray Phillips, men who head black families, workingmen who are very much their children's father. No doubt about it, many black children (and many white children) don't have fathers like Henry Rollins and Ray Phillips, but many, many do — and in this last third of the twentieth century, when one slogan after another is fastened upon over twenty million American citizens, it is well to keep a janitor here, a taxi driver

there, in mind as we go rushing on to the next moment of panic
and despair.

15. *We Are Black, Too*

The so-called "black bourgeoisie" was often mentioned long
before "black power" became (from 1965 on) a rallying cry, first
for disappointed and embittered civil rights activists, and then
for black people all over America. I remember well the mixed
feelings many young black organizers in the rural South had
toward black ministers, doctors, lawyers, storekeepers, insurance
agents, funeral directors, postal clerks, real estate men and
schoolteachers. Here is one member of SNCC speaking, in 1963,
when the fight was most intense, but when the morale of the
fighters was high indeed: "I hate them; they're as much the
enemy as any lousy, rotten segregationist. They exploit their own
people. They lick the boots of the white man. They're the white
man's agents. They work for the white man. They do his
bidding. They run the Negro community and make sure everyone
stays in line, and they hand out little token rewards — just
enough to keep people nice and quiet. I'll tell you: *they* are the
enemy. If we could get rid of them, we'd have our own people
much more up in arms. It would be easier to organize. This way,
I have to try and persuade extremely poor people to fight not
only the white world, the sheriffs and judges and state police, but
the black leaders, our so-called black bourgeoisie."

Yet, at another time he could feel different. He could smile and
be more historical, more reflective, less outraged: "It's a tough
business. You want to *activate* people. You want them to begin
standing up. You want them to say: go to Hell, goddam white
man. That means saying: to Hell with you, all you Uncle Toms
and all you bowing and scraping niggers; to Hell with saying 'yes
suh' to whites, then bleeding your own people of the little they
have. But I know it's more complicated than that. People need
their self-respect. They need to feel they can produce doctors and
lawyers and teachers and the rest. They need to feel that even if
they can't make it, there are other black men who have. That's

why they love Joe Louis and Louis Armstrong and Lena Horne. We may think the average man should be more political, but let's face it, in this country it's hard to get any large number of people to think in a highly political way.

"I go from door to door, and I'll hear these very poor mothers and fathers talking. They want their kids to study and graduate from school and get good jobs and become like so-and-so, who is a businessman or a lawyer. Now, I happen to know how he works and how crooked he is, so-and-so, but what can I do? I can't just knock him down. I can't tell those people — they've barely opened their door to me and the more they hear of my ideas, the more they're ready to close the door shut on me — I can't say: to Hell with the black middle class, because they're pathetic, man, just a big laugh. I've tried that, and people get really put out. They say in so many words: to Hell with *you*, brother. We want our kids to rise up and be somebody. We'd love our kids to be doctors and lawyers and ministers and all the rest. Don't go and take away our local heroes. We need more than a hero up in New York or over in Atlanta. We need our own people nearby, who look and dress and act respectable and nice and are an example to us and make us feel better about what is possible for a Negro in this country. The people I visit don't even have to say something like that; they feel it, and they let you know with a look on their faces that they do. And it takes someone like me a lot of time to realize how a person feels and to learn how to get around the problem. You learn that you have to go along with things to some extent. You pay your respect to Dr. X and you say sure, lawyer Y is a great guy, and that fellow Z, who is principal of the school — and owns three blocks of slum shacks — he's wonderful, and so is the Reverend Jones, who shouts and screams about God coming to separate the sheep from the goats, while he cheats on his wife and splits the profits with the undertaker — and on and on. Then you try to make a point or two by commenting on how few of those people we have, how the white community controls them, and how much more we need in the Negro community: hospitals and schools and legal aid and all the rest.

"Actually, there will be a day now and then when I am tempted to return to school and finish and go on and become a doctor or a lawyer myself. I'm sure one day I probably will. You can't fight like I am now forever — or can you? I'll be waking up in the morning, and I'll catch myself wondering what it's like to have a nice home and an office to go to and be in — a place where you can work and feel you're doing some people good, and you're making a living for yourself and your family. And the fact is that I've met some of these doctors and lawyers and ministers and teachers, and they're not all bad. Some are disgusting — phony and pretentious and full of themselves. They imitate the white world to the point that you can either laugh at them or cry for them or want to get rid of them — drive them out of the country. But there are some good, decent, hardworking people among the Negro middle class. They've fought as hard as anyone can fight just to get the education they've got and to be in the position they are, and they really want to do anything they can. They're afraid, but who isn't? They've got a lot to lose, but not all *that* much, and they know it. In their own way they try to move things along, and some of them have been a tremendous help to us; they've joined the movement. They've split their lives in half, you could say. They're pillars of the community, but they try to overturn the larger community — because it oppresses them, too, which is what I guess they realize, the smarter of our middle-class people."

Nor could that young black activist forget that he himself came from a reasonably well-to-do home, as things go in the "black community." His father worked in the post office, and his mother taught elementary school. True, the family lived in the South, in rural Georgia, which meant that as recently as 1963 they could not vote, however "stable" and "law-abiding" and "respectable" and yes, "property-owning" they were. Nevertheless, his parents preached industry and loyalty and obedience to their children, even as millions of other American children, white children, learn from their parents and teachers and Cub Scout leaders and Boy Scout leaders that such virtues are important. And the boy listened as he grew up: "I can't change myself completely, forget everything I learned as a child. We weren't rich, but we weren't poor; and for Negroes, we did all right, as my dad always put it. So what if he went to college and could only work in the post office! So what if they couldn't vote! So what if they couldn't go into this place and the next one and the next one, or if they had to go to a special water fountain or a special window. They had good food. They had a nice clean house. They had a new car. They had electrical appliances all over the place. My mother had good clothes. My father had his suits. They got us all dressed up for church, and when we left the house we looked as if we had an appointment with Norman Rockwell.

"It takes time; I grew up hearing that. Things could be worse; I grew up hearing that, too. We're making progress; I grew up hearing *that* at least once a week. But then they'd go and ruin the whole thing by letting us know — they had to — where we couldn't go and what we couldn't do, and why it was hard for us and always would be, they admitted. And if we pushed them too hard, as kids do, they pulled out their biggest weapon: look, stop complaining, and stop feeling sorry for yourself. You're lucky and don't forget it. You have a lot more than most Negroes, a *lot* more. You should see how most of our people live. You should see how few of *us* there are compared to *them*. Go talk with the poor colored folk, and they'll tell you how they'd like to be in your shoes, how lucky they'd feel if they were, how thankful they'd be. Yes, go talk with them. And, you know, that's the story of my life, because I did — which is how I got where I am. I'm not sure my mother and dad remember telling me to 'go talk with them' but *I* do."

The more "organizing" he did, the more estranged he became from his own past — until, that is, he came to realize that he could oppose the workings of a particular social and economic and political system and at the same time comprehend the worth of individuals who, to a limited degree, have some edge in that system, which means manage to live fairly well, for all the consequences of being black. In 1970 he emphatically refused to be called a "moderate"; he is as angry as ever, more so even, and he can be as scornful of middle-class people as ever. But he now lives an essentially comfortable life, has gone back to school, finished college, pursued a higher degree, and become of his own admission another member of the expanding "black bourgeoisie." One minute he blames himself for "selling out." Another minute he acknowledges that he might have remained indefinitely an organizer in the rural South — but at a cost he claims that I, a psychiatrist, could easily estimate. All in all he tries to fashion a coherent view of his life, and the view comes to this: he cannot to some extent escape his origins, though he must try to transcend those origins — which means he will inevitably make a living, eat and dress reasonably well, have a certain amount of standing in whatever community he chooses to call his own, while at the same time he will constantly try to be self-critical, aware of his privileges, desirous in a way of undermining them, interested in undermining them, interested in upholding the cause of the poor. In sum, he will be a political radical who yet can be called an intellectual, a lawyer, whatever.

So it goes for one young man — it is like walking on a tight-rope, he declares. Needless to say, many black lawyers, not to mention white ones, don't become so frustrated and challenged by the tensions and complexities they comprehend in themselves and in their surroundings. Nevertheless, I have often found myself, I have to admit, declining the chance to find out just how torn and beleagured are some of the very people the young man quoted above mentions — the urban professional and business-men he himself is now about to join. I could more easily, if after great effort, locate the contrariness of a poor, unemployed man's life, his composure that is undone by his desperation, his dignity that struggles with his sense of ruinous defeat, his cleverness that disappears in the face of superstition or resignation, his humor that in a flash gives way to a deathlike kind of grimness. Yet, when I visit a lawyer's suite or a doctor's office, when I talk with a minister of an established church or a capable, competent but unspectacular teacher — I then find within myself a good deal of rhetoric, a quickness of judgment, a lack of generosity and, worst of all, at least so far as that word "understanding" goes, an im-petuous unwillingness to stay the course. I have had to work a little harder to clear my own head of its dogmatism, its self-justifying arrogance — and do so for reasons I believe not unlike those both implied and stated by the young man just quoted.

That youth is now a lawyer, one of a number of black lawyers I have met in the course of my work in the South and the North. No account of what happens when "the South Goes North" can possibly ignore those law offices, which thousands of poor and not-so-poor blacks visit, or should have gone to visit but didn't, or fear like the plague itself but end up coming to know rather well. If crime and delinquency afflict the slums of our cities, and if the police who patrol those sections are harried and driven and fearful, and if the law courts are way behind schedule, then it stands to reason that many lawyers must have busy offices. One such lawyer is a man I will call Allen Howard. His experiences, his viewpoint, his effort to make do as a lawyer, a black man, a middle-class man, a man in conflict yet reasonably sure of himself, would probably be appreciated even by a skeptical or unfriendly listener, because he is, as many lawyers can be, an emphatic and convincing speaker: "I was born up here. That puts me a generation or two ahead of many Negroes — black people. Damned if I can switch so easily! My father worked on the railroads; the likes of him is gone. He was the Pullman porter; yes, he was the stereotype of the Uncle Tom, if you are to believe our militants. How much contempt they would have for him if they were to see him today at work — and how utterly wrong, and plain stupid, they would be!

"Some of our young *black* students see only what suits them, what they have already made up their minds to see, and the same holds for some of our up-and-coming lawyers, I'm afraid to say. Maybe we need their indignation and political intelligence, and some of their zeal. They sure have that, energy and passion. Maybe at forty-seven I'm just becoming an old man. Maybe I haven't a right to my own opinion — even when I'm talking about myself! But I'm not really going to surrender *that* right, that civil right, you could say; because I really believe that I've done the most I possibly could for my people, *given my experience and training*. I mean, what *was* I to do? Was I to march down the streets when no one else was marching and get sent not to jail but a mental hospital — as some kind of kooky 'nigger lawyer'?

"And then, there's my father. What was *he* to do? He came North from Memphis, Tennessee. I think his grandfather was a sharecropper in the Delta of Mississippi. My grandfather fled Mississippi — he was uppity even then, I gather, and tried the city, Memphis. Well, if you know the South, you know that there's nothing magic about going to a southern city. You go there and you're as bad off as you were before, maybe worse. At least in the North they've been guilty enough, and rich enough, I suppose, to increase welfare payments over the years and try to break down the more obvious kinds of discrimination — in the bus and railroad terminals, the drinking fountains, the restaurants and movies. Until a very few years ago, before federal pressure, southern cities were like southern small towns and the rural countryside. I laugh when I read in a magazine that life has become better for the black man as he's moved into the cities: *which* cities, and since when? Anyway, my father left Memphis when he was only nine years old. He caught a bus and came to Boston. You know why? He'd been given a name and address by a schoolteacher of his and told to go find the man. The teacher said Dad was smart, and he should escape, and immediately. She offered to pay his way and said her brother worked for the railroad, and she would write to him, and maybe my dad could begin to learn how to be a porter himself. Her brother had only one child, a daughter, and he wrote back and said yes, and the next thing my dad knew, he was on his way. I think my dad had eight brothers and sisters, and his mother and father told him to grab the chance as if it was a lifeline — because he was in a swamp and the water was up to his neck and rising every second.

"He became a porter. He served the white men. He took care of their every need. They rang, he was there. They looked for him, and he appeared in a second or two. He was neat — spotless is the word. I've never met a more tidy and careful person. He'd go away for weeks, and we'd not see him, but I could picture him going across the country, becoming friendly in his own way with all those rich white folks. You could say he was almost intimate with them, the way maids and butlers and chauffeurs sometimes get in the South — less often in the North. He never missed a trick, and when he came home he was full of stories for us. I can remember my mother putting me on his knees, and he'd describe the prairies to me and the Rocky Mountains and California. They seemed like foreign countries to a boy growing up in Roxbury, who never did get to travel until he was forty or so — only a few years ago. When I first saw California, having flown there, I realized what a fine story teller my dad was. I couldn't come home to my children with reports like Dad brought to us — about everything he saw and found interesting.

"My mother is the kind of Negro lady Malcolm X describes — the old Negro aristocracy in Boston, I suppose it's been called. He is unfair to them, though. He makes them *only* smug and color-conscious and anxious to be like white people. They were that, but they had other qualities, too. My mother's family had escaped North before the Civil War, and they were hardworking craftsmen. Her great-grandfather had a little farm in what is now Boston's Hyde Park section, that's right; and he also was a first-class carpenter. He could build a home all by himself, we were told. He spoke fine English and was self-educated. He loved to read. So did my grandfather; he used to read to me. My mother was rather light-skinned, the 'high yellow' one reads about. I never once heard her called that until all these sociology-types started influencing Negro college students! She was 'higher' in status than my father, I guess; certainly he was darker-skinned. But as a Pullman porter he was every bit the measure of my mother's father. My mother's uncle was a minister, a man quite impressed with his own importance, from what I remember. He was a leading Republican. In fact my entire family was. My father wouldn't vote for Roosevelt until 1944. My mother always associated the Democratic party with the South. They both died Democrats, though. By the time Truman finished his term they saw the Republican party was no longer the party of Lincoln. But on the state level, my mother and father *never* voted for a Democrat; and I'll admit, I voted against John F. Kennedy when he first ran for the Senate. I guess I'd *like* to be a Republican, even now, out of memory to Lincoln and Theodore Roosevelt. But the Democratic party has more concern for my people, I believe.

"But I want to say something about this Uncle Tom business. Do you think there is any difference between what my father said and what our militants say today? The answer is no. My dad could say the most devastating things about the people he waited on. He knew them for what they were. He wasn't hypnotized by them. Nor was he ashamed of his life or his race. I know. I heard him talk. He was like a preacher with me, an angry preacher at times: fool the white man; tell him what he wants to hear, then get around him; try to do the best you can and be a credit to your people; don't be ashamed of being colored — and that was how he referred to us; be tough and strong and yes, be ready in case someday the black man will be in a position to run things for himself. I heard about 'black power,' you see, a long, long time ago. My father told me that this is a white country, run by white men for white men. He would tell me what America has done to its Indians as well as its black men. He would say that you can't fight against an overwhelming majority, which has an army and navy and all the rest. *But,* he would always add, *the time will come.* He meant that we'll get more and more in a position to embarrass the country and force it to change, and he once even told me that a few riots by black people would probably help things along, though he was frightened that more repression could also be the result. What could you expect of him? He belonged to the NAACP, which was considered a way-out group in the twenties and thirties. He liked Dr. Du Bois, though he disliked some of the bitterness that crept into him toward the end of his life. My father laughed too much and was too much an optimist *ever* to be bitter. He saw how funny things were, and how sad they were; but he never felt things were hopeless. He said he'd seen so much change in his own life that he wasn't going to tell me *I* wasn't going to see a lot of change. And I have seen change, lots of change."

Needless to say, he can list all the changes he has seen. He remembers when Negroes were tucked away in Roxbury and practically everyone was oblivious to their problems. He remembers when Negroes shunned restaurants and theaters, even though they legally could go to them in Boston. He remembers when newspaper accounts of violence in the South were so patronizing to the blacks that one might have thought Alabama was in central Africa, and the people there strange, exotic "natives." He remembers how few of his race finished high school and went to college, let alone graduate school. He remembers lynchings into the fifties, and separate black military regiments into the forties, and the kind of Jim Crow customs up North one associates with the South: no admission here, stay away from there, don't apply for admission to this school or that college, and even if admitted, don't plan to live with a roommate — unless by chance the college decides to take *two* Negroes.

If he goes on and on with his memories, he also is quite able to bring himself up short and discuss broader social and political issues: "Had it been up to people like me, we'd not be as far along as we are, I know that. I was a pioneer when I did so well in law school they had to put me on the law review — after I threatened to leave the school and write up my experience if I didn't get what I knew I deserved. I was a pioneer when I marched on picket lines to desegregate restaurants that kept on turning away the few Negroes who had the money to go out and eat. We were always told there was 'no room' when of course there was. Those were, as we now say, 'the old days.' Thank God for what happened down South in the early sixties. The country really was pushed into the twentieth century — and I'll admit, I was nervous and skeptical at first. I thought the whites would fight back and start a wave of counteragitation. In the twenties and thirties we had the Klan up North, you know. So, when I read about the freedom rides, I thought they'd kill them all. But I was wrong. When I read about the sit-ins, I remembered some we'd tried in the thirties and forties, and I figured nothing would come of that kind of thing — and again I was wrong. When I saw people from up here going South to do voter registration, I

was afraid they'd *all* get killed, and I wondered whether they'd
really ever accomplish anything. Once more I was wrong.

"Of course, I know some young lawyers, black and white, who
have the gall to tell me that nothing *was* accomplished. They look
at the two federal laws, banning segregation in public places and
voter discrimination, as 'superficial.' They keep on talking about
'the power structure' and the 'exploitation' of blacks. Oh, I agree.
I know a rich man controls more than his one vote's share of the
country. The rich rule everywhere. There are rich and powerful
cliques in Russia and China and England and every other place.
And I know that my people have been exploited. I have eyes; and
remember, I have chosen to work right in the heart of the city,
among my people, and not in some fancy law firm or out in the
suburbs. When I was young, the damn law firms didn't want me;
now they'd all love to have me as a choice bit of reliable, de-
pendable window dressing. Well, if I did join one of those firms,
I'd be bored sick. But they'd find out about me pretty fast.
They'd see that I may be gray and more 'mature,' as one former
classmate of mine at law school calls us 'older Negroes,' but I'd
have the same ideas that the younger black lawyers have. When
my old classmates say, 'You're a wise man, and why aren't the
younger Negroes as mature as you older Negroes were,' they
mean this: you pushed us, but we've forgotten; and now these
guys are pushing us, and they make *you* seem sensible. The fact
is those classmates turned me down once. I was going to picket a
few of those firms a quarter of a century ago, but I thought to
myself: why in Hell should I? Who wants to do that kind of work
anyway? Who wants to become a Brooks Brothers stuffed shirt, a
cog in some big law-office machine?"

What does he do? What kind of law does he practice? Where
and how does he live? Though he is unquestionably a well-
trained lawyer and a member of the middle class, he lives in
what is called a ghetto, a section of a northern city where
thousands and thousands of poor black families live. He knows
that he might now escape to a suburb, but he never has sought to
do so, and never will. He lives in an old building, but one well
cared for. He is near his own people, likes being so, and wants

his children to remain where they are rather than try to move into an almost all-white suburb. True, he has second thoughts. He is only too aware how he might live. Years ago, years before the sixties and what he calls "the great push for integration," blacks like him moved into nice, single-family homes, and so long as they were a few, a mere handful, they were, as he puts it, "absorbed." But he stayed. His wife, light-skinned and also a college graduate, wanted to stay. She felt that her children would ironically become more race-conscious in a white suburban town than in a neighborhood within a black section of the city. And so, again, he lives among his own people and is their lawyer. In that respect, too, he turned down the blandishments of the white world. As he has never stopped reminding me, until recently there have been so few black lawyers in the entire country that he boasts he "almost" knew all of them. Now the number is growing, but the need is enormous, and there was a time when he might easily have turned his back on that need. Instead, he became what he calls "an all-purpose lawyer for the ordinary man."

His office is right square in the middle of a busy commercial section of a black neighborhood, and if he does not have a "storefront," he certainly is only one flight of stairs removed from the street. He is in fact a true source of counsel, in the broadest sense of that word, to many, many people. They come to see him all day and into certain evenings, when he stays in his office so that working men and women will not lose time from their jobs, which means precious money. They come to him with dozens of complaints, with fears and worries, with troubles and more troubles: "I don't know where or how to begin to describe the kind of law I do. For years and years I've gone to my law-school class reunion, the one embarrassing Negro in the class. When I graduated they were embarrassed *because* of me. They were scared I'd come to their dance and maybe the management of the hotel would get upset. I suppose they were afraid someone would say something wrong and start a fight. I never *have* figured out why white people worry so about us black people! And now, of course, they're embarrassed because they can't help noticing that I'm the only one in my class, the only one. I over-heard one of my classmates say just that: why didn't we take more then, he asked his friend. Then he said it: Allen Howard is the only one. I was going to turn around and say, 'You're god-dam right, and I could have pointed that out to you decades ago,' but I didn't. I could never do that, shout and scream. I'm not that kind of a militant. But I work with my people, and a lot of them are poor. I've never kept track of the bills I wouldn't think of sending out, let alone those I have canceled.

"Don't get me wrong. I make money. I handle insurance com-pany accounts and business accounts. I'm paid by the court for defending people who can't afford a lawyer. I'm not poor. I'm comfortable. But I'm not a big fat corporation lawyer — and that's what the militants here keep on calling me. They tell me I've been sucking the blood of the poor. They call me a Negro, an Uncle Tom — oh you name it, I've heard it. I'm an old man to them, a lawyer, a graduate of good schools, a man who wears suits and has a secretary and knows the judge and the police — so I'm everything bad. But for a lot of plain, ordinary people here I'm someone they immediately come to see when they're in trouble. Their kid did something wrong. The landlord is after them, and they can't pay him. The police grabbed them and accused them of something they didn't do. They got in an ac-cident. There was a fire in their building and they lost every-thing. They're fighting with their husband or wife or boyfriend or girl friend and the subject of money has come up and the argu-ment has to be settled. They want a divorce. They want an abortion. They want to sue someone who's crooked them: he's white or he's black, it happens both ways. They thought they had insurance, but now the company tells them no, you've been paying that dollar a week for the last twenty-five years for some-thing else. They were in an auto accident. The city has sent them a notice to get out of the building they're in, and get out fast. There's some problem with drugs. There's a civil rights problem: they've been turned away or turned down or told nothing doing, there's no room in this building.

"I work for the Urban League and the NAACP. I've gone into

every court in this state, local and federal. I've fought the police, fought the fire department, the mayor's office — fought everyone in power. Sometimes I've represented young black students who are friendly with me one minute and call me a Tom the next minute; and Hell, I understand. They look at my gray hair and the lines on my face, and they see that I'm a lawyer who's been around a long time, and they say: he must have compromised and watched his step over all these years, and he drives a nice car and he sure isn't starving, so he's a clever, rich Tom. I see their point, but I also think they're blind at times."

He resents having to apologize for his life. He resents having to summon a historical approach to life, which means summoning elementary common sense. How can someone in 1970 condemn out of hand what a man did in 1940 or 1950, particularly when at the time he was being called idealistic and radical and "way out" — for practicing a certain kind of law, taking on indigent clients all the time, defending the "activists" of the day, writing strong letters of protest "all over the place" and joining picket lines himself? True, there are corrupt and mischievous black lawyers (and white lawyers) in every northern ghetto; and true, Allen Howard willingly admits, there is every reason to examine very closely his kind of work, his position in society. Yet, it is, he feels, almost comic the way some critics do so, the way some critics automatically call a man like him all sorts of insulting and abusive names: "I can only laugh. If some black and white youths want to show that lawyers profit enormously in this society from the business they do for corporations, let them do so. They won't find many black lawyers to condemn for doing that! The black middle class is probably as pathetic as our militant youths say it is. I suppose we *have* made a comfortable living while others have been wretchedly poor — which means we are Americans! I worry that other things are overlooked, though. I am not a totally bad man. I know I sound now as if I am defending myself, but I am defending more than myself. For thousands and thousands of black families, whether our militants of both races like it or not, and even whether people like me are pleased about it or disapprove, the black lawyer or doctor or teacher is a person to be admired and emulated. I am speaking of the poor but bright and ambitious child who wants to rise up and wants to feel that some of his people have done so — that it has been done, that it is possible.

"Now we are all being attacked and despised: that infamous 'black bourgeoisie' is what we are, and Uncle Toms, and all that. Why should an already weak and vulnerable and oppressed people, twenty million among two hundred million, surrounded by signs of white power and influence and achievement, systematically assault its own middle class, call them betrayers and exploiters and all the rest? I hear it has to be done, because we need a 'new society.' What is a young black child exposed to such talk, such propaganda, supposed to believe? He is told that he lives in a country where ninety percent of the people are 'white racist pigs.' He is told that the doctors and lawyers and teachers and businessmen of his own race, whom he sees or reads about, are most likely 'tools,' or that awful thing, a *Negro* or a *Tom*. What is left for such a child? He becomes the desperate captive of a small, frightened, shouting group, totally outnumbered and completely removed not only from the white world, but the black world as well. I am not a psychiatrist, but I have been representing a lot of troubled people for a long, long time and I think there is paranoia in all of this. A people needs its past, needs to understand that there is more to becoming a lawyer or a doctor than words like 'exploitation' and 'Uncle Tom' imply.

"It is true, my father made some money — enough to send me through college and law school — by catering to a lot of rich, self-indulgent white people. It is true, I handle cases for the city and for some businesses, and to some extent poor blacks are ignored or discriminated against by the clients I help. All right: the money I earn is tainted. All money, I suppose, is tainted. Doctors profit from illness. Lawyers profit from the troubles people get into. Politicians exploit the fears of people and make a living out of doing it. But for a struggling minority like my race to be told that it must turn on its own minority of professional men and denounce them and see *only* their worst side — and who doesn't have a bad side to him? — is in my opinion crazy, mad, and worst of all, malicious, because a lot of children will pay the price for that kind of talk. And I repeat: I am not asking for a clean bill of health. Let them criticize me or anyone else. At times I'm disgusted with my profession, and with myself for staying in it. But I want the criticism to be sensible and thoughtful — comprehensive is the word. I mean, I want my children and everyone else's to understand why it is that their ancestors, their fathers and grandfathers and great-grandfathers acted as they did.

"Name-calling may help some people feel better, but it exploits the rest of us. For instance, I know full well that the law is white, but the law is other things, too. White people don't know that the law is white, so *their* children need to learn just how white it is. But black children already know that. What black children really need to know is that the law isn't only an instrument of repression so far as they are concerned. Is it wrong to ask that the finer traditions in the judicial system and in our society *also* be held up to our children? Maybe right now I am daydreaming. Maybe right now too many black people like me, not to mention most white people, don't even stop and think that the law *is* white; and so maybe our militants *do* have to keep hitting hard at lawyers and the law."

For such a man there is no fixed position to be taken up and defended against all opposition. He argues with himself. He shifts his stand, given a reason to do so. The "reason" can come from an antagonist, an essay, a book, a newspaper story. A man like Allen Howard considers himself black, worries about his special and particular responsibilities as a so-called "leader" of his people, but also tries hard to keep in touch with his profession. He has wide-ranging interests. He is a man who reads many periodicals, enjoys novels, likes to go to the theater. His is a discursive, ironic mind. He is as comfortable criticizing himself as he is defending himself. He enjoys rational argument and enjoys exposing irrational argument. He will even allow the irrational its place, so long as there is an acknowledgment that such a development is openly occurring, and for certain stated reasons. He is certainly what many of us would call a decent, honorable, fair-minded man, and yet he feels himself under constant attack — at just the moment when his people are doing better than he once ever dreamed possible. He is an open, well-spoken, generous and forthcoming person. He makes one feel relaxed; he tries to be as thoughtful as he can be, and he expresses himself well. One thinks of him not only as a friend and a colleague of sorts, but as a spokesman who could more than do justice to his own words and those of the many poor people we both have seen in a particular neighborhood. Yet he does not claim to be such a spokesman. He disqualifies himself upon occasion, recognizes his blind spots, acknowledges that others are leading the way, are fighting on the frontier of social and political change.

For me Allen Howard has been a constant reminder that although people like him and me can try to understand history, we most assuredly can do little to make history, to change in a thoroughgoing and decisive way the grim facts of that neighborhood in which he lives and which I have continually visited these past years, always to leave. I know that many of the families I have visited hold no grudge against me for that, have indeed been glad to talk with me; I also know that I have done some things, helped particular children and their mothers in various ways. Perhaps in writing a book like this I am helping them some more. (Notwithstanding the fact that I am also advancing my own career as a doctor and a writer.) Like the lawyer just quoted at such length, the turmoil and unrest of our northern cities unnerves me, the earnest middle-class professional man, and if the wild and hysterical and petty and mean-spirited accusations can be dismissed, there are some shafts that do not miss their mark. One is left to cringe in recognition of our condition — Mr. Howard's, mine: we see wrongs we find ourselves unable to oppose — not in the vigorous and open and direct ways that others choose. We say we are ourselves, we are of a certain age, from a certain background. We say we do what we can, do more than others do. But we wonder. Do we do all we might — or more haunting, all we know in our minds and feel in our hearts we ought to do?

16. *What Else Is a Storekeeper?*

The store is one of six on the block. Jews formerly owned all those stores; now two of them are unoccupied, but four are very definitely in use. One houses a federal "antipoverty" agency. One is a drugstore. One is a food market. One is a sort of all-purpose place in which a person can buy new or used clothes, and everything from light bulbs to cheap toys for children, from sunglasses to a pair of pliers, from a radio and long-playing records to an umbrella. That last store is owned by a man in his mid-thirties who looks upon himself proudly as a businessman, an up-and-coming one who, with others, will demonstrate to the neighborhood (and to the white world) that "blacks can take care of themselves and don't need a lot of white merchants coming in here and cleaning up on us." Though he speaks those words with conviction, he also acknowledges how much he learned from a white, Jewish storekeeper for whom he worked as a boy. He acknowledges that he wants to make as much money as he can, indeed has to make more than he is now making if he is to stay in business for very long. And most of all, he acknowledges that he is torn, in a dilemma: "I want the people I serve to be glad I'm here, and not some white man. But I still have to deal with white people all the time. I buy from them. I depend upon them. They deliver to me. They lend me money. They insure me. I'll be honest: I don't trust the local insurance man, even if he is black. You know what his business is? He collects from a lot of people, a dollar here and five dollars there. He's good with life insurance, but he can't handle the kind of insurance I need: fire, theft, spoilage and damage, all that. I have a black lawyer, though. I'd like to be only doing business with blacks, but I can't. There was a time when I'd go shouting that I'd do business with blacks or I'd do no business at all. But that would be it: I'd have ended up doing no business.

"Of course all my customers are black. They are proud of me. They come in here and say, 'You're doing fine, you're doing just fine.' They feel that I'm one of their own — and it's about time!

Until just a couple of years ago these stores and others nearby were owned by white people, mostly Jews, they were. Their own people had moved out, and so did they — I mean their families did. But they kept on driving over here and trying to forget that we want to run our own lives and not be putting money into the pockets of strangers. And one of them, the guy who ran the food store, he was a lousy racist. I'm not exaggerating. He'd make little remarks. He'd say, 'You people should work harder, then you'd get someplace.' Or he'd say, 'If you're lazy, you get nowhere.' That's what our kids would come back and tell us. Once he told a nephew of mine that he'd better watch out, the way he was staring at the candy, because if he stole any, he'd be sent back South. I was going to go punch him right in the face and tell him to go back to Europe, where he belongs. But up until a few years ago we took that.

"Just four or five blocks away from here there was a pawn-broker, and he owned a lot of the buildings near here, too; well, he was always telling us we were lazy, and we had no real brains, and we're slow, and all that. Can you beat that? Hell, if he was around here now he'd be a dead man. *He* sure wasn't slow, though. He saw that he'd better get out of here. I think it was 1965 when some of our kids went to see him. They told him that he either shuts his mouth and becomes respectful to us, or he leaves, and fast. He laughed at them. He showed them his gun. So, they smashed his windows, and they took some of his stuff. The next thing we knew, he was gone. He closed up — lock, stock and barrel. It spread around like a fire: the Jew is gone! And I'll tell you: we'd have burned him out. We were going to burn down one of his buildings. You know why? *He* set fire to his building a while back, and he collected on the insurance. No one was killed, but we could have been. The police said it was arson, but they didn't know who did it. Then the janitor told some people that he saw the boss's son-in-law in the basement just before the fire, and he couldn't figure out what he was doing there, because he never had gone down there before.

"The police came and started to investigate. One of the police told the janitor and some tenants that they had good reason to believe they knew who started the fire — him, the landlord's son-in-law. But all of a sudden they dropped the investigation. And if you want to hear how a plain, old janitor can be a great man: the janitor quit. He told the landlord that he knew everything and that he was quitting. The landlord laughed at him to begin with; then he told the janitor he was getting old, and he had these funny ideas, and it was too bad. Then the janitor told the landlord he was definitely quitting and he was going to the police, because people could have been killed. The landlord changed his tune all of a sudden. He told the janitor he wanted him to stay, please; and he offered to give him a hundred dollars and a paid vacation, because he'd done 'such good work over the years,' the landlord said. The janitor quit anyway. He went to the police. They told him they didn't need his help and to go back to work. He told them he'd never do that. They looked at him as though he was crazy, but one cop was bothered. He gave away the whole story. He told the janitor that even if he was right there was nothing he could do, nor the police, either. The janitor said he didn't care. He couldn't work for people like that. The cop exploded then. He told the janitor that everyone was doing some cheating, and there was no way to stop it, and even if the two of them, the cop and the janitor, tried to stop a man like that landlord or that son-in-law of his, they'd get nowhere, because he's paid off people, the landlord has. That's what the janitor kept saying the cop said. The day the landlord and lousy pawnbroker came to work and saw his store window broke he found a big note on the door. The kids told him they were just beginning. They told him they knew what he'd done, and he'd better get out, clear out, or they'll burn his house up. They'd found out where he lived, and they were going to go and burn the house down, a huge house out in the suburbs someplace. And that was the end of him. He's never once stepped foot in this neighborhood since then."

He goes on to tell me why he still finds himself thinking of such things. It was easier, he feels, for an out-and-out crook like that man to make a living than it is for a somewhat idealistic man like himself — who nevertheless has to put pressure on people to buy things, has to try to profit from an exceedingly harassed and near-indigent clientele. He feels like a bit of a crook himself, he admits. He feels that at times he allows, encourages even, people to buy things they may not really need and really cannot afford. He extends them credit in order to help them, to make it easy for them to buy, and then, of course, he tries to get his money from them. He tries to be compassionate, but he knows he has to be aggressive, persistent, even seductive at times. He has to get those customers to come in, stay in, and buy. And meanwhile his margin of profit is low, prices are going up, and the people he sells to have no corresponding rise in income. It is all very confusing and at times enraging.

He hears and reads that blacks should become capitalists, get "a piece of the action," go into business and rise up, like others have. Then he contrasts all of those words with his actual day-to-day experience. The result is that one day he sounds like a most conservative man indeed, even a bit of a racist himself, but the next day he may talk like a revolutionary, wanting the country to be done with all businesses, certainly including his own. Nor does he really feel the joy some small businessmen no doubt obtain from selecting the stock they will sell and trying to anticipate the customers' wants and needs. He knows only too well the tight circumstances his neighbors find themselves facing. He knows how many welfare checks come into the building nearby, how many men of his generation and acquaintance are either without work or working in menial, low-paying jobs. He also knows how many times he has been asked for a loan, for credit that will never be balanced by payments, for donations to groups struggling for social and political change. "It was easier," he points out, "for others, for the white man doing business here, or the old-fashioned Negroes, who don't give a damn about anything but a dollar. Maybe I'm becoming one of them myself, another Negro exploiter. I'm beginning to wonder if anyone with a soul in him can be a businessman in a section like this. If you make a good profit, you're a success, but you're also a real failure. The fact that you have money means you have taken it from a lot of people who have practically nothing. I know I do a service for them, and I try to please them, but when I see some of them taking out those dollar bills — the way they hold on to them, and then sadly let them go! — I feel as if I ought to be handing out clothes free and giving a cash bonus to everyone who comes into the store.

"When I was a kid I used to run errands for one of the store-owners, the old druggist; he's dead and his son just sold to a black man. The druggist used to give me lectures on how I should save my money. And I guess I listened. My father had tuberculosis, and it went to his brain and killed him when I was eight years old. The druggist liked my dad; he used to sweep up the drugstore every night, and he did a good job. The druggist promised me that I could take over, and he even gave me an increase over my father's pay. It wasn't very much, but it was something, and I was proud to have a job at that age — especially when guys twice eight could find no work at all. I used to keep that drugstore so clean that you could look at the floor and see yourself. I made his counter shine. I dusted everything. And he patted me on the head, he really did, and he gave me extra money, tips. He told me I was like him, neat and clean. He told me I should stay in school and try to get ahead. 'Don't be like a lot of people around here,' he'd say to me.

"Once he joked with me and told me I must have some Jewish blood in me. Most of the Jews had moved out by then, and we were the majority, and he was talking out loud about the changes in the neighborhood. He said he was going to stay, though — for a while. He said he liked the store, and he wanted to be of help to our people, and he knew if he closed down they'd be without a drugstore and that would be hard on them. Then he laughed and told me that I should try to be a druggist. 'You're smart and you work hard; you're like a good Jewish boy,' he told me. I wasn't too sure what he was talking about, to tell the truth. I asked my mother what a Jew was, and she said she wasn't sure she could exactly tell me. She said most whites aren't Jews, but some are, and a lot of the store people near us, they are Jews, and they used to live where we do. She said they didn't believe in Jesus Christ being our Lord, that was their problem, and it was too bad for them that they don't. I was going to ask the druggist whether it was true he didn't believe in Jesus, but I had a little sense in me, even if I was a kid of only eight or so. I remember noticing that he sold all kinds of cards with pictures of Jesus on them — for Easter and Christmas and all that. I told my older sister that maybe the druggist wasn't Jewish after all, but she said no, he was, and he sold those cards because he wanted to make money, that was why. It's funny, but there I was, a little kid, and I sensed that the man was in a real bind: If he didn't sell what his customers wanted, he'd have to go out of business, but a lot of what he sold he probably had no use for himself. I don't only mean the Easter cards, either. I remember asking him about some of the pills he had on display, and he looked right at me and told me never to use them, they were no good. It was only later, on the way home, that I wondered why he sold the stuff. But millions of people all over the country want those pills, and what was he to do?"

He has yet to find an answer to that question, or at least an answer he himself finds satisfactory. He considers himself young, active, progressive, a leader not of the older community but of black men like himself, who want to control their own lives and in essence be free of "white strangers," as he often refers to them. Yet, again, he constantly has to deal with white men; and even more significant, he does not quite in his mind and heart feel as free of whites as he sometimes declares that he and others ought to be. That druggist, for example, was one of the most decisive influences in his life. He won't say something that outspoken, but when he mentions that druggist, he does so in the quiet, unself-conscious way people do when they speak of parents or friends or teachers who meant something to them, meant a lot indeed. If I were to try to persuade him that for years and years the druggist, in point of fact, exerted a greater authority over his mind than any other grown man, I would soon be laughed at or told to peddle *my* wares on some other block. But he has on several occasions and in several ways acknowledged his debt to that old Jewish druggist, and with a drink in him and me he could expand upon all of that rather movingly: "I wish that druggist

was alive, so I could see him and he could see me here, working
in my store. He wasn't as bad as he might sound today when we
talk about 'them' — I know some would say he exploited the poor
and fed off our pain and misery. He was very good to a lot of
kids. He would have his favorites, and if he didn't like someone,
he'd watch them so carefully they'd leave the store in a hurry. I
don't think he was afraid they'd steal anything. I think he just
didn't like a kid who was fresh, a wise guy.

"There was a time when I would have called him a racist, but
now I have a store, and I know how he must have felt: you don't
like certain people, and even if they *are* customers, it's as if
they're in your home, and you want them out, fast. And the
stealing that people do, I know about that. I'm black, and they
steal from me. There are some people I've actually seen take from
the counter and walk out, and I haven't lifted a finger. I know
how they live, how poor they are. But others have money; at least
they have as much as I do. I call the police on them. I've pulled
my gun and held them until the cops come. What can I do? Turn
this store into a public charity? It won't last long that way. Kids
don't realize that I don't own my stuff. I have to buy it from
other people; and if I don't pay them, they come and close me
down.

"You know, a lot that I do now I used to see that druggist do.
He tried to steer the real bright kids along. He'd tell them to go
be doctors or lawyers. He'd give them things from his window
display — to use for fun, or to take to school when they were
writing on some subject connected with 'health.' He used to give
me little pep talks: don't leave school, clean your teeth every day,
use this brand of soap, and take a vitamin pill in the morning.
And he gave me the soap and gave me the bottles of vitamin
pills; they were small samples he got from the drug companies. I
can still hear him; he'd call me over and say 'here.' He didn't say
any more, but I knew what he meant: take these and don't you
forget what I say. Every once in a while he'd give me one of his
wife's pastries or a sandwich she'd make. It was strange food for
me — Jewish cooking, I guess. I recall coming home and trying
to tell my mother what it was that I'd eaten: there was the roll

that looked like a circle and the salty, red stuff and the butter, only it was white and not yellow and real thick. Well, I now know it was a bagel, and that was cheese and smoked salmon. But the poor guy, I asked him the next day what I'd eaten, because I'd tried to tell my mother and she thought I might be getting something bad from him. He said, 'Tell your mother I know what's healthy and what isn't'; and he wouldn't say another word. I think he was really annoyed that we didn't trust him completely.

"He once offered to give me some money. I think he was shy, and he didn't want to boss me around. I told him I was going to finish high school, even if it meant I couldn't bring in the money my mother needed. He told me I was right. His face lit up. He said, 'Look, if I can help. . . .' He had his hand on the cash register anyway, and he pressed it. I didn't know what he was going to do. I half wanted him to give me everything he had in the box, and at the same time I knew I'd never take a penny like that. I think he was a little confused himself — about why he *did* open up the cash register. He looked at me and he must have read me right, because he pushed the drawer back in and said, 'Let me know if I can help you, kid.' The last day he was here I went over to see him. I said good-bye. He said good-bye. He said it was too bad I'm not a druggist, because I could take over his store. His son didn't want to work here, with black people. I knew it wouldn't take the son long to sell. He had to wait until he could find a black druggist, though; there aren't that many.

"I just didn't have the money to go to college. If it were now, and I could get some big scholarship, maybe I would become a druggist. It's better to be a druggist. You've got a profession, you know. Of course, a lot of my people can't afford the prices of those prescriptions. Welfare pays for the very poor, but a black workingman, he gets no money from the city, and if he needs to buy some of those pills, he can lose his shirt paying for them. It's tough selling medicine you know people need when they can't afford it; and it's tough having to buy what you've got to have and you can't pay for. It's like that with me. I see a kid that needs some shoes and a shirt and pants, and his mother can't really afford them. I'm all torn up, I'll tell you. That old druggist, I think I know now what he went through. He said once that running a store is no job for a man who is soft. I didn't even know what he was talking about at the time, but I must have *sensed* what he meant, because I sure do remember him saying it. It's funny how some of those things can stick and stick in your mind, and a lot later you remember them."

And indeed he does. He constantly talks about being soft, about the need to be tough, to be a good businessman, which means *both* make money and please his customers. He is not sure he can do both. He tries hard. He is quick, active, alert, thoughtful, and a knowing person, able to size up people, cater to them, win their confidence. But his customers, so many of them, are down on their luck. And he himself gets all too troubled by the contradictions about him, which cause an almost philosophical rage (I think it can be called that without pomposity). Part of him hails the Black Panthers. Part of him remembers that old druggist with fondness and respect and gratitude. Part of him responds to words like "black capitalism." Part of him simply wants to make a good living and enjoy the comforts that will thereby follow. Part of him feels deeply the troubles of his neighbors, and he admits it, burns with indignation. And all I can say is that all of him is part of the black man today in America.

17. Who Speaks for Us?

There is in what arc called "ghettos" a kind of rage that I fear few of us know about, either because we really don't want to know, or because we simply have no way of hearing the voices of those who feel the rage. I have in mind the thousands and thousands of black people who do not feel themselves to be pathetic and degraded and sick and all eaten up by what is called "social pathology." Nor are many such enraged men and women members of the "black bourgeoisie," unless that phrase is to be ridiculously amplified to include all working people, all men and women who labor hard and are glad to do so and are proud they have done so all their lives. The very word "ghetto," used as it is

by white and some black people offends such workers: they feel
they live in the *city*, like everyone else, and they do not want
their streets talked about as if they are some awful blight upon
mankind. Nor do they want their lives characterized in special
and near hysterical ways. Nor do they like shifting fads that go
from *Negro* to *black* to *Afro-American* — as if whatever a few
outspoken men decide is "right" has to be obeyed by everyone,
lest he be called an Uncle Tom or racist.

As the reader will notice, many of the people I know, of both
races, shift at random from the word "black" to the words
"colored" or "Negro"; and the shifts are not always fraught with
ideological significance of the kind that is often called "deep-
rooted" or "psychological." Sometimes we use words unselfconsciously; they have been used by our parents, and by us over the
years, and it requires time and effort to make a shift, to take up
new words and feel comfortable with them. Nor does everyone
have the inclination to be so concerned with words, phrases and
slogans. Again and again I am reminded in the course of my
work that some of the "issues" and "conflicts" and "arguments"
that trouble me simply don't vex and hound the people who
speak in this book. Why is it that so many of us, who are so
concerned about the "true feelings" of others, be they black or
red or brown or Appalachian-white or whatever, simply cannot
accept on face value some of the things we hear? And why is it so
hard for us to believe that sometimes people don't say things or
believe things simply because they *don't* — and not because they
have some "problem" or are "defensive" about this or "reacting"
against that? I have in mind the unwillingness of some black
people to demonstrate self-disgust, or to ask white self-
proclaimed "sympathizers" for their outrage and pity, or to use
some of the fashionable terms such as "cultural disadvantage"
that one hears among certain white middle-class citizens? Must it
be that those blacks are demonstrating their "pride" in order to
conceal their "inner" hurt? Must it be that those blacks are going
through some "period of self-assertion," some "stage in their
development" as a race or a people?

I believe that thousands and thousands of "ordinary" people

feel things in their bones and speak out of their hearts, and often say what to them almost needs no saying, so obvious and concrete and clear-cut are some matters. I cannot claim to have included here every opinion I have come across, every sentiment and allegiance I have heard. I have done my best to indicate the *range* of ideas and activities one like me sees in certain sections of certain cities. I cannot write about what I have not witnessed or heard. I cannot claim access to the words of those who have their own good and wise reasons to stay clear of white middle-class people, or white observers, or white social scientists, or white psychiatrists.

God knows, when I read some of the things I do in various journals, not all of them professional, I wonder what an observer from another planet, even if he had a sense of humor and the longest historical perspective possible, would make of the pompous, muddled language, the self-serving postures, and, worst of all, the narrow-minded arrogance that passes itself off as "science" or "research." If poor people, of whatever race, have been "exploited" by those who make caricatures out of their lives and want only to rip their words and habits out of context so as to make this point or prove that theory, then many readers have been exploited in another way: their hunger for information (one hopes nothing more sinister is at work) has caused them to take in, it seems, almost anything which bears one or another "authoritative" stamp and say to themselves: interesting, interesting. Who is around to shake us and shout: come off it, man? Where are the men ready to demand that we stop being smug, self-centered "benefactors" who secretly or even openly and unashamedly love blood and gore, who enjoy the sight and smell of trouble, who crave objects to pity, groups of people to support faddishly, causes to embrace, then abandon? I fear I have to admit that I have been so shaken and shouted at; and if I cannot accept all the rage I've heard sent in my direction — because what I have seen with my own eyes and come to believe I will hold to and speak about — I can most definitely share much of what I have heard.

I suppose we all worry that our own very special point of view doesn't get understood; but often the loudest complainers are the wordiest and fussiest people. Still, the four words that make up the question *Who speaks for us?* can often be voiced by someone who is simply and directly annoyed and, yes, even wryly amused. Here, for instance, it what I heard in 1969 from a tall, somewhat heavyset worker; that is what he is, and that is what he calls himself and what he wants to make quite sure I call him: "I get sick when I read the papers or the magazines. Mind you, I don't have time to read a lot, but I do my share, and I tell my wife that my stomach turns as a result. I say to myself: who do they think they are, writing all that about us? And on television, those documentaries and talk shows, I don't recognize me or my family or my neighbors; I don't recognize so much that I have to scratch myself and ask whether it *is* my people they're talking about, right?

"I'm thirty-seven years old. I am called a black man. The fact is, mister, I work in a factory, and I have a wife and three children and we live in an apartment. I used to think there were a lot of people like me, thousands and thousands of them. I used to think I'm a worker, and there are a lot of workers like me at the plant, and some happen to be Negroes and some happen to be white, but we'd all been there for years and we knew each other, and when you come right down to it, we're not that different. We spend our days the same way, and when we talk about what we do in the evening and on weekends, it comes out sounding the same then, too. But these days I'm supposed to believe I'm an oddball, a rare bird, you know. I'm supposed to believe I live in a *ghetto,* and all around me are these *diseased* people, and they are *crazy,* and they are *addicts,* and they are *prostitutes,* and they set *fires,* and they think they're in the worst, most terrible situation anyone could be in, and they need everything, man, everything — because the *racial tragedy* has gone to their heads, and they are in a bad way, a real bad way.

"Well, I'll clue you in to something. I'm not rich, and I'm not special. I'm not a doctor or a lawyer. I didn't even finish high school. My mother and father came up here from Virginia — Dinwiddie, Virginia. They didn't have a cent to their name, and no degree either, or rich relative waiting for them. And times weren't so good. It was in the late twenties and early thirties. I was born under Roosevelt, Franklin Delano Roosevelt, and I can recall my father saying it sure was rough trying to make a living. But he got by. He was a janitor. He was a watchman at night. He scraped up enough for us all to live and eat and have a roof over our heads. And when I was sixteen I'd been working three or four years myself, and then I got the job I have now. It's hard work; I have to keep on my toes. But I get a salary that means we all can eat and have clothes to wear and a car and a phone and television and a toaster and a waffler — Hell, what *more* can a guy want! I help make those appliances, so it's only right that I should own them; but I pay, like everyone else.

"They call this a ghetto. Can you beat that? The building is old, and whites used to live in it; but it's a sound building, and we like it here, and we don't want to live with white people, and we're happy with our own people, and that doesn't mean we're Afro-Americans or for black power or any of that. Hell, I work with white people, and I'd like my kids to go to school with them. But I live where I do, and I'm happy living here, and there aren't rats eating up my kids or cockroaches crawling on them. My kids eat good food, and brother, we're not rich, either. I'm just a plain guy — and there are thousands like me right in this section of the city. Why don't people talk about someone like me? Why don't they call me an American citizen, not a black man or Negro or all the other words? I'm not out to tear the society apart. I get up every day and go to work and come home and I'm not on heroin, and I'm not a two-bit drunk, and my kids aren't experimenting with drugs and on the way to being pimps and prostitutes. You know, it's insulting the way people try to create an image of the Negro as some pathetic creature who can't for the life of him take care of himself and has nothing he can really believe in and be proud of. It's bad enough we get that treatment from those white 'bleeders' who just love to find us in bad shape — the worse shape the better they like it. They'll walk by ten blocks of buildings where we live in order to find one that's bad, really bad, so they can start crying and can say: oh, those poor, poor people, they are

so low, so down and out. Then they'll go home to their big suburban homes and start crying for us, and they'll take up a collection for us and feel as sorry as they possibly can for us.

"But what about the Negroes who talk like that? It's not just
the white ones who bother us, it's our own people who put on a
show about how *bad* it is for anyone who isn't white. Their eyes
fill up with tears, and they start wringing their hands and say,
'Let's feel sorry for ourselves, brothers; let's feel as sorry for
ourselves as we can, because we are the worst-off people you can
ever catch sight of, that's for sure.' I have to laugh when I see
some white guy and some black guy appear on a talk show, and
they tell you that where those Negroes live, it's bad, real bad.
After I hear them long enough I start wondering to myself:
where are all those bodies lying on the street, and where are all
the ruins, and where is the garbage up to your neck, and where
are the mice and rats running down your back?"

He has no interest, by the way, in denying the obvious poverty
and misery many of his people must every day live with and
struggle against and often enough find too much, much too
much. He knows the special burdens his parents had to bear, and
he himself still bears, and his children will no doubt bear. He can
demonstrate impatience and anger and outrage — that still, *still*
it is so hard for so many of his people "to get by, just to get by."
Nevertheless, he knows that all over the city he lives in one can
find black workingmen who do the best they can and make a
reasonable living, and who simply do not recognize themselves as
described by some of their own people or by "concerned" and
"sympathetic" whites. Yes, he has his "problems." Yes, he wishes
things were different in various respects. But like many white
workingmen he feels thoroughly (and by that I do not mean
"defensively") proud of achievements he is quite willing to
specify.

"Hell, it's a long way from Dinwiddie, Virginia," he reminds
himself as well as me. "You can emphasize the poverty you came
from or how you're living now. You can emphasize the good or
the bad in this life. Some people love to find trouble. Some
people can't believe it if they find someone else laughing and

enjoying himself. They feel they've got to find a little bit of misery in the guy, and they go over and over him until they can say: you poor bastard, don't you see how lousy and no-good your life is? My dad used to tell me about Dinwiddie, Virginia. He used to tell me that I should never, never go and see the place. But three or four breaths later he'd be joking with my mother about some fun they used to have back there, and all the tricks they used to pull on each other and their friends, and the games they played and the laughing. They used to laugh a lot, my dad says — even in Dinwiddie, mind you. Now, he's had a hard life. But he's not a slave. And he doesn't want people calling him a beggar and a thief and an addict and a no-good who can't work and drinks all the time. My father has worked all his life, and so have I. He doesn't use drugs and he doesn't drink and he's got a nice place to live and he's happy to be alive and he knows damn well he's made a lot of progress in his life — and I'll say it for him, because he would laugh in the face of people who asked him. He would wonder how they could even ask; if they had any common sense they'd already know. Anyone who talks about those awful ghettos ought to come over here and go from building to building; he'd wake up, then he would. He'd see we're not special and rich, we're just workingmen; but we do the best we can, and we don't want ourselves talked about as if we're all lying in the gutter someplace, or as if we're Uncle Toms just because we try to keep a nice-looking apartment and obey the law.

"I don't scare. I don't scare so easy. Let them call me what they want; I work hard for every penny I make, and no factory would keep me going five minutes if I didn't. Then I come home and turn on the television, and some black man is saying that what he says is what all black people say; and some white man is saying that the ghettos, the ghettos, they've got to be torn down, and the poor, poor black man, isn't he in the worst way! It makes a man want to vomit. A lot of my friends, they just laugh. They think the whole thing is real funny, and I mean *real* funny. But I tell them it's *not* funny. Look at the way we get shown. Look at how the people out there watching see us. Look at what we hear about ourselves. That's not right. That's bad. That's bad news. I want the people of this country to know that there are lots and lots of Negroes around who are doing pretty good. Sure, we could be doing better. Sure, I hope my kid will finish high school and go to college. Sure, we get a raw deal, our people do. Sure, we have to keep on pushing and pushing and pushing. But that's not to say there are only a few rich Negroes, and all the rest of us are — like, living on a plantation, man, or down in some sewer pipe, jabbing our arms with needles, or thinking about which broad to knock up next, or which building we ought to burn right down to the ground. Would you like it if some people came out to your street, your town, and looked around, and then said the town is a ghetto, and its people are in really bad shape, and they're out of it, man, way out of it? Every day I see the buses fill up with people just like me. I mean guys who have their family and their work, and they can smile and get a kick out of life. We don't need someone pointing his finger all over us and poking around until he picks up some trouble and says: here it is, here it is!"

From a black nurse I hear similar thoughts. She lived for three decades in Harlem, then moved up to Boston's Roxbury section because her brother lives there and she had lost her husband and wanted to be near him and another brother. She has two sons, one a teacher and one an engineer. No doubt about it, they are what some call "middle class"; but there is more to their lives than those words were ever meant to suggest, and even if she is a reasonably well-off person as things go for her people, she is still able to look around and talk: "I sometimes think I'm reading science fiction when I pick up magazines or the papers. When I tell people, white people, I lived in Harlem, their pupils dilate. They give me a look that is supposed to say, I guess: oh, how awful for you; it must have been Hell, a living Hell. People *have* said that to me, word for word. They've practically wanted to give me a medal for bravery and heroism. Then they decide: she's a nurse; she must have been special — you know, the black middle class! Life is easier for them, but it's still no picnic! I've heard that line, too. I've heard black people speak the line and watch their white audience squirm more and more with guilt. It's all very well to laugh and say it won't hurt to make whites squirm; it won't hurt to make them bleed and cough up some cash; it won't hurt to 'mau-mau' them, scare them by telling them we're mad, we're fed up — so unless they do this and they do that we'll explode, we'll burn up the cities, we'll go on a rampage, we'll turn the country over to the Russians by starting a civil war or something. But after a while I think we make fools of ourselves, and the worst of it is we actually start losing our heads and believing all that talk.

"We forget. We forget the ideas people get of us, white people, and the ideas so many of us have about ourselves. Why do my own people, who should know better, parrot the line that goes like this: they are so destroyed and so unable to help themselves that we've got to do something drastic — tear down their ghettos and rehabilitate them. I'm so sick of that word *rehabilitate*. When I was studying to be a nurse, rehabilitation meant getting someone who had been sick back on his feet again and to work and all the rest. Now I hear that Negroes are ruined people, and the ghetto is full of pathology, and only 'massive rehabilitation' will work. And do you know what they want to do? These are our *friends*, so called, I'm talking about! They want to take our little children and bring them up away from those 'ignorant' mothers of theirs. They want to tear down Harlem and Roxbury. They want to break the 'cycle of poverty,' which I read is 'transmitted from generation to generation.' Why don't more people talk about changing the American business system, which is also transmitted from generation to generation?

"We are called criminals and diseased and addicted, and we are told that the thing to do is build low-cost housing and get some more medical help to the addicts and alcoholics. All the while I see my people leaving their apartments to work, work, work. They teach their children to be good. They save what they can. They go to church and pray as hard as a person can pray. They buy pictures for their walls and records to dance by and listen to and enjoy. They keep the rooms they have as clean as can be, and the hallways, too. They sweep the stairs and make sure the garbage stays in the barrels and gets hauled off on time each week. And no one comes and notices. No one comes and learns that they aren't rich, and they aren't businessmen or professional men, but they aren't exactly poor, either — not the kind of poor who make people weep and want to send off a basket of food. They have jobs and they try hard and they *want* to try hard. They do not want to have their houses and their streets torn down by some white planner — or black planner — who says: Harlem, it's all rats and roaches and dazed people and terrible, terrible tenements.

"I wish, oh how I wish, more people in this world would go and look around a little before they started sounding off. I mean, I know street after street in Harlem and here in Roxbury where black people live exactly like other people do in white neighborhoods — none of which anyone is suggesting need be razed to the ground, or called 'disaster areas,' or be given 'massive rehabilitation' because the people are so out of it, so deprived and without a culture of any value. I'd like someday to tell people about how *deprived* my childhood was and how *poor* my parents' culture was! I'd like to tell how my father and my mother read from the Bible, and how they read from the history books, and how as children they had taught themselves to read and write, and how they taught us to go and do the same, go and get an education and get ahead. I know, I *do* know, how awful life can be for a black man or a black woman — in the South or up here, too. But it's been pretty awful for all groups, if you go back far enough and see what they faced. I think in America the Negro race has probably had to live with more hardship than any other group of people. But we've come through it, and we're not destroyed by the experience, I don't believe. We are a vital, alive, swinging race.

"Some say it's genocide that America has tried to commit on black people, but if that's been the wish, we've beaten them: we're over twenty million and growing fast. Is that a people facing genocide? And look at those white college kids. They are so 'deprived' culturally that they more and more try to talk like us, dress like us, play our music, dance like us. My God, I hear from my sons that there's no limit to the white man's interest in our habits and our values and our way of doing things! Doesn't that show that we've been busy doing more than feeling sorry for ourselves and complaining that we have nothing? Doesn't that show that we're more than sick, sick, sick? Was it 'sick' of us to learn how to survive and keep our thinking straight and learn how to whistle a good tune and pray plenty and smile and smile and swing, rather than sit and cry all day long? I don't want to hear my mother turned into a huge, smothering dictator and my father into some drunken, doped-up philanderer. Who has come and talked to me, or to my brothers, or to thousands and thousands of others like me in Roxbury and Harlem and any other city? Why don't they know about our good side, our tough side, our damn smart side, our clever-as-can-be side?

"I am a nurse. I've worked in hospitals. I know all the bad side of my people. But is there any group without a bad streak in it? I get sicker by the year of all this propaganda, that's what it is. We're made out to be so bad and so awful and so shiftless that for every white person who cries for us and says give them everything they need, another gets disgusted and says it's hopeless, they're just a bunch of hungry, ignorant animals. We don't need the weepers and we don't need the bigots. We need friends who know that most of us may have our faults, like everyone does, but we're trying, we're working, we're sending our children to school, we're going to church — and you know, we're getting something out of life, too, not just sitting around with our heads in our hands on a drug high. And let any bulldozer come near this street; we'd laugh at the sight of it, and the man driving it would laugh, too. There's not a stockbroker or lawyer on this street, just working people; but we take care of our buildings and our yards like people do everywhere. It's bad on some streets, very bad; but it's bad on plenty of streets where white people live. What I object to is the stories that have all of us at the end of our rope. I don't like our streets thought of as if they were covered with garbage and littered with syringes. The country needs to be more discriminating, that's right! People have got to realize that wholesale words like *ghetto, cultural deprivation, black rage, black despair* — that they can give a completely false impression about twenty million American citizens who are more like their fellow citizens than those fellow citizens may want to believe. But maybe whites have been persuaded to believe what they believe by — of all people! — those who keep on claiming how tolerant they are and progressive and pro-Negro and pro-black and who say how awful it is for us in such a way that everyone begins to believe *we* are awful."

At times I catch myself saying that she and the man I have quoted are lucky; I have with my own eyes for years seen the misery and harshness and meanness and sadness and bitterness of life in Harlem or Roxbury. Yet I think the truth is that those two individuals know full well how far from unique they are, how much they share with others, and how devious and misinformed and sometimes even deluded some of their so-called advocates are. I believe they are onto something about many of us who consider ourselves sensitive and compassionate and interested in serious, thoroughgoing "structural" changes in America's social, political and economic system. Too often we confuse our aims with those of the people whose "condition" we find so "low" or pitiable. Meanwhile, to our embarrassment, if we even care to look around, some of those people, not a handful by any means but a substantial number, say and do things that announce their lives are not as we say they surely must be, or their hopes are not what we say they ought to be.

To keep our faith in our destiny as the wise ones who know how to distinguish the merely apparent from the real, we ingeniously come up with a series of words: they have all been *brainwashed,* or they have been *co-opted,* or they have been *duped* and *bought out by the power structure.* Poor souls, they want gadgets, while *we* know (we've had them all our lives!) how irrelevant and even obscene those machines and trinkets and diversions can be. And *we* will help *them* — tell them, educate or reeducate them, make them want what we want, make them live the better lives they should have, make them over into people worthy of our dedicated efforts, people whose grim, tragic presence justifies every bit of our rage and despair. Are not we the ones who *know* how all these things work, know how the poor live and how the rich live off them? Are not we the ones who *know* about ghettos and about the black bourgeoisie? As for a man like that factory worker or a woman like that nurse, and as for so many other black (or red or brown or white) people whose vision of their lives and their country doesn't quite fit into ours — we can only shrug our shoulders and remark once again upon the way the oppressed are masked and beaten and fooled. But we will eventually show them, organize them, lead them — until, we always add, they are "ready" to take over for themselves. And if that factory worker has the impression he has been quite "ready" for decades, and indeed has been taking quite good care of himself, as have others like him, then we can only sigh, or these days, grit our teeth and dig in for the long haul.

IV

WHITE VISITORS

E VERY single day they can be seen driving into the black neighborhoods of American cities: a white landlord or his white agent, the white police, white schoolteachers, white firemen on their long, awkward, ladder-heavy trucks, white garbage collectors in fat trucks with those wide, hungry mouths that take in everything, white welfare workers, white insurance men or salesmen, white storeowners. They are not necessarily glared at all the time or harassed. Day after day they arrive, they go about their work, and then they depart. Most of the time neither they nor the people they meet up with are noisy or wordy or self-conscious about who has white skin and who has black skin and who are the strangers and who are residents. They get along with one another — though often nervously, fearfully, angrily, suspiciously, moodily. Sometimes, though, they get along quite well. There are moments that even go beyond courtesy, that are more than businesslike and formal — or so one hears from both white and black people. On the other hand, of course, there are moments when words like "distrust" and "hate" only begin to describe the tangle of feelings that can come to expression in a flash and leave outside newspaper readers as bewildered and puzzled as ever, and full of the same old questions: what is going on "over there," and why is there so much tension between people in those sections and the police or the schoolteachers or the welfare workers?[1]

The things I have heard and in turn set down here are not easily forthcoming to an "interviewer," have indeed required years and

years of talking, of sustained acquaintance. Therefore the thoughts
and feelings are of particular if limited value — which means some
light is shed, even if categorical "answers" are not provided. So, I
again have to hope there is some value to a book like this; and I
guess I make such a statement at this point because I especially
feel that many readers simply do not know or understand (or care
to know or care to understand) the people who speak in this section. I am not saying that white, middle-class readers, even those
who call themselves "liberals" or "radicals" know and understand
the blacks in our northern cities, either. But many of them at
least *want* to understand ghetto children, their needs and fears
and wishes. In contrast, policemen or firemen are considered
"enemies" while at the same time other white people look
upon the same policemen or firemen as protectors. The police in
particular are called "pigs" by some; by others they are considered
all that is good and decent and loyal. I wonder, though, how
many of us really try to learn what it is that a policeman does in
a black section of a city, what the blacks see him as doing, what
he feels about his work, what he feels others feel about his work,
and what those others actually say they feel.[2]

I cannot see how I could have gained some sense of cities like
Boston or New York or Cleveland or Chicago without coming to
know some of the people I am now hopefully going to bring in
touch with the reader. When I first started my work in the North
I asked a black mother whom I should go visit and get to know. I
wanted her advice badly, and she thought a long time before she
gave it. Finally, she gave me a name or two, friends of hers she
thought I would very much profit from knowing. Then she jolted
me (and I later realized, herself also) by saying this: "You'd
better go and speak with those visitors we have here, the white
visitors. Ask them some questions and see what their answers are.
Then let me know. I'd like to know. I'd like to hear. We never
can get them to say anything to us. I think they're afraid to talk,
because they might have to listen to us, and they might even say
something they'll be sorry for. Once you start talking, and once
you start listening to yourself, you may change your mind. So,
you go over and see them."

I do not know whether I share her conviction that we change

after we have spoken and been heard (by ourselves and by others) but she is right: many of those "visitors" she mentions talked far less readily than she did. Yet, when enough time had been spent, when we could really relax with one another, there was an outpouring of words and ideas and feelings the likes of which I do not believe I have ever before encountered. Perhaps some of our more sinister politicians have always known that — realized how desperate and uncertain and conflicted are many of our so-called "silent people" or "ordinary people" or "white, lower-middle-class people" or "civil servants." Perhaps no one but a skilled novelist who is also a social historian can do the kind of justice that is required. In the absence of such a person — in confusion and apprehension and despair I sometimes think only a mix of Tolstoi and de Tocqueville will do — one can only call upon the people themselves, and indeed upon what their words evoked in a particular observer and listener.

1. Law and Order: That's All There Is

He is Irish and he wants everyone to know it. He isn't in the least worried that they may already know and that they may feel he is beating a dead horse, saying the obvious, indulging in a lot of silly, trite, ethnic boasting that these days one would not think was done so openly and loudly — especially by a policeman who works in a completely black neighborhood, and a "tough one at that." For eight years he has worked there, which means for most of his career as a policeman. He is thirty-two and has been on the force for ten years. Edward Herlihy is the name we can appropriately give to him, and with sincerity and conviction he will talk about the Herlihys and Ireland and poverty and the need any society has for a certain degree of conformity, for an ethic of obedience and patriotic loyalty. Eventually he will also make it clear that some of his forceful display of self-confidence, his constant effort to identify himself with a mixture of ironic self-deprecation and fierce pride as "an Irish cop," reflects the fear he has that, quite literally, the United States of America is "going to pieces" and that he and his family are by no means oppressors or agents of oppressors, but rather victims of whatever it is he fears is coming into being — a new kind of country, a new kind of world.

One day, four years after I first met Mr. Herlihy, I sat on his back porch with him. While we both looked at his lovely and nicely tended garden, enjoying the late spring sun and the fresh, brisk air and the peace and quiet of the scene, interrupted only by a noisy, bothersome fly or two, and while we had a cup of coffee and everything seemed reasonably relaxed and casual, he proceeded in an almost offhand way to say things that later, as they are read and considered and analyzed, seem almost apocalyptic in nature. I say all this, in a rather long prelude before drawing upon the man's remarks, because I have had trouble at times reconciling Mr. Herlihy's actual words with his genial, kindly, open manner and also with the circumstances that have surrounded some of our talks — circumstances, if he will forgive the allusion, something like those supposedly to be found in a small English country garden.

"What is to be done?" I am asked, as if I were Lenin himself. (But Mr. Herlihy certainly would not like *that* allusion.) He is tall, thin, blondish, blue-eyed, ruddy. His hands are delicate. His fingers could be those of a pianist. He looks calm always, and I have seen him calm under provocations that would unsettle almost anyone. He never twitches or taps his feet or blinks excessively or stutters or raises his voice too much or gets intense and taut; and only rarely does he become emotional and outraged. He smiles rather often. Occasionally he laughs. He likes to talk, but he does so deliberately, in no rush. He has stories to tell, and he will tell them. At first he can appear to be guarded and tight-lipped, but that is not a fair description. He needs time to know someone, he says; but when he does — well, he *does*. When he asked, "What is to be done?" he was as concerned and forthright and candid a seeker as one could wish. He was referring to the rising unrest he sees about him every day, and he was asking how we as a nation can solve some of the problems he has no doubt most of us have every wish, if not hope, we can somehow learn to deal with successfully: "I was born here, and so was my dad. But my grandfather came here from Ireland, and he used to tell me that compared to Ireland and England and Europe we don't have *any* problems here. I knew he was exaggerating; after all, my father had a terrible time making a living during the depression. He was almost forty when he got married, and my grandfather was over forty when he got married. They both were Irish! I'm the first American in the family. When I got married at thirty, my dad said, 'You're only a boy.' He was only half kidding!

"I wonder sometimes what my old grandfather would think of this country now. I don't believe he ever saw a Negro in his life. How could he have seen them? He came here and settled with a brother who came here before him. They lived among their own people, and they never wanted to see anyone else. They hated the English. *Those* were the people I was taught to hate, not the Negroes. I try to tell some of the black kids that, when they tell me I'm picking on them, but it's no use. They're determined to have everyone hate them, everyone be against them. I've never seen so many bigots in my life; I mean it. A bigot is a person who misjudges another person. Right? Well, that's what the Negroes are like. You come to them and try to be of some help, and they're ready to stab you in the back as their worst enemy. So help me; I mean it. I've given up trying to make sense out of it all. There's no point. You can drive yourself crazy. I take each day by itself, and I try to be a good cop. That's what I am. I'm an Irish cop. I'll say this: I used to think I was a *policeman,* an American citizen who happened to get a job trying to protect other citizens from thieves and crooks and murderers and bullies and liars and all the rest. Lately I hear I'm a pig, and good Lord, a lot of other terrible things. I have to scratch myself and say: is that you, Ed Herlihy? Well, it *is* me: I'm the same, but some of our people, they're going wild, and that's why I say to you: what is to be done?

"One thing you can do is keep your respect for yourself. I'm not a pig or a fascist and all the other things I hear myself called. I've decided I *am* a cop, not a policeman anymore, but a cop. I mean, I *have* to be tough. It's tough where I work, and the people there respect toughness. No, I don't think they respect *me*. They just know that I'm not going to be pushed around — absolutely not. I drive my car through the streets and when they see me, they smile, a lot of the kids. A lot of people won't believe that, especially the loudmouthed white radicals. They want all the Negroes to be fighting with the police. They believe that's all I do, insult people and beat them up. How much more of those lies do we have to hear on television? I am sick and tired of those television programs and those news stories — it's always some screaming white kook or a way-out black militant who is quoted and gets his speech across. What about the hundreds of black people — they are kids and they are parents and they are old people — who call me Officer Herlihy, that's right. No one asks those people to speak on television. No one runs stories on them in the papers or the magazines. No one asks to talk with me, either — or with the other police who work near the colored people.

"Look, there are some mean, vicious hoodlums around, out to tear down our entire society. To those people I'm a dangerous cop. I've got to be. If I show them I'm the least bit soft, they'll kill me. I've already been fired at four times this year, and it's only May. Once they really meant it; I'd have been dead if I hadn't bent down suddenly. And you know why I bent? All of a sudden I thought I saw a penny. A penny! I figured I might as well pick it up, though it's worthless these days. They didn't know what I was debating in my mind, all those snipers who saw me standing there. Just as they fired, I started to bend, and they missed. I ran for cover. I was taken in by a black man; he owns a little market. You should have heard *him* talk. He called his own people more names than I'd ever dare. I used his phone and we moved in. Did we! We never caught them, though. We arrested a few kids, and we're trying to track the snipers down. But it's slow work. You can't arrest everyone in a building. All you can do is watch people and question them and hope you can trace them to some crazy group.

"It's not really any worse now than it was a few years ago. There *are* these way-out crazy groups, but most of the Negroes are just like they always were. I've been with them for a long time, you know. I'm no college professor, but I think I understand them; they're not bad people, and if they'd be given a chance, they'd be all right. If you ask me, they're being used by those white radical kids. *They* are the enemy. They get their hands on a few Negro kids and teach them the tricks of the agitator, and they hope we'll have a revolution in our cities. But you notice we really don't have one. Sure, we've had riots, but that's not what these agitators are after. They want the black people, the Negroes in the city, to be their stooges; they want to use them to destroy the country. They practically say as much. I have to listen to all that stuff, one hour after another. I stand there and feel like vomiting. They're a bad, bad lot, I'll tell you."

He does indeed tell me. He drinks his coffee and goes on to say, in one breath, that the country is fine, just fine, and in another, that he wonders how much longer we can stave off an utter and complete disaster, in which violence begets violence, and the nation is no longer a stable and strong democracy. And the more he talks, the less hopeful he sounds: "Look, I'm basically optimistic. I have a nice life. I have a good wife and three good kids. I don't make enough to keep up with this inflation, but I'm not starving either. I could sit back and say everything is just wonderful. I've been saving money, and I could dream of the day we all take a trip back to Ireland. Instead, I watch the news when I'm home, and I feel my muscles tense up. I even get a headache. We're miles here from a ghetto, but it's not far enough. The reason is those poor black people, they're sitting ducks for the anarchists and Communists, the crazy, goddam student agitators. I've never felt about Negroes the way I do about these student types. They're a clever and spiteful bunch. The ordinary colored man isn't. He's not so damn brainy, and all filled up with those slogans. He wants a better deal, and I don't begrudge him one, no sir. But he's going to end up getting a worse deal, that's the tragedy. The people of this country, the majority of us, aren't going to put up with violence and anarchy. Without laws you have nothing; I mean, if people don't obey the law, it's not a society any more. We're back in the jungle. You need law and order. Law and order: that's all there is. Without law and order there is chaos and revolution. This is a rich country, and we're strong, and countries all over the world are depending on us. Should we allow a few crazy kids and some kooks in the ghetto to take over our whole nation?

"Some of those television documentary people ought to stop searching all over the place for the craziest, wildest black militants and go and talk to the ordinary man in the street in the colored sections, and they ought to stop broadcasting one speech after another that the college radicals make. I'm sick of hearing about those kids: they're all 'alienated,' you hear. The mayor's office or the governor's office — who knows? — tried to get one of those college people, a sociologist or something, to give us lectures on 'the ghetto mentality,' something like that, and 'the college student and his alienation.' We thought they were kidding. The guy talked and talked. Jesus Christ! He needed three or four shots of rye and a long chaser of beer. The chief said no to any more of that. *He* wants to select the speakers, and why in Hell shouldn't he? They're freaks, some of those intellectuals! Take one look at them and you can tell. They try to talk plain and simple, but they can't do it. They talk down to us. Hell, we know more about 'the society' than they'll ever know!

"But that's the crowd this country has been listening to — for too long. There's just so much patience that the ordinary man has, though. You'll see people expressing themselves more and more. If the Negroes start killing white people, and the college kids dynamite our buildings more and more, you'll see the government step in. If it doesn't, we'll have to vote in a new government. What else can we do? Is this country supposed to turn itself over, lock, stock and barrel, to its own enemies?"

I find the contrast between those words and his description of his working day rather striking. When he talks about what he does and how he goes about his tour of duty, he speaks with far less rhetoric and terror. Perhaps he can only later, and in the context of a broader, more philosophical discussion, express what he may well actually feel from minute to minute during the course of his car rides through certain streets, or his walks from block to block. Not that he gets half as excited as his words suggest he does, even those strong words just cited. But the calm, matter-of-fact side of his personality most certainly comes across when he talks about "the job, the job."

I have many times, for instance, asked him to tell me what he does; tell me about the small and insignificant things as much as the more dramatic and memorable moments he has experienced — which he naturally enough wants to recount and in a way put to rest within himself. "Well," he begins with a smile, because he is half amused at the remark that is about to follow, "every moment for me is a big moment. It's like you see it on the movies, being a policeman." He knows that I have driven around with him and spent a number of days seeing firsthand what he and others like him do, but he wants to say what I have just quoted for a very shrewd reason: "The public has no idea how hard it is to go down those streets. I think up until very recently a lot of people were inclined to think of us as loafers: we gave people speeding tickets; we were there when there was a parade — that kind of thing. That's why when I saw a movie that showed how dangerous it can be, I thought: good, maybe we'll get some gratitude from people. And I do believe a lot of people are at last beginning to wake up. They're beginning to understand that without the police we'd be back in the Stone Age, and let me tell you, we'd be back there a lot faster than most people would ever believe.

"Every day I have to show myself on every single street I'm in charge of. It's important. They all have to see me. They have to see the car, and they have to see *me*. A lot of people wait for me. They need a ride to the hospital, or they're afraid of someone, or they have a message: a guy is going to beat another guy up, or there's no heat in a building and the people are in real trouble, or there's a hustler or a pimp or a pusher, a dealer who's *bothering* people. Look, I can't go cleaning up a neighborhood like that. All I can do is keep things under control. I can try to make sure little kids aren't being pushed around and scared half out of their minds by the addicts and prostitutes. I can prevent people from killing each other when they're all drugged up and liquored up. I

can push the landlords to obey the law and warn the gangs that
they can go so far and no further. And every day I have to help a
sick lady out, or rescue a kid whose arm is caught on barbed wire,
or something like that. And the poor shopkeepers, they want
protection! They would have me around all day if they could.
The holdups in that neighborhood, the robbery and stealing and
breaking and entering — it's unbelievable. We don't report half
of it. We couldn't. People wouldn't believe it, and there isn't
much we can do about it all, anyway. Like I say, we can try to
keep things under control — but only within limits.

"I'm on the scene early, before eight. Walter and I drive
around for a few minutes. He's more excitable than I am. He
really bleeds for some of the people — and he really would like
to throw a lot of the agitators in jail. I keep on telling him: there's
just so much we can do. We look at the stores to see if any have
been broken into. We check out the hydrants and the street
lights. We go see a few of our friends. If I were to tell you that a
good policeman knows everything, *everything* that is going on in
his district, you would laugh. How can a guy like me keep track
of the Negroes in their ghetto? I heard someone on one of those
talk shows say that the blacks hate the cops; they hate us and
they don't trust us worth a damn, that's what he kept on saying. I
had to laugh. I wouldn't be worth anything; I'd be totally useless,
if it weren't for some black people. And I don't mean the store
owners. I'm talking about young kids and their parents, too —
just plain people, like anyone else; people who want to have as
much law and order as it's possible for them to have. They know
they can't live the way they'd like to. They know they've got to
put up with gangs and violence and stealing and drugs and all
that, to some extent at least. They want our help, though. They
know that if we don't come around and round up a few people
and demonstrate that we're ready to take on any really crazy
types, then they've all had it, the thousands and thousands of
people who live in all those tenement houses.

"Hell, the people in the ghetto are at the mercy of every two-
bit thug and gangster around. And when you have poor people
like they are, the colored people, and a lot of them just up here

from some little town in the South where they lived — I believe it — like animals, then you've got to protect them. And that's exactly what the police of this city do. I could get a thousand signatures of gratitude for all I've done and Walter has done. He's gruff and he doesn't smile much, but he's rescued people from fires and caught kids and made them return what they'd taken — from old ladies and mothers whose husbands have left them, and from some poor kid who suddenly finds a big, tough hoodlum has grabbed a pair of skates his father worked for and saved for and finally bought for him. Why don't the bleeding-heart types worry about that kid? Why don't they worry about the mother who tells us, 'Thank God you're here.' Why don't they worry about the hospitals that serve the poor? Every day some thief tries to break in and steal something and scare the nurses and doctors. If we weren't patrolling the streets nearby, I can tell you what: there wouldn't be a hospital. They'd strip the place bare. They'd strip every store and every building. And it's not the hungry who do it; it's the addicts, who need hundreds of dollars to buy their heroin.

"You know, I'm not the one to tell you what goes on over there in the ghetto. I'm not a crusader, so I'm not so damn sure of myself. I try to do my work, and I'm grateful if I have done just a little bit each day. Walter, my buddy, won't even talk at all. He's so fed up that he's thinking of leaving the force. He'll stay, but it's hard on a man who tries to protect people and be there when they cry for help — it's hard when all he gets from a lot of snotty people is insults and wisecracks and filthy names. Let some of those nice people out in the rich suburbs and the universities come with me for a few days, and see what I see and hear what I hear and do what I have to do. And let them come and talk to the people from my district — the *people,* not the propaganda types, the fast talkers. I give them one day, those nice, kind, sympathetic people who live in quiet streets where everyone has a hundred thousand dollars or so, and they all say hello to each other, and they've got about a hundred or two big, fat books in their houses and plenty of furniture and a car for each kid and summer homes and boats and all the rest. They all don't know what we're protecting *them* from, never mind the poor old colored lady or the young mother I had to rescue yesterday — from her own husband, who came and stole *their own son's bike,* and when she caught him, threw lye at her. That's right! He could have blinded her. He could have killed her. He's no good. He's a pimp and an addict. He's been up before the judge again and again. I'll tell you this: there isn't enough room for them in our jails, and if we doubled, *tripled* the jail space in this country there still wouldn't be enough room to hold all of them. I don't haul a lot of them in. The judge tries to keep a lot of them out on parole, or with their case pending. What else can we do? There aren't enough police, enough judges, enough probation officers — you name it, we don't have it.

"Yesterday I broke up four fights between women and their men. Don't ask me if they were married. I've given up even asking, or God help me, even caring. I told the priest a long time ago: I can't do everything! He smiled, and he told me we'd both have to pray for all of them. I thought for a moment he was kidding, but no, he had a serious look on his face. I couldn't hold my tongue. I said, 'Father Lynch, they don't want our prayers, they really don't. They don't even think they're doing anything bad, living as they do.' He said yes, he knew, but that was all the more reason we had to pray for them. Well, I have! I've been there in church and I've asked our Lord, please, to do something. I sometimes think He's the only one Who ever will, Who *could.* Walt and I agree on that. He's come out of some rough meetings, especially with the addicts when they're desperate for money and they're stealing left and right and they know we're onto them and we're going to take them in, which means they may easily lose the habit once they're in jail. They do smuggle drugs into prisons, I know that. He'll turn to me and say, 'Ed: all we can do is pray to God that a few of the kids will turn out OK.' And I say yes, that's right.

"Neither of us believe one single kid would have a chance, a chance to become a halfway decent person, if the police didn't keep the blocks under some control — at least compared to what the streets would be if we left there for good. And are we tempted! I leave my house in the morning and I ask myself: why should I get the salary I do — barely enough to pay our bills, and plenty of times not enough — in order to risk my life protecting a lot of people from their own kind, their very own 'brothers,' they call each other? And then the college kids call us 'pigs' and 'murderers' and 'oppressors.' Oh, my God, I'd like to lug a few of those kids out to my beat. I'd like them to see what I see and hear what I hear. I'd like them to talk with the people there and hear what they would say about the work I do. Those students, they sit in their campuses and talk, talk, talk. They're full of hate, and if you ask me, they're full of ignorance. They have their ideas, but they don't come out in the world and learn the facts. They insult a man like me, and meanwhile I'm carrying an old Negro lady down five flights of stairs and taking her to a hospital; and I'm protecting a Negro lady from her 'man,' who's drunk and on heroin, *both;* and I'm being rushed to a hospital myself, because I rescued two little Negro babies from a smoke-filled apartment, and they were unconscious and I was also near unconscious.

"Look, I'm not asking to be called a hero. To Hell with that! I'm a cop. I'm nothing more. I'm like thousands of cops all over the country. I try to do my job the best I can. I make my mistakes. And I admit it, I have my prejudices. Everyone does. But I'll tell you this: I'm out there on the firing line; I'm taking it every day. Because those people got a raw deal a long time ago, they're in a sad way now, a lot of them, and it's left to a guy like me to keep them from killing one another and beating one another. I can't count the number of addicts I've found unconscious; I've had to rush them to a hospital to keep them from dying. Now I don't have the answer to all this. That's not my department. I try to do the best I can. But I don't like being called a pig, and I don't think it's fair to the Negroes themselves if those college kids listen only to the Negroes who attack the police. You know, it's the criminals who always attack us and call us names. Like I keep saying to you: what about the poor people in those buildings, hundreds and hundreds of people in my district alone, who call us up all the time for help and thank us for coming and giving them the help they needed and offer us food and all the rest? Who is telling the American people about that? What do our college students, the radicals among them, know about that? It sickens me, the way the truth gets buried. If I didn't know them better, I'd feel sorry not only for myself but for all the other cops in this country. But Hell, I haven't got time for that!"

A day spent with him would certainly convince his most skeptical listener, even perhaps his most outspoken opponent, that he is at least right on that last count. He is indeed a busy man. He has little free time for much of anything. He is overworked and underpaid. He constantly risks his life, and therefore he is quite naturally afraid. He feels as "rebuked and scorned" as the black people he spends his time with have always known themselves to be. Nor is it only those "college radicals" who trouble him and accuse him so sternly and vehemently. He himself has his misgivings — not so much about anything he personally does as about what he calls "the whole damn business," by which he means, in effect, the train of events that began centuries ago and now has reached a crisis, forcing him to take risks all the time, while the wrongs and injustices (again, centuries of them) persist. For the fact is that he strikes out at "college radicals" for *two* reasons: yes, he believes them to be mean and gratuitously insulting and arrogant and self-centered; but he also considers them privileged, protected, secure, on top of all sorts of ladders — which means, bluntly, that their fathers and grandfathers are so often the ones who own or owned plantations, or real estate, or banks and stores, or whatever. He puts it this way: "Who has to keep the whole country from becoming a big battleground? Who's protecting the wealthy suburbs? Who's keeping the Negroes from killing themselves and killing the white people? The white people who own all those tenement buildings, and the white people who are the lawyers to the landlords, and all the rest? No. It's a guy like me; and I'm not sitting here with stocks and bonds, and my kids off in fancy colleges deciding whether they want to be in the Peace Corps in Africa or maybe spend a year in Europe someplace."

From him I hear angry, brutish, callous remarks, some I don't care to set down here, about black people and college students; but from him I also hear a frustrated kind of indignation that I fear many of us simply do not know about, or do not care to recognize as additional evidence that this nation has a lot of political and economic business left to transact. Presumably, many who consider themselves to have "social consciences" refuse to appreciate one group of people at the expense of another, but prefer to see what is shared among an Edward Herlihy and the people he claims to help and the people he constantly offends. What *do* all of those people share? I believe Mr. Herlihy has himself come very close to an answer. They all, though in different ways, feel themselves now suffering from rather than profiting from all that has gone before them, suffering from the painful and grave part of America's history.

2. *Fires, Fires, Everywhere*

We know the words "burn, baby, burn," but we may not know that such literally inflammatory words have a life which is not measured by the hours or days it takes for a riot to begin and end. Fires are not only the work of suddenly aroused people, but of chronically resentful people; and sometimes the heat of biting, snapping flames can stand in a fire-setter's mind for a whole lifetime of disenchantment. It is as if wasted energy and misspent passions suddenly come back again to live, to have their moment, to claim their vengeance.

I would laugh at my own statement as an example of silly romanticism had I not heard, more than once, words such as these: "You bet there are a lot of fires around here. You've seen the buildings. You know they're firetraps. That's what they are. That's *all* they are. Then you have the nerve to tell me that they're people's homes. Well, they shouldn't be. They goddam shouldn't be. If Whitey keeps on choking us, not letting us out of here, pushing us, sitting on us, and all we have left is these brick shacks *he* left — but still owns — then we're going to show him something; we're going to teach him a lesson. He'll see his rotten property burn. He'll see more and more places burn. I'll let you in on something: when I see a store go up, or a building they should have condemned ten years ago go up, I see my people speaking up so that they'll be heard. The black man in America has been burning, burning ever since he was brought here. They branded us, and we're burning to fight them back, fight fire with fire. What else can *we* do? It took until 1965 for them to let millions of us vote, *vote*. And the liberals tell us to wait and go to the polls and be nonviolent. They shot Medgar Evers. They shot Dr. King. But we should wait and pray and sit on those boxes in front of those buildings, with rats jumping all over and roaches crawling on you and the floors with holes and the stoops with holes and the windows broken and no screens and the roof leaking and no garbage pails. Sit there. Stay there. Vote. Trust in God. Obey the law. *Whose* law?

"I say burn it all. Burn it down. Don't riot. Just burn it all down, one street by one. Get the people out, then burn down the prisons, then say: Whitey, we were in jail, and now we're still in jail, but you can't collect your hundred a month any more, and we're going to embarrass you, oh are we! That's it; that's what some of our fires are telling Whitey. And he'd better know it; he'd better get the message soon, because if he doesn't he might find some of his own people standing out there on the street and watching those flames. *Then* maybe they'll start asking themselves what it's all about."

What am I as a psychiatrist to make of that line of reasoning, those sentences selected for their "moderation"? I can call that man "sick"; I can say he is an "aggressive" person who is "disturbed" and "irrational." I can conclude that his thinking is bizarre or disordered, and that surely there must be some "long-term psychopathological process" which accounts for the imagery he uses, the feelings he openly declares, the "attitudes" he expresses. And even if I have a distaste for psychiatric rhetoric — for jargon that conveniently enables one to gloss over elementary injustice, injustice which does not *inflame* the consciences of many so-called "healthy" and "normal" and "well-adjusted" individuals; yes, even if I said to myself that people like me can indeed speak like fools, can indeed speak about utterly compli-

cated matters with absurdly simpleminded psychological formulations, I would still be confronted (and I have been) with the
sight of people, black people, made homeless and injured and
terribly and unforgettably frightened by fires. And I have seen
firemen rescue those people, and themselves be rescued, and in
two instances die, and in other instances require hospitalization
for burns, body scarring and terribly painful injuries. It takes gall
on the part of psychiatrists to ignore the social, political and
above all historical circumstances which the man quoted just
above summons. History has a way of smoldering in the minds of
some people, igniting their passions. But it also takes a lot of
nerve for some people to go about getting even with white people
in such a way that black children and black parents have to run
for their lives, are left standing on streets — if indeed they are
lucky enough to live — because they have had to escape being
burned or choked to death in a smoke-filled building or crushed
to death by a crumbling wall. I recall watching a wall of an
apartment building cave in, and in so doing barely miss three
black children, one of whom asked a fireman standing nearby:
"Did the people who set this fire want us to burn up, just like the
stores they tried to get rid of?"

In that particular instance no one was seriously injured, though
three black children and their mother had to be taken to the
hospital because of "smoke inhalation" and one fireman suffered
a broken right leg. The fireman I knew was not hurt that time,
though he has put in his days of lying on his back while a bone
heals or a burn mends: "It's part of the job. If you're going to be
a fireman, you have to expect that you may get trapped. And
there's always smoke to knock you out, or a wall to fall on you,
even if the flames don't seem too bad. If you work in a nice town,
you don't do all that much. You rescue cats and there *are* fires,
but often they're small ones, in buildings that are well built and
safely wired. There might be a mixed-up kid who sets fires;
usually they do it in a field, and that's bad enough, but at least
you can contain the fire if the wind isn't bad and you get there
fast enough. Of course, there are crazy kids who will go and spill

gasoline on their back door, or their neighbor's, and put a match
to it. They're sick, you know.

"In the ghetto, here, it's different. There are so many firetraps
here, the whole ghetto is a firetrap, when you come right down to
it. The buildings are old, and they're not wired the way they
should be, and they're unsound. The walls of buildings are weak
even without a fire. Steps are broken or full of holes. The heating
systems are old; there's always the danger a boiler will burst. The
plumbing is terrible, and if a plumber comes to repair anything — I say *if* he comes — all you need is a spark from his
torch when he's working on the pipes and the whole building
goes up. I mean, the spark catches something in between those
walls, and *that's it*. I'll tell you the truth, but don't ever say I said
it: there are whole blocks of this city, here in the ghetto, that
ought to be torn down, and new buildings put up. But we don't
do it, and instead there'll be a fire one day, then two the next,
and it's tragic for the people, because they have nowhere to go,
except to friends and neighbors and relatives, and just about
every apartment around here is already filled up, packed with
people.

"All the fires in this part of the city aren't accidental, you know.
It's not only bad buildings that cause fires. We have arsonists
here, professional arsonists they are. I'm not fooling, either. I
don't think the ordinary person knows what we have to go
through on a job like this. I'm a fireman, and I don't get enough
money. It's as simple as that. I have to work when I'm off duty,
and my wife works when the kids are in school. She works as a
waitress. What else can she do? But if I tell people that I'm not
getting enough money, they tell me that a fireman doesn't do
much work, either. So help me, that's all I hear. They say: you
must sit on your rear end all day, so why should you get a lot of
money for that? You'd be amazed at how many of my own neighbors think like that. They picture us lying in bed in some old-
fashioned firehouse. Then every once in a while a couple of kids
pull a prank, a false alarm, and we get up and slide down those
brass poles and get into our spit-and-polish clean engines and
answer the alarm, and come back with the fire chief's whistle

going and our bells going and go back to sleep. Or maybe we go
rescue a cat caught up on a high tree. Or maybe once a year
there *is* a bad fire, in some warehouse, and then, it's true, a few
of us get hurt, and maybe one guy dies. That's how people picture the work. I'm not exaggerating.

"I wish people would come and spend some time with me. I
give them an hour, and they'll want to double my wages, at least!
They'd hear that bell ringing and ringing. They'd see us running
to engines that have just come back from a bad fire and are
covered with mud and water and foam. They'd see us getting
through with a fire and then moving on to another one without
going back to the station at all. They'd see us worn out half the
time, and if we looked spick-and-span, that would be a good day.
Sure, we have cots near the engines, but I don't remember the
last time I slept on one of them. I mean, I come to work and
someone has set a fire in a store, or a house is burning down, or a
building is full of smoke, and we don't know what's gone wrong
to cause it. Or someone is on a roof, out of his mind on heroin,
and he's going to jump, and we have to have a net there and try
to climb up to him on a ladder. That's the day we spend. And
besides there are those gangs; they throw one false alarm after
another at us, and you don't dare ignore them. And when we get
to a real fire, we don't just have to risk our lives saving people
and going into the old buildings and putting out the fire; no,
that's just the easy work! We might be shot dead by a sniper. We
might have a brick thrown at us, which could hit someone on the
head and kill him. We could go into a burning building, and
damn if some crazy guy isn't there screaming that we're killers,
we're Whitey, the enemy, and take this — which is a Molotov
cocktail or a piece of wood that's aflame or a knife. They love
knives and razor blades.

"If we're lucky, if we're real lucky, we'll just get the noise, the
static we call it. That's the shouts, the insults, the crazy, lousy
talk they throw at you. Because I've got white skin, I'm supposed
to be a big plantation owner or something, who owns slaves and
won't let them go. I have been called words I've never even
heard of. They have the dirtiest mouths of any people I know,

the colored do — except for the students, I guess. Thank Almighty God I never see *them!* At least I can once in a while feel
sorry for some of these colored people; they're poor, 'dirt poor'
one of them said to me, and I've never forgotten those words,
because it's true, they're up here from the South, trying to get by,
and you can see it on them, how they really belong in some log
cabin, you know, near a farm.

"I don't know what to say. I'm not prejudiced against any
group. That's stupid, to hate a whole group of people. I'm Italian,
and I know that some Italians are no good, just no damn good at
all. We have our good people, and our bad people, too. Look at
the Mafia. You mention that you're Italian, and probably with a
lot of people, that means the Mafia. What do I know about the
Mafia? I've never in my whole life met anyone in the Mafia. I've
never met a gangster. My name is Capraro, Anthony Capraro; so
I meet someone who isn't Italian and in their mind they're thinking: he probably has a brother or a cousin who works for some
mob, some branch of the Mafia. Isn't that the way people think?
If I had an Irish name they'd be checking on how many drinks I
take, and they'd say I can always get a job in City Hall if I need
one. Dumb, it's dumb to think like that.

"I judge anyone on his merits. I've met some colored people —
I haven't *met* them, I've helped save their lives — and they're the
finest people you'd ever want to know. People say — I read it in
the papers — that we, the Italians, are anticolored, anti-Negro.
Well, maybe some Italians are. All I know is that there are some
colored people I wouldn't mind living right next door to my own
family. That's right; next door to us. And if the neighbors didn't
like it, that's just too bad! But a lot of the colored, they're hopeless. I tell you: there's nothing, absolutely nothing we can do to
change them. And there's nothing that we do that they're grateful
for. You give them something, and they start complaining that
they want more. You'd think they're the only ones who have it
tough. You'd think the rest of us don't have to work and sweat
just to keep our heads above water. I'm tired over, I'm fed up
with their bellyaching — more and more bellyaching. And Jesus
Christ, they can do no wrong! To hear them, everything bad is

the white man's fault. It couldn't be that they're lazy and like children, a lot of them! I see them every day, you know. You drive up a street and they're all on welfare. It's unbelievable. Welfare is what they came here for, and welfare is what they want, and welfare is what they've got. Do you know what I've heard? I swear, on my life I swear, I've been told by plenty of men here that they don't even try to get jobs. They don't care to work. They hide in the closets when the welfare workers come. They *want* large families. It means more welfare money. I have four children, and my wife and I are all torn apart. We're devout Catholics, and yet we think four children is enough, more than enough for the money I make.

"But of all I see and hear, the worst is their moral character. I don't understand it. They have their churches, a lot of them. I've heard them shouting in church. We had a fire to put out in a building next to a church, and you'd have thought the fire was started in Hell itself, the way they talked. They came rushing out of the church and they said the devil had set the fire to distract them or something, and there was a lot of talk about Jesus being black and not white, and the white man being a devil. I don't know. What do you say to them? How can people who are so noisy about their religion turn out so bad? They produce all these addicts. They produce all these illegitimate children. They fill up the welfare rolls, and then you see them spending the money — *my* money! — on pool and those records they buy. Have you ever heard crazier music? If you want to call that stuff music, that is! I'll be frank with you: I think they're a different kind of people. I mean, they're not like us. You take a Polish guy or an Irishman or an Italian, they're all different, but they have some things in common. I mean, they're not like the colored. You go into an Italian section or an Irish section or a Polish section or Lithuanian or Armenian, and you'll find people there who *work*. They want to work, and OK, it's hard to find a job sometimes, but they try, and by God, they do — they do find jobs. And you don't find illegitimate kids in every apartment, with each kid having a different father. You don't find addicts sitting around all over. You don't find welfare women coming into every street every morning — and guys like me, to put out fires *the people set themselves*. You don't find razor blades — kids of seven and eight with razor blades and knives, the longest damn knives you'll ever see. And truants, the kids are all truants. They don't want to go to school. They'd rather stay around on the street and become hoodlums. They go back into town and steal pocketbooks from white women, and then they come back here and they think they're safe, because even the police have to close their eyes to crime in a neighborhood like this one.

"I know the cops. I know all of them that work here, and I hear things from them I wouldn't repeat, not to my wife or anyone — about the prostitutes, men and women they are, and the way they cut each other up. Around here it's just not like in a civilized country. And this is the problem, the big problem — it's the biggest problem in America: people don't really know! Either they don't know, so they weep tears for 'those poor, poor people'; or maybe they have a suspicion, but they're afraid, they're afraid to be honest and speak what's on their mind. I pick up the newspaper, or I turn on the television, and I say to myself: these people are either a bunch of jackasses, the ones who write those editorials or the people on those talk shows, or else they're deliberately deceiving the public and glossing over the truth, or else they're just scared to come out and be honest.

"Now I ask you. I ask you: do you ever see a fireman like me on television, or a policeman? Do we ever get our say? I'll turn on the television, and damned if there isn't another college student with his long hair and his sideburns down to his neck sounding off about this and the next thing. I know this, he says. I'll tell you about that, he says. We've got to free the blacks! They're oppressed! It's genocide, whatever the Hell that's supposed to be. Genocide! They're multiplying like rabbits. They're pushing one another aside in those buildings. There are so many of them — ask the welfare workers! — and I'm supposed to believe we're guilty of genocide, killing them. It's crazy. Then you read in the paper that this here professor, he knows all that's wrong, and we should remember, like he says, that America is no good, and we've done all these bad things, and the good people are the ones who are killing our boys in Asia, and the good people here at home, they are the ones who belong to these gangs, and the ones who use dynamite, and the ones who use drugs and never work and steal from their own and from the white man. *They* are the good people! The Panthers, they're good! They call the police pigs, and a guy like me, who puts out their lousy fires and tries his best to keep people from dying, they call me a pig, too. But they are the heroes — the Panthers and their friends the students who burn the American flag and shout at this country, the country that has given their parents all the money to send them to college, where they sit around and swear at their teachers and demonstrate and burn buildings down and throw rocks. It's crazy. Let me tell you, it's crazy. I come to work and I wonder. I say to myself: what the Hell is this world coming to? That's what I say. And you know, I'm not alone. No sir. There are a lot of people in this country who are in my boat.

"I'd like to make a bargain with a lot of those big 'experts,' and the students, too — I mean the ones who aren't completely out of their minds. I'd like to have them stick close to me for about a week. That's all. Then I'll bet they'll think a little before they come out with their big ideas. The only thing they'd have to do is sit beside me on the truck, and I could tell them some things as we drive by. If they didn't believe me, they could go and investigate. All I'd want is for them to be fair and honest. If I said: they cash their welfare checks over there, and then go and play pool and make bets here or visit the whores here or buy something here from a pusher or buy their cheap wine here — then all the guy would have to do, if he didn't take my word, was get off the truck and go and check up on what I told him. The same goes for the record store. They call it soul music. Well, do you know who pays for soul music? Do you know who pays for the transistor radios they buy? Like I said: the taxpayer. They are like children; they spend their welfare money like children. My ten-year-old girl loves to sit and listen to music, and she thinks a transistor radio is the greatest thing in the world. But you know, she's started baby-sitting. She knows how to save her pennies.

She paid for half that transistor with money she earned herself. And she's only ten!

"Anyway, I don't think I'll get any takers. A lot of the white people in this country have gone crazy over the colored. They are white, and they go around saying it's our fault, *our* fault — the white man's! They say they know how bad it is in the ghettos, and we've got to change all that. Then they say *we're* the problem: the average American guy is supposed to be prejudiced. If people could only go around with me and hear the names I'm called — you goddam blankety-blank white man. Sure, some of my buddies give it right back to them. But I'll tell you something. They're scared; every fireman who comes into this neighborhood is so scared he can't even talk about it. We know what can happen to us. We know that a day doesn't go by that they won't try to shoot us, or trick us one way or the other. They set the fires, then they hope we'll get killed putting them out. One of them said that, he said that in a demonstration, and I heard it on television. That's right, *on television!*

"Do you see what has happened to this country in the last few years? The militants say they're going to burn their own neighborhoods down, and they're also going to start coming to our neighborhoods. Can you beat that? I know all of them don't talk like that. But they've got their leaders, the militants, who do — and the worst ones are the white ones, the radicals. It's the white radicals who love to hear the colored talk like that; they eat up that kind of talk. I told my wife the other day that before we're out of this mess, they'll be setting more and more fires. There'll be fires everywhere in the ghetto, apart from when they riot, and they'll start slipping into *our* part of town. It'll mean a lot of work for me; no fooling. And I won't get time and a half. I won't get a raise. And we'll be lucky if the country sticks together. That's what scares me. There are people who want to destroy this country, and they think a guy like me will just sit back and shrug his shoulders and say: go ahead, go ahead, because anything goes. They're wrong, though. They'll hear from us. Don't write us off. Don't think we're not keeping our eyes open and listening."

I doubt his worst enemy would think that. As it is, when a

meeting takes place between firemen such as Anthony Capraro and black militants like the ones I have described and quoted in the previous chapter, the occasion is a fire. Then the police, often with drawn guns, are on hand, and no one is very intent on paying attention to the ideas and feelings of other people. Then the point is to confront each other and win or lose what on each side is considered a desperate and deadly battle. As for the white students Mr. Capraro mentions so often and speaks about with such vehemence and abhorrence, he certainly has never heard them out, nor have they by and large heard much from men like him. If he is mean and callous about those students and their motives, more than enough students can be thoughtless, arrogant, and utterly ignorant in the way they look at the Anthony Capraros of this world – or indeed, refuse to look at them. If sympathy and compassion for black people, for the oppressed in this land or other lands, can only be purchased at the expense of an insensitive disregard, sometimes even a vicious and provocative disregard, for other "groups," then at the very least no one has a right to be surprised when those slighted and snubbed make their reply, measure for measure.

What is more, the irony is that Anthony Capraro and others like him who get by on a thin margin of comfort and security, men who are as frightened and bewildered as they are angry and petulant and at times, it seems, full of malice, are capable of articulating distinctions and subtleties that ought to be understood by some of "us," the well-educated, relatively moneyed, and not particularly hard-pressed writers and readers of this world. For instance, this is how Mr. Capraro responded to words hurled at him and other firemen by blacks literally up in arms and mad with rage: "I wanted to go kill them, but we had to pull in the hoses and put the ladders back and get the Hell out of there. There might be another fire in an hour or so. I don't mean to say the whole city is burning down, but like I told you, we keep busy – too busy. I was thinking, though, on the way back to the station. I was thinking: what the Hell kind of life is it for them? They're born with a hundred strikes against them. If you're honest with yourself, you have to admit it. You know what my test is? I say to myself: Tony, be fair now and ask yourself a question. The question is this: would you want to be born a Negro? If you start asking yourself that, then you can only feel sorry for colored people. That's how I see it. Look, they don't like me, and I don't like them. That's the way it is. You can't get around that. No one can fool them or me with a lot of talk about 'brotherhood.' We don't trust each other. You just heard what they called us. I could match them, I'll tell you!

"But I remind myself that they've had a lousy deal, and they're not really shouting at *me*, Anthony Capraro. Hell, I just climbed four flights of stairs of that building and got two kids, their grandmother and a cat to get out before the damn walls came falling in on them — and me. To the colored people, I'm just a white man, and they're shouting at the white world. Did *I* cause the troubles they now have? That's a nutty idea. But when I hear some white kids — whose fathers are loaded with money, and the kids are living off that money — tell me that I'm a 'racist,' whereas *they* are so good and wonderful, and *they* are real lovers of the Negroes — then I *do* get mad. I feel like telling those kids: you're wrong, you're dead wrong. You know why? I'll tell you why. I'll prove to you that I'm no racist. The proof is that I hate you white thugs, you white kids so damn full of yourselves, so sold on yourselves, I hate all you a million more times than I do any poor colored man. Now how do you like that? I'd ask them that question. But they're not the kind that will listen. They think they know everything. Mr. Know-It-Alls is what they are. And they treat the colored people like their private property, their stooges. If I was a colored man I'd tell them to get away — fast!"

And meanwhile he gets away fast. He sits on top of a modern fire engine and speeds across the streets, races by old buildings, hastens back to the station or on to answer a new alarm, a new call for help — while children run to look and laugh and applaud, and youths scramble to shout and jeer and curse, and old people open their eyes and move toward windows and sometimes, when the bells and sirens get too noisy, put their hands up to cover their ears and shake their heads.

3. *The Welfare Lady*

Janet Howe, who is twenty-four and well-educated and articulate and anxious to help "her" families, could surely find other, less strenuous ways to earn the approximately ninety dollars a week she now makes as a welfare worker. Yet, Janet Howe would have it no other way; she likes the families she visits, and for good stretches of time they enjoy her visits. They offer her coffee — not to placate her, appease her, ingratiate themselves with her, but because they like to sit and talk with her; they know she comes to them wanting to do whatever she possibly can. Still, even for her, an obviously able and kind and generous and well-intentioned worker, some sharp and abrasive moments come up, moments in which she is subjected to abuse and bitter invective, moments which she tries hard to "understand" and not so much ignore as "survive." Those are the verbs she often uses as she talks about her work: understand and survive. She must understand the angers and frustrations of her "clients." She must understand the way they take out on her feelings "really" directed toward many other people. She must understand, too, the fears and resentments, the continuing prickliness of the "political majority" (as she refers to them): the hardworking, also harassed or edgy or worried people who put in long and not always satisfying hours on the job and bring home just enough, just barely enough to pay those mounting bills and make ends meet. They feel threatened or enraged that others should get "for nothing" what they must obtain by working long and hard.

"It is a matter of envy," Miss Howe says. Nor is she being snobbish and coolly analytical when she makes a remark like that. She really does understand how so-called "lower-middle-class families" feel. She herself came from one of them; her father to this day is a carpenter who is up at six and out of the house at seven and not back home until six or seven in the evening. He works for himself. He is an entrepreneur of sorts who never made a fortune, but also never took a cent of money from anyone, even during the thirties. He detests "freeloaders." He believes that if a man *really* wants to work, *really* is an honest and reliable person, then he will find a job, and "for the life of him," keep it. And he believes in "education," in the importance of saving one's meager dollars so that a girl like Janet Howe can go to college, go to a school of social work, and finally come to be self-supporting. "I hear my father's voice sometimes," Janet Howe says, and then she talks about her own mixed response: "Of course I have a mind of my own, and when his words and philosophy come to me — often it's when I'm driving — I have my answers. I remind myself how fortunate he was. He is white. His family has been around here for a long, long time. He was not a dazed and confused and frightened man from the rural South, or a Puerto Rican never before in an American city and unable to speak English. He was not from a hollow in West Virginia. He went to school; he even graduated from high school. That may not mean a lot now, but it meant a lot forty or fifty years ago. And he has a skill, a 'trade,' as he calls it. He was trained by his uncle; he apprenticed with him, though they never were so formal that they called the work they did together an 'apprenticeship.'

"But I know I could never get away with it; I mean if I said all that to my dad and tried to explain to him what the families I see have gone through, in contrast to the experiences his family has had this past one hundred years — well, he would get angry and hit his fist on the table and say to me: look, where there's a will there's a way. And that's the point, for him that has always been true. Like everyone else in this world, his source of knowledge is his own experience. It would be easy for me, I suppose, to dismiss him, but I don't think it would be fair — even though I realize that a lot of the welfare rules and procedures, awful as they are, have come about in response to the feelings that millions and millions of people like my father have. Does anyone doubt that the majority of the country's people talk the way he does?"

She can go on only so long in that direction. Soon she feels the tug of her clients, her families, her friends. Soon *their* voices are in her mind, clamoring for recognition, craving a word, many words: "I don't know how to talk with my dad, but I do believe from the very bottom of my heart that he is blind to some terribly important facts. I wish some of the people I go to see could sit in his living room and tell him about their lives. I wish they could say: Mr. Howe, you don't know what it has been like for a lot of people in America. You just don't. We don't have anything against you personally. We can't expect you to go and visit all over and take an interest in everyone else's problems. It's just that we *do* have our problems, and believe us, they are *not* yours and they aren't necessarily solved the way you've solved yours.

"I know that my father is never going to hear someone in the ghetto talk like that to him. It takes time to explain what others have to face, more time than anyone has got, I sometimes believe! I myself sometimes have to be convinced! On a rough day, in each home, I hear complaints and more complaints, and requests and more requests, and threats — more than you would ever imagine. I'll be tired and all I can do is say to myself: wait until you get home; a glass of sherry or a gin and tonic, and you'll be feeling better. Instead, I'm in the last or next-to-last apartment, and someone raises her voice at me and tells me I'm not doing enough, I'm not providing enough money, and it's *my* fault, *mine*, because I have to ask a supervisor for permission, or I have to fill out a request and hope — that is *all* I can do — the right decision will be made back at the office. Suddenly I hear myself saying: enough! I've had enough of it. Suddenly I picture myself quitting and going to work in a school, in a hospital, in an office — anyplace where I'm not under this kind of cross fire. And I'll admit it, if I get *really* annoyed, and I'm completely exhausted, my voice gets sharp with the people. Then I obey the letter of the law and get out fast — because I'm tempted to tell them to shut up and stop swearing and stop cursing and leave me alone and *go out and work*.

"I've never said something like that to a person, but I know at times they can read my mood if not my exact thoughts. And I'm one of the young, so-called activist welfare workers. I'm one of the protesters. I've even picketed our own headquarters! I've signed dozens of protests. I've called our regulations inhuman, unfair, condescending, arbitrary — you name it! I've refused to

ask some of those insulting, demeaning questions. I've written
letters to my congressman and senator. I've written to the governor. I've joined new organizations. And I honestly believe that,
day in and day out, I do pretty well with the people I visit. It's
just that the whole system is an impossible one, and the people
who need welfare are in an impossible series of binds. So, when I
come to see them, and they have me right there and available
and ready to listen and not push them around and not scream at
them and not threaten them, they just let it all out on me, the
anger they feel toward the landlord, or the city's garbage department, or the whole social and economic system in America,
actually — and if they don't use the words we do, they come
close enough. They pull themselves together and say it's not me,
they know, but 'everything.' If I ask them what they mean by
'everything,' they let me know — that everything is 'the way
things are run' or 'the way people are allowed to treat other
people.' And I prefer their way of speaking to the hazy, indirect
talk I used to hear from my professors of social work. Some of
them are as afraid as the people in the ghettos. I guess we've all
got our bosses to worry about, me included."

She certainly does have a boss to worry about. Every day
"special situations" come up, emergencies that compel families
already living marginally to cry for help. She hears the cries, but
others approve or disapprove the requests for money subse-
quently made. And rather typically, she refuses to do to her
supervisors what at times she feels being done to her. That is to
say, she tries to understand them, too. She tries to remember that
the laws prevent even the most compassionate and evenhanded
official from doing what he knows ought to be done. She tries to
remember that there simply is not enough money to go around.
Sometimes, no doubt about it, bureaucratic blindness or inertia
or duplicity is at work, but by and large Janet Howe cannot
successfully turn the welfare department into the devil she every
once in a while openly wishes it were: "We have some fools in
that office; and even worse, there are some cold and mean
people, who are everything the families say they are. But the
fools are a minority, a small one at that. It's so easy to turn the

welfare office into the problem, rather than a symptom of the problem. I can't tell you how much I wish the whole problem *was* the welfare department! Then, a change in personnel would be all we'd need. But if you came to our office and spent a lot of time talking with people there, from the top man down, you'd find on the whole a superior group of people. They bend and twist those laws and regulations — which for the most part the state legislature has made — in an effort to help individual families.

"I can honestly say that some people in the welfare department are the biggest lawbreakers in the state. Every day they enter into collusion with the client in order to help people through a bad time. As I've said, we have our share of incredibly insensitive and tightfisted people, but they do not dominate the department, and among the younger employees they are nonexistent. The laws direct us to do only so much, and no more, with certain families and not with others. Even if new federal laws were enacted, we'll still not have the money these people need: they are more than simply poor, remember; they have been living for years and years under conditions that make their problems not only serious but very, very costly. I mean, they had rheumatic fever but they never were treated for it in Alabama or Georgia, and now they're up here and their hearts are badly damaged, and they need not only careful medical evaluations and treatment but help at home because they can't do things, lift things, catch their breath, all that. They can't get to the hospital easily, because for them to go up and down stairs is dangerous, sometimes impossible. They need expensive medication. They need special diets. People don't realize what a welfare department in a northern city has to face: we're supposed to heal and repair each day the damage that hundreds of years of history have paved the way for. We're the ones who see the end result of poor nutrition and diseases never once treated and poor sanitation and all the rest — not to mention the psychological damage."

She will not stop with generalities. She has uppermost on her mind the specific illnesses and hardships with which many families contend, and in any conversation about that abstraction

called her "work" she is more than ready to bring up those
specifics, to talk about everything from tuberculosis to malnutrition to rat bites to parasitic infestations to alcoholism. Alternatively, she will talk about the high rents the poor often have to
pay — for the most miserable of places, or the poor service they
get in garbage removal or police protection. "Everyone talks
about the police and their attitude toward ghetto people," and
then, that said, she pauses as if to say that she too has also talked
about it. When she is ready to resume her line of reasoning she
becomes openly ironic, even sarcastic: "I'm sure a lot of the
people I see wish the police were around more — and would do
a better job of being policemen — rather than be on the payroll
of the racketeers who prey upon the people in the ghetto. We
could start a second complete welfare service on the amount of
money that is illegally made around here: prostitution, drugs,
gambling. And, of course, there are payoffs all the way up and
down. The landlords are always slipping money to city inspectors
and the police. No one comes around and really checks into the
violations of the law, not unless one of the newspapers runs an
exposé, or the people really organize and make a lot of noise. It's
very discouraging to me, and even more so to the people who
have to live in those tenements. People on the outside always
think of a slum or a ghetto as a place where nothing much is
happening, where poor people live and sometimes riot because
they're unsatisfied. But the ghetto is also a place where storekeepers charge outrageous prices they'd never be able to force
upon middle-class customers, who can drive from place to place
and speak out and raise their voices. In the ghetto there is a
network of crime that makes a few black men rich and keeps
plenty of policemen and fire inspectors and plumbing and heating and building inspectors happy with extra dollars.

"That's why I have to laugh when I hear people talk as if the
police drive up and down ghetto streets looking for trouble and
trying to push people around. And I have to laugh when I hear
talk about the white oppressors, the outsiders, who are always
bleeding ghetto people. Some of the police are bullies, yes, and of
course the ghetto is a product of our society, so if we had differ-

ent values and priorities the ghetto might be a lot better place for people to live in. But I really wonder whether many who talk about these problems have ever put one foot into a ghetto, or done more than walked through — or driven through! — on some afternoon. The people I see, black people mainly, are exploited every day by other blacks. The kids I know grow up among black pimps, black addicts, black pushers, black prostitutes, and black salesmen who cheat their customers, sell them worthless insurance, and gouge them with prices far higher than they should be. Whites own some of the stores, but blacks also own a good number of them, and I've not found them angels and public benefactors, those black real estate men and property owners and storekeepers. That's a joke, the idea that a man's skin color makes him more honest or compassionate. Tell that to the people in the ghetto who know! And listen to them talk about the payoffs that a black policeman can take just as easily as a white one does. I learned that from the people I visit. They'll sit me down and tell me to forget all my nice, liberal ideas. They don't say it that way, but the message is clear.

"One tough old grandmother — you would think she is the sweetest, most innocent thing alive until you heard her speak — told me to 'stop dreaming and face the facts.' What facts, I asked her. 'Sister, around here it's kill or be killed, and that goes for black and white and tan and pink and green and yellow and any other color you can think up.' I wasn't convinced then, because I was just starting out, but now she wouldn't have to say that again to me. I've met too many black hoodlums, robbing and stealing from little children or weak and frightened old women, to settle for the notion that it's all a matter of white racists and what *they* do. I've even seen some landlords — everyone can jump on them so easily! — try to keep their buildings in good repair and make sure the trash is carried off and the alleys are swept regularly and the halls kept clean and reasonably well lighted, only to find mailboxes forced open, even ripped out of the walls, and banisters kicked and broken and windows or screens smashed and destroyed and half-full barrels deliberately overturned. It isn't easy to talk about all of that. I hope you've heard black people on the subject; many of them know only too well how their own people, their immediate neighbors, can terrorize a whole block. One of the worst parts of my job is hearing *those* facts, learning how *really* awful it can be *among* the poor — and not only because we continue to deny them entry to 'our' schools or colleges or jobs or neighborhoods."

Maybe she should have *known* such things, she hastens to say. She did take courses. She did read widely. She always has kept her eyes open, and in addition she has had her father's warnings. Still, she went into social work, and particularly welfare work, because she believed that by and large the poor are victims, even if not necessarily saintly victims. Now she knows that she was silly and naïve, at best, when she failed to consider the real price poor people have to pay for such sustained weakness: their susceptibility to all kinds of sad and terrible "temptations," if that is the right word; their vulnerability, which makes them easily tricked and used and abused; their sense of futility, which so frequently unnerves them, undoes them, prods them to turn on themselves vengefully. Now she dwells on such issues so exhaustively that she feels she has ironically come full circle and in so doing lost a good deal of her effectiveness as a welfare worker: "There comes a point in this kind of work when you see too much, perhaps. All the wretched 'facts of life' come upon you with such a wallop well, you become terribly discouraged. I am. Tomorrow I may not be, but today I am — discouraged and about ready to quit. Welfare, anyway, is not the answer. Many of the people on welfare have somehow lost respect for themselves, not for the reasons my father would say, but for other reasons. They are sick, disabled, fearful, brutalized — and therefore able to be brutal themselves. They are dazed and confused.

"I saw a mother today: she has had one illegitimate child after another. She comes from the South, near Augusta, Georgia, I believe; she came up here as a child and promptly lost her mother and was sent from relative to relative and then to a foster home; soon the street became her home. By the time she was ten she'd been 'around' so much that if she came from a rich family and they wanted to shower her with affection and concern and put her in psychoanalysis and do everything else they could, she would still require, as we put it in our jargon, 'a major rehabilitative effort,' and she would still have a 'guarded prognosis.' Meanwhile, she stayed in those tenements, one day after the other, and was tossed around and beaten up and plied with booze and pills. And still, *and still*, she fought to keep her children and make a home for them. And I swear, within the limits of her knowledge and experience and resources, she does well, damn well. She feeds those kids and tries hard to clothe them well. And she takes them to church. She has her lapses. She buys a bottle. She lets a man come and get her pregnant, which means she forgets the pills I got for her — without my superior's approval and yes, with my own money. She wanted those pills, desperately did. But she forgot. There it is. We've 'forgotten' about those people for a long time, and now they've got the habit of forgetting. I give up."

She doesn't really give up, though. The next time I see her she is full of talk, full of concern about another family, another mother, another set of problems — and quietly hopeful that somehow, in some way, at some time, she and her kind will be put thoroughly and completely out of business. That is what she says all the time: the faster there are no welfare workers like herself, the better it will be; provided, of course, the people she sees have their own resources to call upon, have a sense of their own power, have an unmistakable sense of self-sufficiency and self-respect — all of which are transmitted to children and need no boosters from weekly visitors who work for "the city" and who like Janet Howe want to scream, cry, and tear out their hair.

4. My Buildings

He is puzzled by the accusations he has heard only in recent years. He claims he is troubled by what he considers to be an impossible predicament. He is convinced that the worst is yet to come, and he is persuaded that whatever happens he will lose. The aging but sharply observant and skeptical man can only fall back again and again upon sentences which seem to be at once an affirmation of his faith and a warning to anyone inclined to doubt his intentions or his will: "They are my buildings. If they are not mine, whose are they? I paid for them, and I've tried to keep them up. I'll stop owning them when I sell them, and only then — period."

He insists repeatedly that he is no "operator," no " speculator" out to milk property dry, then abandon it. He is fifty-five years old and for thirty years has owned buildings all over the city, *all over* and not just in a black neighborhood. He started buying buildings in 1940 when the depression still lingered and when he had exactly five thousand dollars to his name — and that from his grandfather's life insurance. He had graduated from high school, had not gone to college because his parents had no money to send him and because he had no interest in reading books and writing papers and taking examinations. He was always active, he now says, and always willing to do the unconventional, to take risks and then stand firm. He feels, then, that his life has had a certain reassuring continuity and consistency. It is the times, the times that are out of joint.

Under stress a man may look back and try to make sense of his life, to know just what it is he is fighting for and against. Certainly a man who talks like the man I am now writing about is trying hard to gird himself and say that he stands *here*, and by God, he will not surrender: "Why should I? Why should I walk away from buildings I've put my whole life into? If I'm supposed to do that, then everyone who owns anything in this country will soon be in the same spot I'm in. Someone with a big, loud mouth will come up and say: hand it over, brother. Then the television boys will do their usual one-sided documentary, exposing the owner as no good and heartless and fat and rich and mean, and the next thing you'll see is a few pickets, and then a bigger demonstration, and then the poor owner feels like he's committed the crime of the century. And what is the crime? The crime is that he's owned something, he's had the colossal nerve in the United States of America to take some of his money and buy

something and keep it and try to make a profit out of it! That's
what we've come to these days — you have to defend yourself for
being a businessman and for trying to make a living. And if you
do make a halfway decent living, then you're exploiting the poor
and squeezing them dry and you're a Nazi and a white colonialist
and a murderer.

"I'm tired of it! I ask myself every now and then why I stay,
why I keep coming here and trying to keep my property in good
shape and trying to have a reasonable talk with my tenants. I'm
no illiterate, you know. I read the papers and the magazines; I
read what all those smart-aleck writers say. I know that I'm
supposed to be plundering my property. Even though I keep my
buildings looking good and say hello to the tenants and hear
them say hello back to me — I'm still supposed to be a plunderer.
A lot of guys I grew up with and went to school with had money
behind them, so they went to college. They live 'cleaner' lives, I
guess. One is a lawyer, and he makes his money because other
people have got themselves into trouble. No one calls *him* an
exploiter or a plunderer. Another one is a doctor; he makes his
money because other people are sick and dying. Half the time he
can't do a thing for them: they either get better on their own or
they die or they keep on moaning and groaning because they
want to be sick. But no one thinks the doctor is exploiting anyone
or plundering. I've been to his office: they come in and leave
every five minutes, and they pay him ten dollars in cash, a lot of
them, and God knows how much of that money gets declared on
the income tax forms. But he's a *doctor*, a pillar of the community. And I just own 'slum property.'

"My kids, or at least one of them, is ashamed of me. He's in
college, and he says he won't tell his friends where some of my
property is. He'll only tell them about the stores in the suburban
plaza. I told him he'd better stop telling *me* things — like what
he doesn't want to tell friends. I told him that I'm no crook and
I'm no thief and I'm no drug addict and I'm no traitor to my
country, and I'm sick and tired of hearing about slum landlords,
slum landlords from a bunch of hypocrites! Everyone who has
money in this country is an 'exploiter,' if you want to look at the

world that way; and the more money a person has, or has inherited, the bigger an exploiter he is. But a guy like me, who goes out and works and tries to keep his property going and visits it and talks with his tenants and listens to their complaints, he's the scapegoat. Every doctor or lawyer with money can sneer at me, and every son of a guy with money can call me a name instead of looking at how his own father made money.

"I'm not saying I do everything my tenants want me to do. I'd have to be a multimillionaire to keep them happy. They're unhappy people, you know. When a person is unhappy, he complains. When a person is out of work, and he's just sitting there, and who knows if he's married to the woman or not, or how many men she sleeps with — then that guy will tell you how bad everything is. I know it's bad for them; they don't have to tell me. I'm no bigot. I've always liked the colored people — excuse me, the *black* people. I was talking with them and going into their homes and on a first-name basis with them before this whole civil rights movement got going. In 1950 — how do you like that! — I was given a scroll by one of the Negro churches. They said I was a trusted friend. I've given money to that church for over twenty-five years. 'If only all white people were like you': I've heard those words for twenty-five years, too — for thirty years. But no, those people are just Uncle Toms, I'm supposed to believe, or else they were lying to me, just trying to please me, fool me — I don't know *what* they were supposed to be doing, because every day I hear a new theory about the Negro, and every day he's called by a different name."

The man owns many buildings in a black section of a large northern city, some of which are indeed to any middle-class eye old and crowded tenements, in need of various kinds of repair, and some of which, old though they be, are well kept up and relatively uncrowded. In other words, the man has as tenants both large families and modest-sized families. One need be no social scientist to see that on one street the families are black, but generally headed by men who have steady jobs that yield at least halfway decent wages, whereas on another street welfare workers can be seen knocking on most of the doors in his buildings. He claims that as a landlord he is actually "impartial," so far as his comparative "attitude" toward his better-off tenants and his poorer tenants goes. He claims that all along he has tried to do everything that each of his nine buildings inhabited by black people requires. He claims that he has working for him a full-time plumber and steam fitter and a full-time carpenter, and a more-or-less full-time electrician, and they spend a good deal more of their time in those nine buildings than they do in the apartment buildings and stores he owns elsewhere — that is, in white, middle-class neighborhoods. And finally, he wants to emphasize his personal approach to his work, his effort to go out and see things for himself and instruct his employees quite openly and directly on what he wants done.

Those employees, by the way, include four black janitors, who care for the nine buildings which he sometimes collectively refers to as his "headache." Yet, he will not deny that he makes a certain profit out of that headache, and he has as reward not only the solace of money but a sense of pride in achievement which he feels his daily behavior somehow demonstrates: "I've got respect for myself, and that's one reason I don't sell those buildings. I could have sold them numerous times, and at a profit. I don't sell property, though. I buy property and I hold onto it. I make my living by being a landlord. I'm not a speculator. I bought those buildings a long time ago, when Negroes were there, but also some white people. The whites moved out a year or two later. They just wouldn't live with Negroes, not that close to them. I remember being angry at them. One of them asked me why I don't sell the building he lived in and was just leaving. I asked why. He said, 'You know.' I said, 'No, I *don't* know.' Then he gave me a long look and he said, 'Look, it's not me, it's my wife. She says they're not clean.' I said, 'Do you believe her?' He said no, and what's more, she didn't really believe herself. He said they were really moving out because they just didn't think it was 'natural' for white people to live 'surrounded' by Negroes. Well, I told him I thanked him for being honest, and I could understand his feelings. I told him I didn't live with them, and I wouldn't, for the same reason: I believe you're always happier with your own people. But I had nothing against Negroes, I told him that, and I was going to stay right where I was, so far as owning those buildings was concerned.

"Two banks had offered to buy the building from me, and I felt like this: if the buildings are fully rented and they net a good profit, not a huge one, but over ten thousand dollars clear, which is part of my income, and a good return on an investment, then why should I turn that kind of investment over to a bank? Or to a big real estate firm? That's the way I thought. Sure, I could have made a fast pile of money, but then it would either go to the government or I'd have had to reinvest it. And those buildings are good investments."

He is, then, proud that he bought the apartment houses and proud that he did not sell them. He is proud that he did not become panicky and flee at the sight of more and more blacks. And he is proud that he has maintained a steady, satisfying kind of acquaintance with dozens of black people, who do indeed, in the course of various discussions, affirm their friendship for him — or at the least, their toleration of him. "He's a fine man," one tenant says. "He's no worse than anyone else, black or white," another more guarded tenant says. "What can you expect? He's the landlord. If he was black, he'd be no better. I know worse landlords who *are* black," a third and more cynical or begrudging tenant observes. When he arrives at a building he is greeted cordially and often offered a cup of coffee — although that holds mostly for his better-off tenants. Sometimes he collects the rent from them. Often his agent comes and does so. None of his black tenants mails money to his office, a contrast with the way his white, middle-income tenants choose to do things. Yet, he has no illusions; he knows that even though things *seem* relatively quiet, there is a lot of tension in the air, and he may well one day be in serious trouble, if not face to face with what he calls "a business catastrophe." So he lashes out. He becomes angry. He anticipates criticism, then replies to it. One gets the feeling that he somehow gains a sense of control over an unpredictable destiny by arguing out things with himself. And anyway, in time he will become hurt in some way, he knows that — which is why he believes that the best thing to do is prepare himself: "I know I'll have trouble. Maybe they'll burn one of my buildings down. I hate to think about it, and yet I've got to. I'd be like an ostrich with its head in the sand if I didn't.

"Who will suffer if that should happen? It's so stupid! I'll collect on my fire insurance, but what about the tenants? Of course, arsonists and hoodlums and petty thieves and crazy revolutionaries never care about people. They do what their wild impulses tell them to do. They aren't sincere, kind people who want to help their fellowman. They're exhibitionists. That's what they are. And they're willing to have others suffer so that they can say: look at the fire I set; I'm a *militant;* I'm a *leader.* It's always the poor and the innocent who pay for the theatrical types!

"I know exactly what the militants say about me. And it's a bundle of lies. They exaggerate. They exaggerate the money I make, and they ignore the costs I have: the money I have to spend on upkeep and maintenance, the taxes I pay, and all the rest — insurance, water bills, mortgage payments. I don't own the buildings outright. You should see the interest the bank gets out of me every month. But the public has no interest in all that. They just say: those landlords collect all that money and stick it in their pockets. If you try to explain to them what a landlord has to do, what his bills are like and what the risks are that he takes, they say you're crying false tears. There's no point in even trying to argue.

"The one thing that bothers me most is that the really crooked and dishonest landlords, and the cheapest, tightest, most inhuman owners of property are the ones who never get blamed by anyone, black or white. It's someone like me, who *comes* here, who is visible — he's the one attacked. Who can insult someone never, never seen? Who can figure out who owns some of those buildings? I'll tell you who owns them: banks who have foreclosed mortgages on deadbeats or crooks — guys who took all they could from a building and never paid the bills, so the bank had to come and take the building away, while the guy disappears or claims he's broke or something like that. The other kind of owners are the large real estate companies. They are huge, impersonal firms. No one knows who is in charge of the buildings. There's an agent who collects the rent, and every once in a while someone comes to fix a leak. But it takes a team of lawyers to figure out who it is — what collection of guys or what individual — owns most of the apartment houses around mine. The Negroes don't know. How could they? In a way, they're right when they talk about the big banks being the landlords. The banks *are* the mortgagees in a lot of cases. Or there are a series of 'trusts' and 'corporations' and 'companies,' with all kinds of 'officers' that a tenant will never see, and the buildings are 'owned' by them: the so-and-so trust, you know, and all that. If you did track them all down, the leading investors in the banks and the officers of the real estate trusts and companies, guess what you'd find. You'd find big, prominent families. You'd find the same people who invest in stocks and bonds and everything else. You'd find the most respectable and honored names. Some of them probably have no idea they're 'slum landlords.' Some of them just give their money over to a man or a company 'for investment.' But some are quite aware; they know they own huge blocks of property in the ghetto, and they know that the management company in charge of the property is 'doing as well as can be expected.'

"It's a laugh! It's so hypocritical! I'll bet some of those people give to the NAACP and the Urban League. I'll bet some of them are on the boards of those organizations. In fact, I know that's the case here in this city. I know a man who's on the board of a bank that owns some of the worst property in this neighborhood, and at the same time he's on the board of all kinds of Negro organizations. He's considered a 'friend' of the Negro community. He's a big lawyer. He's a nice man. He's probably never stopped and checked into the various real estate holdings of his bank. Why should he? He's a busy man, everyone says. He's got so much on his mind. He's so generous with his time and money. He wants the colored people to have a better life. Meanwhile, I pick up the bank's reports and whose name do I see on the board of trustees, and who is a stockholder or something like that in the bank — a big depositor, you can be sure? Who gets his interest from the money the bank makes out of its properties in the ghetto? Well, that man of course, and many others — when you come right down to it, thousands of people who would never consider themselves property owners as such. Their hands are clean. They don't know where their money comes from. They feel morally superior. They probably look down on me a little. I'm grubby. That's me: a grubby slum landlord.

"I'd like to tell those holier-than-thou types what I have to do. I'd like to tell them what some of my worst tenants do to my property. Better, I'd like them to come and see. They'd see things done to walls and stairs and mailboxes: dirty words scrawled everywhere, locks broken, screens slashed, windows constantly pushed in, garbage just thrown out the window as if I was there, ready and waiting with my arms wide open. What is a landlord supposed to do? I spend thousands of dollars every year — you heard me, *thousands* of dollars — in order to fix up the damage that those 'poor, underprivileged' Negro kids do. It's part of my expense. I have to figure on that when I anticipate my costs. The police laugh at me when I call them. And I laugh at them. What can they do? We'd have to have a million police in some of our cities if we were going to stop these gangs. They come with paint and smear the walls. They break bottles, one after the other, until the alleys and streets are covered with *layers* of glass. I try to sweep up after them. I mean, I ask my janitors to do so, and they try, they really try. They are hardworking men — like I said, Negro. You should hear what *they* say about their own people. I never dare speak like that, even to my own kids — *especially* to my kids.

"I once asked my son to come and talk with those men, but he said no. He said they worked for me, and so they said what I wanted them to say. I said OK, OK, have it your way. But you're wrong, so completely wrong I'd like to laugh, but I end up almost in tears. Why is it that a boy like mine, in college, prelaw, gets an idea in his head and then doesn't try to find out whether it's right or wrong? I see him reading books about 'logic' and 'reason' and all that, and I say to him: before you call your father an exploiter, and his janitors paid dupes, please come and look around and ask some questions. But no. He's willing to insult those janitors, never mind me — and believe only what he thinks is right. He doesn't even want to test out his beliefs. I guess he's afraid that if he did, life wouldn't be so clear-cut — I'd say black and white, but I'm not trying to be funny. This is no laughing matter, the way a person believes only what he wants to believe, and doesn't bother with the facts."

The facts — more than anything else he stresses the importance of facts: the money he makes, the money he spends, the rents he collects, the cost of maintenance he has to put up with. Like the policeman he calls but knows cannot really help him, like the fireman he has also had to call (so far only for "minor" blazes, mischief done by children or accidents in particular apartments) and like the welfare workers who come to see his tenants regularly, he claims to know things about black people that others do not know. He thinks of himself as the outsider who is also the insider, the white man who really has his eyes on the black man, the heavily scorned person who is really the knowing and courageous person. Again and again he wants that last point made: others talk, but he sees; others use rhetoric, but he takes part in a neighborhood's "action." He uses that word, action. He considers himself a restless, active man, and he says that he is glad he has to take risks, test his willpower and perseverance against the growing danger and uncertainty his work provides.

One thing I must know: he is not afraid. And I do know that. True, somewhere "underneath" or "way down" he is scared and ashamed and guilty and all the rest, as many of us are for one set of reasons or other. But in his everyday life I am quite convinced he knows little fear. He walks those streets, streets in a sense he partially owns, and for all the world he seems almost carelessly casual and untroubled. He likes to whistle, which can always prompt from someone like me the clever observation that at some "level" of his mind he is indeed whistling, whistling in the dark — quite literally so, because he is at large among the darkskinned people who pay him so significant a part of their income. But one of those darkskinned tenants, on welfare and capable of intense anger at white people, finds that landlord no real menace and even laughs at him — with scorn yes, but genuine appreciation of sorts: "He's always smiling, and he'll whistle you a tune if you ask him to. So help me, he will. Now, how can you hate a man like that? I hate him on the first of the month when that Uncle Tom of his comes around for the rent; but when he drives up here, whistling and worrying about a leak in a pipe and pointing out something to his plumber and worrying if the plumber is going to cheat him good by stretching the job out — well, I have to smile and say: the poor guy, he's running scared, too, like the rest of us. I'll save my gun for the bigger cats."

So it is that those two have their moments of agreement, that landlord and his tenant. Only moments, however. Each of them can attack the other, and do so with words and phrases which make one wonder whether there is any hope that somehow this country will keep itself reasonably intact. And yet, and yet; I can only add the "and yet," the qualification those two human beings and others like them require from me — because again, for a moment here and there, and sometimes even longer, they think and talk almost alike, which may never mean a thing, or may one day mean quite a lot.

5.　Their Buying Habits, Their Garbage

Speak long enough with a storekeeper about his customers, or a garbage collector about his work, and soon the people who consume things and turn them into waste disappear; all one has in mind are particular commodities and a sea of bottles, cans and smelly, decaying organic matter. I have talked with the men and women who own or operate food stores and record stores and with the men who take away garbage in poor sections of our cities. Like a black maid in a rich and fancy suburban home, or a storekeeper in a large and luxurious suburban shopping mall or a "man who does the trash" in a spotlessly clean, well-to-do neighborhood, the man who sells soul food or soul music and the man who carries off the litter from tenement building after tenement building has a chance to see and hear people in very special ways. One has to caution, though, that such individuals can be blind and parochial as well as clever and in touch.

The maid whom I have written about in the preceding chapter first put me onto the work, the explorations and meetings and interviews that eventually enabled this section, and I believe I ought to let her advice be read at this point: "The trash man, the missus calls him, comes and I watch him putting all that stuff onto his truck, and I say: Lord, how can you stand it? These people, they throw away more in a week than I buy in a year. It hurts me. It pains me. I hear her opening that huge refrigerator she's got and then I hear her say, 'Oh, dear!' and then I wait, and there's a crash, and I know she's tossed something else into one of her baskets.

"She has baskets all over the house. I've never seen so many. I have only one in my place. I've never been in a place where there's more than one. But around here they have two in a room and in one room there's three. I'll go look at what she's thrown out from that icebox, and I'll want to pick it up and hide it and take it home. But I can't do that. I'd become the trash man myself that way. I'd be taking home so much they wouldn't let me on the bus, I'd have so much to carry on. I tell you, sir, if you want to know about this here family, you just go and study what they throw out. And you'll find out something. You'll find out that they don't know what they want, because they buy everything, and then later they throw out, throw out — a lot of the time without using anything of what they're throwing."

I knew, of course, that such would not be the case in her own neighborhood, and I told her that. But, no, she wasn't so sure of that. People are also wasteful "back home" she insisted — back South and back "across town." The difference in her mind is as follows: "Around here a lady like my missus will get excited about something, or she'll hear someone talk about what is good to buy and then she goes and buys it, too. But she's got so much money she doesn't care whether she'll use what she's bought or not. My neighbors can't afford to waste anything; even so there are some of them who buy more than they can use and throw out a lot. They're mixed-up, you know. They can't think the way they should."

Perhaps we all are "mixed-up" along the lines she has suggested; in this rich, industrial nation waste is everywhere and "consumption" is indeed irrational — and it can scarcely be of great comfort to hear that in this respect our poor people are, after all, Americans. On the other hand, there is a certain bitterly moralistic tone to some descriptions of the "conspicuous consumption" to be found among the rich and poor alike; deliberate understatement ("shabby gentility") can itself be a sly and conspicuous way of signaling one's sense of self-importance. I have to make mention of such matters, so human and so universal, because I have heard more than one welfare worker or social worker or politician say things similar to the following remarks, spoken by a supervisor of certain public health nurses: "We need to educate the poor. To give them money without education is cruel. Many of them aren't equipped to spend money wisely. They buy food that is not nutritious. They injure their children's health that way. They waste their limited money on trinkets. They purchase silly, childlike things — and then they complain that they're without money for the food their children need. It is tragic. They don't know how to be good managers. That's the problem. They buy incorrectly, waste what resources they do have and then wonder why there isn't more coming. Now I know we all do that to some extent. But when a person is extremely poor, she needs to be more careful than some rich woman who doesn't have to worry where the next dollar is coming from. I don't mean to be harsh or overly critical in the way I talk. It's just that for years I've gone to homes and tried to do the best I can for sick children. I've talked patiently, as patiently as I know how, to the mothers. I've tried to give them hints and clues and advice — *anything* to make life better for them and their children. But their buying habits are poor ones, that's a fact, and if you were to go see what they throw out, their garbage — well I think you'd agree that it's education, not just money, that they need."

In a way, but only in a way, she and the maid I have quoted

agree with one another. There is, certainly, about the supervisor's manner a stern quality that comes across to the eye more than the ear, hence cannot quite be conveyed on paper by a record of her words. I do not mean to deny her point — nor do I think we get anywhere by turning her into a caricature of herself, a sort of prim, ascetic, puritanical censor who would deny people some fun, however it works at cross-purposes to their budget. What she has seen she has seen; and it is her sincere wish to improve the health of children obviously in need of medical attention. I cannot be so sure of the motives some politicians have when they take up her viewpoint and use it as grist for their particular mills. Nor can I help wondering whether another kind of nurse, intent on the very mission that supervisor has, might not achieve rather more in the way of improved "education" among our needy families.

I do believe that the maid's advice was good advice, and as a sort of response to her suggestion I would offer here the remarks, first, of a man who sells both food and music to black people and, second, a man who collects their garbage. They are both white men, both among the outsiders and visitors already discussed. They are both nervous men, aware that their days may be numbered, so far as their work goes — but ready, in fact, to dispute that contention when they hear it spoken. Here is the store owner's view of what he will find happening in the coming years: "I'll be here until I die. The reason is that I have a good store, two stores really, and the people want what I have to offer them. If we have a riot, they'll burn me down, I suppose. But during riots they've burned down their own houses and their own stores, owned by blacks. It's no fun owning a store anyplace. I read that college students break into stores near their campuses. But in most black neighborhoods there have been no riots. People remember the big riots in Watts and Detroit and Newark, but they forget that there are hundreds and hundreds of black neighborhoods that have never had a riot and never will have one. So, I've been lucky, but not all that lucky."

He goes on to insist that all is well, perhaps protests too much. Then he takes up the issue of his customers and their "tastes," as he calls them: "I'm a white man — but so are most of the businessmen here on this block. That's how it is in a lot of places. It's always been like that. Things are changing, I'm sure. I know that black people — I call them what they want to be called, and they don't all agree, you understand — are more and more moving into the retail business, and that's fine. But if every white store owner in the black sections of our cities were to drop dead right now, you'd find a lot of people in real trouble — black people. It's easy to say: get out, get out of here. Those militants have come in to see me and told me that. I said to one of them: you come in and try to run a store like mine. You look through the windows of the stores while they're being run, and you say: easy, easy, all you have to do is learn how to operate the cash register and rake in the green bills. Well, the answer is that you have to know more than people would ever dream is necessary.

"I'm a psychologist and an economist and an efficiency expert and an advertising man. That's all part of selling people food and selling them radios and phonographs and records. I have these two stores, and I'm supposed to be a white businessman, but I'll let you in on something: I have to know black people, because I myself have to buy, in the first place, what I know they'll buy later, when I've put it in stock. To run a store you have to know what's going on in the mind of the person who comes in, and how to get her attention, and what she has to spend, and what she has to buy, and what she'd like to buy — it's more complicated than you'd ever dream. I know this: the people who come into my stores see me and they see my salesmen, who are black. They trust us, most of them do. They'll come to me sometimes and say: *you* have soul. Well, of course I do. I sell them soul music. I have a manager who buys what he knows they want to hear.

"I started selling meat and fruit and vegetables and canned goods to colored people nearly three decades ago, that's almost thirty years — a long time. And I've seen a lot. I've seen a lot of changes. But let me tell you something: don't let anyone go into fancy explanations about 'Afro-American' and 'black is special' and all the rest: the people around here are human beings, like you and me, and they need to eat, and they do eat. And since they're in America, they eat American food. The food isn't white and it isn't black. Oh sure, there's soul food. We had that years ago, spareribs and the rest. But people lately have been talking about blacks as if they're a bunch of food connoisseurs all dressed up in African tribal robes. I have hundreds of people go through this store every week, and I'll tell you what they buy: a lot of potatoes, bread, ham, chicken, bacon, sausages, eggs, cigarettes, candy, Coca-Cola, Pepsi-Cola, soap, toilet paper, chewing gum, funny books, TV Guides. They can't afford high-priced fruit and vegetables, but in season they buy watermelon and peaches. They buy beans and okra. They buy a lot of canned spaghetti. If I were them I'd buy the spaghetti and make it myself and make my own sauce; but Hell, they're not Italian, and neither am I — and come to think of it, my wife makes a very poor kind of spaghetti sauce, and she usually doesn't make any!

"All right, if you had to summarize, I suppose you'd have to say that they go heavy on starches. They like the pig better than the cow! It's crazy the way the Panthers call the cops 'pigs' — because black people love the pig; they've always eaten ham and bacon and chitterlings and sausage and fatback. They give their kids too much candy and too many Cokes. I don't think they buy as much toothpaste as they do in the suburbs. My customers are poor people mostly, compared to the suburbs, and toothpaste costs money. The men work as janitors and elevator 'boys' — I don't like that expression — or in buildings, where they run errands or sweep floors, and the women, a lot of them are on welfare. The better-off Negro, I think, goes to a chain supermarket. But we don't have a supermarket around here, and the people here have no cars, so they can't travel all over and shop around, and they have to buy light, because they carry home what they buy. They can't buy in bulk, in other words. And I'm not bragging, but I don't mark up my prices the way I could. They know I could do that, but they read the papers and they see the ads of the chain stores and they see I don't. And I decided long ago that I *would* be beaten up and driven out of here if I tried to take unfair advantage of people. That's why I have good black clerks working, and I do the best I can to be fair."

Across the street from his market is his record store, which he decided to buy about ten years ago. It had been owned by another white man, who became sick and had to sell out: "I bought it because, like I say, I know my people here. I always used to sell some small-sized LP's. I kept a stack of them, usually hit records, near the check-out counter. I noticed that they sold like hot cakes, faster than just about anything else. So, when that store came up for sale, I grabbed the chance. I remodeled the place. I made it look like a completely new store. They started calling it 'the palace' when they saw the fluorescent lights and the modern counter and the booths and the vinyl floors, so I listened to them. I called it Soul Palace, and they really liked that. They feel like somebody when they come in there. We try to have what they want, and they leave feeling happy. They can sit and listen there, and then they can't let themselves leave without the record. They'd feel lonely going home! And if I have to keep on repairing the machines they use to listen, then it's worth it.

"Sure, some of them buy records when they complain they don't have enough money to buy the food they want. Who is all that rational? Why hold it against these people because they want to hear a good tune? You know, life is more than eating vitamin pills and a lettuce and tomato salad! I have a lot of sympathy for these people — though they may not know it, some of them. They may call me 'the white devil,' some of the drugged-up ones, and the fanatics. But most of my customers are plain, ordinary people. They're like anyone else. They want to eat, and they want to enjoy themselves as best as they can. They like potato chips, so they buy them and not celery. They like cookies, so they buy them and not pears. They have musical mentalities, is the way I put it, and so they buy those records. Records are food, too; people just eat these records up! You can practically see saliva come out of their mouths when they listen in those booths. I come home and tell my wife that I wish I could like music! I'm tone-deaf. Music of any kind is a bore to me. But to those people, it's one of the things that keeps them going. They take to music like a big-business executive does to a martini or something. They unbend and feel relaxed and laugh and feel alive again. It's a tonic. And it's the way they have of talking to each other. I've come to realize that. I've come to see that for the black man, soul music, jazz, the blues, the gospels, all of that — it's to them what books and magazines are to us, and like I say, martinis, too."

Certainly his Soul Palace is one of the busiest stores I have ever seen. And certainly one can see tired, burdened people come in there and begin to liven up. They no longer seem slumped over. They start snapping their fingers. They can barely keep themselves from dancing — and sometimes they do dance. They talk and hum, they sing and use their arms and legs and make their bodies move and whirl and arch and bend, "quick and fast and all of a sudden," according to a clerk in the store.

Meanwhile, in other parts of that neighborhood things do not happen with such speed. Rats don't get exterminated, even though programs meant to do so have been announced and "implemented." Decrepit buildings go unrepaired. Playgrounds are planned and promised but fail to materialize. Garbage, the revolting garbage, stands in uncollected barrels and spills over and covers sidewalks and catches in their cracks and makes people watch their step, move away, hold their breath, walk faster, or slip and fall and curse and wonder why, why.

When the garbagemen do come, some are black, but some are white. In the neighborhood near that Soul Palace the drivers of the garbage truck are almost invariably white; they have seniority; they have been with the sanitation department "the longest." One of them says: "I've been doing this all my life. I started in the depression. You know something? We were all fighting to get a job, any job, and this job was for the city and you had a regular paycheck at the end of each week, and you weren't laid off. A guy who worked for the sanitation department was lucky, let me tell you. I had political pull. If I didn't, I never would have got the job. There was a time when I was the envy of a lot of people. That was before the war, up to 1940 or so. I thought of quitting then and trying to get a job in a factory, but I didn't. I figured all the factories would close down again after the war, and we'd be back in the same jam we were in the thirties. I was wrong, but at least there's no one watching over me in this kind of job. I'm near retirement age, and I'll have a good pension. It's no fortune, but I'll get by.

"When I was a kid starting out, this whole neighborhood was white. Would you believe that? It shows you what can happen in a lifetime. My brother works in a bar, and he says to me sometimes that nothing changes. I tell him he's out of his mind, completely out of his mind. He sees the same old rummies every day; but he's inside, and I'm outside. If you want to know what's happening, you have to step out into the street, I tell him. Look at these streets; if you do you'll know all you need to know, mister. I mean it. These people, they're the funniest people in the world. I used to hate them, you know. When they first came in here I didn't trust them for one minute. They'll pick your pocket and hold you up with a knife, and they'd as soon stab you as not, even if you hand over your cash to them, and especially if you're new to them, a stranger. But I got used to them; I guess that's it. They grow on you; it's funny. I'm not telling you I love them. I'm no nigger-lover. Isn't that what they call some of those college kids? But I know them and they know me; it's been years and years I've been coming here, loading the trucks and now driving. I've never been in their homes, and I don't have any of them as friends, even the colored guys I drive around, the guys that do the loading. But I watch them. And you can tell something about people by what they do with their dirty linen — and with their garbage."

There is a lot of work to do, because there are many too many people packed into those apartment houses. He knows that the landlords often fail to provide an adequate number of barrels and garbage pails. He knows that the ideal thing would be incinerators in each building — but only new and costly apartment houses in the other (white) sections of the city have such improvements. He knows that his truck comes around once a week, and that once a week for buildings filled with dozens and dozens of families is not quite the same as once a week for a street lined with single-family houses. Knowing all that, he can be for long stretches of time a quietly sympathetic observer who

is impatient with the rhetoric of some of his brother civil servants, like policemen and firemen. But he can also be very much
like those policemen and firemen. He can forget the warnings he
himself has made, the observations he himself has offered, and
really run amok with wild and hysterical, mischievous and abusive comments. Yet, suddenly and without explanation, he will
reverse himself. He will almost retract what he has said. He will
tell me that it is true, they throw things out of the window, and it
is true, they buy a lot of junk and throw a lot of junk away, and it
is true, they can be ugly, they can deface property and overturn
full barrels and hurl garbage at each other, not to mention
innocent passersby — but, after all, they have a thoroughly unpleasant life in those buildings, and besides, every one of the
buildings ought have been torn down a long time ago.

If the substance of his remarks is not very surprising to the
reader, the man's changes in mood are certainly striking and in a
sense unaccountable, and therefore surprising. I often have felt
that my surprise at his willingness to say some of the things he
does is itself worth examining. We can be condescending to men
like him as much as to black people — those of us who think we
know so much, and perhaps want to find that fact confirmed at
the expense of others. We can hear what we want to hear and no
more. Time and again I have been ready to stop listening to that
garbageman, who is sneered at often enough by blacks, who are
in turn sneered at often enough by him. I have to go someplace,
so I say I am sorry, but we will have to talk again next week.
Once when I did that, tried to cut our conversation short because
I had heard a lot of bigotry and nastiness and could take no more
that afternoon, he told me he had to go on for just a minute
more, he had to say something: "I don't like to condemn all of
them. You shouldn't kick people when they're down. They're no
better and no worse than the rest of us. If I call them names, I
get it back. A little nigger kid will shout, 'Here come the Whitey
garbage men,' and then his friend will say, 'You mean the white
trash.' Well, I'm no millionaire, I sure know that.

"I feel sorry for them sometimes. God must have made them,
like He did us. I look at the stuff they throw out, and it's the

same stuff I'd be picking up in other places: cans and bottles and boxes and paper bags. Maybe they *are* like pigs sometimes. But they haven't the incinerators and why should they spend their money on plastic bags and all that? Why should they be so proud of their backyards? Look at them — a few square feet of cracked cement, and the mice and rats and alley cats and stray dogs run all over and leave their stuff. Hell, you have to have a strong nose. It doesn't get to me, now that I drive rather than collect. But I used to see plenty. They throw out boxes of condoms, and not one of them used. No wonder they have so many kids. You wonder why they want to bring any kids into this world, even if they do get a raise from the welfare people every time they do. I think they look at their kids and figure they'll do better, somehow they will.

"You know, when kids are six or seven, they'll tell you they want to be a garbage collector. They're all excited because of the big truck and the big pails we have. They come and watch you and ask you questions and tell you that it won't be long before they're on with you, working up there on that truck. They think it's great, standing there on top of that garbage, pushing it and shoveling it. I've heard the same thing from white kids and colored kids, so long as they're only five or six or seven. But then the white kids get smart. I've never in my life been told by an older white kid that he *wants* to be a garbage man. Nor have any of my buddies. Even back in the thirties and forties, when the people here were white and we were all in a Hell of a fix and not many people could look forward to much, not the plain working people, the white people you used to find here; even then I could see the ten- or twelve-year-old kids do one of three things: they'd snicker, or they'd look at you as though you're a freak or something, or they'd feel sorry for you — on their faces it was written, the pity they'd have. Well, I didn't want their pity, and I still don't. I'd rather have a nigger kid speaking as mean and fresh as they do. At least they are honest.

"But what I was trying to tell you: I'll get twelve-year-old nigger kids asking me about the work, and older ones ask, too. They're standing around, and they look as if they don't have anything to do. It reminds me of the depression in the thirties. And one of them will come over and ask me — he's serious! — how long it takes to cover my route, and he *tells* me that you probably get used to the work. And I say yes, that's right, you do. The next thing, he wants to know about salary, of course, and the working hours, and how much vacation do you get, and how do they decide upon the route you get. I've spoken with some of them that are all grown up. I never know *how* old they are. I can't tell with the colored. But they're men, maybe fifteen, maybe twenty — the ones I'm talking about. Once I asked one kid if he'd mind working in a white neighborhood. He said no he wouldn't, then he laughed and said there couldn't be much difference, because garbage is garbage. I said it wasn't like that, because if you have money you can buy a lot of fancy barrels and coat them with plastic paper — until you'd think it was diamond jewels they were putting out for you to take away. Hell, in some sections they spray perfumed deodorant on their barrels, so you come near them and you think you're in a bar, and some broad on the make is coming up to you. No such luck here. I tell them that. I say white or black, it's the same if you're working where the people aren't rich. Then later I'll say to myself: damned if there isn't something crazy going on — that some of those kids actually *want* this job I've got. Don't get me wrong: I'm all right; I'm satisfied. But you don't go and *look* for a job like this, not these days you don't. I mean, if you're white you don't. I guess with a lot of colored it's the only thing they can get. I believe if a lot of them tried harder, they could find something. They wouldn't have to stand around here, like they do. But maybe there's a limit to how many of them *can* find jobs. Don't ask me. I just come here a few hours and leave."

Although he doesn't want to be asked about a "subject" like unemployment, or mistaken for a man with answers, he has something to say not only about that problem but about something as imposing as "child development." He has seen side by side in black children and youths things like idleness and apathy and bursts of curiosity and the desire for work and the urge to find something, anything almost, that takes up time and brings in money and a sense of usefulness and competence — a feeling that one *is* someone, *does* something, *has* someplace to go. He has even seen black youths envy him, find his work worth asking about. As a result he can only express the agitated kind of confusion which comes across in that phrase of his: "damned if there isn't something crazy going on."

V

WHITE NORTHERNERS

FOR decades a steady trek of blacks from the South has increasingly brought race as a local, volatile problem to the North and the Far West. But it is only recently that the North has had to face what can be called a "white problem," in contrast to a black one. The historical and political pressures working to liberate the black man have not been confined to the South. Blacks everywhere in America are awakened. No longer do they stay quietly in their bulging neighborhoods, out of everyone's way but their own. Aroused blacks in the South have had a clear direction to travel; there were — and even with reforms still are — voting polls to enter, restaurants to frequent, schools to claim as theirs, too. Blacks in the North have the complaints of the poor. To lodge those complaints, let alone make them effective, requires a direct assault on our complicated, ambiguous, not always equitable social and economic system.

Yet blacks are not the only people struggling for money and position in America. In the South they alone have been excluded from a wide variety of places and privileges, though in that region — and elsewhere, too — there are millions whose white skin gives them precious little more than blacks have.[1] In the North such people have not even had what is any southern white man's consolation. "I'm poor," a fiercely segregationist farmer in Alabama once told me, "but I'm proud of my race, and I'd as soon die as see it contaminated." I can still see his home, a cabin really, "two rooms and a pathway." His farm is small, and so is his income. His children are getting neither the quality of food nor the education this country can well afford for everyone. His wife is a tired but determined woman. Once, a few years ago, they left their farm for the city; but there, too, they saw hardship and a kind of impersonal living they could not bear. "So we're back here. At least we can grow some food, and the niggers aren't creeping in on us." As long as black men were niggers, and niggers tightly kept in their place, the farmer was at least that much a man of property. Millions of blacks were his.

In the North and the West the issue is not a matter of falling into line so that the nation's laws are obeyed, its customs followed. From Harlem to Watts, uneasy, suspicious millions, newly aroused and aware, make demands that cannot be satisfied by compliant voting registrars or the fresh hospitality of restaurant owners. Very poor, and long scorned, they are asking for money and power. In so doing they stand alongside others, white people who have their own reasons to feel shaky, apprehensive, and needy.[2]

Here, for example, are the words of a thirty-year-old woman, the mother of six. Her origins are Irish. Her husband works in the repair shop of a utility company. They live in a mixed Irish and Italian neighborhood in Boston where homes vary from the comfortable and well kept to others in obvious decline. Her young children now have several black children in classes with them, and though the two young boys and the little girl do not seem to mind, their mother is quite upset.

"Why do they do it? I don't understand them at all. They have their own people, just as we do, but suddenly they're not happy together. They want to go here and there, and send their children everywhere. All you hear these days is news about them. You'd think Negroes were the only people in America who have a tough time. What about the rest of us? Who comes here asking us how we get by, or how we feel about what *we* had to go through?

"My father couldn't find a job either, not a steady one, anyway. I remember my mother telling us how he walked and walked, practically begging for work. She said he would almost offer to work for nothing rather than sit around home doing nothing. The day he applied for relief was the saddest day of his life. It broke him. He hated himself ever after. He was always against taking charity, and to have to ask for it was too much for him. When the war came he got steady work again, but my mother said he never was the same. He was always nervous, worried about losing his job, like in the thirties. He became very tight with his money; he even hoarded pennies in a bank. He was plain scared for the rest of his life. To be truthful, I think he died happy. It was like a relief for him. He was very religious. He went to mass every morning. He died with a smile on his face, and our mother, she said he had been waiting for that day for a long time. He used to say to her that whether it was Heaven or Hell the good Lord chose for him, it would be better than the worry and the trying to make ends meet of this world.

"That's the trouble, though, with Negroes. They're a superstitious lot. They have no real faith, except all that shouting they do, and they only know how to ask, not go out and earn. I know they had it bad here, but so did we all, my father and everyone else practically, except for the rich. And it's the rich, out there in the suburbs, who keep on telling us what we should do. They preach at us to take them here and let them live there, and act this way to them, and that, and so on until you get sick of hearing it all. Suddenly they're so kind, the suburban crowd. They stepped all over us and kept us out of everything, the Yankees and the college people over there at Harvard did. Now they're so good. They're all excited and worried about people, but only the Negroes get their sympathy, only them. Talking about prejudice, that's what we face, prejudice against *us*. I think we should start suing in all the courts and marching down those streets, like the Negroes. Maybe if we had done that a long time ago, we wouldn't still be so up against it now."

In nearly every conversation I hear in one way or another certain common themes: we all have it rough, the black man being only one of many in that regard; what the black man calls the civil rights movement in the North is in fact an attempt to crowd out others from schools, jobs, and opportunities of one sort or another; no one is entitled to anything "special," not when others have to sit by and get little or nothing; though somehow the black man is half-witted and immoral, he is also devious and clever, because he has managed to exact sympathy and consistent help from the well born, the well educated, who have ignored the misery of other people for decades.

At least until quite recent times many southern whites lived rather intimately with blacks. Even the poorest white man could keep company with blacks, share jokes and general talk with them. The white child could play with blacks; while growing up he could eat from their hands; as an adult he worked with them every day. The black man's position helped the white man feel on sure ground, above the uncertain social and economic waters that threaten most of us at one time or another with feelings of worthlessness or insecurity. In the particular situations of daily life, however, a given black man could be depended upon, even though, as a race, they were excluded or looked down upon.

In the North, for many white people the black man, perhaps pitied in the past, is now a constant topic of news and conversation. His presence is relatively recent in a region with its own history of religious prejudices and racial antagonisms, at times cloaked perhaps, but no less grim and brutal than those the South has lived with so defiantly.[3] While he has aroused the concern and even the devotion of many, to others his arrival and the widespread solicitous response to his arrival only confirm a number of existing fears and suspicions. Life is indeed harshly competitive; another group is coming, and at a time when jobs may be scarce. Moreover, those who favor the black man and want so earnestly to aid him are the very people who care not at all about the poor (and white) people who have been living in the cities and towns of the North for generations, or at the least before the black man came to stake out his claim.

A young lawyer — an aspiring politician — in an extremely poor section of Boston spoke as follows: "This is a slum — but it's a white slum, so no one cares about it. There's no glamour in white slums, only Negro ones. The suburban housewives and the Ivy League students, they've gone poor-crazy, but only for the colored poor. They've been pushing us around all these years before the Negroes started coming up from the South, and now they have someone to do it for them. They do a good job, the Negroes do. They act as if they own the world, just like their friends out there in the suburbs. It's contagious, you see. The ministers and the students come on Saturdays to tutor the Negro kids and take them to the park. They drive right by this neighborhood without blinking an eye. We have overcrowded schools. We have rotten buildings that should have been torn down years ago. We have lousy parks that aren't half the size they should be. A lot of the people here have jobs that barely give them enough to get by, and the others, I'll tell you, are on relief or unemployment checks or veterans' checks, or something. We have our delinquents and our dropouts — the works. Who cares, though? Who has ever cared about this neighborhood? If we have some alcoholics here, or people in the rackets, that proves we are no good. If the Negroes pull a switchblade on you and rob and steal you to the poorhouse, that means they've been persecuted, and we have to overlook everything they do and treat them as if they were God's gift to America. It's a two-faced business, if you ask me, and it's becoming worse now that they talk about juggling our kids around so that they're 'integrated.' That's when you'll get the explosion here, when they try to move our kids across the city, or bring all those little darkies here. We've got enough, enough of our own troubles."

His voice was strong, sometimes strident. At first I didn't know whether he meant everything he said, or whether he confused me with an audience in one of his campaigns. After a few months he relaxed some with me, and though he never really changed his views, he did become more philosophical: "I don't hate Negroes. A lot of people in this district do, but it's a recent thing, and I agree that the real trouble isn't the Negroes, though they sure manage to irritate people. I think a lot of this trouble between Negroes and whites will last until the whole setup in the cities changes. Probably it's true the race issue has made it better in the long run for the poor white man as well as the Negro. You can't sit here and see others demanding jobs without wondering why you don't have one either, or if you do, why it pays so little, or gives you nothing if you're fired or retire.

"I don't think we'll get through it without trouble, though. My people are really sensitive to this thing now, and unless the whole country changes, and we get as good a break as every Negro seems to think he's entitled to, then there will be resentment, and you'll have what they call the 'backlash.'

"I admit a politician is in a bind over this. He can try to lead his people, try to make them realize what's really going on; or he can ride with the tide, but make sure he wins every election; or he can really work the race thing up into something, so that he makes it worse, but wins bigger and bigger each time. I think most politicians are in the business of winning elections, so they're not going to do the first. But most of them aren't rabble-rousers, either. They just want to get elected, so it's the second choice they take. Just like everyone else does, they try to steer a middle ground, not too much one way or the other."

Through talks with people like him I think I have a fairly good sense of how cheated and nervous many white people in northern cities feel: cheated out of the most ordinary comforts and opportunities, and nervous about losing what they do have in the one war, the poverty program, which is being waged on their home territory. In many ways the poor or the "working-class" white people in our northern cities are going through an experience precisely opposite to that of the blacks. At this time in history, blacks are struggling to be affirmed, while these white people feel increasingly deserted and alone. The black man's excuse for his present condition is everywhere made known: it was not his fault, but ours. We carried him here by force and kept him in bondage for three centuries. He was not simply poor, but singled out for a very particular form of exploitation. The brutality and exclusion that he experienced have now become our national problem because the price once exacted for the black man's compliance lives on in the illiteracy and fearfulness we encouraged in him for so long.

In the northern cities a white man who is poor or barely getting by has no such past history to justify his condition. On his own, so to speak, he has to face the fact that even our expanding middle class has its definite limitations. Those limitations are now shifting in character, but by no means disappearing. While it is true that educational opportunity and the money to secure it are much more available than ever before, we are also facing severe technological problems as machines replace not only men but other machines. It no longer is fatuous to predict an astonishing productivity harnessed to a relative handful of workers.

Meanwhile, we stubbornly cling to an ethic that prefers to reward only those who can find work, while consigning all the rest to charity and contempt. Through no fault of their own, not improvidence, not ignorance, not apathy, many people simply cannot obtain the regular work they want and need. Others may have reasonably secure jobs, but they are jobs that hardly pay enough to guarantee much security against an inflationary economy. "Who can keep up with it?" a mother who was barely able to make ends meet said to me in an aside during a talk we were having on racial tensions in Boston. "The Negroes say they have nothing. Well, we have more, that's true. My husband works, and it's a steady job. We're Irish, so in this city there's no trouble there, I'll have to admit. But it's as hard as can be just living and staying even with everything. My husband has to work extra just to pay the bills. We don't have any money put away. The kids always want something. All the television does is tell you to buy, buy, buy. A few years ago my husband didn't have a job, and we didn't know where our next penny was coming from. Now he has the job all right, but it's even harder in a way. Any raise he gets means nothing compared to what happens to the cost of everything. You have to be an owner of something or a professional man to have an easy mind today."

On another occasion I found her actually envious of blacks. They were on the bottom, and at least had somewhere to go. She didn't think there was much room "up there" for her family. Moreover, the black man gets an enormous amount of sympathy and attention from people and institutions she feels possessive about. As a matter of fact, in one of the bluntest conversations I have had, she said to me:

"They may be poorer than a lot of white people, but not by very much. Anyway, what they don't get in money they more than gain in popularity these days. The papers have suddenly decided that the Negro is teacher's pet. Whatever he does good is wonderful, and we should clap. But if he does anything bad, it's our fault. I can't read the papers any more when they talk about the race thing. I'm sick of their editorials. All of a sudden they start giving us a lecture every day on how bad we are. They never used to care about anything, the Negro or anything else. Now they're so worried. And the same goes with the church. I'm as devout a Catholic as you'll find around. My brother is a priest, and I do more than go to church once a week. But I just can't take what some of our priests are saying these days. They're talking as if we did something wrong for being white. I don't understand it at all. Priests never used to talk about the Negro when I was a child. Now they talk to my kids about them all the time. I thought the church was supposed to stand for religion and eternal things. They shouldn't get themselves into every little fight that comes along. The same goes with the schools. I went to school here in Boston, and nobody was talking about Negroes and bussing us around. The Negroes were there in Roxbury, and we were here.

"Everybody can't live with you, can they? Everybody likes his own. But now even the school people tell us we have to have our kids with this kind and that kind of person, or else they will be hurt or something. Now, how am I supposed to believe everything all these people say? They weren't talking that way a few years ago. The governor wasn't either, nor the mayor. They're all just like cattle stampeding to sound like one another. The same with those people out in the suburbs. Suddenly they're interested in the Negro. They worked and worked to get away from him, of course, and get away from us, too. That's why they moved so far instead of staying here, where they *can* do something, if they mean so well. But no. They moved and now they're all ready to come back — but only to drive a few Negro kids out for a Sunday picnic. Who has to live with all this and pay for it in taxes and everything? Whose kids are pushed around? And who gets called 'prejudiced' and all the other sneery words? I've had enough of it. It's hypocrisy, right down the line. And we're the ones who get it; the final buck gets passed to us."

Can we really solve the racial problem in this country without coming to terms with the worries and fears of this woman? There is an unnerving thread of truth that runs through her remarks. She and her husband do indeed have cause to worry about jobs and money, even as blacks do. It is quite true that our newspapers, our churches, our political leaders have changed recently. Because they have learned new social concerns does not mean that the people who for years followed their leadership can fall in line easily, particularly when there are no concrete, persuasive reasons for them to do so. Moreover, the rivalrous and envious observations made by the people I have quoted ring sadly and ironically true: there is a certain snobbish and faddish "interest" in blacks from people who would not think of concerning themselves with those many white families who share slums, poor schools and uncertain employment with the blacks — all the elements of "poverty" or "cultural disadvantage."

Many of the poor white people or "lower-middle-class" white people I know in both the South and the North envy not merely the attention the black man is now getting, or even the help he so badly needs. While most of them are not aware of it — I have met a few who are exquisitely aware of it — they also envy the black man his success at finding a protest movement that persists and commands a degree of attention. *They* need a protest movement of sorts too; though likely as not they don't know they do, or don't know how to achieve it. They are stymied by the complexity of our social and economic system; it is easier to hate than to think up a way to make more and better-paying jobs available, or make a minimum income for every family into the law and principle of the land.

If such people are frustrated, then so are "we" — the comfortable, well educated, and relatively secure. This nation has yet to settle upon a policy that would aim to distribute fairly our astonishing wealth, including all its surpluses and potential productive capacities. Do we need wars and military spending to keep our economy going, or can we rearrange priorities to provide the schools, houses, hospitals, and just plain food and clothing that millions of us need and don't have? Until such problems are solved, the bitterness and resentment we see between whites and blacks will continue and perhaps increase — a reminder of man's devious ability to conceal, and thus remain at the mercy of, his real struggles.

Meanwhile, the South will continue to "go North," even if the physical exodus of rural blacks to cities like Chicago or New York were to stop completely, which is of course hardly about to happen. Northern blacks will continue to have a struggle up North as they encounter heightening resistance — and the resistance becomes more and more significant in the lives of those who carry it out, who say no to efforts aimed at bringing children to all-white schools or black families to all-white suburbs. I have in the past five years tried to describe some of that white resistance to black demands in essays for magazines, in the text of a book which also offers some two hundred photographs, in technical articles for medical and psychiatric journals, and even in a children's book.[4] The subject is hard to discuss and brings one face to face with America itself, its purposes and achievements and limitations. I can only hope that the white people I am trying to understand and write about in this chapter will not be given one more haughty and snobbishly disdainful write-up by one more observer. An observer can always find what his biases demand, no matter what people he observes, and I doubt that "middle- and lower-middle-class whites" (people I have chosen to call "white Northerners," people who feel themselves freshly caught up in a racial struggle) have been any better portrayed and characterized by social scientists than the blacks of this country, particularly since those white people have received in recent times much less attention from writers and observers of all kinds. Since blacks so often feel victimized by those who *do* observe them and write about them, perhaps the white people of our northern middle-income suburbs have at least on one count been spared more than they realize!

I believe that in work like mine one has to struggle against setting up one's various sympathies in such a way that they compete with one another. The point is not to use one set of allegiances in order to preclude a hard, clear look at those who also feel isolated and ignored and scorned. These people need allies, too — need perhaps to be assured that their problems are being recognized and worked upon. One thing I know: I hear from white people the same questions I hear in black ghettos; I hear people asking *why* or *what* or *how come* or *when*. The questions are not primarily philosophical or abstract; rather, they are questions directed at practical, immediate, concrete matters that have to do with bread and money, with the here-and-now of things. Needless to say, those "larger" issues are always lurking in the background, and sometimes they do indeed get articulated, but mostly it is something quite concrete and quite frightening that precedes the kind of questions I have chosen as subtitles in this chapter. If the handful of people to follow emerge as complicated people, full of ideas that clash, full of contradictory sentiments, full of a mixture of pride and uncertainty, then I will have succeeded in bringing to life some of their tensions and dilemmas and demonstrating how human they are.

1. Why Are They Here?

Again and again I hear her ask me that: why are they here? She doesn't really expect an answer. She knows the answer. She has read the papers. She has been to the briefings held by the school's principal and his chiefs from headquarters — those several assistant superintendents that all large school systems have. She has been "on the line," as she puts it, which means actually involved for several years in teaching black children bussed to the school she has considered hers, her very own, her life almost, she says, for some fifteen years. Still, she asks the question again and again — not in a monotonously repetitive way, but as if she has never before thought to ask, and as if she simply had to be honest and blunt, rather than as cleverly disingenuous as she believes others to be, especially "the liberals": "I'm only a schoolteacher, and that means I may not even have the right to ask

any questions. The only people who have a right to ask questions
these days are the liberals and the radicals. They tear us schoolteachers apart when they answer their own questions because
that means so much more money for them when they write their
next book about those awful schools and those terrible, terrible
men and women who work in them. I'm sick of hearing that I'm
cruel, and I'm a racist, and I don't let the 'true spirit' of children
come out, and I'm stifling and killing children and all the rest. A
lot of the people who say that and write that have never even
gone to a public school; they come into one and spend a few
months looking around, just enough to say they've been there.
The next thing you know, we're being called every bad name
there is — and the worst of it is that we have so little respect for
ourselves. I mean, a lot of us go and read those things and say,
'It's true, it's true.' You can take any profession and do that:
dwell on the bad and ignore the good, or forget to explain what
the causes of some problems are.

"I've made teaching my life. My husband died in an automobile accident, and I don't believe I'll ever really recover from
that. But I love being with children; they boost my spirits, every
day they do — and I try to give them my best. I am *not* a loafer.
I am *not* someone who mistreats a child, *any* child. I am not
'unimaginative.' We're always being called that. It's easy to call
others names. It's easy to dabble in something, write a book or an
article, then move on to something else. I've been in this building
for fifteen years now, and it's my home, you might say. I spend
the most important hours of my life here. I've been known among
the children as a good teacher, as one they want to have teach
them. The principal has written good evaluations of my work,
and I honestly don't believe he has exaggerated. I am not
ashamed to say I work hard and make sure my children learn. I
am not falsely modest.

"We were doing well here; I say we *were* doing well because I
can't say we *are* doing well. Since they brought those children
over here we haven't been the same school. I'm not saying there
hasn't been a good side to all of this; I am convinced there is a
good side because I have now taught those children, so I have

learned what I *can* teach them — which is a lot that they weren't taught, I'll tell you that. But I still find myself in a new situation, and I'm not at all convinced that this experiment has been good for either the black children or our own children who live in this district. Why are they here? Why did the school officials decide to let them come here? I ask you. No one has really answered that question, and the reason is that no one dares ask it. If you do, you're called a racist, and God forbid that should happen. The people who call names can intimidate ordinary, honest people, who have a right to ask why children from one kind of background and homelife are brought all the way across the city to another neighborhood, where the children live differently, speak differently, come from homes where there are different values, and mind you, come from homes where parents emphasize their preference for their own kind of people to their children. Is it wrong to want to live with your own people? I don't know the answer, but I'm not afraid to ask. And as a teacher I have to spend my days trying to prevent tension between children whose parents don't believe there's anything wrong staying with their race or religion and children whose parents want to get them out of their own neighborhoods. That's the way I'd put it, I'm afraid.

"But I live in this neighborhood, too, and I speak as a citizen as much as a teacher. Every time I pick up the newspaper or a magazine I read about the poor schools, how bad they are, and the poor Negroes, how they are having the worst imaginable time. The parents of one Negro child in my class finally came out to visit this school and talk with me, and do you know what they told me? They told me that *they* were sick and tired of hearing how poor the black people are, and how awful their life is, and how pathetic their homes are, and how much help they all need in the way of education and everything else. I tell you, I could have hugged them, both of them. I thought to myself: if only there were more people like them. Of course the trouble is that I haven't met some more of the parents of my Negro children. They just haven't come out here.

"Now I know they probably don't have cars, and probably

they're working late, or they have big families to take care of. It's not easy to take time off during the day or to come here for an evening meeting if you're a maid or a janitor or on welfare and with a lot of kids at home. But some of our Negro children come from homes where the father is a businessman, or he works in a factory or in an office, just like our own people do out here. I believe those Negro parents haven't come because they're shy, or maybe they're afraid. I can understand that. But what I cannot understand is why they don't worry about the fear their children have — and *do* they! Why do they send their children out here if they themselves aren't at ease coming here? Why do they feel that their children have to be in *this* school in order to learn? Why don't they agitate for better schools of their own? We have enough problems of our own out here, to be honest with you, without taking on other people's problems. It may not be the 'liberal' thing to say that, but I've noticed that the leading liberals are people who have a lot of money and send their children to private schools, or else they have a very special public school that serves their children, and because they are rich, they can get what they want out of the school officials.

"Meanwhile, the rest of us, parents and teachers alike, have to suffer. I don't mean to ask for pity. I'm just trying to say what I believe is right. In this school we need things as much as the ghetto schools do. The building is old. We don't have all the equipment we should have. My salary isn't any higher than a teacher's who works in a ghetto school. And why do we even talk about 'ghetto schools'? We could call *this* school a 'ghetto school.' We could call this neighborhood a Catholic ghetto or an Irish ghetto. Most of our children are Irish Catholics. There are a few Protestant children and a few Italians, Italian Catholic. You know, some of our Italian parents have told me that there are times when they think their children would be better off going to a school where they would have more Italian children to play with and talk to. I think of things like that when I watch three or four Negro children whispering off in some corner of the school yard. And I ask myself again: why are they here?"

Asking that question again, she goes on to provide her own

answers. They are "here" because their parents want a better life for them, a better education as a means of enabling that better life. They are "here" because integrationists and liberals and social critics and educators of various kinds all seem to feel that (in her words) "black and white must be together." They are "here" because it is not quite as crowded as it is "over there," in the ghetto's elementary schools. They are "here" because there is "social unrest" all over the country, and a lot of habits and customs are changing. Black people no longer want to be where they always were, in their own neighborhoods. They are "here" because today white people have to accept the fact that the world is different, that black people, or at least many of them, no longer will let themselves be shunted aside and kept in the worst tenement buildings and schools, and in general be denied the rights and privileges that others unthinkingly possess.

All of that she even welcomes, or sometimes feels she does. Sometimes she is not so sure. She has her doubts, about white people as well as black people: "I may be gloomy — though I'm frankly surprised to hear myself say that I am, because I usually call myself an optimist — but I don't think the white people of this country, at least the white people in a neighborhood like this one, are ready to live next door to black people. I don't think they are. We have some Protestants near here, you know; they were here before contractors started developing this area, building all those ranch houses. The Protestants hate the Irish, so they hated to see them coming. I'm Protestant, and I know. And the Irish hated the Protestants. It's better now than it used to be, but there's still some feeling, plenty of feeling, and they don't have anything to do with each other socially. The same goes with the Italian and the Irish. They mingle some, but they stick with their own a lot, too. If the Jews tried to move out here, or some other group, the Polish or the Greeks, I know there would be trouble. I just know there would. Years ago, before all *this* trouble, a Chinese family tried to move in, right near the school actually, and they changed their minds. They saw how the people reacted, the ones that would be their neighbors.

"These racial problems aren't solved by bringing out one

busful of Negro children here, and later another busful, and then calling us racist because we are afraid that soon the school will be different, and soon white children will be bussed into ghetto schools, something a lot of people keep mentioning, so it's not that our parents are letting their imaginations go wild. People around here are afraid that black families will soon be trying to move in. And black families *are* moving toward this section, and some of them *have* inquired. I think they are frankly out of their minds, those black people. What kind of parents could they be, to want to impose that kind of life on their children? I mean, there would be tension all the time, and trouble, too — I'm quite sure. We have trouble in the school, even under the watchful eyes of teachers. You can imagine what would happen if those black children weren't picked up by a bus, with a policeman nearby, but instead had to walk home, like most of the other boys and girls. The suspicion and distrust we already see between our white and black children would be worse; it would turn into outright fights."

She recognizes the other half of the story. She recognizes the familiarity she has seen develop among the black and white children, and she recognizes the respect for one another, the knowledge of one another, that she herself has remarked upon. But she can't find those "gains" as impressive as the "wrongs" she sees being done — though she is willing to talk about things hour after hour. She is a tall, buxom, blond woman, ready in a second to be candid about what she considers important. And interestingly enough, though she says she is a Protestant, her mother is half German and half French and was once a Catholic; and since her father was of mixed English and Scottish ancestry and had both Methodists and Presbyterians in his family, there are, in sum, three religious groups and four national groups in her "background" — a fact she mentions with pride. But what worked in her family would not work in other situations, or so she believes: "There is a difference between being a mixture of English and French and German and Scottish, and being a mixture of white and black. There just is. White people and black people look different, very different. Even the Irish and the Italians don't get along. And among many Protestants and Catholics, marriage across religious lines is still unthinkable. Don't you see that what was possible for my parents is not possible or desirable for many others?

"Should we insist that racial confrontations become the rule of the day? Should we force people into various neighborhoods? Should we ignore the feelings of millions of people and ignore their right to choose their neighbors? What is more, I'm not afraid to be as honest as I possibly can be: my parents actually looked somewhat alike, because they were both blond, and they both came from the same kind of background. In their case the families have been in this country for over one hundred years, closer to one hundred and fifty, and they thought of themselves as *Americans*, not English or German. But the Irish and Italians and Polish people and the Jews are different. They think of themselves as not only Americans, but Irish and Italians and so on. I mean, they have names and traditions and customs that set them apart, and that they like for that very reason. I know this is complicated. I'm not arguing about what is rational; I'm saying that people have feelings, and I'm not going to forget what those feelings are. And how could I, when I hear what I do from my fellow teachers and the parents I see — and the children? If I were to tell you what I've heard said about black people by white people and white people by black people in the last few years, as a result of this civil rights business and the bussing program and the violence and the demonstrations, then you would agree that it is arguable whether bussing is a lovely ideal, a beacon of hope to hold up to all white people who live near here and the black people. I think black parents especially should stop and think a little about some of this trouble, and maybe decide that it's best for them to improve their own condition and obtain the respect of others — and self-respect! — that way."

She wants me to understand very clearly that she is a "moderate." She is not nearly as angry and truculent as some of her fellow teachers, let alone many of the parents she knows and hears talk; they say awful things, can be exceedingly crude — though she understands why. They are people who (she is con-

vinced) have no one to speak to. And they are people for whom
no one really speaks: not the newspapers and not the television
commentators and not the magazines, and especially not "the
educational television network and the university people." She is
utterly and completely disgusted by that latter twosome; they
drive her to unreason, she freely admits, but with good cause: "I
am tired of those prejudice programs, those programs about
black this and black that, and all those sneaky little lectures
meant to make a teacher like me feel like the worst person who
ever lived. I am tired of being told I'm unfair, and I'm against
other races, and I'm not as intelligent and sensitive as those
educational television people and those editorial writers. What
do they know about my situation out here? They have all their
children in the best colleges. They have one son in the Peace
Corps in Africa someplace, or South America, and they have a
daughter who just loves the Indians and works on a reservation,
and they themselves are always lecturing to us about the ghetto,
the ghetto — where they probably go and do some volunteer
work, for all I know. Maybe there's *another* son doing that,
working in the ghetto as a volunteer for six months — when he
isn't throwing a rock at someone or telling us that I shouldn't
even have my children salute the American flag any more, because patriotism is 'anachronistic,' that's what I heard on our
educational television network the other night.

"I was sitting in my chair trying to relax when on came this
long-haired student who talked as if he had a potato in his
mouth. With him was a black man who looked as if he was going
lion-hunting or something. And how his own people would be
embarrassed, except they're probably too smart to watch that
channel! Anyway, the two of them started talking about 'White
America' and how racist it is, and about teachers and how they
are so terrible to the child, who is so 'impressionable,' and about
patriotism and how it is anachronistic now, since there is only
one world, you know. I just switched them off. I said to myself:
they are so full of themselves, so wrapped up in their precious,
smug, little world, with their phony English accents and their
phony African costumes, that I'm not going to sit in my own

living room and take that. I didn't swear at them, as some teachers do. And I didn't have a fit, the way I've seen my neighbors here do. I just said: enough is enough for me. Let them speak to the people that agree with them. They'll all sit and congratulate each other on how clever and modern and progressive they are, and that's fine, so long as I don't have to sit and hear that kind of talk.

"One of these days, though, the television people and the newspaper people are going to get smart. They are going to realize that you can't ignore millions and millions of people; you can't treat them as if they are so much dirt, or little children to be pushed around and lectured to about how bad they are and about how they must grow up and change. I don't do that with the children in my class in school, and no one is going to treat *me* like that, either — like a bad child who has no say in what he can do. I want those people from the universities, the students and their professors, and the other people, the liberals trying to make these social and educational experiments and changes, I want them all to come here — come here instead of going to their swank resorts. I want them to *listen* and *learn,* and stop their endless talk about what *has* to happen and what *must* happen. If these social and educational changes are brought about, who is affected? Rich liberals? The high and mighty in our universities? We hear that you can't go overseas and impose your own values on another nation, and you can't, if you're white, go and impose your values and habits on the blacks. Then the reformers want to do it on us; they want to tell us what we have to do and what we ought to like doing. The ghetto needs 'community control,' they tell you, or an Indian reservation needs to have the right to decide its own destiny, but not *this* community. No one is suggesting that *we* have a right to decide for ourselves if children from a totally different and far-off section ought to come into our schools. No one is suggesting that *we* have a right to say to outside people: leave us alone and let us live the way we want and stop pushing us to do this and do that and stop trying to impose things on us and stop trying to moralize at us. Look instead at yourselves. Look instead at your own hypocrisy and your own dishonesty.

"I really do believe that some of our intellectuals and our rich liberal types look down on the average workingman or the teacher or the nurse or the person who owns a gas station and is trying to make a living. They like to champion the Negro or the Indian or the people in Africa and Asia. And here is the explanation: they pushed their way up to graduate from those big-name schools, and they went on to make their pile of money, so now they are turning on their own past and trying to forget what their fathers were or their grandfathers. They are trying to pretend they love everyone, but the ones they love are the ones who are different from themselves and don't live near them. Well, you don't have to be so smart to figure out what's going on, and if even I get disgusted, you can imagine what a lot of other people feel like. No wonder I hear talk of buying guns, and no wonder I hear some terrible, terrible language from people who usually don't swear like that in public. That's why I ask you: isn't there another way to do all of this?"

As she gets to the end of her remarks, when they are long and full of avowed indignation, she almost invariably asks such a question, which by then is usually put forward with less vehemence and outrage than the declarations that have come earlier. She is, I suppose one can say, quieting down and trying to plead that in the main the people she considers her people have been used as the brunt of criticisms which maybe ought have been directed more widely and sensitively — even directed at those who make the criticisms, those who have at their disposal cameras and typewriters and made-to-order audiences, those who sneer at civil servants and their "reactionary" politics, and at factory workers and their "limitations" or their "bigotry." Certainly, that teacher and others have made a point of letting me know how quickly they can pick up what they call by various names, prominent among them "the pat-on-the-head approach," by which they mean the effort to see them — American citizens, American workers, American parents — as "people who have to grow," as "people who need to change, and will, given leadership." They want leadership all right, they say, and they recognize the need to grow and change and reform and innovate, and in general do a lot of the action that those verbs and others suggest and imply. What they do not want to hear, what enrages them, are observations that in essence make of *them* a special "problem," which others, a coalition of well-to-do intellectuals and agitated students and black militants will somehow "work on" and "solve." Nor do they like it to be stated or suggested that they are prickly or nervous or overly proud or defensive; that line of analysis smacks of condescension.

I think the people whom I charily call "white Northerners" want to be understood as no less in conflict than others. The woman who declares, "People almost never say only one thing" is the same woman who can ask me, "Why are they here?" She is the same woman who asks, "Why is it that human beings choose only to stay with their own kind, and why is it that white people all over the world don't get along well with black people?" And she is the same woman who can state that "black people are not all alike" — something that she discovered recently when black children were brought out to the school she calls "hers," and she for the first time came to teach them and listen to them and watch them and meet a few of their parents.

2. What Have We Done?

When the black children first came to the school her nine-year-old boy and seven-year-old girl attend, she spoke as if she faced something far more awful than a "crisis." I thought, listening to her, that the apocalypse might be finally at hand. She spoke about how ineffective her opposition was doomed to be: "People don't listen to someone like me. I went to our club at the church, and we all said that: no one is going to care about us. The only people that get themselves heard on television are the colored people. They stand on the street and threaten everyone and tell their people to burn down the city, and I have to see that on my television station. And our newspaper listens to any colored man, no matter what crazy thing he says, just because he's colored. But do the ordinary white people ever get any space in the paper? The answer is no."

She says she is that, an ordinary white person; she used to be "just ordinary," but now she emphasizes that she is white. For three years her children have gone to school with some black children who are bussed several miles, so no longer does she feel that the world is coming to an end. But she does continue to have her serious misgivings — about black people in general, and the ways in which one hundred black fellow students affect her children. Nor is she a peculiar or especially disturbed or anxious person. It so happens that I have met, week in and week out, for several years with her and thirteen other mothers like her; they all belong to a community whose men work in factories, work in offices, work as civil servants of one kind or another. The homes are two-family homes, with an occasional single-family one. The streets in the neighborhood are clean and lined with trees, with cars, with street lamps and with carefully tended lawns. To this woman and her friends that street means a lot: it is a quiet and respectable street, I am told by them, and it is near a church, near a school, near a drugstore, near a supermarket, near a busline, near a bank, near a hardware store, near "everything you want and need," is the way it is put. And now everything seems in jeopardy; even with the first scare over, the mothers continue to be fearful.

The mother of the boy and girl speaks her fears passionately and with bitterness: "What have we done, I ask you? Do you know that the city is not only letting these total strangers come over here, but some of them don't go home in the bus, as they should, but just stay around? I wouldn't want my children sent to a strange part of town when there is a neighborhood school for them to attend. All I hear is that in the colored sections the schools are very old and crowded. Well, they are old here, and they're full here. With these colored kids, there isn't a single seat vacant. The difference is that we teach our children to be respectful of property, even if it *is* old, and with the colored people, it's a different story. My son says they are a restless bunch of kids. They are always moving around, and they give everything wear and tear. The colored boy next to him sits there and his leg is jiggling all day, up and down. And he wears sneakers to school, and in recess all he does is run and jump and try every piece of equipment they have there out in the yard. My son says he thinks the kid has ants in his pants, and he's always breaking his pencil and dropping his eraser, and he opens and closes that desk of his a hundred times a day. Now I ask you, what is wrong? I've watched them getting off the bus, and they're just not like our children, and no one, no doctors and no college professors and no politicians, can tell me anything different."

Perhaps she is angry at me, I think. She *is* angry at me, I later decide. In the beginning I tried to listen and occasionally respond - but only to restate her own remarks. After a while I realized that she also wanted to discuss things with me. She asked me frankly for my thoughts, and I offered them, in as respectful and quiet a manner as I could. I have never looked on it as my role to educate that "group" of mothers or get "therapeutic" with them or "change" them; they agreed to meet and keep me informed about things going on in the neighborhood and I agreed to speak up (when they asked me to do so) and tell them what I had seen elsewhere and what I believed I was learning in the course of my work. We always talked rather informally, and I certainly did get a continuing sense of what was happening in the school as well as in their lives. Yet, I am a doctor and from a university. From time to time I have made it clear that I felt close to those political leaders who wanted to make changes, plenty of them, rather than congratulate all of us on how big and rich and mighty we are. So, when the mother talked about "doctors" I wondered out loud whether I had become a stand-in for all the other "bureaucrats and social planners" who were "messing things up," in the words of that same mother who mentioned doctors and college professors.

No, the mothers said, I was wrong. They implied that I was really going mad a little, or at the very least I was just too self-conscious, too worried, too taken up with noticing everything and giving everything so much importance, so much significance. They did not offer me any "interpretations" of my implied "interpretation" — that I was becoming a living representative, as it were, of white, upper-middle-class liberals — but they did say some moving and instructive things. To call upon our same mother again: "No, no. I'll tell you what *is* bothering us. We have been told that we are prejudiced and that we should be taught how to be unprejudiced. Someone in the school department wants us to go and hear a psychologist. He's supposed to clear our minds of bigotry. I went to my minister, because it was his idea, I heard. I told him to mind his own damn business. I think the church should leave us alone when it comes to some of these problems. I get sick, watching the ministers marching in the street, demonstrating, and taking sides against their own government and their own people. There are times when I think our minister cares more about the colored people than he does about us, members of his own parish. I didn't say it to him, but my husband did. He said we don't want any movies and any college people telling us our minds are sick, and we don't want to be told we're bigots and all that, because the fact is that we're *not;* we're not prejudiced at all.

"I wish I could say it the way he did. When he gets excited, he really knows how to talk. He's not afraid. I am; I'll have to admit it. I hear those sermons about *prejudice* and *bigotry*, and I feel as if I've been a bad girl, and I should be punished. Then I go to visit the school, and the teachers, a lot of them, are on our side; but the school department and the governor and the mayor or someone send those psychologists to give us a talking-to — there's so-and-so, and he's connected with around ten universities, they say when they introduce him to us, and he's supposed to make us think differently, I guess. And my God, you can't pick up the paper and you can't turn on the television without reading something about the poor colored people and all their troubles and seeing a documentary on how they're all nice, and they've been punished by us — me! — all these years, and we owe it to them, we owe *everything* to them. I've never been bad to any colored person. I don't know them. But America is racist, they tell you. I'll tell you what I believe: I believe there is an effort on the part of some to make people like us, the ordinary white people of the country, feel as if we're criminals and get an inferiority complex, you might say."

I told her that I certainly hoped I wouldn't say anything that would add to the already large stock of accusations she had just mentioned. I told her that I believe one accusation after another does little to help people see things more clearly; on the contrary, one gets defiant or moody or disgusted not only with oneself but the brazen nerve of others, who display very little good sense (not to mention generosity or breadth of understanding) when they push people further and further into a corner — to the point that they can only yield and hate themselves for doing so, or strike out in what is felt to be self-defense.

She interrupted me to say that each person has a right to be heard, and not any "one group." I told her I certainly agreed, but I said I believed there are indeed people ready to respond to people like her, including some of our very highest and most influential leaders. Well, yes, she did not feel entirely without support and understanding. Nevertheless, she felt increasingly put-upon these days, and she wanted me and the others in that room to hear the sources of her discontent: "Everywhere you turn, there's a poster or a commercial on television that says the colored people are like other people, and we should have them next door, and we should apologize because we had them as slaves, and it goes on and on. On my mother's side my grandparents moved down here from Canada; on my father's side they were farm people in Maine. They never had any slaves. They were working people, and so were my parents, and so am I. What is all this business about racism, racism? Am I supposed to spend my whole life thinking about the colored, the colored, the colored? I never gave them a thought at all, one way or the other, until the last few years, and now I'm told I'm a racist, and I'm trying to kill off all of them, and a lot of other nonsense.

"I believe that every single person is fine, no matter what his color or the church he goes to, so long as he doesn't bother other people and cause a lot of trouble. I'm not against colored people. I've never had anything to do with them, one way or the other. The same goes for my husband. He works for the milk company.

He delivers milk. He gets up at five o'clock in the morning. He comes home dead tired. He never sees colored people, and he doesn't have a thing in the world against them. All we want is peace and quiet. We bought the house, and we'll be paying for it the rest of our lives. We'd be crazy if we said we'd like colored people to move in here, and then we'd have a house that was worthless, but we'd still have to keep up the mortgage payments. Do the people who write those editorials, do they think we ought to let this whole neighborhood be a colored neighborhood? Should I stay here if the colored move in and surround me? Is it wrong for me to want to live near people like myself, and near my husband's cousins, two of them?

"It seems to me that the people who do the most talking on this subject have a lot of money, and they can live wherever they want. Even our minister, his house goes with the church. He can change churches, if worst comes to worst. And the church, that's been a great disappointment to us, the way the church has behaved lately. All my life I've gone to church. My uncle is a minister, himself; he's a Methodist. He was the bookish one in my father's family. I've been in many churches and heard many sermons since I was a child. It's only in the last few years that these churches have gone crazy over the colored, and they're also against the government more than they're for it. We still have the American flag in our church, but I really wonder whether one day I'll come and it'll be there no more. My uncle says you can't just suddenly switch on people and expect them to go along so easy, and he's right. I was brought up to expect a minister to give you support and lift up your spirits, not to tear into you and make you feel so low and bad that — well, that you don't want to go back next Sunday and hear it again, how you have these prejudices, and the colored people are suffering, and white people don't give them a chance.

"Who gave my husband a chance? He made a chance for himself. He works so hard that I worry for him. He even does carpentry on the side. We've got to meet those bills. I was trained as a nurse, and I have been putting in some hours at the hospital or on private cases since the kids are in school. Now, all of a

sudden, our kids have these strangers in school with them. I don't
know what the colored kids are actually learning here that's so
much better than what they could be learning where they live, in
their own schools. The teacher told us it's not the same. Before,
everybody was relaxed. Now if kids fight, like they always do,
and one is colored and the other is white, there's no telling what
will happen. You might have one of those colored parents phon-
ing the principal; or worse than that, some snotty white minister
or college student will come and say he's over here 'on behalf of'
the colored people. My boy says that a lot of the time he forgets
about the colored kids even being there, and my girl says they're
a nuisance, but they don't bother her, and they mostly just keep
to themselves. Well, they could keep to themselves much better if
they'd stay where they live.

"I'm sure they are going to try to move in here. They'll hop,
skip, and jump their way toward us, inch by inch they will. I
have a cousin in Connecticut, and it happened to them — the
first thing it was children brought in to the school, and the next
thing it was houses they wanted, the colored. It's got to the point
that you have to look ahead and try to figure out if you're safe for
one year or five years or what. I tell my husband: we should sell
the house while we can get a good price, and then rent someplace. That way, you can get away fast. It's terrible when you're
in America and you have to think that way. I suppose if we had
more money and could afford to live way out there in one of
those plush suburbs, we'd be all right. No colored person can
afford to live with the rich, and that's why the rich can afford to
give us all those sermons on how they favor integration and they
believe in treating everyone equal. I believe in treating everyone
equal, too. It's just that no one's fighting for my rights, only me.
The colored have the papers and the television behind them, and
the professors and the college students and a lot of the politicians
and a lot of rich people who like to *help* the poor out but make
sure they're far enough away from them — and from people like
us, too."

Am I to point out to her the various inconsistencies she has
expressed, and pursue her and pursue her until she agrees that

through her opinions runs a streak of obstinate unreason? Am I
to listen as best I can, and see how worried and fearful she is,
how hard she fights for what she has, how nervous she is about
what the future holds, how confused she is by events which move
along rather fast — events for which she was never prepared by
the schools she attended or indeed the churches she went to or
even the particular newspapers she read? As she points out, the
churches and newspapers have only recently begun to speak out
so loud and clear on certain issues. And anyway, she doesn't read
a lot of magazines and books, or "analyze" events and take "positions" with respect to them. But she and her hardworking and not
enormously well-paid husband and their young children live with
and are involved in and worry about those events — to the point
that what we call "events" or "issues" she calls "the biggest
danger we have ever faced."

I have been pressed to make my observations and comments,
and maybe they will have their place and their value. But that
woman and others next door and across the street and "over on
the avenue" and "down near the square" all continue to feel
apprehensive and ignored, even, in cloudy moments, betrayed by
ministers and newspaper editors and others who "change their
tune and expect everyone else to come running along." As I hear
in those meetings we have, "people have their limits" and "you
can ask only so much of people." I hear that last statement rather
often, and sometimes when I am driving home I say to myself
that I have seen people change a lot, an incredible amount, but I
have to add that when people don't want to change so much as
hold their own, they will let anyone who has other wishes for
them know exactly what they think.

3.   Where Are We Going?

Look buddy, you tell me, you answer me: where are we going?
Now, I ask you, is a guy like me supposed to sit back and watch
this country sold down the river by the crazy people? Take the
Negroes: I never used to mind them! I used to feel sorry for
them. If someone came up and talked to me ten years ago, he

would have said that this-here guy is the kind who says: live and let live. I still say that, but when people won't let me live, I'm not going to sit back and let them walk all over me without a fight. I read in the paper that there's "tension" over at the school. I read that the white kids and the black kids are fighting all the time. I didn't need to read that. I know that. I have a boy who's there. He's told me what goes on. What I need to know is how long will the white people of this country sit back and be pushed around by two types, *two:* The Negroes, always wanting more, more welfare and more neighborhoods to take over, and the rich crowd of do-gooders who never live in the city, or if they do, they're up in some penthouse and their kids are hundreds of miles away in some fancy private school.

My son Walt is a good kid, and he wouldn't make anything up. He comes home, and he's scared. He says they can be tough, the Negroes. He says some of them will tell the white kids that they'd better watch out, or they'll find a knife inside them. What the Hell is a white kid from a good family supposed to say when he hears that? I'm afraid. I wish I had more money. I wish we could move out, way out, into a nice country town where there are no Negroes, and where people see the American flag flying and they say: good, it's the best flag in the world, and I'm proud to call it mine.

I used to wonder why we're having all this trouble. I used to say: it beats me — that was my answer when a guy would ask me what in Hell is happening right before our eyes. But now I think I know. Now I think I can answer my own question. I know where we are going. We're going soft, that's what I think. We're becoming a country of bleeders and weepers and groaners. Everyone worries about the poor Negro. I'm not poor, and I'm not rich. I'm a salesman, and everything I make comes out of my own sweat and blood. I'm middle-class. And let me say something real surprising: I don't want a cent of help from anyone, and even if I lost my job I wouldn't want any help, and what is more, I don't want sympathy or pity or a lot of special breaks. My father didn't have one single penny to give me. Everything I have, I worked and paid for. I'm on the road day in, day out. I'm on the line: I have to sell myself and then sell my product. And no one does me a favor. They buy what I sell because they need it. They buy from me because I get their ear and they listen and it clicks with them — what I say and what they know they need anyway. If I was a Negro, if I was a black man, if I was poor and living in some slum, I'd say to myself: this is no good, no good at all, and I'm going to do something, I'm going to get out of here, so help me God.

What's happened to good, old-fashioned willpower, that's what I want to know. I'm not so old. I'm in my forties, but that isn't being eighty — and yet I'll be having breakfast, and I'll hear my son Walter talking about high school and what's going on there, and I say to myself that this is terrible, absolutely terrible, what is happening. The Negroes have moved into what used to be a quiet, old neighborhood, and their kids are in the high school, and they don't get along with our kids, and the grown-ups, I don't think they get along any better. My son says there are tables where only black kids sit and tables where there's only whites. When I was in school there wasn't a single Negro. Now, my son goes to a school and they're a quarter of the total, and *rising*.

They have large families. I can't figure why. If I was poor, I'd want to keep my family small. As it is, we only have three: two boys and a girl. Walt says the Negroes who are more polite are like us; they're the better-off ones. He can tell. They dress better. They bring better food for their lunches. Walt says he talks with them, the higher type, you could say. But a person is a person to me, even if he's very poor. I'm not against anyone before I know him. With Negroes, I'll admit, it's something else: they don't want to make friends with white people, just as we stay away from them. They stick with their own. My son says he even tried once to sit with them, because he was talking to this guy, a Negro, and they didn't finish their talk while they were in line waiting for the milk, so Walt kept walking beside the guy and talking and the next thing, Walt was sitting down and he was still talking and he was starting to eat his lunch — when all of a sudden he noticed everyone at the table was staring at him, and boy, did he know fast what was wrong! What did you do, son, I asked him, naturally; and he said that he didn't for the life of him know what to do. I guess he weighed the alternatives and decided to stay. He said he gobbled his lunch down so fast that his stomach hurt for the rest of the day. He said he didn't really *decide* to stay at the table or leave; he was too scared even to move, so he stayed. Later he got a razzing from his friends. But the worst of it was that the Negro kids weren't friendly. They didn't say a word while he was sitting there, and later on, he says, in the class, they looked at him as though he was some goofball.

Well, the kid learned something. I told him that. I said: we learn by our mistakes. I said: what's a life for, if you don't stumble and then pick yourself up and keep moving? I said: I know how it is; I've slipped and kicked myself for it later. This is a strange world we live in. Things are moving so fast that you have to run just to stand still. Look at what's happening to the dollar. Look at the Communists and how they keep us on the alert all over. Look at this race problem we've got. There's not a city in America where the Negroes aren't testing us. That's why I say that if a country is going to be on top, it's got to draw a line and say: this is the limit, this is as far as you can go, and no further, unless you want to fight. That's what we've got to let the Communists know. And the same thing goes for us here at home: if any one group starts trying to get special and preferential treatment, then they've got to be reminded that there's only so far they can get with that tactic.

I'm not in favor of force or violence. I don't like these crazy demonstrations. The whole country is in danger. We've got to have a return to a lawful society. I'm against racists, too. I can't stand the cheap, loudmouthed types; there's some good to what they're called in the South: poor white trash. I was stationed in the South during the war, the Second World War, and I saw them, the red necks they are called, and the word fits them. We have them up here, I know. We have our northern red-necks. Some of those labor people, they push for higher wages with no respect for the country and its problems. They're like the Negroes, a lot of the labor unions are: they just want more for themselves, and the public be damned. In this town we try to live respectable lives. We're out of the control of the city and all the crooked politics there. But I guess we're close enough! I guess we're too close. They started crossing the town line, just into that one little section, and the next thing you know, we had a problem here, a race problem.

Now, where are we supposed to go? I ask myself that a lot when I'm driving that car of mine. Just where? If I made the money a big industrialist does, I'd have an estate way out in the country, and then I could be safe. But I'll never be rich, just pretty well-off. I'm no ordinary salesman. I do better than most. I make as much as a lot of the people I sell to. I do better than some doctors and lawyers do. We're all in the same jam in this town, the doctors and lawyers and business people. What do we do when our kids go to high school, and we've got this problem that comes out of one section of town? I'm not too worried about our neighborhood — because, Hell, let's be honest: there aren't that many Negroes that can afford the house I have. I've put a lot into that place. It's the best hedge against inflation I know. If one Negro came in here, I'd say: let's see what he's like; and if he's an OK guy, and he hasn't got any crazy, way-out ideas in his head, then fine, let him stay. Now, if they started trying to mass on us, you know, and drive us out — and I hear they'll do that, block-bust, it's called — then we'd have to get together and decide what we're going to do. Do we stick together and fight them? Do we go our separate ways and all lose out in the end? It's like a war, when you come to think about it.

I went to college, then I graduated from business school. I was educated to be thoughtful. I don't like to talk about a lot of this. I mean, I don't like to sound as if I'm losing my head, the way a lot of the Negroes do. And I'll admit, we have our cheap element of whites. They hate the Negro. They're probably threatened by them. But here in this town we've always tried to be fair. When they came in, they bought houses from our poorer white people, and believe it or not, I thought it wasn't such a bad idea. There's a certain kind of white person who's no good, and there's a certain kind of Negro who is quiet and respectful. They know how to work, too — if only they decide they want to.

Now it's different, though. The Negroes say they want "equality," but really they want a part of everything. I told the boys at the club: one day there will be a knock on that door, and you'll see, you won't be able to relax and play your golf game, either. That's the way it's going; that's where we're headed. We've got to keep our heads and not run wild. We've got to remember: this is the best country the world has made. Let those who criticize it do half as well — someplace else. Let them go where they want. And with the Negro, he's going to have to learn that he can work and get all he can get, a million dollars if he's lucky. It's up to the individual. But damn if this country should be turned into one big socialistic ant heap, with handouts for every colored face and every lazy white man. I hope and pray we're not coming to that. I hope and pray.

We've got to save America, not destroy it. That's what I say, and nobody can make me change my mind on that; I don't care what he says about this "civil rights" business. The country is more important than the demands of any one group. Doesn't that make sense? And why is it that some people see it otherwise, and march and demonstrate and make all these demands and succeed in tearing us all apart?

4. Laura

Laura was seven when her school became the subject of considerable controversy. "Seven is a good age," Laura told me when she was seven years, eleven months and five days old. She wasn't sure what it would be like after her birthday, after she turned eight, but she did make a point of letting me know that she hoped the third grade might prove to be "easier" than the second. I asked her to write out her own prescription, tell me exactly what she would want in the way of improvement, exactly how things might get "easier," if she could have an important say. Word for word, I said: "If you could have your way, how would you make sure the third grade would really turn out to be easier?" She replied with a long silence. Eventually she raised her head a little, darted with her eyes toward my face, then quickly turned her head away and spoke. She spoke as if to an audience, as if she was making a public statement, as if her mother's words had finally achieved a certain power over her that could no longer be stayed. Indeed, she spoke like her mother, and the words she used were her mother's: "If the school went back to normal, and they left, the colored kids, we would have it good again — no trouble."

Laura is the only daughter and youngest child of a man who works as a foreman in a factory and a woman who on occasion, now that Laura is in school, works for a secretarial pool. The mother describes her work and her family this way: "I have two sons, and they're growing up fast. John is twelve, and he's becoming a real man. Ted is ten. He has a lot of friends, and I don't see him much, what with school and his baseball or football after school. Laura is our favorite I guess, being a girl. Her dad adores her, and I must admit, after two boys, I was glad to have a girl. They're easier to bring up, I believe. Even now Laura helps me take care of the house. I try to make some extra money by doing typing. There's a company that takes in work, and they call me up and I go there and type a few hours, I'd say three times a week. Laura is very good at taking care of herself. She dusts and she loves to use that vacuum cleaner. I'll come home and she'll tell me she's 'done' the living room, and when she says she has, she means it. Our next-door neighbor keeps an eye on her if I'm not around when she comes home from school."

All of that sounds pleasant and not very remarkable. But when she used the word "school" she came to the end of one train of thought and began another. The word "school" started this off: "This past year has been awful, and there were days when I really wondered if I should ever be away when Laura comes home. We had a nice school, with no trouble at all there, and then the next thing we all knew, the school wasn't normal any more. It was a different place, because the colored said they wanted to come over, and our school officials tried to stop them but failed. Now, all we have is trouble."

Later on she would qualify that observation. Less pressed by her own anger and rhetoric, she could almost casually acknowledge that things had not been "all bad," that from day to day Laura had not witnessed "racial trouble," that maybe over the long run "a few colored" in the school would be all right — but no more than a few, she hastens to add. Nevertheless, Laura has gone through a difficult time in school, that she knows — and that she finds unforgivable: "I'll never forget what a year that child had; it's a shame when a child can't even have a quiet time in the second grade. I shudder to think of what it'll be like in this country when she gets up to high-school age."

Laura herself had all along been quite able to talk about what she saw and heard during that eventful year: "They brought them over in a bus, and some of the mothers were there, right in front of the building, and they were trying to get the colored people to go back home. But they didn't. There were the police there, a lot of them. One of the police was the head, and he kept on telling the other police what to do. They had to take the colored kids into the school, the police did. My mother didn't go there. She wasn't one of the mothers standing there. She said she agreed with the mothers, but she couldn't bring herself to stand in the street with a sign, but maybe she should have, she says.

"Now the colored kids come every day, and there's no policeman around. We have some trouble sometimes. The teacher has to tell them that she can't understand what they're saying. They must go home and tell their parents what the teacher says, because a man came to the school, he's a lawyer, and he complained to the principal that there's prejudice. That's happened maybe three times, I think. I hear the colored kids talk, so I know all about what's going on.

"I like some of the colored kids, and some I don't like. They are like us; they look different, but after a while I forget that they're colored. There's one of them, he's a big kid, and a lot of the boys are scared of him. He pushed two kids, two white kids, and they fell down and had to go see a doctor. Then the teacher said there wasn't going to be any more of that, and we're not animals, and this isn't a zoo. So, then the kid stuck out his tongue at the teacher, the colored kid did, and then the teacher told the kid to get out of the room and stay in the hall until she called him back in. Well, a little while later she did, but he was all gone, and do you know: he's never returned to us. The teacher told my friend's mother that she was very glad, because he was really tough, that boy, and he was always looking for trouble."

Laura, like her mother, wants to observe rather than take part in things. She has managed to keep her distance from the six black children in her room; that is, she has not fought with them, as some children have, nor has she played with them, as other children have. She has two friends, Mark and Sally, and together they keep themselves busy during those recess times and lunchtimes, when there is indeed a chance to talk a lot and have fun with other children. "I was told by my mother," Laura once reminded me, "that it's best to stay out of people's way if you don't know them, and the colored kids come from another part of the city, and there's none of them living where we live."

Does she think those children would want to live near her? Does she think they like being at school with her? And in general, what does she make of them? How are they doing, now that she has had a chance to watch every day for a number of months? Always the first answer, rather naturally, is a noncommittal "all right I guess" or "I don't know" or "maybe" or "pretty good." But Laura likes to talk, again like her mother, and so she can be depended upon to amplify her terse characterizations. What she needs to do is hear yet another question, because the second inquiry tells her that the listener knows she has some ideas and wants to hear them and, indeed, would be disappointed if he did not hear them. Then comes the story or two, the expression of amusement, the question of her own to ask, the statement of doubt or the admission of error or the declaration of pleasure or the inscrutable remark which is elaborated upon and unraveled and made quite clear, all by the girl herself.

"They've been OK, pretty good, the colored kids," Laura told me one day after school. I decided that after six months of talking with her I could get a little pushy with my questions, so I asked, "How good?" She was properly confused. Did I want a

grade for them, some exact evaluation? How is she supposed to
know "how good?" She sat in her chair and puzzled over my
question until I decided I had been dumb, and I had better pull
myself together and demonstrate more intelligence and tact to
the young lady — who must have been thinking, so I thought
later, that it was not her place to make quantitative judgments
about her classmates. (And what is wrong, anyway, with that
man? How can he possibly believe that a question like his can be
answered?) In any event, I next asked Laura whether she could
think of some good moments she's had in class and some not-so-
good ones — hoping thereby to bypass for a while our previous
discussion of her "colored" classmates. We certainly hadn't always talked about racial issues, and now was a time to speak
more broadly about school and home, I felt. Laura at times
wanted very much to discuss how things were going with the
school's new students, and at other times — *this* time, I believed — wanted no part of such a discussion.

"Most of the time it's good in school," she said right off. She
seemed pleased to have, at last, something she could dig into and
expand upon: "We all play, and then the teacher tells us to hush,
and then we do. The best time comes later, after we've done our
work, and we have juice and cookies. She lets us get up and walk
around and talk — but no games and no fooling around, and we
have to keep our voices low. Janice is one of the colored girls,
and she always goes across the room to see her friend Henrietta.
They won't leave the room without each other. The teacher asked
them one day if they were related, and they said no, but they live
near each other."

She had on her own moved the discussion toward one that had
to do with the "adjustment," as some would have it, of "colored"
children like Janice and Henrietta; so with only the slightest
prodding from me I could hear her sharp and sharply worded
observations: "They seem scared. That's what I think. They don't
talk to you unless you talk to them. Sometimes they do, I guess.
But mostly, Janice and Henrietta and the others stick together.
When they forget, they'll break up and play with us. If the
teacher tries to get them to scatter, they obey her. The teacher

says, 'Now I want all of you to scatter and meet new people!' She's kidding us, but she means it. She gives us a talk sometimes about not sticking with only one person at recess.

"There's a boy in our room who is very nice. He's colored, but he dresses very good. He wears a bow tie every day. I asked him if he knew how to make the knot. I told him I said to my daddy one morning when he put on a bow tie that we have Jerry at school, and he has a bow tie on all the time. Daddy told me to ask Jerry if he had a real knot that he made himself, and he probably didn't, Daddy thought. I asked Jerry and he said yes, he did. The teacher heard him, and she said, 'Jerry, that's not a knot you made yourself, is it?' Then Jerry said it wasn't, and he showed me he could pull the tie and it would snap back, because there was an elastic, and he just put it around his neck, like an elastic band, and it looked like my daddy's tie, only Daddy stands before the mirror and it takes him too much time, because he has to have the tie 'just right,' my mother says, and it's not easy to do.

"I try to stay out of trouble. Jerry fights with some of the boys. He's strong. The other day he said one kid called him a nigger. He went and told the teacher. The teacher told both of them they should stop fighting and she didn't want any noise. She wanted them to shut up and stay shut up, she said. Then Jerry talked anyway; he turned and talked with his friend Richey. Richey is colored, too. The teacher sent them both out of the room. But she must have been afraid they would go and leave like the big colored boy did after she put him out in the hall, because no sooner were they out than she called them back in — and they came. They didn't cause any more trouble that day. She kept on walking up and down the aisles, and when she came to their desks, she stopped and looked at what they were doing. She told them they were doing OK. She had her ruler in her hand. We know she means business when she walks around with that ruler. She'll tap you on the shoulder if she likes what you're doing, and if she doesn't, she tells you what's wrong. The colored kids are scared of her, I believe. I've heard them say so. They call her Miss Whitey. Her name is Miss Cunningham, but they still say

Miss Whitey. My mother says they're rude if they do that. I told her that if you're colored, you notice the skin color of the white person. I think the teacher notices their color, too — and that's why they call her Miss Whitey. If she's against them, they become against her."

Shortly after that conversation, Laura drew for me a picture of her school. It was one of some twelve pictures of that school she has done for me in the course of the four years (as of the time I write this) I have known her. Sometimes when we have nothing much to talk about, or indeed sometimes when we have all too much to discuss — a particular incident at school may have aroused the girl's imagination — I suggest that we both sit down and use the crayons or paints I carry around with me. I rarely have to suggest a subject for Laura, though she often tells me to do a particular sketch: a home, a college building, a doctor's office, an airplane, a dog, her school building or the school building my children go to, among others. I do the best I can, and as Laura tells me often enough, so does she.

This time she worked extra long on her picture, done carefully with crayons. Meanwhile, I did my work. I was asked by her to do a picture of a tennis racket. I had a few weeks earlier told her, when she asked me, that my favorite sport was tennis. She pointedly had let me know that her brothers liked baseball and football, and that they don't play tennis at all, and that her father doesn't, and that she wasn't even sure she knew how one plays the game. I had told her that when I was her brothers' age I, too, played baseball a lot and not tennis, but now I love to play tennis. I had explained the game to her. She wanted to know where the game is played and how one learns, and I told her that there are indoor courts and outdoor courts, and that I knew a good tennis player, who was about halfway between her age and mine, a college student, and he was right at that time doing a great job at making me a better player, and perhaps someday she would be able to meet a teacher like him and learn how to play.

Now, a few weeks later, she wanted that racket drawn, and I tried my best. Meanwhile, she did her best. When I asked her about what was happening, as I often did when clearly something *was* happening in the picture, she said this: "It's a school day, so we're all in the building. The only ones outside are Janice and Henrietta. They think they'd rather stay in the yard and talk than come in. But the teacher will go get them. Maybe they should stay at home, if they like to talk so much. But I guess you can't be at home all the time. I guess they should stay here, and then when they get home there will be plenty of time for fun."

So it goes for Laura — and for Janice and Henrietta. The two girls have stayed — and not done so badly, after all. Laura continues to take note of them; they are special in her mind, two close "colored" friends who quite obviously rely upon one another and have demonstrated to Laura and others their pluck, their determination, their ability to keep on coming to that building. As Laura has noted, they could probably have a better time elsewhere, but again, they "can't be at home all the time." I later asked Laura whether she in fact thought Janice and Henrietta desired to stay home rather than come to the school they are now attending. "No," she answered immediately. "I think they really do want to come to our school. They say it's *their* school, too, and I think it's right they say that. I'm not for more and more colored kids coming here, because pretty soon we wouldn't have any room, the white kids wouldn't. But if they send over Janice and Henrietta each year, and some of the others, I think we'd all feel good, because it's like our teacher says: there is every different kind of person in the world, and if you don't get to meet them all, you're not going to know what they're like. The teacher told us she thought she was learning herself, now that we have new people coming from different places in the city, and we should, too — we should learn, too. My mother said the best thing is to let everyone be polite toward everyone, and we try to do it."

From all I have seen they indeed are polite; girls like Laura and Janice, or Laura and Henrietta are not very friendly to each other and not unfriendly. They keep a certain distance, yet talk in an open and cordial and familiar way. At times as I talk with Laura or with Janice or with Henrietta, I think that for all the world the year could be 1962 or 1963 — and I am back in the

South, talking with young southern white children and young southern black children, who likewise gradually learned to get along, to stay somewhat apart but also move step by step by step toward some familiarity, some capacity for mutual recognition and acceptance.

5. Gangs

Only two blocks from young Laura lives an older boy, who goes downtown to school every day on a bus. The high school he attends has a very good "preengineering course," and the young man hopes that in a year or two he will be in a college where he can major in aeronautical engineering. He has loved planes since he was a child, Laura's age or even before — in any event as far back as he can remember. At sixteen he described high school as follows: "It's not bad. I'm doing my work. I'm going to graduate. I know what I want, but it sure takes long to get through. A lot of high school is a big bore, and a lot is a stupid waste of time, and a little part of it is OK — when you really pick up some useful information. And now it's getting rough around the school. The black guys watch your every move; if you sneeze near them, you're insulting them. They are really out of their minds, a lot of them. They give you a look as if you are poison one minute, then they try to be friendly the next. But you can't talk with them; they're only comfortable talking with their own.

"There are some here, white guys, who say they can sit down and have a good time with the blacks — maybe over lunch, or if they're on the basketball team together. But I rarely, if ever, see white and black guys eating together. The blacks stick together and so do we. I never used to think of myself as *white* — until I came to high school, and here they were, those black guys. I'll let you in on something: they run like lightning, and some of them are big, tall bruisers. They stick together, and a lot of them belong to gangs; I mean when they're at home they belong to a gang, and when they come to school, they will try to stick together, the guys from the same gang. If you ask me, they're one big gang, all of them. If they pass each other in the corridor, even if one doesn't really know what the other's name is, they nod and say hello. Then, they keep on talking about how they're brothers, and they talk about 'the Man,' which means the rest of us, the white man.

"Thank God we outnumber them, and by a good margin. I'd hate to think what it would be like if I was in a school and they were the majority. As it is, we have some tough people of our own here — you know, white boys — and they call themselves the Eagles. I guess they think the eagle is real American, and they say they're out to protect themselves now, and then they'll go in the Army and protect America. The black guys have one gang called the Black Stars and one called the Sharks. The leaders of both gangs are in the school here with me. I know them. You haven't seen anything until you've seen them: dark glasses, except in the classroom, when they can't get away with it, and crazy clothes, real crazy — every color in the rainbow. They're like actors, that's what they are. I think it's a show they put on. They have other black kids scared, because there they are: the big leaders, the four top Sharks and the five top Black Stars. I guess the other members are little fish or small satellites.

"Before I came to high school I never laid eyes on a Negro. We didn't have them in the elementary school or the junior high. They're bussing them in there now; I've seen the bus bring them over. It's a shame. Everyone is upset. My dad says in his day there were very few dark faces here in high school. He doesn't know where they used to live in those days. We had them in the city, but maybe they never wanted to finish school. During the depression, Dad says, even a lot of white kids didn't stay in school to graduate. Now the Negroes want an education I guess, and we've got more and more of them up here. I'm not against them, but I don't feel comfortable with them, it's like that, and they don't feel comfortable with us.

"The worst thing is how cliquish the blacks are. Gangs, that's all they know. They take sides on everything. Some teacher will say something, and the next thing you know, after the class, they're saying they're for him or against him. Then we'll hear that when the blacks left school and were on the bus or got home, they had a huge fight. And when they fight, they fight! I've seen them playing basketball, and they have scars on their arms or body or legs, and it's not because they had an appendix out or something! I'll be honest: I try to stay clear of them. I'm headed for college. I'm not the kind of guy who wants to fight, anyway. But we have some white kids who can take them on. They can't run as fast, but they're big, hulking bruisers, and boy oh boy, when they get mad, the blacks *do* run. The white guys aren't a gang. They hate the 'niggers,' they call them, and that's what brings them together. The blacks fight among themselves, so they're no match for the white guys.

"Our chemistry teacher, Mr. Thompson, has been teaching in the school for thirty years, and he says he's never seen anything like it, what's happened the last five or six years. The school is going to Hell, he told me once. He's a real friend to me. He talks to me like I'm his age. He asked me what I thought of the Negro students, and I answered that some were OK. He said, 'How many is *some?*' I said, 'A quarter of them, maybe.' He told me I was generous and that's what he liked about me! I agree with him, that a lot of them don't belong in school at all. They want a diploma and then a job, but they don't know how to concentrate, and they don't think too fast, a lot of them. My dad hates them all; but I think that's a wrong attitude to have. I try to be fair, and there are two or three I really think are great guys. One wants to be a pilot, and he's serious about it. He and I talk a lot. He can't stand his own people. He's told me so. I tell him I don't agree with him; I don't think he'd like to hear *me* saying what he does. But actually I *do* agree with him. With those black gang leaders around, if we didn't have a real smart, tough principal and the police right nearby, this building would be turned into a battleground. The police station is only two blocks away; it's the one thing that keeps us safe, Mr. Thompson is convinced. And even if we haven't had any big fights, a day doesn't go by that someone doesn't get hurt during the lunch hour. It may be a black guy, or it may be a white one, but it's someone."

The more he talks, the more angry he gets, and the more like his father he sounds. At sixteen he feels hemmed in by blacks and cheated out of a quieter life by their presence. He sees them as big, swaggering bullies, demanding and provocative and gang-prone. He does not talk much about the frail, sensitive, hard-working blacks — not directly at least. They are mentioned almost accidentally: the black who is the "exception" and wants to go to college and fly airplanes; or the black whom Mr. Thompson admires because he does so well in Mr. Thompson's tests; or the black who wrote a good story in the school magazine, "the best science-fiction story ever." Nor does that white youth mention the dozens and dozens of black youths whom he really notices very little: they come there to class; like him, they try their best at schoolwork; and then they leave for home. By the same token, when he talks about the school he doesn't speak of the ordinary white students. He mentions white youths whom he doesn't really like or admire, but who fight with the blacks, keep them some-what fearful, "even things out," and in truth add their fair share of brutishness to a school not yet destroyed by such tensions and hatreds, but certainly as a result kept under constant strain.

The problem is, as he himself puts it, that "you can't forget what race you are." He and his black classmates, way up North, are as conscious of their skin color as any Southerner, and a lot more racially conscious than many Southerners I know. Indeed, at times when I hear him and his friends I again feel I am back in Alabama or Mississippi, listening to white people struggle with their various feelings toward black people — and of course, toward themselves. And, just as I have heard worried, fearful white yeomen from Mississippi time and again define themselves (ever so sadly and pitifully it so often seemed) by what they were *not*, namely black, so in that New England high school I heard this, from the same young man: "When I first came here I was confused. I didn't know what I wanted to do. You know, these black guys, they can give you a real shock. You think of yourself as tough, and maybe you never did want to study much. Then all of a sudden *they* are here, and you're looking at them, and like I told my dad, you say: wait a minute, *wait a minute*. I'm not going to turn out like them. I don't want to be in some gang, and on drugs probably, and in jail. White kids try drugs too, but not the way the black kids do, I don't think. My father says it was the colored people who introduced the idea of drugs to people. Then some of their white buddies caught on, and now it's spreading like a fire gone out of control.

"I've learned to keep my eye on the future: no drugs, no beer except on the weekends, and a lot of studying. I feel sorry for the good Negro people of this world. I know there are some. In my school there are some. Negroes have to fight all the time just to get a square deal, but what I've seen is this: they have worse enemies right in their own backyard, worse than any white person can be. The one or two black kids I can talk with tell me how they have to watch their step, and how they are afraid of the black thugs in the ghetto. When I see a riot on television it just all clicks in my head: these guys in my school, they'll soon be doing that. A gang is a gang.

"The country probably has gangs like the ones I've seen in every city. I'll bet there are thousands and thousands of guys like the Black Stars and the Sharks. I'll bet there are a lot of blacks ready to rob and burn buildings down. That's the great danger in America now. That's what we've got to fight against. We can't just sit back and let them take over, can we? We can't just say, look: take all you want; we're too scared of you to fight back. I think it may come to a war. My dad used to say that, and I thought the old man was getting a little soft in the head. Now, I don't even dare tell him all I see in school. If I told him we have big gang leaders there, and I know who they are, he'd go into a rage. Then he'd want me down at the police station and the FBI, telling them everything. My mother says to keep quiet. Dad has a heart condition. But even she said that they're all one big gang, the colored people, and probably they'll only be stopped when the white people start pulling together for themselves and form their own gangs and don't give in all the time. You'll be seeing more and more gangs in the future, black and white both."

Whether that near-Armageddon will come about or not, he personally is not taking his mother's words too seriously. He is rather a loner. After school he stops at home, then works in a gas station for a few hours, again goes home, eats and studies. He is too busy to *worry* about black people, though he does *think* about them. He shuns clubs, let alone gangs, and he is convinced, when he stops and analyzes things at length, that "the country is too big and strong" for those gangs to take over, however powerful and pervasively influential he sometimes thinks them to be. In fact, he believes that his high school situation is not unlike the nation's state of affairs right now: there are a lot of restless blacks, increasingly cohesive and angry, and there is an alarmed, combative group of whites, still in control but worried about a future of fights and more fights, and in between there are people like him — mostly white people but, as he occasionally points out, a number of blacks too.

VI

IN THE PLACES WHERE
THE MOUNTAINS ARE GONE

FOR the title of this chapter I owe thanks to a man from McVeigh, Kentucky, whom I met in Cleveland; one of his sons had gone North, to Dayton and then Cleveland, and he had followed, but only for a while. He went back to a hollow near McVeigh and swore he'd "sooner die hungry than spend his last few years in the places where the mountains are gone." He didn't really think he was going to starve to death in McVeigh; he knew his son could be counted on to send him money each week. I believe he went back to Kentucky because he had known another kind of hunger in the city; he felt sad and lonely and bereft. He hungered after those mountains, and finally he went back to them and to his sister and his brother-in-law, who like him, now exchange letters with a son "up in Ohio."

In a previous volume, *Migrants, Sharecroppers, Mountaineers,* I tried to describe the kind of life common to thousands of Appalachian men and women and children. In recent decades many mountaineers have had to leave that kind of life for Ohio or Illinois or Michigan — but still they yearn for, pine for, dream about, think about, talk about the hills, the great and lovely hills. In a sense, then, Appalachian life lives on, in cities like Dayton and Cleveland, Chicago and Detroit, in the minds and most especially the hearts of people who have gone to the cities for work, but who would, if they could, choose without a moment's hesitation to return to the Appalachian hills and mountains. Back there they would be sitting, gabbing, picking the guitar, sewing, fishing and hunting, doing some planting, and as one hears again and again *getting along,* which is not meant to be an economic or social or political description but rather a way of conveying one's essential contentment — however difficult the external circumstances of mountain living may be.

Men and women in eastern Kentucky and western North Carolina and West Virginia have tried and tried to make do, have defiantly claimed they can manage, they are getting along — only to decide one day that it has to be done, it just has to be; and so they pack up and drive downhill and catch a road, which joins a bigger road, and then one still bigger, and then keep moving — until there she is, the city they have expectantly and nervously sought after. And after the flatness of those streets is believed, after the crowds are accepted, after the air is got used to as "the only air there is, bad as it may be," and after the look on people's faces, the indifference and outright unfriendliness is understood to be no personal thing, "just the way a person is in the big city," after all that and so much more is absorbed and understood by the mountaineer, he must go about justifying the trip, the state of exile he has voluntarily felt compelled to assume. (Yes, he feels he has chosen to do what he also has felt he must do.)

If it is a woman, she must settle in, get things put away, and in one mother's words, "cradle ourselves as best we can for as long as we have to." As for the children, they can be seen looking around or talking in muted tones — as if someone unfriendly if not sinister might be nearby, watching and listening. Children feel their way into a new world, which they have less reason to dread than their parents do. To quote that mother again: "With the kids, it's a new place to explore, and they don't have all the memories we have to make our eyes watery." In the following sections I hope to indicate how women like that mother do what they say has to be done, and how men like her husband go about their quest for work and self-respect, and how their children take to and look at their surroundings, and how in those cities various individuals get to know mountaineers, strive to work "with" or "for" them, or conversely, make their life difficult indeed.[1]

1. Gone, Gone

I want to begin with the daughter-in-law of the man whose words stand as the title of this long chapter. If he talks about the mountains as "gone," he is only echoing his daughter-in-law, who is a smiling, friendly, affable person, but who all of a sudden (when reminded for some reason of what is gone) will openly have herself a cry. She is quick to recover, though. She has five children, four sons and a daughter, and she wants to be a source of strength to them. They are all under ten; and they need, she knows, more than tears and a dour face. Nor does she feel sad and lost exclusively. She has money, more of it than ever before, and she lives in a house that, if old and somewhat broken-down by some standards, for her is an enormous improvement: heat comes more or less regularly, even though it takes the form of a blast of hot, dry air that dries up everyone's nose and throat; water can be had by the turn of a wrist, even though it tastes so very bad, so ugly almost compared to stream water; and during winter one can easily leave home, come and go as one pleases, even though there is not much to see outside.

Life is less hard and mean, then, if also less enjoyable. Mrs. Bowman is not one to forget the bright side of things; in fact she tries very hard to gloss over the disadvantages of city living. For one thing, she is a devout believer, and so she believes that whatever she is now going through has a meaning, is for the best, and will lead to what she always calls "the good." Her moody times come as a surprise even to her, let alone her children, who cannot understand why, all of a sudden, their mother "fills up," as one of the boys describes it, and then goes and "sobs herself out." She is soon back, though, and her children have come to realize that she has her memories and her attachments and her longings, even as she can suddenly take note of how lucky they are, when a blizzard comes, to be living in Cleveland rather than up the hollow.

I think more than anything else I have been struck by Mrs. Bowman's struggle for balance; her struggle is, I believe, very characteristic of the struggle of many Appalachian women who are now city women: "My mother taught me that when you're in trouble, try to think of the best that can happen. I tell my children that we're in trouble, or else we wouldn't be up here, but its not all so bad, and when we go back home we'll have more stories to tell than there will be ears to listen, so we'll have to keep talking for a long time until we're plain heard out by the kin left there in Pike County. I'm glad we're here, and I wish I was back there; that's what I tell my children. They'll come over to me when they feel me sinking into a mood, and they'll say, 'Ma, should we stay or should we go?' They've heard their father and me ask each other that question so many times, it's only natural that they would be wanting to ask it. Then they sit back and wait for me to answer them. I always try to answer the same, but I guess when they see me losing my nerve or just getting tired and pining away, you know, for a hill and kin up the road — well, that's the time they'll come and ask me their question again, and I say the same thing as always.

"I don't just pretend for the children's sake. I hated to come up here, and a day doesn't go by that I forget my home up the hollow, and my mother and my three sisters still there. But if it wasn't for Jack's money — my husband always got on especially good with my mother — there'd be no money for them back there. And of course, my sister's husband is right here with us, though I don't think it's right that she isn't here with him. I wasn't going to stay back there in Pike County, Kentucky, while my husband was wandering his way through Ohio, looking for a good job. And now that my husband is up here in Cleveland, it's some distance from McVeigh, and he couldn't drive it every weekend. What would come of us as a family if I just sat there, and he was up here, and all I could do was go to the store once a week to hear his voice coming in on the telephone from long distance? Up here I say to myself they're gone, gone; I mean, the hills are. If I was like my sister, I'd be in Pike County and saying that my *husband* is gone, really gone, and I'd be in worse shape than I ever am now.

"Of course, my mother couldn't have lost two of us daughters at once, so I guess Alice had to stay. You see, one of our sisters, Caroline, is slow; she's like a child. Mother has to care for her all the time, and our oldest sister, Betsy, helps her out. But Betsy has her own baby — he's her husband. That husband of hers is all the time sitting with his liquor, and he's just a waste of a man, a God-awful waste. So Alice and I were the two anchors of my mother's life, because our men are good men, and we could help her with Caroline, and she could lay her eyes on the grandchildren and feel there was a future ahead, and not just all of us sitting and crying over what's happened to Pike County, Kentucky. I think if Alice took her girls and boys — three of each — up here, my mother would try to come with her, and bring Caroline, and then Betsy and that husband of hers would have to come, and lo, it would be a lot of trouble up here, I'll tell you. I don't know how we'd manage up here with Caroline. Back in McVeigh we could sort of put her out in the field, and she'd sit and have a good time in the sun. I'd see her laughing and running about and making funny noises, and then smiling at her own noises, and she'd try and catch a butterfly or poke grass into an ant pile. I'd think to myself that even if she's twenty-four, it doesn't make any difference, because God must want her here the way she is, and He must be smiling at the sight of her smiling, and with all His troubles, having to watch over us, He must need a rest for Himself.

"If Caroline lived up here and had to leave this apartment building, we'd have to go with her. I think it would be too much for her, the change. She's not really the child she seems to be. A child can leave and forget and find comfort in the new place to stay. For Caroline the hollow is the whole world. She's dug in there, and God forbid, if she had to leave I think it would be the end of her. We send her picture cards, and they show them to her and tell her that Cleveland, Ohio, isn't so far that we can't drive home sometimes, and of course we do, especially on holidays. I think by now Caroline believes in her mind that we're going to be away for most of the time, but we're going to come back now and then, and so she'll be seeing us. Of course, when we go she can't say good-bye. She just can't bring herself to do it. She gives us a look and then goes running out to where the chickens are, and then she must be upset, because she gets them going, making such a lot of noise. My mother will shake her head and say that poor Caroline gets the chickens to do her crying for her. Later, we'll be in the car, and my Jack will tell the kids that we're entering Ohio now, and all of a sudden I'll hear those chickens in my head!

"I do believe it's gone, the time we'll stay in Pike County. Jack says that if we could save some money we might go back one day, and we'd be able to live down from the hollow, in a nice new home we could build on the road to town. Some old people come back and do that. They'll give their lives over to living in the city, and they'll put aside some money, no matter how hard it is to do, and even if they can only save a little. When they're old and they have what they need to live on — with social security, you know — they come back to Kentucky and they die in peace. They have a happy last few years. I used to see them tracing paths up the hill, and they'd nod and say: it's the same, it's the same. I used to wonder why they'd ever want to leave for so long, when they didn't want to leave at all, you could just know that. But now I understand. We left, and we promised everyone we'd be back inside of a year at the most, and I mean back for good, not a weekend visit. Poor Caroline, we all thought she was so slow she couldn't make out what we were saying. My Jack got impatient with her and said we should shout out real loud: we're going for a year, a year, a year — and the word would sink into her head, and she'd know that it meant from winter to winter, you see. She said over and over, 'Only a year?' It was as if she didn't believe us. But it turns out she was the smartest of all of us. Jack himself said so when we stopped and realized that we'd been up here three years, three whole, long years. He said Caroline knew; she just knew.

"I think my own children knew, too. I didn't let them say all they wanted to say. They'd start, and I'd tell them to hush. A mother can sense what's in her child's head, even if she doesn't hear him speak it. You can look in their eyes; you can see the words on their faces. My children say things to me without making a sound, and a lot of the time I'm grateful to them for not speaking. It hurts to hear out loud what you're trying to push out of your thinking. Once you hear something said, you keep on hearing it inside your head. That's the way it is with me, anyway. I know the same goes for Jack, too. He and I will be sitting there, and we'll be so low in our spirits that it's best not to say a single word out loud. That's when he has his beer and watches the television, and I do my sewing. Then I'll ask him what he saw, and he said he was only watching, but he wasn't listening, so I shouldn't ask him anything. Then he'll ask me what I was sewing, and Lord if I don't have to take a look myself! I've been doing the work but my mind has been far off."

If her mind sometimes wanders down the length of Ohio and over the mountains of Kentucky, her mind often stays home. She tries to keep the five-room apartment clean. She likes to cook big, hearty meals for Jack and for the children and for her brother-in-law. She and Jack and their daughter sleep in one bedroom. The four boys sleep in another bedroom. Alice's Bill, as Mrs. Bowman sometimes calls her brother-in-law, has his own room. And she calls that room "his own place," as if the man is entitled to more than a room's worth of privacy. Jack and Bill, who happen to be distant kin, are fortunate enough to have jobs in a factory, the same factory. They are like brothers, and obviously of considerable support to each other. They get up very early, but not too early for Mrs. Bowman, who always has a breakfast of hot cereal, eggs and bacon, toast and jam and coffee for "the men." They are tall men, once lanky, now a little filled out. They work six days a week and are glad to do so. When they can't work on Saturday they tend to get glum. It's a little too far to drive to Kentucky in two days, and time really hangs heavy. Bill gets lonely, and Jack starts looking for something to do.

On weekdays after the men have gone, the children wake up, and they also eat well. I have never seen children eat better.

They seem to sweep the food off the plate. I have spent the night on the Bowman living-room sofa, and by the second breakfast have been awake enough and hungry enough to pitch in, but the food seems to disappear before I can really get to it. Mrs. Bowman gladly prepares me what she calls a "special plate" and apologizes for her children's vigorous appetites. She loves to put food for the children on one large plate and let them fend for themselves, and she also loves to watch her children eat. They only seem greedy, though; they actually demonstrate considerable thoughtfulness and tact and self-control: the bacon is evenly divided, the eggs go to everyone, no one fails to get three pieces of toast. Both coffee and milk are had by all of them, and the children do love the taste of coffee — at six or seven or eight they crave the hot cup with its special aroma the way older people do. But there is also a bus ride and long school hours, so one needs all the energy one can find.

Mrs. Bowman makes clothes for herself and her family. She makes dresses for her daughter. She buys cloth and makes pants for her husband and her sons and her brother-in-law. She writes brief daily letters home, and two or three times a week much longer letters. They know in Pike County, Kentucky, what is happening up there in Cuyahoga County, Ohio. Newspaper clippings are sent back, and their range is interesting — from dramatic news and pictures, such as of a fire or an explosion, to recipes and funny stories or bits of advice, such as one encounters in the so-called "back section" or "women's section" of the paper. And in return come simple, direct, open-hearted, giving letters — full of news about the hollow, the weather, kinfolk. Those letters are read and read again: "I feel that a few words from my sister or from Mother take me right back home, almost like a trip itself does. When Jack and Bill come home I'll tell them there's a nice letter waiting for them, and their eyes light up, as though an airplane just landed on the roof of this building with the whole family in it. Of course, Bill gets his special letter from my sister. It's hard on him, but he says it was harder on him back home, sitting and having nothing to do, and so he's better off and so is everyone else with things as they are.

He says he misses his wife and children, but they wouldn't want
him back the way he was before he left for Ohio. All he did was
drink. There wasn't a job he could find, and he lost all hope, and
I think he was expecting not to wake up from one of those long
whiskey sleeps of his. Now he takes just a little more beer than
my Jack does, and why wouldn't he need a little extra, sitting
there trying to write a few words down on paper? Writing
doesn't come easy to him, or my husband, either. I tell my sons
that they can't be like their father, not so far as reading and
writing goes. And they're not going to be like him, I can tell.
They go to that school, three of the boys do, and the teachers
make them learn everything, it seems. Not that we didn't have
our good teacher back in Pike County. She was a wonderful,
wonderful woman, that Mrs. Farmer, but I guess she wasn't
under the pressure they are up here to make children study.

"That's the big difference, you know. In the city everyone has
to do the best he can. There's a clock in everyone's mind. You
have to be here at this time and there at some other time. My
Jack says that the entire plant is run by the clock: he checks in,
and checks out for his lunch, and he checks back in, and he
checks out to come home. I've had to think more about what time
it is myself. I'll be doing my sewing, and I'll say to myself: what
time is it? The children will come home, and they will tell me the
time. They know. They look at the clock near the shopping
center, or they ask the driver, because they want to keep up with
the right minute and right hour. They asked me for their own
clock last Christmas, to go in the boys' bedroom, and I was glad
to get them one.

"I have to think back though; I love to think back to the days
we lived up in the hollow and neither Jack nor I cared what hour
it was. We knew what we had to do, and we went and did it.
There was the sun, of course; the sun's time was enough for us.
Up here, we never see the sun. I will wonder to myself sometimes, what has happened to the sun and to the moon? I can go
for weeks and never see any sign of the moon, and the stars are
always behind some cloud. And the sun doesn't shine into our
windows; we're at the wrong angle, it seems. My little girl hears

me complain, but she doesn't really know what I'm talking about. She was two when we left home, and she doesn't remember those evenings with stars so low you could hold out a cup and sweep it full of them, my mother would say, and the moon perched over a tree smiling down at you. And in the morning suddenly you'd hear the birds begin, and you knew they were shouting their hello to the sun, and it was trying to get to your territory — from China is it? That's what our teacher told us, that at night the sun was in China. Sometimes the sun would be slow in coming to us, so the birds seemed to get louder and louder, because they get impatient after a while, waiting and waiting. But then she'd come, and the whole cabin would be a different place. If I had to say one thing I miss most, it's the sunrise. And the second thing, that would be the sunset. In the apartment it doesn't really make much difference if it's day or night outside. I see why everyone has to have a watch and a clock nearby. They'd never know otherwise whether it's light or dark in the street.

"Another thing I miss is the walking. There's no place to walk. There's no place at all you can call *outside*. My Jack will drive me to the supermarket, and that's the furthest I go outside, but I feel as if I've never been but inside after I come back from a trip like that. Back home I'd walk for the longest time; I'd go visit a neighbor way up the hollow, or way down. It wouldn't even enter my mind to estimate how *long* it was I'd walked. Now, if my kids are going someplace, they want to know how far they've gone, and how many miles it is, and is it longer than the last time they went someplace, or is it shorter than the time last year they went over there. I have to tell them to stop thinking like that, and then they tell me to stop thinking the way *I* do, and then I think they're the ones who are correct.

"It all comes down to recognizing that we're up in this city and not back in the shadow of those mountains. My daddy told me something when I was a little girl — and I still do remember him saying it: don't ever leave the shadow of these mountains here, my girl. I told him I never would, and he told me he was sure I wouldn't, but just in case I was tempted, he wanted me to hear his advice. Well, he was wrong, and so was I. My Jack says he never would have believed it, if someone told him when he was a kid that he'd end up clocking into a factory every morning at eight o'clock and coming back to this apartment house we live in, with not a hill in sight anywhere. But that's what happens in a life, I tell him. And you know, he comes back and reminds me that until we left Kentucky and moved up here, no one in either of our families had ever done such a thing — since they first came out to Kentucky, and that was so long ago I couldn't give you an exact number, but maybe two hundred years, more or less."

She switches back and forth in her estimates; sometimes she will rather casually say that they haven't really left their Appalachian home at all. They are in Cleveland, true, but they go back home often, or at least as often as they can. And one day, one fine, beautiful day they will hear, maybe, of some new opportunities in Pike County, or they will stop and realize, maybe, that the few thousand dollars they by then may have saved up can go a long way in McVeigh and its nearby territory — all of which will mean it is time to head back, pull up those tentative stakes in that dingy but adequate building and drive South until the hills loom up. But on other occasions Mrs. Bowman is far less hopeful, and, as her remarks immediately above indicate, almost apocalyptic. The city casts its own shadow on the history of her family and on her life. The city is a place of exile, a place where one has to be, where one can at least have bread and gravy and meat and potatoes and eggs and bacon and coffee, plenty of it, high as the price is on the beans. (She calls them that, coffee beans, though she actually buys ground coffee.) But she can get worried and self-conscious about her speech. The children are picking up "city talk," she muses, and they are probably noticing her ways of saying things — and smiling a little.

Perhaps later children will be less tolerant, she thinks to herself. Perhaps they will be ashamed of their parents and their family. Perhaps they will want to stay in Cleveland. There is no knowing. There is no telling. But actually, come to think of it, bad as things are, they could be worse, and besides, there is something else she can say to comfort herself: "I don't really believe my children will ever be ashamed to tell people where they'd really like to be living. Every time we go back, they forget all their city habits and go running in the woods, and I say to their father that it's in their blood, those hills, and all we have to do is somehow get them back there, and then they'll take to the woods and the hills without needing a single word of advice or encouragement from us."

It is not for me to say how she "really" feels. I have never understood how a doctor can possibly make that kind of exact, categorical judgment — in the face of the deeply felt and conflicting sentiments that patients or for that matter all of us have in the course of our lives. I suppose that one minute Mrs. Bowman "really" feels she is up in Cleveland for good, and another moment she "really" feels that the three Cleveland years have been an interlude, a significant interlude, no doubt, but a "spell," a finite span of time.

I remember an evening when she and her husband were not in the best of spirits. Word from McVeigh told them that Caroline was sick with pneumonia, and Bill's Alice was also sick with a cough and fever and chest pain. It was winter; and if they could imagine how cold and unpleasant it was up the hollows near McVeigh, and how "bad" the weather was for those two sisters, they could take little comfort in the dreary weather they were also experiencing: the cloudy days that became cloudy weeks; the dirt-covered snow and ice. I had heard a lot that evening about how soon they hoped to be back home, and how long it had been since they left for Ohio. Yet, suddenly Mrs. Bowman looked up from her sewing and had a change of heart: "We'll be all right here. I do believe we'll bring up the children so they have clothes and plenty to eat, and they've got a good education in their heads. That's why I hope for their sake that we stay here a little longer. I was thinking to myself just this morning that I have a dream for my sons. I'd like them to be pioneers, just like our ancestors were — and you know what *they* did! They chopped and cut their way out to Kentucky, and they loved it so much they didn't want to go any farther. I'd like my boys to go through school here and get a first-class city education for themselves. And they'll be big and strong and husky and healthy boys. They're getting the best food I can buy for them, and Jack brings me all the money I need, and there are no long, long spells of going hungry every winter, like we had back home. When they're all safe and grown and with their education, then I'd like them to go on back home and be pioneers again. I'd like them to build up Pike County somehow, the way a real educated person can help in doing. Today we need another kind of pioneer; I guess that's the truth of it. I guess our boys will have to go back there and show people what they know, and hopefully they can get jobs for themselves in a town — and it doesn't have to be in McVeigh or Pike County, so long as it is somewhere in Kentucky, or maybe West Virginia. I mean, so long as it's near the shadow of one of those mountains!"

She went on to dream, picturing her sons as teachers, or perhaps lawyers or businessmen. She even went on to mention out loud that she was going to have a baby, and he or she would be born in Ohio. She knew it would be safer and better for her to deliver the child in a hospital, a good city hospital. She was going to write that news home, she said, and she was going to prepare her family, because it would take some getting used to, the idea that she wouldn't come home a few months "before," but rather stay put, and feel quite pleased about doing so. Not that she doubted she would have her second thoughts once she was ready to enter the hospital, or once she was actually in the building, but now she knows what is "best." And often she reminds herself that what is "best" is what she has to think about, has to keep in her mind as she goes about her life.

2. Work and No Work

The states of Illinois and Ohio are familiar to him. He also knows the southern part of Michigan. Breathitt County, Kentucky, is where he's from, though, and like so many others, he gets back to Kentucky a few times a year, mostly on holidays. He is six feet three and muscular and blondish; his face is prematurely lined. He has gray eyes. His arms and legs are long. I believe a lot of people would think of President Lincoln when they saw him: the angular features, the heavy eyebrows, the untamed hair, the heavy, sad look on the face. In Chicago he talks about his mountain life ahead — after he strikes it rich. There is a pleasant glow to him when he speaks about that future, but the glow fades fast. One believes in his self-knowledge without his having to put his despair into words. Though he cannot give his "realistic perceptions" the brutal force of language, no sensitive observer would need him to construct a wordy analysis of "the muck of life" he feels himself struggling through.

He tries hard to get through that life, as hard as any "realistic" observer could ever expect him to try. Yes, he has a huge appetite for beer and whiskey, which are supposed to push people into a "dream world" or bring on "depression," if not a "manic" attack. Here he is, though, sober as can be and utterly "oriented" and thoroughly clearheaded — two days after he has lost a job, an hour after he tried to find another job: "The trouble with me is that I've got my body here, and it's willing to work, and I've got my head, and it tells me to go to work, and I can take care of a horse and goats and chickens and I can grow crops, but I'm not good for a single thing up here, except what they call 'day labor.' When they run out of day labor, that's the end of me. In Breathitt County I couldn't make a single penny. There was no work at all; and that's why we've all come up here to Chicago: we thought we'd go get work, and then we could buy our kids shoes and our women would have shoes, too. But you get up here, and there's work one day and no work the next, then work again, then no work. How long can a man stand it? I try to talk to myself. I try to tell myself that this is a good country, and I've not seen the end of my life yet, and one of these days a man like me, who's strong and willing, will be able to go into a place and say: here I am, and all I want to do is give you every ounce of energy I've got, and do anything I can, and all I want back is a fair wage, enough to give my woman some money to buy food and my children the clothes they need, so they won't go cutting their feet all the time and shivering come winter.

"I wish I could go back to Breathitt County. If only I could get work there! Up here I can at least tell my wife to say I've deserted her, and she'll get money from the city. But I don't picture myself doing that. I couldn't swallow my pride that way; nor would my wife ever be able to say something like that. She says she tried to say it, just to herself, and she broke down and cried and cried, to the point that my little girl, Mary Elizabeth, thought she was crying because something bad happened to me, and when she told her mother what she thought, of course her mother broke down even more, and I think the child was really scared quite bad.

"I don't know what is going to become of us. There was a time that I thought God would take care of us. I used to hear my mother pray, even when she wasn't in church, and what she said was this: it's hard, living on that patch of land by the creek, but if God had any other ideas for us, He'd let us know. Well, how long can a man put up with that way of thinking about the world? I tried — until I found myself cussing at the Lord so hard I figured He'd rather I stopped relying on Him at all than saying yes, I'm waiting for you, but then giving Him a piece of my mind when nothing ever happened. I really had to leave Breathitt County. What was there for me to do? Nothing, is the answer. And how many of us brothers could live off that one little farm we have? I was glad to go. I thought I'd do well in Cincinnati, but there wasn't work there. A minister told me to try Chicago. He said this is a bigger city and there's more work up here.

"It sure is a bigger city. I hear on the radio: Chicago, Chicago, a wonderful town; that's a song. I never want to sing it. I'd like to know who wrote the words. He never talked to us who are here from the hills; I know that. Like my wife said when she heard the song: wonderful for those who have it good, and terrible for those who have it bad. Bad as it is here, we have to stay. We've tried Dayton, and we've tried Detroit. I've had jobs for a week or two, and I've tried to save a few dollars each time, and when I heard I might get a permanent job in Detroit, I took us all over there. But they're not making cars the way they used to. Things are slow, so I couldn't find a job. Thank God for the church missions. They help you eat, and they try to get work for you. But when I saw that there was less work in Detroit than Chicago I took us all back to Chicago. Thank the Almighty Lord for my car; and if I didn't teach myself a long time ago, in Breathitt County, how to make an engine go, I do believe we would have ended up in some ditch by some road, and we never would have gotten out. We would have sat there and waited for God to say: OK, come on up here, because you people are really stranded now."

He goes on to tell how he's had that 1959 Dodge for years, how his older brother and he bought it together with money they both got when they came out of the Army, how his brother reenlisted and is still in the service. Now the brother has a new car, while he drives the old Dodge and cares for it and tries to keep it running, because he may have to move on to another city or he may want to go home. And anyway, the one thing he really looks at and feels proud about, feels to be *his,* is that car. Memories, too, go with the car: in it he and his wife and four children left Breathitt County; in it they drove up Route 75 to Cincinnati, crossed the state of Ohio, headed for Chicago, went over to Michigan, returned to Illinois; and of course in it they all go back there to Kentucky "oh so many times a year, whenever it's a good time."

What does he mean by those few words? Is he nostalgic, incurably and ruinously so? (There is a touch of the skeptical moralist in the listener because he wonders whether the man's remark might just possibly "give away" something that explains his trouble finding or keeping a job.) Does he really get tired of the work he finds, leave it, go home, then come back homesick as well as on the look again for employment? I fear a question like that last one is too readily asked by someone who knows something, but not enough, of what actually goes on when many mountaineers try to find work in cities like Chicago. All one need do is go to certain bars in that city, or in Dayton or Cleveland or Detroit, and listen to the men dreaming about the next trip home and talking bitterly and sadly about the disappointments they have met in the city — and the conclusion seems obvious: their hearts are elsewhere, so that they never really stick with whatever possibilities or opportunities may be forthcoming; indeed, after a while they either return once and for all to the mountains of Kentucky and West Virginia, or they live in limbo, not quite settled in the city, but not quite back home either.

All well and good, such explanations; and I suppose one can add the observation that many mountaineers are "naïve" and "gullible" and easily persuaded to accept almost anyone's promises. And of course mountaineers are also poorly educated people, unsuited for most skilled jobs, and by their "cultural tradition" prone to "passivity" and other "traits" that a big, booming, buzzing, business world can do little with except exploit in its own relentless, unthinking and rather automatic manner. Meanwhile, there is a man's life, his personal experiences, his history as a particular human being, and his narrative history, too — which, as it emerges, gives the listener a thing or two to think about before he accounts for everything in a life: "When I was a boy I'd ask my dad what I'd be doing when I was his age, and he said that most likely I'd be doing what he was doing, trying to stay alive by squeezing what he could out of the land. But there was just so far we could go on a few acres of land. And there were more and more of us hungry for those odd jobs my dad could always find — and hungry for food, too! I hated to leave Breathitt County, but let me tell you something right now: I was also *glad* to leave. I recall saying to my dad: if I can find work up there, I'll be the happiest man that ever lived. He said: son, I know how you feel.

"Since then I've been looking. I've been looking for work, and I guess looking for happiness. I'll never be happy until I find a job and it lasts; and the way things look, that means I'll never be happy. The first thing I found out in Cincinnati was this: if you have only your strong arms, it's no good. They want you to be a carpenter or a plumber or an electrician. I can build a house, but I didn't have the references they wanted. I've never been an apprentice to anyone, excepting Dad. And the last few years they've been cutting down on construction in the cities, so even if I was a certified electrician, something like that, I might have trouble finding work. I take jobs washing dishes and floors and all that. I've tried to hold on to each job, but no luck. Once the owner said he didn't like a white man doing that kind of work; it was for colored, he said. He said I was being too careful with my work, and I took too much time. Another time they got a machine and didn't need the three of us with the mop and pail. I almost had a job a few times elevator-operating, but they seem to like the colored for that, too. They always complain, the colored, but the way I see it, white people want the colored in a lot of jobs. The people at the employment agency kept on telling us that white people like us, from the hills, don't stand much of a chance in Cincinnati, because some jobs are reserved for the colored, and there are so many of us white people coming in. I had a job washing cars, but it was the same story there; the man said I cleaned each car like it was my own, and that's no good. He said I should go back to Kentucky because I was too good a person for the city; so I told him I would, if he'd only tell me how I could find a job there. He shook his head and said he didn't know.

"In the beginning we were all in one room, the children and my wife and me; and Cincinnati is a hot, sticky city in the summer. We fought for air all day, and at night we were so tired we gave up; I would fall asleep and it was bad, because the last thing I'd think was: maybe I'll never wake up, and *then* I'll be happy. I decided to go farther north. I heard it would be cooler, and besides, I kept hearing we'd have a better chance to find work in Chicago. Well, I heard right and I heard wrong. In Chicago we get it hot and sticky, too — come summer. It's true there are plenty of temporary jobs here, but none that I can keep and hold onto. I get up at four in the morning and I go and try to find something. They'll take me for day labor, like I say, but they tell me right to my face that I'm not an educated man, with a degree from a high school and all that — and with a lot of jobs the people will tell you they have to hire the colored, or else the government will get after them, and all that. It's no good. The factories take people who've got friends and relatives, and now it's slow for the factories anyway; they're laying off, a lot of them, not hiring. Things have been getting worse the last couple of years, and here it is, 1970, and there's no sign of the country having jobs for a man like me.

"The ministers try to help us out. They have missions. They have people looking out for us. They try to find work for us. They do all they know how. There are some good people in this world, I'll say that: young students and some people that work with the churches. Thank God for their help. They've given us food and helped us find a place to live. We go over to a place they have and we meet other people, and they're just like us: they can't really go back, because you can go for a year and not see a dollar bill up there in the hollows, and they hate it here, but at least there's day labor, so we're not starving.

"I've done so many jobs. I've cleaned places and helped people move and done some raking or shoveling, and I've had some good jobs before Christmas, loading and unloading and keeping stock moving in the warehouses. I wish Christmas came once a month and not just once a year. Between all the part-time work and the busy seasons in the fall and the spring, and with the help we get from people up here, we manage to keep going, and I'm grateful, I really am. I'm sure my kids eat better up here, for all the uncertainty we have from day to day. It's no joy living in these old buildings; there are too many people around, and the halls are as bad as can be — pitch-black, and holes in the stairs. My boy tripped and fell and his arm was broken. My wife tripped and fell and she was bruised and it hurt bad. We all crawl and scurry upstairs like we are frightened squirrels. We stop and go. When we've made it to the top we're safe for one more day!

"I have my beer. Sometimes I have a shot or two of whiskey. I'll tell you why: maybe I've been taken out in a truck to do some moving, and I've been lifting all day, and now I'm through with work and my arms are sore and my hands are red and my back hurts real bad, but I'm home at last. It's been hot all day, and we've been stuffed into that dark truck as if we were pieces of furniture, too. I didn't eat anything, because I get a stomachache when I eat fast and then go right back to lifting. I'd sooner not eat and just work right through. Then the truck finally gets us back to the agency, and they check us out and give us about two-thirds of what we make — the rest goes to them — and then I've got my money. I'm hungry. I'm parched. I'm tired. I'm thinking: what will I do tomorrow? I'm thinking: if I was back in Breathitt County, what would I be doing? The boys say, 'Let's stop and have a beer.' I say, 'Yes.' I think to myself, 'I shouldn't have a beer; I shouldn't have two beers.' But a man has to relax a little. I feel tired enough; if I didn't stop and listen to the music and nurse along my beer, I think I'd explode. I feel like dry powder near a fire, come five or six o'clock in the afternoon. And when you've been going since four or five in the morning, you're ready for a rest.

"We all sit around and talk about the old country, that's what some of us call it, back in Kentucky. We talk about going back, until you'd almost think we *are* back, to hear us. I'll close my eyes sometimes in the bar, and by God I can be right up that creek — sitting there, deciding whether I should go hunting or go visit my cousin Jim. He was killed in Korea, you know. If I keep my eyes closed too long, someone has to nudge me, because I fall asleep. It's in between being awake and falling asleep that I like the best. I'm not really in Chicago and I'm not dead to the world. I'm in the woods, or up one of the hills, or I'm in that store, with some of my 'Chicago dollar bills,' Mrs. Perkins who runs the store calls them. When I come there and pay her for something with cash she says that right off.

"I do, I certainly do, look forward to going back on visits. It's a lot of driving, but we arrange to go when it's really slow up here and I wouldn't be missing any jobs I might otherwise get. We go on holidays, too. We drive through the night. We drive and drive. The old car holds out. I can fix almost anything, if I can get the parts. I try to keep good tires, all four of them. Here in the city as long as I know there's that car outside, waiting on us to tell it where to go, I'm not too unhappy. I can always go back, I say to myself. But I never do, except when it's a good time. A man has to dream, and I do. I see myself finding a real, lasting job, and then I save up money, and we go back to

Breathitt County, and I buy the store from Mrs. Perkins. She's getting on. She's over seventy. She would sell, but there's no one to buy. She has no children. She doesn't trust her kin. She'd sell to a stranger first, I believe. But how could I run a store? I'd know everyone, and I'd trust them for the money, because they wouldn't have any. Soon, I'd be owing to the people that supply me, and I'd have to close the store down. She's tough, and she can scare people. It's not in me to be like that. So, like I say, it's a dream I get now and then.

"Up here I can rest on Sundays. I try to find work on Saturdays, if there is any. If there isn't I come back and sleep a little and have a beer and sit and talk with some of the neighbors. I'll throw a ball with one of my boys. I'll watch the television, and that puts me to sleep again. There sure is a lot of talking that goes on in this country. No matter what hour it is, there's someone talking away on the television. And the news, they keep telling you the news, and how bad it is for the country. I don't understand why America is always having trouble on its hands. If we're the strongest, we should be winning all the time, not having everyone talk back to us. But what the country takes is what I have to take: people say bad things to you, unfriendly things. They'll say you have no education, and you haven't the right way of talking, and you're too careful, and you spend too many minutes trying to be perfect — they say the same thing all the time. Then they'll tell you they've driven through the mountains of Kentucky and West Virginia, and they thought it was pretty there, and they want to know if there wasn't *something* that I couldn't find back there. I tell them no, there just isn't. They don't understand, though. They think jobs are around, if you really look. They think we're lazy, or something, and we didn't have the brains to stay in school, and we're running away from some crime, you know, or we've done a bad deed — otherwise we'd be back there.

"There's no use explaining things to people. They believe what they want to believe. They want to think ill of us; it's easier for them to do that than think there's something wrong with Chicago. One man told me that; he said Chicago is his hometown, just like Breathitt County is mine, and he always thought that anyone who comes here can find a good job for himself and settle in, and he's sorry I haven't found what I was looking for up here, but maybe I'm a special case, he said. I told him he could think so if he wanted, but the truth is that I'm like my friends and my kin — we have some kin up here, too. I told him to go check us all out, but he said he had a lot of other things to do, and I said I wished I was as lucky as he is."

Actually, he does feel lucky at times, because he remembers worse hardships than those Chicago presents. He knows that he is up in Chicago because there he can obtain work — even though it is intermittent and not highly paid; but still it is work, and the result is money, food, clothes, and a place to live. To a man who used to go for days and weeks without seeing a single dollar bill, such a state of affairs is not a disaster. And for such a man the world was never expected to be an ideal place, or a place without substantial pain. The years in cities like Chicago can only remind a man that if he has it rough, so do others; and if many have a relatively good life, then no one is without tribulations. Here, for instance, is what might be called a philosophical statement, an exercise in reflection and introspection: "I never thought I'd find Heaven up here. I've been asked whether I'm disappointed. Are you disappointed, a minister asked us one day. I said, 'Hell, no.' I shouldn't have sworn, but I forget myself. Of course, I *am* disappointed; I won't say I'm not. I'd like to be making a regular living. I'd like my kids to be able to say their dad has a job, and his work is something that has a *name* to it. In school they ask them what I do, and they don't know how to answer. I don't blame the kids. They get to feeling sorry about themselves. I tell them not to worry, we'll be fine, but they'll worry anyway. One of my boys asked me if we were on relief. I said no. He said a kid had told him that all of the hillbillies are feeding off the welfare department. I told him to go ask the kid to come home, and I'll straighten him out. I wouldn't hurt the kid. I wouldn't lift my voice at him. I'd just tell him he's mistaken, and I'm sorry he is.

"I'll be walking, and I say to myself: there's something wrong in America, and I wish the government would make the country better. I'll be on the truck, coming back from work, and I see people all dressed up in their suits, you know, and driving good cars, new ones, and even so they look to be in real bad shape. I look at their faces and I say, 'Oh, it's not a good day, is it!' They glare at each other. On the road they use their horns at each other, and they go cutting into each other. If my dad ever saw me use a horn, he'd stop me from driving. He said a horn is for real bad-mannered people. And I've never used my steering wheel the way they do up here. They mean to kill, the way they cut out of line, then cut back in. Then they all catch up with each other, because lights make them stop and go and there's no figuring them out, no matter how clever you try to be.

"There's a lot of good about the city of Chicago. I'm not one of these people who always say bad things. I'm not ungrateful. I saw a television program a few months back. They told me at work to be sure and see it. They said it was about the hillbillies. I felt like telling them to go to Hell, but they're foremen, and they pay you, and it's not worth it, fighting. You never change anyone's mind when you fight. But I remembered what they said, and I watched the program. They had some nice people there — talking and speaking their minds — but there was too much belly-aching, if you ask me. Just because it's not easy for us, that's no reason to keep on complaining and asking for more of everything. I want more work; I could use more money, but I'll be damned if I want someone else I don't know to turn on a television set and see me there saying that it's all bad up here in Chicago. The truth is it's bad everywhere, if you're not making any money.

"If I had money, I'd drive back home. But if I was born here and never knew anything else, I guess I'd be driving all over those big, superhighways, just like the people here do, and cutting in and out, and stepping on the gas with all my might just to move ahead a few feet, and cussing at the next guy because he won't move out of the way — when it doesn't make any differ-ence, because ahead of me is someone else, and then someone else, and then someone else. The way I see it, a city is like a forest, only the people are trees and bushes, and they're all over, and you learn to live with them. I'll be walking down the street, and I see people cutting into each other, like they do in their cars, and they run and bump into the next fellow, and they push someone else to one side. They're just trying to make a path for themselves, I guess. I'll be thinking to myself that it's like in the hills, when I want to be in a meadow but I'm in the woods, and I get caught by a bush, you know, or I nearly trip over a fallen branch, and I say: I've got to keep pushing through here, even if the path gives way and it's hot and the bugs are all over me and I get scratched and I'm afraid I'll lose my bearings. If you want to hunt, you have to push into the woods. No animal is going to stand out there in the meadow and say: here I am, and there's nothing to hide me, or protect me, and go ahead, enjoy yourself walking through the grass, and I'll be standing and waiting on you to come across me and lift your gun and fire. Like I say, if you want to hunt you have to make your way through the woods, and if you want to get someplace in Chicago you've got to force yourself through the crowds.

"I'm not as God-fearing as I guess I ought to be. When I was a boy my mother taught me I might have to wander for a long time before I found my God. I always thought that would be after I died, and not before I go to my grave. We've been doing our share of wandering since we left home, and there may be more ahead. I should pray harder when I'm in church. Maybe God is signaling us. Maybe He wants us to go someplace else. But Chicago is the best we can do, I believe. I told my wife the other day that if there's to be more wandering, like the minister says, it'll probably come later, when we've departed this earth. We're alive here in this city, and if a man can say he's kept his family alive, I don't believe he ought to be too bitter, you know. I moved with my wife and children because there just wasn't another thing to do, except throw ourselves on the mercy of the county officials, and they would have laughed and told me my family is no friend of theirs, and why don't I leave right away, before I'm carried into jail. I have a friend who keeps on saying that these cities are like the Hell you would hear the ministers back home talking about, but I look him in the eye and I say, 'You're here, aren't you?' Then I say, 'I'm going back home in a

month or so, and you can squeeze in with us. Would you like to
go? Would you like a one-way trip for free back to Kentucky?'
He'll show a big grin then and say no, and then I say that I feel
like he does all the time, but you can't let yourself forget why
you're up here. My wife is the one who reminds me, and I keep
her words in my head. A woman can make a man stop and
think."

He likes to stop and think. He likes to talk and reminisce. But
most of all he likes to keep busy. If he can't find work, he walks
and goes to a bar and talks, and he goes to a "center" and sips
free coffee, and he goes to his car and looks at it and checks on
the motor and makes sure it sounds right and runs right and
looks to be responsive and ready to go and able to last the
journey. More and more, though, he doubts there will be any
more long journeys. Trips, there will always be trips back to
Breathitt County; but his children will grow up in Chicago, and
it may even be that he and his wife will die there, rather than in
Breathitt County. He has to accept such a likelihood, come to live
with it and find it not unbearable. He has to see in the coming
years hardship and struggle, but also a life to be lived, day after
day and concretely. The alternative is endless dreaming about a
distant and unlikely future in which the prodigal son returns
home in triumph. "I'll stay here; I'll stay here and work here and
die here." He says that after he has put in a long day's work and
has a beer or two in him and has had a thought or two about the
old days "back home" and now has to pick himself up from the
chair and walk out into the streets, Chicago's streets, and make
his way "back home" — to his family in a nearby building.

3. Sights and Memories

I am an old man, and I don't do much but sit and smoke my
pipe. I do other than that, actually; I pick a guitar, and I'm good
at showing my daughter how much I like her food. My daughter
is my life. Since my wife died I've wanted to go join her a lot of
times; I've wanted to die. But my daughter is good to me, and
she says she doesn't know what she'd do without me around, and

I believe her — so here I am. And I'll tell you this, there are days when I have to go touching things and saying to myself: it's true, it's true, you *are* here, you've left Logan County, West Virginia, and you're in Pittsburgh, Pennsylvania, and it's a big, big city, and it's not a quiet town like Whirlwind was.

They say to me I'm getting a little deaf, and I say to them that a man can't get very deaf in a noisy city, because even if he loses some of his hearing, there's more than enough noise to make up for it. When I was young I could hear everything in the world and still have the quiet a man needs to hear himself, but up here in the city you want to protect your ears even if they aren't smart enough to take care of themselves. I imagine I'm losing my hearing because my ears told themselves one day: we can't let all this commotion keep hammering away at us, so we're going to learn how to say no. But those ears listen all right when I pick my guitar; they hear the music, and if my daughter calls me, they catch her words too.

I left Whirlwind — thereabouts it is, five miles away — an old man, you might say. I was fifty-five. I'd worked in coal mines. I'd helped my daddy with his crops. I'd gone over to Beckley, West Virginia, and tried to work. We had people over there in Raleigh County, kinfolk, and they were always telling me when they came to visit that the city is the place, and I could get some kind of job there and then I'd see regular money and wouldn't have to be pleading with the county people and always asking the minister for a little help. It's been hard in the state of West Virginia for a long time, you know — ever since they cut back on men in the mines, because of the machines. I didn't want to keep taking my wife and kids from place to place, so I went to Beckley myself and worked there a while. I got a job through my cousin; I worked in a market, keeping the stock on the shelves and like that. But I missed my family, and I didn't want to bring them with me, and finally I decided to go back home and try to get along as best I could. I had a friend who owned a gas station, and he would give me a little work time. When he went home I filled in; and when he took a day off, and when it was lunch and suppertime. Between the money he paid me and what we grew and the help we'd receive every once in a while from the church, we got by. I wasn't happy being so in need all the time, but we did get by, and neither my wife nor I were ever people to complain. Today on the television you see people always demanding one thing or another, and you wonder what gives them the idea that they can get all they want. Maybe they can. Maybe they're right. But it's not in me to be like that; it's not in me to push and shout and make a nuisance of myself. I suppose if some of us in West Virginia had been noisier a long time ago things would have gone different. But a man can only be what he is, that's my philosophy. I tell my grandchildren not to listen to me all the time, just some of the time, because people my age made mistakes. They put up with a lot — too much, I think. Thank God my grandchildren aren't growing up in the world I did. I do believe the country has changed a lot for the better since I was a boy.

We did what we could, my wife and I. We brought seven children into the world. We lost three of them as little children. My daughter tells me we needn't have lost them if there'd been a doctor to see them, but I say to her: that word "if" is the longest word in the language, and the hardest to forget. We lost a boy in the war, the Second World War. He was our oldest. He bore my name. I still think of him. I wonder what he would have done with his life if he'd have lived. Now I have a grandson, and he's over there in Vietnam. I don't know what to say about that war. We've got to win; we can't let the whole world push us around. But I wish we'd get out of there. I wish they'd send our boys back to us. It doesn't seem right, the way this country has to go fighting battles for every other country.

My three children alive are good children. I have two daughters up here in Pittsburgh, and they are the best girls you'd ever want, the best *women* they are, and their husbands are sons to me, real good sons. I have a son back home in Logan County. He's not doing much. I don't like to think of him, but I have to; he's my boy, no matter what. He was a good boy, but he got himself into trouble. He couldn't find work, and he went into the Army. He did fine there, but when his enlistment was up he came out. That was a mistake. He'd gotten used to the high living you have in the Army. He'd been eating all that good food they have, and he wasn't any longer thin and wasting, you know. He'd saved money and got himself the best clothes I've ever seen a man have, and he bought himself a real good car, a Pontiac, and he loved to drive and go like lightning, he'd say. When he came back I thought I had a millionaire for a son. I asked him where he got the money, and he said he'd been a soldier, and Uncle Sam pays his soldiers. I'd forgotten that!

Back home he just slowly fell into pieces; that's about the only way I know to tell what happened to the boy. He tried to find work, and of course I knew there was no point even trying, but I thought to myself: he's got to go and learn that, and it's not up to me to go setting him straight. I guess he was spoiled by the Army. I guess he thought: once well-off, always well-off. He asked around for work, and then he looked all over, and then he began to get discouraged, I could see; but he tried to keep his pride, you know. He'd come back, and I was watching, and I'd see the look on his face when he got out of his car. He'd look sad; I'll say he did! Then I could see him trying to cheer himself up. He'd walk around the car and look at it and start patting the hood, you know, or one of the fenders, and I'd see him smile to himself. At least he had that car. He took to calling her Millie. Then he'd walk up to our house, and he'd try to keep his smile on, and his mother and I, we would drive ourselves near crazy trying to make talk, so that he wouldn't feel we wanted to ask him anything. We knew the answer. We knew what the story was. There just wasn't work.

After a while, of course, he couldn't hold on to his spirits. He got sour, and he didn't want to eat, not even his mother's cooking. He wanted to drink instead. He kept on looking for work, but how many no's can a man take? I told him he was asking for trouble. I told him there's no point in knocking your head up against a brick wall: blood comes; you get weaker and weaker; you can end up killing yourself. I told him to stop looking for work that doesn't exist and stay with us and help me out with the vegetables and maybe we could put in some new land for crops;

it's hard on the side of our hills, but with enough hands working you can do a lot. He kept asking me about the mines, and I told him: God forbid. He said he'd do anything just to make some money. I told him they were cutting down on miners, because they have machines now; but even if they weren't cutting down, I told him, it's no good down there. Then he blew up and said I shouldn't tell him what to do. I told him what I'd already said. He answered that he'd been out in the world, and he'd seen the country, and he had his car, and he didn't want to be like me. I didn't say a word to that. What was I to say? I didn't want him to be like me. When a man is down and out like me, and barely able to keep his wife and children alive, then he doesn't want his son to live the same kind of life as that.

His mother told him to mind his tongue; she told him that if he turned out one-half as good as I was, then she'd be proud of him. He got angry at her, though. He said he was as good as I was already, and she had no right to say he wasn't. Of course he was choosing to read his mother wrong. She only meant to give me a helping hand, to stand up for me. He was so upset, the boy was. And we all were. My daughters, they were growing up, and they sat and heard the talk, and they started to cry. I tried to get them to go on outside, but they wouldn't leave. They insisted on hearing everything.

My son left us that day, and I don't know when he got into trouble, or how; all I know is that he must have gone into a store and tried to take something, and they caught him. He denies he meant to take anything without paying. He hit the man who accused him, the storekeeper, and the man fell over and got hit worse — on the edge of the counter, I believe. My boy drove off, but a customer got his number, and it wasn't long before the sheriff had him, and the boy had plenty of liquor on his breath, from what I heard later. That was the beginning of his ruin, I can see that now. He never has been the same since then. They put him away in prison, and even though they tried to keep his sentence down, he became a different person after he was let out. He was a hard man. He didn't have that smile on him; practically never did I see him smile. He chased after some girls, but each one he dropped, and they were heartbroken. One of them came to see my wife and me, and she told us our boy was a cruel, cruel man. At first I didn't believe her. I thought: look at the way she is, so mean and spiteful herself. Who is she, that I should listen to her? But my wife said later that she was convinced that the girl was one hundred percent right, and that it pained her to say so, but we'd best accept the truth and not try to blind our-selves.

So, I began to change and see my wife's argument, and when the boy came to see us, I stood up to him, and I told him he either straightens out or he doesn't come and see us any more until he does. He lost his temper and said a lot of bad things to us. He went after me first, but he wasn't easy on his mother either, and he called my two girls a few bad names. He said we were all plain dumb, and he was glad he'd wisened up. He said he wasn't going to sit back and be poor all his life while a lot of business people kept on making more and more money. I told him to go ahead and make all the money he could. I wasn't against that. I haven't anything to be proud of, so far as my own life goes, and I told him so. I told him he could call me all the names he wanted; all I hoped was that he'd go and get rich, like he said he was going to do. And I told him that when he did get rich I wanted him to remember one thing, please: I don't want any of his money; I want him to go and enjoy it, all he will ever make.

He never made much of anything. He looked for a job some more, and found one, lucky that he was. He was helping a man who had a chain of five-and-dime stores, four of them. They were going to make him a salesman, but first he had to clean up for them and help them unpack their stock. It wasn't too different from what I did in Beckley. The trouble was that the man began to lose more and more money, and he had to close the store my boy was working in. Have you ever seen a man just begin to get better from a bad sickness, and everyone is so happy, and he looks better than ever — and then all of a sudden he goes bad again, and this time you can tell there's nothing that can save him, because he's used up all his energy fighting the sickness, and now that he's failed, he's really gone? That's what happened to my boy. He was fired. He started drinking, and he never stopped, he never did. I'd have to say he's married to the bottle. He has a wife, and she's a patient woman. She tries to keep her husband on his feet, but it's not easy. She has only one child, thank God. She got an infection, and she can't have any more, I guess. She takes in work; she makes clothes and quilts and rugs. She's very good at keeping the three of them fed. He goes and gets his friends to give him one drink after another. He always was a nice boy to have around, and I guess his friends think so, too. They make their liquor, you know. If they got caught, they'd all be put in one of the government's prisons, but if they caught all the people in West Virginia who make their own liquor, they'd have to build a few extra places to house them.

I'd rather think about my girls and their husbands and their children. I can't always be recalling the bad things in my life, the sorriness and the heartache. My wife died a few years ago; it was her heart, and the last thing she said to me was: don't think of the past, just enjoy the few years you have left. She was always right. She knew how to do the best she could, and then she always said: the rest is up to God. I thank God for my two daughters. They are close to each other; that's why they live in the same apartment building here. Their husbands get on very good. They're almost like brothers. They were the ones who decided to come up here. They came up together, and left me back in Logan County at first, with my two girls and the grandchildren. The men decided they *had* to get out of Logan County, and they figured if they were going to leave Logan County, they might as well go all the way and leave the state and try to find some good jobs in one of those big cities. But they did try first to stay in West Virginia. They went to Charleston, even though they'd heard that for men without much schooling, it wasn't so easy there. They couldn't find much. They got discouraged. They drove back home, and they weren't going to try anymore. They told me they'd as soon die as live in a city, and I could see what they meant. I told them Beckley was bad enough — the streets and the cars and the traffic lights telling you to stop and go every minute or two. Charleston was worse, I knew that. They said they were thinking about a move to Pittsburgh, but they'd decided not to do it. They would stay put.

After a while, though, they changed their minds. They had a friend who was up there, and he had a job in a hospital; he was an orderly, and they'd trained him while he worked, and then they put him at a desk, and he took care of people when they showed up with their appointments. He made sure they got to the right place in the building. He said he'd try to get a job for them; he is kin of my younger girl's husband. So, they got in the car and drove up there, and one thing came to another, and that's how I'm here right now. My girls aren't living it up rich, but they eat, and they have enough for a car and television and clothes, so they're not cold in the winter. That's all anyone has a right to ask for. I wish everyone in the state of West Virginia was as lucky!

I'm the kind of man who's too old now to do much but live from day to day. I'm nearing seventy. Because of sicknesses I must have had a long time ago, I'm not as strong as I could be. My stomach isn't good, nor my heart. But I get on. I take walks. I look at the city. I've come to like the city. I'm glad we're up here. Maybe it's my son who haunts me, but I think back to all the trouble we had, my wife and I, just in staying alive, and I say this: it's a terrible shame, and if the people of the state of West Virginia have to leave so they can make a living, then I guess they have to leave, and the sooner the better. I'll be taking a walk, and I see the buses go by, and the trucks and all the cars, and I see the people, so many of them, and the big signs you see, lit up in the day as well as the night, and the big buildings — and I say to myself that there's a lot to see, a whole lot, in this world, and if you're in the cities you stand a chance of seeing more of all there is to see than if you stay back in your place up a hollow or a creek. If I had all the money I needed, I'd probably propose to my daughters that they and their husbands and children all come back to Logan County, but I'll never have money, and with that as the way it is, I'm glad we're up here.

I go back home in my mind. I have my memories. I think of my wife; a good woman she was. I think of us dancing to my brother playing the guitar. That was a long time ago. I think of the walking I used to do, how peaceful it could be back there. But up here you can keep yourself interested in what's going on in the world, and that's good for you, the doctor told me. He said I should go on a walk every day, and I should keep my mind interested in everything I see. I told him: thank you, Doctor, and I'm grateful to be able to go see a doctor, but I've tried to keep my mind interested in the world ever since I was a little boy, I believe, and I'll keep doing so. My eyes are in good shape, so I look at as much of the city of Pittsburgh as my feet will let me — and my heart. It's a sight to see, the city, a sight. My grandchildren are city children, you know, and *that's* a sight to see! They say they wouldn't mind going home to West Virginia on vacations, but their favorite state is Pennsylvania and their favorite city is Pittsburgh. Now it shows you: a child likes what he knows, so long as he's not suffering and feeling cheated out of something.

I go for a walk, and my grandson is with me, and he's like one of those city slickers — I used to call them. A city slicker is someone who is real fast on the draw. My grandson knows where the buses stop. He knows all the fares you have to pay. He knows when the lights will change, and when to cross. I don't even notice the lights, but he does. He knows where to go if you need anything. He'll take me in the drugstore, and I've never seen anyone who knows his way around like that boy does. I tell him that he reminds me of a beaver; the child goes scurrying around all over the place, and he's so fast I'm afraid he'll disappear right before my eyes. I have to look at him twice or three times, and remind myself that I saw him being born, and he's named after his uncle back home, even if his uncle isn't the best person now. This boy will make us proud of the name. He told me a little while back that he wanted to grow up and own a drugstore and make the medicines up for people, and he wanted to be a doctor, too because that way he could make the medicines he told his patients to use. I told his mother what I'd heard, and she said she was always hearing that sort of thing. I told her she had a boy who really kept her hopping, and she said it wasn't the boy, really, it was the city and what it does to a child. She said he played around the neighborhood, and he saw everything. Back home she used to know where each path went to and when the birds would come and when they'd leave and where to go find the animals. Her children here in Pittsburgh know the city that way. They take in the neighborhoods — into their heads!

More than anything else I like to go sit in the park and watch the children. Mostly they are children like my own grandchildren. There are a lot of us from the hills in West Virginia in this neighborhood, and you'll find us in other cities. I know because I watched men I knew leave; they told me that one day I'd have to go myself, and I laughed. I wouldn't have gone, either. It was what happened to my boy that gave me the push, and then I was glad to leave. In the park I sit and watch the kids play. I'll see a boy, and he'll remind me of my oldest son — dead over in France, I believe. I'll see another boy, and he'll remind me of my younger son, as good as dead. I'll be honest: I wish he'd die. I do. I think to myself: it's good to see the children up here. The sight of them is enough to raise a man's spirits high as can be; they have shoes and socks, and they have good jackets, and they have scarves and hats and gloves. I look at their clothes, and I remember what my own children *couldn't* wear, never wore, never had, never dreamed they'd have. And the kids aren't slow and tired. They're eating good, and they're full of fun.

Sure, I say, that cement is no match for a good stretch of meadow, even if it *is* on the side of a steep hill. Sure, the young ones do slip and fall and tumble down a little and get scared and get hurt. They fall on the flat cement and scratch their legs real bad, and I wish they were back home, that's all I can think. But I'll stop myself. I'll remind myself what we had to go through each winter, and I'll see those boys and girls, and I'll be glad they're up here, cement and all, steel pipes and all. You can't compare steel pipe to a tree. You can't compare a swing to our hills and creeks and animals and birds and fish. You can't compare the cement and the little grass they have here to all the land a kid can get to know back home. I think we bring up a man who's better able to be on his own — back home we do. But the trouble is that we've been getting poorer and poorer. I hate to admit it. I never did call myself poor, not once in my life while I lived in Logan County. The minister back there would call us poor sometimes, and we'd all go up to him and tell him, please sir, to stop saying that about us. He said it was no shame to be poor, but we never wanted anyone feeling pity for us. That's no good, a man stretching out his hand to you just because he thinks you're in a bad state, and he'd like to give you a few crumbs.

Up here there's some begging that goes on. I know. The colored, I hear, are on relief a lot, welfare. Some of our people are, but we don't take to charity, not if we can help it. Maybe we should, though. Maybe we should start *demanding*, the way you see people doing these days on television. So long as my daughters and their husbands have enough money, they won't ask for anything special; but I think now they're different than they would be if they were back in Whirlwind, West Virginia. Yes sir, if they had no money coming in, they'd *have* to start demanding, or else they'd be on the street and with no food to eat. In the city you have to pay that rent, and you have to buy that food every week. In the city money means a lot more than back home. You can't catch a fish or kill a rabbit or a deer around here. My grandchildren go to school, and the teacher tells them about all those animals as if they live up on the moon. Of course, we go home a couple of times a year, and I show the children real, live animals, and they come back and tell the class what they've seen.

The worst thing about going back is the sight of my boy and his wife and their girl. They're lost people, if you ask me. I'm afraid I'm going to fall dead one of these days when I'm there, and I'm looking at my own flesh and blood. All the way back to Pittsburgh I hear his mother's voice, and she's crying. I don't cry. I've never cried in my life except twice: once when my boy was killed in the war, and they came and told us, and once when my wife died. I guess I should be crying all the time for my son that's alive, but he makes me too upset. I ask him please to come back with us; they have a good hospital up in Pittsburgh, I tell him, and they could help him out. They could maybe get him to slow down on the liquor. The girl, their child, she's a nice person, but she's so shy I can't believe it's a grandchild of mine. She favors her father, and she reminds me of her grandmother, my wife. But that's only her looks I'm talking about. She won't talk. She's smart enough; I can tell. But she's against us people coming to see her. She knows it makes her daddy angry, the sight of us does, and that's why I can't blame her at all. I have memories of the girl being born, and I came and looked at her, and I prayed to her. I said, "Please little child, help your daddy; he was once a good boy, and if he'd had some luck he would have stayed that way." But you can't expect a baby to hear a prayer like that and to change her daddy's life. I know the one thing that never, never should have happened: my son should have stayed in the Army and not left, not come home here with his money and his big hopes. If he'd have remained one of Uncle Sam's boys, he'd be today the fine man he once was.

Maybe if I'd have known how to find work myself in a city like this one and taken us all up here a long time ago — maybe then my boy would have turned out better. I often wish I was back home, but I know for a child it's better here, unless you've got money and can live real high back in Logan County. Some do, but people like me don't; they just get by, or to be exact, they just stay alive. "We don't die" — that's what my father used to say when he'd hear a man start complaining. But my father was bragging and boasting, when he said, "We don't die." A lot of people did. Today my daughters ask me why my father didn't go and fight with the sheriff, or demand that the county officials give all the people up every hollow some welfare money, if there was no work. I try to tell them that it's all very well for them, in Pittsburgh, to talk like that, but what about my father? He wasn't in a city with a job. He'd never been out of Logan County in his long, long life. And he didn't have a television set with the man telling him all the news and showing pictures from everywhere in the whole world — with people demonstrating and demanding things. He was lucky to be alive; that's what he knew. In every family a lot of children didn't ever grow up, and you felt you had to accept hardship. My two girls are the first ones I've ever known that take their children to a clinic and get the doctor's help whenever something goes wrong.

My dad and my grandfather would say that if you stay alive you're as darned lucky as can be, and anything beyond that is like the gravy, don't you know, on the meat and the potatoes. And did we grow potatoes! We'd also go hunting and get our meat. And we could go catch a fish. And we grew vegetables. I can see the tomatoes, the carrots, the radishes. But come winter we'd still be hungry. My mother couldn't pickle and store away more than we grew, and it wasn't enough for the long, cold months, and so she'd be sighing and worrying instead of whistling and singing while she was preparing her preserves over the stove.

I have a memory. I can see her putting the tomatoes up; she had her jars, and she was working as hard as can be. I guess I came in, and she thought she was alone, and she was crying. I asked her what the matter was. She said nothing, but then she told me. She said come February or so, we'd all be sitting in the cabin, and the jars would be empty, and all she'd have for us would be some corn bread and the tea, and more tea, and it would hurt her every morning to look at our faces. I don't recall what I said back to her. A child can't grasp certain things, you know. It's in a child's nature to smile, even if he hasn't got a reason to smile. I believe my mother told me to forget what she said, and I did — promptly, I'll bet. But I didn't really forget. I'll be sitting at the playground sometimes, and it'll be winter, and the children are running around all over, and they're nicely bundled up. Then they take out some candy they have, and that gives them more strength. Then they say they've got to go home to lunch, so I take my grandchildren home. It's Saturday, maybe, and they're home from school, and their mother gives them all a big, big lunch. The sight of all that food being eaten in the month of February — well, it gets memories in me going, I guess. I can't help thinking my mother is smiling down on us from someplace and saying: you did real good to go where you are.

4. Settling In

Automobiles are hardly anything new to America's youth. Up the remotest hollows one can find them, often enough broken-down and abandoned. But they are used, too — and in the course of my work with young Appalachian men I have often wondered what we would have talked about had there not been an automobile to mention, then discuss at some length, then go over and look at, and finally drive in. I suppose before there were cars, men talked about horses. When one first begins to spend time in Kentucky or West Virginia the roads seem thoroughly dangerous. If one is like me, possessed of and sometimes victimized by a particular vocabulary, thoughts begin to assert themselves: am I crazy or suicidal to be on these roads with these drivers, or are *they* all crazy or suicidal — or "aggressive" or "antisocial"? The roads are narrow and winding and at times tortuous beyond all others in the nation. Asphalt can without warning turn into sand or mud. And the drivers: they seem so casual and vigorous; they move along as though lanes and lanes of road were on either side of them, and no cars were in sight for miles ahead — even when only a few inches separate them from the steepest of hills, or a curve approaches around which totally unseen, a car or huge coal truck may be coming in the opposite direction. Yet throughout the years of my work in Appalachia, I have never seen an accident — which is not to say accidents don't occur, but simply to suggest that my fearfulness must have had something to do with the limitations of my own experience: as a driver I took for granted certain road conditions, consequently I was made nervous when I found them lacking.

By the same token a youth from, say, Leslie County, Kentucky, can find superhighways and most especially city traffic puzzling if not terrifying. All that space and all those cars and all those traffic lights and traffic signs! So many distractions: horns blowing, stores with things in the window and pictures of wine and women! And the turnoffs, the constant intersections, the warnings which insist this highway has now become something else, or is about to join with yet another road — all of that is confusing, as are those constant reminders that one is so-and-so miles from such-and-such a town or city, not to mention from some state line. Then, there are the restaurants and gas stations: how can they all stay open? How can there be so many people eager to use such places? How can there be so many people at all?

For Larry Walker, age seventeen and a half, who is originally from a creek near Thousand-Sticks, Leslie County, Kentucky, but now lives in Dayton, Ohio, those questions are not openly asked. They are very much on his mind, though; and after a beer or two they come to expression. Larry has been in Dayton for five years, but he is not *from* Dayton. His little brother and sister may have the notion at times that they are from Ohio, that Dayton is their home, that their future is to be found in a growing city, but not Larry: "I'm from Leslie County, and I'll always say that's where my home is. When I turn eighteen I'll probably go into the Army. I hurt my arm once, broke it, but I don't think they will hold that against me. They'd be fools to; I'd make a good soldier, I believe. I've always dreamed I might one day go into the service and maybe stay there for a while. If you stay in twenty years, you can retire, and you have a good pension, and then you can go back to Leslie County and there's no ache over money. We only left the county because we had to leave. My father's brother left first, my Uncle Jim. He got a job here in a factory, and he came back with all those green bills in his hand and told my father he had to come up to Ohio, too; so here we are. My mother says it's like in the stories you see on television: people go away for a while, but then they come home, and they're glad. She means they go on vacation. Like my dad says: it's a vacation having a job and money; you don't have to stand around all the time and worry if you're going to survive the winter.

"If I had my choice, I'd go into the Navy. I know it's strange, because I've never seen the ocean, only a lake or two in Kentucky. But I saw a movie once about the Navy when I was real little, maybe seven, I'd say. I've wanted ever since to join the Navy. The Navy people might decide I'm no good, being from the mountains. I'd probably get seasick. I'm going to wait to be drafted; I'll have a chance to go back to Leslie County then and take my physical. The government will pay for my travel home, I believe. The Army can tell me where they want me to go, and I'll be glad to serve my country — even if it means Vietnam. There's too many people these days who don't salute the flag the way they should. This is the greatest country in the world, and if there's going to be a great country, there has to be a great Army.

"Until we moved to Ohio I never realized how *big* the country is, and how you can go from one place to another, and it all changes. I knew we had these cities, these big cities, but like I tell my friends when we go back home and I can talk with them: seeing is believing. If I'd stayed there and seen pictures of Dayton on the television, I wouldn't know much, not compared to what I know now. I mean, you have to drive in a city to know it. You can't believe it's like it is until you try to drive from one place to another, one street to another; then you find out. The guys back home, kids I grew up with, they say a road is a road, and that's all there is to it. I tell them they don't know what they're talking about. I have my car, and I've got to keep my foot on the brake more than on the gas — that's what it means to live in the city. Living in the city for a guy like me is learning to brake the car all the time, and wearing the clutch out, and using gas like it's water that's come down the mountain and is waiting to be picked up in buckets and poured into the tank. Living in the city means you have to turn your head every other minute you're driving and keep your eye out for almost anything — when all you want to do is push that gas pedal to the floor and take off.

"I love my car. She's a beauty. She's a Chevy, the best car there is. The motor is good. The tires are good. I think there's no use driving a car if you can't have good tires. Have you ever had a flat on a city street? That's no fun. I'd rather have to fix a flat right in the middle of a curve up one of those hills; there I could hear the car coming and flag it down. Here in Dayton no one pays any attention to the next guy driving, and it is so noisy you can't hear your own voice speaking. They tell me it's even worse in Cleveland. I can get around here, though; now I can. And if my car goes bad, I can take it off the road and fix it myself. I've learned everything I can about car engines. I like new cars and I like old cars. Don't you love the old Thunderbirds? They were some car — 1955 or 1956, I believe. I was only a baby then. When I was a little older and just beginning to go to school I remember a big shot, someone from Hazard, coming up to the little schoolhouse we had; and it was a Thunderbird he drove. I think they were talking about closing down the school and sending us someplace else. I think a mine company bought the hill nearby, and they were going to tear it up for coal. I recall telling my friend Carl — he was my best friend — that I hoped one day I could drive a car like that, a Thunderbird; then I'd have everything I wanted. I still don't have a Thunderbird, but now I don't think I'd buy one even if I had a huge bankroll on me. I'd buy a Mustang or a Cougar, maybe. But for a beginner like me, this old Chevy is a good car to have.

"I've taken the motor apart three times. I painted the car myself. I know how. I know how to spray the right way. If I go into the Army, I hope I can be near some of those jeeps and trucks. I wouldn't mind driving them; I hear they're something to drive all right! I'd rather work on the motors, though; that way I could learn more about the different kinds and how they all work. If I could only get a job back home working in a garage or a gas station! But it's not easy to do. I don't know anyone who owns a gas station, and if I did he'd want to use his own son, I'm sure. Jobs are scarce back home. That's why we drove here, and that's why my car is going to spend most of its life in Ohio. The poor car will suffer plenty on that account, but that's just how it works out. I'll be driving — and stopping and starting and stopping and starting — and I can hear the motor saying: stop it, and get me out of here, fast. So, I just talk back to it. I say: motor, take it easy and just keep going, because there's not a thing in the world you or I can do anyway, except keep going. Then I baby her a bit; I go easy on the brakes and try not to shift more times than I have to — and the old motor seems happier.

"I get nervous when I'm in a crowd of cars; that's when I guess I keep shifting the gears back and forth, and it's not good to do. But how are you supposed to live with all those other cars? I never knew there were so many real, live, honest-to-goodness people in America until we came up here. To this day I can hardly believe it. In school they taught us that it was New York City that was most crowded, and next Chicago. But I asked the teacher if it could get much more crowded than Dayton, Ohio, when the factories were letting out, and she said no, she was sure it couldn't, because there are hundreds and hundreds of cars all over the road, and they're coming in and turning off and switching from one lane to the other, and the horns are going, and you get the meanest looks, and all you're trying to do is mind your own business and not get yourself in a giant of a wreck.

"I've had two accidents. If I'd have been driving only in Kentucky I'm sure I wouldn't have any accidents to my name. They weren't big accidents, just small ones, a fender each time. I fixed them myself, did the straightening and sanding and painting. I knew how to do that from watching my dad. He learned as a boy himself. He'd hit the car into a tree going up or down the creek sometimes. Mostly he's a good driver, though. He never had an accident in Leslie County, but he's had one up here, and that makes three in the family — two for me and one for him. It's different, driving in Kentucky. There aren't all the other cars. There aren't a lot of signs every mile or so, confusing you, always confusing you. They'll drive me to wearing glasses, those signs will, I do believe. And I don't mean to say anything against the people up here, but I think it's friendlier back in Leslie County, and it comes out on the road, because at home people will be more helpful to each other.

"I'll drive out away from Dayton sometimes. I'm not going anyplace special. I'm not going to see someone. I just want to give my Chevy a rest from the city. I want to give her a good time. I want to take her on a road and let her roll along, and not stop and start. I don't want to have to clutch her and shift her and brake her and idle her and get her so tired and hot she's ready to explode or go dead on me. Out in the country I can bring her up to sixty or seventy pretty fast. She holds the road good. She's no new racing car. She's no big new car. She's light and six years old. But she's got pep in her, a lot of life in her. I hope I'll be like her when I'm that old. A car is like a dog, you know. Each year is six or seven. I figure my car is getting on to forty-five, and that's old.

"My dad says it is not old, forty-five, but to me that's a long way off. I can't picture what it's like to be twenty-five, never mind forty or forty-five. You must begin to feel real tired. I get tired myself. I'll be in the stockroom, handling all those crates, from eight in the morning to five in the afternoon. When I punch my card, and it says five minutes after five, I ask myself where the day has gone to, and my muscles answer that they can tell me, they surely can. Then I come home and have my supper, and I go and drive around. I rest that way. I'm sitting in my car, and I have a good, soft blanket on the seat, and that rests my back. I have some friends I take for a ride — a few of the guys I know up here. And I have two girls I take out. I switch to one, then I switch to the other; they're both from Ohio, born here, and I don't know if I want to get serious with a girl who isn't from Kentucky. I don't have to marry a girl from Leslie County, but Kentucky is my home state, and I want to be going back there someday, so I don't see why I should get myself married to a girl who has other ideas in her head, you know. I've heard them talk, the girls from around here. A lot of them are spoiled. They want everything. They *expect* everything.

"I went to school until last year, until I was sixteen. I didn't graduate from high school, but I went there, and you get taught a lot. My friends back home, a lot of them never bothered going beyond sixth or seventh grade. They said: what's the reason to? I can see how they think that way. I wish I'd gone and finished high school. It's just that I had this chance for a job, and I couldn't turn a good job down. The job means money for all of us, and I save some for a new car. In school that's all the girls wanted, a guy with a new car; they didn't care much what the guy himself was like. I always thought it showed something about the girls, the way they looked at you for your car and not yourself. I don't believe a girl in Leslie County would be like that, though my mother and dad say they would, because it's only natural. I guess a girl is going to like a car, just like a toy, and that's why they ask you right away: what are you driving?

"They want to know your *plans*, the girls do. I tell them I don't have any. I tell them I may one day get into my car and drive and drive and fill the tank and empty it, until the road ends, and I'm somewhere, but I don't know where. Then, wherever it is I stop, I'll settle down. I'll get settled in, settled into a house, and there'll be a garage for my Chevy, and another garage in case I decide to get a second car, and I'll work in a job — I don't know what kind. The girl will be waiting for me to mention her. They don't know how much they tell about what's on their mind by the way they look. I try to keep myself from laughing, and I keep talking — but I never mention getting married. They always ask me why I may get myself a second car, and I tell them it's nice to give one car a rest and use the other, and then switch back again. You can get attached to a car. You have driven it so long and worked on it all that time, so it's yours, and you don't want to lose what's yours. The nice thing about living in Dayton is you stand a chance of making money, all the money you need. Then you can treat your car right!"

He thinks about it more than he talks about it, the money Dayton, Ohio, permits him to make, the money he cannot make in Leslie County, Kentucky. With each year he is more and more a city dweller, an owner of property, a worker — hence, less likely to return for very long to his home in the mountains, unless things should drastically change there, which is highly unlikely. He is no longer a child, yet not quite a grown-up. Almost half his childhood has been spent in Ohio, but with each month the balance changes, and he feels increasingly "settled in." He often uses that term "settled in," uses it as he did just above, in connection with what I suppose can be called a daydream or a fantasy — or an utterly exact way of describing what is on his mind and what he at least presently intends to do. He cannot really go back home, he knows that, yet he is not very happy living in even a medium-sized city like Dayton. He dreams of the West, the open and endless West, perhaps in the way his ancestors dreamed of what stretched ahead as they left the eastern seaboard. But he may actually spend the rest of his life in Ohio.

As one talks with him it becomes quite apparent that he finds a life without automobiles inconceivable, and a life without a decent home and a garage and suitable clothes and enough food also impossible to contemplate. He very much enjoys buying himself a sporty new jacket, unworn by someone else, not handed down to him to be used for a while and then in turn handed over to a brother or a cousin. And he likes to do other things that in sum reassure him how well he is coming along, how able he is to take care of himself, put away a little cash, and feel like what he calls "a going business." His father always had wished he could raise the money to have just that, a gas station or a garage, "a going business," he also puts it when he reminisces. The son now has those same dreams, but of course knows that if his business is going to grow, or even survive, Dayton will have to be the address and not some very small town in Leslie County.

So, step by step, innocently but decisively, the young man thinks things and dreams things and says things and decides things that commit him more and more to the life of a northern city, or maybe a far western one — and commit him, perhaps, to a girl who does not come from home, from the mountain country of eastern Kentucky. He does not say out and out what I have just written. How many of us at seventeen (maybe at any age) want to say exactly what we will be doing, come five or ten years? But we do at all times have certain assumptions, silent but influential, and during his five or so years in the city Larry Walker has become a different youth than he would be had he not been brought to Ohio as a child by his parents. He especially notices those various differences when he goes back home on a visit, and when he returns to Dayton he is most likely to talk about such matters. He is most likely to observe what he does in the day, and contrast all of his activities with those of his friends he knew as a small child. He is most likely to notice the way he dresses and the way others who live near Thousand-Sticks, Kentucky, dress. And yes, he is most likely to look at those girls he once knew and had crushes on and fought with and felt close to, and then think of the girls he met when he went to school in Dayton, three or four of whom he has courted in an offhand fashion, then forsaken, then gone back to, then again withdrawn from.

What distinguishes those girls from the girls in Kentucky, what distinguishes him from the boys in Kentucky, is something he finds hard to find words for, yet very much wants to clarify in his mind — hence the effort of language: "It's my home, my folks' home, Leslie County is. When I go back there I feel like I'm back where I belong. I can sit back and enjoy myself with the best people the Lord ever made. But after a few days I don't mind it too much if I have to leave. I begin to hear myself saying: it's near time to go, Larry, it's near time. There will even be a time when I start having a talk with myself. I say I'm ready to leave. Then I say why on earth are you actually looking forward to going, when you know full well how you'll soon be complaining about Dayton?

"I guess that the more you live in a place, the more it grows on you. I don't mean to say I like living here in the city rather than up in the hills, but a man has to earn a living, like my dad says. And if I'm going to get married and have kids, I can't see being so down and out, the way a lot of people in Kentucky are. I don't want my son to see me just sitting on a porch and carving wood and maybe picking on my guitar. My dad said he'd never have stayed alive, if he had kept on spending his days like that. He came up here, instead, and he was lucky to get a job for himself and hold on to it, and I've been lucky to get a job for myself and hold on to it — and that's why I don't think either of us can go back to Leslie County for more than a few days. There's no work, compared to the work you get here.

"But I do admit work isn't the only thing good up here. I talk a lot about my job, because I'm grateful to have it, and the money is good; it's sweet, real sweet, that money. I like Dayton, though. There are the movies, all of them; I've never seen the number of movie houses we have here in all of Kentucky I've been through, not just Leslie County. There are restaurants, good ones. You can live it up here. You can take a girl out on the town. You can have a good supper, any kind you want, then go to a movie, almost any kind you want. You can go bowling and you can go play pool and you can hear a good singer in a club and have a few drinks. It's not bad living in a city. There's a lot you miss, but there's a lot you have, too. I guess it's a matter of what your philosophy is, and where you can get the money.

"I'm not sure I could bring a girl up here from Kentucky,

though. It might be real hard on someone to live here — a person who hasn't grown into the place, like I have. I think the kids I grew up with, they'd have a hard time coming up here now. The reason I don't mind a lot of things, and like living here, at times, anyway, is that I was brought up here when I was much younger. I wasn't a baby. I was over twelve. I was growing fast. I was outgrowing everything, I can recall my mother saying. But I was still a kid, and I wasn't set in my ways. I'm getting set now; my dad says so, and he's right. I might want to get married soon, except that I may go into the service in a few months. Sometimes I think I'd be smarter to come back to Dayton after two years in the Army, rather than make a career of it, go regular. I'll have to wait and see.

"If I meet a real nice, pretty girl from here in Dayton, I might just marry her, if she'd have me. I once asked my favorite girl in Leslie County, Sylvia is her name, if she'd think of coming back with me, just for a week or so. I told her she could stay with us, and she knows my folks. She's distant kin to us, I believe. No, she said; she didn't want to leave the county. I asked her why. She said she didn't have anything against me or my folks, no sir; she'd love to stay with us, she said, and for longer than a week, she said. But to go all the way up to Dayton, out of the county and out of the state, that was too much for her, she said. She gave me a long look, right into my eyes, and I could see she really wanted me to propose marriage to her then and there, but I believe she knew, like I did, that I had to go back up North, and there wasn't any two ways about it. I said to her: Sylvia, just come and give it a try; come and travel through Kentucky and cross the river, the Ohio River, and look at Cincinnati, and then go up into the state of Ohio and get to know Dayton a little. But she kept on shaking her head. She didn't answer me. She just turned her head to the left and to the right, and I knew what she was telling me. Maybe the reason she couldn't speak her thoughts out loud was that she really did want to go with me, and she couldn't bear hearing herself say she wouldn't.

"I came home and told my folks what I'd said to Sylvia and what her answer had been. I never mentioned the word *mar-*

riage, or anything like that, but my mother said she thought that since we all are settling in, me included, and we're not going to leave Dayton for a long time, then I might have better luck if I chose a girl from Dayton, provided she's a good girl, for my wife than someone like Sylvia from back home. I was mad as I've ever been. I told my mother she was talking out of her head, because I wasn't thinking of getting married now, and when I did think of marriage, that would be the time I would go home to Kentucky and by God I'd stay there until I found a wife, and if my wife wanted to stay there and never leave, I'd stay that long myself and be glad to do it. Then my mother told me to cool myself down, and she said the way I was talking, she was sure I wasn't going to get married in a long, long time, not if I meant every word I'd said to her. Well, I had to smile then. I saw what she meant."

He not only saw what his mother meant; he knew it in his bones, her message. He is glad in so many ways to be in Dayton, bothersome as its traffic is, hard as his car finds the going, crowded and anonymous and noisy as the city, any city, can always be. He is glad that he is not living in a cabin up a hollow or creek. He is glad he does not live in a small town whose "unemployment problem" is severe and chronic and to a youth like him discouraging beyond the power of words to convey. Still, he does straddle two worlds, does go back and forth, feel divided loyalties, dream of one place while he lives in another. At seventeen nostalgia can be as powerful and summoning as at any other age, but at seventeen the meaning of a job and money is no less influential. What an observer like me has to watch very closely is the temptation to take a young man like Larry Walker too seriously *at any one moment in his life.* One day he can sound utterly convinced that he will soon, very soon, be a mountaineer again — a real one, not a distant, would-be one. The next time we talk, all of that seems not gone or buried or forgotten or "repressed" or denied or contradicted, but gently and tactfully put aside.

It is in such moments of "adjustment" to Dayton that a youth like Larry feels most alert, most challenged, most sure of himself

— and most at loose ends. What indeed will he do and where — now that he has ("sort of") decided that his destiny is to be found in Ohio's industrial cities, or perhaps in Illinois, or (who knows?) California, to which the Army might one day order him? And will he, therefore, slowly lose contact with Leslie County? Will he less and less think of those hills and valleys, those waterfalls and high trees and soaring birds, those clever animals and those dumb animals, those innocent but ever so swift and elusive fish? Will his car lose forever the feel of a narrow mountain road, with the sharp rises and the sudden falls, with the exciting twists and turns and curves? Will traveling by car become a bore, a nuisance, a tedious necessity? Will he one day say good-bye to that Chevy and good-bye to the notion that motors are wonderful, demanding, endlessly stimulating puzzles — objects of interest, exploration, and passion? Will he instead find his woman, his wife; find his job that lasts and lasts; find his nice, comfortable home, near others, near dozens and dozens of others? And for his two cars will he have no proud old two-door Chevy, no Mustang or Cougar, but a station wagon and perhaps a brand new Chevy four-door sedan? At seventeen one often doesn't *ask* such questions; instead, one does things — and so Larry's actions gradually will supply the answers to those questions.

5. Driving Around

Mountain people can go east as well as north and west; can leave West Virginia for a city like Washington, D.C., and its suburbs, or Norfolk, Virginia, or Baltimore; can find work in such cities and feel reasonably happy — but like their counterparts in Chicago or Dayton cling to memories and songs and certain foods and certain styles of cooking and certain forms of worship. Nevertheless, nostalgia has its limits, even among notoriously nostalgic "southern highlanders," the mountaineers or hollow people of Appalachia. A man like Ken Stevenson, a cabdriver in Washington, D.C., a resident of Arlington, Virginia, can tell exactly what the limits of nostalgia are. He can also sense what others think he is like: "I drive a cab in the nation's capital, so I hear a lot. I read the paper. I watch television. I know what I'm supposed to be. I'm supposed to be a hillbilly, a guy who used to drink liquor he made up some hollow, and now he's here in Washington, going from job to job, a lot of the time without any work. I'm also supposed to be crying every day because I'm not back in West Virginia, sitting on the steps of some log cabin and singing a song — with no shoes on, and overalls maybe, and a corncob pipe, and a dumb but happy look on my face. I don't know how these stories get going, but they do. You can't just be yourself. There's always someone who's trying to tell you you're someone else.

"I drive this cab ten hours a day. I pick up a lot of people. I like the job; it's interesting. I get to talking with the customers. I don't push myself on them, but if they look like they want to talk, I oblige; if not, I turn on my little transistor radio. They'll ask you where you're from, some people will — I guess because I don't talk as fast as a lot of people do who grow up here in a city like this. I'm in no hurry even when I drive. I like to get people to their destinations, and I like to get home alive each night — and I like to keep my license and not pay fines or go to jail. But no sooner do I mention that I'm from West Virginia, that I was born there and grew up there, than I hear about 'the hillbillies' and 'the miners over there.' I hear that we're nice people, just as cute as can be, 'darling people,' one lady told me. They ask me when I'm going back. They tell me they know my heart is back there in West Virginia, and isn't it a *beautiful* state, full of the *nicest* scenery. They want to know if I can sing songs, or if I play the guitar. They say they've heard we speak *very special English,* that's what a man told me once, and he said he was an expert on the subject — though to me he sounded from England, not America.

"One man said the liquor in Washington must be like soda pop to me, because he knew how strong the liquor is they make 'in those mountains,' he called them. And there's the man who wanted to know if I go home every weekend, and in Washington do I live 'in a settlement of your people' — that's how he talked. I told him no. I told him I live with my wife and my two children. I looked at his face through my mirror, and he was looking at me as if I was lying to him. 'Only two children?' he asked me. I said yes, and did he have any, I asked. He said he also had two. He didn't say anything more. I think he could tell I wasn't put in a good mood by his questions. I came home and told the wife what he said and what I said, and she said it was obvious he pictured us living with eight or ten children, dressed in rags, in some awful place, and counting the days until we could get home and throw away our shoes and eat the roots of trees or corn bread and drink whiskey from the still in back of the log cabin up the hollow and then throw cans and all the garbage we could find into the creek running down the hill — while we sang some song that told how we're idling, we're idling, and ain't that good, ain't that good. My wife is right; she says the colored people don't get any more prejudice and discrimination than we do. A lot of people in this world just like to see people the way they want them to be, and not the way they are.

"Let me say this, too; it's not only some of my fares who talk like that. I read worse about us in the papers, and I see worse about us on the television. There's always someone with an angle, trying to make us out as dumb people, as simple as can be, and never really happy until we're back in the cabin where we were born. I saw a program, and the program had us miserable all week, then speeding home every weekend to get away from some city we went to. I read in the paper that someone said the people from West Virginia and Kentucky, they're a strange bunch, and they don't trust anyone that's from the outside, and if they go away to a city, like I did, they won't stay away, but go back as fast as they can. And the story went on to say that we fight a lot in the hills, and we get nervous as can be in the city, and we're poor in West Virginia and poor in Chicago and all the other cities, including Washington, D.C., and Maryland and Virginia. I told my boy, my ten-year-old boy, that he'd better let me read the whole article to him, so he'd know what to expect whenever he starts reading newspapers. He once told me he'd like to be a newspaper reporter. He'd seen a fire, and he heard a reporter going around talking to people and writing down what they'd said. He came home and said he'd like to do that. I said fine. I hope he learns to talk with a lot of people before he comes to any conclusions. I hope he learns to report the truth, not a lot of stories.

"I told someone I was taking over to the State Department that the trouble with this country is that the people who run it don't see anyone but themselves and their friends, and meanwhile the ordinary man in the street doesn't get a chance to tell his ideas to anyone — and it's supposed to be *his* government. That's the trouble all over; you get people who are supposed to know things about the rest of us, and they say they do; they say they're all filled up with ideas, but they don't even let it worry them that the rest of us feel we're being double-crossed and cheated and made fun of. If a man wants to talk about hillbillies, he'd better go talk to enough people so he won't come up with all those crazy ideas that make us look like a bunch of circus freaks, you know. And I'm tired of the people who knock us down all the time and keep on saying we're so bad off that the only answer is to put us on permanent relief and cry over us every once in a while."

The facts are otherwise, Ken Stevenson hastens to state — otherwise for him and otherwise so far as many others he knows are concerned. The facts are that he and his wife are glad to be living where they are, glad to have money coming in, glad to be away from the difficult and burdensome life they formerly knew. To the Stevensons the hill country of West Virginia was, very simply, a home that had become unbearable, whatever its long-standing virtues. And to the Stevensons a city and its suburbs can be a pleasant and lively and interesting place to live in and work in. Mr. Stevenson and his wife believe their children are better off living in Arlington, Virginia, than Raleigh County, West Virginia; they not only live in a better house, eat better food, and get to go to a doctor when they feel ill, but they became more aware and more ambitious and more worldly and in general "better prepared," their father says. Better prepared for what? His answer is not quite what one may expect — something he himself realizes: "I don't mean that I want my boy and my girl to become city-slicker types. I don't want them to be like a lot of the people I pick up: full of a lot of talk and so in love with themselves that a guy has to wonder how they ever got that way. I picked up a guy yesterday, and he was combing his hair most of the way across the city. He'd take out his comb and put it through his hair, and then a couple of minutes later there'd be a breeze in the car, so small a breeze that it wouldn't have moved a speck of dust, but there he was, combing his hair again and putting his handkerchief all over his face, and looking at his fingernails. I thought to myself: I'm glad I don't have to worry about myself like that, and I hope my boy doesn't ever get a job where they judge him by whether he's got a hair or two on his head out of place.

"I'd like young Kenny to finish his schooling and amount to something. I don't care if he becomes a newspaper reporter or a teacher, or gets a job in an office or works in a factory. All I want for him is to be able to know his way around and not to be taken in by the crooks that live in the world; they're in West Virginia, and they're in Washington — and some of them are big people, too. I mean, the state of West Virginia was robbed of its coal by companies that didn't care what they did to the land and tried to pay the miners as little as could be. And here in Washington there are people who talk from sunrise to sunset and don't say a single honest word; all they're trying to do is put something over on the people. I want my boy to be smart enough not to be tricked and fooled by Washington politicians, or some of the crooks we've had in West Virginia; and the West Virginia crooks are the worst, because they take and steal money from a state that's already poor. I tell Kenny that because he's growing up here in Washington he'll be on the alert. He won't believe everything he hears. He won't trust everyone who shows up at the door, or collars him with a speech and a pitch to buy something. I have to laugh when I hear we're supposed to distrust everyone, the people who live up the hollows. The truth is up the hollows we never knew how crooked a lot of people are, and we were too easily ready to believe a guy who came along selling and talking up a storm and trying to pull a fast one. My son knows a lot of different people, and he knows his way around Washington, and most important he knows how to take care of himself. He can fight with his fists. He can run fast. He knows how to watch out and not end up in some strange street where he might be robbed and beaten.

"I take the boy back to West Virginia once or twice a year. I have a brother there. Kenny has some cousins there. After a few days we're all glad to leave and come back to Arlington. My brother is still up that hollow, and he thinks I'm crazy, driving around Washington. How can you just drive around, he'll ask me; and I'll tell him I'd rather be driving around than sitting around, and that was what I used to do. My boy likes the woods, and playing with his cousins, and of course he would. But on the way home he always tells me that he's glad we're leaving and he's glad I left a long time ago, a year after he was born, and I tell him that I'm glad to be going myself. My son would rather ride his bike down the street we live on than go running through the woods up a hollow; that's the truth. And he likes to go into Washington with his friends and walk through the Smithsonian; they have everything in the world to see, it seems, and Kenny is always telling me about something new he's discovered there. He's good in science, his teacher says, and maybe he'll be a scientist. When I compare all he's learning with the little my brother's kids are learning, I know I did right to come to Washington and get a job driving a cab. I've been getting an education myself, driving around, and I do believe my children will grow up to live a better life than I ever could have — and that's the main thing a parent hopes for when he sees his children growing up. He thinks to himself: should I go someplace else, to give my kids a better chance, or should I stay where I am? I look at my kids, and I can't help feeling I did right by them when I brought them to this 'terrible city,' my brother calls it — and he's never once come here, no matter how many times I've invited him and tried to get him over for a visit."

He goes on those visits, though. He wants to see his brother, and underneath his air of indifference one does sense some lingering attachment to his birthplace, however stoutly he denies any "interest" in West Virginia, only a loyalty to his family. His wife has two brothers who live only a few miles from his brother, and she definitely wants to take those drives westward across Virginia "every once in a while." But she, too, is not overcome by a need to be up in the hills. She likes her all-electric kitchen, and she loves to move a switch and find her whole house warm and cozy. She sometimes thinks that when her children are grown up she will be lonely and more homesick, but then there is a lot her husband has told her about Washington that she would like to go see for herself. And she fully anticipates staying in the ranch house she and her husband now are paying off year by year; she expects that after her children grow up and marry, her grandchildren will visit her there. Why should she ever move? Why should she return to West Virginia? Why indeed, her husband says rather than asks. The past is the past, they both say.

On one visit to their home I heard about an even more radical break with the past that young Kenny might someday choose to make: "I came home and told my boy I'd picked up some South American type, a general and his aides, at the airport. I think they were supposed to have a limousine there for them, but something went wrong. They were talking in Spanish, I guess. They kept on talking about Brazil, Brazil. There was an American with them, and he'd been there in Brazil, and he seemed to know everything about the place. They asked the American where he came from here in this country, and he said Pennsylvania. That's next to West Virginia, of course. I thought he was probably from a big city, Philadelphia maybe. But he told the generals that he was born in a little town called New Salem, and it wasn't far from West Virginia, and his grandfather was a miner, and his father was so smart that he got sent away to college on some special scholarship, and now he was working for the Defense Department, I guess. He looked as fancy as the rest of them. He talked as fancy, too. He was all polish, a smooth guy. But he seemed to get more honest, the more he talked about his grandfather and his father and how they were *real* Americans, he kept on saying. I could see what he meant; a lot of Americans who live in Washington don't impress me as real *anything*.

"After I left them off, I thought to myself that I wouldn't mind if Kenny had a good job in the government and got to visit other countries, like Brazil and the ones over the Atlantic — England and France and the rest of them. Kenny wouldn't ever start talking high and mighty; he's a good, honest kid. I'm glad I have this job; I like my cab, and I like to drive around this city. But I'm not my son Kenny. I was born and brought up in a little place no one here has heard of. People I'm driving ask me where I was born, and when I tell them they quickly change the subject. But Kenny has grown up here, even if he was born in the exact same room I was. He doesn't talk the way his mother or I do. He knows a lot more than I do. I tell him he does. I'm glad he does. I'm not the kind of father who wants his son to look up to him all the time and never once dare disagree on any subject. I tell Kenny: I came here so that starting with you there'd be a change in the family. I mean, someday there may be a Mr. Kenneth Stevenson who will be taking a cab all the time, and there will be a cabdriver like me, just here from over in West Virginia, and he'll be giving Mr. Stevenson a ride, and he'll think to himself: that guy in the back seat, he sure knows a lot, and he's sure lucky to be in the job he's in, and he sure talks as though he's been in every country and on every continent.

"Of course, I don't want my son to be anything he doesn't want to be. And all I want for my daughter is that she find a man who's a good person, no matter what part of the country he comes from and what his job is. But I hope both of them won't be poor. I'm not poor any more, I'd say. And I don't really believe my children will be poor. If it took coming here to stop some Stevensons from being poor, then I've never done a smarter thing than I did when I went to see my dad, and he was sick then, dying then, and told him right to his face: I'm going. He looked at me, and you know, he wasn't sad or upset at all. *He* was going, too, and he knew it. That's what he said to me. He said he was leaving West Virginia, too, and he wasn't ever going to come back, he knew it, and maybe when I got over to Washington or some other city, I'd find that there wasn't much reason for me to come back, either.

"I was surprised to hear my dad talk like that, but my wife told me my dad had told her the day we got married that we might have to leave the hollow, leave the whole state, and go find some other place to live. She never wanted to tell me he said that to her because she thought I should decide to leave on my own — and besides, until I did decide to leave, she was scared to go. She got the shakes every time she heard me mention the idea that I might, just might, pick us all up and go. But when I actually said I'd made up my mind, and the time had come to leave, she was glad, and she told me what my father said. I can see us now saying good-bye, my dad and me. He said he wished me well, and he was as happy as he could be that I was on my way. I told him I'd see him soon; I'd come back in a few weeks; I'd be back as regularly as I could. He told me not to bother, and I was hurt. I thought he meant that he didn't like me leaving, even if he said I should go. But then I got it through my head that he knew he was going to die soon, so there might not be another chance for us to see each other.

"He did mean that, I'm sure; but he had more in his head, too. He came over close to me and held on to my arm and told me that he knew there wasn't much of a future at home, no future at all, and I owed it to the baby, to Kenny, to get up my nerve and go find some other place to live. Then he almost had me crying. I *did* cry — as soon as I was out of his sight. He told me how he once thought he ought to leave West Virginia; it was long ago, and he was about the age I was when I left. He told my mother, and she was with him. She told him she'd do whatever he wanted. But I guess he got scared. He kept on thinking that things were bad all over the country, so he'd better stay where he was. And he said they still had the idea back then that if you went to the city you'd almost be killing yourself, it's so bad there, even if you did get a job and make some money. It's like thinking the doctor's medicine is worse than the disease you have. So, he stayed right where he was, and he said that a year didn't go by without him saying to my mother how wrong he'd been for staying. I think I can even remember them talking like that when I was young. My mother would always say that it was just as well,

but I don't believe she really believed her own words, and I
know my father couldn't ever trick himself into believing something he really knew better than to believe.

"When we drove off I had tears in my eyes, though I was
fighting them back; but my father was smiling, and I'll tell you,
the last words he said to me were, 'Good going, son'; and then he
turned around and went back inside, and I gave the car all the
gas I could. I waved to my mother a last good-bye and soon we
couldn't see them, any of them, any more. A week later my dad
died all of a sudden in the middle of the night. We came back as
fast as I could drive the car, but even then I felt as if I'd been
away a year or two, and not just a week, only a little over a week.
And ever since I've felt like a stranger when I go home. I look
upon myself as someone who's going to die in Arlington, Virginia,
or Washington, D.C., and not in West Virginia."

Wherever he happens to die, he certainly does enjoy living
where he now lives. He takes excellent care of his ranch house.
He mows the lawn carefully. He plants flowers and helps his wife
do the weeding. He washes windows. He builds things: a bookcase for his children, a table for them, a desk for them, chairs for
them. He is proud of his name, as it hangs from a small post in
front of the house. And he is proud to hang out his American flag
from another post, a flagpole, that stands in front of the house.
He believes in that flag, in his nation's worth, in its need to
maintain a strong army. He distrusts those who demonstrate for
anything — an end to the war or a change in the country's
policies toward blacks. He is against the rich, the snobbish, the
elegant and self-centered, the powerful, in sum the important
men and women a Washington cabdriver inevitably sees, listens
to, in his own way gets to know.

Kenneth Stevenson wants a better deal for the kind of man
who is like himself — the man who works long hours and doesn't
boss others around and doesn't want to be bossed around himself. I think it can be said without exaggeration that he sees
himself to be the pioneer his ancestors were — and an entrepreneur, too. He knows that Washington is full of people who spend
their lives importuning others for favors and privileges, and so he

wishes that somehow he, too, might "get some of that gravy" —
which means the promise of a good social security check, a
medical plan that would keep him from ruin in the event anyone
in his family falls sick, and a guarantee that if "things really get
bad," he and his wife and his children will not go hungry. I
suppose he can be called a puzzling mixture of the patriot, the
worker, and the proud, almost anarchic, self-employed worker.
(He in fact works for a company, but of course, as a taxi driver,
is also very much on his own.)

At times I hear him trying to make sense of ideas that he
himself knows don't easily fit together. At times, like some of his
kinfolk back in West Virginia, he shouts his populism, his contempt for the rich, the well born, the well educated — and all
their thoroughly deceitful and hypocritical ways. But then he can
shout with equal passion at the "crazy liberal types," whom he
has also carried around from street to street in the nation's
capital: "I can spot those liberals, I truly can. They're always
attacking the country. They're always talking about how bad
things are and how wrong the government is — even when
they've got the President on their side. They'll talk about the
colored people and how bad off they are, and I hear them talking
about Appalachia a lot, too. I keep my mouth shut. I want a tip
from them. They're not so generous with their tips as they are
with the taxpayers' money, I'll tell you that from nearly ten years
of driving a cab. When I hear one of them saying how bad it is
for the poor, I figure he's probably going to skimp on me. I've
figured I should really go and tell them that I'm one of those
poor, poor hillbillies from their Appalachia, and please, won't
they give me an extra quarter, because those quarters do mount
up, and it's a chance for them to help a poor, poor man. But I
don't want their lousy money. I'd rather take from the rich, who
don't give a damn about Appalachia or any other place, just
themselves. At least they're not pretending.

"I think a lot of the liberal types, they've got all the money they
need, and they love having a man like me to feel sorry for. They
want to go around patting people on their heads. I picked up one
the other day, and all he could talk about with his friend was

how the country was going to Hell and should they go to Australia or Sweden, or all those other places. They both looked dressed in two-hundred-dollar suits. I picked them up in the fanciest part of the city, where the homes are nice and big and loaded, I'll bet, with expensive furniture. I've seen them from the inside. I've gone and rung those doors and stood and waited and had a chance to look in. I was going to tell both of them to go and try a little hard work once in a while, and stop worrying about people like me — or my brother in Appalachia. They were talking about a friend of theirs whose wife has a lot of money, and how wonderful he is, because he uses her money to do a lot of good things. I thought: I'll bet if they had their way they'd tie me to a leash and clean me up and call me the greatest pet they ever had. But they ought to know something: the American people don't want the country run by a lot of high-class guys, all full of themselves and living off their wives. We don't want the country run by these college types who say that the United States is no good and it needs to be changed over completely. I love this country, and I don't want it changed over. I want America made better, and I'll vote for the man who'll do it; but I'll be damned if I'll vote for some guy who talks big about what he wants to do for the poor people — when you can see that he's never talked to a poor person in his life, and he wouldn't give a guy like me the time of day if I tried to speak with him as an equal. And I'm anyone's equal; that's what I believe."

He not only believes what he says, he lives out his passionate sense that there is yet room in this increasingly crowded country for a man who comes down from a mountain, finds a job in a city, buys a house, turns it into a proud and attractive home, and dreams of his son's future. Again and again he tells me that he looks ahead, not behind, that America ought to look ahead, that he wishes more people in Washington would look ahead — people he drives around and tries to "figure out." But he knows he can't quite figure them out — or change the direction of their thinking. He can only stick to his own principles, he observes a little fatalistically, and over the years I have had no reason to doubt that he will do just that.

6. Organizing the Whites

Some call the people who live up the hollows, up the mountains of West Virginia and Kentucky "hillbillies"; others refer to them as "poor whites" or "Appalachian whites" or indeed "whites" and nothing else — in contrast, say, with blacks. I chose to use the word "mountaineer" in the previous volume of this series because again and again I heard men refer to themselves as "men of the hills" or "men of the mountains," or "mountain people"; from several men I heard: "We are mountaineers, that's what we are." But in cities like Chicago or Dayton many political activists I know insist on using "poor whites" or "Appalachian whites." By "political activists" I mean men and women who "work with," do "organizing" with families once from West Virginia or Kentucky and now settled at least for a while up North. And to a certain kind of organizer there can be all the difference in the world between a word like "mountaineer" and words like "poor white." One organizer, not the man whose ideas I am about to present, put the difference this way: "*mountaineer* sounds nice but tells you nothing. *Poor white* emphasizes class and race."

A doctor like me, intent on making his own particular observations, must listen carefully to the political organizer's thoughts, his ways of seeing things and talking about what is seen. As I must constantly insist, it is alarmingly easy for a child psychiatrist to emphasize his concern with the fantasies and dreams and feelings of children or their parents or grandparents or teachers — and do so in such a way that the powerful effect of an actual social and economic system on a child's mind somehow is never really noticed. Yes, in our clinical conferences we mention "socioeconomic factors," or the "sociocultural" ones or the "psychosocial" ones — but between seeing the society as a "factor" and seeing it as the heart of the matter there is quite a difference in degree of emphasis. From the very first day of life, and indeed before that in the womb, a child's "class," his or her social and economic condition, affects what and how much is eaten and what diseases will occur or, once contracted, will be treated or left to run their harmful course. In a number of books and articles I have tried to show what it means to be a hungry child, a migrant child, a child whose parents are sharecroppers in Mississippi or inmates of a concentration camp or middle-class professional people suddenly and arbitrarily overcome by a serious and often enough crippling disease like poliomyelitis.

Still, one cannot escape a given conceptual or philosophical approach, as many organizers have constantly reminded me. I emphasize the mind's maneuvers, its tensions, hopes, fears, ambiguities. The organizer emphasizes how a particular society compels acquiescence, enables some to live well indeed, while others barely stay alive. I am not saying that the issue is one of right or wrong, nor am I apologizing for my work, or defending it, or attacking what others do. I simply feel that an earnest, open, hardworking political organizer's view of the people I call "mountaineers" and he calls either "poor people" or "whites" or "Appalachian whites" deserves more than the usual disclaimer: he is doing his job and I am doing mine — an altogether different one. I am not doing the same work that John Ashley is doing, nor should young John Ashley, an avowed political organizer working in a midwestern city, require me to talk or think as he does. Yet my work does require me to gain some understanding of his work, because he has a daily influence on certain families; in addition, there are others like him who also are struggling to win the ears and the minds and the energies of people like those I am writing about in this chapter.

So, here is John Ashley talking to me about his work and his ideas and his dreams for America: "I've been at this for five years; I'm no novice. I started out in Kentucky, in Harlan Country, near Coalville, that's right, Coalville. First I tried just going and living with some families. I wanted to do whatever they wanted me to do. I helped build a bridge. I taught the children. I helped make a road better. I wasn't clear in my own mind what I was out to do. I mean, I liked the people; I was born in Tennessee, near Knoxville, and I can even say I'm one of them, except that my father is a lawyer in Knoxville, and I never even knew what a hollow was while I was growing up. And my parents sent me off to prep school when I was fourteen; I guess they thought at Phillips Exeter I'd be far away from all those poor hillbillies who live near Knoxville. They wanted me to be polished and bright and Eastern and Ivy League and all the rest. They sent me to Europe. They have all the 'right' magazines in their home. My mother goes on shopping trips to New York and Chicago. They never wanted me poking around in my own backyard, any more than they poke around themselves. The one mistake they made is letting me get too involved with the Boy Scouts — yes, the Boy Scouts. We'd go on long trips, and that's how I first met mountain people. I saw the hollows, the creeks, the cabins, the kids my age with those rags for clothes and the gaunt, hungry look their faces had. I came home and asked my parents why, why, why. My dad said they were lazy and mostly slow — retarded and genetically inferior, that's his view of them and of Negroes, I'm ashamed to say. Poor people can't measure up, he says. If they could, they'd push their way up and ahead, the way people do who have *initiative* and *intelligence* and *imagination* — he's always shouting those three words at me. My mother, she's a sadder case; she has some gentleness and compassion in her, but she's overawed by my dad, and she basically defers to his judgment. She was brought up by *her* father to think the same way my father does. My grandfathers on both sides were lawyers. How do you like that!

"Anyway, my mother used to tell me that she felt sorry for the poor, wherever they are, but there wasn't much she could do, except pray for them in church — in that rich Episcopalian church she goes to every Sunday, except in the summer, when they're in Europe or on a cruise someplace. She would have the cook make cupcakes and brownies for me, so that I could give them to the kids I'd meet on our Boy Scout camping trips. And the kids were glad to get the food! At the time I didn't know *how* glad they were. All I knew was that I became more interested in those kids and what they were like than in accumulating credits to be an Eagle Scout. And the scoutmaster began to worry over me. He told my mother that I was 'too wrapped up' in the people of the hollows and not worried enough about the names of trees or animals or flowers. She told him I was a 'kindhearted boy,' but I'd grow out of it, she was sure. Can you imagine that! I was listening in. Even then — I was only twelve, I'd guess — I felt myself listening to something wildly funny and something awful and crazy, too. I felt like running into the room and telling my mother that I was sorry I was kindhearted, and I'd try to 'grow out of it' even faster than I ordinarily might. I'm not sure she would have been able to laugh at me or herself or the whole lousy setup, which to this day she accepts as 'natural.' That's what she always says to me: 'Why don't you live a normal, natural life?'

"My mother wanted to send me to a psychiatrist in Knoxville. When I was older I went three times to oblige her — and I *did* want to talk with someone about my parents and myself and the people up the hollows in Tennessee and North Carolina and Kentucky. But the psychiatrist kept on asking me what my 'plans' were, and why was I so 'hostile' to 'my parents' way of life.' I told him about the poor people I'd met, and how I wanted to do what I could to help them, and he said — I'll never forget it: 'You think it's up to *you* to change things; you think *you'll* be their savior.' I told him no, I didn't think that. I told him I didn't think I was Jesus Christ. I told him I wanted to help, just help. He asked me why I couldn't help later on, when I was a lawyer or a doctor. I told him I didn't see many lawyers or doctors doing that kind of work up those mountain hollows. He said, 'Do you feel anger toward your father for not doing that kind of work up the hollows?' If I'd have said yes, he'd have been so happy, and if I'd have said no, no I'm not angry against my father, but against the whole society for the way it is set up, then the doctor would have thought I was dodging the issue and refusing to give the real, true answer. They've got a nice system, those psychiatrists: heads, I win; tails, you lose.

"I stopped after three visits, like I said. He was a self-satisfied, boring man; he spent his time raking in fat fees in exchange for trying to get kids like me to shape up and live the way our parents do. He told me that I had to be 'realistic,' and that I was 'rebellious,' and 'we will have to find out why.' I asked him whether he would want to explore with me why *he* isn't *more* rebellious, given the way millions of people live in this country, including a lot of children only a few miles out of Knoxville. He got red at that, and he squirmed in his big, fat chair. He said he was concerned, but his job was to help me 'focus' on the way I 'distorted things.' I told him that I thought he was capable of blurring things, too — and rationalizing and forgetting what it's inconvenient or embarrassing to think about. Then he wanted to know why I was so angry at him. I wanted to tell him that he really was a dumb son of a bitch, that he refused to discuss *issues* with me, including the issues of his own relationship to our society, and the uses to which his time is put, at a rate of twenty-five and thirty dollars for forty-five minutes, and that all he did was try to push and bully people into a fool-proof system. If his patients disagree with him or question him or try to ask him something difficult and maybe upsetting, then they get slapped down with name-calling labels he's got — they're angry, they're hostile, they're disturbed, and on and on. After all, he's the doctor. He's the authority. Why should he discuss certain sub-stantive issues — especially when only *he* is to decide what is 'relevant' to what he keeps on calling 'your problems'?

"The fact is my parents sent me to him because they wanted him to straighten me out, so that I'd stay at Harvard and go on to the law school there and eventually come back and join the family firm. At least my dad finally admitted that to me. He's an honest man and a rich man; the psychiatrist isn't half as rich, and he spends his life tricking himself with words and concealing from himself the basic fact that he works for people like my father. When he got a little drunk once my father told me he'd sent me to the doctor because he figured the guy could outtalk me and persuade me to stop 'ruining a good life,' all for the sake of a lot of people whose troubles are their own business, and not mine. Now, maybe he's right — I now realize. But at least the man put his cards right on the table. He told me he knew I wasn't crazy. He said: 'You're wrong, not crazy. I don't agree with any of your ideas. I'm sorry that doctor didn't make you see the light.' I told Dad the doctor saw the problem differently. He felt I was mixed-up, and the 'roots' of my political ideas had to be 'traced,' and maybe I'd change then. My father was wonderful when I told him that: 'Hell, I don't give a damn what he said. If he'd convinced you to stop bucking the whole American system, I'd have paid him triple his fee, and now that he's not got to you, I can only call him a failure, so far as I'm concerned.' I told Dad I wished he'd call up the doctor and tell him that, but he told me to stop being funny. I don't think the doctor would have thought my father very funny if he *had* called up. He would have been called 'hostile.'

"That's all so long ago, it seems to me now. I stayed in college. I finished. I forgot about a lot of my 'preoccupations' — the doctor called them — with the hollows and the people up there who barely get by from day to day. I even applied to law school. But then I had a summer off, and there was this program tied up with VISTA, and I signed up, and they sent me near home: to Appalachia, they called it. I'd never really thought of Knoxville or Harlan County, Kentucky, as part of Appalachia; they were *home* to me, places I knew, places I'd grown up in and traveled through. Now I was back in a 'poverty-stricken' area, and it was like the Boy Scouts, actually, only instead of piling up credits for tying knots and spotting birds and hiking up the mountains, we were trying to prove how nice we could be to those poor people, and how much of their 'culture' we could learn, and how much 'good' we could show we'd 'done for them' by the time the summer was over — when, of course, we would leave, go back to school, tell people what we'd 'done,' and be looked up to as real idealistic guys, who are kind and self-sacrificing and 'tomorrow's leaders,' that's what they had the gall, the incredible gall, to tell us we were, the newspaper that wrote us up.

"Those newspaper editors knew. They knew we weren't going to do anything too drastic, too vigorous, too touchy. They knew we'd no sooner dig in and find our way around than we'd have to leave. They knew the government was paying us, and government bureaucrats would keep their eyes on us — *or else*, meaning or else those same newspapers would start talking about 'agitators' and 'Communists.' No, even my dad thought the idea was good: a summer is a summer. If I had signed up with the Peace Corps or with the regular one-year or two-year VISTA program — however long it is — my dad would have adjusted to *that*, too: two years is two years. What he worries about is a whole life of commitment to some of these struggles — and not only because of the time I'd lose, or the money I wouldn't make, or the loss of social position. I think he's smart enough to know that the longer a guy like me spends in this thing, the longer he is with the poor and learns what it's like for them, the more he learns about the *real* America, the America that permits these injustices, the America certain individuals and corporations own — that's right, *own*.

"At the end of that summer I came home and started asking myself *who owns Appalachia?* But I was even scared to put the question to my own mind, and as for my dad, I think he nearly died when I first put a question like that to him. 'What do you mean?' he asked me back. He wasn't kidding. He wasn't stalling for time. He never in his life allowed himself to think in that way, even though he knows the answer better than anyone, because he represents some of the companies who *do* own the region. But in polite circles one doesn't dare think about such things. They are companies, and he does their legal work. If they strip the region's land, destroy the homes of people, extract millions of dollars worth of coal and pay back nothing to whole communities whose land and water are ruined forever — then that's something my father for all practical purposes doesn't ever think about. As for the poor up those hollows, they should go get jobs. If there aren't any jobs to be had, my father can only scratch his head, take another martini, and say what he actually did say to me once: 'I guess they should get the Hell out of where they are and go to some city where they can find a job.'

"The people have done that. They have been fired by some coal companies, which have mechanized, and pushed off the land by other coal companies, which want to strip-mine. So the people have gone to the cities. After I finally got wise and decided to live up the hollows for a good long time, a lot longer than the summer it took to help build a bridge over a creek, and later, after I finally came North, up here to his city — well, several times I reminded my dad that the poor people have done what he suggested, gone on the road to find work. Once after we talked he said this: 'It's tough, being poor in this country. I know it, son.' That's all he said. I could tell he didn't want to speak another word. He turned his head from me and looked out of the window. He went out of the room to go get my mother. It was the closest moment I've ever had with him. A man like him, he can't dare let himself think like that, *feel* like that, too often. He wouldn't be able to work. He'd stop 'functioning,' to use that psychiatrist's word. Then he'd have to go see him, the doctor — and you can imagine how quickly he'd tell my father to come off it and stop getting himself all tense, all obsessed by those worries and doubts about the poor. But my father isn't one to get obsessed like that, and he's not one to visit a psychiatrist. He's a man who can see everything as clear as can be for a few seconds, then shake himself right back to 'normal,' as the doctor would call it."

John Ashley is able and willing to talk at great length about his recent past. The more he talks, the older he seems, though in fact he was born in 1942. He is a young man who has struggled. Whether or not one agrees with his various positions and premises, one cannot fault him on honesty and directness and moral candor. Though I very much have wanted to hear what he has come to know about the particular "community" he hopes to "organize," I have only gradually come to realize that John himself is part of the very region whose people he so admires. True, his parents are rich and would not want to be considered "Appalachian whites." But if one goes back in time they turn out to be of white yeoman stock, from the foothills of the Appalachian Mountains. Their ancestors went into a city several generations ago, and in time prospered. Their son has abruptly changed the family's direction, its history really, and in so doing has forced his parents and one surviving grandparent to look a little more closely at their own region, to worry a little less exclusively about when the J. Press salesman will bring those Ivy League clothes to

Knoxville and what might be the "best time" for a "trip East."
Nor is John Ashley's "family background" all that unconnected to
the way he looks at the people whose fate he at least to some
extent has chosen to share. As one listens to him one hears his
tough, unyielding highly political ideas, but something else can
be heard, too — something that is impressively personal, something that may have first cropped up when a Boy Scout from a
well-to-do Knoxville family couldn't quite ignore certain things
he saw on a "field trip" with his fellow scouts.

For example, we once were talking about his work and my
work, and he had this to say: "I have to admit it; someone like
me can become more arrogant than he ever knows. I've gone on
and on about some of my professors, how blind and smug they
are, and I've talked about that poor, half-witted psychiatrist I
saw in Knoxville — how all he wanted to do was make a good
living and help people like me stop being too 'bothered,' so they
can settle down to making a good living themselves! But I feel at
times that I'm as manipulative as that doctor ever was. I mean,
I'm organizing the whites up here in the big city, but often they
don't know it. They see me as a nice, helpful young guy, who is
always around and ready to go on errands and offer advice and
run interference with city officials or employment agencies or
landlords. I have a car, and I take people places. I speak well,
and I know how to confront bureaucrats or real estate people. I
know lawyers and can get them to come and take a case for
nothing. I can go to a school and ask a teacher about a kid or
demand that certain children get free lunches. It's all very noble
and idealistic, and a lot of the kids and a lot of the parents call
me 'our John' or 'Johnnie' — and I sure can feel the affection
when a child says, 'Here comes our John.'

"But all the while I'm trying to organize them. I'm trying to
make them more conscious of the *political* problems, their *class*
position in American life. They go from little issue to little issue,
and never stop and put the whole, damn, rotten thing together.
They know they're being charged exorbitant rents for the lousiest
of places. They know they work from day to day like dogs — for
long hours at hard, backbreaking jobs. They know they have to

split what they make half and half with a guy who sits in an office and contracts out workgangs to people who need what is called "cheap labor." They know what the coal companies did to their homes, their land, their lungs and backs and arms and legs. But they can't take the next step; they can't look at the way capital was accumulated in this country and the way the rights of workers were consistently ignored — *until* they organized and joined unions and fought for their rights. Not that unions — take the mine workers union! — can't also exploit workers or bargain away their true interests. It's hard to get things like that across in such a way that the whole society is seen for what it is — interested in making and selling products, rather than achieving for all people a certain standard of living *as their right*. There are days when I want to scream at the people on this block and all over the neighborhood: don't you see how exploitative this society is, and don't you see how you're being used, and don't you see what might happen if you all pulled together — and joined with the blacks and the Chicanos and the Indians and a lot of other basically dispossessed people who, like you, plod along and get cheated every day in one way or another?

"I suppose I have *ulterior designs.* I really do want my neighbors here to *fight,* fight for their rights. But *they* want something else, a lot of them; they want a little money, a little security. They want jobs and a car and some appliances. They're unhappy because they've really had a raw deal back home in Kentucky or West Virginia, and they're getting a raw deal here. But they can so easily be bought off by the system. Those who get good jobs in a factory — not many these days! — quickly lose whatever critical spirit they had. They are now "in"; they now can get things, buy things, have things — so why worry about the others? Why protest, and risk sinking back into the pool of the unemployed? Even the services a city provides — a hospital, welfare, school lunches — take the edge off the extreme poverty and brutality these people experienced in those rural areas; the result is people are made less critical of the overall society. Sure, up in the hollows they can also be conservative, God-fearing, quite willing to take suffering, to submit, to die rather than organize and march and protest and demand. But up those hollows I've also heard the most radical kinds of statements about county officials and coal companies and the whole way the country works. In the city, people like Appalachian whites are too confused and fearful and vulnerable to criticize anyone, or aim a musket at anyone, as they sometimes do back in the mountains. And they can always get a little — a little cash from welfare and a little surplus food and even a little temporary work. So, why sweat it and look too carefully at things and risk trouble? And besides, at school and at church they've learned all their lives to sit back and take it, take it, take it.

"That's why I try to remind them at every turn that they are a political group, that they are *Appalachian whites,* and like *blacks* and *Chicanos* and *Indians* and *migrant farmers,* they have got to pull themselves together, become a force, become their own advocates and lobbyists, just as other groups in this society have learned to do. The word 'mountaineers' may sound nice, and they may want to call themselves that, but it's an antipolitical word, I believe. It's a word that encourages people to think about themselves in a pleasant, almost romantic way: we're mountaineers, proud mountaineers. The problem for the exploited, poverty-stricken Appalachian whites is that they have been thinking that way for generations; it's an opiate, a word like 'mountaineer.' I know they have a right to call themselves anything they want, and I respect their pride. But when people have pride, and their kids are born and die without medical care, and they don't even have electricity in their cabins, and they are hungry, and they are denied welfare and can't find work — then there's something sad and tragic about the whole business, and their pride is self-deluding, it really is.

"I am not saying that I'm immune to the same kind of thinking. I feel real love for these people. They are my people. I'm of their stock. My ancestors once were farmers in the hill country of Tennessee. When I was a kid and first went into the mountains, I never could forget the people I met; they seemed so tough and sturdy and honest and unpretentious. I loved to hear them pick those guitars and sing and tell their stories. I loved to watch them sew and knit and make things — a jug, a jar, a bottle, a quilt. I loved to see those old miners, full of talk about what it was like to go down and cut that coal out of the earth and get it up, haul it up to the outside world. They were so kind and polite, too — decent and courteous people. And they never felt sorry for themselves. Suffering to them is a part of life, is inevitable. I'd come home and realize that my parents worried more and felt sorrier for themselves and complained more and could be ruder and less polite to strangers than those 'poor, poor people,' which is all the scoutmaster could call them. He'd never dare say that some of the richest people in Tennessee are pathetic, pathetic people — but that's always the way it is: if you have no money, you get a lot of contempt from people, masked as sympathy; whereas if you're rich, you get envy masked as admiration and respect! I guess I'd like to help the people I work with to feel genuine respect for themselves, which would mean they'd have to be strong, have money and work, have political leverage. I'd like them to be the same people I met when I was a kid trying to be an Eagle Scout, but I'd like them to have nice homes and good jobs. I'd like them to be free of corrupt, dictatorial county officials — they are all-powerful czars — back in Kentucky, and up North I'd like them to be free of the cruel ties of the labor market system and what it does to people who want work but either find no work, or get brief jobs that pay outrageously low money, most of which then goes to private agencies and labor contractors."

One can predict that young John Ashley doesn't stop there. He is outraged at the values which he insists most of us willingly or reluctantly embrace. In his mind most of us are not deliberately evil persons, as is the case with the slum landlords and labor contractors and county officials and mine company officers and mine union leaders he rails against. We are, even those of us who study social issues and write about and proclaim our concern for "the poor," being sustained by a "system" which rewards those who investigate "problems," but still does nothing to change life up in the mountain hollows or in migrant camps or on Indian reservations or in those vast stretches of tenements and more tenements now called "ghettos." At times I argue with him about the use of abstractions like "the system." I try to emphasize a long-range and historical view of things. I try to emphasize a complexity I feel he ought to share. I tell him he makes things too dramatic. I tell him he simplifies. Then, I see him going from door to door; I see the look of affection his eyes show toward family after family; I see the look of affection he receives from mountaineers, from Appalachian whites gone North — and I find myself in awe of his spirit and integrity and decency, and wondering whether he needs any warnings or advice after all.

7. Those Proud and Set Faces

I don't know how many times I have used the word "proud" to describe the mountaineers of Appalachia and their city cousins, even as I have heard it used again and again by others: "They pride themselves on their independence and ability to get on, no matter how difficult their lives may be." I suppose that some would want to say that pride is only a cover, that underneath a proud man can be a worried, frightened man, particularly if he is hungry. The fact is, however, that some deeply troubled and poverty-stricken people demonstrate pride, even as they struggle desperately to stay alive, while others, similarly afflicted, appear more openly apathetic or apprehensive or sad. Do we get very far by turning every coin over and saying that "really" this is that, and what seems to be one thing is "secretly" or "deep down" something else? Everyone's behavior masks something, even the insistent desire to pin psychological labels on people can itself be shown to be the product of something other than scientific curiosity or therapeutic zeal. Perhaps the apparent pride of the mountaineers can for once be looked upon as evidence of deep-seated pride.

Yet, it is only natural for a harassed and earnest welfare worker to be a little skeptical about the pride mountaineers up North show in the face of the hard lives so many of them live. She knows about their disasters, their hardships, their illnesses and periods of joblessness, and she wonders how it is possible for people to contend with such a fate and still be so tight-lipped and defiant and long-suffering — so proud. Since *she* is unnerved by the stories she hears, the situations she meets up with, she wonders why "they" seem to be so stolid and quiet and controlled and (sometimes even) so able to smile and demonstrate a light touch. Maybe, she wonders, there is something wrong with "them." Maybe they are "depressed," badly so, and therefore they only *seem* proud or resolute or unyielding. Underneath, underneath where everything *really* important *really* is, there must be another story, far different from what usually meets the eye. In her words: "Underneath I believe they are anything but proud. They are probably terrified."

I tell her yes; I tell her I am sure "they" are terrified — though I think they are quite aware of the terror they feel. But she tells me no; she tells me that there is something almost startling and certainly inappropriate about "those proud and set faces." How *can* they be so proud, she asks, she exclaims almost, in view of the hurt and pain they have had for so long and *must* realize they will continue to know just about indefinitely? I reply that I am puzzled, even as she is. I reply that like her I see the proud and set faces she talks about. I reply that people, particular people, develop their own special ways of dealing with the world's turmoil and injustice — which is hardly a very original idea. And in reply she talks about her daily experiences, which in fact may contain answers that both of us seek. For her those experiences are exhausting and confusing and at times quite maddening. Yet, she can recognize that she is not as hopelessly bewildered as she sometimes feels: "I go to homes, poor homes, and I want to help, I want to help so badly. The people need help, too. A minister may have called me to suggest I go see a family. And there they are: the tall, quiet, shy man, and the gracious wife, and their lovely children — lovely to look at and sad to look at. It's an American stereotype, I guess, that blond, blue-eyed children are supposed to be neat and clean and healthy and perky and in the best of spirits. Some of the children look lovely, and they try to be nice and pleasant, but I can see how sick they are; I can see what living up a Kentucky hollow in extreme poverty has done to them and to their parents.

"Every time I go to a home I try to figure out a way to help the people. I find myself wanting to tell the father that if he would just go away, or pretend to go away, things would be so much easier, so far as relief goes. But I could never say that, not to families that have come here from Appalachia. It even turns out often that a family doesn't really want help from the city. The city is trying to be flexible; I am allowed to go out and take a look at 'problem families' whenever a minister or a policeman or someone like that calls us up. Yet, time and again I'll go and meet the people and decide they need emergency help and all kinds of medical services and help in a job-training program or whatever — only to be told that no charity is wanted, none at all. They are not beggars, they say, and when I reply that I know that, they really watch me, to make sure I really mean what I say. If they detect an ounce of pity in me, they gently show me to the door.

"I've finally begun to realize that the very fact they can be gentle and polite in showing me the door proves they are genuinely, honestly, through-and-through proud. If they were putting on an act, if they thought they could get more by pretending to be self-reliant and denying their need for assistance until I pressed them hard, if they wanted our help but didn't quite know how to come out and ask for it, or if they were afraid to ask for it, but were hoping eventually they would get up the nerve — well, I think they would be disappointed if I somehow let them down, showed pity for them but failed to 'force' money or food on them. Then they would get rid of me fast, or turn sullen and crabby or completely silent. Instead, they treat me as a guest. They are obviously sorry they can't be even more hospitable. They offer me tea or coffee. If it's hot weather, they offer me water. And I leave feeling as rotten and guilty and amazed as a welfare worker can be!

"I'm supposed to be watching out for con artists, for people who want welfare but shouldn't be getting it. Instead, I find people who don't want what a lot of them call 'free money.' They want medical care for their children, yes. They'll take food, especially free hot lunches for their children at school. They'll sign up for job-training programs. But welfare checks, those pose another problem. They want work, that's what they want. They don't want 'a lot of everything in exchange for doing nothing.' That's how welfare was described to me by a man from West Virginia.

"Some of them *do* want welfare, of course. I don't mean to paint a total picture, with every Appalachian family alike. Some of the men do in fact desert their families; they become drunks, serious alcoholics, broken and wasted men — 'hillybilly lushes,' I've heard them called. And some families will take, take, take — the way you read in the conservative editorials welfare families are supposed to do. But I'd like to bring along with me the most niggling critics of our welfare program and have them meet some of the families I meet. I do believe in a short while those critics would be as troubled as I can get; they might feel like begging those parents to take money, just a little money, for themselves and their children.

"I don't know how to explain such things. Is it a special kind of honesty in them, almost perverse honesty? After all, they really are entitled to as much help as we can arrange for them, within the letter, if not the spirit, of the law. Is it that pride we keep on talking about? What kind of pride encourages parents who need money for their children to turn their backs on that money, or at any rate put obstacles in the way of getting the money? Are we talking about *shame,* the shame that people feel when they have to ask for something and take something? Are they *angry,* so angry they can't accept help? I've thought of that often — that the proud look on their faces actually is a way of expressing hostility. They must resent people who have more than them, but they are quite inhibited by their culture, and so they don't feel free to express their resentments. And just when I'm ready to consign all the Appalachian families I know in this city to one big 'group therapy' meeting, I remind myself how lovely and genuinely hospitable they are, those people I call hostile and resentful and about a dozen other names. Then, I begin to wonder if it's not *me* who's hostile and resentful, because 'the poor' don't come running to me and begging for everything they can get. It's a hard job, this one — making sense of the people I meet and making sense out of my own reactions to them."

She has had some psychiatric treatment. She prides herself on her ability to look inward and say what is on her mind. She finds herself uncomfortable with people who prefer to keep silent, watch rather than pour forth ideas and feelings. When she gets nervous she starts analyzing herself, describing her behavior, categorizing what bothers her and what bothers others. When she meets people and they do not immediately fit into one or another psychological scheme she has learned (and learned to use in her various "relationships") she starts out with the words: they are "defensive," or they are "overreacting," or they are "really" trying to say not what they mean but something different. God, it can be a bore to hear such a mind wordily grind human beings up — and yet, I have to remind myself that the young woman is a sincere and hardworking person, perhaps hindered by a lot of stupid and fanciful jargon, a lot of terminological drivel, but also utterly intent on doing what she can to bring money and food to people who badly need both.

Those men and women and children she meets seem to have more patience than Job even could have had. They seem to be stubborn to a degree no mule could ever match. They have the resignation, it almost seems, that Kierkegaard wrote about and envied and singled out as man's highest task and least common achievement. Since, over the decades, they have challenged and confused any number of people and held fast to certain distinctive customs and habits, no wonder various efforts to understand mountaineers have been made, among them resort to biblical allusions and allegorical stories and philosophical formulations, not to mention psychological and psychiatric ones. Because so many mountaineers are themselves very devout Christians, and because they look eligible, given the right clothes and environmental background, for a photograph aimed at expanding the consumption of Coca-Cola or family-size station wagons or outdoor cooking gadgets, an observer or a welfare worker feels in contact with two strands of American life: the tradition of religious piety, which until recently was very much present, especially in the South and Midwest, and the secular, materialist tradition, which clothed itself in advertising stereotypes, such as the clean-cut blond family, with the eyes staring right at the reader or television-watcher. Yet, mountain people are not just formally religious; they are dead serious about God and His presence among us. Nor do they behave like the "typical" Americans they so often appear to be — all of which confuses people like that welfare worker and me, strangers to a region and its traditions.

Here is the welfare worker again, struggling hard to see clearly what it is that unsettles her so: "I worked with black families for a while, and despite all the talk about how hard it is for white workers like me and black people in the ghetto to trust one another and speak frankly, I found that work far easier than the work I'm now doing. The blacks came up North to get away from southern sheriffs, and to get money either by working or through welfare. They want help; they need it and they ask for it. They would welcome me — so long as I behaved myself and didn't start pushing them with a lot of insulting questions. They would laugh and joke with me, and they made me feel I was doing a lot of good: I helped hundreds of children eat better food and wear better clothes. I would hear 'thank you' all day and if some people laughed behind my back and snickered at 'the dumb welfare lady,' as I accidentally heard myself called once, I didn't mind. I knew I was being conned sometimes. Why *shouldn't* they con me, I thought. I was on their side, and I knew just what their side was. They have been cheated for generations in this country, sold into slavery, then treated like animals; if they now try to squeeze their due from a tightfisted, regulation-crazy welfare department, that's just fine, I felt.

"One day I was told the department needed a real good worker to try making contact with Appalachian families up here, and even though they kept on telling me the work was very difficult, I thought the supervisors must be kidding either themselves or me — because I believed that nothing could be tougher than working in the ghetto. I was tired, and I felt the need for a change, and I was curious, too; I'd never been to West Virginia or Kentucky, so I thought I'd have an interesting time meeting new people and learning about their way of life — you know, all we're told we're supposed to do when we're in social-work school. I was always the rebellious student, who wasn't going to be an ordinary social worker, who wanted to go out into the community and visit homes rather than stay in a clinic or a hospital. So, I became a welfare worker, not a social worker, and I decided to try visiting Appalachian families rather than the black families most people like me work with.

"At first, I expected to have an easy time, because the people seemed so easygoing and so *familiar* — you know, very American-looking. They didn't speak my kind of English, but I could understand them better than I could a black woman from rural Mississippi or Alabama. And to be blunt: they were white, and I wasn't always worried about the race thing, the race barrier, the race problem. I'm white, and my parents weren't rich, and I'm from the Midwest, so I thought I wouldn't have too much trouble making good contact with families originally from Kentucky or West Virginia. I should have known better, though. My supervisor told me that there were 'serious problems,' but the people concerned tended to deny their difficulties. I asked her why we were going out and *looking* for new clients. If people don't want help, then what can we do? I asked her that. She said there had been complaints from ministers and community organizers and political pressures as a result of newspaper stories. What's more, some people in the state administration believe that it will help the welfare program and the blacks if welfare payments weren't so heavily going to blacks in so many cities and towns.

"I started by going to talk first with a minister, and then a reporter who originally came from Kentucky. I got the names of families from the minister, and I started visiting them alone. I didn't want any previous introductions. I told them the truth! I told them I knew they had serious money problems, and we in the welfare department want to do the best we can to help people in need. I told them that sometimes people don't know about us, or don't have a way to get to see us — so I was coming around to talk with some people the Reverend so-and-so suggested I go visit. They always smiled and asked me in and offered me coffee mostly, tea sometimes. They would often tell me right away that things are bad, yes, but they are managing, and they hope to keep on managing. I would ask them if they perhaps need some emergency food, and they would say no. In fact, often the mother would get angry when I mentioned food — as if I was accusing her of some crime. They don't go and fling open their refrigerators and show me how little they have. They don't tell me what they've been eating — so little their stomach hurts and they feel weak and all the rest. Instead they look hurt and tell me that they're doing fine, just fine, and they don't want to be taking, always taking.

"All they want is work. That's what I heard when I first started, and that's what I still hear. All they want is a chance to be independent and make their own way through the world. I tell you, after hearing that for a year, I can almost recite the words by heart. I've almost come to think that way myself. It got so bad that I went on 'rounds' with a friend of mine; she works among the blacks, and we'd go into a house, and I'd hear a complaint about how inadequate the welfare payments are — and they *are* inadequate — but instead of nodding in agreement I could feel my face tightening up, and I could just hear those voices inside my head, saying: all I want is a chance to work, and I don't want money I haven't worked for, and I'll as soon die as take what's not become mine by the sweat of my brow. It's interesting, though: they will let the church help them. I think it's because to them God and His church are friends, whereas city or state agencies are like the county officials back in Appalachia — the enemy."

Perhaps one reason black families don't feel the way she describes mountaineers feeling is this: blacks have had no land of their own, no hollows and creeks of their own to defend and live on and cultivate with gardens and in general fall back on for survival. Blacks have always had to depend upon the hated and feared and envied enemy. In contrast, the poor in Appalachia have had sanctuaries of their own that no authority would dare approach. Within those sanctuaries people hunted, fished, grew vegetables, took care of chickens and goats, and maintained their sense of themselves as aloof, self-protected, defiant, ingenious, inventive people — as proud people who will survive, come what may, with God's help. It must be remembered that for a long time after mountaineers recognize they will have to leave for the cities, they hesitate and stay put. They never really have had to "go asking," as they say it, or "go begging," or "go on hands and knees for anything." Proudly and with set faces they have, rather, withdrawn and worked hard on their own and learned how to fend for themselves. The price they paid was a stiff one, but they had no real alternative. Their county agencies are hated and distrusted, and in a poor region they have only so much to give, even to friends and allies. And the strip-mining companies, what have they done for mountaineers? The moral, then, is to be wary of outsiders, and perhaps especially those bearing gifts — like the strip miners. The moral, then, is to stand on one's mountain territory, however bleak and unpromising it may seem, and guard it, and not suffer entry into it lightly.

No wonder the welfare worker talks this way about those who have left that mountain country for the city: "They are in those apartments, and they don't want to move. They're not always shifting from one place to another, like poor blacks do when they get into the city. Instead, they almost burrow in and help each other out as best they can. If one man gets a job, he tries to find a job for his neighbor, often his kin. They have their emissaries — the men who work, and the women who get to know a minister or a worker up here from one of the Appalachian organizations. I've never been up a hollow, but one child told me the apartment building was a hollow, too. He was joking, the way children joke when they want to say something very important!"

I told her I had heard that remark, too — from several children. I told her one child even let me know that his parents had always been the highest up the hollow back home, and now were happy to be living on the top floor of a building in which their kinfolk predominated. And it was important to the child's parents that the front door of that apartment house be kept locked. Poor as they all were, and old and broken-down as the building was, the fact remained that the families were living together, felt together, felt as one, and they wanted no outsider, ostensibly friendly or obviously on the prowl, coming up those stairs and asking questions or trying to suggest something or sell something

— or "talk a fast line and end up fleecing us." I will in another chapter let that child describe at greater length how he and his parents look at the building they now live in — at the world they once lived in and the world they now inhabit. Here I can only emphasize that before we name such people "passive" or "masochistic" or "suspicious" or more ominously, "paranoid," we had better understand their historical fate in Kentucky or West Virginia, their economic and political experience over the generations with respect to an assortment of powers and principalities, their social customs and their religious beliefs, their long-standing and intensely shared values, ideals and habits. I believe that both the welfare worker and I have quite similarly had to learn, learn thoroughly and not forget, what I have just written. Unfortunately, to this day there are moments when I do forget, when my eyes narrow, my brow wrinkles, my ears perk up, and my mind gets ready to take note of yet additional evidence of the mountaineer's "psychopathology." But then a child will casually remark upon how he did this back home, or heard that up in the hollow, or was told something a year or two ago by his uncle or his grandmother — and I find myself saying to myself: slow down, wait, hear more, and above all, keep your psychiatric mouth shut.

8.   Doing the Possible

I shall wait till the last chapter of this book to discuss the religious faith of black and white immigrants to our northern cities. In this section I would like to convey something of the work done by white ministers outside the churches — the "community work," the "organizing," the "urban ministry." Mountaineers in certain midwestern cities have become the beneficiaries of this work at first hand — often, if not always, done with remarkable and edifying absence of ideological propaganda, be it religious or political. I have met ministers who have remained ministers, but very much become social and political activists. At their best they come across as good teachers, or just good citizens, rather than politically self-conscious organizers or socially concerned clergymen or effective "links" between bureaucracies and individuals.

It was Terry McAllen whom I first heard refer to himself as "a minister in khaki pants." He was not being coy. He himself is from Kentucky, from Wolfe County, and he knows his people. He knows they want from a minister a certain "standard" of behavior. Mountaineers may wear overalls or dungarees or khaki pants, but a minister dressed like a slob, who shuffles up to them and slaps their backs and tries to guzzle a beer or gulp a shot of whiskey is not going to be "accepted" as a nice, unpretentious, "regular guy." No, Mr. McAllen's manner of dressing came about as a result of an uncontrived and accidental chain of events, which he recounts without being unmindful of the significance so-called "accidents" can sometimes have: "I know to this day that I am a minister, even if I don't have a church now, and even if my parishioners never hear me give a sermon. The people I visit don't like to talk about religion in their homes, so I can't go and chat with them about their faith and hold on to my sense of myself as their minister that way. I guess I remain their minister because they feel I am, know I am, want me to be, their minister. Some of them know me from their childhood back home, and others know me from my work in Kentucky. They all know me from my work up here, and they know me as a man from the mountains, a man whose family has been there from as far back as their own families have been there, and a man who went to school and became 'one of the Lord's people.'

"I've been doing this work up here for five years now. I came because I knew there was a need; there were too many people leaving Kentucky, then coming home on weekends and talking about how 'bad' it is 'up there.' I would ask them what they meant by 'bad,' and of course — I should have known better! — they wouldn't say, because they *couldn't*. They *knew*, but it isn't in them to talk about themselves, to put their experiences into words. To do so has always been the responsibility of a man like me: on Sundays I would talk about life in Wolfe County, the good moments and the hard times, and connect all of that with Christ's life — *His* good moments and *His* hard times.

"After a while, though, I decided I had to go see for myself; I had to go up with a family when they returned from their holiday weekend with us in Wolfe County and see what I could see and hear what I could hear. They said yes, the people I asked if I could accompany them; and so I went. I didn't really see all that much, not the first time. I saw that they lived in Ohio and not Kentucky, and they lived in an apartment house and not a cabin, and that the man went to work in a small factory rather than take care of his crops or go kill an animal or catch a fish. I saw that they all kept pretty close, the family I knew and some other families — and it turned out that I knew most of them. They all seemed really settled into the city, and yet I had the feeling they'd be gone from that place in ten minutes if suddenly they got a thousand dollars — or maybe even a hundred dollars! It was a little strange for me, seeing people who were so proud of their land living in buildings they obviously didn't feel very attached to. I'm not saying they went around wrecking property or saying bad things about the building. It's just that they really hadn't made themselves at home; I could tell. They had boxes here and there, full of things which they'd take out and use and put back. I mean, out would come the pot or pan, and then back it would go, as if in a half an hour — no telling! — they might all have to 'get up and go,' and you can just guess the direction they'd be traveling in. I'm speaking now of people who'd been living in Cincinnati for three or four years, not a few weeks or a few months.

"Well, anyway, I found the week I spent very upsetting. I came back home and told my wife that I felt compelled, absolutely compelled — *called*, if you will — to go back there and do whatever I could. Of course, I didn't know at the time *what* I could do. All I knew was that I had to try staying in Ohio for a while, just like those people I went up with from Wolfe County were planning to do.

"I went back home. I told my people the following Sunday what I wanted to do. I told my wife first and she said yes, and then the people at church said yes. I got in touch with some other ministers, and they steered me to the group I'm with now. When

we first came to Cincinnati, and later, when we moved up to
Dayton, I had trouble knowing how to be of help. My people
don't want 'help.' They don't like the idea of someone standing
over them and saying, 'Poor souls, I feel sorry for you, and let me
give you something.' They are a very tough people; they've sur-
vived hard winters, one after the other, and they've learned how
to take care of themselves. The only sustaining work they've ever
had was down in those mines, and that work was also hard. To
them nothing comes free, nor ought a person expect handouts
and gifts and charity. With our people it's different than with the
colored people: we've always had those mountains to fall back
on. Poor as we are, there are streams with fish in them and woods
with deer and rabbit and land on which to grow some vegetables
and keep a goat or cow and some chickens. Outsiders should
know that, but they forget it. I go to meetings now, and I keep on
hearing people say, 'Look at the Appalachian whites, they don't
go flocking to the welfare people the way the colored people do.'
I answer that I don't know much about colored people, but I
know why my people stay clear of welfare; and I don't believe
the colored people ever had little cabins of their own and land up
their own hollows. They were owned by others. They never had a
gun and a hollow between them and the outside world. It's
different.

"My work has been important. I don't mean to brag; I'm just
telling the truth, I believe. I go from door to door and building to
building. I ask how things are going: 'How's it going?' I say. I try
to put welfare in a different light. If a family needs help, I try to
show them that they're not doing anything wrong or foolish or
insulting to themselves by asking for assistance. The people trust
me, and they listen. They don't always heed my advice, though.
No one is going to push them too far — or any farther than
they're ready to walk on their own. When I first started my work
it was summer, and hot and sticky in Cincinnati. I was talking
with a family, and their little baby needed a doctor, I could tell. I
wanted to take the mother and child to the hospital, but the
mother was obviously afraid of going there; she thought 'the
hospital people' would keep the child, and that would be more

than she could bear. She asked me what to do, and I was honestly frightened myself. I knew the child needed a doctor, but I also knew how hard it would be on that family to go to a hospital and see their child 'taken away,' that's what they'd say and feel and think.

"Finally I decided to encourage them to get the child at least seen by a doctor. I offered to go along, and they were glad to have me. We went over, and the doctor was very good. He examined the child and said he was feverish, but it was probably due to the heat and a cold he had. He needed more fluids than he was getting, the doctor said. He gave us all a lecture on what the body needs during a hot, muggy spell. He told us to leave the baby uncovered and give him cool baths and get plenty of water and juice down him. Then he looked at us, the mother and father and me. I'll never forget that moment, because as he looked at us, I suddenly found myself looking at us, too — out of his eyes, a stranger's eyes. We were dressed formally. The parents were dressed as if they were going to church, and so was I. After all, if you're going to a doctor's, even if he's located in the emergency room of a public hospital, you don't just relax and wear pleasant, loose-fitting clothes. The doctor didn't say anything, thank God. If he had told us what his face indicated he felt, I believe all three of us would have felt hurt, and then we'd have become angry, 'mighty angry' is the way some of us in Wolfe County would put it. Who is *he* to remark upon us and our habits, the child's father would have said.

"The doctor's good sense in keeping his thoughts to himself enabled us to get talking. On the way home the mother was holding her baby and feeling much better, and she suddenly told her husband and me that we should also 'dress cooler,' and she said she should, too. Then, she told me that she'd wondered even before how I could stand the heat of the city, since I always had on a suit. I asked her what I should wear instead. She said, 'Some nice, loose-fitting khaki pants,' like her husband does at home in the evening. I told her that was a good idea, and I'd follow her advice. She said she was glad, and then she said something that showed what it all had meant to her, that visit to the hospital, and the weeks before she'd been spending in the city: 'I guess we've got to remember that we're up here, even if it is only for a while. They do things different up here. They dress different. And down from the mountains the weather sure is different.' I told her yes, and I realized only then that I had as much to learn as the people I was supposed to be working along with. When I showed up there the next day to ask after the baby, and she saw me with my khaki pants on, she said, 'Good for you, Reverend, good for you.' I told her I surely felt more comfortable, and she told me her baby was feeling better, too."

Now he often wears those khaki pants, and he rarely has on a necktie, except when he goes to church. He is hard put to describe, even to himself, exactly what his work is meant to accomplish. He is capable of using rhetoric, but he laughs at the words even as he uses them: *liaison, communication, agent of change, community organizer, resource person, interpreter, supportive individual, urban ministry, neighborhood consultant.* "It's talk and more talk, what I hear at some of those meetings," he observes, though he acknowledges from time to time that he does indeed learn a lot by hearing what other people, doing other work, have to say about the various problems that continue to plague our cities. I think he more than anything else objects to any effort to pinpoint his tasks and responsibilities, and his objections are not arbitrary, gratuitous or egotistical. Rather, he knows how prickly and sensitive the families he visits already are, let alone can become. The last thing he needs to do is become self-conscious with them — or talkative and assertive because he has heard and read that he should be doing one or another thing he so far hasn't done.

We have spent hours with each other, and the upshot has been that both of us do get talkative, assertively so; and certainly we get self-conscious about ourselves and the work we are doing. We get worked up over the "Appalachian whites" as a "problem," as an "issue," as a "challenge." And then the moment will come when we have had enough — enough of ourselves and our words and our theories and our formulations. We stop. We laugh. We change the subject. Then when we resume our "discussion" somehow things seem for a few minutes more hopeful. Perhaps long discussions, formal or semiformal or even "relaxed" or "open," bring out so many "questions" and "difficulties" that the people being talked about and looked at and analyzed end up being not *themselves,* but the inhuman mass of "problems" we have turned them into, treated them as, talked and talked about.

At any rate, if mountaineers are notoriously silent upon occasion, ministers (not to mention psychiatrists) can be quite voluble, and one day as the two of us rambled on with our talk the following thoughts came forth from a minister who does more than he cares to say he is doing and enjoys far more affection and trust from his fellow mountaineers than he will ever find it seemly or wise to acknowledge publicly, or even privately: "I try every day to start fresh. I don't want to become one of those 'programmed' people. I couldn't if I tried, and even if I started out being like that, the families I visit wouldn't let me get away with it. They're all different, the people I see; they're not as alike as I used to think they were. In the beginning I was their minister, so they responded to me as a minister; they came up to me and asked me to pray for them and come visit them. When I did, they were ready for me, dressed up and with the Bible there. Now I'm a friend. I'm a familiar face. I talk like they do — more or less. There are times when I honestly feel I have to speak forcefully and authoritatively, and I do; I know something, and it's important to get it across. At other times I am so silent that people begin to ask me if I'm 'hurting,' or if I have anything on my mind, troubling me. Then I speak: no, and how about you? Since they brought the whole thing up, they don't feel I'm reading a lot of problems into their lives.

"I'll be going to a family I know well, and just as I think I've got them all figured out, they'll fool me. They'll announce they're going to become legal residents of Ohio — when I think they're getting set to go home. They'll decide to pick up and go home — when I think they're really up here in Ohio for good. I'm not saying they're all unstable or unpredictable; I just mean this: you've got to watch yourself when you start talking a lot about a lot of people. I went to a conference in Chicago a few months ago, and they kept on speaking of 'Appalachian whites,' and how they all think, and what their 'culture' is, and what my 'role' should be. My role — all I know is that if I became too decided in my mind about my 'role,' I'd stop *having* a 'role.' I hate these articles and books that try to fit people into 'types.' I actually heard one man talk about the 'Appalachian personality.' I almost got up and told him to sit down and stop being so silly. I almost got up and started describing all the people I know, from back home and up here, and how they *don't* always see eye to eye on a lot of things, and they *don't* always say the same thing and do the same thing. But I guess I'm 'passive' and 'silent' and maybe 'depressed,' the way the man said a good 'Appalachian white' is supposed to be up here in Ohio. So I said nothing.

"As for what I hear those 'experts' say about the people who live up in those hollows — 'suspicious' and 'apathetic' and all the rest of the words — it's a shame, a real shame, educated men get to talking so. The people who talk like that never take the trouble to show that for everything they say, there's another way of looking at the picture, which means you can come up with another story: the mountaineer is full of energy and as friendly and kind and generous and trusting a person as you will ever meet in this world. I think when a man talks about a whole lot of people, he owes it to them — and to himself — that the words be very carefully chosen. I know a man up a hollow in West Virginia is not the same as an Indian or a colored man or a traveling salesman from California or a business executive out of New York City. But I also believe there is a lot more to my people than outsiders give them credit for — and insiders, too. It's taken me years up here to realize how clever and resilient the mothers and fathers are. Sure, they stand there and seem uninterested in your ideas. Sure, their faces are stony, and you don't for the life of you know what's going on behind those eyes. But, I'll let you in on a secret: a lot is going on. They come up here, and everyone says they're homesick and bored and anxious as can be to go back home. And you hear how superstitious they are, and how they like starchy foods, and how they'd just as soon sit back and listen to country music and play those guitars. I'm tired of hearing all that and reading all that. I don't say the explanations of mountain people are wrong; I just say there's more, much more, to the story than those explanations will ever really account for.

"I'll give an example. I've been going to see a man who's about thirty-five and has a wife and four children. They've been up here about seven or eight months. Each time I come to see him, he seems lost in his dreams. He drinks too much beer, and he thinks of the 'old days' back in Kentucky. He always seems stern with me, as if he didn't quite trust me. He knows I come from not too far away from his own creek, but up here he told me once: 'It's a big city, and you lose yourself, everybody does, and you can't trust anyone, it seems.' He meant, I think, that he couldn't even rely on himself, let alone me; the city cheats people of themselves, their distinctive qualities. Anyway, I have kept on visiting that house. The children badly needed dental care, and I arranged it for them. The wife had some trouble with her stomach, and I got *her* to the hospital, too. The husband wants to work, but has found himself more and more discouraged, because the jobs don't last for long — or when they do, he simply can't take the work. He had a job with the sanitation company, hauling in garbage from restaurants and office buildings, and he came home and was near tears. He told his wife he was sorry, but he couldn't take the work. He wanted to go home and die up that hollow — starve to death there, he said. His wife told him she wouldn't have him going home to die, and she wouldn't have him picking up garbage every day and coming home and looking so bad.

"When I came to see them they were wondering what he *would* be doing. I was ready to bet they'd go back to Kentucky. He had already started to pack his belongings. She, too, was packing. They had his brother and his family 'place' back there, and they could move in with the brother. The kids were excited — because they sensed they were moving, and kids welcome any move, a move up North, a move back to the mountains. We sat and talked, and all of a sudden the man looked at his wife and said, 'I believe we'll stay.' She told him he'd said that earlier, and she hoped he meant it. He said yes, he did. Now, they didn't run to unpack. They didn't run to do anything. Nor did they say anything more. They just went about having coffee and listening to the radio and its 'hillybilly music.' A day or two later when I came by the man asked me if I knew of any 'schooling' he could get, so he might find a better job than the one he had working on that garbage truck. He'd never before asked me for that kind of help, even though I'd offered it and been given what I then considered a cold, unfriendly glance.

"Actually, I now realize that he had simply been listening to me and waiting for the right time to ask. Do you know how I know that now? The wife told me something afterwards, after her husband was well settled in an on-the-job training program directed at men like him; she told me that every time I made a suggestion, her husband told her later that he was listening to me, and he thought I had my head firmly on my shoulders. In other words I had completely misjudged that man! I had decreed him to be a heavy drinker, a slow sort of person, exceptionally silent and suspicious, *surly* is the word I kept using in my mind when I thought of him. I was convinced that he'd never be able to stay in the city, that the trip here had worn him down completely, and he would never recover from his 'despair.' It wasn't just the look on his face, but everything: his body appeared so tired and bent over and he kept tapping his right forefinger on the kitchen table — and never stopped, never. He made *me* nervous!

"I don't know what really happened. I mean, his wife has never been about to give me an 'explanation' of why her husband has become so much better 'adjusted' to the 'urban condition' up here in Ohio. She said one time we talked that 'things were settling down,' and she wouldn't for the life of her think of going any further than that. As for her husband, he has learned and learned, and recently he got a good job for himself in a small factory. He drives a truck and moves the products to a shipping depot, but his employers have promised to put him on the assembly line soon, and his salary will then go up. *Any* salary is for him an improvement over the kind of setup he had to face up in the hollow; but what interests me is that the man is obviously taking life up here in stride, even if he has his ups and downs. And he won't be moving back.

"I would never have predicted that he could go through all that 'culture shock' I keep on hearing about. The more I bear down hard on a man like him and think about his 'values' and his 'culture,' the less hopeful everything seems, and the more I predict the wrong thing about his future. I was talking with another minister, and we decided we feel this way: according to what you read, the poor 'Appalachian white' is doomed; he is doomed up the hollows and doomed up here in the city. The only exception to that rule is the individual families we happen to have met. *They* look doomed, too; but they are complex people, and some of them, believe it or not, manage to stay alive and find work and become to a certain extent like anyone else in an American city — sometimes within a matter of months.

"I'm not saying there aren't memories and visits back home and special ways of cooking food or talking or all the rest. It's just that too much can be made of those differences, much too much. I do it all the time; I see a man who looks just overwhelmed by the streets up here — by everything. I hear him reminiscing. I see the glint in his eyes as he talks about the best times of his life, back home in Kentucky. I see the sad look on his face as he looks to the future. I see him staring out the window toward the sidewalk or the cars moving along and honking their horns. I see him staring at the trucks and the fire engines, maybe, or an ambulance speeding along, or a plane overhead. Then I see him beginning to pick at his ear, or he rubs his forehead, and I'm convinced I should offer to drive him back to Wolfe County or Harlan County, Kentucky, myself. How *can* he stay up here, I ask myself.

"But they do. A lot of them do. A lot of *us* do. We find we've got a lot more going for us than we ourselves ever dreamed. I'm speaking of myself now, not just the men and women and kids I go see every day. I think I know something of the terror they feel, because I've been miserable up here myself. I walk down a street, and dust and dirt fall on my face, and people are pushing at each other, whether they're walking or whether they're driving, and I decide I must be out of my mind to be here and to let my children grow up here. But they love it at school, and they love playing with the kids on the streets — and I now find that when I go back home I like the quiet of the hills, I still do, but I also miss the city, I miss it bad. And that's what I've eventually heard from all these 'displaced' families, these 'refugees,' I've even heard them called. They like to go home, but they like to return and make a week's pay, and then they like to go home again. But it's not just the money. I think that's a big misunderstanding; all the time I hear the mountain people are 'hooked on the dollar bills they get.' I'm sure they *are*, but I'm also sure that they get used to living better, and they get used to feeling easier about life.

"One mother told me she realizes, *now that she's up here*, how hard her life used to be. In fact, she is convinced that she could never go back to the old ways. She first came to me because she thought somehow it was sinful of her to feel like that. She wanted me to tell her that there's nothing wrong in being away from thin ice, and that's exactly what I *did* tell her. I told her that she was doing fine, and there was no reason for her to feel bad because she could smile in the morning and smile in the afternoon and smile in the evening, which was her delightful way of describing her present life. I'm sure she also smiled often when she lived in Kentucky, but there were tears, too, lots of them, and she remembers *them* as much as she remembers the beautiful weather and the woods and the little country church and the gathering of the kinfolk on a Sunday or holiday. When I told her I thought she really was doing just fine, she said she thought so, too — but she wondered whether the Lord didn't want more from her, more sacrifice. I told her I thought the Lord was happy knowing that she was eating and wearing warm clothes and feeling in pretty good health. There's always the impossible I said to her; the Lord could always ask the impossible. But He never asked that of His disciples or of anyone, and I don't see why He would begin with people from Kentucky who have crossed the Ohio River because they want to see some money every week and see good food go down their children's mouths and nice wool jackets on their children's backs. She listened, nodded, and smiled. As she turned to go she shot back a comment to me, though: 'God *did* ask the impossible of us; sometimes back home every day seemed impossible.' She wasn't fooling when she spoke. She was dead serious, and I was quite surprised. For a second I even thought she was a little fresh, a little too outspoken, a little sarcastic. Well, if she was, she had a right to be. And I realized, as I thought about her remark, that in all my years in Kentucky and now up here I'd never quite let myself be aware of the other side of all that acquiescence and calm and love of the hollow and pride in one's situation. In a second, on her face and through her quick reply, she'd told me how rotten things had been, how enraged she'd been all along, how happy she now was. And I needed to be told."

And I could only tell him what he already knew — that he was not alone in needing to be told. It is so hard to be prepared for the kind of moment he described. We learn and study and observe and are ready and waiting for that woman's guilt and fear. In our better moments, we are even prepared to recognize the joy she feels now in a city — for all the nostalgia she also can genuinely feel for the hills of eastern Kentucky. But the pain and bitterness she long kept inside her are harder for us to look at and accept and fit properly and decently into her life's history — by which I mean know how resentful she must all along have felt. But she never was prepared, never will be prepared, to allow that resentment to take over her mind and heart and dominate her spirit. We who hunger after ills and ailments, who make a virtual business of identifying people's resentments, had best keep that woman's manner of 'adjustment' in mind. She waited for just the right moment to say just the right thing to just the right person — and, in so doing managed to educate at least two people who would like to have thought they knew a good deal about individuals like her.

9. *Sally*

Ten years is a decade, I was told by Sally three days after she became a decade old. In Chicago a child learns things like that,

Sally also hastened to tell me. I asked her whether there was something special about Chicago that enabled her teachers to be so fine — because, after all, Sally was always telling me how "very good" those teachers are, and how "poor" (she was sure) her teachers were back home. Not that she can really remember that one year of school she had in the little school near Burning Springs, Clay County, Kentucky. As we talk I find her constantly struggling to forget the past, or else happening to forget it, or else pretending to forget it — then all of a sudden remembering it with a vengeance.

I fear I had better explain my language and my various qualifications. Sally likes to think of herself as a native of Chicago, even though she knows full well that she was not born in the city. About three years ago her teacher asked the class who was *not* born in Chicago. More than half the children in the class raised their hands, Sally told her mother later — but Sally didn't. She said at the time that she didn't know why the teacher would want to ask such a question, since it seemed "stupid." Her mother told her she was right: "I said to Sally that there are a lot of poking, prying people up here in this city. They want to know everything. They're worse than the sheriff and his people in Clay County, that's what I believe."

More recently, Sally likes to joke with her younger sister, tell her that they were both born in Chicago, and they will one day go to New York City, which is even bigger and "more of a city" than Chicago. Sally hears her teacher talk about New York or Los Angeles, and then tells her sister Anne what has been said — but, again, she confuses her sister by mixing in with all sorts of facts and descriptions the remark that Chicago is their birthplace, when Anne knows otherwise. Is there something wrong with Sally? I mean, is she at the very least becoming swept up with her own fantasies? Is something even more ominous at work? Does she, in fact, know where she was born; and, if so, does she have a very good reason for amusing herself and perhaps her sister with her story?

I have no intention of turning little Sally into a psychiatric patient. Her "problem" is that she is a very imaginative girl who likes to march up before the class and tell them stories. When she was in the second grade, and not long in Chicago, her teacher asked various children, including her, to come up front and talk for a minute or two about anything the child wished to share with other children. Sally apparently obliged. She said that she had been born in Chicago, then moved to Kentucky for a while, then returned. She said that her father loved to drive bulldozers and once owned a mine, but now had given up on that and instead had brought his wife and children to the Windy City, as Chicago is called. Then she sat down — amid applause. Later, she came home and told her mother what had happened, what she had said, and her mother laughed and laughed, and her usually taciturn father also laughed. So, Sally decided, one gathers, to keep on amusing her parents, keep on trying to make them laugh — and she has succeeded.

Her mother can give a chronology: "Sally has become better and better with her jokes and her stories. She makes us laugh more than anyone. Her dad comes home and he is tired and he doesn't feel any too good. His heart is poor, you know. He always asks for Sally. She comes and laughs at him. She says, 'You're no owner of Kentucky horses.' She says, 'You're no owner of coal mines.' She tells him he'd better go wash up fast, or else she'll *begin* to believe he might be a plain old workingman, just as he says he is. Sometimes she talks like one of her teachers, I guess — I've never met any of them. She tells her dad that she has big hopes for him, but he'd better go and put on the best clothes he has and try to speak the best possible words he can think up. So, her father laughs and laughs and goes and scrubs his face and hands and puts on another shirt, and if he'll have another beer in him before he gets home, and he's not too tired, he'll take up with the girl. I mean, he'll come away from the sink and announce that he had a good day inspecting his mines, and they really are producing. Then he'll tell her that he decided to ride a bulldozer or two, just so he could show the men how good he was, and how good *they* ought to be. She comes right back at him and tells him she still wonders about all those horses he owns. I guess the teacher told the class that Kentucky is known for all its fast-running horses. Well, her daddy says he rode two or three of them in the morning and turned them over to one of his 'men.' Sally says she wants to ride a horse someday, she really does — and then I get a little frightened for the child, because I'm her mother, and I can look in her eyes and see the tears she's fighting back and see what's in the back of her head: she is wishing with all her might that she *could* be riding a horse, and be out in some pastureland and not here in this neighborhood. I'll have to agree with her, but I never could say so. I think it would break the girl's heart to hear *me* say that it's too bad we're not back home — only with some money, enough money so we could own a horse and not be hungry all the time."

Sally can also turn her attention toward others. Yes, she is partial to her father, but she is also close to her mother, and the mother depends on the child for the same kind of affectionate reassurance the father often gets upon his return home. If the mother can describe what goes on between father and daughter, the father can describe what his wife and child say to each other at certain moments: "They're like on a television program, that's how I'd describe them when they get to talking and laughing. Sally tells her mother that she's going to Washington, D.C., and when she gets there she'll send a postcard back home. Then my wife asks the girl what kind of postcard, and Sally says it will be of the White House, and she will say on the card that she's visited the place and talked with the President. Then her mother asks her what she'll tell the President when she gets to see him. Well, damned if that little girl hasn't got a long story figured out in her mind. I don't know where she gets those ideas from, but she sounds like the old union men I knew back home, some of the time she does — and great story tellers they were! Then at other times she just seems funny, like a comedian, you know. Maybe she will get herself a job one day on television, they have a lot of nice ladies talking and letting you know all kinds of things when you turn on to listen to them.

"Sally will say she wants the President to know that we're the best people in the world. She tells her mother to get ready, because the postcard is going to be a huge one, and there will be a big, long message on it, with the White House for a picture on the other side, like I said. Sally says she'd write like this: Dear Mother, I'm here in Washington, and I saw him, the President, and he's a nice man, but he hasn't come to Kentucky to visit our people there, and he hasn't seen us in Chicago. We're doing fine in Chicago, but we need help. He should make sure everyone in Chicago has a job, or else there will be trouble. I told him so. I told him he's got a nice house, and there are nice buildings in Chicago, too. So, *we* should have a nice place to live.

"She has a new message each time, and her mother surely does laugh. She tells Sally that she started talking the day she was born, and she's never stopped and never will. I have to say that the girl is a puzzler to me sometimes; she's got a very strong imagination, our minister said, and her teacher back home said the same thing after the first day the child spent in school. When we left for Chicago the teacher said we should tell Sally's teachers up here that Sally was the best storyteller in the mountains. We never have met any of Sally's teachers, what with city living being as it is, but I think they know, they know about Sally. We got a note last year that said our daughter might turn out to be an actress one day. I told my wife: she'd make a lot of money, a lot of it, and we'd have our problems over that — spending the money. The truth is that Sally has a good sharp ear, that's all. She can listen to me or her mother or a kid she's playing with or a teacher, and then what she does is come home and start talking like she's heard the person talk, imitating the person. I believe I could do the same, but I'm too shy. My brother, he'll get a drink or two in him, and he starts picking away on that guitar of his, and soon he'll stop and tell one story after another, and he has everyone laughing so hard they're pleading with him to stop, but when he does, they plead for just one more story, please. The thing that gets to them is the way he'll take off after other people; he uses their voices, and he makes you think that it's them, and not him, who's the one talking. Now, Sally has been with him, and I told her mother: it's catching, like a sickness can be, except that I'd rather make people laugh than get them sick. Sally caught her uncle's storytelling gift, the minister told me, after I said she'd sit on his knee and listen to him.

"Sally's uncle, my brother, is dying. He should be up here in Chicago. They'd fix him if we took him to a hospital. He can't see a doctor back home. He's got no money. They only care for money, most doctors do. They have all that talk about helping people out, but if they don't get those dollar bills, they say, 'Sorry, mister, I'm too busy for you.' Sally says we should bring my brother up here, and she'd go with him to the hospital and between the two of them all the doctors would be laughing, and they'd become a friend to him and cure him. She's always seeing the good side, that girl is. I tell her, she was born in the middle of the day. I remember. The sun was out all the way. I think the result is that she's a very happy child, and she likes to make everyone else happy."

Does the girl get carried away with herself? Does she know the difference between fact and fantasy, between the stories she tells and the actual, day-to-day life she lives? Is she "basically depressed" or seriously fearful and anxious — all of which she "denies," or "projects" onto the people in her stories? Is there something "bizarre" about her behavior, something seriously "hysterical" or "prepsychotic" — and on and on? I have to emphasize that Sally has not been sent to a child-guidance clinic or any other kind of clinic by her teachers or her family's minister. Nor does she make people nervous or apprehensive or worried for her or about her. Nor is she out of touch with what psychiatrists call "reality." She knows exactly who she is and where she lives and what her prospects are. Perhaps she knows all that a little more acutely and vividly than the rest of us, who spend a good deal of our own time using psychological mechanisms like "denial" — to protect ourselves, for example, from thinking "too much" (or at all) about the fate of people like Sally and her family, including her uncle, whom I have met, who worked in a mine for twenty years, who was fired without a pension and now is dying of pneumoconiosis, so-called "black lung" disease. The coal dust is choking the man to death, but still he struggles not only for breath, but a chance to entertain, make people laugh, keep his own spirits up. As for Sally, she also is struggling with the darker side of life — and she also tries to push aside her worries, many of them quite real, or "objectively based," as I sometimes hear it put in conferences.

Here, drawn together from many conversations — because, of course, children of ten, even those natural-born talkers and entertainers like Sally, don't go on at such lengths without interruption — is the sober and undramatic side of the girl, the side, I suppose, that would reassure one like me, who always has to consider how "appropriate" various forms of "behavior" are, and how "well-integrated" or "pathological" a child's "defenses" are, and how successfully the child is moving along up some "developmental scale," which means how "normal" the child can be considered — perhaps *judged* is the word: "I don't believe everything I tell my friends, no I don't. My daddy told me once that we don't have to sit and stare and feel glum all the time. He said I should never lose my smiling face, so I try to smile, and if I tell him a story, then he smiles. I've seen my daddy cry. He hasn't the money we need. He tries to work, but the jobs close down, and he has to look again. He has a bad arm from working in the mine. But at least he can breathe OK. My uncle, he tries so hard to breathe you just sit there and hold your breath and hope he'll catch *his*.

"When I grow up I'd like to live in a nice, big home. I'd have a lot of food in the kitchen, and anyone who wanted food could just knock on the door, and I'd ask them to come in, and I'd tell them they should eat all they want, because it's no good to be hungry. I'd give people work to do. They could work on the house to make it look nice. My daddy had a job cleaning out a place; they had torn down a building, and they were going to build a new one. Daddy helped get all the wood and pipes and bricks into trucks. It's too bad they won't let him do work on the new building, then he'd make a lot of money, he says. He can build anything, I think. He says he can. But he's not in the union. All they let him do is clean up and load the trucks.

"I don't think I'll ever live in a mansion, no. The teacher showed us some pictures of big homes, and she asked which we

liked best. I said I'd like to go and see them, and then I'd decide
on my choice. The teacher said that was what she expected me to
say. She said I was always wishing I'd get a peek at the rich
people. I didn't answer her, but I was almost going to say that a
peek would be all I'd ever get, I know for sure. Daddy said that's
right, and so did my mother. It doesn't seem fair that only a few
people have houses like that, big ones with a garden all around.
If we had a garden, we could play on the grass. I think my uncle
could breathe better if he lived in one of those houses.

"I wish we'd go back to the mountains. I like my teacher and
my friends, but I think we'd all be happier in the mountains. My
daddy says if only we had a little money, he wouldn't stay here
one minute. I tell my friends I was born here, but I'm fooling
them. I'm from Kentucky. Maybe I'll live there when I get older.
I told a boy that I was going to Washington and to New York,
and he believed me — until someone told him I was fooling. I
don't think I'd like going so far away from home. My mother says
that if you don't know a politician, there's no reason to go visit
Washington. All the politicians from all over the country live in
Washington, because it's the capital. Daddy says the politicians
get the money that's collected in taxes, and they fight over who is
to keep the money. He says that no one in Washington or any
other place sees that people up the hollows get much of anything.

"If I had one wish, and no more, I know what I'd wish. I'd
wish my uncle got better. Then, if I could have another wish, I'd
wish that my father found a good job. He says it's in Kentucky
that he'd really like to be working — so, I'd wish he had a job
back in Kentucky. Then, if I still could wish things, I'd ask for a
new dress and some shoes and a doll and a pair of roller skates.
I'd ask for a bicycle. They are expensive. They cost more than a
man can make in a week, even up here in Chicago. Of course, if
you live up the hollow, there's no need for a bike. Even a car can
only go halfway up the hill; that's how it is if you live in a
hollow.

"The saddest thing I see is when my mother has to go shopping, and she's afraid she hasn't the money she needs, and she
starts crying. I try to make her stop. I come near and tell her

something funny. If I can't make her smile, I keep on trying. I make up a new story, one she's never heard, and she pretends she's not listening, and her head is still down, and she's sniffing and wiping her eyes, but I know she's heard me. Yes sir, I know by the way she turns a little to me, and I can see her face, and there's a smile beginning on it. When I finish, she takes me round and says, 'God bless you,' and I can see she's more smiling than anything else. The tears are mostly gone."

I am not sure that the description Sally offers of what goes on between her and her mother doesn't apply quite exactly to what goes on between Sally and some of her friends, whom she so ambitiously and warmly and generously entertains. For that matter, I am not so sure that Sally doesn't do her share for her teachers, too. They also get weary and discouraged — and as I try to show in a long section of this book devoted to schools, a classroom can be a scene of great sadness, and therefore present a child like Sally with a particularly strong challenge. And so, when I went to see Sally's fifth grade teacher I got from her the following response: "She's a lovely child. Her mind fairly races along. No, I have never felt her to be particularly troubled. I suppose all my children here in this school are in a bit of trouble. They come from poor families. Their parents would much rather be back in Kentucky, up those mountains, than here in this big, sprawling city. They all get confused, the parents do, and the children naturally try to help them out. We forget sometimes how much a child like Sally can do to comfort her mother. Sally is a born nurse, that's my opinion of her. Miss Florence Nightingale, that's Sally. I've called her that. She looks embarrassed, but she loves me for giving her such a nice, long, impressive name. I told her that Florence Nightingale was a nurse who helped soldiers who got hurt in war. Sally said her father had been in the war, the Korean War I believe, and he'd been in the mine union and fought with the bosses — the bosses of the union, I'm quite sure, as much as the bosses of the coal mine. They're all corrupt, you know — labor and industry both. It's people like Sally's parents, and us, the schoolteachers, who get caught in the middle.

"Anyway, when Sally once told me that her father had been in fights, I told her that we never stop fighting, one way or another, until we die. After I'd said that, I bit my lip. I thought to myself: she's ten years old and too young to hear that kind of talk. But she knew exactly what I had meant. I'm afraid that she's probably heard much worse at home. She said, 'I know. My daddy says he has to fight all the time.' I asked her what she meant — as if I didn't know! — and she told me how he has a bad arm, but he goes out every day and uses it and uses his good one, too; he shovels and rakes and lifts things and pushes things and moves things, and then he comes home dead tired, but glad to have the dollar bills. I felt my eyes filling up, so I turned away from the child. That was all she had to see. She's a bright little one. She doesn't miss anything. I think a lot of my children are like that. They live close to much suffering, so they keep their eyes wide open. True, some of them close their eyes and keep them shut tight for the same reason — they've seen so much, and they don't want to expose themselves to one more thing. But a girl like Sally is too smart; she's going to keep on noticing all the troubles in her world, and then she's going to do her level best to heal as much as she can. The first day in this room, she asked if she could bring her daddy over to plaster the walls and get rid of the cracks. I was taken aback, and then I thought to myself: there's a girl who's trying, really trying!

"I was saying — I was saying I almost broke down and cried before the child. I turned away, and there she was running up to me and telling me that her daddy was a funny, funny man, and when he got started on one of his real funny stories, she knew the clock would go around and around until at least a whole hour was gone. Then she told me how her father knows more songs to play on his guitar than anyone she's met, and how he makes faces at her, and she makes faces back. By that time I'd forgotten everything sad I'd heard. The child is so full of life that she makes you want to take her aside and ask her how she does it, become so charming and vivacious. I believe some children are born that way, and their parents have a godsend when they get such a child. I just cannot imagine Sally's mother or father becoming *too* sad, not with a girl like her around. She's like a soldier. She stands guard over people so they don't sink too low, so they keep their morale as high as possible. And she is not a mixed-up little girl. She's not constantly worrying over something. I've seen children worry about their parents and worry about the entire neighborhood they live in. They may also try to cheer their parents up, but they never do — because they're not very cheerful themselves. With a child like Sally — she's not the only child I know who's so sensitive and thoughtful — the good humor in her soul, the lighthearted quality she has, simply comes across and lifts up a person's spirits.

"Don't ask me where she gets those qualities. I told you I thought one either has them or doesn't. I think children are born different. Some are going to live, and some are going to die. I believe that. Some look sickly from the first day, and some look as if they're ready to leap into a boxing ring and start fighting. I'm no mother, but my sister has had four children, and I've been working with children and meeting their mothers and talking with them for twenty years now — so I think I know a little. When I get my new class each year, I look at the boys and girls, and in a few minutes I've moved from face to face, and I can almost count the children with spark in them and the ones who have given up. That's what I'll catch myself thinking with a child. She's *alive,* or she's *given up.* Sally will never give up. She's like her ancestors. They were tough people; they battled their way into those hills, and they've managed to stay there despite all the suffering they've had to face. I've taught all sorts of children, not only children from Appalachia, and I do believe there's a special sadness some Appalachian children feel — and a special liveliness and strength they have. In a girl like Sally I think I see both of those qualities; she's very wise, the way a tired and old and disillusioned grandmother can be, but she's also as sprightly and gay and lovable as the young and vigorous child she certainly is."

I was told more, all of it essentially the same thing: Sally is a somewhat extraordinary girl, but then every year there are to be found a few children like her because, in the teacher's words, "that's the way the human race is." Sally herself admires a boy who is not in her room but is in her school and her grade; her reasons for admiring him and considering him special and extraordinary tell a good deal about her: "Tim is always trying to run fast and hit the ball as far as he can. He says he could climb up every mountain in Kentucky if he could only have the time. He says he wants to be a pilot, and then he would fly over the mountains and find the tallest one. He would land the plane in a valley, and he would go climb right to the very top. Then he would go down and help get his grandfather to the top, because his grandfather is very sick, and he says that before he dies he'd like to go up the tallest mountain in Kentucky and sit there and look. Afterwards, he could die happy. I told Tim I'd like to go with them. We could see for miles and miles, in all directions. Tim says here in the city you can't see anyplace, just a few houses ahead of you, and the streets have big trucks, so you can't even see across to the other side a lot of the time."

She goes on to describe Tim as an active, bright boy and she admires him because he is very much able to manage things in Chicago, but at the same time he has not forgotten the mountains and their importance. And Sally, who can blithely deny being born in those same mountains, how can she so admire Tim for talking so much about Kentucky and its hills and rivers and fields and animals and creeks and hollows and small towns and winding dirt roads and ponds and lakes and flowers and animals and fish and single-track railroad lines and small bridges one can casually walk over — right down the middle and with no fear of traffic? Sally is not in the least worried by the apparent incongruities some fastidious grown-up has noticed and seen fit (had the gall) to mention: "I like to get some of my friends real mad at me. Almost everyone in my room was born in Kentucky or maybe West Virginia, my daddy says, or if they weren't, they just barely made it to Chicago. My mother says a lot of people from the mountains have been here for a long time, so they could have been born in Chicago, a lot of the kids in my room, but their mothers usually have gone home to be with their families when they found out they were going to have a baby. In my room most of the kids admit they were born in Kentucky. No one wants to be born in Chicago. This is no city to be born in! So, I go and say *I* was born here, and they all laugh and say you never can tell what Sally will come up with."

She can actually go back and forth about Chicago: the city is awful, noisy, too big, or the city is full of secrets and mysteries and nice, nice people. There is her schoolteacher; there is her best girl friend; there is Tim; there is the janitor, who is kin of hers, and is very much taken with Sally. "I guess I haven't made up my mind," Sally says, speaking about Chicago and Appalachia and urban living and the rural life and her future: "Sometimes I think one way, and sometimes the other. Sometimes I think I'd like to live in a new apartment building right here in this city, on the top floor; other times I want to be back with my uncle and grandmother in Kentucky. I know my daddy's heart is there; he says so. I know the same is true of my mother — she stays here because we all have to stay here, she says. And she doesn't agree that we should go back home to Kentucky all the time. My mother says if she was going to have another baby, she'd be glad to go into a hospital right here. When my daddy worked in the mines they had money, so we were all born in the hospital, and my mother had a doctor when she needed one. But after he got laid off they didn't have any money at all, and my mother lost two babies soon after they got born."

For Sally, life goes like that: one measures advantages and disadvantages; one sees the good and the bad; one doesn't quite know; one tries hard to find and then emphasize the enjoyable and amusing side of life; one does what a person can to keep going, to be animated and of a sunny disposition; and all in all one manages, even at ten, to inspire in young friends and older parents or teachers a certain "gladness" about life. That is the word Sally's mother uses to describe her child's influence upon her particular world: "The child gives us a little gladness when we sorely need it." The mother said that and moved her long, thin, bony fingers toward the child; quickly the fingers worked their way up the child's short arm and reached her shoulder and clasped it; then the child rocked a little, in response to the mother's pressure to do just that; and the child smiled, obviously delighted to be having such a good, close time. And the mother smiled, too.

PART THREE

THE SCHOOLS

VII

THOSE PLACES
THEY CALL SCHOOLS

PEOPLE like me visit a large number of schools, talk with the principals and assistant principals and teachers and children, then leave and soon have our say: this school had some interesting things going inside it; that one was awful; the children over here are learning practically nothing; the children over there may be picking some things up in the classroom, but the price — psychological, emotional, spiritual if you will — they pay for the achievements is much too high.

Meanwhile, the children keep on going to school. Sometimes we learn what they think: their poems or compositions are published; their words, spoken under a particular set of circumstances, are reported. Their "attitudes" are elicited and are analyzed and are declared to be statistically significant so far as one or another "variable" goes, and are then summarized and written up and discussed. For all the effort that goes into those studies, and for all we find out from them, I am not sure we don't miss a lot, miss a lot that we want to know and need to know. I realize from my own work how much I miss — how the drawings I ask children to do, because I have in mind certain things, often disappoint me, simply because a few moments earlier or later I hear something or see something that reminds me once again how ambiguous and inconsistent and contradictory and ironic and frustratingly, delightfully unpredictable the human mind can be. So, I have to place those drawings and paintings alongside other "data": the observations I've made of the way children play, the talk I come upon, the things that are done (or indeed not done) in the natural course of a child's life — a part of which, it happens, I'm around to witness.[1]

Yet, I also have to give those drawings or the words I hear spoken an authority all their own, not subject to all the qualifications and interpretations and explanations and translations that in this age have made any statement, however clear-cut, direct and to the point, something to be deciphered only by a certified oracle. I think one of the children I am soon to quote put the matter very well when he took me to task this way: "I don't know if I meant anything — except what I said. I listened to what you asked, and then I thought to myself that he wants a straight answer, so I'll give it to him, and then I thought of what I thought, and then I tried to tell you."

In this account — a brief prelude of a chapter to the long one that follows it — the children will, I hope, be allowed their leeway. They are so-called "elementary school children." They are black and white. They either live in the black ghetto of a large northern city or they live in sections called "white lower-middle-class" by sociologists and (so I have heard since around 1968) "backlash-prone." As I write this I have known them, the boys and the girls, for at least three years — some of them for four, going on five. I have visited them again and again and I think we get along. We dig each other. We laugh and get suspicious and talk about a lot of nothing and about a lot of something and about a lot of everything and about "a plenty lot," as Margie put it once. In the autumn of 1968, I asked Margie "a plenty lot" about her school, about the building in contrast to the usual questions about the things going on inside the building — the teachers, the lessons taught or not taught, the way things are done and not done.

Margie is concrete. She talks about "those places they call schools." She talks this way: "I don't know if you need to have schools in buildings. Those places they call schools, they're really no good. You know why? It's because they're *not* schools; I mean, they're a place where they force you to go, and you sit there, and the teacher, she's tired and all she wants is for the clock to go round and round until it's time to leave. Maybe if the teacher was different, then she could come and help us out right here. My mother says there are enough of us in this building here, so we could have a school — maybe in our kitchen, it could be. Then we could get a cookie sometimes — no, they don't have them, and no hot lunches either, or anything like that — and we could be doing something, not just sitting there and each of us laughing at what a joke it is."

Well, if she had her say, what would she do to make the school better, the school she now attends? Or, alternatively, what kind of school would she suggest be built for her and other children all over America? The question is asked again and again, in the same or slightly different form, and over time a number of responses are made: some enthusiastically, some tentatively, some for sure, some skeptically at best: "I'll tell you one thing, I'd tear *this* building down. There's nothing to do but that. Then, if I could build a new school, I'd make it pleasant-like. I'd get rid of all the desks, every one of them. I'd have us sit around a table, and maybe we could have cookies. I'd have the teacher be better. She could laugh a lot, and there wouldn't be a clock up there, making noise every minute that goes by. We could open and close the windows, and they wouldn't be stuck like now. We could have a big rug here in the room, so if you fell down you wouldn't get hurt, like I did. And they could have some places, some big sofas maybe, where if you didn't feel too good, you could lie down, or you could just sit in them sometimes, and you'd be more comfortable.

"I'm not sure why they have us go to school. Do you know? Is there anyone who does? I know it's to learn things, how to read and do arithmetic and like that, but most of the time it's just a waste, and you'd think they might want to change it around and have us spend the day better. You'd think they might try to change a lot of things themselves. The principal himself, he complains to us that the big hall, it's too big, and you can't hear good, and the corridors, they're just too long, and you practically should have a car to travel from one part of the building to the next. My older brother, he's in the sixth grade, and it's like he's across the country from me. I never see him except when school is out. Then everyone wakes up."

Margie's brother, Arthur, is old enough to be well into junior high school by the standards of many suburban schools. He seems at first glance very shy, very timid, very silent, and yet another "slow" student — full of all the "disadvantage" and "deprivation" we keep on hearing ascribed to him and thousands like him. Outside school, from a distance, when no one is taking notes or asking questions or recording grades, when no one is teaching or doing his research, making his observations, Arthur's mouth can be seen working overtime: speaking, saying things, issuing orders, asking questions, making replies, shouting, crying, laughing — the banal word is "communicating," and yes, communicating what is "relevant" to Arthur: "Well, I'll tell you; the whole place, it's pretty bad. I'll tell you why, I will. My sister said it was like a jail the other day, but it's not a jail, because you can leave, and if your mother will let you, a lot of the time you can just stay home, and they don't really care, anyway. But when you're in there, in that building, I guess it does get pretty bad, like Margie said. I step and fall, because the floors are no good; they're too smooth and you can hear everyone walking and it's like in a war, in a battle, the teacher said. The windows, no one ever looks in them or looks out of them. My friend Jim put his finger on one, and there was so much dust he could write his name, and then the teacher got mad. What's the window for, though? We'd have to climb up on ladders to see through most of it. The bathroom, like Margie said, it's no good. They should have one for our homeroom, one for each one, and then we wouldn't be walking all over, and it would be ours, and that goes for eating, too. I mean, why couldn't they have a kitchen for us, like at home? My mother said if they can build these fancy apartment buildings so you can each have your refrigerator and your bathroom, they could do it for us in school, and then the whole place would be better, because we'd have a nice room and you wouldn't have to go a mile and then find a big bathroom and you can get lost in it and by the time you get back you've missed everything they've been talking about. Then if they send you out for the recess it's a joke. They tell you to watch out for the glass and the cracks in the cement, but they never do anything to get rid of them.

"I'd like comfortable chairs, like ones that have cushions so your back doesn't hurt and your bottom, either. I'd like us sitting around — you know, looking at each other, not in a line, not lined up. I'd like a sink, where you could get some water to drink, and you wouldn't have to ask the teacher to go down the hall, and half the time she says no. I'd like for them to have Cokes, not only milk, and they could have them cold and we could have our cups and there'd be a table and it would be a lot nicer homeroom than it is now. We could have our books in a bookcase, and we wouldn't have to sit in the same place all the time, and you feel it's like you're glued to the chair, and the chair is glued to the floor — it is — and you can't move around, and if you do she'll shout at you to sit down and shut up and mind your own business.

"You know what? I'd like to be able to take off my shoes and relax. The floor is so cold, you can't do that now. And they could do better than having the room like it is — you can't put anything anyplace except where it's supposed to be, inside your desk. She'll give you something to read, the teacher, and then she'll have to take it away and put it in the cabinet and lock it up. If I could do what I'd like, I'd have TV and popcorn and you could put our books on a table, spread them out there, and it would make a nicer room."

In his homeroom there might even be curtains and a magazine stand and lamps "like at home" and not only schoolbooks but other kinds of books and "better pictures" on the wall, and a teakettle and of course a stove and some candy and a lot of doors that opened up to the next rooms "on either side" and plants and flowers and "most of all, really most of all" a window in the roof so you could "just look up and see the sky and the clouds and the sun and when the rain falls you could see it falling and you'd like it better, being in school."

So say Margie and Arthur and others like them: older and younger, all from their school, which they call theirs yet also disown with a scorn equal to that of our harshest social and educational critics. Perhaps it is because they are black children, hence particularly dissatisfied. Arthur himself, in a way, took the responsibility of discrediting his own complaints: "Even if they built the best school building they could, it wouldn't mean much if those teachers were the way they are, and if it kept on being the way it is — a pain, I think. My uncle, he says you'll have to change a lot more than buildings if you're going to make it easier for us to get by. That's the way I think, too. Maybe I'm too hard on my teacher and that school — the building, I mean — because like I say, the school, well it's not the real enemy, that's what my uncle says. He says we could take that school, bad as it is, if it wasn't that a lot of other things, they're even worse, even worse than it."

Miles away on tree-lined streets that no one would ascribe to a ghetto, live children as old as Margie and Arthur, but white and from homes that are called "single-family" and "middle-class." The fathers who own those homes are office workers, firemen and policemen (who frequently hold down two jobs and whose wives often work as well) and, not the least, schoolteachers. The children go to a relatively new school, but still have their criticisms to make. Susan, for example, is Margie's age: "I'm pretty good at school. My mother says if I keep it up, I'll get to college, and it's not easy for a girl, not in our family, because there's just so much money, and it has to go for my brothers, if they can get in. If I could build a school, I guess play make-believe and do it that way, play magic, I'd make the school warm and small and not big and too hot one minute and you're shivering the next. I'd have a lot of little schools. I'd have every homeroom a school, separate from the rest. Then there wouldn't be all those big buildings, and you get lost in them. My mother says I got scared, the first time I went to school, because it was so huge, and you couldn't see to the end of the hall; it just went on and on. And it's too dark in school, way too dark. And once you're inside, you never see the outside until the big bell rings and you can leave, if the teacher says yes, it's OK.

"A lot of the time, I think, if they put on the radio, like we have at home, it would be better than not hearing anything but your-self and the clock. The teacher, she always coughs and says it's time to do the next thing, and you can tell when she gets angry, because her chair squeaks a lot, because she moves around more. They should get rid of that chair. And they shouldn't have us go to the bathroom way down the hall, and they told us that the lunchroom, it's too big and everyone gets lost in it. My mother says we could have little sun-rooms, with plants in them, and we could go and eat there, a few of us in each one, and it would be cozy. And I think we could have places to play, not just the halls and the classrooms and nothing else. Yes, we have the gym, but that's for games, and it's too big, and I mean a room like we have at home, a playroom, for our class, and other classes, they could have theirs, too."

Billy, a couple of years older, lives across the street from Susan. He supported her view and added some other things, too: "They should divide schools up, so you get to know the part you're in, as if it was your home or your friend's home. They should have a movie theater there, and we could watch TV and it wouldn't be in the big auditorium, where it's too big and the seats are no good. They should have a fireplace or something like that in the room, so we could sit around it, and that would be better than those desks, especially if you're put in the back row like I am. They should have it more like home when you eat lunch, and not like it is, with the cafeteria, and everyone trying to eat at once, and a lot of the time you can't get a seat, and when you get one, it's no good anyway — those benches! And worst of all is the stairs — climbing them all the time, and you feel you'll get lost trying to find out which floor you're supposed to be on and where the right room is. They could build buildings that are better: nicer and friendlier and the kind you can get to know every corner of it in a short while. I'll bet I could."

I took Billy and the other children up on that; I asked Billy to do exactly what he said he could do; and he did indeed sit down on several occasions and draw his school (Figure 1). As he drew and after he had drawn he talked. He told me how important it was that a school building be strong and able to survive snow and rain and strong winds and the wear of thousands, of millions of footsteps. He told me that buildings should beckon and welcome and reach out and say hello and a big good-bye and in general be something more, much more, than the word "building" implies. He put his feelings like this: "This school I'm doing, it will be liked by everyone in it. They'll say, 'Isn't this a great place.'"

Billy and his friends build huts and hideouts and tents and cabins and forts — and do things to make those buildings livable, even lovable. They arrange and rearrange. They decorate and embellish and add and subtract: wood, leaves, rags, sticks, rocks, all the "materials" that architects and designers and engineers talk about. They struggle for privacy, yet they want to make themselves and their choices and preferences and works and constructs apparent, very much so. They insist on the integrity of their own decisions and judgments, yet at the same time they constantly call upon the authority of their parents — and not necessarily out of begrudging obedience or fear.

A month later Billy and his friend Gerry got together and Gerry, more of an "idea-man," as he calls himself (he got the term "on television") told Billy what to draw (Figure 2) because, in Gerry's words: "I can't draw, not even a straight line with a pencil and a ruler to do it. A good school would have a road going right through it, or under it, and you could see cars and stores and people, and they'd be looking at you, and then you wouldn't have to take a bus and go way out into nowhere, just because you're going to school. They shouldn't drag us all over the city just to see some pictures in a museum and places like that. They could have a big room in the school, and we could go and look at things all the time, if we wanted, not just once a year. They could even hang our pictures, and the teacher, she should try drawing, the teacher should. She told us she wasn't any good at it, and neither am I; but some teachers are good painters, I'll bet, and they would probably like everyone else to see what they've done."

Margie draws her school reluctantly (Figure 3); she is bored and in time is outspokenly annoyed. After all, she isn't drawing what might be, but what is: "There's nothing to draw, except those big walls. That's all school is, a big brick building, and all the stupid stuff inside. Half the time I'm ready to fall asleep, and half the time the teacher is just as sleepy. If you want me to make up a *good* school, then I could try. I think the best thing to do is tear down the old school and let it be a place for us to play, the land. Then we could build another one, and it would be better. Outside it would have statues of our people, black leaders, like I saw on the news they had someplace, in front of some building. And you could walk right in the building without steps, and it would be good inside. They'd have a garden, with rocks and water and flowers, just like they had in the museum, and there'd be a bridge over the water, like there is there, and you could walk inside a room like in the other museum, and they'd have a map of the world on the walls, all around everywhere, and you could stand and see all the continents and the oceans."

Margie's brother, Arthur, has a hero, a youth named Jack, a tough more-than-youth: at fifteen he is a "child" — still required to attend school — who is also very much a grown man. Jack talks, talks a lot. Jack is in junior high, and at sixteen will certainly leave school. For Jack the ghetto has other schools, schools that offer him something, maybe everything he has decided he wants. He stays on not because school officials pursue him and compel him to stay, but because his father, his stepfather in fact, insists it is necessary and desirable: "The old man, he's up against the ropes. He's broke. He used to have some money, but they cut him off, the people he worked for. Now, he's got nothing, and he thinks I'll get nothing, too, unless I go to school — which is crazy. His brother, he finished high school, and he never could find a good job. They say now you can, because they want the black man for display, and they're scared, too. But man, we're too many, and they only want a few.

"These schools, they're real old, like all the other buildings here, and even when they build a new one, they know it'll become just like everything else, in a day or two it will — because it can't help being like that. The rat that bit my kid sister, he's not going to stop and say, 'Well, well, what a nice school, I think I'll stay clear of it.' And anyway, there'll always be those teachers, driving up in their cars and looking both ways when they get out and locking their doors with triple locks and making a run for the building. Don't they know we can take any car we want? They'd be better off not locking them. They forget that a man like my stepfather, he can't afford the gas, even if he drove off with the car. But I'll have a car and there'll always be gas in it, I can bet you on that.

"As far as school buildings go, they're all no good, any I've seen. I told Arthur they should forget the whole thing. Let some of those teachers come over here and talk with us — I mean, in our homes, or at the pool hall. As soon as they get together under one roof, even if it's all glass, like Arthur says it should be, then you're sunk. It's no good. All they want is for us to be quiet and polite and mind them. Then are they glad when school is out and they can get away from here. And what they teach you, it's enough to make you drowsy, drowsy all day.

"Arthur says if they changed the way the schools are, then he'd stay. But how can they? They'll never do it. You think they'll tear down that school of Arthur's and build one like he drew over there? That's a joke."

VIII

TEACHERS AND THE CHILDREN
OF POVERTY

1. *Pygmalion in the Classroom*

THE moment a child is born he or she joins a particular kind of world. A doctor has done the delivery in a hospital, or a midwife has done it in a rural cabin, or the baby emerged almost unassisted, except perhaps by someone who just happened to be nearby.[1] As the months and years pass, that baby learns all sorts of things: how to sit up, walk, talk, play, dress, and take full responsibility for eating. Though genes have a lot to do with the child's appearance and appetite and growth, things rarely happen to anyone, infant or grown-up, solely because they are ordained by the laws of nature. Put differently, man's laws give shape even to our biological destiny. A child might have it in him to become a tall, strong, energetic man, and another child might have it in her to become a woman of unusual beauty; but without proper food neither of them will survive infancy, let alone reach adulthood.

When a subject like what goes to make up "intelligence" is debated, some very concrete and practical issues may really be awaiting the outcome of the dispute. If intelligence is considered to be something fixed and precise, a biological given that is either substantially present or relatively missing, then teachers are right to separate the quick-witted child from the slow one, and both of them from the ordinary plodder. In fact, teachers are right to look upon themselves as agents of a sort, or as mates for a particular kind of child: the child comes to school with a good, fast mind, a rather average one, or a relatively slow one, and the school's job is to find out which it is and then act accordingly. This teacher works well with fast learners; that one has a place in her heart for the dull child; and so-and-so in room X has an uncanny knack with those in the middle — who respond to her and go as far as they can as a result of her attentive ear, her light, gentle touch.

"Intelligence," however, can also be considered not a distinct entity, a thing that has an exactly measurable reality, but instead a highly complicated and variable kind of activity by which the mind, under certain circumstances — and clearly what is favorable for one person can be just the opposite for another — encounters facts and situations and comes to understand them, act upon them, gain some measure of control over them. Such a view places great stress on complexity and variability, because people behave in strange and inconsistent and unpredictable ways.[2] Idiots can have astonishing powers of recall. Geniuses can be dumb about so very much. Writers can barely know how to count and any number of brilliant social scientists can't write a straight sentence to save their souls. More to the point of our present national problems, children can be stubbornly, impossibly backward in school, but then at home, or more likely, on the streets and in the alleys, those same children appear shrewd, imaginative and resourceful — in other words, as intelligent as can be.

At this point the anthropologist and the psychiatrist (and perhaps the merely intelligent teacher or parent) wants to speak out and remind us that some children grow up in a family, a neighborhood, a whole town, where schools mean a lot, where the child's achievement in them means just about everything to his parents. Such boys and girls learn that it makes a difference, it counts, if they pay attention to the teacher, do what she says, and become regarded as "good" or "smart" or "cooperative." In contrast, other children literally learn not to learn. Perhaps a boy's parents are well-to-do and ambitious, but for some hard-to-fathom reason of his own, the son is afraid to learn, and so has what child psychiatrists call a "learning block." That is to say, the child's brain seems normal enough, but his mind won't, for any number of reasons, take in all those facts, put them together in various ways, and offer teachers the result, a kind of coherence about the things of this world. Somehow a blurred, indistinct world seems safer.

Many other children have no such psychological problem, but also don't do well at school — because they come there, as it is now put, "disadvantaged" and "deprived."[3] They come from very poor homes. They don't eat good food; and indeed many physicians and nutritionists and neurophysiologists would argue that a faulty diet, low in critically important vitamins, minerals and proteins, causes serious damage to an infant's brain, so that eventually he comes to school retarded, not by an accident or disease or injury, but the repercussions of a nation's social and economic problem, which becomes a very personal, everyday problem for millions of families. Yet even if poor parents can provide their children with decent meals and adequate medical care and suitable clothes — which is not usually the case — there remains the larger issue of a family's spirit. Does the mother give her children a sense of confidence, or do she and her husband feel discouraged about life most of the time? It takes a lot of conviction — which can take the form of subtle suggestion, persuasion, charm and even force — for an infant to become the kind of child teachers tend to like: well-scrubbed, eager, obedient, responsive. Mothers who live in broken-down, rat-infested tenements, who never quite know when the next few dollars will come, have little energy left for their children. Life is grim and hard, and the child simply has to find that out. He does, too; he learns it and learns it and learns it. He learns how to survive all sorts of threats and dangers. He learns why his parents have given up on school, why they may have tried and fallen flat on their faces. He learns about things like racial hatred, about the state of the economy, about technological change. He learns whether he is an insider or an outsider, whether people like storekeepers or property owners or policemen treat his family with kindness and respect or with suspicion if not out-and-out contempt. By the time a child of the ghetto first arrives at school he has learned so much that his knowledge might perhaps be credited to an account called "the intelligence of the so-called unintelligent as it appears in sly, devious and haunting ways."

The average teacher may know all that, but find little time to dwell upon the social and psychological forces that make children so very different before they have had one day of school. To the teacher those differences are a beginning, not an end. Yes, years go into making six-year-old children what they are; but they are what they are, and they are quickly found to be fast learners or slow learners or something in-between. They are found so by experienced observers — teachers and school psychologists — and they are found so by "objective criteria," by all those intelligence tests, of which there are dozens, each with its own twist, its own special, prideful, reasonable (or extravagant) claims. In thousands of schools all over the country those tests are employed and the results used to separate children into "tracks": fast, medium, slow. In theory the distinctions and separations are meant to help each child: the able and gifted ones will not be on hand to intimidate the fearful or slower ones, nor will the latter cause the former to lose their right to learn just as much as they can, at a speed they find congenial. Yet, what often happens? Rather obviously, those who score well in the tests take an active interest in schoolwork and become known as first-rate students, whereas those who find teachers and the work they assign a big bore or a big fright soon become the "problem child," the "disruptive child," the slow-witted or stupid one — no matter how bright they all may be "underneath."

Well, what can the poor, overworked, underpaid teacher do about all that? Can the teacher be responsible for our nation's injustices, for its history of racial strife, for the regional circumstances that doom white Appalachian children and Indian children and Mexican-American children as well as black children? Can schools make up for lacks and shortages and cruelties experienced in homes? Can a few hours in a given classroom, even one run by the most capable and best-intentioned of teachers, really change a sullen, troubled child's destiny, make him something he would never otherwise be? Can it even be that teachers in dozens of ways, for dozens of reasons, decisively determine which children will eagerly absorb their lessons and which ones will say maybe or positively no? Can the child's performance in school be considered as much the result of what his various teachers' attitudes are toward him as his native intelligence, or his own attitude as a pupil?[4]

Questions like those cannot be answered easily, concisely or unequivocally, but a book with the dramatic and suggestive title of *Pygmalion in the Classroom* has a lot to say about the whole issue of who learns what and why — and so ought to be discussed at some length in this book.[5] The authors are Robert Rosenthal, a social psychologist, and Lenore Jacobson, a school principal, and their study has to do, in the pedantic words of the book's subtitle, with "teachers' expectation and pupils' intellectual development." Dr. Rosenthal and Mrs. Jacobson began their work in the spring of 1964, when they gave the "Harvard Test of Inflected Acquisition" to most of the children of an elementary school on the West Coast. The only ones not tested were sixth graders, who would no longer be in the school a year later, when another round of observations was to take place. The test was supposed to have prophetic powers, or so the school's teachers thought: "As a part of our study we are further validating a test which predicts the likelihood that a child will show an inflection point or 'spurt' within the near future. This test which will be administered in your school will allow us to predict which youngsters are most likely to show an academic spurt. The top 20% (approximately) of the scorers on this test will probably be found at various levels of academic functioning. The development of the test for predicting inflections or 'spurts' is not yet such that *every* one of the top 20% of the children *will* show a more significant inflection or spurt in their learning within the next year or less than will the remaining 80% of the children."

There is actually no such thing as the "Harvard Test of Inflected Acquisition," though Dr. Rosenthal and Mrs. Jacobson clearly knew how to go about impressing teachers. When people out of Harvard provide a means to estimate "inflected acquisition," a lady who struggles to teach boys and girls their letters and numbers can only be grateful for the mysterious ways of those twins, Progress and Science. The children were really given a somewhat obscure but well established and useful intelligence test, Flanagan's Tests of General Ability, or TOGA as it is abbreviated and called. Flanagan's TOGA is one of, say, a hundred such tests that teachers don't usually know about. Many teachers do know, however, that social scientists are very smart about finding things out, about asking questions and studying the answers to them and coming up with all sorts of new ideas referred to as "conclusions" or "results." So, in that California school the teachers had reason to believe they were helping serious research along by lending their children to an experiment. Naturally, the teachers also believed that they would become privy to some very interesting and important information.

As the school year began, lists of children's names were given to teachers in all grades. The school divided each grade into fast, medium and slow tracks, and there were lists for all three tracks of each grade. TOGA apparently could spot "bloomers" anywhere and everywhere. The teachers were, as a courtesy, let in on the secret — or more accurately, in on part of the secret. They were cautioned not to tell any of the children or their parents what the tests had revealed. In fact, Dr. Rosenthal and Mrs. Jacobson had arbitrarily, by random choice, selected the names for those lists of "bloomers." The TOGA scores had nothing to do with the selection of "bloomers," who amounted to almost a fifth of the school's children. The individual lists that went to each teacher varied in length. A third grade class made up of fast learners might have supplied one or two children to the honor roll of the "Harvard Test of Inflected Acquisition," and a first grade class whose children seemed slow, slow, slow might have done exceedingly well — with eight or nine of its members headed for better things indeed, if Harvard and its scholars were to be believed. Yet, all along Harvard's scholars had other things in mind. They had prepared a school's teachers for the fact of "inflected acquisition" by testing all their schoolchildren in the spring, and in the autumn listing the results, class by class. The truth was that the children on the lists were in no sense "special." Their names were in essence pulled out of a hat. If they were different, it would be because their teachers were told they were, or rather, told they were going to be.

Needless to say, lists are lists, names on inert paper, and teachers have a lot to do in the course of a year besides reading and rereading the names of a few children who just might receive a kind nod from fate. All during the autumn of 1964 and the winter and spring of 1965, the Oak School, as it is called, went about its business, interrupted here and there by holidays — and by two more bouts with TOGA: in January and May of 1965, all the children were again tested. Then a year later, in May 1966, TOGA put in one final appearance — and the Harvard social scientist, along with his collaborator from the West Coast, repaired to Cambridge with the "data." They also brought other bits of information to Cambridge. Teachers routinely grade and make comments about their pupils — how they are getting along in each subject, how they behave in class, what their "attitude" is. All of that, for each child in the Oak School, was sent East to the computers. Toward the end of the school year the teachers were even asked to make detailed descriptions of and judgments about their children. How successful might they be in the future? Were their achievements in class the result of native ability asserting itself or, say, a capacity for pure drudgery? Was this child "appealing, well-adjusted, affectionate" or that one "hostile and motivated by a need for approval"? It even came to this: "Each child was rated by the teacher on nine variables on a scale that went from 1 ('Not at all happy') to 9 ('Extremely happy')."

What did they discover — the social scientist and the school principal and their research assistants, who no doubt labored long and hard on a most substantial collection of scores and ratings? *Pygmalion in the Classroom* is full of charts and graphs and statistics and percentages and very carefully weighed and guarded statements, but the reader is also treated to some striking and thought-provoking conclusions which clearly have a great deal of significance for this nation, preoccupied as it is with severe educational problems of many kinds. For example, among the children of the first and second grades, those who were tagged as eventual "bloomers" made astonishing gains on later tests, far more gains than the others in the school (the "control group") could claim: "In these grades about every fifth control-group child gained twenty IQ points or more, but of the special children, nearly every second child gained that much."

The authors call that development a dramatic one, and in a way it is their central finding, though they made many others. When the reader finishes looking at several tables and lets the large amount of statistical information sink in, he is left with the following lesson: all sorts of young children, whether they were slow learners, ordinary pupils, or very bright students, did very much better in school than others like them — did so presumably because their teachers *expected* them to do so. In other words, a prophecy became fulfilled in such a way that hard-line social scientists, bent on accumulating objective measurements and calling things statistically significant or insightful found themselves surprised, even startled. They were taken aback by other results, too. They found the greatest gains among Mexican-American children, who in the Oak School were considered a "minority group," hence afflicted with "cultural disadvantage" and "cultural deprivation" and God knows what else. Despite all those clumsy and condescending labels, the poor Mexican-American children in that school became much better students, both in their teachers' eyes and quite "objectively" on a very reliable intelligence test. What is more, the children who looked classically Mexican did better than those who looked a little "Anglo," which prompts the authors to speculate rather drily that "the teachers' preexperimental expectancies of the more Mexican-looking boys' intellectual performance was probably lowest of all. These children may have had the most to gain by the introduction of a more favorable expectation into the minds of their teachers."

However, although the very Mexican-looking children may have in fact jumped way ahead of themselves and their classmates, the teachers of the Oak School were by no means won over by the remarkable improvement. The Mexican-American children still were judged as before, still rated low in "adjustment" and intellectual curiosity. Yes, those people with their tests might have something to say about a few boys and girls, some of them Mexican-American, but from day to day a class is a class. It is as if the teachers believed that miracles would indeed come about through divine intervention, or in any event not because of anything to do with them and their attitudes as educators, as men and women who believe in some children and view others right from the start as nearly hopeless. Maybe the dark, hesitant, awkward Chicano children sensed the surprise their teachers felt when they were told that a boy here and girl there would mysteriously, wondrously "bloom." Maybe a teacher can silently let a child know that good things are — incredibly — around the corner, because the experts say so. The teacher's faith is apparently not needed, only her loyalty to experts, the secular gods of the twentieth century. Dr. Rosenthal and Mrs. Jacobson were quite aware of the effect a pair of scientists, armed with carloads of paper, can have on a school, but what obviously surprised them as investigators was the substantial and persisting nature of that effect, obtained almost in spite of the long-standing prejudices of teachers: "One wonders whether among these minority-group children who overrepresent the slow track and the disadvantaged of Oak School their gains in intellectual competence may not be easier for teachers to bring about than to believe."

Sadly, the prejudice of teachers — and the effects those prejudices have on the learning of children — are revealed on almost every page of *Pygmalion in the Classroom*. When bright children were designated potential "bloomers," they were found more pleasant and attractive by their teachers. When slow children were designated as "bloomers," their teachers begrudgingly viewed them as "more autonomous but less affectionate." When a few children from the lowest track inexplicably improved, even though they were not called "bloomers," the teachers became thoroughly confused and angry: "The more such a child gained in IQ, the more unfavorably he was evaluated by his teacher in almost every respect." As a result the authors find it necessary to make this ironic suggestion: "If a child is to show intellectual gains, it may be better for his intellectual vitality and for his mental health as seen by his teacher if his teacher has been expecting him to gain intellectually. It appears that there may be psychological hazards to unexpected intellectual growth."

What actually happened in the Oak School? The authors of *Pygmalion in the Classroom* don't exactly know, and are frank to admit it. Before they tell about their own carefully designed and controlled project they devote sixty pages, a full third of the body of the book (there are another forty or so pages of statistical tables and references) to a more general discussion of what I suppose is best called the self-fulfilling prophecy, as it takes place not only in everyday life but in the practice of medicine and psychiatry and in the education not only of children but of animals. Banks have failed not because they were actually in trouble, but because frightened, panicky people have *believed* them to be in trouble. Throughout history particular groups of people have been considered by nature inferior and uneducable. Treated so, they have appeared so, behaved so, and confirmed in every way the beliefs of their oppressors. In medicine the so-called "placebo effect" is well known. Patients feel better, even get better, because they are persuaded that a given pill will really do its job well. No matter what the pill is made of, faith, belief, conviction do their work — even to the point of relieving severe pain, the product of utterly real and discernible disease.

Like their patients, doctors in many instances have good reason to wonder exactly what does make sick people feel better. A new drug arrives; the doctor reads rave reports about it in the medical journals; he prescribes it to his patients with assurance and optimism, a spirit his patients quickly pick up; they take the "new kind of medicine," as it may well be put to them by the physician, and feel much better. In time, though, the doctor's enthusiasm wanes. He has read about "side effects," or inadequacies and limitations. Anyway, an even newer pill has come on the market, and it surely deserves a try. Again there will be hope, followed by disappointment.

As a matter of fact there is evidence that even something as concrete and tangible as a surgical procedure draws upon all sorts of suggestive (psychological) overtones for its success. In 1961 Henry K. Beecher, professor of anesthesiology at the Harvard Medical School, described an operation to relieve the persistent and terrible pain that goes with angina pectoris, a disease caused by hardening of the heart's arteries.[6] In Dr. Beecher's words the benefits of the surgery were the result "of what happened in the minds of the patients and the surgeons involved." How could such a thing take place? Dr. Beecher reports on carefully controlled experiments which revealed that the surgeons who believed enthusiastically in the new surgical method brought relief to their patients about four times as often as the more skeptical surgeons did. Even more surprising and disquieting, it turned out that a feigned operation, a mere nick in the flesh, done under anesthesia and believed by the patient to be a complicated surgical procedure, was an equally effective way to treat angina pectoris. No one ought draw the lesson from Dr. Beecher's important research that appendectomies work because patients (and their doctors) are convinced or persuaded that they work; but we all are suggestible, even the most stubbornly rational of us, perhaps more suggestible than we care to know.

Certainly a field like psychiatry has not even begun to settle the issue of which treatment works for what reason. Entire mental hospitals have been suddenly turned into different places by the arrival of a new drug or new "technique" — and just as soon have the old despair and gloom reappeared. Psychiatric theorists argue fiercely, attack one another in dense, muddled language — often enough to conceal from themselves, let alone others, the ever-present hunch that the mind is healed not only by rational explanations, however intricate and compelling, but a whole series of experiences (in the doctor's office, outside his office) that have to do with things like faith, reassurance, suggestion, persuasion, all of which a doctor can first inspire or offer out of his heart, and later nervously dress up in elaborate language that sounds respectably scientific.

Even experimental psychologists, who run rats through mazes or pigeons through Ping-Pong games, cannot shake off the kind of self-fulfilling prophecies Dr. Rosenthal and Mrs. Jacobson are writing about. In fact, Dr. Rosenthal's earlier work, also described in his book, reveals that when experimenters are told a group of animals is brighter or more capable than another group — which in fact is not the case — the pretended distinctions become actual ones: "To summarize now what has been learned from research employing animal subjects generally, it seems that those that are expected to perform competently tend to do so while animals expected to perform incompetently tend also to perform as prophesied." Dr. Rosenthal not only found that his students taught supposedly "bright" rats to negotiate mazes faster than "slow" ones; he also found that the students declared the "bright" rats "more likable." And in a description of one of his experiments he connects animals with children in a way every teacher in America might want to think about: "At the beginning of that study experimenters assigned allegedly dull animals were of course told that they would find retarded learning on the part of their rats. They were, however, reassured that it has been found that even the dullest rats can, in time, learn the required responses. Animals alleged to be dull, then, were described as educable but slow. It was interesting in the light of this to learn that of the experimenters who had been assigned 'dull' animals, 47% believed their subjects to be uneducable. Only 5% of the experimenters assigned 'bright' rats were equally pessimistic about their animals' future. From this result one wonders about the beliefs created in schoolteachers when they are told a child is educable but slow, deserving but disadvantaged."

In the Oak School those "disadvantaged" children suddenly came to life and made astonishing gains — in IQ scores, in ability to read and solve various problems. Yet nothing was done for them: no crash programs, no special tutoring, no trips to museums. Their teachers were simply told that they bore watching, those particular children, because something would happen, because possibilities so far concealed would come to light. Rather obviously, after the teachers were "simply told" something, a quite subtle and complicated chain of events followed. Another research project is needed if we are to know how teachers go about letting children know they have a special destiny. No doubt dozens of signals are made: gestures, postures, facial expressions, a manner of approach, a choice of words and the way they are spoken, a look in the eyes, a touch of the hand. Soon the child gets the message, perhaps in the best way, unself-consciously. He begins to feel the teacher's feelings, begins to feel a bit differently about himself, about what he can do, about the whole thing — school. He gets a nod here, a longer pause there, followed by a slight beckoning smile; he begins to have hope, to study harder, to experience the pleasure of approval, and in fact, to learn more. Obviously there comes a point when the issue is not only emotional but intellectual, when a teacher's expectations become a child's sense of prideful achievement, which in turn enables *him* to expect more — of himself.

Pygmalion in the Classroom was not meant to be a popular book, though as books written by social scientists go, it possesses an exceptionally accessible narrative style. The writers make plain that they are not afraid to write a readable and lively sentence, and they almost uncannily mix blunt social comment with the most complicated and hard-to-fathom statistical equations or tabulations. Without attempting eloquence the authors have achieved a matter-of-fact eloquence that goes with an original, imaginative study tied to people and their doings with one another, to men and their shared fate. In addition, the authors constantly remind us of the ethical dimensions to scientific work. After all, they might have persuaded the teachers of the Oak School to think less of certain children, to despair more about them, to expect just about nothing from them, or to feel reassured in expecting nothing, simply because scientists had lent their imprimatur to raw prejudice. All of that the two investigators refused to do, and for the best of reasons. There is even a limit to what is permissible for the sake of that messianic secular enterprise, the "research project."

What enables some children to live, to live and learn and stay alive as students, and what in the classroom — as well as elsewhere — dampens the desire of children to pay attention and remember things and for that matter stay in school at all? Dr. Rosenthal and Mrs. Jacobson have given us many possible answers; and in a sense the purpose of this study, a study within the larger study that goes to make up this book, was to begin where *Pygmalion in the Classroom* left off — to spell out exactly what a clinical observer, trained to talk with people and listen to them and get some sense of their thoughts and feelings, could see happening between children and teachers, between teachers and principals, and in a way, between schools and the various cities of this nation. *Pygmalion in the Classroom* offers us yet another confirmation of what most of us believe anyway — but don't often enough remind ourselves: we are not born to be what we are. We become what we are. We are raised to expect a lot or to expect virtually nothing. We are given hope or taught fear. We live in a time of progress, or we live amid a century's moment of chaos. And finally, we send our children to a school system full of experiments and inquiries or to one that is set in its ways and unwilling to budge much for anyone. Dr. Rosenthal and Mrs. Jacobson point out again and again that ability and achievement in children appear and develop when recognized and encouraged by a given society, which in their experience was mediated by teachers. (Societies send out many ambassadors to children, beginning with parents, of course.) Other studies much discussed these days have emphasized the same sort of thing: the so-called Coleman Report,[7] prepared for the United States Office of Education, stressed that boys and girls probably do better in school when they are taught by first-class teachers, rather than when the building is new and fancy or the curriculum is clearly constructed and up-to-date. A recent report by the United States Commission on Civil Rights[8] claimed that the child's classmates in school are very important: if they are full of ambition and are brought up to take school seriously, they will influence others who are sitting in nearby desks and are not so sure about the value and purpose of an education.

2. Questions

What do teachers and school administrators in this school and that one, in this city or that one, think about their students' abilities and liabilities, their possibilities and faults and limitations? How do they look at poor children, ghetto children, the "deprived" or "disadvantaged"? What do they expect of those children, and what do they see their future to be? What hope is there for those boys and girls — and how much effort, care and attention do they require? Indeed, is there any hope, any real hope, or are things hopeless so long as the world is as it is, so long as the ghettos are as they are? Can anything be done, and if so, what? What will it be like five or ten or twenty years hence — for today's schoolchildren and for *their* children and for the ghettos and for the schools that ghetto children attend? What, if anything, works in the classroom with "low achievers" and "disruptive children," with the "disadvantaged" and the "deprived"? If something does work — some technique or philosophy or method or rule or plan — well, how does it work?

And the children, what do they see happening around them, to one another and to their teachers and to the world? What does the future hold? Of what use is school, and why do children go to it, except because they must? What is interesting in school? What is boring, or worse? What are the teachers like? Are they pleasant, friendly, helpful, kind, ready to lend a hand, ready to smile and speak words of encouragement? Or are the teachers rude, surly, unfriendly — or fools? That is, are the teachers no good *apart from* what they do or say, no good because they are white, or well off, or powerful? And you — who are, say, eight or ten, and in the third grade or the fifth grade — where would you like to be living, and what would you like to be doing later on? As a matter of fact, how do you feel about things right now? Are you happy with most things at home and at school? Do things bother you about school? How would you *like* things to go at school? Where would you like to be, or who would you like to be — if all wishes and dreams, however silly and make-believe, were granted? One more thing: is there any teacher you've ever had who somehow really turned you on, really made an hour or two of school seem OK, or even better than OK? And if so, how come? What was he or she like, and why aren't more teachers like him or her?

Those are some of the questions I had in mind as I went to

schools in thirteen cities, located all over the country, and talked to dozens and dozens of elementary-school children and their teachers and principals. In doing so, I have tried to give a clinical dimension to complicated social, political and educational problems. Now, that may sound both pompous and obscure, but it comes down to something like this: history sooner or later (as Tolstoi knew long before any social scientist said the same thing more intricately) has to do with particular men and women and children, whose lives become history.[9]

Today, when people enter a social-scientific discussion, it is because they have been stopped and asked to answer all sorts of questions, and the answers have been fed into a computer and emerge as one number or another. Of course, today we need every scrap of information we can get, and there ought to be room for all kinds of scholarly (and not so scholarly, but thoroughly practical) efforts. I suppose it can be said that this particular effort, in its entirety, is merely aimed at looking in a new way at what others have looked at. The difference is simply this: I have handed out no questionnaires, done no "statistical sampling," made no effort to ask "standardized questions" of "representative interviewees." I have visited schools as a physician, a psychiatrist, a child psychiatrist — who is trained to work with and study individuals and arrive at some reasonable idea of how they think and what they feel.

Perhaps at this point I had best simply describe what I did and when — the "method of research." I selected for study schools in thirteen cities, located in every section of this country: the Atlantic seaboard, the Midwest, the upper South, the far West. The cities (large, medium-sized, or small) were chosen because they have, or claim to have, schools which are making some headway, some substantial progress with — well, the boys and girls are called any number of names: "ghetto children," or "culturally disadvantaged children," or "poor achievers," and many other euphemisms. The point was not to document once again how awful it can be in school for ghetto children, or how frustrated and finally enraged many of our teachers have become. Rather, I hoped to discover what hope there is, and to compare one kind of effort against another, and thereby see which educational achievements seem to offer most promise for children, for teachers, for principals.

So, I traveled the country, and I took the schools at their word, letting their claims determine which ones I studied. If a school declared or even tentatively suggested that it was *doing* something, then I asked if I could come and see and listen and learn what I could about what can be done to make better students out of apathetic or distrustful or merely indifferent or dazed ghetto children; about what changes have to take place — academic, institutional, psychological — if children are to learn more than they have and remember more of what they learn; about how those changes, when made, actually affect children, and others, too — since teachers and administrators may also change, may also feel themselves on the one hand more useful, or perhaps on the other disappointed or even betrayed, to use a word not at all out of keeping with the depth of feeling I eventually encountered. Throughout, I hoped to learn whether something was actually happening in schools said to be places of improvement, of reform and uplift. I looked at everything in the school that might make teachers teach better and expect more of their pupils, or make children feel better about themselves, their studies, their destiny. I tried to take into account for each school its past history; its present policies; its architecture; its facilities; its curriculum; its personnel and their background, their training, their reasons for being there and not elsewhere; and most intangible but very real, its "tone" — a product, immediately, of a particular principal and set of teachers and group of children, and even the climate of opinion that characterizes a given region, a state, a city, a neighborhood, then a street, a school, a classroom, eventually emerging in a teacher who teaches in a certain way, and across the room, a child who responds to it all in a certain way.

The study's "methodological procedure" was not very elaborate.[10] I traveled to each of the thirteen cities and spent days, sometimes weeks, visiting a particular school, or more than one. Though I was primarily interested in what went on in school between *teachers* and children, I also talked to parents, mainly to

hear what children said about school, about this or that teacher. I
talked with children individually and in groups of three or four
or five. We also played games, and drew pictures and then discussed them. I asked children to draw pictures of their schools,
of their teachers, of themselves, of their best friend in class. In
each case I started off the same way: "I'm here to find out how
things are going in this school. I'm a doctor, and I'm doing a
study, and I hope you can help me learn something."

For the scientifically oriented, I think it fair to say that I have
been developing methods of interviewing children (and
teachers) for a long time — asking them to draw the school they
attend, or talk about the children they teach — and therefore
have some basis for comparative analysis, description and discussion.[11] Qualitative and quantitative studies are not antagonistic, and indeed can be nicely complementary. Sometimes we
rush prematurely to the quantitative and forget that not enough
preliminary work has been done, not enough thickets have been
cleared away. If that is the case, and it well may be so in the field
of "compensatory education for ghetto children," then this study
aims to help out a little — with concrete descriptions, and it is to
be hoped, only those analytic conclusions that can be tied to
specific observations. Needless to say, the reader also has a right
to expect not only my ideas and comments but my "data" — the
actual conversations (some tape-recorded, some noted down)
and also the drawings or paintings, with the *children's* interpretations of their own work (tape-recorded) as well as mine.

3. *Observations*

Again I must emphasize that this book contains what I saw
and heard, not what ought to be or might be or should be. My
eventual purpose was to learn whether, in fact, there was anything general to be learned from a series of particular instances.
What made those classrooms differ from one another?

The more obvious differences, which need not be established
by any further study (there are already too many of them, and
their futility, so far as educational reform goes, must haunt the

men and women who wrote them) have to do with many "factors": the school's neighborhood; its location in a given city, state, and region; the kind of children who go to the school — that is, the parents those children have, the homes they live in, the traditions and customs and values they have learned allegiance to; the principals and teachers in the school, with all their purposes, hopes and doubts; the particular building, which itself, inside and outside, may inspire, in children and grown-ups alike, a whole range of impressions and feelings. Yet, how does all that translate itself into activity, into experience, into an atmosphere, into IQ scores, reading achievement levels, school dropout rates, and other objective indices by which one school is distinguished from another?

Though I interviewed a wide range of children — black and white, from rich and middle-class and poor homes — I was chiefly interested, first, in the educational difficulties that face poor children (and their teachers), and, second, in progress made, however minute, rather than yet another examination of how bad things are. In three cities the schools were clearly in ghettos, were almost totally made up of black children, though in each instance the faculties contained both white and black teachers. In five cities a bussing program was in operation — bringing black children, and even on occasion, white children from relatively poor districts to schools set in the middle of well-to-do neighborhoods. In the remaining five cases, whether by deliberate design (districting and redistricting) or by fate (mixed neighborhoods or adjacent ones) children of both races and varied "socioeconomic levels" studied side by side.

I found among teachers three consistent sets of attitudes and expectations; and I found among children three consistent views of themselves, their position in the world, their future. Moreover, in most instances, what the teachers predicted and deemed possible for the children about what life in the long run would bring them, about what schooling meant and will mean to them, had come true. The children had already, even at, say, six or seven, acceded to their teachers' judgments about themselves, about what would happen to them, sooner or later.

4. *Ghetto Schools*

The teachers I interviewed, by and large, had come to terms with what they one after another described as the "reality" of the world outside the schools. In word and deed, in gesture and posture, in outspoken statements during our interviews or in dozens of less direct ways, those teachers revealed at best a hesitant optimism about the force of education, but most often a grim determination to fight the odds — in the touching words of one earnest, idealistic and dedicated teacher, "to stem the tide as best you can, and hope maybe a few kids will be spared." Spared what, I asked. "Spared everything that goes on around here, across the street from their classrooms. It's tough out there, and I don't see how our kids can escape, most of them, no matter what we do — and we probably work harder trying to do something, anything, than most teachers in this country."

By her own description she feels, "generally," less than hopeful about the value of her own hard work. And so do the other teachers I interviewed in similar schools located in other American ghettos. Generally, they see little hope for most of their pupils, except for a few "breakthroughs," as the teacher just quoted put it. Generally, they consider themselves hardworking, sincere and competent teachers, laboring under difficult circumstances for little enough reward. Many would like to be elsewhere, and expect someday to be elsewhere. Some love the work they do, and would go nowhere else. A few consider ghetto children more alive, more vital, more challenging, even brighter than other boys and girls. For a handful of teachers they are a "last hope for a decadent society, these kids." That same teacher, whom we shall later quote once again said: "I grew up in the middle class, and it's death. Those kids here, they're at least different. Sure, they don't want to go to college, but the best college students, they're fed up with colleges, too. I don't expect my kids to be nice, well-behaved, studious boys and girls. I try to take them as they are and help them to learn what *they* find important, what will help them make it in their world. Of course, we're not supposed to do that. But in one way or another I think *all* of us do. Some don't admit it. Some will put it to you differently, more indirectly or more politely. But it comes out the same — they're not going to walk out of this school, most of them, and go study for college. We'll be lucky if they stay within the law and get themselves a job, any job, never mind a half-decent one."

The many ghetto children I saw do not disagree with such statements. If their teachers expect them to acquire — to want to acquire, to be able to acquire — only a limited amount of conventional, academic knowledge, the boys and girls of the ghetto show (and draw and paint) their agreement. Often they see themselves as direct heirs of their parents' lives. Very often they do not expect to graduate from high school — or indeed even *get* to high school. They speak all too clearly their scorn for books and classrooms and often enough teachers, who have the crazy idea that it makes a difference, the grades and the achievements and the promotions and the diplomas. Ahead there is a "deal," or a "good time," or "a lot of trouble, I guess — that's what my mother says." Ahead they imagine a big car, maybe, a huge number of dresses or suits, maybe, and some unidentified circumstance that will enable the presence of — in fact, everything from television sets, soft, silky couches, furs and jewels to motorcycles and leather gloves and wallets and belts and scarves and snappy, sporty, cool shoes, plenty of them, and always, cash.

Yet, ahead there may be other things: the cops, jail, a tough time making it from day to day, idleness, sickness, and a quick and sad death. Despite what social scientists have recently told us, it is still hard to believe that young boys and girls can be so awfully, brutally, precisely clear about themselves, their present and their future — about the kind of lives they now live and the kind of lives they expect to live.[12] It is hard for doctors and lawyers and teachers to believe that some children see them not as kind and honorable and helpful, not as men or women to be watched, imitated, and followed, but rather as utter strangers at best, and most likely as enemies: "The teachers in this school, they're a joke. Yes, the black ones, too. They're here to collect their money. They're putting in time, man, that's all. You know what one of them told us last year? She said we were not to be blamed because we come from upset homes. 'Upset homes,' she kept on telling us about our 'upset homes' all year. I'd like to 'upset' her, boy would I. She drives here in a nice big convertible. We could get her speeding and make her car turn over and then bang, she'd die on the spot. There'd be no roof to stop her head from heading straight for the road."

That is rather strong talk, strong imagery, strong "fantasy material" — whatever. More of it will be included in the specific descriptions to follow. I can only say, as a child psychiatrist, that the young boy, nine years old and in the third grade, was not an unusual or "sick" child. He is not crazy. He is not out of his mind. He is shrewd, observant, by turns sullen or ingratiating, and capable of a good deal of charm. Whatever his tests may declare his IQ to be, he comes across, for all his faulty English, as intelligent — very intelligent indeed. His teacher made a point of asking me to talk with the boy: "He's one of many we get every year. They're as sharp as can be when they want to be, about the things that interest them, but they just don't want to learn. The first day they come to school you can tell. They just don't want to learn, and anything we try will never really make a difference. Yes, they may get a little bit of education. They may even find out how to read pretty well and write a half-decent sentence, but they won't ever be hungry for information — you know, become students, kids who want to play ball with the teacher and learn as much as they can. We can't get them to be 'good,' to accept school as a good thing, even when they've obviously got the mental raw material — when you can see it, in a boy like that one. He's only nine years old, but his mind is on other things than books; it's on the street, and what he's going to pull, the first chance he gets, as soon as he's able to."

Perhaps that boy is particularly assertive, even at times fresh and nasty. Perhaps he, more than most, is headed for trouble, and perhaps he is indeed unusual, not representative of others his age and background who attend the same school. But from child after child I heard remarks that in sum indicated an aware-

ness that one's destiny has precious little to do with one's education, one's schooling, one's achievements as a student. And, as I
shall try to show, the very ways these children of the ghetto drew
and painted their schools is of interest — especially when con-
trasted with the drawings of other children, from other neighborhoods and other schools. Try as the teachers tried in the specially
staffed and equipped schools I visited, the children somehow
failed to feel special. Instead, children and teachers alike reported uninterest, skepticism, indifference or worse: sullen annoyance or open contempt. Scores might go up a bit with
coaxing. Classrooms might quiet down with a decrease in their
size or an increase in the size of the school's staff. The children
might feel they were getting a better deal, and the teachers might
feel more hopeful about things. But, as recently as the last months
of 1970, in cities which have begun serious efforts to improve
their ghetto schools, a great number of teachers and children
remain unpersuaded that the changes make any real difference:
"In the end — I'm afraid to say it but it's what I believe — in the
end most of these children just won't make it, not if you judge by
middle-class standards. I just don't believe they will, no matter
how hard we try here. It's a slow thing. It takes more than one
generation. Maybe *their* kids will be a little better, will feel less
defensive about the schools because of what we're doing, and
maybe their grandchildren will come here without a chip on their
shoulders and feel open enough, *interested* enough is the word,
to come to grips with us, which is what a child has to do if he's
really going to learn, rather than be coaxed and forced to
memorize a few things and a few techniques, so that we can test
him and tell ourselves that we're at least doing something,
accomplishing something."

What that teacher said, children have also said: "I know it's
supposed to be the best school around — that's what the teachers
keep telling you, and my mother, too. They went and visited her
and told her she should cooperate and make sure I do the best I
can. So, she said, 'Listen, do the best you can,' and I said, 'Yes, I
always do, Ma,' and she said, 'Yes, I know!' That was all we said;
but I heard her tell my dad that they were coming around

checking on us, and the next time, she'd tell the teacher to go away and leave us alone and do her work in school, and that's enough. Later when I told my dad the school wasn't so bad, he said that was good, and I should stay clear of trouble. Well, I don't want any, no trouble. I just want to get out of here. You don't make any money in school, and everything costs money. My father, he can't find a steady job. We need the money real bad. My father says if it gets worse, he'll leave, then we can go on relief and get that much, at least."

When I told the principal what that pupil of his had said, he gave me a reply that could well summarize much of what I saw and heard in ghetto schools: "That's the story. How can you separate our school from that kind of life? Children like that bring all those experiences to school, and we try to pay a little more attention to them, push more facts at them. But when they look around, they see other kids who are going through what they're going through, and when they look out the windows they see the same old thing. No matter how nice and new our building is, the other buildings are right across the street. Maybe we can do a lot more here than we're doing, maybe we can. But we're trying as hard as we can right now, and I'm just not sure it'll all work. The kids here need real experiences inside school to balance what they go through on the outside. I mean, they've got to see and hear and feel something — call it 'hope' or anything you want — that proves it's possible to get something out of school, and like it, and then live better because of the work, because of — you know — the energy put into learning."

5. Mixed Schools

In one group of cities I visited, both teachers and students had access to those "experiences inside school" mentioned by that principal. In those cities ghetto children were going to distinctly middle-class schools, either located within a city or in a nearby suburb. Buses carried the children across the tracks, through a series of streets and neighborhoods, and into a very different country. Sometimes, whether by chance or design, a neighborhood school served very distinct and separate groups of families. Teachers in such schools, or indeed in any set of schools, obviously cannot be lumped together, made all of a piece. Yet, I did find that common circumstances and shared struggles made for certain *trends* — in thinking and getting along and acting, on the part of children as well as teachers.

So far as teachers in this second group go, I found more hopefulness, more confidence, about the future of the poor children they taught. But at the same time, many of the same teachers were plagued with doubts, worries, uncertainties, and yes, angry feelings. They had learned how to work with one sort of child; now they had to come to terms with another sort, even though the majority of their students continued to be from better-off families. Some teachers welcomed the arrival of new, "different" children — who were seen as a challenge. Other teachers were far less interested in what was happening, and indeed opposed to a "lot of this," as one of them put it. What did she mean by that? "Bringing together such totally different children, from such different backgrounds — it's impossible to do and be fair to both sides. They've been doing more and more of it, all over, and now we have to have it. To be honest, I love to teach bright, hardworking children. Here, you've always been able to assume certain things about most children: that they want to come to school, and they want to graduate from school, and they want to do as well as they can, and they share some of your own habits or values — however you'd put it. Then suddenly, they bring in others, and it's completely different with them. They just don't belong here, not until they've had much, much more orientation, not until they're more like the rest of our children — and I guess that's how I feel."

She is a very good teacher, and she tries hard with her new children. Like other teachers she feels impatient and at times very, very upset. Something called "desegregation" or "bussing" or "redistricting" has confronted her and many teachers elsewhere with a classroom they do not understand and do not quite know how to handle. Some teachers like her go to a course here, an "institute" there, a series of meetings meant to help clarify "the desegregation process" or shed light on "the disadvantaged child" or the "culturally deprived" one. Yet, as I shall try to make clear by example, the teachers in this second group of schools don't quite know what to expect — of themselves or of their new pupils. Everything in their own lives, in their own background and training and experience, prepared them for the middle-class urban and suburban children they almost exclusively, up to now, taught. Suddenly of late they have met new children, children who come to school with unfamiliar ideas and anticipations: "You don't know what to expect of them, or *from* them, either. I try to understand them. I attended one of those institutes. I read five books, all about race and poverty and prejudice. But a lot of good all those helpful hints, those suggestions they tell you, a lot of good they do when you're trying to teach different kids in the same classroom. I mean, the kids bussed in here don't trust me, even when I try to be of help. I don't think they feel very much trust at home, and I know it affects them here. But there's just so much I can do with a child to earn his trust, especially when he's not about to give it to me or anyone else, probably not his mother, either. So, you try to be good with them — good *to* them — and you hope they'll relax and loosen up and work with you and work for you, but you can't be too optimistic; that I've discovered. A lot of those boys and girls just aren't going to put much faith in us, in school, and we teachers will have to get used to that. Yes, we'll try to change things, *get* them to do better here and feel better about school. I think we've got to do that, at least *try* to, I mean. But I don't think we can be too optimistic, that's all I say; not from what I've seen so far."

In a sense it can be said that teachers like her expect trouble because they have had trouble. How circular the whole thing is cannot be precisely known. Undoubtedly each school, even each classroom, has its own special conditions. In some schools I visited little was done to recognize the special problems that would confront both the teachers and their new pupils. In other schools a lot was done, but somehow not enough to give the teachers (or the children) a strong sense of confidence that

things would work and could change in the lives of those involved in the program. Still, again and again I saw how a particular teacher's assurance and enthusiasm could mean everything to
the children: a style, a manner of approach, a subtle and hard to
describe attitude somehow was sensed and believed. Indeed, the
purpose of the particular descriptions to follow will be to make
explicit, insofar as it is possible, those subtle things — that have
to do with a look, a tone of voice, a gesture, as much as any
formal, observable "technique" or curriculum.

Nor were the teachers in this middle group of schools alone in
their mixed feelings. The children, too, were not quite sure how
they felt, what they thought, about their new schools. Nor were
they sure what to think about their teachers, their classmates,
and as one eight-year-old put it, "all this." To her "all this" was a
school to which she and a number of other children are now
being bussed. But of course "all this" is much more: "Well, it's
like you go out from what you know, and you find yourself
someplace else, and you don't know what to make of it — the
people, the kids and the teachers. One day I'll feel real good
about everything, and the next I'll think this is bad, real bad, and
we shouldn't be out here, because it's a waste of time, and it's
just the same old thing."

"The same old thing" to her is school, any school, every school.
School is where one spends time for a few years; school is miserable, stupid, boring, dumb, useless, insulting. School is a joke.
School is Whitey's way of making a person feel lousy all day
long. School is for those nervous, shouting, silly teachers, who try
to act big and strong and important, but who are scared and who
don't know a thing worth knowing. School is part of "them," is
"theirs," is "time wasted," rather like what happens in jail.

Yet, from child after child I heard other remarks, which indicated that all is not so settled and fixed in their minds. It was
interesting to see how others live and study. It was *fun* to travel
into strange, unknown territory. It could *lead* to something, the
new and better school, and the teachers who seemed so serious,
so concerned, "so worried about you," one child said. He was
picking up the teacher's anxiety, but he was also picking up her

genuine and obvious concern. She wasn't sure what to expect of the children, that teacher, but she did show what she wanted: a better life, a better education for him and others like him. And he picked up that extraordinary event — for him: a teacher's evident interest, hesitant though it was, in his welfare.

His drawings, and those of many children like him, reveal a similar blend of apparently antagonistic themes: suspicion and scorn and bitter anger and sadness and loneliness, together with humor and hopefulness and even on occasion a driving ambition to move on, move ahead, move up, get out of something — a trap, a mess, a very unpleasant or unrewarding state of affairs. Although many of us fancy ourselves social critics, and particularly critics of the schools, we are not very likely to appreciate how sensitively children examine the world around them, and how precisely they take stock of things. They can spot a tense, doubtful teacher, and indeed a tense, doubtful school or school system. As I hope to make clear, all the conviction and determination and fear and uncertainty and resentment that characterize the top of an educational hierarchy ultimately make their way down to schoolrooms and the individuals in them, young and older alike. And in pictures, often more than in words, changes, however relative and tentative, begin to appear: a little grass here, some flowers there, outside a sketch of a building, a building that looks more like a building — in other words, a building that seems solid and inviting and somewhat attractive, in contrast to one that is ugly, littered, and often enough, grotesque; skies that have sun, or that are blue rather than cloudy or rain-filled; yards where one plays rather than fights or runs in flight or takes revenge; and of course, teachers who appear on paper as at least half friendly, as reasonably human and accessible and well intentioned. Moreover, all of that can have a bearing on the child's drawing of himself, or a drawing of his that is meant to show his idea about the future: the legs and arms become sturdier and more appropriately drawn; the eyes are there, working and involved with the world; the ears are also to be seen; and even the mouth seems in working order. ("Here in this school you talk in class, because the teacher wants you to. She even *tells* us to talk to each other some of the time. It used to be I'd never once say a word until the lunch period, I mean except to whisper. It's different here.")

6. Committed Schools

Finally, I come to quite another group of schools — which may be best called thoroughly committed schools, committed to proving that poor children who come from poor neighborhoods can learn much more than they ordinarily do — and in fact learn enough to keep up with eager, bright, competent children who come from surroundings far more favorable to learning. In such schools I found most teachers determined at the very least, and often actually enthusiastic, convinced, curious. There were, of course, extremes on either side. I met teachers whose alertness had become a caricature, so that they seemed openmouthed and on tenterhooks — ready for Nirvana, which was expected tomorrow or at the very latest next week. I also met teachers who once had been buoyant, cheerful and within sight of the promised land, but, alas, their hopes had been dashed, and now they could only say something similar to what this one did: "I do everything I can, but I'm not sure it's possible — to bring up a disadvantaged child, in a few years of school, to the level of most other children. I think you can improve their reading and do a lot else for them. But you can't do the whole job. I don't blame the children, and I'm sure no school in America is doing more than we are. But there are limits, that's all. If a child comes from a certain kind of home, where he hasn't learned much and learning is not valued, at least the kind of learning we call learning — well, then, it's hard for that child to keep up with our comfortable suburban children. We can narrow the gap, but I believe it will take more time to close it."

Yet, most of her colleagues are neither whistling in the dark nor quite so guarded or hesitant or doubtful or discouraged. Their principal, their school board or board of education have persuaded them not only that they have a job to do, but that it can be done, it has to be done, and every possible bit of help —

financial, educational, psychological — will be forthcoming to make sure it is done. Put differently, these schools have teachers who expect a lot from their children, all of them, and believe that what others say is impossible, or hard to achieve, or only distantly possible, can actually be accomplished now, each year, each day in fact — step by step. In this regard, it is interesting to compare the second and third groups, as I have just described them. Among the former one hears the past and the future evoked; among the latter it is the present that matters. Among the former, mention is made of serious injustices and handicaps, of an inheritance that will only be overcome through years and years of effort. Among the latter it is all now: "We've got these kids here, and we're going to do something. We're going to show them and ourselves that they're able to learn as well as anyone else. A lot of them are shrewd and clever, and they need some help in becoming smart — in school, I mean. That can't be impossible, and I don't believe it takes 'years and years,' as you hear some people put it."

She and others have a different sense of time, so far as the education of poor children goes, but there are other differences, too. In mood, in choice of words, in imagery, in behavior with the children, the two sets of teachers are quite distinct, quite different. One group feels glad to be taking part in an important, contemporary social struggle. One group tends to use passive verbs, or weak constructions. The other uses active verbs, an intentional and deliberate manner of speech. And the children are approached differently: they are soothed or reassured or quietly overlooked or treated as special and nice but full of difficulties and "problems," or they are encouraged, prompted, sought out, even confronted. In the words of a fourth-grade teacher: "You may think I'm a little cruel, but I really bear down on them. I don't coddle them, or feel sorry for them, or tell them how I understand, I understand, I understand. That's the way all us liberals were brought up to feel, and if you ask me it's wrong. It's unfair to the kids. It's condescending. It's a way of justifying our own pessimism — coating it with sugar, you might say. I

don't think about it when I'm doing it, but if you asked me to put
it in words, I'd say that I go after those children and let them
know that I believe in them, and I'm not going to take no for an
answer. They have something inside of them, a lot, and I'm going
to bring it out — here, in this school, right now. And if we have
to fight a little, while I coax and goad it out of them, then it'll
come to that, too. One thing I won't do, though: sit back and feel
sorry for them. I hate people doing that to me, and I'll bet they
can spot it a mile away when we do it, the teachers."

It so happens that she is right, that the children can do just
that. They can sense who really wants to help and who only says
he or she wants to help. Put differently, they can distinguish
between pieties and action, between sympathy and a determined
businesslike effort to forge a working arrangement: "There's one
teacher who says she knows how bad we've had it, and there's
another who won't let you get away with anything. She's after
you all day long to get your things done and keep up. So, I try to;
I do." He is one of many children whose words and drawings
show not only hope but in a way certainty: "Well, I figure we'll
all make it, everyone from this school will. The teachers tell you
that now that you're here you've got to work, but there's a lot
going for you, and no one gets let down. No sir. So, I think it'll be
real good later on. I might even get to college. That's what I
think. I might."

From children like him one hears about high school and
college, about jobs and achievements and specific, concrete plans.
In manner such children are less casual than children in the other
two kinds of schools, less outspoken, less bold, less willing to
resort to the put-on at the slightest provocation. They tend to be
more serious, rather silently assured, and a bit proud. They are
less ingratiating and sly with an outsider bent on "interviews,"
but that is because they seem more involved with their work,
their classroom, their school. They are not glad to be excused to
talk with the doctor, to joke with him, to get away from "that
room." Rather, they want to know how long they are to stay
out — and when they will be able to return. They are happiest
talking about what they did, are doing, or will be doing in

school — and not what they plan to do "this afternoon" or "next vacation" or when they are "head" of this or that: a gang, the Army, the Air Force, a baseball club, or the United States. They are occupied, busy, trying; not idle, inert, patronized and preoccupied with wild and extravagant flights of fantasy, preoccupied with rich, subtle ironies and asides and ambiguities, but also with fears and doubts and hates. In sum, these children attending our third group of schools work (and are asked to work) more thoroughly than those in the first and second. In turn, they seem fitter, more likely to stay in school, more in control of themselves and their future. They speak of themselves more seriously and consistently and modestly, and they draw themselves or their school or their teachers and parents more coherently. They look ahead less nervously or outrageously; but most of all, in school they seem very much taken with and absorbed in the present — of learning and getting along with others near at hand, their classmates and their teachers.[13]

7.   The Cities

We now come to the thirteen cities, divided into the three groups (A, B, and C) noted above. (The names of the cities are somewhat disguised — and I had to agree I would do so in order to be granted admission to several of the school systems about to be described.) We will be moving from more hope to relatively less of it, and from somewhat manageable problems to problems that sometimes seem altogether unyielding. Yet each city, each school, has plenty of children who against great odds are nevertheless winning out, and children who in spite of all that is being done for them are getting nowhere.

GROUP A
Green River

Fifty-five thousand people live in this eastern city, a suburb of one of the nation's largest cities. About a quarter of the population is black. The schools serve eighty-seven hundred pupils,

*seventeen percent of whom are black. School officials have been
alert to the problems of racial imbalance longer than most of
their counterparts in similar communities, and they have moved
to correct the imbalance without prodding from civil rights
groups. The city has one high school, and in the mid-fifties, when
overcrowding seemed to compel those officials to build a second
one, they hesitated, fearing the presence of two high schools would
easily lead to segregation. They finally built one new school large
enough to house all high school students and turned the old
building into a junior high school. In 1957 they closed an elementary school because the student body had a disproportionate
number of blacks and built a new school on a site that would
insure racial balance. Finally, in 1964 they had to close another
elementary school for similar reasons. School officials wanted
more certain guarantees against segregation, so they decided to
build another school in a better location and also to set racial
quotas for all schools in the district and to bus children, if
necessary, to meet these quotas. Each school was required to be
no less than ten percent and no more than thirty percent black.
Some district lines were redrawn, but three hundred students
still had to be bussed to accommodate the quotas. Bussing has
continued at about this level since 1964.*

In Green River I met first with the town's superintendent of
schools, and indeed with his entire staff. Right off I learned of
their interest and concern, of their willingness in fact to look
at themselves, change things around, experiment — in the words of
the superintendent, "do anything, anything we humanly can to
reach these children and let them know that if they are confused,
then so are we." His remarks seemed not only self-effacing but
self-critical, and he seemed anxious to do more than pay lip
service to a series of fashionable educational clichés about "disadvantaged" children. For several hours I heard an American
school system unselfconsciously analyzed by its own administrators. "It's hard for some of our teachers to understand the
deprived child," said Green River's superintendent of schools.
"They've never taught them before, and it takes time for people

from different cultures to communicate." One can, of course, be suspicious of that kind of talk. All the right words, the current words, are there: "deprived," "cultures," "communicate." And the sense of perspective can be questioned, too. *How* long a period of time does it take — several generations? "I hope very soon," said the superintendent. How soon? "Oh, if we really work at it, if we convey urgency right down the line, from me to every single child — then in time for the children now in school to get an education worthy of the word."

Well, how does *that* happen? He wasn't so sure, nor were his deputies and assistants; but they did know what they wanted, and they did make the effort to convey their ideas to others: "We try to have more than a chain of command here. We try to have a chain of shared purposes, of things we all wish and can talk about and do talk about. I know that talking won't solve these problems, but the individual teacher, out there on the firing line, has got to know that he or she isn't alone, that we all want the same thing, and we all know it's not so easy to get what we want, not when some of our children have no reason at all to believe in us, in white people and the white schools and the white world. *We* may know that their suspicions are unfounded, but no one person will persuade *them;* they'll need one experience after another — and only all of us, pulling together, can provide that atmosphere."

He kept on talking about an "atmosphere," which is not so easy to measure. In an elementary school located in a pleasant suburban neighborhood, I asked the principal how things were going. Several dozen children were bussed every day to the school from what amounts to the town's black section, about a ten minutes' ride. Of course everything was going well, he said, though in time a few problems were indeed mentioned. The black children were at times uncertain, aloof, suspicious. They tended to stick together, to resist the friendly overtures of earnest, well-intentioned teachers and children. A number of them for a long while had been "difficult" in class: they were noisy, or sullen and too quiet; they were indifferent to their work or only sporadically and unpredictably enthusiastic about it; in many instances their parents never appeared in school, unless they were telephoned, even visited at home, and asked to visit or attend a meeting; they used words hard to understand, or spoke in accents difficult to comprehend; often they seemed not so much anxious and frightened — that, too — but bored or sullen or even, to use one teacher's description, "vastly amused."

"I tried for a long time to think of those children as — well, as just like any others," said that teacher. "I kept on saying to myself that we're all equal, until I realized one day that we're not, that some children come here all ready to go, to trust me and follow me, to listen to me and learn from me. For other children it's very hard, and it's hard, too, for us, the teachers. They're put off by our skin color, our background, our assumptions, by everything about us. When I finally allowed myself to look at them — well, I learned how closely they were looking at *me*. I'd catch them staring at something I was wearing, or I'd catch them straightening up and even bristling at some remark I'd make. I don't mean that I said something directly aimed at them; I mean that somehow, in some way, they became offended by my attitude, my assumptions, the tone in my voice — it's hard to be precise, and yet they sense things and react to them *very precisely*. Often they seem amused, vastly amused, as I said. It's as if they don't take everything as seriously as the rest of us do — the work and the grades given and the promotions, the whole ladder, I guess you can say. Some of them do, but even the very serious and good students only half believe us, and often I feel they are waiting to find the *real* truth — I guess the kind that will show 'us' all to be hypocrites and worse.

"One day I asked one of them, one of my best — she is very bright, but does not work as efficiently and enthusiastically as I think she would if she were from a white, middle-class family — what she expected to find here when she came, and what she hoped to get out of school. I was surprised to hear her reply: 'nothing much.' That's all she could say. Mind you, she wasn't being particularly cynical or unfriendly. I could tell by her manner that she was simply her usual, friendly, guarded self. She was telling me the truth, that she didn't expect much, when all was said and done — 'just more of the same, fixed up in nicer dishes.' Do you know who said *that* to me? Her mother did. When I finally got to meet the mother I frankly told her of my worries and doubts, and I appealed to her for help. She didn't say a word, didn't give me the slightest encouragement, until I asked her what her child *hoped* to find here — and then she said that, those words. I don't think such mothers and such children can take many things for granted, the way we can, and I don't think teachers like me realize how they feel, what they believe possible for themselves.

"Some black children I've taught here these past two years have surprised me by what they've said or done — and then I've realized that I never expected them to be that bright, or that shrewd, or that imaginative or responsive. Now, perhaps they *saw* the surprise on my face, or *felt* my surprise. What do you think that would do to them, to their 'attitude,' as I hear it said? I think we have to learn a lot more about these children, about their assets as well as their liabilities. I think we teachers need help in that; we need to be encouraged to give these children the benefit of a few doubts, to bend as much as we ask them to bend, to learn from them about ourselves, our values and even our prejudices. I'll have to admit one thing: I've learned as much as I've taught the last two years. I've been frustrated and annoyed, but I've also learned."

She and others like her have been encouraged to do that, to learn. The atmosphere in her school, in the system of which her school is a part, has in a sense sanctioned her learning, through meetings and conferences and lectures and discussions. She also learns from a hard to describe but very real atmosphere that can be found at all "levels" of the school and in the larger administrative setup in the superintendent's office — all of which children can sense. I asked children about the teacher just quoted, and indeed about other teachers. Briefly and not so briefly they answered me and drew pictures for me. Yes, teachers are different. Yes, some of them inspire trust, some of them don't; some of them try to be nice, and some *are* nice. How can one tell the difference?

"Well, she gives you a look, and you know she's on your side, and she wants to help you. Some, they may be polite and nice and all that, but you can tell, you can tell."

But how can one tell, the observer insists.

"I don't know. It's just something you decide. I'll ask my friends, and they all agree with me, most of them do. One teacher, (Figure 4), she'll give you the idea that she's with you all the way, and you're glad you're in her room, and even if you do have some trouble, she'll be there to help you, and like they'll say, they're here to learn, too. But the other kind (Figure 5), they make you want to look at the clock and count the minutes until the end of the day. They've decided you're a zero, and maybe a one or two, but no more. The good teacher, she thinks you're one hundred or a thousand — as big as anyone, if you can just catch on and keep going."

What does a "good" teacher look like, and a "bad" one? Do they come at you differently? Can you see anything in one teacher or another one, in the way this one or the other one teaches, that makes it better to be here and not there, with Miss X rather than Miss Y? What do you see yourself doing in ten years, and will this school, its teachers, affect that — your future?

"Well, I think if all my teachers were good, I'd be better. But my mother, she says we have it real hard, no matter how good the teachers are, and I'd better not forget that. But I think most of the teachers here, they're trying hard, real hard. My mother, she says she's convinced; so I am too. The other school, they were tired, the teachers. They told us so. They said we came ready to give up, and so they would give up, like us. Here, there's some like them; but not Mrs. A, and not in Miss B's room. There, they're all excited, and they carry you along, yes sir. The other day the teacher said we all could be up there, a mayor or something like that, and I thought she was kidding. Now she keeps after me. She cuts out things from the papers and shows them to me. She wants me to believe her, I guess. No, I don't a lot of the time, but she could be right, maybe. I don't know. I'd rather be here, though — in this school. They seem to want something for you — that's how I see it."

East Park

Two separate municipalities combine to form this small north-eastern community of twenty-four thousand. Before 1966 each ran its own elementary and junior high schools, although one high school served them both. The smaller of the two towns integrated early and easily: in 1948 all kindergarten through fifth grade pupils were assigned to one elementary school and all sixth through eighth grade pupils were assigned to one "middle" school. The larger town could not find so simple a solution. Since it had only one middle school, integration was guaranteed on that level; but the four elementary schools served neighborhoods of varying racial makeup, and the townspeople were reluctant to bus children to relieve racial imbalance. In 1966 the two munici- palities decided to put all students under the control of a single, elected board. The board immediately faced the touchy problem of bussing children, and despite opposition, favored bussing. Today fifty-one hundred students attend the town's schools; nine percent are black. There are four elementary schools, one middle school, and one high school. Elementary pupils are bussed daily to assure balanced enrollments.

Sometimes true wisdom takes the form of doubt, confusion, uncertainty. Eastern Park's superintendent of schools is a young, vigorous, exceptionally well-educated man who has the intelli- gence to speak clearly and directly, without resort to the jargon that all too many schools of education have borrowed from the social sciences and pressed upon thousands of students. I did not have to ask many questions before he was able — pointedly and exactly — to state the purposes of this study: "You want to know what our teachers *want* for our children, what they have in mind as possible and probable when they enter the classroom and look at those children, mostly white and well-to-do, but some black and far from well-to-do. We've been wondering that, too. We've been wondering whether something doesn't happen almost right off between the teacher and the children. It's hard to put what I mean in words. I guess you have to talk about an 'atmosphere' or a 'climate,' or, if you're an experimental psychologist, perhaps you could say that 'cues' are given back and forth. The teacher comes in and says something or does something, or doesn't say something or doesn't do something — and pretty soon the children have her sized up: what she likes and dislikes; what she thinks about all sorts of things; what she thinks her job is like; how she expects them to behave and learn and get along together in the classroom. And the teacher — she's doing her own sizing up: this kid over here said something 'bright,' and that one over there looks 'dumb' or 'stupid,' and it'll be a long, hard struggle with some of 'those' over there, and this group right here, near the window, they all seem eager and smart and ready to learn. In a month, maybe a week, and I sometimes think in a day or two, the children and their teachers have it all decided about each other — who's who and what's what and how the whole year will go. It's all frightening, and we don't like to think about what it all means."

Yet, in fact, he *was* thinking about what "it all means." In his town black and white children have gone to school with one another for years, but the academic and social problems persist, and he had no desire to let the school system he headed relax and enjoy a certain national distinction that had come its way. In his words: "We moved the bodies together years ago, and we thought that would solve our problems; then we started worrying about the curriculum, and we thought some changes in that would solve the problem. Now we realize that we have to go way back to the most fundamental thing in all education: the teacher. If he or she can't teach certain children, then no matter what else we have here in this town — well, it's just not enough."

He and his deputies regularly meet with the school principals, and they meet with their teachers. They all talk about life in the South, life in the ghetto, life in East Park — for themselves and for poor children, almost all in this case black. They feel it important that they understand various social, political and historical matters before they ask their schoolchildren to do so. In one meeting I heard a principal talk about an "undertow" that exists in every school — one that is "either positive or negative." Later, I visited his school and spent several days there talking to him and his teachers and a number of children. What did he mean by "positive or negative undertow"? What did he think could and could not be done by the schools, in contrast, that is, to the home, the business world or the voting booth? How did his teachers see things going with the slow learners, the "difficult black children," to use an expression I had heard him use — sardonically.

"Well, that's the problem. As I said at the meeting, when a teacher talks about 'difficult children' she's in trouble and so am I as the principal — because she's lumping together a lot of girls and boys; I know she is. In a way, you know, a lot of our teachers, in a progressive school system like this, have learned too much sociology and psychology, or maybe learned to use what they've learned in a very self-defeating way. They read and read and take extra courses on Negro History or whatever, and then they take all the phrases they've picked up and do the same thing with them that supposedly ignorant people do with blunter words — discount, discredit, and even slyly insult black people. It's not easy to say something like that, but I see it happening, I hear it happening, all the time. I have some teachers in this school who obviously like clean, quiet, well-dressed and obedient children who do just as they're told. They don't even like the more active and 'wild' — their word — white child, no matter how intelligent he is, and no matter how 'important' his father is. They are a little aloof and self-contained themselves, the teachers, and they don't take to children who are 'fresh' or 'undisciplined' or 'unpredictable.' If that kind of boy or girl is white, and if they *do* manage to make some kind of peace with him or her, they'll call the child 'zany' or 'zestful' — but in need of 'control.' If the child is black, and they're honest with themselves, they'll say they don't like him; if not, they're liable to fall back on a lot of lingo — he's 'immature,' and he comes from a 'culture of poverty,' and he's 'disruptive,' and he's one more 'difficult black child.' That's why we have to meet a lot, all of us, and I have to say — what I've just now said to you."

One of his teachers seems not to hear his message. She refuses to attend many of his meetings and is frank to say that she "looks for excuses." Yet she has an astonishing record of success with those "difficult black children" — something her principal and vice-principal both know. In the words of the vice-principal: "If all our teachers were like her, we wouldn't have to have those meetings. She's considered an oddball, and she is — but for other reasons than those who call her that realize. They think she's brusque and outspoken — and, of course, she's from the South. Actually she's odd because she really makes those kids work, and sometimes she makes them do more — come out of themselves is the way I'd put it."

So, she skips the meetings, but in class somehow gets "slow" children to speed up. I watched and watched her (and them). I asked her how she did it, realizing all the while that she was not disposed to put the whole business into a few phrases. But she did: "I'm a kind of intense person, emotional you might say. A lot of these kids, they come from families like that — where the mothers shout and scream and cry; you know, let out their feelings. I don't do that, but I let the kids know how I'm feeling. I lean on them, you might say — and I let them lean on me. I don't ever want them to think they can't come up and hold to me, or have me hold to them. And I *look* at them — eyeball to eyeball. I tell them what I want and tell them that they're going to do it, and no nonsense, no messing around. I've lived with colored people all my life, you know. In the South they're no strangers to us. We may not have treated them as our equals, but we lived with them, right beside them and sometimes closer than that. Up here, they don't know the Negro. They don't know where he comes from and how he *is* — in his mind, I guess you'd say it. They don't know how they talk and think and — everything.

"You know what I do. I say, 'Hey, there,' and I say, 'Come on now, y'all go and get that done, and I mean now, or I'll paddle the life out of you.' I'd be ashamed to have some of our teachers hear that — they might call me mixed-up, some of them might. They do, I know. But I'm trying to make these kids feel at home so they can get with it! I talk about the South — many of them have relatives there. I talk about music, *their* music. I show them

I'm not afraid of what *they* know, what *they* can do well: music and art and athletics. I show them I know about their history, their speech, their everything, I hope — and they catch on. Oh, it's not even all that deliberate. It sounds it, now that I'm talking, but the truth is that I feel close to a lot of those children, and I guess they pick that up. Then, they also pick up that I want them to move on, get ahead in the world. I tell them that. I say it right out loud. I say are you going to mess around and amount to nothing, or are you going to take notice and get your work done and *be* somebody?

"They want to be somebody, too. They want to read. They're hungrier for education than most teachers realize. We should change our teachers, that's what I sometimes think. We should recruit different kinds of *people* to be teachers. It's what you feel that counts, not only what you've learned in education school — I never went to one, thank God. I might have been ruined for life. I'd be afraid of my shadow — and afraid of theirs, I'll tell you. I'd be afraid to speak up, to give it back to them when they're messing things up, to let them know I'm alive and they're alive and we're going to make something out of it. I'm so tired of all this introspection, this analysis, analysis. You get to the point you watch yourself breathing in the classroom — and of course you get nowhere. The kids can spot that — spot that nervousness, the self-consciousness that takes over. It's terrible, I think. I like to teach. I like these children. I want them to learn, and they get the message. I believe it's as simple as that. Yes sir, I do."

Whether things are as "simple" as she would have them or not, she does indeed reach her children. They study hard, and by everyone's acknowledgment (even those she annoys and antagonizes) she "gets results." Her children speak of her with pleasure and warmth and a proper bit of awe: "She makes you work. She wants you to work, and she'll not stop until she wins you over to her way. She's real friendly, though, at the same time."

To one of her black children she is "the best kind of person, because she won't settle for less than everything. That's what she says, and she makes you believe it yourself. One day she asked me what I wanted to be, and I said I didn't know. Then she said,

'What do you mean, you don't know?' Then I said I was sorry, and I did know: I wanted to be a — a teacher. Then she leaned down, and she looked right at me and said, 'I know you're saying that because you haven't really thought of what you're going to be, and you should.' And then she said I had a good kind of mind to be a lawyer — because I was always figuring out the puzzles and asking questions and things like that. So maybe I will be one."

I asked him to paint a picture of her (Figure 6), and to paint one of any other teacher he knew (Figure 7) — and, if he wanted, to tell me how they were alike or different. He would indeed make a good lawyer. He talked as he painted, and he outlined his case rather insistently — in paints and words. I noticed during my stay in that school that his ideas and feelings — about that teacher and about other teachers — were shared by many children.

Central Park

Over a century ago blacks came to this midwestern town as they headed north toward freedom on the legendary Underground Railway. The townspeople shared a strong commitment against slavery and were generous hosts to runaways, who thus stopped often at this depot and stayed on. Since then the town has grown to a city of eighty-three thousand, an eighth of whom are blacks, and it has prospered. The mean annual income is $11,400, sixty-four percent above the national average, and the chamber of commerce proudly bills the city as "the national and international headquarters of many companies and organizations."

The city annually elects two members to the seven-man school board, and every third year elects an additional member; each member serves three years. The board appoints the superintendent. Together they oversee the city's seventeen elementary schools and four junior high schools. The city's single high school is run by its own group of administrators and belongs to a district officially independent of the elementary and junior high school district, though geographically coterminous with it.

In 1961 the board began to take note of segregation in the elementary schools. A quarter of the eleven thousand pupils are blacks. At that time eleven elementary schools had, with rare exceptions, only white pupils; one school had only black pupils, and at another, two-thirds of the pupils were black. The other four schools were relatively integrated. By 1963 the board adopted a "free transfer program," allowing students to attend any school in the district, though problems of transportation, special registration, and ordinary loneliness discouraged parents from sending their children to different schools. The next year the board resolved to end de facto segregation of the schools. That sort of resolution generally gets bogged down and often forgotten in the years of "study" and "research" that can precede "well-considered action"; but the board didn't waste much time. By the fall of 1967 its members had gone through the entire routine of study and planning and community meetings and polite explanations, and they were ready to desegregate the schools completely.

In accordance with the proportions of the total school population (white to black, three to one), the board required each school's student body to be one-quarter black, three-quarters white. These requirements were applied even to individual classrooms; average classrooms have twenty-seven students, so six or seven should be black. District boundaries were altered to minimize bussing. The formerly all-black school was turned into an experimental school and closely affiliated with the local university, thus becoming more attractive to white parents, despite its location. Indeed, the school is open, by application, to pupils living anywhere in the city, though racial balance is insisted upon. One embarrassing irony during the first year of desegregation was the unexpected problem of segregated lunch periods. Since white pupils often live near their schools, they could walk home for lunch; black pupils, who were bussed to school, found themselves dining in the city's "Jim Crow" lunchrooms! But the program, on the whole, has worked extremely well and could serve as a model for other communities. Still, one must concur

with the superintendent's modest admission: "Even the combina-
tion of desegregation and compensatory education is not enough
to achieve the goal of individual fulfillment for all children."
What is?

"We are not doing enough, because we still have children who
just don't take to school. Some of them are obviously bright, but
don't trust us; others could be doing much better, but don't seem
to care." It was a surprise to hear that during a visit to one of the
best, most progressive and successfully integrated school systems
in the nation. The speaker was the superintendent of that system.
I soon realized that his very frank and honest manner, his unself-
conscious humility, helped make Central Park's schools as impressive as they are. He had no intention of letting the city become smug, self-contented and self-righteous. He had no desire,
in his words, "to sweep our very real problems under a rug that
appears nice and has all the good liberal patterns in it."

His leadership emphasizes the things that still have to be done,
and the principal and vice-principal in the elementary school I
visited took the same tack with me. As I went from classroom to
classroom with the vice-principal, he made sure I knew the
trouble he faced every day, as well as the obvious achievements
the school could lay claim to: "I'd like you to meet some of our
more troublesome teachers. We have them. Every school does, in
my experience. It would be easy to show you the best teachers
we have, the ones who somehow get across to the black kids
we've had come here through redistricting, but there are others
who are good teachers, very good ones, but not for those kids.
They've been used to bright, ambitious upper-middle-class children, and they can't take any other kind, though it's hard for
them to admit it or talk about it. We try to approach the subject
indirectly — gently but firmly. We've tried every way, too —
workshops and meetings and lectures and discussion groups and
conferences, you name it. We've bought 'audiovisual' equipment
and kits and 'packaged materials' — the works. Sometimes I'm
optimistic, and sometimes not. A teacher will tell us that at last
she's beginning to see something, that it's not *whether* poor black

children learn, but *what* they learn — the lessons of the street or the lessons we offer them here in school. Then she'll go on. She'll say what she's heard in a lecture or something — that kids bring their neighborhoods right into the building, that all the values and ideas and assumptions of the ghetto are brought right across the railroad tracks to this new, beautiful building in the middle of this nice suburban neighborhood. It all sounds great until you find out that the same teacher is actually scared of those black kids, and really, scared of us liberals, too. So, she doesn't discipline the black boys and girls. She lets them get away with everything, and then complains that she's trying desperately to 'understand' them, rather than punish them — though they *are* destroying her classroom."

I spent several days with a teacher like that and found her a fascinating mixture. She is an earnest, intelligent, attractive woman in her early forties, the mother of three children. She speaks excellent English and has real and obvious warmth, which many of her schoolchildren sense immediately: "I know you well enough now to tell you that it's not always like this. With you here, they were better behaved. We've had a lot of trouble here since they sent us the Negro children. We have to admit it and see what we can do. They're behind our children — everyone knows that — and to tell the truth, I believe they're not the natural students that our children have always been. You've got to start there — by admitting the obvious and seeing what you can do to change things. I think a lot of them have an innate shrewdness, but they can't apply it to books, to learning in a classroom. That's the problem. They can't go from the concrete to the abstract. They can't generalize, the way the other kids do. And they're very, very touchy. I've certainly learned that. They take offense for almost anything, half the time I don't know for what — a word here, an expression on someone's face, anything. I've tried to ignore that and keep them busy. I don't want them to think that I'm against them, or punitive. I've walked out of the room *myself* several times, rather than explode at them.

"But it wears on you, I'll admit. There are times I wish we were back in the old days. Every year we'd have a real good class, and there'd be none of this watching every step you take, everything you say, and all the meetings we have, one after another, and the same old things — race — to discuss. Maybe we brought them here too soon, without better preparation. Not that I believe they'll ever get anywhere until they get a better education, and they certainly weren't getting that over there in their own schools. I know *that* now. So, I'm in favor of doing everything we can to help them, and yes, they should be brought here. But I just wish sometimes we could teach them more easily, so that all of us could have a better time in school — the teachers, the children from this neighborhood, and the Negro boys and girls.

"I'm for equality, but I'm for common sense, too. You cannot overcome three centuries of poverty and persecution in one generation. Sometimes I think we should have an 'intermediate phase' — in which perhaps the ghetto children would have intensive education in special schools. Then they'd be ready for a school like this — I guess *their* children would be — and then it would probably work out much better than it does now."

How *is* it working out now, so far as the children she teaches see things? One white child, a nearby doctor's son, a very bright student and in fact one of her obvious favorites, had a few words of appraisal: "It goes OK a lot of the time, though some of them, the Negro kids, they speak out sometimes. They'll say they don't want to do an assignment, because it's dumb, or like that. One of them said there weren't enough black faces in the book, just one on each page and that was a big joke. They'll say bad things about the teacher, and they say it so loud you can hear it, and you know she can. She's a real nice lady, the best teacher I've had so far. She works hard all the time, and you know she's got your best interests in her mind. She must spend every night preparing for the next day. My dad says I'm lucky to have a teacher like that, and that I'll remember her later on, because she'll really prepare me for high school. I don't think the others — the Negro kids — they trust her so much, as much as I do. I can tell. She'll be trying to win them over with something she says, and instead they take it the exact opposite, the wrong way, and they start talking and making noise, and she gets angry — you can always tell, she flushes, and her face gets redder and redder — and then she tries to change the subject. My dad says she's under stress, and it causes her blood pressure to go up, and that's why her face looks like that. But I like her a lot. I've never had a better teacher. I think some of the Negro kids will learn to appreciate her after a while. I hope they will."

That is how he sees his teacher — and himself. One day I asked him to draw a picture of her; the next day I asked him to picture himself twenty years from now, and then, if he could and would, draw the result. He could and would (Figure 8).

As for those "Negro kids," they found the same teacher "dumb" and in one case "a mean one." Why was she mean? "Well, she doesn't really care about us, only the others." I was talking with five black children — three boys and two girls — in a group, and there was some disagreement and spirited talk: "No, she's not mean, and she's not against us. She's just dumb. Half the time she'll go and say something that sounds real bad, but she doesn't know it. That's what my dad said when I told him. He said you have to keep quiet, because she probably doesn't know what it's all about. The way I see it, you can't come here and expect them to know how we feel. I don't expect that. My mother said I should just watch myself, don't let my guard down, do what they ask in the tests they give, and it will be fine. She lets you make noise, though — so she's not so bad, just a little slow on the draw. She looks scared to me. That's how I see her. She's trying to be nice and good, but she's afraid she's going to fall down flat on her face any second now. The way it looks, we could be teaching her almost as much as the other way around. She admitted it the other day. She said we knew all about Africa, and we should tell the class about it; but I don't know what she means. Africa is someplace else, that's what I said, and the whole class laughed and she turned red like a beet."

As I listened to more and more such talk — the scorn and anger and sarcasm masking fear and anxiety — I could only remember the teacher's message: black children (so she believes) don't easily go from the concrete to the abstract. One

thing was certain: these black children were finding it hard —
even dangerous or futile — to go from their concrete neighborhood to another one. Perhaps the abstractions they seem to shun
stand in their minds for a whole, distant world — both envied and
ridiculed and held in contempt. One thing I did learn from their
drawings: they certainly made some kind of generalizations or
abstractions about both their teachers and themselves, even as
their white classmates did (Figure 9).

West Park

*This west-coast city has perhaps led the nation in an effort to
desegregate its public schools. In the fall of 1968 it became the
first city of more than one hundred thousand residents to achieve
total desegregation. Some northern cities have closed ghetto
schools and bussed black children to schools in other parts of the
city or to those in the suburbs, but only this city has combined
that sort of bussing with the bussing of white children to former
ghetto schools. School officials had to fight hard to do so; board
members had to face a special "recall" election when they introduced their initial plan; but they did, and won.*

*The city has a population of about one hundred twenty
thousand: seventy percent white, twenty-five percent black, and
five percent Oriental. Many retired people have made it their
home, and since they usually have no children of school age, the
school population, sixteen thousand, is small for a community of
its size. Among the students, fifty percent are white, forty-one
percent are black, and nine percent are Oriental. Local chapters
of national black organizations — CORE, NAACP and others —
are numerous, articulate, and active. They started desegregation
as early as 1958, though not until 1964 did anything tangible
result. That year school board members decided to desegregate
the city's three junior high schools. They changed one to a ninth
grade school, essentially an annex to the nearby high school, and
they had seventh and eighth graders use the other two. In 1968
they were ready to desegregate the fourteen elementary schools.
This has required bussing thirty-five hundred of eighty-nine*

hundred pupils daily and takes a considerable slice from the budget, but local citizens have complied with little fuss. Besides, the federal government pays almost half the fare. So, today the entire system is desegregated, down to individual classrooms.

Unquestionably the city of West Park wants to do more than most cities even dream to be either possible or desirable: "We want to do *everything* — everything that has to be done so that black children and white children can go to school together, learn, and learn from one another. That's our purpose, and we spend long hours trying to achieve it." He is a forceful superintendent, no stranger to social struggle. He is surrounded by equally stubborn and bold deputy superintendents and associates of various kinds. He wants, in his words, "more than the appearance of change." He wants "real change," which he defines as "a mixture of academic improvement and psychological transformation." What sort of psychological transformation? "Well, a child's sense that others who are different matter very much, and a child's sense about himself — that he can do a lot, a lot more than he once may have thought possible." Then comes the elaboration: "I'm talking about white children as well as black ones. A lot of black children don't think they can live easy with books, and a lot of white children are afraid of something else — any world except the one they know and own. I'm not sure which fear is worse, but I believe we can help *all* our schoolchildren feel less afraid and more sure of themselves and the world — and of us, as a matter of fact, the teachers and principals and officials in the school system."

So it is intended in West Park's schools, at least at the top. What happens to such intentions as they work their way down the ladder — as commands struggle for obedience, as programs encounter daily events, as outlines seek to become action? The principal of an elementary school gave me some answers to that kind of question. He told me that he was in charge of a "completely and carefully integrated school," and that "every day we see things happen here, important and worthwhile things. We've tried to do away with 'tracks' and 'grouping,' at least the kind that separate children by race or class or even achievement. We try to mix children and teach them not only how to read and write, but live with one another — the rich with the poor, the quick with the slow, the confident with the fearful. I don't mean to sound pious, though. It's not just a matter of being 'good' or 'democratic.' We've seen how children learn from one another and become better students as well as better citizens. And it doesn't only go one way. I mean, I've seen bright white kids from well-to-do homes learn a lot, a real lot from some of our slower kids that came here from what is in comparison a ghetto. I hope you'll ask the children about that — about what they've learned from one another. They might end up telling you what they've *learned,* period!"

I talked to the children with that in mind — did so before I spent time with their teachers — and found the principal's suggestion a very good one indeed. A rather properly dressed white girl had this to say: "My mother was going to take us out of this school, me and my brother. She said she was in favor of integration, but we're very good at school, and we need a school that can keep up with us, she said. My brother, he has an IQ that's so high he's in the genius range, the lady told my mother. But my father said we should stay for a year and see how everything goes; then if we're wasting our time here, we could always go to another school, because there are some real good private ones around.

"I can't say I've made real close friends with any of the Negro kids, but a couple of them, yes; we're pretty good friends. Last week I went over to one girl's house with her. She invited me, and my mother was real worried. When I told her I was invited, she said no, how could I possibly go over there. I said, 'You could drive me, Mum,' and she didn't say anything — except that she'd talk it over with my father when he came home. I don't know what they decided, but later the next day my mother said OK, I could go, and she would drive me, and she'd come and pick me up in a half hour or so. I think it was my dad who told her to stretch it to an hour, though.

"I had a real good time. Sally, she seemed real different in her home. She wasn't so quiet. She was telling me this and that and — everything. She showed me around and had me meet her friends, and she took me to the store, and I met some people there, and she played me some of her records, and I had a good time. She has four brothers, and they think she's the best person that ever lived. They'll do anything for her. They all seem real close together, her and her brothers and her baby sister. They don't have the things we do, they sure don't, but they're real good to each other. I told my mother that on the way home, and she said that's right, because they're poor, and they have to stick together or they won't have anything at all left. But I told her — I told her they *liked* sticking together."

Could she draw a picture or two of her home (Figure 10), and perhaps one or more of her friend's home (Figure 11)? Yes, she could, but before she did and as she did she wanted to say one more thing: "If you go visiting, you see a lot you'd never know about. Now when I see Sally come into school, I know where she's coming from, and it isn't as if she was just Sally, and from nowhere that I've ever seen."

Her teacher had some similar thoughts. Like most of her students and their parents she was also "in favor of integration," but has had her doubts, too. She saw, every day she saw and struggled with, "the great disparities between ghetto children and middle-class children." She remarked, on the favorable side, how obliging and cooperative many black children are, compared to some of the provocative, snobbish and self-centered children who at nine or ten already know they have inherited the earth: "You hear a lot about the noise that ghetto children make in class, and how unruly they are, fresh and combative. I wonder how many articles have been written about our spiteful, spoiled suburban children, who *also* cause us pain in the classroom." Yet there are, finally, those academic problems: "There is no doubt that the black children we get here are a real challenge to us. At first I tried hard to ignore all differences and simply teach, teach them hard so they would catch up with the rest of us. Then, for a while, I'll have to admit, I became very discouraged. I began to believe that it wasn't hopeless, but it certainly would take time — more time than we have in an elementary school, or maybe any school. But one day I decided to visit several black parents in their homes — they'd asked me several times — and it was the best decision I've ever made as a teacher, yes sir. I saw where those children live — but it wasn't only bad news that I found. I realized how *many selves* there are in one person. The children were different in their own neighborhood. Now they could show *me* things, explain things to *me*. They talked more, were more alive and alert. They seemed friendlier, more trusting. Oh, they were shy and scared, too, but they did something with their shyness and fear — because they felt able to. After all, they could entertain and teach me!

"When I spoke with their parents I realized that we had to do more of this, more visiting back and forth. The black children come home and say things that are picked up and distorted by parents who are as cut off from our school as they are from the rest of the middle-class world. The result is the children's fear increases tenfold in the mother's mind. She becomes angry and resentful. An incident here or there becomes something much larger — and there's no way to talk about it, certainly not in a large, public, formal P.T.A. meeting. In those private conferences with each parent that we have — well, they're held on our home ground, and they can be pretty brief and formal, too. Somehow we've got to bring these families and our family, the school family, nearer. I did it to some extent that day, and I've continued to do it ever since. I think it has made a difference. I *know* it has; the black children come toward me in a more open and direct way. They don't mind being pushed and prodded. They know I'm doing it *for* them, not *to* them. I've seen how smart they are — and smart they can be, in a way, at acting dumb! They know how to frustrate teachers. They know how to be polite, then rude, then nasty. If they see that I'm convinced they're hopeless or worse, they act accordingly. If they see me giving them a lot of excuses, they give them right back to me, plenty of excuses. But once I asked one of them to do something and he said, 'No one ever asked me to do that before.' Then I knew I was at last getting someplace. At last I'd had the sense to tell that child that he *had* to do something, that he was *going* to do something. He had seen that I knew he could do a lot more than seemed to be the case. The reason I felt he could was I'd been to his home and seen what he could do there — take care of his sister and help his mother and deal with the storekeepers and all the rest, even help out at a cafeteria."

She did indeed seem to know her children and get them to respond to her. "Oh, yes, yes you can" were words she used — unselfconsciously and with feeling — over and over again as I sat in the back of her class and watched things move along. The children heard her and seemed to believe her. They tried one more time, and often they succeeded. And then — well, she promised to call up their mothers and fathers and *tell* them they'd succeeded, or, if there was no phone at home, go visit them and tell them the same thing in person. "Why should we only call parents when there's trouble?" she asked me. I had no answer to that.

South Park

One school system serves the two, small, neighboring communities that make up this upper South town. The schools serve almost five thousand children, twenty-seven percent of whom are black. About twenty-five thousand people live in the two communities. The larger of the two communities accounts for twenty thousand of those citizens, around fifteen percent of whom are black; it also houses a university where fifteen thousand students are in residence most of the year. There are other large and small universities and colleges in nearby towns, making this section of the state its academic center and a major academic center of the entire South. These schools have helped bring a spirit of questioning and openness to racial problems and have clearly effected progress towards desegregation.

Until 1966 schools were pretty solidly segregated. There was a "Negro high school" and a "white" one, which people at least acknowledged frankly by those names. That year a new high school opened for tenth, eleventh and twelfth graders, the "white high school" became the junior high school, and the "Negro high school" served all sixth graders; so the schools had desegregated from the sixth grade on up. The next year district lines for elementary schools were redrawn, so today they have student bodies that range from twenty percent to thirty-eight percent black.

The South and the so-called "border states" are not without islands of significant educational ferment. In South Park I encountered one of the most extraordinary school systems in America — an unusual one not only for the region but the entire nation. The town's superintendent and his immediate colleagues gave the first hint that something of a surprise was in store for me: "It was here, in the South, that words like 'desegregation' and 'integration' were first used, and maybe it'll be here that we move way ahead of them and think of school as a lot more than a place where black and white children learn side by side with each other, or even become friends with each other."

What did a superintendent who spoke such words have in mind? When asked that I heard in reply ideas that sound a bit vague — until, that is, I visited a school where those ideas were being turned into a whole set of events. The principal I met was a tall black man — in charge of a school that is attended by reasonably well-off white children, who constitute far more than half of the total enrollment: "Yes, I'm black, and most of the children here are white — and we're not up North, either; not bad, don't you think! There are times when I don't even want to call this a school. I want to call it something like a 'center where children spend a lot of time and learn a lot and get good medical and dental care and grow and have fun and *do* all kinds of things, as well as sit back and learn their lessons.' Now, that's a long, long name for a school, isn't it!"

The visitor wants to know exactly what all this talk about a "center" means. I saw children who were not only learning how to spell and read and write, but having their teeth repaired and any number of ailments treated — all in a school. Their parents were also attending classes in the school — classes aimed at correcting medical, nutritional or psychological problems of one sort or another. In sum, families as well as children came to the school, which for its part had many kinds of "experts" and "services" to offer. A philosophy was also offered by one of the school's teachers: "We try to let the children know that we believe that they can learn and they will learn and they must learn. You ask *how* we let them know that, how we convince them of our intentions and our belief. Well, I say it out loud, and I say it in about a dozen different ways every single day. I tell them, the ones who need telling, that we've got to learn, that it's no fun not knowing things, and that by the time the year is out — well, I mean it, we *will* learn, all of us. I won't let the children fall into groups or cliques either, any more than I think teachers should. That's what will happen if you don't be careful: the white kids and black kids separate, and so do the white teachers and black teachers.

"A lot of our Negro children, they come to school frightened — and not only of a white teacher like me. They've been hit and whipped and all the rest by their mothers, just as they're often hit in the Negro schools. Liberals don't like to talk about that — about what Negroes do to one another, and if someone like me is forceful with a Negro child, because that's what he's used to, and if I ease him into a new kind of experience with his teachers — well, then I'm called a segregationist or something like that by some of our liberal parents. I believe I can get a child, a Negro child, to respond to me by touching him, by putting my hands on his shoulders, or holding his arm. They are much closer with one another, physically, than we are — parents with children and children with one another. They're not so dependent on words, on all sorts of talk. A look, a gesture, a glance — and I can tell a Negro child that I mean business, that I'm depending on him to get down to work, that I understand him and am — oh, 'simpatico,' you might call it.

"Our white children are more independent, of course, and they are more distant in a way. They don't touch one another as much. They go off on their own more. They don't look at you and watch you; they listen for your words, your statements. There's a difference in the way children of the two races respond to teachers, be they white or black. I believe that you either feel that difference or you don't. If you don't, I think you've got two strikes against you before you start. The Negro kids will tend to become wild and silly unless they're given control as well as kindness. And the white kids will become pretty scared and confused if you grab them with your hands and give them a good firm look. Why, they'd go home and tell their parents that their poor teacher has gone and lost her mind."

The white children, in fact, consider her a very fine teacher, and the black children in her class call her "the best woman in the world." Several of them said she was "like the sun." She was described as "lighting up the room" every time she enters it. Her humor is attractive to the children of both races — and they all talk to one another about her. I met with a group of children of both races and heard this, first from a black child: "She's a real tough one. She means business. She doesn't allow you any edge; she's right there, down on you for not doing all you should have. She's on your side. You can tell by how she acts. She'll be tough with you, but she won't be mean. She's wanting you to work and learn the stuff, and you know that's what she's after. She's just nice, that's what I think. She doesn't ignore you. She's there, on the spot, if you want to know something."

A white child put it this way: "She's very honest. She lets you know exactly how she feels. If she doesn't like something, she says so. If you've been sitting back and not doing your work, she's not going to let you get away with it. She'll just come right toward you and tell you to *get going*. My mother says she could be more tactful with us, but then she said that maybe each teacher has to go and do things her own way. I like her, though."

A black child had some further observations: "She's the best teacher I've ever had. She knows how to get right to you. She'll come in and stare at me and say, 'Harold, why are you sitting there and wasting God's time waiting for me to talk with you like this?' If I'm talking, she won't tell me to stop; she just stares me down and holds her hand over her mouth — and I know. Once I kept on, and then she came over and held my arm and put her hand under my chin and made my mouth shut. She's pretty fast, the way she moves toward you. How old do you think she is? Fifty, I'll bet."

They went on and on and I gained a sense of a *person* — quick, earnest, stubborn, crusty, at times perhaps old-fashioned and cynical. Yet, the children "took" to her. That was the word one of them used: "You get to know her after a few days, and you really take to her. She seems too hard at first, always wanting you to do this and do that, but it's like she says — if we sit around doing nothing, there are better places to do that than in a school building. So, we'd better go through the books and things here, and then go outside and enjoy God's earth. That's what she calls it outside, God's earth. My mother, she said if every white person was like her, we'd have been having a lot better time here, and there wouldn't be so much hate around. She wants us to really learn and get ahead, she said, and then she'd feel like she was a good teacher, and she was doing her share for the South. She told us the South needs the Negro, and none of us should go North. We should stay right here and get a good education and show the rest of the country that we had it worst of all before down here, and now we're having it best of all."

GROUP B
Upstate City

According to the 1960 census 216,038 people live in this north-eastern city; six percent are black. In 1959 the city's median family income for whites was $3,308, and $2,566 for blacks. There are many major industries in the city, and electronic and indus-trial machine industries alone employ over a quarter of the labor force. More than eighty percent of the black population lives in a small "ghetto" area in the center of the city.

About thirty thousand pupils attend the city's schools; twenty percent are black. In May of 1962, CORE picketed the school board and organized a one-day boycott of a highly segregated elementary school. This provoked some response: meetings, con-fessions, promises. But in 1962–63 fifty-eight percent of all black elementary-school children attended two of the city's thirty-three elementary schools, and most of the other thirty-one were solidly white. Since then school officials have made various efforts to eliminate segregation and improve the education given to black children. They have closed "ghetto" schools and bussed black children to predominantly white schools. They have redrawn district lines to correct racial imbalance; they have transformed "ghetto" schools into special, experimental ones — open and attractive to applicants from all over the city. They have also recommended that schools be no more than thirty percent black and no less than ten percent, and they have started a voluntary *transfer program and paid for bussing to help implement their recommendations. Still, segregation persists in certain schools.*

The principal in the elementary school I visited has a quiet, old-fashioned charm. She admits to feeling "behind the times," but in fact has very much tried to keep up with them. She has tried very hard to keep the size of the school's classes down. To do so she has brought in aides, helpers and part-time teachers. To do so she has worked long hours, read everything about "the disadvantaged child" she could get her hands on, and by her count, attended fourteen institutes devoted to "teaching the deprived." She considers herself a fighter, a veteran of all sorts of battles, not all of them won: "I'll be honest. The city isn't much interested in some of these matters, not really interested. Some are, a lot of those who live near this school, but you lose a lot when you can't fall back on your own superiors, on the school system as a whole. Sometimes I go to meetings downtown and the others there — they look at me as some sort of curiosity. 'Are you *still* trying?' one of the assistant superintendents says to me almost every time. I know he means well, but it doesn't help my morale. And every once in a while I begin to ask *myself* that question."

Most of the time, though, she pours her heart and soul into her school. She is proud that when the city was plagued with riots, her school was ignored. Black people live near the school but traditionally used to go to another one, in the heart of the city's ghetto. Now, through a combination of a bussing program and a change in school-district lines, her school is integrated, and considered "progressive" and "experimental" by school officials. Much of that reputation is due to the principal's efforts — aided by those of some white, professional people whose children make up a large percentage of the school's population. Integration brought troubles, but the principal and her assistant made a series of responses to those troubles: "I had always been interested in retarded children. Amid all our very bright and able children we get some slow ones — who make their eager, intelligent parents feel very frustrated. I know how stubborn such children can be — and how much they can be persuaded to learn, if only we reach them and convince them that there is a *point* to learning. So often they've already learned something — about themselves. They've learned that they're "slow" or "retarded" and that they can't do this or that or whatever. No wonder they're afraid of school, or they become angry and agitated here. I found that teachers who really liked slow children, and believed in them, in what they *might* do, they *could* do, did in fact do wonders. If the teacher feels she can succeed, if she says to you, 'I love the work,' if her face shows her real interest and concern — then the children feel it and respond to her and learn from her. I know that. Of course the entire school system rarely encourages such teachers. Bureaucracies don't usually encourage much of anything — ideas, people, a philosophy. Bureaucracies just exist, I'm afraid. When I was developing my program with retarded children I never went to the bureaucrats. I went to the parents of those children. I invited them to come to the school. I called them 'aides.' I had them all over, learning with their children and learning what their children could learn and — just learning. You'd be surprised at the difference it made. They'd go home and feel better about their boy or girl, and at school they'd help our teachers."

Her teachers need help. They admit to feeling troubled, uncertain, even in despair: "I feel confused. A lot of the time I feel worse than that. I think it's just hopeless. I used to come to my classes full of enthusiasm and pleasure. Now it's different. You never know what new kind of trouble will face you each day. We still have our bright, ambitious children, but we also have these new children — and their whole way of looking at things is different, totally different. I try. Lord knows, every day I try. If it weren't for our principal I'd probably have given up a long time ago. But almost every day she gives us a pep talk, and I take an oath with myself to keep on trying. The trouble is they just don't seem to want to learn — mainly the Negro children. They look bored, or they start getting spiteful, or they turn on the other kids. I don't mean *all* of them, no, but enough to make every day a new source of worry, real worry for us teachers."

She and others in the school cause some of the children to worry, also. One black child in her class, the brightest in fact, the source of least worry to her teacher, spoke these words: "It's a joke here a lot of the time, because they keep telling you they want to help you, but they're all out for their own kind, the white, if you ask me. She keeps giving us those talks on how everyone is created equal and all that, but she's trying to convince herself, that's what I think. She thinks we're dumb, and we need all the help we can get — that's how she's always saying it, 'all the help you can get.' How about her? She could stand some help, too. She gets annoyed at us, and then she tells us we should just keep quiet and behave ourselves until lunchtime. One time we went down to get lunch and she was with us and she saw the woman throwing the food at us and shouting and I heard her say to her friend: 'How can we expect the children to behave, when they treat them like this in the cafeteria?' And her friend, she said they were Negroes, the people in the serving line, and that's what we're used to at home — getting bad treatment, I guess. If I was bigger and out of this school for good, I would have said something. But I didn't. I went home and told my mother, though — and she said that's the way it can go, and you have to close your ears a lot of the time, and your eyes. That's right."

His friend also closes his eyes and ears: "I don't pay that much attention to a lot of things around here. A lot of the kids, they've got so much they don't know what to do with all they've got. I can tell. I listen in. They'll be talking about this thing they have and that thing. So I just pretend I don't hear, and I think to myself that I could take most any one of them and knock him flat down, if it came to anything. The teacher, she'll be giving you these lectures on how we should all be friends and like that

(Figure 12). But they keep on pressing you down, and trying to get you to talk like them and act like them. You know what I mean? They're unhappy because we don't speak like them, and they want us to cut it out and step along the way they do, but as I see it, we've got our own lives to live. That's what my daddy says all the time — 'Don't you let them give you the idea it's all their ball game, and we have to play according to their rules.' That's what he says, but I'm not sure he's right."

A white student isn't sure either. He comes from a very liberal home. His father and mother "favor civil rights." He has been told again and again that black children and white children are "all the same" and "learn just as well as each other, if only given a chance." So he thinks and so he speaks. Yet he also says other things: "The way it looks, the Negro kids, they're just not prepared like we are. They don't speak up, and the teacher can't understand them a lot of the time (Figure 13). She'll lean over and tell them to say it again, only this time go slower. But they're already talking slow. I think she does understand, but she wants them to speak like us — that's what my dad said — and they can't right off. It'll take a long time — maybe our grandchildren, my mother says. A lot of the time I think the Negro kids would like to be like us and speak the same way and have the same things, but they won't admit it, and they get mad if you say so. The principal, she's trying to make everything go smooth — but she can't do it all alone, and my father says she's fighting a losing battle because of the riots, and the white people, they're just fed up now and won't stand for much more trouble. I asked one Negro kid if he thought integration would continue, and he said he never thought about it one way or the other. But his friend said he hoped not, and he wanted to know what I thought, and I said I was in favor of it, but we had a long road to go yet. My parents say it will take years."

Capital City

Seventy thousand people live in this New England suburban community. Almost thirteen thousand children attend its public *schools; until 1966, fewer than twenty-five were black. That year local citizens agreed to accept eighty black students from schools in the nearby city, where the population is one hundred sixty-five thousand and over half the schoolchildren are black. In the city the median income is $6,000; it is twice that in the suburb. City children were taken from schools where the black population exceeded eighty-five percent of the total student body and were assigned to suburban classrooms with vacancies. Most were elementary-school children, though some junior and senior high school students found places. Officials studied the experiment with care and great thoroughness, finally deeming it "successful." Today the program operates on a somewhat larger scale.*

"I have to say to you that I never would have dreamed a few years ago that something like this would happen, that I'd be standing out here in front of this school and watching Negro children come here from the city. Sometimes I wonder what they think as they get off that bus, but I suppose by now they've stopped thinking. They just get off and go in the building and go to school."

So he thought — and he certainly knows children, if not black children, quite well. For two decades he has worked with children in a small town near Capital City, first as a teacher, then as assistant principal, and finally as principal. He speaks forcefully, even brusquely, in a way that an older man can sometimes get away with — indeed, in doing so even gain a bit by being considered a man who is "kind underneath." What does he think of the bussing program? What does he think about the black children, about possibilities that they may possess — as pupils and students and future citizens? Does he have any thoughts about how they think of themselves, about their view of what the future holds? How do particular teachers influence the kind and amount of learning that their pupils acquire? The questions are put forth with unusual speed and candor because he seems to invite that kind of pointed, direct conversation. He has strong opinions, he says almost immediately, and he is quite willing to make them known: "I was against this in the beginning, like a lot of people who are now willing to give it all they've got. I'd be fooling you if I told you I said, 'Bring them all out here!' What ran through my mind was — well, 'how can this possibly work?' I kept on asking myself that, but the town didn't want to wait and think. They said they wanted to *do* something — and sometimes I think they didn't care *what*, so long as they felt less guilty. One mother came to see me and practically got hysterical. She kept on saying that we'd done bad things for three hundred years, the white people, and we had to start making amends. After about ten or fifteen minutes of that I told her to stop, please. I asked her what *she* had done to any Negro — she or anyone she knows. Well, of course, the answer is nothing. Then I asked her why she was getting so *emotional* and putting the whole thing on a personal basis. She said she didn't know what I was talking about. So, I said that the way she talked, anyone who had reservations about this bussing program or anything else having to do with Negroes — he's just no good. They call you every name in the book. Talk about 'tolerance' — have the liberals ever looked at their own intolerance? I wonder."

He went on in that vein, and then had the courage and honesty to go further: "I frankly don't believe this is the answer. It will only work for a handful anyway, and it's hard on everyone, the Negro kids and our own. I believe Negro kids need a kind of schooling we just don't offer here — because our children are different. The Negro child brought out here needs discipline, firmness and patience from teachers. I don't believe they take easily to the kind of freewheeling and imaginative atmosphere we encourage here for our children. Yes, they are stimulated by things here, and some of them have done very well indeed. But some of them have had a very difficult time here, and so have we — with them. They have trouble academically, then they become angry and even violent. Rather than face their own inadequacies, they start striking out, provoking people — teachers and children alike — so that they can have someone to blame other than themselves. It's a very sorry business, and I frankly don't know how to solve it. One thing, too: I know I'm blunt, and I know some other principal will talk a lot differently

FIGURE 1

FIGURE 2

FIGURE 3

GREEN RIVER

FIGURE 4. The good teacher has open eyes and ears, and opens her mouth (perhaps so she can talk), and has hair and a dress and fingers and somewhat substantial feet.

GREEN RIVER

FIGURE 5. The bad teacher, according to the same child, "is always asleep, really." In this picture she seems to be doing just that, dozing. In addition, she is drawn in a hurry—and denied arms, hair, a dress, and halfway usable legs and feet.

EAST PARK

FIGURE 6. "I can't draw, but I'll try to show you how good a teacher she is—she's with you all the way; you can see it on her face."

FIGURE 7. "Now a bad teacher — I can't even draw them because they're all alike and they're no good — so, there, the best thing to do is cross them right out, the way they do to us."

CENTRAL PARK

FIGURE 8. A white child draws himself and his teacher as best he can, using crayons.

CENTRAL PARK

FIGURE 9. A black child shuns crayons, except for a black one, and turns himself into a somewhat bizarre Oriental; he can only start his (white) teacher's face, then make her appear Negro, then in a sense destroy her with a grid placed on her profile.

WEST PARK

FIGURES 10 AND 11. One house is a grim tenement, and one house, obviously, has a lot to make it pleasant.

UPSTATE CITY

FIGURE 12. A black child shows the teacher with a pointer and on a stool. "She's always over you and on you to do something, and she gets annoyed too quick. She's too nervous about us, I think. She always lectures at us."

FIGURE 13. *(Right)* A white child says the same teacher is "friendly" and "likes to hug us a lot."

CAPITAL CITY

FIGURE 14. A black child from a ghetto in a northern city draws the school bus (owned, he says, by "white people") that takes him and others like him to a suburban school. His face can be seen amid the dabs of black. The white bus driver literally blends into the bus, which is the same color as the driver's face.

FIGURE 15. (Below) Another black child draws his bus, and himself and his brother in it, and his (white, suburban, sun-drenched, yellow-colored) school.

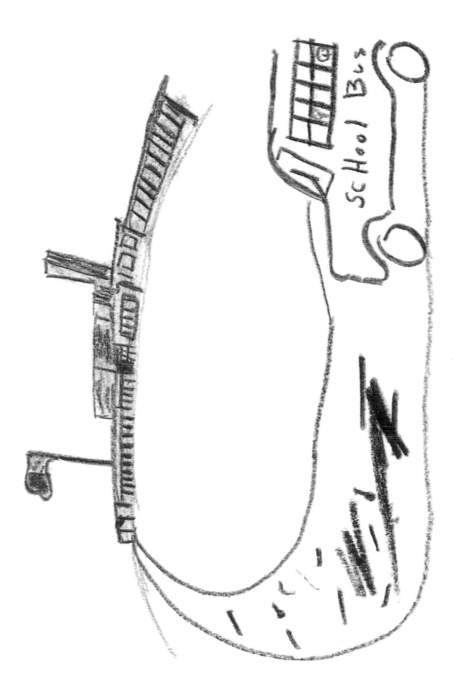

FIGURE 16. "Here I am now. It's raining, and I have an umbrella, but still I get wet."

FIGURE 17. His teacher.

FIGURE 18. "Here I am when I'm grown up. That's a cowboy hat. I'm on top of a hill. The school, it's way down there. I could fly in that plane. The kid, he still has to go to school, but I thought I'd give him a cowboy hat, too. That's a crow. She's saying: 'Why don't you kids fly away from school and get yourself a deal

WEST CITY

FIGURE 19. His school: "It's just an old brick building, nothing else."

FIGURE 20. "I'll be someone big, and they'll have a picture of me, and kids will have it on cards—like with baseball players."

FIGURE 21. "There's the school, and me in it."

EAST CITY

FIGURE 22. "And there's me later — I'll be as big as can be, and I'll be able to take on any white kid around — in football or anything else. In football my shoulders won't need any padding, no sir."

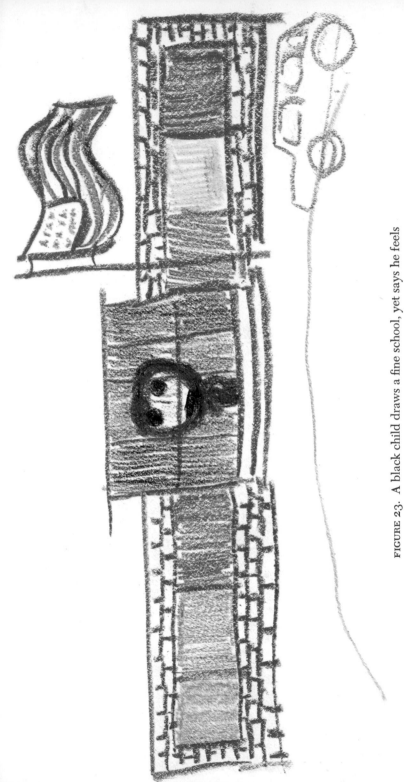

FIGURE 23. A black child draws a fine school, yet says he feels lonely there and is seen as lonely there by his teacher.

BORDER CITY

FIGURE 24. (*Below*) "The school and the buildings around here."

CENTRAL CITY

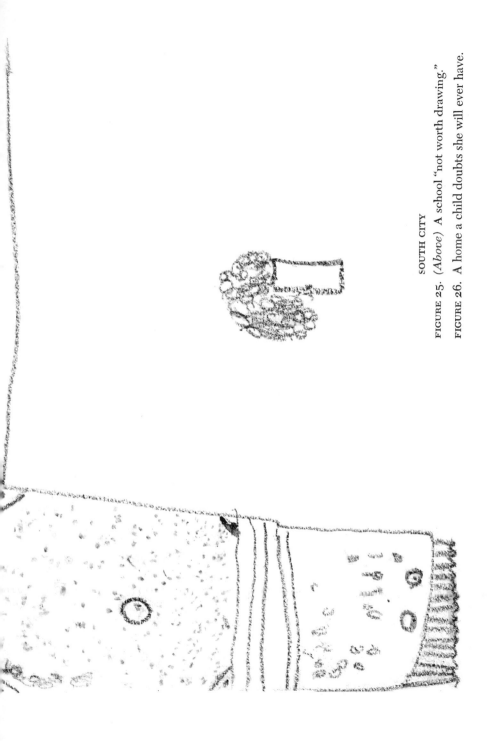

SOUTH CITY

FIGURE 25. (*Above*) A school "not worth drawing."

FIGURE 26. A home a child doubts she will ever have.

to you. But they're all facing the same problems I am, even if they put the whole thing in different words. One of my friends in the next town over — they have the same program we do — keeps talking about 'stages' and 'understanding' and 'working out the tensions in time.' It'll take a long time. I think the Negro children know that better than we do, much better. We can fool ourselves, but not them."

One of his teachers disagrees with him. She has heard him say that black children are for all practical academic purposes "different" — which he did indeed say to me — and she has even challenged him at a staff meeting: "One good thing about him is that he can say outrageous things but not hold a grudge against you for disagreeing. He even likes arguments. I do believe the Negro children respect him, too. He is gruff and stern, but he's very personable with them, and they feel that and look up to him. I suppose he's a lot better than the smooth-talking types who smile all the time and say the 'right' liberal things — but really don't like the Negro children one bit. We have some of those, you know.

"The thing that bothers me, though, is that because of our principal's attitude we're not doing all we could, not by a long shot. Actually, I shouldn't say that. Sometimes I think his attitude is good. He makes us stop and think about what *we* think. He makes us question the conventional wisdom, I guess you'd put it. He dares to say a lot that some of us think but are afraid to say. The trouble is that *he* misses a lot, too. He doesn't see the positive side, the slow changes in the attitudes of both our white and black children. He doesn't see how white children from suburban homes learn things from these black children, and how the black children learn — oh, they learn a lot. They learn academic things, and they learn to feel some of the hope that our kids feel. It's hard to put your finger on hope, but if you have it you've got the most important thing in the world, and if you don't, you're in real trouble. I think our black children are doing quite beautifully, for all their troubles here. *They* tell me they're learning better, and I *know* they are, most of them. Bussing is no panacea, I admit that, but something has to be done, to begin with. In the long run maybe we'll have a more metropolitan kind of school system; towns like this one and the cities will join together. We either do that or we tell black people they can have their America, and we'll have ours out here. Our children look to us for signs, too — signs to tell them we believe one thing or another. There are times I think we teachers should be graded. We should pass or flunk, depending on how our children do. I've had some Negro children who would confirm every one of our principal's opinions — and yet I've said to myself that they're going to do better, they're just going to. And it's not the class size or the equipment that *made* them do better. I hesitate to say it, but it was probably me, me and some of the children I enlisted to help me. I called them in, five of them, my best — not my smartest, my *best* — and I said we had to work together and help some of our new students, and yes, we had to let them help us. I didn't know exactly how to put it to the children, and maybe I was condescending — I realize that now. But I wanted something to happen between all the kids, not only between me and the Negro children. So, I told some white children I wanted them to work with the black children: show them around the school and the town, and tell them things, and *be told* things. I had the class divide itself up, so that one child could tell a story to another and be graded — for *interest*, for the power in the story, not grammar. It's not easy to tell you all this, but I think it worked; the children caught on to one another, that's how I'd put it. No matter what their parents thought, or the principal, or after a while maybe even me, they proved they could do things side by side and be teachers, almost as much as I am, I sometimes believe."

One of the white children she mentioned was even more vague, if just as touching to hear: "They're all right. That's what we discovered. And they said we are, too. They told us they wanted to grow up and buy some land out here and build themselves a huge, big house, and we could all go swimming together in the summer. They said they might want to go to high school and get their diploma, and go to college and pick up one there, the same. They said it was fun a lot of the time where they lived, but a lot of the time it wasn't, either. I didn't dare ask what was the matter, and my mother said they probably wouldn't have said, and I did right to keep quiet and mind my own business and try to be friendly. She said a lot of people who live near us, they have a lot of trouble, too."

The black children generally felt glad to be at the school, glad to be "on the inside," one of them phrased it (Figures 14 and 15). He went on: "I don't like everything here, and some of the kids and the teachers, too — they turn you off. But I've made some good friends, and they have a lot of nice things here: it's better in the building, and they give you better food, and they really try to make you learn your lessons. Back at the old school, all they wanted was that we keep quiet and don't make any trouble and sit still. They told us we'd never amount to anything, anyway, and they weren't going to let us cause them any pain. So, if you squeaked your chair, they looked at you as if you'd gone and killed someone, and they were going to kill you back. Here, they're better to you. I believe I'll stay with it, and maybe get myself one of these fat jobs like my friends, their fathers have got. It's getting easier for us; that's what my mother said. So it's worth the ride on the bus, I believe."

Border City

This upper southern city lies on the eastern edge of the Piedmont near a major governmental center, where many of its residents work. One hundred twenty thousand people live here. Thirteen percent are black. The schools serve eighteen thousand five hundred students; eighteen percent are black, and they are in general kept well to themselves. The city has fourteen elementary schools; five have black enrollments ranging from fifty-five percent to ninety percent, and the remaining nine are almost solidly white. The city also has three high schools; each is paired with one of the three middle schools. Two pairs are twenty-five percent black; the third barely one percent. There has been some shifting of white and black students to assure that no schools are one hundred percent black or white, which would disqualify the system from federal aid.

The school is a new and lovely building, well-designed, full of sun and light and space. Nearby live black families, and also nearby live white families. The black families live in a "project" and are not so very well off. The white families are quite comfortable — headed by eminently successful lawyers, a number of doctors, and some writers and journalists and architects. The school was once all black, and now is thoroughly integrated, because its white children no longer go to an all-white school about a mile away. The school's principal is the same lady who has been in charge of things for years, well before the recent past, with the desegregation and redistricting that have come along. She is black and originally from South Carolina. Her assistant is white, and arrived at the school when the white children did.

At first acquaintance the white assistant principal seems far easier to talk with, far more perceptive, observant, in tune with the school's problems. Yet in time the older lady, the dark lady, emerges as a wise, shrewd and able person, who has lived through a lot and expects to live through much more: "I went to school in a one-room shack in South Carolina, in the low country. I was lucky to live, stay alive, let alone get an education. I remember once we had a bad cold spell in winter, and our cabin had no heat except the stove, and we lost one of my brothers from pneumonia, in a day or two, and then lo and behold another one from the same thing about a week later. I can never forget that. When people, our nice white people coming here now, ask me about 'what it means to be black' — well, that's what comes into my mind, every time it does. The other thing that does is the teacher we had there in that one-room school. She *taught* me, oh, did she. She did more than the word 'teach' can ever convey. She reached out for us, for any of us who was willing to respond to her — to her intelligence and her conviction that somehow, somehow we had to rise up and become educated and more in control of our fate. To this day I think of her when I go into a classroom. I think of how *she* influenced us and changed us and taught us and made us learn and — you see, she did everything to make us feel there was a point to it all, to being a Negro in South Carolina. I don't know how to tell you she *did* it, but it had to do with her spirit, her hopefulness. There we were, out in that rural section, in a one-room schoolhouse. We had nothing, nothing really but her. But she was something — was a lot more, I'll tell you, than any school of education or teaching technique or machine could ever make her or turn her into. I've gone to about five of those 'institutes' for desegregation and for 'better teaching' and such, and every time I just sit back and think of her and how she'd come over and look right into our eyes so that you thought she could read every thought you ever had, and how you'd blink and blink and get scared, but she'd always hug you or touch your shoulder — and tell you to 'perk up' and 'get down to learning before it's too late.' She meant it, and we knew she did, and no matter how bad it was then, she could make us believe there was a point to school; she could inspire us, I guess you could put it. I wish more of our teachers in this city and in others — I wish they could inspire our children, bring out the life I know they have inside them. Sometimes I look out this window and see the children coming toward this building, and I can almost see their faces begin to frown or become somber, and then they leave in the afternoon and they start coming alive again. You can see by the way they move, and you can hear by the sounds they make, the excitement they feel at being out of school — at last! For one more day!"

She and her white assistant have tried very hard indeed to bring about changes in their school, to make its teachers more inspiring. The white assistant principal meets with teachers, meets with parents, meets with other principals and assistant principals: "We have a problem here, and whatever I do we'll have one. We have well-to-do whites and relatively poor Negroes sending their children to a school that's trying, but has a long way to go. We *are* trying, though. I think the children will tell you that — tell you that we're giving up on rules and regulations and tests and rote memory, doing everything we can to get our privileged white children to teach — and learn from — our black children. They each have things to offer. And their parents have things to offer one another, too — we've learned that at our P.T.A. meetings. One lawyer, from a big Washington firm, got up at the last meeting and started talking about Nebraska, where he was born on a farm — and how much he had, poor as he was, compared to southern sharecroppers. But the thing that really struck us teachers was the introspection that he had found in himself. He said so publicly. He said that really for the first time he'd sat back and thought about his life and its assumptions. He said that he could see now that his little boy comes to school all ready, all set to do well, and other children, they believe school means very little and maybe nothing. Do you know how he came to realize that? He met a Negro father at a P.T.A. meeting, and that man had gone to college and for years the best job he could get was that of a postal clerk! Yes, things are changing now, for some young blacks. But as the lawyer said, 'How long does it take for three hundred years to be forgotten?' That's what we teachers ask, too."

The children in that school, not to mention their teachers, know what that lawyer was asking. A white child, distinctly well dressed and well bred, openly talked about his black classmates: "They've had a harder life than us. They'll probably have a harder one in the future, too. I'll be honest; I'm glad I don't have to look ahead to a lot of trouble like they do. The boy who sits beside me, Arthur, he told me that down South a white man kept on saying he'd kill every Negro around, the way things are going. I think the white man, he didn't like Negroes asking to vote, and things like that. So, Arthur's dad and mother decided to move closer to the North, but now they think it's the same all over, even in Canada, even in the North Pole, and my daddy, he says they may be right. Arthur, he tells me that today everyone says the Negro should study hard and get ahead, but he's not so sure it'll pay off very much. He said they're running out of 'showcase jobs,' and there might not be room for any more Negroes soon. I didn't know what he meant by 'showcase jobs,' but he explained it to me. My dad says he may have a good point."

Arthur doesn't insist upon that, but simply has his doubts, and he admits that he also has his difficulties: "Learning, it just doesn't come very natural to me. I'll have to say that. Maybe it could have. Maybe. I don't know. A lot of these white kids, they've been primed for it, primed. It's in their blood. I've been to their homes and their rooms. They look like schoolrooms to me. That's a fact. I told one kid. I said, 'How can you stand it, being in school all day long and the night, too?' He didn't get me. So, I explained myself. Then he did. He said that he could see what I meant, and if he was like me, he said, then he wouldn't swallow everything they dish out in school, either. But I try to learn what I can. It just isn't my style. That's what my older brother says, and I agree. It's not easy to walk in to school cold and catch up with these kids — the white kids. I think I'm improving a little, though. The teacher says so. But a lot of the time I feel lost; I feel lonely" (Figure 23).

The teacher does say he is improving. She says that Arthur continues to be taciturn, suspicious and slow, but actually has been learning quite a lot and has about caught up with "the national average" in reading. The teacher adds a few interesting details: "The other day he said he was glad we 'changed things around' and mixed races and class here. He said he's made a few friends, a few white friends, and he's found out 'they're not any smarter than me. They're just better trained, that's all.' Arthur also told me a few weeks ago that he used to think he wanted to be a boxer, or a baseball star, or a marine guerrilla fighter in Vietnam, but now he wouldn't mind being a lawyer. He said Negroes need lawyers, and now that he can read better, he might one day take up 'reading the laws,' that's how he put it. I was impressed. I thought he meant it. But he also admitted that he feels real lonely here at times. Maybe that's what he meant in that drawing he did for you. Maybe the face is his, and he feels there aren't any others here that he really trusts." I think she is right.

North City

Some black families have made their homes in this northerly midwestern city for as many as five generations. They accompanied the United States Cavalry, which came to set up forts and outposts and keep watch over settlers, working as stable boys *and attendants. Later the city became a major railroad center and blacks took jobs as porters on Pullman cars. Like the cavalry, Pullman cars also disappeared, and left many unemployed. In 1960 the median white family income in the city was $6,543; for blacks it was $4,641, almost a third lower than the city median, despite the many black women who work and add their share to the "family" income. At the same time, three percent of the city's white workers were unemployed; for blacks the figure was twice that, six percent.*

According to the 1960 census, the city has a population of 313,411; 8,240 or 2.63 percent of the total population, are black. About seven thousand, or eighty-five percent, of these citizens live in a mile-square area within the city. Two busy main streets form its outer boundaries, and the freeway, which manages to bypass other residential areas, runs right through its middle. Because of its size and shape, inhabitants of this "ghetto" area can easily walk to different sections of the city, and their children could easily walk to different schools. But then, they'd have to cross busy streets, which some local officials insist is dangerous.

In April of 1964 "minority groups" accounted for 6.9 percent of the 44,835 pupils in the city's schools. Mexican-Americans and Indian-Americans made up a small portion of this figure, but most were blacks. Nearly all attended schools in or near the "ghetto." Within the "ghetto" three elementary schools had the following percentages of black pupils: ninety, sixty-four, and thirty; one junior high school had thirty-two percent. In the surrounding area three elementary schools, one junior high school, and two high schools were from ten to fourteen percent black. The remaining schools had few, if any, blacks.

Pressure for desegregation began when black organizations approached the school board and asked for an assessment of racial imbalance in the schools, and actions to correct it. They got the usual results: admissions of de facto segregation, a district line redrawn here and there, an "open enrollment policy." A group of women from a better part of town decided to show the board that something more could be done. They raised money to bus children to schools in their neighborhood. In 1965–66 they

bussed seventy-five black children to their schools, and the next
year, they bussed one hundred thirty. Though pleased with their
program, they feared board members would use it to excuse their
own inaction. So the women gradually ended their program and
waited for the board to move, but so far it has hardly budged.

There is a consistency to the black man's American experience
that unnervingly defies space. In North City, so far removed not
only from the South but from those large metropolitan centers
that now figure prominently in the nation's racial struggle, the
ghettos once again appear — both familiar and ironic. The
mother of one boy I met — he is bussed daily to a pleasant
suburban school, once all white and now *almost* all white — had
this summary to make: "We came here because my husband said
there must be someplace in the United States where you can be
black and be like other people. In the South you're a nigger,
wherever you are and no matter what they've done in the last
few years with those laws. I go back every year and see my sister.
She's in North Carolina, and it's supposed to be better there. And
in the big cities up North — well, all you have to do is look at
them, and how we live up there. But we heard that up here in
this state there were only a few of us, at least compared to other
places, and we thought why not try it. So we did, and here's
where we have to stay, and you just try to do better than in any
other place. You just try. Even up here they call our neighborhood a 'ghetto,' and I do believe they're right. This place is run-
down, and they won't work on it, the way they do with parks and
lakes out in the countryside. They won't let us out, and no one
but us comes in, and so we're just here, in the old, broken-down
part of the city that everyone else has used and left behind. It's
pretty bad, yes sir, for us and for our kids. They ask me why,
sometimes, my kids do, and I don't know how to answer them —
about why we live here and all the other kids in America live on
the outside, you know in those suburbs. It's hard to explain all
that to your kids. I'd like to see white people try. Maybe if they
did, they'd understand a little how we feel."

Her boy goes to a lovely school, and the teachers in that school do indeed try to "understand a little" how black people, and especially black children, feel. The school's principal has it all figured out: "People are people. Children are children. Yes, there are differences. But don't you think the similarities outweigh the differences? I know that Negro children suffer because for a long time their ancestors were discriminated against. I know about the psychology of prejudice — what it does to the mind. I tell my teachers that there's only one way to straighten all this trouble out: treat every child equally; forget skin color; forget who is white or black, who came here from Europe and who came from Africa. If we could only do that, the whole race problem would go away, here and everywhere else. Two of my teachers came to me a couple of months ago and wanted special discussions held. They said we had to talk about the ghetto and race and prejudice and the disadvantaged child. I told them there were *no special problems* here, just children: not black, not white, not smart and not disadvantaged. I've been principal of this school for twenty years. I've worked for civil rights here in this city since way back in the forties. I believe the only way we're going to solve this problem is to forget skin color and go ahead and live with one another. I don't want this school to be separated into white and black, and I don't want our teachers spending hour after hour talking about one small group of children. I want those children to be like all the rest, and I believe they are like that already. Some of them are fast, and some are slow. Some come here all dressed up, and some get off that bus looking pretty bad. Well, you ought to see how some of our kids from over there, across the street, look when they walk in here — they're as neglected as any of the bussed children are. I've said over and over again: don't talk about groups of children; talk about the *individual*, the particular child."

Does she think a black child has the same prospects as a white child, most other things being equal? Aren't we right in making a *few* generalizations based on obvious distinctions that hold in person after person, instance after instance? "I believe — and I think I can say I speak for the superintendent, because I've talked with him many times about this — that the only reason we bus children here is to show them and ourselves that in *any* group, of whatever origin, race, color, or creed, there are all kinds. I don't think Negro children have to come *here* to learn. That's nonsense. They don't need white teachers, either. Some of them would learn beautifully if they were all alone, or with purple children and taught by green or red, white and blue teachers. Some of them won't learn well no matter how many white people, children or teachers, sit near them and talk with them and try to help them out. But *we* feel bad because there are no Negroes living near us, and for a long time the Negroes have felt they're missing something because they're not sending their children to schools with white children in them. They don't know how bad we can be, for all our wonderful white skin! There are times when I wonder why anyone would want to send their child over here, to be with some of our spoiled, self-centered children. But of course you can find spoiled, self-centered children among all people. Anyway, we're doing the best we can, and hoping that in the end the children will feel they can relax with each other and not pay attention to skin color but choose their friends on the basis of other things."

How about the children in that school — are they becoming good friends, regardless of race? In fact, have they learned to disregard race, to become, black and white, unmindful of that one "thing" and draw to each other "on the basis of other things"? A very bright black girl gave me her answer: "I'm glad to be here. The school is a good one. They have new books, new desks, new everything. You get to see how the rich people live. I try to mind my own business and study, like my mother said I should. Yes, I have several friends, but not like my real friends at home. No sir, I don't think it's because I've not been here long enough. Sometimes I think I've been here too long, because I think it's not as much fun as with your own people; but I do think I'm getting a better kind of schooling, and that's important, everyone says. My daddy, he says if I don't get to learn now, I never will, and that will be real bad for me later. He says that the white people, they know how to get through school, stay until you graduate, and go to college, and like that. I'd like to be a nurse someday, and that means I've got to stay in school, so I'm glad I'm here. But you have to stay on your toes. In the old school you knew what to expect, but here, it's not always clear."

What did she expect in the old school, and what does she expect to get out of this new one? She doesn't know. She's not sure. She can only say — well, she can only say: "Over there, we all knew there was so far you could go, so there's no use trying. Over here you know most of the kids, they're going to grow up and be like their fathers — rich, you know." How about her and her brother, who also rides the bus with her to this new, suburban school? "Well, we might be helped and get a little rich, too. That's what my daddy says. But I'm not betting on it. A lot of the kids, they ignore us, and the teachers, some of them are friendly, but some don't care much about us. The other day a teacher said we should close our eyes and forget what we look like and treat everyone the same. But I can't just do that, close my eyes and forget, and afterwards I heard a white girl say that she couldn't either. Then she saw me listening and she tried to pretend and smile, but I knew what she was thinking in her mind. I did."

It so happened that I was able to talk with that white girl, and she turned out to be a thoughtful and sensitive child, perhaps a little more observant than at least some of her teachers: "I think it's different for them than it is for us. They're not used to a lot of the things we are, and we're not used to the things they are. I can tell when they serve food in the cafeteria that some of them haven't eaten some of the food. They look at it as though it's new to them. I'm in favor of being as friendly as you can to them, but they're silent, a lot of them, most of the time — except when they go off by themselves. Then you can see them laughing and snickering and being funny with each other. I think if one of us went and sat with them — in the lunchroom — they'd stop talking right away. The teacher says we should just be natural with everyone, but you can't be natural unless you know the person and you feel that way with her. My mother says it takes time and you need to work hard to do it, get to know a — a stranger. And

because of all the trouble in the past, a Negro girl from downtown, she's going to be a stranger to us, almost for sure."

GROUP C
West City

*This northern California city has a population of three hundred
seventy thousand; about thirty-five percent is black, and about
five percent is Mexican-American. The unemployment rate
among blacks ranges from fifteen to twenty percent, and dissatisfaction with the squalor and uncertainty of daily living has
turned many blacks toward militant leaders, who have considerable power in this community. Fearing "another Watts," the
federal government has anxiously responded with aid, studies,
"pilot programs" — and with some success; but the sad, explo-
sive mixture of apathy and rage still infects the air and casts a
shadow on the city's future.*

*The majority of schoolchildren are blacks. Schools, like the
neighborhoods they serve, are pretty thoroughly segregated. Officials have tried only a small number of "experimental" bussing
programs.*

He was in many respects the kindest, most sensitive principal I
met: a black man, a man capable of firmness and kindness both, a
man very much respected by the white parents he met and spoke
with every day. (Their children make up over half of his school.)
He was born in the South, but brought to West City as a child:
"My parents came here to escape. I think they were smart enough
to know that there's no escaping the South in some of those
northern cities in the East, but the West, maybe there it would
be different. They were wrong, of course. This city, West City —
well, we're known all over the country for our racial troubles. It's
a hard thing to say, but sometimes I wonder whether the long
trip across the country was worth it. We're not segregated like we
used to be in Alabama, but a lot of my people came here penniless, dazed, confused, at a loss to know what to do. And their

children, they don't have much going for them at home. When they come to school they're hungry and weak, and a lot of them, they're sad — sadder than anyone really knows, I'm afraid."

He knows how sad those children are. He also knows how much hope those same children have: "They're already suspicious, a lot of them, but they're looking for something better, too — something better than what they see all around them outside of school. The way I see it, we can try to offer them a little here in this building. We can try to show them other people — me, my secretary, the teachers, the nurse, the doctor, the people who come to help with speech problems. We can try to show them how we take care of ourselves, how we appear and act and talk and all the rest. It may be a long way from here to some of those tenements, even if they're nearby in distance, but we can try to bring things closer together, at least a *little* closer together, in the child's mind. That's what I want to do, as well as see the children learn how to read or count or whatever. But it's not any easier for me, I'll tell you, than for them. They have their problems, the children, and I have mine, too — plenty of them."

He does indeed have his problems. As a principal he feels lonely and embattled. His is in many respects a "showcase" school, one of the city's best, the city's only "really integrated" school. By "integrated" he means something quite specific: "I don't mean bodies whose skin color varies. I mean children from different backgrounds *learning* from each other. I also mean parents learning, too. I try to get the black parents to put pressure on me, to demand things from me, to go downtown and tell the school board they're not happy with what I'm doing, because I don't have enough to offer their children. It's not easy to do — to get them going and to take the risk to myself of getting them going. But I must, as I see it. Our white parents feel that there's a *point* to school, that there's a good reason to keep their eyes on what we're doing here. Many of the black parents aren't at all sure. In fact, they either *know* things are hopeless — and tell you why — or they *feel* things are hopeless, no matter what I say, no matter what they say to themselves. That's pretty bad, isn't it? And that kind of attitude gets across to children very quickly. One black girl was sent down here for being fresh to her teacher, swearing at her when she tried to be helpful. I asked her why she'd done that, and she didn't pause a second before she gave me her answer: 'There's only room for one of us who's black. The rest of us, we have to live different from you. That's what my uncle said. He said school won't get you far, and there's only room for a few black people up top. They'll never let us have our own schools, unless we build our own, and we haven't got the money.' That's about what she said, and you can imagine what she really heard at home. Why *should* she study, if that's what she believes, if that's what she's told every other day of her life, now that she's growing up and finding out about things?"

Children like that child move about, too; from school to school they go, as their families wander within the confines of the ghetto. Children like that child or her brothers don't want to be secretaries, teachers, nurses, professional men, or even big-name sports heroes. A teacher told me how those children think: "They don't really have anything in mind about the future, not when they first come here. They're not accustomed to thinking about the future, about next year and five years from now. With them it's minute to minute. One of the things they learn here, I know, is how to plan ahead, think ahead, and *anticipate* things — I mean, count on them as well as wish for them. They learn that from some of our better-off children as well as us."

It is not easy for those children to learn, though. So I was told by the principal and by all his teachers. The school has a reputation for being "a good apple in a basket full of pretty bad ones." The school's white children come from rather liberal homes, and as a result, this state of affairs, described by one teacher, is what holds: "The white parents have kept their children here, and as a matter of fact, kept *themselves* here, in this neighborhood. In the beginning they did so with a good deal of fear, but out of principle. Now they're not afraid, and they realize that. *They've* gone through something, *they've* learned something. I know I have. I've learned what black children have learned before they ever step foot in a school. I've learned to redefine the word 'learn.' That's how I'd put it. Many black children learn all the time, but don't learn in the schoolrooms. It's not only that they aren't 'motivated,' as we say it. There's something else: they come here afraid. Sometimes the fear is obvious, but sometimes it takes other forms — boasting, gloating, noisiness, insolence, belligerence, silence you cannot penetrate, a sullen look that never leaves the child's face, or in one case I just thought of, a half smile, a half scowl, really, that haunted me for weeks. I thought the boy was disturbed and needed to see a psychiatrist. But one day I asked him to stay after school, and I just held my breath and *told* him — how he looked to me and what *I* thought that *he* thought. Then he straightened up and smiled, really smiled, and said one word: 'Yes.' He wasn't yessing me, either. He *meant* yes. After that he started doing better in class. There were no miracles, but he paid attention and asked for my help and improved — improved and improved and improved. I'd like a lot of other teachers to hear about him — but I'm sorry I can't prove exactly how it all happened. I only know that he was a troublesome, distant child, and then at long last he and I came to an understanding with one another, and then his work in class improved a hundredfold."

The young boy she talked about is quiet but constantly on the watch. His eyes follow his observer around the room. His eyes never stay anyplace for too long. His eyes are open but not exactly trusting. "I like it here," he says, "but you don't stay here after the sixth grade. So I won't be here after that." His family moved from Mississippi all across the country, and since then have done a good deal of moving about — from tenement to tenement in West City. It is "no picnic" moving a lot, and "no picnic" going to school — though he does indeed, with no prompting, describe his teacher as a "good lady." He drew a picture of himself (Figure 16), and of himself twenty or thirty years from now (Figure 18). When he had done that he wanted to know whether I had asked any *teachers* to do drawings — of, say, a pupil like him. No, I hadn't. As a matter of fact I had never thought to do so. Why? Well, actually, for no reason — except that often grown-ups talk easily whereas children may prefer to keep quiet, but draw and sketch and paint their ideas and feelings. Maybe so, but still it would be a good idea to ask this one teacher to draw this one picture of this one person — him. I complied with his request, and his teacher complied with my request, but insisted that she keep the drawing she did. She said she was not very good at drawing, which is precisely what her young pupil said, too, as he did his work with the crayons — drawing a picture of his teacher (Figure 17).

East City

This northern seaport city has, on a grand scale (a scale proportionate to its size), almost all the problems that threaten or afflict other major cities. Twenty-five to thirty percent of its residents are nonwhite (Blacks, Puerto Ricans, Chinese, etc.), as are roughly sixty percent of its schoolchildren. In the past ten years it has lost almost fifteen percent of its white schoolchildren and gained a similar number of nonwhite children. During the same period the politics of these "minority" groups has changed. In the fifties they demanded integration with the white majority, while today they demand "community control" and virtual isolation from the white "minority" running the schools. This change mirrors the general change in black politics from hope for nonviolent association to the militant cry of "black power" and racial solidarity. The reasons behind these changes are especially apparent in this city, where ethnic differences sharply distinguish various racial, religious and national groups.

Several elementary schools, five to be exact, had to be visited and visited again in East City if any sense of its school system's educational difficulties was to be gained. Interviews with various kinds of officials and authorities, various kinds of superintendents and administrators, even with the city's board of education itself, revealed no absence of genuinely felt and openly expressed concern for the thousands of schoolchildren in East City who go under the name of "disadvantaged" or "deprived." The principals and assistant principals were even more strongly concerned than

the superintendents. In one school the principal expressed all his
emotions: "I can't tell you how I feel about the success of this
program for the disadvantaged. Every day I feel so many things,
and they're all contradictory. One minute I'll talk with a teacher
or a kid and hear about some progress being made, and I tell
myself that we're winning, slowly, yes, but winning. An hour
later I'll see or hear something that makes me think it's all a
waste of time and money. If I had to take a stand, though, I'd
put it this way: we're working against great odds, tremendous
odds, and we really don't have many weapons. We have a little
more money than before, but not nearly enough. The kids are
locked into this neighborhood and don't see much except what it
provides for them — and I don't have to tell you the details. This
is a ghetto, a real bad ghetto. There are plenty of ordinary,
decent, hardworking people who live here, but there's also plenty
else going on around here, and the kids can't help seeing what it
is: the drunks and addicts and prostitutes. And most of the
people here are very poor, and basically are strangers to the city.
They're here from the South or from Puerto Rico, you know.
There's no point going on and on about all that. Everyone knows
it; or at least *we* know it. The point is that we have to take what
we've got, here in this building, this neighborhood, and turn it
into a place of hope and sunlight for these kids, and I'm not sure
we can do it. A lot of the time when I stop and think about the
odds — well, frankly, I think we can't do it."

His colleague, the school's assistant principal, was similarly
worried. He gives all of his time to the "new programs," the
various efforts to "compensate" for this and that "disadvantage."
He enumerates those efforts: to make sure the children are well
fed at school, get adequate medical care there, receive the closest
possible attention from the best teachers available, who use every
new book, technique, approach, method, whatever — then he
stops and asks for questions and because they are not quickly
forthcoming, he asks one of his own: "Is it possible? That's what
I keep on asking myself, and honestly, I'm not sure it is. There's
too much we have to overcome — all the history of these people.
In a way, the more we think about it and the more we *do* — well,

the worse things get for us, the principals and teachers. Years ago we did what we could, and a few of these children worked themselves up, and the rest just didn't, period. Now we're trying to use the schools to further a social revolution. Mind you, I'm in favor of the whole idea, but I'm also a very practical man, and I've worked with these children and their parents for a long time — a lot longer than most people. I was here when no one cared about the ghetto — and I was doing what I could years ago before those college kids arrived full of slogans about how bad you are if you're from the middle class and trying to teach in a school like this. You've got to be black, they say, and then the children will sit up and take notice, and you've got to throw the whole school system into chaos. Well, you go and see some of our black teachers and tell me what you think! I'd like to know what the kids tell you, too. I mean, I'm interested in their views. I go around and try to talk with them, and I ask them if they have any suggestions — for subjects to teach, or books, or anything. But they look at you as if either you're crazy, and they feel sorry for you, or they're angry but not quite ready to assault you, or something like that. It's very discouraging. I cannot deny it. Sometimes I think it's going to take us at least another century, at the very least that — and even then we'll be having trouble with children like these. It goes from one generation to another — poverty and ignorance and segregation and all the rest. I'll admit there are times when I wish they were more like other immigrant groups, but you have to understand the difference, and I make sure we teach all that in this school. We're quite up to date in our curriculum. I feel that if we can just attract the *attention* of some of these children, then maybe they'll *want* to learn, and they will. But it's hard to do, very hard. We offer them the best books, the best materials in the country. We use audiovisual here, and the best social studies manuals you can get. We emphasize racial identity, the Afro-American heritage — the works. And *still* a lot of our kids are bored, that's the word, *bored.* And us? We're discouraged!"

One of the black teachers he told me to see turned out to be rather a surprise to hear talk: "I've been teaching here, right in this school, for eighteen years. I was born near here, born as poor as anyone ever was. I worked my way up. I went to school and *paid attention*. I didn't expect everyone to be doing everything for me. I didn't get a lot of government money to go to college. These kids, they'll speak back and behave like spoiled children, and then throw a fit if you try to discipline them. The white teachers who come here, they're kids, naïve kids. They let bedlam loose in the classroom and think that's progress. They mix politics with teaching. They're more interested in the sociology of the ghetto than in teaching these kids to mind their manners and sit up straight and obey the teacher and most of all *learn* — learn what they're told to learn. I'm sick and tired of all this damn pampering, all this 'psychological approach,' and all the radical politics that have come into the school system. And I'm tired of people saying you need to be black or white or blue or green to *teach,* to make kids learn what they've got to learn. There are plenty of Negro teachers around, and Negro parents around, who are like all other teachers and parents: all they want is to work and get along in the world and feel they're getting someplace. But no one pays any attention to them, particularly white people, I'm afraid. They give their newspaper space and television time to any Negro crackpot around, and they make our good Negro children and Negro teachers like myself seem either nonexistent or that most insulting of epithets, 'Uncle Toms.' Well, I'm me — and I'm not going to let anyone decide who I am because of my skin color or my job or how I teach or anything else. I believe most of these kids are going to get nowhere fast, but I believe they could get somewhere, somewhere very good, if they were made to obey their parents, and obey their teachers, and use their minds to study rather than become little lawbreakers when they're six or eight. One thing I do with each class — I make them sit quietly and I make them either learn or repeat the year through. I can only *try* to do that, because they overrule me in the office. They're afraid of the parents, is what they'll say. Well, I'm not. The parents are afraid of me. They don't even dare come see me. They know that I know the score!"

In that school, near his room, another teacher talked — and she is very much like others I saw in the various schools of East City: "Oh, I don't think being white is all that much of an obstacle. It's being middle-class that separates you from these kids. You have to remember how little these kids think of school, how meaningless it is to them. Middle-class children have learned something more important than any particular lesson *before* they come to school: they've learned that school *matters*. These children have learned just the opposite. That's the lesson of their history in America, and that's the lesson that's been transmitted to them over the years. We have to teach them *hope*. We have to teach them that school *enables* — work, comfort, a degree of prosperity, a better life, all that. We have to teach them to harness their imagination and cleverness and resourcefulness and all the rest to schoolwork. It's no easy job, and frankly, I'm not sure we can do it *here*, in buildings like this, practically right next door to those bars and the addicts and hustlers and all the rest, and worst of all the tenements that surround us like a terrible wall. That's how I feel about it. I just get discouraged a lot, I guess."

In another school a very young and energetic black teacher was very far from discouraged during most of our talk: "The kids swear, use bad language. But a lot of it is very forceful and emphatic speech, and I try to show them that. I accept their statements rather than be shocked by them, and I go on from there. They've got a lot of humor in them, these kids, and they're full of songs and shrewd stories. With a camera in their hands, or crayons, they say a million things — nonverbal of course. It's *us* who are hung-up on words. I think we've got to have a sequence that fits with their history, their experience. In the South black men learned for generations to keep their mouths shut and look carefully and sing and shout their hearts out — in churches or in the fields. We've got to keep that in mind when we teach these kids. A lot of them, they're only one generation out of Mississippi and Alabama and South Carolina.

"Our programs here aren't so bad. They're not all they could be, but we're trying. The worst of it is that they're already being diluted before they even get going. I admit if we could mix up the classrooms a little, so some of these kids could imitate other

kids and learn from them and make friends with them, it might
be good. But that's impossible. Anyway, we've got to help these
kids realize what's *inside them* — how for all their poor grammar
and swearwords, they're full of strong purposes and, I believe it,
ideals. They *want* things. They haven't surrendered, though I
admit this school may not be the place to persuade them that's
true. Some of them are very angry kids, but you know, they'll be
angry, and at the same time they won't let you go — the teacher.
A lot of them could stimulate us, yes, the teachers, if we'd let
them. They could make us more flexible and original and enthusiastic. The kids seem to be daring us to make them learn, and
we could take up the dare, if we had the guts."

His principal agreed with all he said. Both asserted a degree of
success for all the special programs in their ghetto school:
vandalism went down, a sure indication that both within and
without the school a certain respect for the teachers' efforts had
emerged; attendance went up; a number of children came to
school better dressed; the children seemed less suspicious; and
some of their parents became more involved in the school's activities, and for that matter, so did many *teachers,* who for the first
time felt at least *something* was possible. "But it's only a beginning," the principal insisted, "and I'm afraid that for the school
department as a whole, it's an end. They never stick with these
programs for very long. They start them in a few schools, then
dilute them and spread them thin over the whole city — no
money is the reason — and then we're called failures, which in
the end I'm afraid we do become! It's very sad to think about,
but you can't help thinking about it. Even our best and most
enthusiastic teachers do. They'll come up to me and say: we're
getting someplace, not very far, but someplace, but I'm sure it
won't last long, not in this system. It just can't. What do you say
then? I try to point out a kid here and there that's making
progress and get them off the larger picture and turned toward
the individual child!"

One such child, whose work has definitely improved as a result
of the school's various programs, had this to say about school,
himself and his future: "I've liked it better here. They've been at

you to do more than sit around and wait for the bell to get out of
school. So, I figure if they're all that eager to help you out, then
I'll go half the way with them — that's what my momma said you
should do. She said if they go and offer something, you go and
take it. I'm still waiting to get out of here, though, and spend my
time better. You don't need school to be a big-time baseball
player, or maybe play basketball. I know a guy, he makes a
million dollars a year, they say, and no one knows where he's got
it put away, and the government can't get a penny from him. He
pays a lot to the cops, and *they're* working for *him*. Maybe I
could try to work for him later, if I can't make it in baseball. I
don't think the books they give you will do much for you. My
uncle, he tells us you can't eat words. The teacher heard us
talking like that the other day, and she said true, but you can get a
good job and money if you know how to read and write good.
But I'm not convinced. I asked her where, and she said downtown. That's a long way off, my uncle said, and they're sure as
Hell not going to let us all out of here, he said — only a few at a
time, to make everyone happy."

He gladly drew a picture of his school (Figure 19) and a
picture of how he would look "later on" (Figure 20). (He had
been asked whether he wanted to picture himself a few years
older, doing some of the things he had talked about.) A friend of
his also drew a picture of their school (Figure 21), and also drew
a picture of himself, "maybe ten years older than I am now,
which means, I guess, eighteen or so, I think" (Figure 22).

Central City

Civil rights groups pressed long and hard to obtain improve-
ments for the black poor in this city, one of the largest in the
Middle West, which contains a vast and populous black ghetto,
one of the largest in the country. They asked for better housing,
for better streets, for playgrounds and parks, and for better
schools. They also asked for school desegregation and eventual
integration, which very few of the city's schools have.
A third of the city is black, as are over half the schoolchildren,

but only three blacks, and until recently only two, represent them on the eleven-man school board. Eighty percent of the schools are "segregated," with a student body at least ninety percent black or white. Even the twenty percent labeled "integrated" are not quite that: many of them are simply changing from white to black, as blacks move into a neighborhood and whites leave it for the suburbs, ending such "integration" quickly. Most black teachers and administrators end up in nearly all-black schools, segregated like their pupils. Of seventeen black principals, sixteen run such schools. These schools are more often overcrowded, understaffed, and ill-equipped than white schools; for instance, they average thirty-four pupils per class compared to twenty-nine in white schools.

"We are trying everything, everything we can find, everything we can come across, to help these kids." Again and again that theme made its appearance in conversations held with deputy superintendents and assistant deputy superintendents — and in fact a whole array of administrators and educators and social scientists, all working on Central City's educational problems. What is "everything"? After visits to several elementary schools "everything" comes to a strong emphasis on relatively small classes (wherever possible) and "intensive" teaching through the use of "new and imaginative curricula." In one school the principal talked and talked and talked: "I've got a lot to say, because we're trying to do a lot; though how much we *are* doing, I'll admit, is debatable. We've brought in more teachers, and we've been provided with special services for difficult children. We have a speech therapist, a psychologist, and the doctor spends twice as much time with us as before. We've been holding a series of conferences for our teachers, and we've really tried to get the community involved. I was told a few weeks ago by a young man — he went to school here — that if ever a riot broke out, our building would be spared. I'm not so sure. We've got some of the best reading materials in the country here for our children. What we're attempting to do is saturate the children, saturate them with pictures, books, movies, everything audiovisual we can get our hands on. They've been deprived of that, and need it, a lot of it, if they're going to make it in our society.

"And we also hope to get the parents more motivated, because without their help, it's hard to turn these kids on. They come in here sometimes looking as though they'd been working all day in a factory or someplace. They don't have good clothes, many of them don't. More important, they haven't had breakfast, we've discovered, or at least a good number of them haven't, or if they have, the breakfast can't be considered adequate. I really believe that one thing we should do that might help our children a tremendous amount would be provide nutritional education for their mothers. I know we're a school, not a service center for the neighborhood, but when a child hasn't had anything nourishing for breakfast, and maybe something not very healthy the night before for supper, he's not going to be alert and responsive during the day. Sometimes I go through the school and see those lovely pictures we have posted on the walls — of glasses full of milk and big oranges and pineapples and grapefruit and eggs and bacon and children brushing their teeth — and I feel we either have to make those pictures more a part of the lives of our children here, or take them down from our walls and put up something that really speaks to these kids and doesn't make them laugh or get angry. Yes, they do get angry and outspoken, too — more so than an outsider can believe possible, considering that they're seven or eight, that age. Every time we try to do something for them they get fresh and nasty instead of grateful. It's hard for some of my teachers to take. The parents are like that, too — in fact it's the parents who say things, and the children of course, repeat what they hear at home.

"The other day one child, he must be nine, or maybe ten, told one of our best teachers that we were all wasting our time and trying to patch up a broken-down mess when a whole new thing has to be built — words to that effect. I asked the teacher what she said in reply. She hesitated for a while, I gather — she did with *me*, too — and then told the kid he was right, basically. You know what the kid said? He said that he knew she'd say that, because she was their favorite teacher, and that was why, be-

cause she saw things the same way they do. And that kid is slow
in reading! The same teacher told me a few weeks ago that the
whole business of learning and teaching in this school has to be
reexamined. 'Some of the brightest kids, clever as can be, just
don't *want* to learn. They mock learning.' That's what she said,
and she's right. Not all of our kids are like that, but enough to
make us tear our hair out. And get this: Negro teachers, black
teachers, have no more success with them than we do, no more.
It's not only a race issue; it's a class issue. Many of these children
have learned from their parents that there's no hope, that if you
have hope — hope about getting ahead in the system is what I
mean — you're a fool, a real jerk. The kids come here and live
out that conviction — that school is a jail, a place of temporary
confinement, a place where the white world rubs the black boy's
history into his face.

"If you question some of our kids closely you'll hear that, hear
their embarrassment at the little heritage they have, at the
poverty of their homes — *cultural* poverty as well as the economic kind — and their sense of futility. Oh, they're smart about
their world, but to them ours is way off, and meaningless. And
under the present circumstances — well, there isn't much I can
do to persuade those kids that they're wrong. They know how a
lot of people in this city feel about them. They know they're not
wanted. They know who runs things here — and they also know
what some of our leading *school* officials have said in the past. I'll
be honest with you: it's only because we've had a change up top
that I can talk as openly with you as this. What happens at the
top gets right to the bottom. We feel every vibration. But there's
only so much that even the best school system in the world can
accomplish when it has to contend with the things that go on in
this neighborhood, and the things that each of these children live
with all the time — before school and after school and on weekends and vacations, and for their entire lives, I'm afraid."

The children did indeed respond to the "close" kind of questioning he urged. They spoke more directly, openly, and
brusquely than others did in many other cities visited in the
course of this study. They seemed almost waiting for a half-

interested ear: "The teachers, they want you to read, but I've got a lot to tell you, mister, and you won't be able to read what it is, because no one writes books that talk the way we do, I'm sure of that. The teachers, they keep on telling you tomorrow it'll get better, and then the day after it'll get even better than better, but they're not even kidding themselves — we know that. You can see them driving in here from where they live, and they have that look on their faces when they park their cars, and they lock their doors and check them, and then they come into the building, and you can tell they're worried. My dad, he says he's worried, just like them. He can't get a job, and someone came and stole our TV. The lock on the door didn't mean anything. They just picked it as easy as that. They have to lock the school doors here. I don't blame them, but then they drive away and we're here all the time, and that's the difference."

"Me?" said another boy. "Me, I'm going to get myself some kind of a deal just as soon as I can. I don't want to be like my dad. You know what his trouble is? He thinks if you sit back and try to be a good guy, that it'll pay off one day. That's what's wrong with him. The other day he said I should be a doctor, like the guy who gave him medicine in the hospital, and he was black. That's right, there are some, like the teacher says, doctors and lawyers and all that. But that's just a few, and around here there aren't many who can go and become someone like that. You have to have someone backing you, yes sir. The teacher says if you just read and like that, you'll get ahead, but my dad says you can read every book there is, and they'll still step on you and keep you out if they can. I'd like to read, though, I would. I'd like to read faster than anyone, and I hope someday I will. And I hope I can have a car, and someone could drive it for me, and I'd be sitting back there and reading! Boy, would that be a deal! A big Cadillac, and me in the back seat with a book!"

His friend is much less dramatic: "The way I see it, there's not much you can do in school but try to get through it, and when you do, hope for the best so far as a job goes. I'd like to have one, a job, when I get through with school, but I'm not sure I'll be able to — to get one. So, I'm just trying to learn all I can here, yes sir, I am. The teacher, once she said she knew how we felt, that it was hard for us people. And we all said — we all said amen to that. Yes, we did. Then she said it was too bad the school and the buildings around here weren't as nice as in other places, and we said amen to that, too." A little later he drew "the school and the buildings around here" (Figure 24). Some buildings were crossed out with a brown X, and the sky was brown rather than blue.

South City

According to a special census taken in March of 1967, this upper southern river-port city has 536,585 residents; forty percent are black. Like many large northern cities (Chicago, New York, Philadelphia, Detroit, for example), the majority of its public-school children are black. In 1969, fifty-two percent of one hundred twenty-five thousand students were black. Although the city calls its schools "integrated," most students are isolated in their own neighborhoods and in their own neighborhood schools. School officials have gone so far as to approve a "free transfer" program, but no one has made any genuine effort to balance enrollments.

The city's economy similarly isolates and confines black citizens. As one report maintains: "They [blacks] hold only eight percent of the government's customary white jobs. Such jobs include everything except sewer, sanitation, and street maintenance, in which blacks hold seventy-four percent of the jobs." Due to such good workers, the city has four times received national acclaim as "America's cleanest city" and has also been nationally acknowledged her quietest. Only recently have street violence and disorder occurred, surprising local citizens.

"We are a progressive southern city in some respects, almost northern in ways, but we're certainly not Atlanta, and our progress hasn't really reached into the schools, I'm sorry to say." So spoke a high official of South City's school system. Born further south than South City, born to fiercely segregationist parents, he speaks almost too quickly of his origins, his past, his recent struggles. He assures his listener that they are on his mind, those struggles, and so he *has* to talk about them: "It was hard for me in another way, because I'm moving a lot faster than some others here in South City's schools. I've seen too much evidence to let me sit back and say that everything is just fine here, and we're moving along 'at a good pace' — that's what they keep on saying, some of my colleagues. What do they mean, I'll ask them, and they say something like, 'The nigras are slow to move along, and we can't hurry them or we'll lose them.' Imagine that, from school officials with advanced degrees in education! Of course, I'm not so sure a lot of people up North don't think that way, too. They may say what's on their mind a little more carefully, but the basic ideas are often the same. I've been to a few of those 'desegregation institutes' up there, and I could tell. Here, we've just failed to adjust our language. We call the nigras slow and a problem, and up there they say they're 'disadvantaged' and 'disruptive.' Now I ask you, what's the difference, really?

"A while back at a meeting, I said we can't settle for any of that, our words and the Yankee ones. I asked for a real, strong program for just one of our Negro schools, just to see what could be done if we put everything we have into the effort. Well, they voted for the effort, but not the *real* effort. I mean, they set up a 'name program,' but they said they couldn't afford this, and they couldn't afford that, and they'd have to see about this later, and that later, and by the time the whole thing was over I decided we had a lot of fancy frosting, but no real cake.

"But we tried, and we got every possible mileage out of that experiment. We have a wonderful principal over in that school, and we put her in charge, and a few of us went to a few private citizens, well-to-do people who are liberal and have an interest in the school, and we got some more money from them. And we did everything we could — to give the teachers the idea that this was a really important first step for South City."

The principal he mentioned is indeed wonderful — full of intelligence, determination and a kind of guile: "You have to be tricky with those people downtown — if you're a black principal of a black school, that's the only way. I go there and talk with them as if they owned a plantation, not a school system. I ask and beg and plead and threaten only indirectly. And they think and think — and try to figure out how little they can spend to get a little peace and quiet from us."

She admits that she is angry. For several years she has been trying one "remedial" program after another, much of it enabled by federal funds of one sort or another. Each time there was hope and anticipation and enthusiasm, followed by progressive disenchantment: "It's not that we haven't accomplished something. We have. But it's a beginning, and we never really do half of what we ourselves know could be done. It's not only money, either — though that's a lot of the problem. It's the whole attitude of the system to us — and I guess we feel it ourselves. I mean, I *know* we feel it. I sit in those meetings with my staff and I hear my teachers, *Negro teachers*, talking like someone in the Klan. Oh, it's not that bad, but almost that bad. You see, our assumptions of what is possible — for us as teachers and for the children we teach — are constantly being shaped by the assumptions they have downtown, in the offices of the board of education. Look at this building. Look at what they give us. Look at our salaries and the size of our classes and — well, just look at the books, the old books and the books full of white America, with a smiling black face here and there in one or two of them. On paper they could show you that they've given us more these past few years than ever before, and that's true. But you can't start at zero and go up to one or two, then congratulate yourself; not when white kids are up to ten on the scale — getting ten of the things they need at school, let alone at home. The other day a girl in the fifth grade — the teachers call her sassy — came up to me and said we were kidding ourselves with all these new programs. Well, there are three of them, and she's been in all three. She reads better, and she has a little more hope about the future, but she's also bitter. She feels she's being 'used.' It's not rational, but that's how she feels. She's right in a way, too — because like a lot of children here, she could be doing much, much better than she is. The improvement she's made is a mere beginning, and she knows it, and we know it, and we feel discouraged about — I guess about what we know but can't seem to change yet."

The girl she mentioned is indeed outspoken, if not sassy. She thinks school is a "farce," even though she does her work rather well. She openly criticizes her teachers, her school, her city. Nor does she see much point in moving to another city. She is "plain unhappy" about some things, "plain angry" about others. She is also, curiously enough, rather resigned — for all her candor and outrage, prematurely resigned. She draws a picture of her school (Figure 25), then says it's not *worth* being drawn. She draws a picture of the kind of home she would like to have, say, twenty years from now (Figure 26), and she laughs at what she herself has drawn — and lets the observer know that "it's a joke." In an afterthought she qualifies herself: "It's not a joke, it's maybe something I'd like to have. But it's a joke, too. You can't have that, not us."

How does she like school? What would she like to do when she grows up? Have there been any changes in this school recently, and if so, what have they been and how have they worked? She listens to questions like that, so carefully and nervously contrived and posed, and then smiles faintly and knocks them down impatiently as though they were as much "jokes" as the home she drew: "They're trying here, a little. The teacher, she said we shouldn't just get promoted anymore, regardless. We should work and get to know the books and read real, real fast. So, you learn to read real, real fast, and you fall asleep reading what you read. That's how I see it. They come and give you those books, and you want to laugh. You can tell even before you read them that they're just a big joke. I told my momma that it was all funny, and she said I should shut my mouth and do what the teacher says. And the teacher, one minute she tells us we should say what comes into our minds and try to have imaginations, and the next time she's telling us to shut up and obey her and stop being pests. Once she came up and grabbed me, like they used to, and then she said she was sorry, and why didn't I learn as fast as they want us to? I asked her, 'Learn what?' She said, 'Learn what's in the books.' I said the books were a joke, and she must know it, being as smart as she is. She said I should mind my mouth, or I'll get in trouble. I told her we were all in trouble, anyway, and there wasn't a thing we could do about *that*.

"Then she said I was talking out of the back of my neck, and I'd be sent home for good if I didn't watch out, and just because I was quick with my thinking was no excuse. And why don't I apply myself to the reading and writing and arithmetic, and not be fresh. And she said I was *cynical,* and did I know what that means? Well, I told her that she wasn't any more sure of what use the school was than I was, and I said as long as she was asking me, then I'd tell her. And I did. So, I told her my momma just wanted us to get the best education we could, but she hoped we'd soon be old enough to work and help her pay the bills. And right now we're in bad trouble, and I don't believe going to school will help out. Last week I couldn't come because my shoes needed to be fixed, and we couldn't get it done until yesterday. Yes sir, the check came then. Yes sir, from the city. My momma says we're lucky to be in the city. She says maybe we should go farther north. Maybe the farther north you go, the better. But I don't think she's sure."

CONCLUSIONS

The preceding observations, interviews, and drawings or paintings were not randomly selected, but rather amount to, I believe, a representative selection of what seemed to be happening in each school system studied. I have also tried to emphasize the diversity and ambiguity of all the situations I studied. In the schools that seemed "best" — full of hope and achievement, as seen and felt and put into words by both teachers and children — there were despairing teachers to be heard, and children who viewed themselves and their futures with a good deal of doubt. In the "worst" schools — where many teachers wondered what the point of *any* school was for their schoolchildren, and where the children in turn more than shared such a viewpoint — some really luminous and inspiring moments were to be had: this teacher beautifully drawing children out and prompting them to striking levels of performance, and that child forging ahead against what seemed like an impossible fog of instructional apathy, resignation, boredom, condescension and on more than one occasion downright malevolence.

My "conclusions" are not sweeping, categorical or easily translated into one or another "program." I can only say some things that are distinctly modest. No school, no teacher, no pupil exists in a social and political vacuum. What a school system does (or does not do) a teacher and a child can recognize — and either defy or acquiesce in. Children (and teachers) vary in "background," in character and purposefulness and temperament, but so do school systems — which are, of course, complicated social institutions that have strong links to the political arena, to the marketplace, to the religious, philosophical, and ideological forces at work in a community. I have, I hope, made clear the extent to which a school responds to nonacademic and noncurricular forces and influences. We have also seen the extent to which children learn in school a lot of things that teachers don't necessarily know they are teaching, even as teachers also learn a lot of things not easily spoken or formulated or even admitted to consciousness about the assumptions held by a particular school system, indeed a city or a nation. Finally, what about those vague, hard to measure and hard to say things that live perhaps in a man's heart rather than his brain? In three cities I heard children make reference to the "heart," not because they are aspiring poets or self-conscious or prissy or cloudy thinkers or, in today's language, "put-on artists." One child said: "Are you trying to figure out if school makes any difference to us? Because if that's it I can tell you, man, here in my heart, it doesn't. You learn a few tricks with the numbers, and how to speak like someone different, but you forget it pretty fast when you leave the building, and I figure everyone has to put in his time one place or the other until he gets free, but my friend, he says most people get caught and they're never themselves, just parrots for the teacher or someone else. That's bad, real bad, but you don't hear them telling you that, here in this school. They just want you to say your words like the next guy."

What can a school system do to inspire more confidence, more hope, more passionate conviction in its students *and* its teachers? We *expect* because we have *learned* — learned that there is something to expect, learned that there are gifts to be had in this world, that something once was given and that, accordingly, more just might (on the basis of experience) be forthcoming. Put differently, we expect satisfaction because we have once been satisfied; we want and anticipate because we once have been appeased, offered a nod, a touch, a smile, received some immediate and tangible nourishment. There is a disguised and symbolic and "higher" kind of nourishment that some of us also take for granted, but we never remind ourselves for what reasons: why we find all that memory work and compliance and industry so pleasant, so stimulating, rewarding, and advantageous — *there's* the word. So, if expectation arises from the past, and if the future is tied up in the past, and if the present, in a way, is the past being lived out, what hope can we expect to arise in certain children? I believe that many of the children quoted here, and indeed the teachers too, have supplied us with some answers to those kinds of questions. They have told us that because they seem slow, indeed act slow and difficult and silent and hard to teach, because they are thoroughly disadvantaged and deprived and retarded and handicapped (and God knows what else they will yet be called) does not mean that at the same time they are not looking around, even looking ahead — yes, *expecting*. What do they expect? What might they expect? What do their teachers expect for them? What might they expect, were "things" different? *What* "things"? The answers are more or less implied in the foregoing personal statements and in the pictures, with their accompanying comment; but (so we are told) the blunt truths, the honey and acid that tincture the heart's blood, must all be turned into "action programs" and "agendas" and all the rest.

We all want to know how we can interest the indifferent, turn them on to our ways, lest they become not only further removed and more angry than they already are, but instruments of our undoing, not to mention theirs. (The undoing of *their* ancestors, of course, is *our* history.) Here are the clues one gathers from these thirteen cities: children become deaf, dumb and blind if a school lacks hope — the insubstantial hope that has to do with the mind's ways and the heart's, the incarnate hope that can become realized in particular buildings and corridors and neighborhoods and books, but most important, in particular persons, both young and older. A cell or two of a new philosophy cannot be grafted onto an old philosophy with its very own set of assumptions. To take refuge in a child's remarks — a very studious child, it should be added: "Here it's one thing, and pretty soon the bell rings, and it's time to leave, and you can see the teachers smiling for the first time." Apparently both children and teachers get the point — they comprehend futility even as they work against it.

In the words of one principal: "What are we to do?" He followed that question with another one, and then his own answer, which was quite a fine one: "What are we to do if we know that our teachers practically tell kids how much can be, or even ought to be taught them, and if our kids get the message fast and go on strike? I suppose we can bring the whole thing out into the open; we can show our teachers what they're doing, and we can signal a lot to the kids — that we know how we've been doing things, but honestly, honestly, we're setting new sights for ourselves, first for ourselves, and then we're asking the same from them, the kids and their families both, I guess."

"What do *you* suggest?" I was asked again and again, tactfully and eagerly and angrily and sullenly. Discussions? Courses? Yet more "institutes" and yet more readings to go through? Billions more poured into the schools? Changes in our schools of education, in our school boards, in the places we send children to get what we call an "education" — and also changes in what we choose to call an "education"? More changes in which children go to school with which children? Changes in the way schools are connected to the neighborhoods around them, to the parents who live near the schools? Changes in our society, in the way bureaucrats handle human beings, in the way man the doer and maker becomes so sadly man the cog, the acted-upon, the done-in, the made-and-packaged, the inert, the dead — hence dull, hence unquestioning, hence all too obliging. Or, alternatively, hence fretful and spiteful and agitated and insolent and violent and sometimes murderous or self-murdering? We have heard a lot from the social critics of our schools, and a lot from those who criticize the critics, but not so much from those who are in fact caught in-between. Often those latter people are teachers. Sometimes they are children — who want to go on, want to "get ahead," want to "make it," but also feel annoyed or disgusted or put-upon or just plain bored.

These feelings somehow will have to be reckoned with if thousands of American children are to stay in school, to get anything worthwhile out of the experience, and to go on to any kind of fulfillment as persons, as workers, as citizens.[14] Interestingly enough, the very presence of those feelings, their very articulation, proves that there is a lot for us all to fall back upon: the anger and dissatisfaction and idealism of teachers — even their apathy, which in a very real sense can mask a kind of moral outrage that has been surrendered; and so far as our "victimized" and "deprived" children go, *their* apathy, their guile, their wit, their shrewd ability to adjust themselves to their world, and to make sensible, realistic appraisals can only impress those of us who, though much better off, are similarly loyal to the virtues of common sense and realism. This kind of study can perhaps only be successful if it prompts questions rather than answers. Let us conclude that there is a little value to hearing others complain, boast, put their sentiments and notions and hunches and rages to word or (through crayon) to paper. So, here are some recommendations from some children and some teachers and principals, recommendations I was lucky enough, privileged enough, to have offered me.

"I'd get the teachers and the kids in one big room, and I'd have them let each other know what's on their mind. They should level, but they won't. But after a while, maybe they would."

"I'd bring the home into the school more, and the school into the home. Why do we make such clear distinctions between the two? In the suburbs, actually, we don't. But here, we sure do. It's not necessary, though."

"I'd pour everything we have into a few schools, and prove what we *could* do. Then maybe we could shame the public into doing more for the other schools. I'm not sure, though, it would work. The public might just say: all very good, but we don't want to raise the money, or divert our money from where it's going now."

"I'd teach our teachers how their expectations affect the learning of their children. And I'd try to get our children to expect more for themselves — by showing them what others have done against great odds, and in the end, if we could manage it, by exposing them to other kids, other neighborhoods and other schools, schools where there are kids who *do* expect more from life, from this society. But don't ask me how you could do that — with this ghetto and all its kids and its schools!"

"I'd tell those teachers to cut it out, kidding themselves and trying to kid us. If they admitted what it's like, I mean the way they treat you, the cops, or the people you work for, if you can get yourself a job, then they'd be on our side, and we'd like it better here and we'd listen to what they say. Most of the time it's in one ear and out the other, and that's how it should be. That's what my older brother says, and he's right."

"We need more of what we have, more money to keep what we have and build upon it, and an *absolute guarantee* that what we have won't be taken away in a year or two. No compensatory education scheme has ever really worked in the ghetto, even this scheme, because no American school board has ever really had the resources and the will to try it and keep trying it, and no school board has really *committed* itself to the idea and communicated that commitment all the way to the teachers and the kids *and* their parents."

"We need, oh, that tired old word, *integration*. We need our children, the children we teach, to see how others have come to think about school, to see how others live and think and study and — well, everything. How can these kids believe there's any chance in this world when they live all the time here, here in this prison? It's all right for me to come here, teach, and leave — though even *I* have lost a lot of my faith in what's possible, for me as a teacher as well as them as kids. When you lose your *own* sense of confidence, your own belief in what you're doing and what it means, how can you expect the kids to do *anything?*"

"The way I see it, if Whitey really wanted us to make the scene, he'd clue us in that he did, and brother, we'd get the message. Right now, I think he's kidding us, Whitey is. And he's even kidding himself, that's what my sisters say."

"I've been teaching for twenty-five years, and I believe that every child I've taught *could* have done more, could have done better, and I believe that I as a teacher could have, too. But both the teacher and the child need to think there's a *reason*, a reason to do more or better. In the suburban schools those kids have that reason — whether you and I think it's a valid one is another point, I admit. In this kind of school they also have a reason — *not* to do more or better."

"They tell us be like this one or that one, like Henry Ford or Booker T. Washington, and like that. Then they say if the others could get to own their own homes and stores and be doctors and lawyers, then so can you. But my dad, he went to college and he works in the post office. He couldn't get a job a while back, not the kind he wanted. That's all changing now, they say. But are we supposed to be turned on and off like a light? They're taking more black people to work in places, but my dad says you can't make twenty million people think they've got to Heaven because suddenly a thousand get to the top of the skyscrapers, and even ten thousand."

"The children come here from trouble, trouble, trouble. Their parents were born to trouble in the South and up here they live in trouble all day long. Then we're supposed to, we teachers, make the trouble evaporate in their minds, just like that — with a few books and a lecture on the American Dream."

"I figure someday I'll get there, way up, with a lot of money and a job everyone else wishes he had. And I'd feel great. And I'd want to work hard, and I'd tell everyone, 'Look at me, what's happened to me.' But I'm not sure it'll happen, and when I told the teacher, she said she wasn't sure, but we had to keep hoping, and move along inch by inch. I'm no sap, so I'm going to sit, and I'll stay alive somehow, I hope."

PART FOUR

THE WAY IT IS

IX

THE WAY IT IS IN THE ALLEYS,
THE WAY IT IS ON THE PORCHES

A THOUSAND MILES and only the Lord knows how many "social" and "cultural" differences and how much psychological distance separates the two Peters from one another — even though they share certain kinds of experiences. Yet, they both occasionally talk about how things are going in their lives, and I have heard from both of them those words "like it is." One Peter is black; one Peter is white. One Peter's family came to the Northeast by way of Alabama; one Peter came to the north central region of this country by way of some mountains that straddle the East and Midwest. (Even now those Appalachian Mountains are a sort of frontier, defining two sections of a great nation.) One Peter's family was, long ago, slaves; more recently they have lived under the constant domination of sheriffs and plantation owners. The other Peter's parents boast of their family's long-standing independence; no one, absolutely no one, could ever tell them to do or believe anything they didn't want to do or believe. Today the Peters live in buildings that are quite similar, and both Peters hear their mothers make mention of another kind of life, a kind that is gone and yet seems curiously attractive, even as it was "awful, awful, awful." Both boys know poverty, have felt the state of exile and the consequences of upheaval.

The boys were both nine years old when I sat down to write about them. They were both in elementary school, in the fourth grade. Neither Peter was (or is) a particularly good student, which is an understatement; in fact, each boy has never liked school, which is another understatement. I leave it to them, a little later on, to put their feelings into words. Yet, for all their troubles at school, and for all the critical things I have heard about the boys from their teachers, the fact is that each boy, each *young man,* has his own kind of intelligence, guile, sharpness of vision, breadth of understanding. And each Peter has a rhythm to his mind and body that is partially his and his alone, but also partially of a kind he shares with other children like him.

I cannot, I have no wish to, define words like *rhythm* or *grace* or *style* as they apply to something called "the personality" of a child, any more than I quite know how I would define what runs through me when I come to feel that a child's *spirit* is hurting, is faltering, is in jeopardy. At times I have found myself wishing that the two Peters were patients, or research subjects or, yes, characters in a short story or a novel I was trying to construct. Then maybe I could capture the spirit of the boys and feel satisfied that I know just what to say and just how to say it.

All one like me need do to lose his smug sense of professional competence is keep on going back on those home visits. Both Peters have told me in dozens of ways, direct and indirect, to watch myself and not be so sure about what I decide to conclude and assert and insist upon as "right" or "the answer." Their message is, I suppose, every individual's eventual message to the observer, be he professionally sanctioned or driven by those "inner" and "private" rages or compulsions or desires that prompt writers and artists to seize from the world events they find significant and give them all the coherence or illumination they as particular human beings can summon. I refer to the message implicit in this remark the black boy named Peter made to me, perhaps because he sensed that I had been thinking days before *how much* I knew about him and others like him, now that I had spent four or five years in their neighborhood and knew my way around: "You're learning, man. You're learning. But I haven't started telling you about a lot of things, a whole lot of things. Then, when I do, there'll still be something else that I've got to bend your ear about."

I suppose as a psychiatrist I have always known that the mind's preoccupations are as endless as time itself; furthermore, given half a will on the part of a given speaker and a corresponding degree of responsiveness on the part of a genuine listener, what Peter called "a whole lot of things" can come to light, only to be followed by a whole lot more, and then yet more, until either or both parties say *enough* — with reluctance or relief or out of weariness or boredom. It is necessary at times to mull over "things" at very great length and to make statements and formulations and "diagnoses" which have about them a flat, unequivocal, authoritative spell that no one dares dispute, not the patient, let alone a somewhat doubtful colleague. It is necessary, I mean, the way death and taxes seem necessary; it happens and happens and happens — so one cannot envision a profession, never mind *a kind of existence,* in which each person is seen and responded to as *himself* or *herself* and, further, discussed in words that he or she evokes, as a very particular and special and individual human being. The other Peter, the white boy, has said it in his own special way: "I heard the teacher talking about all of us from Appalachia. I never heard us called 'from Appalachia' until I came up here from Letcher County. First they told me I was from Kentucky, and I tried to tell them no, I was from Letcher County. Then they told me I was 'from Appalachia' and I tried to tell them no, I was from Hot Spot, that's where we lived in Letcher County. But they never do listen to you."

When he spoke he didn't emphasize that last word, that *you;* he had obviously almost given up trying to emphasize such a word. He had learned that the more he will pull himself away from Appalachia and Kentucky and Letcher County and Hot Spot and realms more familiar to *him,* the more his teacher (and all of us) will start tugging him away toward the ever larger generalizations those geographical names symbolize. Peter's mother, when she heard what he had told me, turned to him: "Well, even if they don't listen to you, don't you stop listening to yourself. No matter what anyone says about you, there's more to tell than they'll ever know. My daddy would say that to me when I was a girl. If I got a compliment or if someone said something bad, he'd always tell me I had the last laugh on them, because I could always think to myself and come up with something that would contradict them plenty."

And with that warning, I will try to say something relatively brief, but not so general, about alleys and porches and two boys and two mothers — testifying to what I have witnessed of how it goes, how it is for them.

"In the alley it's mostly dark, even if the sun is out. But if you look around, you can find things. I know how to get into every building, except that it's like night once you're inside them, because they don't have lights. So, I stay here. You're better off. It's no good on the street. You can get hurt all the time, one way or the other. And in buildings, like I told you, it's bad in them, too. But here it's OK. You can find your own corner, and if someone tries to move in you fight him off. We meet here all the time and figure out what we'll do next. It might be a game, or some pool, or a Coke or something. You need to have a place to start out from, and that's the way it is, like it is, in the alley; you can always know your buddy will be there, provided it's the right time. So you go there, and you're on your way, man."

Like all children of nine, Peter is always on his way — to a person, a place, a "thing" he wants to do. "There's this here thing we thought we'd try tomorrow," he'll say, and eventually I'll find out that he means there's to be a race. He and his friends will compete with another gang to see who can wash a car faster and better. The cars belong to four youths who make their money taking bets and selling liquor that I don't believe was ever purchased and pushing a few of those pills that "go classy with beer." I am not completely sure, but I think they also have something to do with other drugs, and again, I can't quite be sure what their connection is with a "residence" I've seen not too far from the alley Peter describes so possessively. The women come and go — from that residence and along the street Peter's alley leaves.

Peter lives in the heart of what we in contemporary America have chosen to call an "urban ghetto." The area was a slum before it became a ghetto, and there still are some very poor white people on its edges and increasing numbers of Puerto Ricans in several of its blocks. Peter was not born in the ghetto. His family are Americans and have been here "since way back before anyone can remember." That is the way Peter's mother talks about Alabama, about the length of time she and her ancestors have lived there. She and Peter's father came North "for freedom." Americans, they moved on when the going got "real bad," and Americans, they expected something better in the new place. They left Alabama on impulse and found Peter's alley by accident.

Peter's mother believes that "something will work out one of these days." She believes that "you have to keep on going, and things can get better, but don't ask me how." She believes that "God wants us to have a bad spell here, and so maybe it'll get better the next time — you know, in Heaven, and I hope that's where we'll be going." Peter's mother, in other words, is a pragmatist, an optimist, and a Christian. Above all she is American: "Yes, I hear them talk about Africa, but it doesn't mean anything to us. All I know is Alabama and now it's in Massachusetts that we are. It was a long trip coming up here, and sometimes I wish we were back there, and sometimes I'd just as soon be here, for all that's no good about it. But I'm not going to take any more trips, no sir. And like Peter said, this is the only country we've got. If you come from a country, you come from it, and we're from it, I'd say, and there isn't much we can do but try to live as best we can. I mean, live here."

What is "life" like for her over there, where she lives, in the neighborhood she refers to as "here"? Her answer provides only the beginning of a reply: "Well, we do OK, I guess. Peter here, he has it better than I did, or his daddy. I can say that. I tell myself that a lot. He can turn on the faucet over there, and a lot of the time, he just gets the water, right away. And when I tell him what it was like for us to go fetch that water — we'd walk three miles, yes sir, and we'd be lucky it wasn't ten — well, Peter, it doesn't register on him. He thinks I'm trying to fool him, and the more serious I get, the more he laughs, so I've stopped.

"Of course, it's not all so good, I have to admit. We're still where we were, so far as knowing where your next meal is coming from. When I go to bed at night I tell myself I've done good, to stay alive and keep the kids alive, and if they'll just wake up in the morning, and me too, well then, we can worry about all the rest come tomorrow. So there you go. We do our best, and that's all you can do."

She may sound fatalistic, but she appears to be a nervous, hardworking, even hard-driven woman — thin, short, constantly on the move. I may not know what she "really" thinks and believes. Like the rest of us she has her contradictions and her mixed feelings; and there are some things that she can't say to me — or to herself. Sometimes she doesn't tell me something she really wants me to know. She has forgotten, pure and simple. More is on her mind than information I might want: "Remember you asked the other day about Peter, if he was ever real sick. And I told you he was a weak child, and I feared for his life, and I've lost five children, three that was born and two that wasn't. Well, I forgot to tell you that he got real sick up here, just after we came. He was three, and I didn't know what to do. You see, I didn't have my mother to help out. She always knew what to do. She could hold a child and get him to stop crying, no matter how sick he was, and no matter how much he wanted food, and we didn't have it. But she was gone — and that's when we left to come up here, and I never would have left her, not for anything in the world. But suddenly she took a seizure of something and went in a half hour, I'd say. And Peter, he was so hot and sick, I thought he had the same thing his grandmother did and he was going to die. I thought maybe she's calling him."

Actually, Peter's mother remembers quite a lot of things. She remembers the "old days" back South, sometimes with a shudder, but sometimes with the same nostalgia that the region is famous for generating in its white exiles. Now, she has moved from the country to the city. Her father was a sharecropper, and her son wants to be a pilot (sometimes), a policeman (sometimes), a racing-car driver (sometimes), and a baseball player (most of the time). Her husband is not alive. He died one year after they all came to Boston. He woke up, in the middle of the night, vomiting blood. He bled and bled and vomited and vomited and then he died. A doctor does not have to press very hard for "the facts": "I didn't know what to do. I was beside myself. I prayed and I prayed, and in-between I held his head and wiped his forehead. It was the middle of the night. I woke up my oldest girl and told her to go knocking on the doors. But no one would answer. They must have been scared, or have suspected something bad. I thought if only he'd be able to last into the morning, then we could get some help. I was caught between things. I couldn't leave him to go get a policeman. And my girl, she was afraid to go out. And besides, there was no one outside, and I thought we'd just stay at his side, and somehow he'd be OK, because he was a strong man, you know. His muscles, they were big all his life. Even with the blood coming up, he looked too big and strong to die, I thought. But I knew he was sick. He was real bad sick. There wasn't anything else, no sir, to do. We didn't have no phone, and even if there was a car, I never could have used it. Nor my daughter. And then he took a big breath and that was his last one."

When I first met Peter and his mother, I wanted to know how they lived, what they did with their time, what they liked to do or disliked doing, what they believed. When particular but not unrepresentative or unusual human beings are called in witness, their concrete medical history becomes extremely revealing. I cannot think of a better way to begin knowing what life is like for Peter and his mother than to hear the following and hear it again and think about its implications: "No sir, Peter has never been to a doctor, not unless you count the one at school, and she's a nurse, I believe. He was his sickest back home before we came here and, you know, there was no doctor for us in the county. In Alabama you have to pay a white doctor first, before he'll go near you. And we don't have but a few colored ones. I've never seen a one. There was this woman we'd go to, and she had gotten some nursing education in Mobile. No, I don't know if she was a nurse or not, or a helper to the nurses, maybe. Well, she would come to help us. With the convulsions, she'd show you how to hold the child and make sure he doesn't hurt himself. They can bite their tongues real, real bad.

"Here, I don't know what to do. There's the city hospital, but it's no good for us. I went there with my husband, no sooner than a month or so after we came up here. We waited and waited, and finally the day was almost over. We left the kids with a neighbor, and we barely knew her. I said it would take the morning, but I never thought we'd get home near suppertime. And they wanted us to come back and come back, because it was something they couldn't do all at once — though for most of the time we just sat there and did nothing. And my husband, he said his stomach was the worse for going there, and he'd take care of himself from now on, rather than go there.

"Maybe they could have saved him. But they're far away, and I didn't have money to get a cab, even if there was one around here, and I thought to myself it'll make him worse to take him there.

"My kids, they get sick. The welfare worker, she sends a nurse here, and she tells me we should be on vitamins, and the kids need all kinds of checkups. Once she took my daughter and told her she had to have her teeth looked at, and the same with Peter. So, I went with my daughter, and they didn't see me that day, but said they could in a couple of weeks. And I had to pay the woman next door to mind the little ones, and there was the carfare, and we sat and sat, like before. So, I figured it would take more than we've got to see that dentist. And when the nurse told us we'd have to come back a few times — that's how many, a few — I thought that no one ever looked at my teeth, and they're not good, I'll admit, but you can't have everything, that's what I say, and that's what my kids have to know, I guess."

What *does* she have? And what belongs to Peter? For one thing, there is the apartment, three rooms for six people: a mother and five children. Peter is a middle child with two older girls on one side and a younger sister and still younger brother on the other side. The smallest child was born in Boston: "It's the only time I ever spent time in a hospital. He's the only one to be born there. My neighbor got the police. I was in the hall, crying I guess. We almost didn't make it. They told me I had bad blood pressure, and I should have been on pills, and I should come back, but I didn't. It was the worst time I've ever had, because I was alone. My husband had to stay with the kids, and no one was there to visit me."

Peter sleeps with his brother in one bedroom. The three girls sleep in the living room, which is a bedroom. And, of course, there is a small kitchen. There is not very much furniture about. The kitchen has a table with four chairs, only two of which are sturdy. The girls sleep in one big bed. Peter shares his bed with his brother. The mother sleeps on a couch. There is one more chair and a table in the living room. Jesus looks down from the living room wall, and an undertaker's calendar hangs on the kitchen wall. The apartment has no books, no records. There is a television set in the living room, and I have never seen it turned off.

Peter in many respects is his father's successor. His mother talks things over with him. She even defers to him at times. She will say something; he will disagree; she will nod and let him have the last word. He knows the city. She still feels a stranger to the city. "If you want to know about anything around here, just ask Peter," she once said to me. That was three years earlier, when Peter was six. Peter continues to do very poorly at school, but I find him a very good teacher. He notices a lot, makes a lot of sense when he talks, and has a shrewd eye for the ironic detail. He is very intelligent, for all the trouble he gives his teachers. He recently summed up a lot of American history for me: "I wasn't made for that school, and that school wasn't made for me." It is an old school, filled with memories. The name of the school evokes Boston's Puritan past. Pictures and statues adorn the corridors — reminders of the soldiers and statesmen and writers who made New England so influential in the nineteenth century. And naturally one finds slogans on the walls about freedom and democracy and the rights of the people. Peter can be surly and cynical when he points all that out to the visitor. If he is asked what kind of school he would *like*, he laughs incredulously: "Are you kidding? No school would be my first choice. They should leave us alone and let us help out at home, and maybe let some of our own people teach us. The other day the teacher admitted she was no good. She said maybe a Negro should come in and give us the discipline, because she was scared. She said all she wanted from us was that we keep quiet and stop wearing her nerves down, and she'd be grateful, because she would retire soon. She said we were becoming too much for her, and she didn't understand why. But when one kid wanted to say something, tell her why, she told us to keep still and write something. You know what? She whipped out a book and told us to copy a whole page from it, so we'd learn it. A stupid waste of time. I didn't even try, and she didn't care. She just wanted an excuse not to talk with us. They're all alike."

Actually, they're all *not* alike, and Peter knows it. He has met up with two fine teachers, and in mellow moments he can say so: "They're trying hard, but me and my friends, I don't think we're cut out for school. To tell the truth, that's what I think. My mother says we should try anyway, but it doesn't seem to help, trying. The teacher can't understand a lot of us, but he does all these new things, and you can see he's excited. Some kids are really with him, and I am, too. But I can't take all his stuff very seriously. He's a nice man, and he says he wants to come and visit every one of our homes; but my mother says no, she wouldn't know what to do with him when he came here. We'd just stand and have nothing to talk about. So she said tell him not to come, and I don't think he will, anyway. I think he's getting to know."

What is that teacher getting to know? What *is* there to know about Peter and all the others like him in our American cities? Of course, Peter and his friends who play in the alley need better schools, schools they can feel to be theirs, and better teachers, like the ones they *have* in fact met on occasion. But I do not feel that a reasonably good teacher in the finest school building in America would reach and affect Peter in quite the way, I suppose, people like me would expect and desire. At nine Peter is both young and quite old. At nine he is much wiser about many things than my sons will be at nine, and maybe nineteen. Peter has in fact taught me a lot about his neighborhood, about life on the streets, about survival: "I get up when I get up, no special time. My mother has Alabama in her. She gets up with the sun, and she wants to go to bed when it gets dark. I try to tell her that up here things just get started in the night. But she gets mad. She wakes me up. If it weren't for her shaking me, I might sleep until noon. Sometimes we have a good breakfast, when the check comes. Later on, though, *before* it comes, it might just be some coffee and a slice of bread. She worries about food. She says we should eat what she gives us, but sometimes I'd rather go hungry. I was sick a long time ago, my stomach or something — maybe like my father, she says. So I don't like all the potatoes she pushes on us and cereal, all the time cereal. We're supposed to be lucky, because we get some food every day. Down South they can't be sure. That's what she says, and I guess she's right.

"Then I go to school. I eat what I can, and leave. I have two changes of clothes, one for everyday and one for Sunday. I wait on my friend Billy, and we're off by eight-fifteen. He's from around here, and he's a year older. He knows everything. He can tell you if a woman is high on some stuff, or if she's been drinking, or she's off her mind about something. He knows. His brother has a convertible, a Buick. He pays off the police, but Billy won't say any more than that.

"In school we waste time until it's over. I do what I have to. I don't like the place. I feel like falling off all day, just putting my head down and saying good-bye to everyone until three. We're out then, and we sure wake up. I don't have to stop home first, not now. I go with Billy. We'll be in the alley, or we'll go to see them play pool. Then you know when it's time to go home. You hear someone say six o'clock, and you go in. I eat and watch television. It must be around ten or eleven I'm in bed."

Peter sees rats all the time. He has been bitten by them. He has a big stick by his bed to use against them. They also claim the alley, even during daylight. They are large, confident, well-fed, unafraid rats. The garbage is theirs; the land is theirs; the tenement is theirs; human flesh is theirs. When I first started visiting Peter's family, I wondered why they didn't do something to rid themselves of those rats, and the cockroaches and the mosquitoes and the flies and the maggots and the ants and especially the garbage in the alley which attracts so much of all that "lower life." Eventually I began to see some of the reasons why. A large apartment building with many families has exactly two barrels in its basement. The halls of the building go unlighted. Many windows have no screens, and some windows are broken and boarded up. The stairs are dangerous; some of them have missing timber. ("We just jump over them," says Peter cheerfully.) And the landowner is no one in particular. Rent is collected by an agent, in the name of a "realty trust." One day I went with three of the tenants, including Peter's mother, to see if someone in the city administration couldn't put some pressure on the trust. I drove us to City Hall, which is of course all the way across town. After waiting and waiting, we were finally admitted to see a man, a not very encouraging or inspiring or generous or friendly man. He told us we would have to try yet another department and swear out a complaint, and that the "case" would have to be "studied," and that we would then be "notified of a decision." We went to the department down the hall and waited another hour and ten minutes. By then it was three o'clock, and the mothers wanted to go home. They weren't thinking of rats any more, or poorly heated apartments, or garbage that had gone uncollected for two weeks. They were thinking of their children, who would be home from school and, in the case of two women, their husbands, who would also soon be home. "Maybe we should come back some other day," Peter's mother said. I noted she didn't say *tomorrow,* and I realized that I had read someplace that people like her aren't precisely "future-oriented."

Actually, both Peter and his mother have a very clear idea of what is ahead. For the mother it is "more of the same." One evening she was tired but unusually talkative, perhaps because a daughter of hers was sick: "I'm glad to be speaking about all these things tonight. My little girl has a bad fever. I've been trying to cool her off all day. Maybe if there was a place near here, that we could go to, maybe I would have gone. But like it is, I have to do the best I can and pray she'll be OK."

I asked whether she thought her children would find things different, and that's when she said it would be "more of the same" for them. Then she added a long afterthought: "Maybe it'll be a little better for them. A mother has to have hope for her children, I guess. But I'm not too sure, I'll admit. Up here, you know, there's a lot more jobs around than in Alabama. We don't get them, but you know they're someplace near, and they tell you that if you go train for them, then you'll be eligible. So, maybe Peter might someday have some real good steady work, and that would be something, yes sir, it would. I keep telling him he should pay more attention to school and put more of himself into the lessons they give there. But he says no, it's no good; it's a waste of time; they don't care what happens there, only if the kids don't keep quiet and mind themselves. Well, Peter has got to learn to mind himself and not be fresh. He speaks back to me these days. There'll be a time he won't even speak to me at all, I suppose. I used to blame it all on the city up here, city living. Back home we were always together, and there wasn't any place you could go, unless to Birmingham, and you couldn't do much for yourself there, we all knew. Of course, my momma, she knew how to make us behave. But I was thinking the other night, it wasn't so good back there either. Colored people, they'd beat on one another, and we had a lot of people that liquor was eating away at them; they'd use wine by the gallon. All they'd do was work on the land, and then go back and kill themselves with wine. And then there'd be the next day — until they'd one evening go to sleep and never wake up. And we'd get the bossman, and he'd see to it they got buried.

"Up here I think it's better, but don't ask me to tell you why. There's the welfare, that's for sure. And we get our water, and if there isn't good heat, at least there's *some* heat. Yes, it's cold up here, but we had cold down there, too, only then we didn't have any heat, and we'd just die, some of us would, every winter with one of those freezing spells.

"And I do believe things are changing. On the television they talk to you, the colored man and all the others who aren't doing so good. My boy Peter, he says they're putting you on. That's all he sees, people 'putting on' other people. But I think they all mean it, the white people. I never see them, except on television, when they say the white man wants good for the colored people. I think Peter could go and do better for himself later on, when he gets older, except for the fact that he just doesn't *believe*. He doesn't believe what they say, the teacher, or the man who says it's getting better for us — on television. I guess it's my fault. I never taught my children, any of them, to believe that kind of thing, because I never thought we'd ever have it any different, not in this life. So maybe I've failed Peter. I told him the other day he should work hard, because of all the 'opportunity' they say is coming for us, and he said I was talking good, but where was my proof. So I went next door with him, to my neighbor's, and we asked her husband, and you know, he sided with Peter. He said they were taking in a few here and a few there and putting them in the front windows of all the big companies, but that all you have to do is look around at our block and you'd see all the young men, and they just haven't got a thing to do. Nothing."

Her son also looks to the future. Sometimes he talks — in his own words — "big." He'll one day be a bombardier or "something like that." At other times he is less sure of things: "I don't know what I'll be. Maybe nothing. I see the men sitting around, hiding from the welfare lady. They fool her. Maybe I'll fool her, too. I don't know what you can do. The teacher the other day said that if just one of us turned out OK she'd congratulate herself and call herself lucky."

A while back a riot excited Peter and his mother, excited them and frightened them. The spectacle of the police being fought, of white-owned property being assaulted, stirred the boy a great deal: "I figured the whole world might get changed around. I figured people would treat us better from now on. Only I don't think they will." As for his mother, she was less hopeful but even more apocalyptic: "I told Peter we were going to pay for this good. I told him they wouldn't let us get away with it, not later on." And in the midst of the trouble she was frightened as she had never before been: "I saw them running around on the streets, the men and women, and they were talking about burning things down, and how there'd be nothing left when they got through. I sat there with my children, and I thought we might die the way things are going, die right here. I didn't know what to do: if I should leave, in case they burn down the building, or if I should stay, so that the police don't arrest us, or we get mixed up with the crowd of people. I've never seen so many people going in so many different directions. They were running and shouting and they didn't know what to do. They were so excited. My neighbor, she said they'd burn us all up, and then the white man would have himself one less of a headache. The colored man is a worse enemy to himself than the white. I mean, it's hard to know which is the worse."

I find it as hard as she does to sort things out. When I think of her and the mothers like her I have worked with for years, when I think of Peter and his friends, I find myself caught between the contradictory observations I have made. Peter already seems a grim and unhappy child. He trusts no one white, not his white teacher, not the white policeman he sees, not the white welfare worker, not the white storekeeper, and not, I might add, me. There we are, the five of us from the one hundred eighty million white Americans who surround him and the other twenty million blacks. Yet, Peter doesn't really trust his friends and neighbors, either. At nine he has learned to be careful, wary, guarded, doubtful, and calculating. His teacher may not know it, but Peter is a good sociologist and a good political scientist, a good student of urban affairs. With devastating accuracy he can reveal how much of the "score" he knows; yes, and how fearful and sad and angry he is: "This here city isn't for us. It's for the people downtown. We're here because, like my mother said, we had to come. If they could lock us up or sweep us away, they would. That's why I figure the only way you can stay ahead is get some kind of deal for yourself. If I had a choice I'd live someplace else, but I don't know where. It would be a place where they treated you right, and they didn't think you were some nuisance. But the only thing you can do is be careful of yourself; if not, you'll get killed somehow, like it happened to my father."

His father died prematurely, and most probably, unnecessarily. Among the poor of our cities the grim medical statistics we all know about are encountered as terrible daily experiences. Among the black and white families I work with — in nearby but separate slums — disease and the pain that goes with it are taken for granted. When my children complain of an earache or demonstrate a skin rash I rush them to the doctor. When I have a headache, I take an aspirin, and if the headache is persistent, I can always get a medical checkup. Not so with Peter's mother and Peter; they have learned to live with sores and infections and poorly mended fractures and bad teeth and eyes that need but don't have the help of glasses. Yes, they *can* go to a city hospital and get free care, but again and again they don't. They come to the city without any previous experience as patients. They have never had the money to purchase a doctor's time. They have never had free medical care available. (I am speaking now of Appalachian whites as well as southern blacks.) It may comfort me to know that every American city provides some free medical services for its "indigent," but Peter's mother and thousands like her have quite a different view of things: "I said to you the other time, I've tried there. It's like at City Hall, you wait and wait, and they push you and shove you and call your name, only to tell you to wait some more, and if you tell them you can't stay there all day, they'll say, 'Lady, go home, then.' You get sick just trying to get there. You have to give your children over to people or take them all with you, and the carfare is expensive. Why, if we had a doctor around here, I could almost pay him with the carfare it takes to get there and back for all of us. And you know, they keep on having you come back and back, and they don't know what each other says. Each time they start from scratch."

I took Peter to a children's hospital and arranged for a series of evaluations which led to the following: a pair of glasses; a prolonged bout of dental work; antibiotic treatment for skin lesions; a thorough cardiac work-up, with the subsequent diagnosis of rheumatic heart disease; a conference between Peter's mother and a nutritionist, because the boy has been on a high-starch, low-protein, and low-vitamin diet all his life. He suffered from one attack of sinus trouble after another and from a succession of sore throats and earaches, from cold upon cold, even in the summer. A running nose was unsurprising to him — and so was chest pain and shortness of breath, due to the heart ailment.

At the same time, Peter is tough. I have to emphasize again *how* tough and, yes, how "politic, cautious and meticulous," not in Prufrock's way, but in another way and for other reasons. Peter has learned to be wary as well as angry, tentative as well as extravagant, at times controlled and only under certain circumstances defiant: "Most of the time, I think you have to watch your step. That's what I think. That's the difference between up here and down in the South. That's what my mother says, and she's right. I don't remember it down there, but I know she must be right. Here, you measure the next guy first and then make your move when you think it's a good time to."

He was talking about "how you get along" when you leave school and go "mix with the guys" and start "getting your deal." He was telling me what an outrageous and unsafe world he has inherited and how very carefully he has made his appraisal of the future. Were I afflicted with some of his physical complaints, I would be fretful, annoyed, petulant, angry — and moved to do something, see someone, get a remedy, a pill, a promise of help. He has made his "adjustment" to the body's pain, and he has also learned to contend with the alley and the neighborhood and *us*, the world beyond: "The cops come by here all the time. They drive up and down the street. They want to make sure everything is OK to look at. They don't bother you, so long as you don't get in their way."

So, it is live and let live — except that families like Peter's have a tough time living, and of late have been troubling those cops, among others. Our cities have become not only battlegrounds, but places where all sorts of American problems and historical ironies have converged. Over the past ten years I have been asking myself how people like Peter and his mother survive in mind and body and spirit. And I have wanted to know what a twentieth-century American city "means" to them or "does" to them. People cannot be handed questionnaires and asked to answer such questions. They cannot be "interviewed" a few times and told to come across with a statement, a reply. But inside Peter and his brother and his sisters and his mother, and inside a number of Appalachian mothers and fathers and children I know are feelings and thoughts and ideas — which, in my experience, come out casually or suddenly, by accident almost. After a year or two of talking, after experiences such as I have briefly described in a city hall, in a children's hospital, a lifetime of pent-up tensions and observation comes to blunt expression: "Down in Alabama we had to be careful about ourselves with the white man, but we had plenty of things we could do by ourselves. There was our side of town, and you could walk and run all over, and we had a garden, you know. Up here they have you in a cage. There's no place to go, and all I do is stay in the building all day long and the night, too. I don't use my legs no more, hardly at all. I never see those trees, and my oldest girl, she misses planting time. It was bad down there. We had to leave. But it's no good here, too, I'll tell you. Once I woke up and I thought all the buildings on the block were falling down on me. And I was trying to climb out, but I couldn't. And then the next thing I knew, we were all back South, and I was standing near some sunflowers — you know, the tall ones that can shade you if you sit down.

"No, I don't dream much. I fall into a heavy sleep as soon as I touch the bed. The next thing I know I'm stirring myself to start in all over in the morning. It used to be the sun would wake me up, but now it's up in my head, I guess. I know I've got to get the house going and off to school."

Her wistful, conscientious, law-abiding, devoutly Christian spirit hasn't completely escaped the notice of Peter, for all his hardheaded, cynical protestations: "If I had a chance, I'd like to get enough money to bring us all back to Alabama for a visit. Then I could prove it that it may be good down there, a little bit, even if it's no good, either. Like she says, we had to get out of there or we'd be dead by now. I hear say we all may get killed soon, it's so bad here, but I think we did right to get up here, and if we make him listen to us, the white man, maybe he will."

To which Peter's mother adds: "We've carried a lot of trouble in us, from way back in the beginning. I have these pains, and so does everyone around here. But you can't just die until you're ready to. And I do believe something is happening. I do believe I see that."

To which Peter adds: "Maybe it won't be that we'll win, but if we get killed, everyone will hear about it. Like the minister said, before we used to die real quiet, and no one stopped to pay notice."

Two years before Peter spoke those words he drew a picture for me, one of many he has done. When he was younger, and when I didn't know him so well as I think I do now, it was easier for us to have something tangible to do and then talk about. I used to visit the alley with him, as I still do, and one day I asked him to draw the alley. That was a good idea, he thought (though not all of my suggestions were). He started in, then stopped, and finally worked rather longer and harder than usual at the job. I busied myself with my own sketches, which from the start he insisted I do. Suddenly from across the table I heard him say he was through. Ordinarily he would slowly turn the drawing around for me to see, and I would get up and walk over to his side of the table, to see even better. But this time he didn't move his paper, and I didn't move myself. I saw what he had drawn, and he saw me looking. I was surprised and a bit stunned and more than a bit upset, and surely he saw my face and heard my utter silence. Often I would break the awkward moments when neither of us seemed to have anything to say, but this time it was his turn to do so: "You know what it is?" He knew that I liked us to talk about our work. I said no, I didn't — though in fact the vivid power of his black crayon had come right across to me. "It's that hole we dug in the alley. I made it bigger here. If you fall into it, you can't get out. You die."

He had drawn circles within circles, all of them black, and then a center, also black. He had imposed an X on the center. Nearby, strewn across the circles, were fragments of the human body —

two faces, an arm, five legs. And after I had taken the scene in, I could only think to myself that I had been shown "like it is in the alley."

"On the porch I can sit, and my friend Gerry can sit, and we can use our jackknives, and if there's a lot to sweep away, we can just wait until we're all through, and then we do the sweeping. I have a broom, and my mother told me, when my dad gave me the knife, that if I can cut wood I can sweep wood up. So I do. Gerry's mother isn't so good on that score. She says the porch is for sitting and not cutting. That's why we're always here cutting and never there. I can make almost anything, if I can only be patient. I can carve out wood and keep my mother guessing as to what I'm making. First she'll say a boat, maybe, or a little toy for my brother, or an animal, a dog, maybe, but then I come up with a car, you know, or a little pistol for myself, and she has to admit I've fooled her pretty good. If I had a lot of money I'd get a bigger knife. I'd have one with five blades, and I could work a lot faster."

Peter's mother worries about him. She finds herself saying things like this: "He's only nine. He finds his way all over this big, big city. I never thought I'd have a child of mine so smart about a place like this. When we go back to Kentucky I look at him and wonder if he's going to be like a fish out of water back home, back at his own people's home, but he does fine up the creek with his cousins, and funny thing, he's their hero, because he can tell them all the stories about the city. Then we come back to the city, and I do believe the boy turns sad. I think he misses our old place, even if he can't remember living there, because we left when he was three, I believe. That's why I worry about him. I feel he's betwixt and between, you know."

At first glance, and actually for a longer stretch of time than that, Peter seems anything but sad or caught up in the kind of conflict or tension or uncertainty that his mother has several times and in several different ways described to me. He is tall for nine, thin but not bony thin; there are muscles on him. He has long arms, long fingers, long legs, and big feet — and his mother hates the very word shoes, because they are so expensive, and Peter's feet grow so much each year, and in a city he can't run around barefoot and worry only on Sundays about squeezing his feet into a pair of shoes, or about letting his feet swim in another pair. Peter's hair is also long, and blond, and falls over his forehead and comes a little over his ears. He has never been to a barber. His mother cuts his hair. He doesn't like those scissors, though — and so by agreement they hold off until it really *is* time, and then his mother goes easy on the cutting.

The boy's father must once have looked like Peter, but he is a sick man and looks much too old for his thirty-eight years. His name is also Peter, but he is called Pete by his wife, and Peter is Peter to everyone, which means a sister of fourteen, a sister of twelve, a sister of ten, a sister of seven and a brother of five. When the last child was born, the mother nearly died. She bled and bled. The delivery had been done up the hollow that was home, that still is Peter's grandmother's home. The family returned for a "visit," which on that occasion meant a stay at home long enough for the child to be born and the mother to rest and prepare herself for the trip back North to "the building" — her way of combining mention of an apartment house and the city in which the apartment house stands. The child was delivered by a great-aunt of Peter's — his grandmother's sister, his mother's favorite aunt, a woman who radiates self-command and who has delivered many children in her sixty-two years. But after the boy was born there was a near tragedy. An already anemic woman was losing blood fast, had a high fever, was in pain, and had to either see a doctor or die. They drove and drove and got to a hospital, and first had to put their money down, all they could raise from their neighbors and their minister, then the mother was admitted and treated with antibiotics, operated upon, given blood, fed intravenously, and eventually discharged.

Peter's mother talks about such experiences and how they fit in with her life and her husband's life and Peter's life: "We'd only left the creek a year before my youngest child was born. My husband was sick then, and he's sick now. His back was hurt bad in an accident down the mine. His breathing is bad from the coal dust in his lungs. They told him he was no longer good for work, the coal company did, and they gave us one thousand two hundred dollars for Pete's trouble — a payment, they called it, for his injury. We spent it on special treatments at the hospital for his back, and for clothes the children needed. Pete was too honest, that's what our minister told us. Pete was against the coal company, and he was against his own union. He said the union bosses are as bad as the gangsters you see on the television. They'll kill you if you fight them, he used to tell me — and then he'd go to the meetings and argue and argue. I asked him once if he wanted to die. He said no — then he thought and said maybe I was right, maybe we shouldn't stay in Letcher County, Kentucky. That was the night he began to think of going North, and it wasn't a month later that we were up here. We had kin here, and we just came to them.

"Peter was a child of three, and he got over the change easier than the older ones. He even did better than his younger sister. She was very attached to me, and because I was fretful, she became fretful. Peter made friends in the building, and he kept on telling me he was glad we'd come up here. But I wasn't sure then he meant what he said, and I'm still not sure I ought to believe him. He'll *tell* me he's fine up here, but his head starts dropping when we leave Hot Spot, and it never does rise once — not the entire way north on that interstate road. I believe the child half sleeps and half thinks of what he's just been doing up the creek with his cousins.

"Peter's dad tells him all the time that no one's going to help us out in Kentucky. Not the county people. Not the coal-mine owners. Not the union. The county people say they don't have money. The coal-mine people say they don't need too many men, and they gave us the dollars they did, one thousand and two hundred of them, and that's all they can do. The union, they cry poor, and like I said, my husband never was one to wink when he saw a hand in the union till or people fixing up relatives with phony jobs. Up here in the city he's tried to work, and the officials have been good to us. They said we could be on welfare, because he's got a bad back and his breathing isn't the best. So we get by. We're not rich, I'll tell you, and there's a lot we lack, but if we'd have stayed in Kentucky we would have no money, not a cent coming in, and that *is* being poor. Here we're plain poor; back home we'd have been bad, bad, terrible poor. That's what Pete says. And not long ago I heard my boy Peter practically repeating his father's every word to one of his friends. I was going to pull him in and tell him off; but he repeats his father's every word, he likes him so, and I didn't have the heart to punish the boy when all he was doing was being a good talker, like his daddy can be when he wants to."

Peter certainly does admire his father, and he can "go on a bit," to use the expression the father uses when he feels he has talked rather a lot. Peter will even talk about becoming a miner one day; he heard in school about copper-mining in Arizona, and came home and told his parents he might try that. They wondered whether he would want to be so far from Hot Spot, Letcher Country, Kentucky, and when he learned how far off Arizona is, Peter also wondered: "I don't think I'd want to go clear across the country. I like going home. I also like it here, though. In the city you can see a lot of people, and they don't scare you, after you get used to them. My daddy never saw so many people as he did when he first came up here, and he had to go into town, to an office building, and there were elevators going up and down, and they were packed full with people. He took me there, and I was scared. I guess I cried. I don't remember, but he says I did. That was a long time ago. I wouldn't cry now, I know that. I can get home from school four different ways. I've stayed on the bus and gone all the way over to the other side of the city, and then come back. I'll bet on a jet plane I could get to Arizona in the time it took me to cross the city. I'll bet I could get halfway around the world in a spaceship in less time. But there are so many people here, and that's why there's a lot of traffic.

"It's not very far to get to a playground. I go there, and we fool around. We do our carving, and there's no worry about cleaning up the pieces of wood. They've got a few trees there, and we mark them up a little with our knives. The man who's in charge gets mad. He says it's a small playground, and there aren't many trees in the whole city, and we're ruining it for ourselves. I told him I see a lot of trees when we go home, and I'll bring back a few on one of these trips. The man said we should stop bragging about where we *used* to live. He said we're here, and we'll never go back, because we couldn't afford to — we'd starve to death, he said. I asked my daddy, and he says that could be half true. We'd eat what we grow, and people would help us, but it would be close, he'd have to admit it, and up here we get enough money to keep eating, but not much more.

"My mother says we never were meant to live with a lot of money. She tries to hide from my father the cost of everything. After she pays the rent, she says there's barely enough for food. She says she wishes my brother was as big as me, and I was as big as my father, then we could all share the same clothes. She wishes my sisters were all the same size, too. My father wishes he could find work and keep work. He wishes he didn't have the pain he does in his back, and he wishes he could breathe better. He hates to take a penny from the city, but we'd be living on the street and begging for food there on the street if we didn't turn to the city sometimes. We'd go back to Hot Spot, I guess. My folks would like to go back, but they know we're wiser to stay here, Daddy says. I'm glad we go home, and I can see my cousins, but I'm glad to come back here, mostly. Sometimes I wish we'd just stay in Hot Spot, but it's no good that way, Daddy says, and he knows."

So does Peter; he knows exactly why he is living in the city, and why thousands of others like him live in cities north of Kentucky's eastern counties and West Virginia's neighboring mountain counties and North Carolina's western counties and Tennessee's eastern counties. He knows words like "Appalachia" and "poverty" and "disaster area" and "mechanization of the mines." He has a young teacher who often tells the children in her class that she is interested in their "special problems." She has yet to go (or be sent) to the mountains, but she has read a lot and has on her classroom walls a lot of pictures and some maps and a list of products and industries and natural resources and state flowers and state mottoes and state capitals. So, Peter comes home and talks about "the Appalachian region," and how it is an "area," and his father laughs and says this: "Most of the people on one side of Letcher County wouldn't waste their time trying to get to the other side, and why should they? They are settled down where they have lived for a long time — and if they are going to leave and suffer the heartache of moving, then they'd as soon go all the way to California than try another part of the county, or the region, like the teacher calls it. Why she talks about a 'region' I don't know. There are a lot of people in Letcher County who think the county should be divided up, never mind called part of a region."

Peter doesn't want to go back and report to the teacher what his father has said. He senses his father's despair and cynicism and not too friendly amusement, but he also senses that the teacher may be onto something, or those from whom she has drawn her information might be — even if his father may *also* be onto something. I mean to say that the boy gains from his teacher a picture of what a nation must do to help a beleaguered stretch of territory, whose hills and valleys and waterways are beautiful, whose people love what they consider to be almost sacredly theirs; but he also hears from his father the native's just disdain for an outsider's unblinking acceptance of various surveys and studies and analyses that look convincing on paper but ignore things a graph or a chart or a map simply cannot convey. In the words of a nine-year-old boy named Peter, a city boy and a mountaineer's son: "I hear my father talk, and my mother, and when we go home my grandmother and my uncle and aunt, and I have a cousin — his name is Peter, too — and he was in the Air Force, only now he's out. They say there's nothing wrong with where they are, and all they need is work. They say if they're going to be told they should move across the county and halfway across the state to make a living, then they'll move all right, and we'd better find a place in our building for them, because there's no point in halfway moving; you move or you don't, and the bigger the city the better, if it's going to come to that.

"My kin don't want to live in the city, and I know they wouldn't like it in a big city. They might like it better in a town someplace in Letcher County or Harlan County or Perry County. But they say once they're pushed out, they'll quit altogether. My uncle says that he'd like to see anyone come up the creek and try to tell him to move on down some new road they've built to a place over yonder. The man would have some guns trained on him, and no fooling. Like my uncle says: we don't get pushed too easy, no sir, and if they say they're out to help us, let them prove it — because we've heard a lot of that 'help' promised before. That's the way he talks, and I was going to tell our teacher what he says after I came back from the creek a few weeks ago, but I didn't. I think the teacher is a good lady, and I told my daddy, she's always talking about us, about our people. Daddy said that's nice to hear."

Peter and his father do a lot of talking about their people, and they do so on a porch. Not that the porch is what they would like it to be, wide and just above the ground and leading to some rocky pastureland with a vegetable garden and some flowers at the edge to set things off, and then the woods. Not that the porch has a swing on it which goes back and forth, a swing boys like Peter can rush at, jump on, fight for control over, and then exhausted at last, simply lie upon and enjoy. And not that the porch has years and years of initials cut into it and maybe a tire or two and maybe a cabinet or a gun and maybe an old license plate — all just standing there or lying around. No, the porch is a "city porch" — which is what Peter knows to call it. But something is better than nothing, the boy has heard his father say and now reminds me. At least we can sit there, he tells me. Sitting means a lot to Peter's family. Though Peter himself is as active and energetic as other nine-year-old boys are, he does like to sit down on a chair on the porch and talk, rather as his father does. And, like his father, he can whittle away at a piece of wood, even aimlessly whittle the wood down to a mass of chips.

The porch is small and old. The building is four stories tall and is of wood and the porches face a backyard which is all cracked cement and contains barrels and two old and abandoned cars. There are eight apartments in the building, four on one side and four on the other. Open stairs serve the back part of the building

and there are two rear doors on each floor. The doors open up on
the porch and the porches connect, or it can be said that two
families share one porch. The fact is that there used to be
wooden fences of sorts to give each tenant family at least a
semblance of privacy outdoors, but long ago those partitions
were pushed down or collapsed. Indeed, the porches look as if
they might collapse; they seem almost to hang loosely from the
building proper. For several years the city has been planning to
tear down a whole neighborhood of such buildings but has not
done so. Peter, who sometimes says he might one day want to be
a carpenter, or a builder who puts up "good buildings and skyscrapers, too" can talk about the building he knows best this way:
"The man who built this building built a hundred others like it, I
think. Every house on the street is the same. The teacher told us
a lot of people have come through here before us — all different
kinds, she says. A girl asked her if some of the buildings here
were built during the American Revolution, when George Washington was President. The teacher thought the girl was being
fresh, but she wasn't at all. She told the teacher she was sorry,
but she heard her mother say the buildings must have been built
hundreds of years ago, and she didn't know if her mother was
correct and how long ago they were actually built, so she thought
she'd ask the teacher. The teacher said she didn't know either,
but it was a long, long time."

The building should indeed be torn down. It is a dangerous
building, as the city's fire department has publicly stated. The
wiring is old. The coal-burning furnace is old and not always
reliable. The radiators are old and often useless. The stoves are
old gas ranges that go back thirty or forty years. The hall is
unlighted, hence dark, and its stairs are hazardous to climb: a
plank is missing here, a section of the banister is gone a little
further on. One imagines the things that can happen to small
children negotiating their way past those empty spaces to the
side of the steps. Since Peter's family has rented an apartment in
that building, one child has fallen down, fallen through, properly
speaking, and been seriously hurt. Another child did so, but only
from half a flight up, and was "only" bruised and frightened.

Every day mothers worry about recurrences, but then, as Peter's mother put it: "There's so much to worry about in this world; one thing pushes out another from your mind."

Here are some of the competing worries her mind must contend with: the water that leaks into her apartment from the one above; the cockroaches and mice and rats that get into the building and try to get into her apartment, however tidy she is; the stench from the basement that comes up a well the height of the building and works its way into each room of the entire house; the mosquitoes and flies that come in during the summer when the windows have to be opened but screens are not available; the flat roof of the building high over the street, to which children have access through an open staircase; garbage, at best irregularly collected, and so always visible from her kitchen window; broken glass all over that neighborhood, on every stretch of sidewalk; the black, sooty smoke that the chimneys emit, the result of old, thoroughly inadequate heating systems. Still, the building is home to her, and I know full well that Peter's mother and father would not like me to recite such a litany of complaints. They make their objections infrequently and one at a time, and not with great bursts of indignation. They pride themselves on their ability to see the bright side of life, even though at heart they feel (and admit to feeling) discouraged.

And Peter — he is their son. He knows that there are other, better places to live; he has traveled enough, within the city and back and forth from Hot Spot, to have a clear idea how it is possible for many Americans to live. Still, his parents live where they do, and he loves them and they love him and that is that — all of which he has his own way of declaring: "I like to sit here on the porch and do my carving and sometimes I bring pebbles up here and see how far I can throw them. My daddy and I have a contest: the one who throws the farthest can throw one more as a bonus, then we throw against each other again and the guy who gets rid of his pebbles first wins. We get the pebbles from the roof — it's covered with them. My mother says she doesn't believe there's anything else on that roof but pebbles, but Daddy and I try to tell her there's black tar and the wood underneath. In the summer the whole building roasts because of the flat roof, and when it rains a big puddle collects in the middle and then it leaks through. I'm not supposed to go up there, and I don't really go anymore. It's no fun going after you've been there a hundred times. You see the same thing from our porch. You see the other buildings. My sister and I count the chimneys. We count the television aerials. We count the skylights, then we count how many are broken and how many have the glass unbroken. My sister said if you imagine hard enough, you can turn all the roof and the chimneys and the aerials into a big forest, and we're here sitting and looking out at the trees, and we rock in Daddy's rocking chair."

That rocking chair was brought up from Hot Spot, from the house up the creek. Peter claims it when his father is not around. Lately, as Peter's young brother has become older and more assertive and more demanding and more fearless and combative, he offers Peter real competition, and their fights over the father's chair go on and on. During warm weather, there are three other chairs on that porch. Often I have sat on one of the three chairs and talked with Peter. On a card table his mother provides we have been able to draw and paint, which the boy says he cannot do well, but enjoys doing. As we have worked he has recalled an uncle, a great-uncle actually, who can draw just about anything, it seems, and who used to draw pictures for Peter when he was three or four — before the family moved away. Peter is not sure of such things — of exactly how old he was when he first started living in the city. He asks me how anyone can be sure. A person can't remember exactly, he tells me, when it's over a year or two in the past that one is going back to, searching for as best he can. Do I agree with that? More or less, I say and hedge. I fumble for a remark that will reassure him and allow my nervous, well-informed mind to relax. Finally, I tell Peter that two or three years back is for him a long, long time; that it's the equivalent in my life of about ten years. He tells me that he sees what I mean, but then I am not sure I do myself. That is to say, I really don't know whether his forgetfulness is the same as an older person's. His older sister remembers very accurately things that happened to her when she was three or four — so the mother maintains. Peter, on the other hand, was always hazy when it came to remembering details, his mother will say — and then go on to give her explanation of why some people, regardless of age, retain the details of their various experiences right up in the front of their minds, so to speak, while others let almost as much as they can sink into a "background" that we call "distant memory." Very briefly: "The good Lord made us all different. You'll meet people who remember everything and people who remember practically nothing. I believe He has to make sure we don't all turn out the same in our thinking. It would be no good, that way."

I think Peter is inward, likes to think about, to savor, what is on his mind, and therefore he has more and more each year to push back and *not* think about. As a very young child he was called "dreamy" by his mother. Now the boy is described as liking to be "by himself" sometimes, but not all the time by any means. He simply likes to use his slingshot by himself and sit on the porch in his father's chair by himself and, when back home on a visit, go exploring by himself. He has friends. He is quite open and charming with his sisters. He looks up to his father and heeds his mother's words and is considered polite and "responsive" by his teacher — but, again, he likes to be alone upon occasion, and when he talks about such a preference, he does so indirectly but with great candor and simplicity: "When I go back to our family in Hot Spot I ask my daddy if I can take off. He says yes, because I know the woods all right. So I find a path and I'm gone. I whistle and try to fool the birds. I chase a butterfly and let it go. I chase a toad and let it go. The turtles are too slow. They think all they have to do is poke their head inside and they're safe. Then I'll pick them up and they start peeking, just at the wrong time. You can hear the squirrels running out of your way, just ahead of your steps. You can hear the birds warning each other, and even when you stop and don't make a move or a sound for as long as you can stand it, they seem to know you're still there. When I come to a clearing I lie down and I can see the moon sometimes, as well as the sun in the sky if it's clear. There are mosquitoes. There are grasshoppers. There are ants crawling up your leg, but it's no use moving, because they'll follow you. The bees are looking for honey — all of a sudden they smell me! I can see the bigger birds circling; then they land on a tree and look right at me. They're just keeping their eyes open, my daddy says. And suddenly, before you know it, a pheasant takes off into the sky, or a rabbit goes so fast you'd think he was shot out of a gun. My daddy used to take me through the woods, and he'd tell me to soak up everything, so when we left for the city I'd have it all to recollect. Now I go out by myself; like he says, it's a plenty big change from what we have around us in the building."

I mentioned that Peter and I have done some drawing and painting. Peter in general likes to draw animals, animals he has seen in books. He and his classmates were taken by his teacher to the zoo, and for weeks afterwards I saw Peter's version of an elephant or a lion or a zebra. Sometimes Peter draws a turtle or a rabbit and lets me know the obvious, that no such animals are going to be found around "the building." Sometimes Peter draws his dog, his family's dog, Wally. And through Wally I hear about life in the hills and life in the cities: "My father says he's glad Wally is old. When we came here Wally was four or five. He's a little older than me. They weren't going to take him with us. My mother says my father was near tears at the thought of bringing him and near tears at the thought of leaving him behind. She says she heard my father trying to say good-bye to Wally. He was talking to him. He was saying that we'd be coming back and we'd be seeing him, especially around holidays, when we always try to have something special for Wally. Then he started crying, and my mother says Wally did, too; he just cried the same as Daddy did — and I guess my mother couldn't stand it any more. She says she almost started crying herself, but then she got as mad as she could be, and she came out from hiding and told both of them, my father and Wally, to stop — because Wally was coming up with us to the city and that was all there was to it.

"On the way up, though, Daddy kept changing his mind. He's told me a lot of times how he reasoned things. He figured Wally was no pup, no baby; since he was five or so, he'd lived nearly half his life. He figured Wally would miss us as much as we'd miss him, even if a lot of our kin are still back there, and the house won't be empty, not with my grandmother and aunt and uncle and cousins there, and planning never to leave, come what may. He figured Wally might forget us, and he'd sure be better off running up and down the creek and through the woods and across the meadow over to the rocky part of the hill, where he'd all the time bark and bark at something, and we'd never know what it was. But we'd never forget Wally, and Daddy said Wally was our dog, and we were going to keep him, and we did. I don't remember too much of the first trip we made up here; I was a little kid then. But I can remember Daddy talking with Wally, and I can remember once he stopped the car, and he told Wally to go and have a good run for himself, because the field next to the road might be the last one he'd be running over in a long time. Then he told us kids to go out and do the same, because we weren't any different from Wally, he said — we'd have to get used to the city.

"I think Wally doesn't mind the city too much; he'd rather be back home, but he's old now, and mostly he just lies around the house and sleeps. He doesn't hear very good. He doesn't see very good either. But every time we go back home he turns into a puppy, practically. His tail starts going, the nearer we get to Hot Spot, and then by the time we're at the turnoff from the road and going up the creek, Wally is crying for us please, please to stop the car — just for a second to let him out — even if we have to drive a little further on. We do, and then he's off. Look at him go, my daddy will say, and we all watch. Then he seems to be away so long that we take to worrying; maybe he's forgotten where the cabin is, or maybe the sudden run was too much for him at his age. But he always shows up and then he takes a good long sleep for himself. And you know what? He sleeps better. He doesn't snore so much, and he doesn't have a lot of bad dreams, and he doesn't wake up and cross the room, and fall asleep, and then five minutes later wake up and cross the room — and the same old thing over and over again. He just falls down on that floor near the fireplace, where he used to sleep when he was a puppy, and he's dead to the whole world — except if we get some cooking going. Then his nose wakes him up, and he's after us, staring and begging in the way he looks at you, but not jumping or whining, because we won't let him do that."

Peter worries about Wally's last moments. He wishes the dog would die when they are back home and not in the city, in the building. He feels certain Wally somehow would be happier that way. He sees other dogs, city dogs, who don't at all seem unhappy with their lot — but he knows why: they have never known anything better. As for Peter himself, he is like his father; unlike old Wally, a boy of nine has a lot of curiosity and enthusiasm, and so can find his way all over a neighborhood. He can see men standing in front of houses or sitting on stairs and talking. He can see men going in a bar for a beer or two. He can turn an old abandoned car into a hut, a cave, a hiding place, or he can sit there in that car and hold the steering wheel and imagine himself driving south, south on the interstate, south across the Ohio River, south on the interstate again, and then at last south down the "regular road" to the creek — and now *on* with the gas and *up, up, up* to the cabin. Peter lets it be known in no uncertain terms that one day *he* will do the driving back to the hills. He already knows a good deal about automobiles, and he knows the way back, from the streets he has to take in order to get out of the city itself to the various turnoffs on those interstate highways. He may not have actually driven a car, but his father has taught him what does what and even taught him a lot about motors and how to change oil and where the battery is and what spark plugs are and where the wires from the windshield wiper go. And if I needed proof of Peter's road knowledge, I got it once when I traveled with the family, went "back home," and heard the boy tell his father each turn to make. They were having a fine time, the driver waiting for his instructions and the boy utterly annoyed by the long, long waits on those interstate highways — until, again, he could let his father know exactly where to go and what to do.

Once Peter told me he'd draw the whole trip for me. I couldn't for the life of me figure out how he was going to do that, but I soon found out. He started with the porch, and I thought he would get completely taken up by that particular "scene," which meant we'd never get out and into the countryside. But he knew what he was going to do — make a road map of sorts. Suddenly he just took us right out and had us on the main highway — and now he could accelerate things, emphasize the crucial twists and turns of direction, and indicate to me not the long distance involved, the miles and miles of the same thing, but the changes of pace he knew so well. And when we did at last arrive, there was no mistaking it: the hills, the trees, the water, the grass, the bushes, the birds. Then he had something to tell me. (I often asked him, after he drew, what was going on: if people were being portrayed, I might ask what they were doing, and if an animal or a bird appeared, where they lived or came from.) Did I know, he wondered, where those birds go in the winter? No, I didn't. Well, they go South, perhaps to Texas or even Mexico. Then in the spring they start coming North again, but they stop in Kentucky. Why should they go any farther, after all? Why should they go North to all those cities in Ohio and Illinois and Michigan?

I told Peter what he knew anyway, that birds can be found all over those three states and into Canada, come summer. Yes, that is so, but not in the cities. All he has ever seen are pigeons and a few sparrows, and only at the playground and at school, and only there because they're probably on their way to someplace and the peanuts "draw them down." As we talked some more he admitted that birds may live in a big city, some of them, though in nowhere near the numbers a place like Hot Spot attracts. We agreed on that, and then he proceeded to remind me in the course of an afternoon how smart birds are, how many things they can do that we cannot: they can build a home on a thin branch of any tree anyplace; they can fly all over, move around at will; they can seek out the best places, go South, come North, avoid extremes of weather; on the ground they can hop and skip; they can sing enviably, soar into the heavens, and dive down at high speeds; they can find food almost anywhere; they can escape all sorts of predators with a flap of their wings; they can keep good company, cross the country in the most amazing formations, warn one another of impending danger, get up easily and automatically at the first sign of morning, and go to sleep safely and mysteriously in the stillness of early evening. They look so attractive, too; they have bright colors, a fine and decorative set of clothes on them, as it were. They are cheerful, and they inspire cheer in others, maybe envy.

I am not saying that Peter said all of that as I just have done — one, two, three. He has more patience, likes to wander through a conversation, let his ideas slowly emerge, then repeat them, then drop the whole subject, then come back again with a thought, and be surprised himself at what he has said. At the end of that particular afternoon — an afternoon in which I had seen a road map drawn and heard birds acclaimed — the boy brought up Wally's limited future and wondered out loud what his own future held in store for him: "My little brother asked my father the other day if there was anyone luckier than Wally, because all Wally did was eat and sleep and, at least in the city, take a short walk. Daddy said Wally was Wally, and we're not him. Think of all the things we can do he can't do. He asked us to start mentioning them. So, I said drive, and my brother said ride a bike, and I said carve wood and play music on the guitar and whistle — and then my brother started talking about how he can climb a tree, and Wally can't, and he can pick up a ball and throw it, and all Wally can do is push it with his nose, and then go chasing after it." And before I left we talked for a few minutes about giraffes, and how tall they are, and how they can eat off trees, according to the books Peter has seen in school, but they have trouble bending; and of course with fish, it's great the way they swim, but on land they're dead almost immediately.

So it goes. We can only be what we are. Peter's father has given Peter and his brother that message in many ways and upon many occasions, something all parents have to do — as their children grow up and notice who can do what and who cannot possibly do what, and who has what and who lacks what, and who goes where and who stays put and who does move around, but only so far. Certainly Peter has no illusions; he knows very well that his father was a coal miner, that he was hurt down in the mines, that he left Kentucky reluctantly, that he looks back upon his life with mixed bitterness and (from the distance of a northern city) a good deal of nostalgia. Peter also knows that his own prospects are better than his father's — maybe. Here is how the boy talks about his future: "I won't work in a mine, I know that. Daddy says to stay in school, and I might get a good job if I go all the way through. I don't know if I will or I won't. Sometimes Daddy says he may just drive us all back for keeps, and we'll take our chances from day to day. He says there's no room up here for us; the people don't like a man who's from the mountains, and he's honest, and all he wants is a good job and a fair day's pay. A lot of the older kids on the block, they say the best thing is to go into the Army. That way you have good food and good lodgings and good uniforms, and they'll send you all over the world, and otherwise you'd never get to see so many places. My mother says that when the time comes, I'll know what I want to do. Meanwhile, she says I should do the best I can, from the start of the day to the end of the day."

He does just that. He is up early. They live in a four-room flat, so the children are very much together in a room. They are awakened by their mother, who needs no alarm, has no alarm to awaken her. They get dressed, usually in the very same clothes they wore the day before, and help their mother put together breakfast — cereal, hot or cold depending on the time of year, and half milk, half tea, or coffee with less milk, about a quarter of a cup. Eggs and bacon are expensive and served for a Sunday, a birthday, a holiday. The children don't drink orange juice, and their mother can't really stand the sight of it herself, so any thoughts a visitor has about vitamin C and the need the children have for a balanced diet meet up with a family's firm preferences. Then comes school: the approaching bus, the ride, the hours in that classroom, the moments of recess outside in the yard, the time spent in the cafeteria, and soon enough it is time to go home: board the bus, sit and look out at those streets lined by old buildings, most of them wood, some brick, all inhabited by people "from Appalachia," as Peter has heard his teacher mention. Then comes play on the streets, play near the roof, perhaps on it (*that* stoutly denied, if a parent should inquire) and always, every day, a bout of sitting on the front stairs of the buildings or sitting on the porch in the back of the building — and whittling and maybe (in warm weather) listening to the country music which comes out of the windows of various apartments. By six Peter hears his name called, or one of his sisters comes to fetch him and bring him back for supper: a homemade soup, bread, potatoes, beans, gravy and sometimes chicken, sometimes pork. I have heard Peter's father say, upon completion of such a meal: "It's good, eating regular and every day and until you're not hungry any more." Peter hears the words and says yes to himself. Later, he watches television, sees cowboys riding, thinks *that's* good country, too — not like Hot Spot and Letcher County and Kentucky and the "region" called Appalachia, but also not the city, not the place where one eats regularly but dreams of another kind of life. Or, as Peter puts it: "Out West, the cowboys never left the ranches, and they really like their jobs, I think."

In fact the city has been kind to Peter's family, and perhaps as the boy grows up, or certainly as *his* son grows up, the city may seem less a temporary necessity and more a land full of its own pleasures and adventures and promises. I suppose it all depends on what the city itself will become like — on whether our cities ever become anything different for boys like Peter. I sometimes think that Peter's mind is where the changes will have to take place: he will have to give up dreaming of Hot Spot and dig in as one more full-time member of something called a metropolis. That he do so is more "realistic," and "practical," and even a matter of life and death, as the older Peter says often enough, perhaps to justify his day-to-day life, perhaps to squelch any silly, "romantic" thoughts or "fantasies" he may find pressing upon him. In any event, on behalf of both young Peters, the Peter who knows alleys and the Peter who sits on those porches, I hear prayers, the prayers of mothers. I hear the same emphatic, passionate, urgent words, too. I hear. Bless the boy, my God. I hear: Smile upon the boy, dear God. I hear: Find him a life, please do, Lord. I hear: Love him and keep him. And yes —

upon many occasions God, the Lord, Christ Almighty are left out, maybe accidentally, or maybe because somewhere in their minds the mothers of such boys know that before the New Jerusalem arrives there is one day after another ahead for a child of nine, one day after another in the cities we now have, in the world we now have. Perhaps on occasion such women can be too religious to call directly upon any authority, secular or divine, for the kind of help they know their children need, or perhaps they know better than to do so. Perhaps when their calls to God are spoken, they are really calls to themselves, a notice and a warning they give themselves that somehow they will have to struggle along and survive on their own, as has always been the case for people like them.

X

VITALITY AND VIOLENCE,
LIFE AND DEATH

THE reader may emerge somewhat confused from the present chapter. In it I am trying to combine some contrapuntal, even contradictory themes. I am trying to place the families I am writing about in a larger scheme of things than the particular neighborhoods they happen to call their own. I am trying to make some connections between middle-class homes and poor homes, between "us," the book readers and "them," the men and women and children who often cannot take the next meal for granted, let alone find time to read and argue over social theories. I am also trying to contend with a number of ironies and ambiguities, none of which I can "resolve." Side by side in all of us are the psychological achievements we have wrought and the vulnerabilities we have accumulated. We are all at times and in ways inconsistent. We all struggle to subdue the mind's frictions, to tame what is discordant or incongruous or incompatible in us. We are all to a greater or less extent tempted by violence. That is, we are the same, but we differ. We are human, but we are black or white, well educated or just about able to sign our names, possessed of ample money or little money or penniless.

In the next pages I try to deal as best I can with certain questions that have persistently plagued me as a physician and a child psychiatrist. I hope that one day medical students will find the last part of this chapter completely outdated. But I am reasonably sure that the subject matter of the first section will never cease to command our attention.

1.   Death of the Heart in Ghetto Children

In a way, the twentieth century can be called the "century of the child." More than ever before children are watched, studied — and turned into our one hope, our great purpose in life. We work hard so they will have a better chance. We sacrifice so they will be spared suffering. We try to win so they will never lose, never know what it means to be defeated, to surrender.

We claim to know a lot about children. Psychologists and psychiatrists have names to describe just about every year in a child's life. Teachers have learned in course after course how children grow, how they think, how they feel, what they desire, what they fear. And for millions of American parents the baby doctor, the pediatrician, is very much like a particularly inspired oracle who can say nothing wrong, do nothing harmful. As human beings we may have our common sense, our native intuition. But as earnest, well-meaning, dedicated middle-class mothers and fathers we feel it necessary to call upon the doctor for just about everything — that is, if we can afford to do so. The doctor not only will heal our boy's wounds, or treat our girl's sickness. He is the one to let us know what children ought to eat, how long they should sleep, where and how they should play, when they should go to school, and which hobby or game or activity they should be encouraged to take up outside of school.

Yet, despite all this interest in and devotion to children, there are some questions we don't ask our doctors — or even ourselves. And as is often the case, the hardest and most painful questions are very easily stated. What do we really want for our children apart from good food and good clothes and a good school and, later, a good college and a good job? What do they really need if they are to be intelligent as well as smart? Generous and tactful as well as successful? What is our purpose as parents apart from the conventional and necessary purpose of being a protector, an adviser, a guide? A guide to what? Toward what values do we want to guide our children? Put differently, what kind of parents do we want the future world to have?

At this point the honest doctor has to stop both himself and his patient and ask to be excused as an expert. Are children to be protected as much as possible or encouraged to know all sorts of troublesome, unsettling, yes, fearful things? Is wisdom teachable, or charity, or good sense, let alone common sense? Or for all the facts and experiments that twentieth-century scientists have recorded, must parents essentially fall back on the kind of fate Henry James urged upon the writer: "We work in the dark; we do what we can; our doubt is our passion and our passion is our task; the rest is the madness of art."

One need not be a writer to know what it is like to work in the dark, and even live in the dark. For all the experts, we as parents know how awesomely unpredictable children can be. We try hard to meet their needs. We give them everything we've got — and often try to get more, so that we can give them more. And then time and time again we are surprised and silenced. They seem to ask for and want things we may never have thought about. We have done what Henry James suggested, done everything we could, and still as parents we face not the satisfaction that comes with victory, but the very doubt that James mentions — doubts about whether we did the "right thing," doubts about ourselves as parents and our children as children, doubts about our success as mothers and fathers in a nation and a century that have provided us with hundreds of new medicines to cure children's diseases and hundreds of new facts to make what we call "child-rearing" easier.

I am not alone in believing that children have needs that go unmet in America. While some of our children obviously need food and clothing and medical care, others suffer just as much because they have everything — everything except a sense of purpose, a sense of direction, and yes, the kind of passionate doubt that Henry James mentioned. The black maid who speaks at some length in a previous chapter knows what "our" children have to struggle with — the aimlessness and self-doubt and malignant self-centeredness of their parents.

If we would only stop and think, we would realize that children are the world's great skeptics. More than anything else they are seekers. What do they seek? When do they start seeking? And why should their quest be of concern to us as *citizens,* rather than parents? To answer questions like that we have to break down the separations we usually make between the home and the neighborhood, between the nursery and the marketplace, between the living room and the courthouse or voting booth. Each child of two or three is already well on his way to becoming a fascinating and unique mixture of follower and leader, fighter and peacemaker, activist, negotiator, arbitrator, recluse. It is on streets and alleys, in backyards and playgrounds, that children learn what can properly be called the politics of the classroom. There, we as parents and teachers, and they as future citizens, come to terms with one another more decisively than we may care to realize. There, children learn to cooperate with one another, to respect one another; or to use and abuse one another. There, children are encouraged to respect older people but feel free to disagree with them as a right, indeed a human obligation; or there, children learn obedience at all costs — fearful obedience, unquestioning obedience. There, children learn to share their intelligence or to exploit it for themselves and themselves alone. They learn to master themselves, or to beat upon the nearest available neighbor.

In a sense, then, before children even start school they have begun to acquire what philosophers call a "world view," and what psychologists call an "inner sense" — a sense of themselves as worthwhile or as thoroughly expendable. They have learned that food is around when they want it; or, possibly, that food is simply not to be had. They have learned that the winter brings warm coats and jackets, sleds and toboggans, plenty of blankets and plenty of hot chocolate and hot soup; or they have learned that in winter the rats do go in hiding, but only because the ice and cold of the outside has come inside — to add frostbite and the shivers to the hunger that exists in any season.

Children learn other things, too. They learn that their parents work, or that they can't find work. They learn that their mother feels reasonably happy and contented, or that she is really up against it, and afraid from day to day of one or another danger. They learn that their fathers bring home no money, or barely enough money, or so much money that they don't know what to do with it all. They learn that their fathers feel like failures or, to some extent, feel successful. They learn that they don't have a father, or they do have one but he dare not come home if the "welfare lady" is around. They learn, in short, just about everything economists or political scientists talk about.

I suppose it could be said that children learn both the joys and hazards of existence — and no region or class or race has a monopoly on either joy or hazard. The politically and socially weak often produce desperately ambitious children, as history proves. In contrast, well-to-do parents have more than occasionally tried to figure out why their children lack all ambition and even spirit. In the ghetto small children learn to negotiate their ways through dark, broken-down buildings and incredibly dangerous streets. And in our well-to-do suburban communities parents worry because their children seem confused or bored or unwilling to take on or negotiate anything. It is no great discovery that life is ironic, but it can be a tragedy for parents and for a country when the ironies begin to pile up — and in the wrong direction.

One day we may realize that, above all, human beings need a purpose. We are born; we live; we die. It is only a moment we are here, and the mystery and ambiguity of life are always about us, ready in a second to confuse and surprise and frighten us. As children grow they start bombarding us with questions, and we nervously try to comply with answers. Often we are made nervous not because the questions are silly, or absurd, or even unanswerable, but because for a second, in a flash, we have been brought up short. Years of lame excuses, sad rationalizations, and whistling in the dark suddenly are ended by a child's innocent, humiliating curiosity. Why do people kill one another? Why do we live this way and other children that way? Why is it that on television you keep on hearing that people have headaches and stomachaches? And why are they so nervous? What is it, being nervous? Can't we clean up the smoke in the air, the way we clean up the house? Why is the river so dirty? What would you really *like* to be doing, Dad? Why do you say one thing outside the house and something else when we're alone? Is it true, Mother, that we're in trouble, and the world might get all blown up? Why should they make me cram all those facts inside my head and then keep testing me to see if I know how to take tests? I mean, why don't they let me think and say what I think? The teacher says it's so I can get into college someday. She says you have to start early. And when I ask her why, she says so I can be successful. But I want to know why — why be successful if someone can't think for himself or have his own say.

So, the questions keep coming at us. There are brief questions that children of four or five share with philosophers of all time. And there are larger questions, asked by ten- or twelve- or fourteen-year-old boys and girls who are trying their hardest to make sense of all sorts of puzzling and often enough senseless conditions. What are we to do in the face of such trouble — trouble for us as American citizens as well as parents? We can always shrug our shoulders and tell our children to hush, to go off and play. And they listen, too. They hear and sense our silence, our annoyance, our resigned indifference. Often enough they do not dispute us for too long. They do as we suggest, as we urge. They leave us and go out to play. And there, on those carefully tended lawns, or in those alleys littered with debris and vermin, they begin to become *us*. All too often they begin to fight and squabble, hate and retaliate. All too often they stop asking questions and come up with instant, dogmatic answers which they try to force down everyone's throat. Confronted with something new, different, and challenging, they hunch their shoulders and narrow their eyes. Why should they exert themselves, flex themselves, take a risk, make a dare?

Yet, America was founded by people who said no to others and yes to themselves, by mothers and fathers who were willing — more than willing, even anxious and determined — to expose their children to danger, to trouble, to exile itself in order that they might live not more comfortably, but *free*.

Eventually we may persuade and even compel our boys and girls to stop asking, stop thinking, stop wondering. But the price is high — on them as human beings and on us as a nation. Simply put, the price is *the death of the heart* — the title of Elizabeth Bowen's novel, in which a young girl slowly becomes disenchanted with a comfortable but hypocritical world. Her passions seemed futile to her because she judged others unworthy of them. And, of course, she came to feel herself unworthy, too. We cannot feel good about ourselves if we have learned to shut out or distrust others. And to do that, to live peacefully and respectfully with others, we need a certain kind of moral order, a certain kind of social order and political order. It is, therefore, no step at all from the nursery to a city hall, a state capital or the halls of Congress. Children live in particular nations, and nations have particular climates of opinion and stand for particular goals.

A child's passion for excellence, for justice, can be killed at home, or in a school, or even, in fact, by public officials. By the same token, those passions can be encouraged, nourished, and most important of all, given coherent, visible expression in the daily life of a child's nation. A child who sees excellence and justice all around him will not need to learn about such virtues. He will know them in the sure, quiet, unostentatious way that reflects a living, continuous kind of knowledge. Our children desperately need that kind of knowledge, that kind of familiarity with excellence and justice.

All this has to be said before the so-called slum child or ghetto child is singled out for discussion. Children of the ghetto are first children, then particular children who have to learn things no school will ever credit them with learning. If all children learn about the place where they live and what they can reasonably expect of life, ghetto children do so rather precociously.

How is it done? Are six-year-olds taught the ghetto's facts of life by their parents? Do elementary schools brief them on how to fend off large, insolent rats, or how to deal with the mosquitoes and flies that enter windows unprotected by screens? Do those children learn in Sunday School about narcotics and prostitution and alcoholism so that when they walk to a nearby store (and pay higher prices for food than the rest of us do) they can recognize, be unafraid of, and maneuver their way around the drunks and pimps and streetwalkers who frequent certain ghetto streets?

I can vouch for the old-fashioned kind of morality that large numbers of ghetto children are exposed to. Again and again I have wished some of our most conservative citizens could hear the things I hear, see the things I see. I am not now referring to the wretchedness and hunger and squalor, but to the almost desperate (alas, often enough mindless) puritanism to be found among very poor mothers and fathers. We picture them as "loose," immoral, thoughtless, those parents — as lazy, as spendthrifts. We say they don't know how to control themselves, work, save, plan for the future, sacrifice today for tomorrow. And yes, so many of them are wayward, have *come to be* wayward.

But what about the beginning, the first years in our urban or rural slums? Were all those children born criminals? Were they *told* to be criminals by their parents? Is there perhaps some *lumpenproletariat* ideology, some ethic this nation's Mexican-Americans and Negroes and Indians and Appalachian whites have all conspired to believe in? Do they all tell their children to ignore school, loaf around, violate laws, cause trouble, take part in riots, appear disorderly or sullen or apathetic? Is the "welfare road" (as one ghetto resident describes his fate) chosen cynically and opportunistically by able-bodied men and women who simply don't want to work?

I have no universally applicable answers to those questions, but my observations lead me to believe that ghetto children are treated, if anything, more strictly and punitively than their middle-class counterparts. They are shouted at more. They are beaten more. They are trusted less. They are preached at more. They are given more specific and rigid rules to follow — and less leeway in the following. At the age of four or five they often are quiet, all too accepting and accommodating and fearful in the presence of their elders, particularly their mothers. When they first come to school they are ready to be still, to take it on the chin, and indeed be sternly rebuked — whipped, pinched, screamed at — if they dare go astray. Slowly, however, in the words of one teacher I have interviewed — a woman who has worked in a ghetto school for fifteen years — "the whole thing comes apart."

What "thing" comes apart? "Well, everything," she replies, and then spells it all out: "They're told to obey, obey, obey. Their mothers scream at them all day long, and beat them at the drop of a hat. Not all of them, but a lot. They're tired, those mothers, tired and desperate. So they suffer and the kids suffer. And the worst of it is that they keep on telling those kids to shape up, be good and all that, and then they'll get ahead and be rewarded, by God and their country. Imagine that! It would be funny if it weren't so tragic.

"And finally those kids get the score, you know. They see that this school, it's a detention center. They see that we don't care, that we've given up caring. All we want is silence, quiet, just like their mothers; that's all they want, a moment's peace. So, we tell them to 'mind their manners,' and they get the point. They know we're running a 'holding operation' here, a delay, a period of time between their childhood and their grown-up years which, let me tell you, come when they're about ten or twelve, when they start *doing* what they've *learned about* at six or seven: how to live in the ghetto and stay alive.

"So, that's about the story. They 'get wise,' as they put it. Oh, I've heard them say it, exactly those words, a million times these past years. They realize that every word they've heard pronohed at them is silly, foolish, not to the point. They realize that their mothers shout the American dream at them but are themselves, in their very lives, living proof of some terrible nightmare. They realize 'it's no use,' as we hear them say. And so they get stubborn and difficult and 'recalcitrant,' we call it. And they wait and wait and wait until the streets claim them, and the courts and the jails and the insane asylums and the hospitals, and pretty soon, death. But, you know, by that time, they've been dead a long time — deep inside."

Her "deep inside" is in the heart, the soul. And we who live, and die only late in life never quite can "understand." We keep on wondering why, for God's sake, they "behave" like that. But can the living *ever* understand the dead?

2. *Vitality in Ghetto Children*

When I read about ghetto children in psychiatric journals and educational reviews — not to mention the public press — I do not recognize the boys and girls I meet and observe every day. From the psychiatric quarter I hear about the mental illness that plagues the poor (though none of us has noticed psychiatrists — or any other kind of doctors — rushing in large numbers to practice in Harlem, Watts, or Chicago's South Side). I read about how apathetic or unruly ghetto children are: the "culturally disadvantaged," the blacks and Puerto Ricans, the surly, suspicious, "deprived" whites who come from Appalachia to northern cities, or the older southern immigrants who still live in the slums. One report mentions the "poor impulse controls" of lower-class black children; another, the "personality defects" of slum boys who, at five or six, are destined to be "sociopaths," delinquents, or worse. The picture is bleak: untended or brutalized children threaten teachers, assault one another, violate school regulations or city ordinances, and in general show themselves bound for a life of crime, indolence, or madness.

Educators confirm what their brother social scientists have noted: ghetto children do not take to school; they are nasty — or plain lazy. I wish they at least were frankly described that way. Instead one has to wrestle with the impossible jargon of educational psychologists who talk about "motivational deficits" or "lowered achievement goals" or "self-esteem impairment." We are told that slum schools must be "enriched" with programs to suit children who live in a vast cultural wasteland. Machines, books, audiovisual equipment, special "curricula," smaller classes, trips to museums, contacts with suburban children, with trees and hillsides — the ghetto child needs all of that and more. He needs personal "guidance." He could benefit from knowing a VISTA volunteer or a college student who wants to be a tutor or a housewife from the other side of town who wants to give poor children the things her own children take for granted.

Though some of those assertions are obviously correct, their cumulative implication is misleading and unfair. It is about time the lives of ghetto children were seen as something more than a tangle of psychopathology and flawed performances in school. Children in the ghetto do need help, but not the kind that stems from an endless, condescending recital of their troubles and failures — and often ignores or caricatures the strength, intelligence, and considerable ingenuity they do possess.

As I have already indicated, for a long time I, too, looked only for the harm inflicted on the boys and girls who grow up on the wrong side of the tracks. I found plenty to point to. Yet, while I was busy documenting such conditions I failed to see the other side of the picture. Determined to record every bit of pathology I could find, I failed to ask myself what makes for survival in the poor; indeed, sometimes for more than that — for a resourcefulness and vitality that some of us in the therapy-prone suburbs might at least want to ponder, if not envy.

My dilemma was not too different from the one that many civil-rights workers — particularly the white middle-class kind — have come to recognize. In 1964, when by the hundreds we went south to Mississippi, the emphasis was on setting free a cruelly oppressed people. Again and again the black man's plight was analyzed, his suffering emphasized. We had come to put an end to it all, to fight with the weak against the strong. At that time a writer like Ralph Ellison — who for years has insisted upon the rich culture that Negroes have created for themselves — was summarily dismissed by "liberators" who could not imagine they had a lot to learn from the victimized rural blacks of the South.

However, one by one we had to face the ironies in our apparently clear-cut situation. "It's not so easy, the longer you stay down here," said one northern student who had been living with a black family for a few months. "They're poor and beaten down. They can't talk right, and they can't write at all. There aren't any pictures on their walls, and the cabins they live in — you wouldn't even use them for a summer hideaway. They're scared out of their minds when a cop comes near them, like in a police state. But something starts happening to the way you think, because you like the people, the poor, downtrodden Negro, and the more time you spend with him the more you begin to admire him, and even wish your own family were more like his."

"If I talk like that up in Cambridge," he went on, "they'll tell me how romantic I am, how naïve. They'll say it's fine for me to talk — with my white skin and my father's bank account and my ability to leave any minute I want. I know, because a few months ago if I heard someone like me talking about 'the dignity' and 'real character' and 'integrity' of the people down here, I would tell them to get their kicks some other way, not by going native with the people who live the way they do because they have no other choice. And most of all, I would tell them to go ask the sharecropper in the Delta if he wants to stay the way he is, with his 'dignity' and 'integrity,' or get what the rest of us have, the cars and clothes and washing machines and everything else.

"It's a fact that a lot of the people we've met down here are stronger than we ever assumed. And a lot of them really do treat their children in a different way than we do — and sometimes it's for the better. The kids are close. They sleep together and help one another. They don't go off by themselves, the way we do. They're respectful to their parents, and to grown-ups, and very good to one another. They have a real warmth and humor and a natural kind of directness or honesty — I don't know what to call it, but I see every one of us noticing it, and I hear them all trying to describe it, even the hard-nosed social science types. They're ashamed at what they see; they don't want to be troubled by finding anything 'good' in people they came to save from everything 'bad.' "

The longer we talked in our all-night "soul sessions," the more we found ourselves in agreement. We had shared similar experiences and found them surprising and worth considering. I think more than anything else we felt chastened by the sight of our own arrogance.* Late one night, a black man who lived nearby spoke up, confirming our feelings. "The people who help us, we're grateful to them," he said, "but I wish they wouldn't keep

---

* I have tried to document our experience and our dilemmas in the first volume of *Children of Crisis* and especially in its sequel, *Migrants, Share-croppers, Mountaineers*.

on telling us how sorry they are for us, how bad we have it. And I wish their eyes wouldn't pop out every time they stay with us and see we're not crying all day long and running wild or something. The other day a white fellow, he said how wonderful my home is, and how good we eat and get along together, and how impressed he was by it all. And I was sure glad, but I wanted to take him aside and say, 'Ain't you nice, but don't be giving us that kind of compliment, because it shows on you what you don't know about us.'"

Of course people under stress can develop special strengths, while security tends to make one soft, though no one in his right mind can *recommend* hardship or suffering as a way of life, nor justify slavery, segregation, or poverty because they sometimes produce strong, stubborn people. The issue is one of justice — and not only to the black man. The black man deserves to be seen for who he is and what he has become. If giving him his due — as a citizen and longtime victim of all sorts of exploitation — requires first calling him destroyed, "sick," a psychological cripple, or a moral menace, then perhaps we should recognize our own political bankruptcy. If psychological or sociological labels are to be pinned on the black man, then those who do so might at least be careful to mention the enormous, perplexing issues that plague the white suburban middle class: a high divorce rate, juvenile crime, political indifference or inertia to match any rural black man's, psychiatric clinics and child-guidance centers filled to the brim and with waiting lists so long that some are called only after two or three years, greed and competitiveness that worried teachers see in the youngest boys and girls and accept wearily as a manifestation of the "system."

There are, to be fair, some observers who have consistently remarked on the considerable energy and "life" they see in slum children. They have seen openness, humor, real and winning vitality. Many ghetto children I know have a flesh and blood loyalty to one another, a disarming code of honor, a sharp, critical eye for the fake and pretentious, a delightful capacity to laugh, yell, shout, sing, congratulate themselves, and tickle

others. Their language is often strong and expressive, their drawings full of action, feeling, and even searing social criticism.

One thing is certain, though: ghetto childhood tends to be
short and swift. Those fast-moving, animated children quickly
grow old rather than grow up, and begin to show signs of the
resignation accurately described by writer after writer. At twelve
or thirteen these children feel that schools lead nowhere, that
there will be jobs for only a few, that ahead lies only the prospect
of an increasingly futile and bitter struggle to hang on to such
health, possessions, and shelter as they have.

"They are alive, and you bet they are, and then they go off and
quit," said one mother, summing it up for me. "I can tell it by
their walk and how they look. They slow down and get so tired
in their face, real tired. And they get all full of hate, and they
look cross at you, as if I cheated them when I brought them into
the world. I have seven, and two of them have gone that way,
and to be honest, I expect my every child to have it happen —
like it did to me. I just gave up when I was about fourteen or so.
And what brings us back to life is having the kids and keeping
them with us for a while, away from the outside and everything
bad. But there comes a day when they ask you why it's like it is
for us, and all you can do is shrug your shoulders, or sometimes
you scream. But they know already, and they're just asking for
the record. And it doesn't take but a few months to see that
they're no longer kids, and they've lost all the hope and the life
you tried to give them."

The vitality of each new child restores at least the possibility of
hope in a parent, and so life in the ghetto persists in seeking after
purpose and coherence. Mothers tell their children to do this or
not to do that — even as they hold their breath in fear and doubt.
Meanwhile, many of us comfortably on the outside hide our
shame by listing the reasons we can't change things in our
society, or by making the people who need those changes utterly
dull and deteriorated.

Though we may console ourselves with some of the programs
we offer the poor, others are not only condescending and self-
defeating, but they overlook the very real assets and interests of

ghetto children. It has never occurred to some of the welfare workers, educators, or Head Start teachers I have met that "their" programs and policies bore, amuse, or enrage children from the slums.

Consider, for example, one ghetto family I visit twice a week. They are on welfare. Two children were in a Head Start program for a summer. An older son took part in an "enrichment" program. A teen-aged cousin has been in the Job Corps. At school the children are told by their teachers what they already know, that their school is "inadequate." The building is old, the corridors are packed with many more students than they were intended for, and the teachers are disciplinarians at most. The head of this family is a woman not much over thirty who regularly calls herself "old." Once she added that she was also "sick," and I immediately took notice, expecting to hear about an ache or pain I could diagnose. But she went on to say that she was "tired of everything they try to do to help us. They send us those welfare checks, and with them comes that lady who peeks around every corner here and gives me those long lectures on how I should do everything — like her, of course. I want to tell her to go charge around and become a spy, or one of those preachers who can find sin in a clean handkerchief.

"Then they take my kids to the Head Start thing, and the first thing I hear is the boys' fingernails are dirty, and they don't eat the proper food, and they don't use the right words, and the words they do use, no one can make them out. It's just like that with the other kids. They try to take them to those museums and places, and tell them how sorry life is here at home and in the neighborhood, and how they are no good, and something has to be done to make them better — make them like the rich ones, I guess.

"But the worst is that they just make you feel no good at all. They tell you they want to help you, but if you ask me they want to make you into *them* and leave you without a cent of yourself left to hang on to. I keep on asking them, why don't they fix the country up so that people can work, instead of patching up with this and that and giving us a few dollars — to keep us from starving right to death? Why don't they get out of here and let us be, and have our lives?"

I can think of many things that could be done to take advantage of what that mother already has. The city might help her take part in a school she felt was hers, was sensitive to her feelings, her experiences, her desires — as indeed schools are in many other communities. There is work in her neighborhood, in her building, that she and her family might want to do, might be paid to do. Her children might be encouraged to use the strong and familiar idiom they know. Why should they learn the stilted talk of people who continue to scorn them? They might be appreciated for their own dress, their own customs, their own interests and energies — their *style*. They might read books that picture them, their lives and their adventures. Perhaps, then, some perennial "observers" would be surprised. With work, with money, with self-respect that is not slyly thwarted or denied outright by every "public" agency, the poor might eventually turn out to be very much like — us.

3. *Violence in Ghetto Children*

When I worked as a child psychiatrist in a children's hospital, I spent most of my time with middle-class children whose parents very often seemed earnest and sensitive; certainly they were worried about their children, at times excessively so. The boys and girls, for their part, were usually quiet and controlled. They were suffering from "school phobias" or the various fears and anxieties that have been described by a generation of psychiatrists. If they were disobedient and loud, usually it was a specific form of disobedience I saw, a very particular noisiness I heard, all responding to something they dreaded or dared not to look at. In a sense, then, the unruliness I noticed only confirmed my impression of a general restraint (emotional tidiness, I suppose it could be called) that middle-class children by the time they are two or three years old are likely to have acquired, never to lose.

Yes, there are the usual signs of aggressive tendencies in the "latency years" (the years preceding puberty when sexual urges are quiescent) — the bold and even nasty games, the play that seems involuntarily brutish. But a long look often reveals how curiously formal, even restrained, the unruliness of these children actually is. Despite all the "drives" one hears psychologists and psychiatrists talk about — the surges of desire, spite, and hate that continuously press upon the child's mind and in dreams or daytime fantasies gain control of it — the fact remains that by the time middle-class American children first reach school, at age five or six, they are remarkably in control of themselves. As a result, when the violence in such children erupts in a psychiatrist's office during a session of drawing or in the midst of a game played by the psychiatrist and the child, it is almost a caricature of violence — violence so safe, so exaggerated, so camouflaged, and so quarantined that the very word seems inappropriate.

We in psychiatry are often accused of seeing only the drab and morbid side of human nature. If it would be any comfort to people, I suppose we could easily make partial amends for that morbid bias by letting it be known how overwhelmingly law-abiding a certain kind of middle-class man is: if he is vindictive, he is likely to be so toward himself. Psychiatrists spend most of their time helping people take a look at violence removed far enough from their own recognition to be, in effect, somebody else's property. If in time the patient, whether child or adult, owns up to what he secretly or temporarily senses, he will be in greater, not less, control of himself. Thus, I remember treating a ten-year-old boy who drew wild and vicious scenes, filled with fire and death or at least an injury or two. When I wanted to know about what was going on, he let me know the score rather quickly by pointing to the people in his pictures and saying, "I don't know; you'd have to ask them."

Not everyone in America is brought up to disown violence so consistently that its very presence in his own drawings can be adroitly (that is, innocently) denied. As I have worked with children in both southern rural slums and northern "ghettos," I have come to appreciate how useless it is to think of, or judge, the growth and development of the children of the depressed poor in the same way I ordinarily view the development of middle-class children. It is, as one boy in a Boston ghetto recently reminded me, "a different ball game when you're out in left field, instead of in there pitching."

If we consider what a child of the slums goes through, from birth on, and if we keep a special eye on what in his experience may make him "violent," even at the age of seven or eight, we may well gain, rather than lose, respect for the upbringing he receives. To begin, I have seen how much childbearing means to poor women: it is the one thing *they* can do, and do creatively. It is the one chance they have to show both themselves and others that there is hope in this world, as well as the next. By pointing this out, I am not arguing against keeping families to a sensible size, nor overlooking the impulsive, dreary background that is also commonly associated with pregnancies among the poor, whether in or out of wedlock. I am simply saying to others what a mother once felt she had to let me know: "They all tell us to cut down on the kids, cut down on the kids, because you can't keep up with them as it is, and even a few is too much if you're on welfare for life, the way we have to be, like it or not. I try to cut down, and I want to, but it's not so easy. You have to watch your step all the time, and we can't afford the pills they have for the others.

"Anyway, it's the one time in my life I really feel like I'm *somebody,* like I'm doing something. People come around and expect me to feel ashamed of myself, like I've done something wrong, and I'm adding to crime on the streets — that's all you hear these days, *our* crime, not anyone else's — but, instead, I feel proud of myself, like I can at least make a baby, and maybe he'll have it better than us — who knows? — though I doubt it."

Another time she spoke the following words, and for some reason I felt the need to arrange the words this way.

Both Ways

They say no, no, no
No more kids
The welfare worker

She tells you you're
  overpopulating the world
  and something has to be done
But right now one of the few
  times I feel good
  is when I'm pregnant
And I can feel I'm getting somewhere
At least then I am
Because I'm making something grow
And not seeing everything die around me
  like all the time it does in the street

I'll tell you

They want to give me the pill and stop the kids
And I'm willing for the most part
But I wish I could take care
  of all the kids I could have
And then I'd want plenty of them
Or maybe I wouldn't
I wouldn't have to be pregnant
  to feel some hope about things

I don't know
You can look at it both ways, I guess.

If we want to help that woman keep her family small, I hope we also want to give her what she needs to feel like the somebody she still desires to be. I know her children, and already I have seen them readying themselves for what their mother herself calls "the goddam street." Each one of those children has been held and breast-fed in ways I think some middle-class mothers might have cause to envy. Though the flat is cold and rat-infested, there is real and continuing warmth between that mother and her babies. "Symbiotic," some of my colleagues — who have a name for everything — might call the relationship of that mother and her children; it is also a bond that unites the fearful and hungry against the inevitable day when the home has to yield to the outside.

Slum children do not always go unprepared when that time comes. As I indicated earlier in this chapter, the chances are these children receive specific and brutal instruction about the "realities" of life at the age of two, three, or four — so that when they emerge from the home the police, the hoods, the addicts, the drunks are already familiar. The disappointments in the schools or on playgrounds are already expected. The mother I have already quoted has also testified to the morality and lawfulness she tries to inspire in her children: "I don't know how to do it. I don't know how to keep my kids from getting stained and ruined by everything outside. I keep them close to me, and sometimes I feel like everything will be OK, because they know how much I want for it to be, and they'll go make it be, the way I thought I could. But after a while they want to go out. You know how a kid is when he's three or four, and he wants to *move*, no matter where, so long as he keeps going. And where can he move in here? So I let them go, and I stop and say a prayer every morning and ask for them to be saved, but I have to say it, I'm not expecting my prayers to be answered, not around here. And when the kids come back upstairs, I give them a look, if I have the time, to see what's on their face, and what they've learned that'll make a mess of everything I try to teach. And I can tell — I can tell from day to day what's getting into them. You know what it is? It's the devil, and he tells them to give up, because there's no other choice, not around here there isn't."

She is a churchgoing woman, as are many of her neighbors. I have found that she knows her Bible better than me or my neighbors, and in fact she doubtless puts more store in prophetic, messianic Christianity than most Americans do. When her children start walking and talking, she starts teaching them rules and fears — enough of both to satisfy anyone who is worried about the decline of "morality" in America. At least in that home, and others like it I have visited, children are not allowed free rein. Instead, they are told to obey, and they are swiftly slapped or punched if they falter.

Over the years I have learned how loyal slum families can be to America's ethic of "rugged individualism." Children are taught through the ubiquitous television to seek after all the products of our proud technology: the cars that can speed faster than any law allows, the records and clothes whose worth can only be seasonal, the bright and shiny places to frequent, the showy, gadget-filled places that not only shelter people but also make statements about their power, influence, and bank accounts. At five and six years old, ghetto children in today's America share through television a world quite similar to the one known by their wealthy age-mates. I find it almost unnerving when I see drawings from a child not yet old enough to attend school that show the appetites and yearnings our advertisers are able to arouse. Precisely what do such children do with such wishes and fantasies, besides spell them out on paper for someone like me?

When a child of six or seven from the ghetto encounters the politics of the street or the school yard, he brings along both the sensual and the fearfully moral experience he has had at home. Slum children live at close quarters to their parents and their brothers or sisters. They are often allowed to be very much on their own, very free and active, yet they are also punished with a vengeance when distracted or forlorn parents suddenly find an issue forced, a confrontation inevitable. They face an ironic mixture of indulgence and fierce curtailment.

Such children come to school prepared to be active, vigorous, perhaps much more outgoing on an average than middle-class children. But they are quick to lose patience, sulk, feel wrong and wronged and cheated by a world they have already learned to be impossible, uncertain, and contradictory. Here are the words of an elementary-school teacher who has worked in a northern ghetto for three years and still feels able to talk about the experience with hope as well as bitterness: "They're hard to take, these kids, because they're not what you think when you first come, but they're not what you'd like for them to be, either. I don't mean what I *used* to like for them to be, but what I want for them now. They're fast and clever and full of life. That was the hardest thing for me to realize — that a boy or girl in the ghetto isn't a hopeless case, or someone who is already a delinquent when he comes into the first grade. The misconceptions we have in the suburbs are fantastic, really, as I think back — and remember what I used to think myself.

"I expected to find children who had given up, and were on the way to fail, or to take dope, or something like that. Instead it was in a lot of ways a breath of fresh air, talking with them and teaching them. They were friendlier than suburban children, and they got along better with one another. I didn't have to spend half the year trying to encourage the children to be less competitive with one another. We don't call middle-class children 'culturally deprived,' but sometimes I wonder. They're so nervous and worried about everything they say — what it will mean, or what it will cost them, or how it will be interpreted. That's what they've learned at home, and that's why a lot of them are tense kids and, even worse, stale kids, with frowns on their faces at ages six or seven.

"Not a lot of the kids I teach now. They're lively and active, so active I don't know how to keep up with them. They're not active learners, at least learners of the knowledge I'm trying to sell them, but they're active and they learn a lot about the world, about one another. In fact, one of the big adjustments I've had to make is realizing that these kids learn a lot from one another. They are smart about things my kids will never understand. They just don't think school is worth a damn. To them it's part of a big outside world that has a grip on them and won't let them get anyplace, no matter how hard they try. So what's the use, they ask themselves. The answer is that there isn't any use — so they go right on marking time in class until they can get out.

"We teachers then figure they're stupid, or they're hopelessly tough and 'delinquent,' or their homes are so bad they'll always be 'antisocial' or 'incorrigible.' I've found that when they're playing and don't know I'm looking they are different kids — spontaneous, shrewd, very smart, and perceptive. Then we go back into the classroom, and it's as though a dense fog has settled in on all of us. They give me a dazed look, or a stubborn, unco-

operative one, and they just don't do anything, unless forced
to — by being pushed and shoved and made to fear the authority
they know I have."

We have compared notes many times, this teacher and I. One
child we both know is a boy of eight who does very poor work in
school. He is a belligerent child, a troublemaker. I see him in his
home because his brother is going to a predominantly white suburban school, one of the very few children in the neighborhood
who does. Their mother, living on public assistance with six children and no husband, has her hands full. She finds her "difficult
child" smarter than her "model" one, the boy I watch riding a bus
that takes him away from the ghetto.

The teacher and I agree, the "difficult boy" is a smart boy, but
an impatient, agile, and provocative boy. He is headed for
trouble, but as I talk with him I find *myself* in trouble. I have
asked him to draw pictures — of himself, of his school, of his
home, of anything he wishes. I get from him devastating por-
trayals: schools that look like jails, teachers whose faces show
scorn or drowsiness, streets and homes that are as awful to see on
paper as they are in real life, "outsiders" whose power and mer-
cenary hostility are all too obvious and, everywhere, the police,
looking for trouble, creating trouble, checking up, hauling people
to court, calling them names, getting ready to hurt them, assault
them, jail them, and beat them up — even though they are
children.

Once I asked the boy whether he *really* thought the police
would hurt someone of his age. He said: "To the cops, everyone
around here is a little bad boy, no matter how old he is or how
many grandchildren he has around." At moments like that my
psychiatric, categorical mind finds itself stunned and for a
change ready to grant that boy and others like him freedom from
the various diagnostic, explanatory, or predictive schemes people
like me learn so well and find to be (in our world) so useful.

Welfare workers, in the pictures ghetto children draw, stand
near the police like dogs, with huge piercing eyes, ears that seem
as twisted as they are oversize, and mouths either noticeably
absent or present as thin lines enclosing prominent and de-

cidedly pointed and ragged teeth. To ghetto children, as to their
parents, the welfare worker is the policeman's handmaiden, and
together they come, as one child put it, "to keep us in line or send
us away."

I have listened to public welfare workers and their "clients"
talk, and I recognize the impossible situation they both face, the
worker often as insulted by the rules and regulations as the
family he visits. I often compare the relationship between the
workers and their clients with one that develops in psychotherapy,
as for a while powerful forces pull both doctor and patient backward in time toward those early years when parents check up on
children, trying to keep them on the right side of a "line" that
constantly puzzles the child and perhaps also the parent more
than she or he realizes.

One welfare worker recently summarized the situation for me:
"They behave like evasive kids, always trying to avoid getting
caught for this or that. And me, I'm like a child myself, only an
older one — always trying to take care of my poor brothers and
sisters, but also trying to get them in trouble or find them in
trouble, so I can squeal on them."

I find in some of the children that worker sees a vitality, an
exuberance, that reminds me often of the fatally ill I once treated
on hospital wards: for a long time they appear flushed with life,
even beautiful, only to die. I remember hearing from a distinguished physician who supervised a few of us who were interns:
"They're fighting the battle of tuberculosis, and they're going to
lose, but not without a brilliant flash of energy. It's a shame we
can't intervene, right at the critical moment, and help them win."

4. *A Doctor Can Keep a Poor Heart Beating*

To understand the medical problems of the urban poor one has
to keep going back to those rural counties which still send immigrants to our cities but, just as important, provide experiences
men and women later find unforgettable, no matter how many
hundreds of miles they have moved. It is nice, it is lifesaving to
be away from the sheriff in Alabama and the courthouse gangs

that run parts of Kentucky and West Virginia with an iron hand
— one that quite naturally holds the keys to a generous larder for
a certain few. It is nice to be in cities, where electric lights can be
had so easily, and clean water so readily. But it is also, briefly,
like this: "These streets, and all that you see here, and live with,
it's like Hell, like what the preacher told us Hell would be like. He
always did say Hell would be more comfortable and more terrible, both at the same time, and now I know what he meant."

She is a newcomer to a northern ghetto, the woman who spoke
those words, and if she is now very much better off than she was,
she has recently been tired and weary, and as a matter of fact,
sick — very sick to a doctor's eye and ear. She has been thin,
much too thin in view of the starchy diet she holds to. A short
while back her skin appeared wet and in places markedly wrin-
kled. She always seemed short of breath, and a few steps compelled her to stop and breathe heavily and finally "catch up," as
she puts it. While she was doing that, doing exactly that physio-
logically, as a matter of fact, catching up on the oxygen she
needed, she invariably would put her right hand to her chest. If
asked why, she would tell why: "I get the pains." If asked more
she would tell more: "I've been getting these pains ever since I
can recall. I was little, and I'd have the pains over here in my
chest. That was in Sweet Water, Alabama, yes sir, in Marengo
County. They were growing pains I used to call them, because
my momma told me that was what they were. When I was all
grown, and the pains didn't leave, I decided they would be with
me all my life, and there wasn't anything I could do but accept
them, like you do the things, the lots and lots of things that come
to you all of a sudden and don't ever leave."

Unfortunately, her resignation, her sad but philosophical acquiescence, only lasts so long; at times she becomes quite frightened and fears she will die. The pain in her chest becomes stab-
bing, the shortness of breath severe, palpitations begin and stay
and stay until she concludes she is about to "go," a word she uses
in place of "die" — and I have never heard her use that word, not
in some six years of talk, a significant part of which has had to do
with illnesses and with the serious, even crippling effects those

illnesses have visited upon various members of her family. She can remember "that feeling" in her chest as a child, and now she still goes through what she remembers: "I'd have that feeling coming all over my chest, and I'd think God was calling to me, this time He was, and I'd better get ready to go. I'd say to myself that my little sister that departed, I'd be seeing her, maybe in Heaven, so I wouldn't be lonely. I'd be ready. I'd take a breath, and I'd think it was the last one, the last breath I'd ever breathe. Then another breath would come, and I'd have to get ready all over again to say good-bye. After a while God must have changed his mind. He still hasn't made up His mind. I get my spells, and sometimes I'm sure I'm at the end of my stay here, and I'll soon be gone, all gone, and sometimes I'm sure — by now I am — that I'll get through and last until another time, because it's not so bad this time, it doesn't hurt so much. There are people that God calls right away, real sudden-like, once He's decided to do so, and there are people He just can't be sure about, and He waits and waits, and I'm one of that kind, I guess."

As a physician I long ago made some reasonable guesses about what ailed her. When I first met her and got to know her — in Alabama it was, in 1963 — I decided that she might well have a thyroid condition, hyperthyroidism to be exact. Her eyes were large, a little shining, and demonstrated a certain stare that one can see in such cases. She was thin, tense, highly sensitive to heat and very much troubled by profuse sweating, hence the wet skin I mentioned above. For all her thinness, her frail appearance, her nervousness, she ate quite well, even heartily, though she had an appetite for the wrong things, I in my lofty wisdom kept on noticing — and to make matters worse and more complicated, she couldn't afford a lot of the sounder, healthier foods she might have eaten were they there for the asking. She was eating voraciously of candy and bread and potatoes and pork that was more fat than meat, though she did insist that given the opportunity she would eat better pork — of course she would! — that is, pork with a lot of meat to it, "except that it costs, it costs and costs."

Besides her thyroid I thought a doctor ought to evaluate her heart, her "cardiac status," as it is put. Her stories about her childhood suggested to me that she had as a girl contracted rheumatic fever, which in turn had caused damage to her heart, enough damage to give her rather classical symptoms: chest pain, cough, shortness of breath, palpitations, swelling of her ankles, which she remembers getting from time to time "thick and heavy and real puffy" — then gradually becoming better. Her more recent nervousness, her tendency to perspire excessively, her marked loss of weight without any concomitant loss of appetite all suggested the thyroid difficulty; indeed, a daughter had noticed "something about Mother's eyes — they stick out at you." I could not be sure about any of this, any of the diagnoses I made. I only remember thinking to myself that here was yet another person in a ghetto who as a child had gone through repeated bouts of severe illness and as a grown-up was still troubled by illness, seemingly more complicated illness — a person who nevertheless had never gone to a clinic, a hospital, a doctor's office, had never been visited at home by a school nurse or physician, had never in her life even seen a physician.

That is right: at the age of thirty Rosa Lee Welch had gone North, having never once laid eyes on a doctor, and at the age of thirty-one had still not had the medical work-up she so obviously needed — mind you, after a year in Boston's Roxbury, after a year of living within a few miles of some three medical schools and some hospitals that are the world's finest. I urged upon her a visit to a clinic. I told her how much concerned many doctors are — yes, concerned about people like her. I told her about America's younger doctors, especially about them; they are trying to involve themselves in the lives and problems of the poor, and she, Mrs. Rosa Lee Welch, of Sweet Water, Alabama, she was just the kind of woman those doctors would welcome, would want to help, would try to help, *would* help. She listened and nodded her head, but she also shook it, and interestingly enough, she did the latter at just the point I least expected to elicit her misgivings. Certainly doctors up North want to help me, she seemed to say with her face, her look, the movement of her head. Certainly they are around here; they must be, because if they're nowhere to be found by the likes of me in Marengo County, and if they are not in Boston either, except for the rich, then a poor person in America will never find them anywhere. Certainly they would try hard, those doctors. In her words: "They wouldn't be good doctors if they didn't try to beat an illness when they see it. Like you say, they have the colleges up here, the good ones, and they'd probably want to help me out. I know they would. At least I hope they would."

For all her assurances she didn't quite believe what she accepted as true, what she had to say she hoped rather than knew for certain. Still, that kind of doubt was not the one that really bothered her, and as it turned out, very much surprised me. What most of all kept her away from an active pursuit of medical evaluation came to this — and no words of mine can match hers, do justice to the range and complexity of fears and hesitations and expectations and beliefs that side by side struggle for acknowledgment and expression in her mind: "I'd go if they'd be of help, like you say. But I don't believe they can do much, the doctors. They'll mess you up, a lot of the time they will. My aunt, she was someone special. She worked for the bossman's wife. She took care of her room and her clothes, and she cooked for her. She was her favorite, of all the colored that worked for her, she was the one that the missus liked the most, and she told Leona so. She said she couldn't live without Leona because she had 'the best temperament in the world.' Leona would come over and tell my mother that it doesn't make any difference if she gets a lot of money or a little — she got a little! — so long as the missus spoke so much good of her all the time. My daddy once asked her, Leona, if she could eat all the 'good' that was spoken of her, and feed it to her children, but Leona started crying, and my mother told my daddy to get out fast and not be so bad-tongued.

"One day Leona took sick. She'd been having headaches, you know, like everyone has. She'd been having bad digestion, like I do. Then all of a sudden, right in front of the missus, she got a bad headache and her stomach started hurting something terrible, and then she threw up all she'd had over there to eat, and she fell to the floor and passed out. I guess she'd told the missus her head was hurting bad and her stomach, and the next thing she was down, right beside the refrigerator, we heard. The missus acted as though someone of her own was sick. She called her husband, and he called the hospital, and they made a special case of it and took Leona right over and put her in a room, all to herself. There were no colored there, and the room Leona had, it was reserved for the rich ones of the whites.

"Well, it was an awful thing. They wouldn't let us come visit her, only the missus. My daddy lost his good sense and started being funny with my mother. He said Leona had suddenly turned white and that was what had happened — she'd collapsed on her face and turned white and so naturally they won't let us see her, because she's all locked up there in the hospital with the white people, while they try to figure out what to do. He never should have talked like that, because Leona died — it was hardly a day or two after she fell sick and went there, went to the hospital. We never learned what it was that happened to her. The missus told us she wasn't sure, either. She said the doctors told her that Leona had about a dozen things wrong with her, that's right, and maybe even more than that.

"She was called by God; that's what I believe. She must have been upset there, in the hospital. She never was inside a place like that, I'm sure. It was a brick building, large and with glass doors. We went and looked at it. We asked them if they please wouldn't just let Leona look out of the window, so that we could see her and wave to her, and she could see us and wave to us. The nurse told us to go, and the faster the better. So we did. Leona went too — do you see? Leona knew the doctors wanted to help her. The missus said Leona told her she knew that. I'm sure she did. But Leona never before had asked anyone in this world to help her but God. I do believe that she must have prayed extra-special hard to Him when she woke up and found herself in that place, all by herself, in a room she was, with the white people doing things to her — to help her, I know, to help get her better. Now she's *really* better, thank God."

The longer she talks the more apparent it becomes that she is not to be immediately judged as afraid, pure and simple — afraid of hospitals and doctors through "ignorance" and all the

other things one could so easily ascribe to her. Of course her
aunt's quick death in a hospital that barred her and other visitors
cannot be forgotten. Of course she has no real awareness of how
doctors and hospitals work, especially in a city like Boston. Of
course she is badly educated, in fact barely able to write her
name and unable to read. Nor can I deny her the suspicions and
superstitions that go with her particular sort of life. Yet, for all
that, I do not believe she keeps herself away from doctors and
hospitals *only* because she is uneducated, behind the times,
benighted and misinformed. When she can be persuaded to talk
about herself more generally, talk more broadly about her life,
she omits mention of Leona and that terrible event; she doesn't
even talk about doctors and hospitals. She does talk about life's
burdens, though — and she does make it rather clear, after a
while, how, for her, sickness and all that goes with sickness have
never been absent, have been so much a part of daily living that
only a fresh start, a new life, could conceivably do away with "the
miseries, all the miseries you feel."

Now, is she talking about specific aches and pains? Would not
a complete and thorough medical checkup, followed by first-rate
treatment, do away with those complaints, make her feel better,
give back to her the good health she has lacked for so long? Here
is how she might answer those questions, even if the questions
she actually happened to answer merely had to do with such
ordinary and broad (and apparently unrelated) matters as how
she spends her time and what she wants out of life: "I've been
hurting all my life, and I don't ever expect to stop hurting. All
day long there's one thing or another to put up with. When I was
a little girl I asked my mother once if she couldn't do something
that would stop my pains, and she didn't ask me where they were
or how bad they were; no sir, she said there wasn't anything that
could be done, except by God Himself, because He's the only
Healer Who can really heal. She used to take us to the minister
and his wife, and they'd pray over us and put their hands on us
and try to drive all the devils away, but they told us the same
thing my mother did, that you mustn't expect too much, because
God has his own ideas when He'll accept you and use you.

"A doctor, what can a doctor do to change our lives, even if he would come here, right over here to our building, and give us all the medicines he had? Could they make him fix those stairs and get rid of the garbage? Could they help us with our children, so they can find jobs and earn the money they need? I don't blame anyone and not the doctors, not them. We never heard of them in Alabama, and we've only been up here a year, and maybe it's real different up here, but it's not all *that* different. The welfare lady, she tried to make that landlord come here and kill all those rats, those rats that bite my children all the time, but she can't get him to lift a single finger of his big fat hand. Could a doctor get him to be a better Christian man? I don't believe it. Landlords, a lot of them, have the devil in them, like the bossmen down South. I sure have the devil in me. The landlord won't do what he should, and I want to go kill him, like he should be killing the rats. The Bible says we should forgive; we should be forgiving. I can't be; I can't feel that way. I guess that's one reason God makes me suffer, and my children, too.

"I was hardly born before I almost died, so maybe God was keeping his eye on me way back then and trying to warn me about being bad and losing my temper. I threw a brick at the man who collects the rent. I missed. He said he'd have the police here, but he didn't call them. He told the next-door people that he didn't blame us for the way we felt, but all he does is collect the rent, not own the place.

"Like I said, I don't remember anything, but they tell me I nearly went several times, I nearly did, as a baby. I can remember later on, when I was my Mary's age, when I was six or so, I guess — then I can remember my mother looking over me, and the minister and his wife, and they prayed and prayed and prayed, and my mother just kept on holding my hand in her hand, and I do believe she got me better that way. When a child of mine falls ill, I hold him, I hold her. I hold them and hold them. I pray for them, and God will listen — sometimes. I remember being hot, and the sweat was coming out all over me, and it was summer out, down there in Alabama, but I was so hot my mother said I was hotter than the sun was, even then, in the middle of the hottest day you could want. She had my daddy bring the water in, a pail at a time from the well, and she'd wet the cloth and then cover up my forehead with it, the cool, cool cloth. After a while I stopped being so hot. Then I got better, I guess.

"I can remember other times. I hate to think of them. I'm going through the same troubles with my own children. They get the chills. They get the fevers. They get the rat bites. They tell me they're not getting all the food they want to eat, just like I used to tell my mother the same thing. Up here you can get welfare if there's no work, but only if your husband leaves you. My husband won't leave. I don't want him to go. The welfare people give us emergency money, they call it, and they're always trying to get work for my husband. But even when they do get him work for a while, then they don't need him any more, the people he works for. So, we don't have the money to keep up with the food prices and to buy clothes for my children and pay all that rent, and it's as bad as it was down there in Sweet Water, Alabama, yes sir.

"Oh, I hope everything will get better someday, I do. I'd like to be able to get up in the morning and not be tired and not be worried and not have my body hurting, hurting, all the time giving me hurt to feel. I know there are the doctors, and I know they are smart, as smart as can be. Now that we're up here in the North we have a television, and we can see the doctors, how they come and do their work on the people and be of use to them. There aren't the doctors near here, though. I've not yet tried the other part of the city. I've not yet figured out where to go. They say you can get the welfare people to help you; they'll call a taxi and take you, if the worker is good. Some of them are; some of them aren't, the welfare workers. But we have tried to stay clear of welfare. We have tried to be on our own. We tried that in Alabama, too. We were tenants there. We paid the bossman for using his land. By the time we finished paying him there wasn't much left. There was nothing left, I'll tell you. Here, there's nothing left, too. My husband will get a job doing sweeping, or it'll be washing cars, and when he brings home the money, it isn't hardly enough for us, just enough to let us eat something and keep them away from us, the court people that try to throw you out if you don't give over your rent money.

"No sooner is there a job that seems all right, than they tell my husband they're closing shop, or they have to cut down on things, so we're without money again, just like we always were down South, except that here there's no vegetables to grow, and there's that collection man knocking on your door all the time for rent. I never thought I'd wish for the sight of the old bossman from Sweet Water, Alabama, but I do, every time that rent-collection man comes, I do.

"My children have troubles. In school they tell them they need to have their eyes looked at, and their teeth. They say I'm not feeding them the right food. That's what the teacher told my Mary. She said we're new to the North, and we should pick up the way people live here — we should take better care of ourselves, that's what she said to Mary. I'm trying, I am. I'm going to do it; I'm going to get the children looked at someplace, in a hospital, and buy them the clothes that they need. All I lack is the money, then I can go and do those things they tell you to go do: take the taxis, and visit the teachers, and go to the hospital, and demand your rights at the welfare office, and all that. The way I see it, though, is that there's not much you can demand when you're someone like me. The civil rights people come and tell you there's a lot you can demand, and maybe they're right and I'm wrong. But I can see with my eyes; we have people in this building who have been here years and years, not a little time, like us, and they're no better off than us. They even go to the hospital and get pills to take, and they're still no better off. They hurt, and they tell me they do. I said to one of them, I asked her why she kept going to the doctor and fighting with her welfare worker. She said because the doctor might help, and the welfare worker, too. Then I said she looked to be in trouble with her breathing, like me; and her heart and her stomach, the doctor told her they're both ailing her; and her boy got hit, like mine, by the rats. So, there you have it; there's the proof that she shouldn't expect much from the hospital and from the city hall, where she goes. She told me the doctor agreed with me. She told me he told her that a lot of us, we've got a lot of things wrong with us, and we haven't seen them, the doctors, all our life, and when we do get to see them, when we get up here, it's too late, and there's a limit to what they can do, a limit."

Perhaps that mother, Mrs. Rosa Lee Welch, that relative newcomer to a northern ghetto, is a little more sad, a little less hopeful, than other ghetto mothers are — or at least should be, say we doctors or lawyers or teachers or activists, who believe that things are getting better, slowly perhaps, but definitely. Perhaps that mother will find out how significantly different Roxbury, Massachusetts, is from Sweet Water, Alabama, and especially different with respect to the kind of medical services offered. Yet much of Mrs. Welch's despair is shared by her neighbors, even those who have lived in Roxbury years longer than she has. I could easily call upon psychological words like fear and depression and suspiciousness and skepticism to explain such attitudes, such lack of hope and confidence, and I could, of course, add the familiar sociological or anthropological facts that give external justification to those "internal" matters, those states of mind which in this woman's case, and in the case of hundreds of thousands like her, reflect what is real in their particular world. I would much rather, however, use her own words and her own medical history and her husband's and children's — as nearly as they all can be reconstructed by a listener.

In Sweet Water, Alabama, a family such as the one Aunt Leona and her nieces and nephews come from learns to deal with birth, illness or death on its own. Aunt Leona's sudden ending, for all the examinations done on her, the tests taken, the equipment brought into her room, was clearly an exceptional, surprising and fearful experience, and one not easily forgotten by those who came and looked at that hospital building — as outsiders not only at that particular moment, but also as permanent outsiders, who would have felt no less overwhelmed had they, after all, been admitted to the dying woman's room. Aunt Leona's niece, whom I have quoted at such length, was in fact delivered by Aunt Leona and another aunt, Josephine, who herself later died giving birth to a baby. To slip into medical language, a child's destiny in Sweet Water, if he is black and poor *or* white and poor, is to be born to a mother who has received no prenatal care, to be born outside a hospital, in a rural cabin, attended either by a midwife (with various degrees of experience and training) or simply by a relative. Then the newborn infant gets no pediatric examination, no injections or "shots" to prevent this or that disease, no vitamin supplements, no evaluation, no treatment of any kind. The heart is not heard, nor the lungs. Abnormalities are not noticed, nor are attempts made at correction. Advice is not given, nor reassurance. Worst of all, accidents and injuries and illnesses are part of life, and either "take" the child or "spare" him or her. Fractures heal or they don't, often without the benefit of splints or casts. Infections go away or they don't. Burns and lacerations and cuts and sores and rashes either "clear up" or "stop themselves" or "leave the child" or they don't, with obvious results: worse and worse pain, more and more incapacity and disability — and always those complications, which themselves get no more care and attention and treatment than whatever kind of "pathology" caused the "sequelae" in the first place.

I find it hard at a moment like this to list some of the untreated diseases I have seen — both in places like Marengo County, Alabama, and in places like Roxbury. Indeed, among infants and children and their parents in rural areas of the South or Appalachia, a visiting doctor need only recall the various "systems" of the body he learned in anatomy and physiology, and the various classifications of diseases he learned in those medical and surgical clerkships — and then one by one take note of what he sees: cuts and bruises and infections of the skin; unrepaired injuries to bones due to accidents, or the bowing and bending of bones that rickets causes; weakness of muscles; evidence of hemorrhages or anemia; abnormal neurological responses, like the sensation of tingling or numbness or burning. Symptomatically one hears everything, and clinically one sees everything: fatigue; pains and spasms and cramps and itches; indigestion and vomiting, with the food often enough blood-streaked; headaches and backaches and a throbbing or pounding in the chest, or a sharp, piercing

kind of hurt there; loss of appetite, loss of energy, loss of alertness, loss of ability to sleep and "just plain loss of everything," a
nondescript and unscientific summary that usually can be heard
spoken quietly rather than angrily, and tied to all sorts of concrete diseases, ones easy to document were there doctors in
Marengo County, Alabama, or Wolfe County, Kentucky, of a
mind to do so, and were all those law-abiding, out-of-the-way,
utterly penniless individuals to become patients.

The fact is that information about such individuals is nowhere
recorded in our nation's rich accumulation of statistics. Aunt
Leona's birth was never registered, nor was her death. Her illness, her income, her very existence as an American citizen were
a matter between her and a bossman or two and her and her
family, her kin, her neighbors — but not her and Washington,
D.C., or Montgomery, Alabama, or Linden, where Marengo
County's courthouse stands. If our federal government's statistics
show the infant mortality rates for such counties to be double
and triple what they are for other American children, I fear we
have to conclude that matters are even worse than all those
numbers and percentages can possibly tell us. There are people
in this country who never see officials from the Census Bureau,
who never see registrars of this or that or county officials whose
job it is to keep track of things. They are people who are migrant
farmers, hence live everywhere and nowhere, or sharecroppers
and tenant farmers, hence a particular bossman's virtual property
and out of everyone's sight but his, or mountaineers, hence up a
hollow and beyond anyone's range of concern or even awareness.
And in the cities they are those very same people, some newcomers to streets and alleys, some who move about from place to
place, apartment to apartment, neighborhood to neighborhood,
and some who hide themselves with a degree of success hard for
the rest of us to imagine, so proud are we of where we live, what
we are, whom we know and depend upon and visit and welcome
as visitors.

Here, for example, is one landlord, a slum landlord I suppose
he could be called: "I wouldn't even try to tell you how many
people, how many families, live in my buildings. I couldn't find

out even if I wanted to. I couldn't find out if I was working for the United States Government, for the census people, and if I had some soldiers with me when I knocked on those doors. They come here from far away usually, because there's a relative or a friend here, a contact they have, and they move in, and their idea of a crowd isn't yours or mine. All I do is collect my rents. I wouldn't dare try to poke inside those doors. Of course, one day an apartment will be full, packed full, and the next they're all gone, *all* of them. I'd like to see the FBI track them down, that's right, the FBI. What could they go on, any of those detectives? These people aren't recorded anyplace. No one has ever taken their fingerprints for a job or anything else. They don't have birth certificates. They've never had a 'residence' up here. It's hard to explain all that to people. You drive by and all you see is the fronts of the buildings. I'm supposed to know what goes on inside them, but I don't. I try to keep the heat going in winter, and the water going, and the hallways lighted; I even try to install screens every summer and take them out in the fall, but as for that, the screens, it's a ridiculous business, because they ruin them — in a week or two they've been torn and punched and pushed out. It's terrible, what they must have gone through before they came here, but it's our cities that have to pay the price. I guess it's the price of everything that used to be wrong, everything that happened *before* — long before they ever came here. I read someplace that the ghetto is one big disease. I've owned property here for twenty years, and until five years ago this was no ghetto, this neighborhood. I should have sold my property then, before that. If it's one big disease here, landlords like me didn't cause the disease. No one in this city caused it; the disease was brought in from other places, and it was a real bad disease."

To be sure, he was speaking metaphorically, but many diseases have literally been carried into his buildings by the latest newcomers. Aunt Leona never made it North, but her niece and her niece's children and their many, many cousins did. They brought with them parasites and anemias and chronic sinusitis and rheumatic heart disease and teeth in poor repair and congenital diseases and vitamin-deficiency diseases like rickets and beriberi and pellagra. They brought with them scars and lumps; they brought high blood pressure and kidney infections, swollen ankles and joints that don't quite work the way they were meant to work. We each of us get sick, of course, but the illnesses I have just mentioned are not even considered sicknesses — not by those in our ghettos who have always had them, and expect to have them until the end, until that Healer they mention so often with one sweep of His hand does away with all of a person's troubles, all that has gone wrong in body and mind.

I do not deny that in rural areas ("primitive areas" they are called by some who shun the notion that "plundered areas" might be more to the point) efforts are made to do away with all those complaints. Remedies are indeed sought and taken — herbs, roots, mixtures of things. Old ladies possessed of healing powers are visited, and they all the time reach out for those victims, "lay the hand on them," on sufferers and their enemies — sore spots and ailing limbs and bodies that seem seized by "a thousand million devils," as I once heard it put in Marengo County. For solace and reassurance and, just possibly, relief of some sort, there are even the mysteries of voodoo, of curses, of snakes held and danced with by desperate people willing to remind themselves of the Bible, each and every part of it, willing to do anything, say anything, call upon anything, lean upon anybody, all in the hope that a little, a very little might be done to change things, to make the body feel better, to make the breathing easier, to make the heart feel steadier and less fitful and less ominously pounding, to make the pus stop, the worms go away, the stomach settle down, the "soreness" leave. That is the word I hear in Marengo County and Wolfe County, the word used by white and black people, poor people driven from the land; they say it all in the "soreness" they claim to feel, or the "sorriness" they talk about, which is what we would rather more awkwardly, more pretentiously, call the "psychiatric component" of their various sicknesses. Those words "soreness" and "sorriness" are also the two words I have heard in Roxbury, Massachusetts, and in Cleveland's Hough section, and in the west and the south and

the north sides of Chicago, heard used by former sharecroppers
or tenant farmers, by mountaineers, by the descendants of slaves,
by the descendants of yeomen, Scotch-Irish yeomen who are now
"up in the city for a spell" and quite openly willing to say they
"have come to naught," but also at the slightest sign of pity ready
with a flash of sullen and unyielding and thoroughly combative
pride.

Now they are all in the cities, and there to stay, however much
they dream of the return, however often they make those brief
pilgrimages back. Now they live not far from us doctors, more or
less within our sight; they live near us and near us they struggle
to live — not only to make a living but, literally, to catch their
breaths, to get through another day. And often enough they fear
and shun us doctors — to our frustration and sadness, because
many of us, many more I believe than an overly critical public
would acknowledge, really would like in some way to reach out,
be of help, offer our skills to them. That is the problem, though; I
refer to "them." They feel to us like a "them," even as we, well
intentioned or not, feel the same — also a "them." History has
made for the distance between "us" and "them," through generations and generations of experiences, some of which I can only
try here to suggest or cite. We cannot wipe out that history with
a wave of the hand, even the most dedicated hand, cradling a
stethoscope or pointing to the finest, best-equipped, most concerned and responsive of hospitals, of clinics, of newly thought-
out urban medical settings. But to quote a phrase often called
upon both by John F. Kennedy and Robert F. Kennedy, two
Americans who meant so very much to all those people, black
and white, "we can begin." We can begin by looking at what has
happened to the people whose aches and pains do eventually
lead them to the hospitals of our cities; and what has happened
to make for suspicion and withdrawal and apparent unconcern
and even hate; what has happened, medically, to destroy good
vision and good sense.

Fortunately, Aunt Leona's niece did at long last take herself
and her children to one of Boston's hospitals, not at my prodding
but at her own initiative. She did so reluctantly, fearfully, with

little expectation that any real cures would be the result; but she did it. She and her children caused their doctors to be seriously confused, appalled at what they found, troubled and annoyed with the "attitudes" of such patients; but she and her children have kept going to those various doctors. Months later, she could say this: "It's not a new life I have, but I sure feel like the old life is easier to live. A doctor can do that; a doctor can keep a poor heart beating. He can keep the heart alive, so you're alive. I can breathe better. I'm not so jittery. I'm up to facing the day, and my children, too, they're in better spirits. It's the same old troubles we have, you know, but they're not on top of us, just all around. If you can stand up and not be hurting all over, then troubles aren't on top of you any more." She went on to thank the doctors profusely for what they have done, and I would imagine that they have good cause to thank her for what she allowed them to learn — about her and her kind, and about things and conditions and situations we all somehow never heard of, never realized existed, never counted as immediately present and pressing, matters of life and death for doctors, and for a great nation, too.

XI

THE LORD IN OUR CITIES

HERE briefly, soon enough gone, we who are fairly well off and consider ourselves well educated ask why and what. Why are we here? What is "life" all about? Here out of nowhere, soon aware that awareness lasts only so long and can mean only so much, some of us pray for answers to questions like those — and occasionally feel the glimmer of an answer or two. The answer often enough has to do with a sense of destination. And how much we want it, need it in our proud, self-conscious, cleverly humble, thoughtlessly arrogant and presumptuous minds: the conviction we are on a journey that matters, the sense that we have something ahead of us, a place waiting.

Like us, men and women who are poor and desperate and at best barely literate also hunger for a permanent home, a some-where in which an arrival is never to be followed by a departure, "a guaranteed setup" is the way I heard it put by one of West Virginia's mountaineers now become a citizen of Chicago. He called upon a familiar and congenial "frame of reference,"[1] and in so doing he could give his head and his heart and his voice and his arms and his hands all the rein and sway he wanted and needed: "Before I came here to the city, I prayed; let me tell you, I did. I prayed and I prayed until I was so tired I thought God would just enter my head, all prayed-out like it was, and say something like, 'Listen, Mr. Allen, the way to go is that way, and when you get there, it'll be all right, so don't you worry yourself

one bit more.' But I know my religion. I know God hasn't gone
and wasted His time by putting us here just so He can always be
whispering little hints into our ears and telling us all the answers
before the game is over. You have to close your eyes sometimes.
You have to trust in what's ahead. He did, on the Cross He did.
His eyes were lowered, you know. I told my wife all the way up
to Chicago that I'd rather not look too hard, I'd just rather not.
I'd rather keep my eye on the road, so we'll be spared death; to
look, to see what it's like as we got near to the city — well, that
wasn't for me. I might have turned around. I might have lost my
nerve and got to thinking like the devil wants you to — and
according to the devil there's no Heaven, there's no rest in store
for us, there's no guaranteed setup, even if God tries to build one
for you. I might have stopped the car and sat there and shook
and shook, while she was crying the way she always does,
Clara — soft it is, and she lets the tears go all the way down, and
they fall off her face, or some of them find a way of getting onto
her neck, and she doesn't seem to mind.

"We had none of that on the road. I said to Clara and all my
kids that they should say good-bye to those mountains — good-
bye, period, the end. We hope to go back, of course. But you
can't come to the city unless you've *decided* to come. You see
what I mean? I'll tell you how it is: you don't want to leave
because of the strangeness ahead of you, but you know you leave
or you near die, just about, and you know that your kids might
find something in the cities, though God knows what, so you
wrench yourself away, you tear yourself and force yourself and
pull upon yourself, and finally you're loose and floating — driving the car, it is — and soon you're there. And here we are and
here we've been for a couple of years, but don't ask me if I was
right or wrong. Do we ever know, any of us, what's right and
what's wrong? I say no — but I could be wrong, you know."

And he went on; and he went on; and he told me that it is true
that his mind catches itself wandering back, but most of the time
no, most of the time he is in spirit where he is in fact — which
means in a white ghetto of sorts just north of Chicago, where he
has decided to "seek salvation," or less grandly, to "make a

struggle," or more personally, "to throw everything, every ounce of energy, toward staying alive." Not that he actually can do so, summon all his abilities in the way he once hoped he might be able. Often he complains that he feels useless, hopeless, idle, ill-used, at a loss about things, worried in general as well as over the specific and obvious difficulties in his and his family's way. Often he wonders whether another city might not be the answer — since, again, he believes he has thoroughly convinced himself that there is no real turning back to West Virginia. But does one do that, go from city to city? Or are not all cities alike, places of what he calls "strangeness," places at best of the thinnest hope, places where one barely gets a hold on things and feels no more than safely arrived — rather than utterly and explicitly condemned, as was the case "back home, up the hollow."

Now how can that be? How can he feel so, a man who loves Down Bottom Creek, West Virginia, and hates Chicago, Illinois, a man who pines for those hills, yearns for his old cabin, mourns dozens of things left behind and who could, he insists, leave the city tomorrow and miss nothing? In his own way, with his own words and his own "perspective" that mountaineer has asked those questions of himself: "I've asked myself everything there is to ask. There can't be a single question I haven't put to myself. Lately I've been sick, and when you get sick, it makes you stop and think, and you ask yourself even more questions. Sickness can break a man's pride; that's what our minister used to tell us back in the hills. Here we have a minister, too, and thank God for him, because if you have questions nagging at you, it's a minister who can help you with the answers.

"There's one answer I do believe I've found for myself: it's better for my children up here. In a city you can get some money; it may not be a lot of money, but back there we got no money. Here I work. I don't make much, but I make something. I make enough to feed my family, and my kids get some food in school, and there's no courthouse gang out to starve us to death like there was back there. I love the mountains, but look what goes with the mountains — the crooks in the courthouses, and the robbing they do of you and the cheating, if you so much as lift an eyebrow on anything they say or they do. In the city you're able to wake up in the morning and know you'll make it through the day, and so will your wife and kids. Here in Chicago I'm not saying to myself that I don't know if we'll ever eat again. Here I live in a building that has running water and electricity and heat. The snow and ice outside don't mean sitting day and night in front of a fire and knowing that it's only a log or two that keeps us all from dying."

So, it was exceedingly grim in the past, and now it is still grim, but not quite so grim; and never forget it, small differences make a great deal of difference. Over and over again one hears that said: it's no great pleasure in the big city, but it's a little better there in certain respects and, accordingly, life itself can take on a somewhat changed meaning. Not that memories fade and all the good things about the past are forgotten, nor do the noisy streets and crowded tenements of America's "second city" grow and grow on newly arrived white yeomen from the hills of Appalachia, so that a return to the hollows gradually becomes inconceivable.

Maybe the man's wife can say what they both have in mind. Maybe she can find the words, the Clara he mentions all the time as the one with the "good sense and courage" to make him leave: "I never know what to say. I'm no good at saying anything. But I know one thing: it's good to be here in the city, as bad as it is here. And I believe God was the one who told us, finally, that we had to go. He came to us, God did, and He told us that He'd done it before, asked people to move across rivers and deserts. It used to be I could hear God in church, don't ask me how. Sometimes I'd hear Him in the woods; I'd hear His voice in the wind, or I'd hear His voice go washing down the side of the hill, bubbling and gurgling along, right inside the creek. I told the minister that, and he smiled, and he said that of course it will happen, because that's what God did it for, provided us with all of Nature's things, so we could have them, and sometimes we could listen to Him through them. Here in the city there's not much of Nature, only us folks, a lot of people. I see people everywhere, and in church it's so crowded. I'm not in West

Virginia any more — but I still can hear Him, only it'll be the knock of our radiator or the street traffic that sets me to thinking about Him. I've wondered since we came to the city if Jesus hasn't actually come down here to stay with us. I mean, there are so many people in Chicago, I would think He'd be able to hide among us all, and that way get to know a lot about His poor flock down here.

"In the city you see just about everybody in the world, and you're reminded of the Bible. I never did understand a lot of those people in the Bible; they're not like us from the hills. But when we came into the city I began to see that it was a bigger world than I'd ever known, and God has a lot more on His shoulders than us in Down Bottom Creek. That's what the city has taught me. He's not only everywhere, but He's got to be busy, and that means He wants us to be more on our own when we're in a place like Chicago. There are times when I say to myself that right here is the place you really meet God the way you will later, when He's going to decide about you, about where you stand with Him. When I was a little girl I was always hearing my daddy and our minister, Mr. McArthur, talking about the next world, the next world. Well, you know, I say to my husband sometimes that I do believe we may have started on our way to the next world. We've left home. We're in this big city. Everywhere you turn it's new and strange, and so we're being tested, just like it says in the Bible the Lord wants to do with His people, so that He can make up His mind what He thinks about you.

"Since we've been living here I haven't relied upon the Lord the way I had to back there, when we could have just disappeared one of those winters, because of no food and no strength to fight the winter — just pieces of coal my husband and the boys would carry home and wood they'd go cut and bring back. No, here I worry about the Lord, and I'm not so sure of His intentions for us. I ask myself sometimes: what does He have in mind next for us to do? We can't go anyplace farther. This is the last stop before we meet Him and He judges us. Back home I'd say to my husband on a real bad day: let's go, let's leave, let's take ourselves out of here and up to Chicago or Detroit or someplace where we won't see our children so hungry and so sick all the time. Well, he'd say to me that maybe we *should* go, but let's stay just a little longer, and if the good Lord says we should pick up and move, then we will. One day we did, of course. And now that we're here, we yearn for the hills, especially in the summer. But the way I see it, God wanted us to be tested. In the city you're tested. Up in the hollow we were tested, too, yes. But there we knew what we could do, and we did it, and it was our soil, and our people have been living on it for so long back you can't count the years.

"In Chicago it's different. In Chicago God isn't right by your side, giving you a lift here and extending His Hand to you. In Chicago He's saying to you that there's no place to go now, and you've got to dig your heels in and try and prove yourself, and it's hard, real hard, but if you're to be saved you have to earn it. I tell my children now that when they pray to God here in the city they'd better remember that it's not like in our church back there. He could know each of us back there. I still believe He knows each of us, wherever we are, but I believe in a city He's put us more on our own. I can almost hear Him saying to me: now Clara, you've come a long way, and it's been hard, but now is the time to show what you and your family can do. I asked our minister if he thought that sounded right, and he said it did, because it has to be in a place like this city that the Lord makes His choices. Up in the hollows He is there to help us; here, He is there watching us and seeing how *we* do."

As I have listened to her and her husband and others like them I have found myself over and over again taking note of the virtually apocalyptic quality in their descriptions of city life.[2] These refugees of sorts are people of faith who at last have faced up to what to them seems like a bit of luck but also a terrible moment of trial, and maybe a prelude to disaster. Needless to say, we all have our hopeful and gloomy sides. We all can feel thoroughly challenged one minute and at another time either bored, or shackled to an irresistible destiny. For a family like Clara's, a change of scene, a move to the city, has served to sharpen just such alternative moods. And for such people changes in mood bring about changes in faith, changes in religious conviction or sentiment. Once God was immediately present, an ally. He offered a distant promise, even as every single day He could be called upon, talked with, beseeched and implored — and upon occasion gently or slyly or impatiently taken to task. Now God is more removed, harder to reach. Now He has become not only the occasionally stern judge He was always known to be, but a consistently demanding observer who is reluctant indeed to become active in the world's business. Now, though He is no longer quite so uncompromising and harsh, yet He is farther away.

If God is felt to have left such families more to themselves, they are not quite as alone as they believe to be the case. They know that they have kin nearby in Chicago. They know there are thousands like themselves in other cities. But they certainly do not know how much they share with many others whose religious beliefs are not so very different, and whose lives are also comparable in a number of ways. I have in mind the blacks who have also immigrated to our cities, the blacks who like Clara and her husband and children have brought God with them — and in so doing come to feel "changed toward Him," even as they themselves have changed, have found a new place to live if not a New Life.[3] In Boston's black ghetto I hear from Mrs. Josephine Williams how and why she has, in her words, "changed toward Him." Mrs. Williams is a Baptist, and the Baptist Church commands the allegiance of more American blacks than any other organization. Millions and millions of Mrs. Williams's people go to Baptist churches all over the countryside of the South, and in cities those churches appear wherever blacks move in and settle down and try to make sense of the world and their position in it.

"We're different now that we're here and not in Georgia," Mrs. Williams says, obviously sure of herself and ready to be put to the test. "I'll tell you why. It's because up here in the city everything goes faster. I feel as if my whole life is going by at sixty miles an hour. We came up here five years ago, and in the bus we hit sixty. I guess it was on one of the turnpikes, and I got real scared. I've never seen so many trees and houses go by so fast. Now that I'm up here I never go anyplace very far, and in the city a bus can't speed very fast anyway. But everything seems fast. Like I say, my life seems to be rushing away from me and I can't catch hold of it. That's why I feel changed toward Him, our Lord. It used to be in Waycross, Georgia, I'd sit in church for hours, and we could have a good long talk for ourselves, God and me, and God and my sister. We'd always sit together, and she'd pray and I'd listen, and then I'd pray and she'd listen. Now my sister is ailing, and it's real bad. But even if she could carry herself to church, it wouldn't be the same. We went together when we first came up here, before she got sick, and we both said the same thing: up North is not down South, and God has to treat His children according to where they live. Working in the fields, we could stop and talk with Him, you know, wherever we were. Now I can't always feel Him near me, even when I'm right up front there in the church."

Why, exactly why, does she feel so differently about God? Is she "estranged"? Has city living got to her mind? Is it the ghetto's fast pace that her self-described "slowness" can't in any form accept? When she talks about God and His church is she in fact talking about man and his society — or is she saying that once she was happy, if desperate, and now she is better fed and clothed, but unhappy and still desperate, though spiritually desperate rather than hungry? Mrs. Williams has indeed gone through a psychological shock of sorts and, as a result, the nature of her religious faith has certainly changed. Yet, a good deal more has to be said about what goes on between Mrs. Williams and the God she very much wants near her, the God she misses, "looks out after," and yes, of all things, worries about, for the first time in her life even feels sorry for — not out of rudeness or blasphemy or clever intellectual contrivance, but because her heart compels the effort of sympathy. Here she is, talking about the "sorriness" God has to see in Boston, and talking about her sorrow, and talking about God, and again, *His* sorrow: "I never stopped and thought about God and how *He* gets over all of this. I guess I used to take Him for granted. We're His children, you

know, and He must follow us right into this street, and busy as
He is there must be a few seconds during the year when He
shakes His head and asks Himself where they're going and what's
happened to them — us, the black folks, here in a building like
this one.

"It's good to be here; I'm not saying otherwise. Every time I
look at my little girl, my Ruthie, I know that. She gets food she
wouldn't get, and the welfare lady sends a taxi over, and we go
to the hospital in it, because Ruthie can't walk too good, and
neither can I. The doctor tells me I have a bad heart, and if
someone had given me medicine a long time ago, the valves in
my heart — they are like doors, he said — wouldn't be so worn
out, the way they are. I told him God chooses the way we'll all
go, and I'd sooner die of a tired heart than have a heart of stone.
The doctor said he couldn't go along with me, because it's his job
to fight every illness he sees, all day long. I told him I was sure
God wouldn't hold that against him, and he laughed, you know.

"God sees a lot of trouble up in the city. There's sorriness here,
too much even for Him to keep His mind on all day long, and
into the night. In Georgia you could always take your mind off
yourself and everyone else. I would sit myself under a tree and
all I'd listen to would be a few flies or mosquitoes talking away,
or those birds that are always on the lookout for you and forever
reminding themselves to be careful and don't get too close to
anyone, be it a man, a woman or even the littlest of babies. I
remember once Ruthie was asleep and they forgot themselves,
the birds did. They were hopping and skipping and jumping all
around her, and suddenly she woke up, the little one did, and she
let out a cry — some cloud must have crossed over her forehead — and then the birds just scattered, so fast it was like an
umbrella opening up in a real hurry because of rain. I said to
myself that Ruthie has got more strength than she knows, because just look what she could do.

"Up here, though, you never can know what your child will be
able to do, even when she's bigger, and that's because it's not
God's world; it's all built by man, the city is. That's why I know it
must be hard for Him to be patient with us. I do believe He must

pray for us, just as we do for Him. In Georgia I never thought like that, because all you had to do was step out of your house and there He was, all over. Here you can't see anything but a lot of people, and you hear the noise they make all day long, and they're always ready to cross you up — if it's not the landlord wanting his money, it's the welfare lady telling you to straighten yourself up and do as she says or you'll sure enough be in a jam fast, or it's someone on the street who wants to steal from you or get you and your children into trouble. And Lord, there's more kinds of trouble in just this street than I ever saw in all of Georgia, and I've been up and down the state because my aunt moved into Atlanta. I came up here because I had another aunt up here, and I figured if I was going to move to the city, I might as well move out of the South, too. But there's no difference between Boston and Atlanta. They're cities, that's what they both are, big cities.

"I know my Bible, yes sir, I do. To my way of thinking, God suffered so we wouldn't be the only ones who suffered. Because He suffered, we can fall back on His example, and we can say to our kids that it's bad, it sure is, but Jesus Christ Almighty our Lord, He walked all over, and they didn't accept Him, a lot of people, and finally they sure did do Him in bad. And maybe we had to leave Waycross, Georgia, and move here. Maybe it's up here that God gives us a chance and says we've got to try and save ourselves, like He did, and if we but try, He'll remember us when we finally come to meet Him.

"A little while ago our minister talked to us about Judgment Day. Now, I've been hearing about Judgment Day since I was a child back South and old enough to sit there in church, 'The Church of God the King' my aunt always used to call it — by the whole name. But the new minister was saying that Judgment Day might be every day, and I thought he was wrong there, as wrong as he could be. Then I got home, and I got to thinking. I said to myself that maybe he was right, after all. Every time I open the door and walk down the hall and go out into the street I expect I may have all I can do to stay alive and not lose something to a robber: it could be my life or it could be the few dollars I have on me. That's why you have to pray that you won't lose faith in God. It's harder to keep your faith when you're not sure what to expect from day to day.

"My oldest boy, he's fifteen, and he sure knows how to say things that are true. He says you can do a lot more for yourself in the city than back home in Georgia, but only if you move fast; and it's all up to you. That's what I think the minister meant. God has said good-bye to us, for most of the time while we're up here, and He may be watching over us, but He wants us to move along on our own steam, and that's what we have to do, I know. Jesus did the same Himself, didn't He? He walked the Holy Land. He tried to do His best, but it wasn't enough. Even God the Father couldn't save Him, except after Jesus had gone and died. When I'm really down I know it's no use; whatever we do, we'll lose, at least here on this earth. When I feel up, I say we have to work hard, and the world may be a lot better one of these days, a lot better. But we'll never know, will we? I'm not sure God Himself knows what we'll come to, hereabouts, and that's the biggest worry I have. But I'm afraid to tell my minister what I think. I did once, and he got himself all excited and was cross as could be with me. All I said was that God couldn't be as sure of Himself when He looks down upon Boston as He is when it's time for Him to worry about Waycross, Georgia. That's all I said. And I think I was onto something, even if that minister says no."

She believes she was onto a lot. She believes that, for her, religion became much more complicated and difficult and impersonal after she moved from a rural life to an increasingly sophisticated urban one. She believes that her children are "learning so much new up here that they are forgetting the most important thing to remember, God's wishes." She believes that "the city is a place of temptation." Before, there was only extreme hardship and the daily surrender to God's inscrutable will. Now there are "promises, a lot of them, and people whispering into my children's ears."

Many things are whispered into her children's ears, not all of them bad or wicked or sinful or insulting or demeaning. Yet, even opportunities bring their dangers — and for people brought up to expect nothing (or risk death for expecting much of anything) it is by no means easy to sit back and welcome God's grace as at last within grasp. God was tricked, remember. God was arrested, arraigned, condemned and killed, remember — just as He was beginning to make a dent on people, to make His way, to obtain a responsive following through the attentive ears of believing men. Life always was and always will be treacherous, unpredictable, uncertain. God must not be doubted, but men and their promises, cities and their blandishments, are quite another story. Maybe someday it will be different. Maybe someday our cities will bring for Mrs. Williams and others like her glimmers of the New Jerusalem. But right now it is memories of the old Jerusalem that haunt such people, the Jerusalem of rural cabins and cottonfields and watchful, heavily armed sheriffs, the Jerusalem one entered with hope and just about nothing else, the Jerusalem one soon learned to know all too well — hence the dreams of another chance, a New Life, this time in a City of God's.

By no means is Mrs. Williams without any hope; nor are the Allens, once of West Virginia and now of Illinois, totally in despair. They have put behind them their past and not a small part of their heritage precisely because they do indeed have hope, a kind of hope, it seems, America's cities alone can offer them now. Still, they worry — and not only about the obvious, concrete, explicit problems that go with everyday life. They worry, too, about just those matters any "urban planner" thinks about, not to mention whatever social philosophers our cities still manage to have around. Will the city, some form of it, bring the good life to more and more people? Is there ahead of us some "golden age" that bricks and mortar and wise social policies and plenty of money and well-designed programs will all manage to usher in? Will old, dying cities become bright and swinging, full of all that man has dreamed is possible, full of much that many have never dared dream to be possible? Can we somehow save ourselves from fear and hate and revolution by arranging things, enacting new laws, raising up buildings, tearing down others, and in schools and places of business and on streets and avenues achieving what words like "desegregation" or "integration" or "social justice" or "radical political change" are meant to convey?

Far be it for Clara Allen or Josephine Williams to take up such broad and speculative issues quite that way. They are no social theorists, no "experts," no students of America's "urban dilemma." But they are not completely immune to big and significant questions, and at times they can be as grandiose or messianic or prophetic as any of us. If we advocate Reason, a Better World, a New Society, New Towns, Cities of the Future, they continually wonder just what it will be like in the New Jerusalem ahead of them. They wonder, as a matter of fact, how one is ever to distinguish between the New Jerusalem and the Jerusalems that have always been with us, waiting to receive all sorts of visitors, strangers, exiles, wanderers, refugees. That is to say, how does a believer know God's will? For Mrs. Allen the answer goes something like this: "God is awaiting us, and when we get to Him we'll know, and until we do, we'll worry. We came to the city so we could have enough food every day. I never expected to find God and His Kingdom here, though to hear some people on the radio and television talk about Chicago, you'd think God built this city for His favorite children. We left the happiness we had back home so we could stay alive here. Sometimes I really believe God sent us here so we'll be away from Him for a while, and more grateful when He calls us back."

In many ways her disenchantment is nothing new to her: "Before, we were in the wilderness, and it was touch and go if we'd make it. When we decided to come up here, I had a dream that we'd find the Holy City, but it's not a holy city, this one, that's for sure, though we eat better here. I have nightmares, and in them it's always the same: we're falling way down, down, down, the whole family, and we're bad off and there's no welfare check. Then I wake up and I know what a fool I was to think we'd ever reach that Holy City until we're dead and gone from this city here. But meanwhile my kids have their food in them. That's something."

And so it goes in our cities. Perhaps Mrs. Williams is being unwittingly blasphemous when she compares her travail with that of Jesus. His stay in the wilderness, His hunger, His time in the Holy City, the temptations He knew there at the hands of the devil, are not exactly those Mrs. Williams or Mrs. Allen have known. Not divine, indeed only too human and terribly needy, those women would doubtless welcome any stones that might come their way to be turned into bread. Yet, like Christ, they continue to believe that there is more to life, much more, than the comfort that material possessions provide. Some would say they *have* to believe so out of desperation. Others would want to raise them high, make of them superior spiritual people, who see further than the rest of us do, who have a wisdom we lack. They themselves make no such claims, nor do they ask for the clever and condescending "explanations" of their beliefs, their religious faith, that various observers are tempted to offer.

Mrs. Allen and Mrs. Williams speak for no one but themselves, and have nothing to recommend to others. From childhood on they have heard Christ's story, listened to His experiences, memorized His words — though they would be declared "illiterate" by us, the knowing and articulate ones. In Mrs. Williams's words: "We live on God; we wait on Him. After I've prayed to Him, I'll just think of Him, and sometimes I'll say to myself the words He said — that my momma told to me back in Georgia." When the New English Bible came out I told Mrs. Williams that I had been reading it, and she asked me how it differed from the Bible she has never read but heard and heard quoted and can recite by heart with passionate conviction, for all her "ignorance" and "poor education." In the course of things I found myself calling upon Matthew's account of how Jesus was tested and tempted — because she herself knew the story so well. I told her that the New English Bible had Jesus speak this way: "Man cannot live on bread alone; he lives on every word that God utters." She waited maybe four or five seconds, long enough for the words to be taken in and tasted, long enough for me to get a little curious, then a little worried. But there was no reason for apprehension. She is an old veteran of biblical translation, even of exegesis. When she at last responded she spoke to the spirit, not the letter: "Yes, that's right — *every single word*. And we need them real bad, God's words; we need them more than anything else in the whole world."

From childhood on, people like Mrs. Allen and Mrs. Williams have understood how famished Christ must have felt those forty days, and known what he fed on. For them He very much lives as Jesus Christ, the Son of God, Who walked and wandered and knew the countryside and eventually knew the city, and was badgered and importuned and made light of and mocked; Who was judged suspect, dangerous, an outrageous dissenter, a threat to an empire's sense of law and order; Who was put to death; Who yet lives on in the mind and heart and soul of a Mrs. Williams or a Mrs. Allen; and Who thereby does indeed walk the streets of our American ghettos.

Observers like me are devilishly tempted to take the hard, tough lives of ghetto people and somehow make them over into whatever kind of bread we traffic in: the bread of a particular ideology, the bread of a given theological or psychological viewpoint, the bread of those theories intellectuals feel they must have and proclaim if they are to be self-respecting. I have to warn the reader (and myself) repeatedly, and at no point more than now, that there is a good deal more to the religious life of people like Mrs. Allen and Mrs. Williams than words like "rationalization" or "projection" or "opiate" or "illusion" can ever convey. I have no doubt that all those words have much to commend them; they prompt us to look at the world in occasionally suggestive and illuminating ways. At times I certainly have felt Mrs. Allen justifying her impoverished and embittering life to herself by quoting some reassuring passage from the Bible, a prayer or a hymn or a story Matthew or Luke or Mark long ago told for the sake, so she believes, of people like her. And as for Mrs. Williams, she can be superstitious and melodramatic. She can talk as if she is now going through very much what Christ went through. Some theologians would say yes, of course, that is the whole point — to know and understand the more general significance of Christ's life. Psychiatrists certainly have a right to schematize the workings of the mind, suggest how Mrs. Williams has come to connect her life with Christ's, her suffering with His. I had best acknowledge that I believe the relationship between Mrs. Williams's early life, her current life and her continuing (and yes, developing) religious faith is for me something of a miracle. That is to say, I am as much in awe of what I see (her convictions and their effect upon her) as I am driven to explain their existence.

The fact is that a woman like Mrs. Williams has managed to find in Christ's life some meaning that makes her own life bearable, and more than that, worthwhile. She cannot read or write, but she has always been able to listen, to retain in her mind what she has heard, and to make sense of what she has retained. She is no religious philosopher, nor would she lay claim to being anything as "high and mighty" as a scholar or a social scientist or a psychiatrist. She is so intimidated by the "high and mighty" that she has shunned them. In Georgia they were schoolteachers, and they told her she was ignorant and so were her children, and she was bad — a bad, bad woman for keeping her children away from school. But she hadn't the clothes her children needed (the shoes and socks, for instance) if they were to attend school — though she did take them to church on Sundays, and the minister didn't mind if they came there barefoot. In Massachusetts the "high and mighty" are welfare workers and landlords and, again, teachers — and also the doctors in a city hospital who treat her and her children. She can often be grateful to them for the favors they sometimes grant her. Nor is she ever sarcastic or slyly contemptuous or as put out as her words read when she is quoted as calling so-and-so "high and mighty." There is, rather, a matter-of-fact quality to her way of talking: "I was brought up to know that I'll never amount to much, I'll never be high and mighty; but Jesus Christ, our Lord Jesus, He wasn't either. So, I tell my kids what my momma told me: there is hope for us, because He died for us, and He knew what it's like being poor — He did, He did."

So, again, I am trying to describe something — which in this instance is all I believe one like me can do, or for that matter, has any right to do. I am trying to describe a certain intimacy that exists in this world, an intimacy between a Life (some would say Life Everlasting) and certain lives I have come to witness in their day-to-day unfolding. I feel words fail me here, but fortunately they never have failed Mrs. Williams. "I was born poor and I'll die poor," she can begin. And in a flash the Lord is summoned, thereby moving us both from matters sociological and economic to a philosophical and theological discussion of time and God's Will: "But there's no reason to feel so bad. I don't want to be poor, but if I'm going to be, I'm going to be. I once asked our minister if he thought Jesus liked being poor, and he said he couldn't answer me: it was up to each person to believe what he believes about something like that. I told him I'd heard about the Lord since I was a baby. I told him the first thing I recall is my momma telling me about the infant Jesus and Mary and what a hard time they had, and no one wanted them. So, I think the answer is that He didn't mind, no sir, He didn't.

"The Lord has his eye out for us, and the reason is that He lived for us and He died for us. But you mustn't forget He lived just as we do. When I'm feeding my kids, nursing them, I sing them the songs we sing in church. And I talk to them; I do. I tell them about the Infant way back a long time ago. If I was to tell you that every time one of us asked a question of Momma or Daddy, they'd bring in Jesus, would you understand? I'm not as good as they were. I forget my Bible stories a lot of the time. But it all comes back when we go to church. Suddenly I hear the words, and I start singing them. Suddenly I recall the lessons, and I start reciting them like I should. It seems as if God can be there, inside of you, waiting to get you going.

"I teach my children about how Jesus lived and what He tried to do. He was the best teacher there ever was. Why don't some of those schoolteachers take after Him? Back South they'd read the Bible to me and my sister when we went to school. Here in the city there's no Bible allowed. They never talk about Jesus. My own people, they are forgetting Jesus — a lot of us are. A lot aren't, though. Our church is full, every Sunday it is. I also go in the evening in the middle of the week. I sit there and get myself rested. I'll be looking around, and I see people begin to look better. Their faces seem happier. He can do that, He can; He can lift your burdens. He carried a lot of burdens in His lifetime. He died young, you know. They didn't like Him; they turned on Him, the high and mighty. They said He was no good. They said He was a bad one, yes sir. They said let's go kill Him. Why do people behave like that? I never went to school much, and I can barely get my name down right on paper, but I couldn't go after a good man trying to preach the Lord's Word, whether He be Jesus Christ or anyone else. I guess you can get pretty big and important in this world and still be a mean, mean person. My neighbor, she's all determined her boys will go through every grade and then go to college. I tell my boy he should be like her boys. But if he brings home good grades, and he does, I say good, good — and then I tell him not to let it go to his head. You can get a big head in this world, and that's the worst thing. They must have thought that Jesus was no good and a begging man and a crook, that's why they killed Him. They knew so much, the people who killed Him, that they didn't know a thing! That's how I see it. My daddy said to us every day: don't get carried away with yourself. The white folks, he said, have got carried away with themselves, and they'll pay for it one of these days, even if it won't be here and now on this earth.

"The older I get the more I see what it's all about, the life we have. You have to prove to God that you're with Him, and you're not against Him. I was always told that, but more and more I see it's true. I'm not like some people you see in church. They're all the time praying and going to church, every day and twice a day and all that. If I go twice a week I'm lucky. I can barely find time to stop and think, but I do try every few days to stop myself and say, now I'm me, Josephine Williams, and my husband was shot by a white man for getting uppity one day. And so I'm up here in Roxbury, Massachusetts, and it's a long way from Georgia, but I'm not so far from God, I hope and pray that I'm not. The welfare lady asks me where my husband is, and I've never told her the truth. She might think we're no good, and then we'll get no money at all. She thinks my husband is somewhere around,

and hiding, so that I can collect. I just stare at her, though
sometimes I want to cry. But I mustn't be weak. We're born to
find out if we can become strong, and then God will take notice
of us, yes, He will. He was strong Himself. They thought He was
a weak one, and they thought they could push Him all over, and
they had the power to, yes, they did, like in Georgia and like up
here, too. But He fooled them. I don't say we will. We're not like
Him. How could we be like Him? But He'll help us out; He does.
I get low, real low, and I hear His words and His songs, and I
feel the way I used to back South: there'd be a hot, hot day and
it was sticky as can be, and the mosquitoes were all over you, and
before you knew it the wind would rise up from the pond over
yonder and freshen up your spirits, oh would it! Here in Roxbury
there'll be a rainfall, and we'll get a breeze, and then it's not half
bad, bad as it is it's not half bad. I do believe it must have been
the very same thing for Jesus. He could have given up and sat by
the road and stopped doing what He had to do, and stopped
being Himself. But He didn't let that happen. 'There are a lot of
breezes even in the worst of places,' my daddy would tell us. My
husband believed the same. He said God didn't have it much
better than we do. He always told me he'd do what he believed
right, and if he got killed for it, then he'd not be the first. And we
both would think of the Lord God, but we'd not say it, what
came to us, because I guess you never really do want to die, not
when you're still young and you have your kids to bring up."

She does talk a lot about death, though — as indeed do some
of her neighbors, whom I also visit. Sickness is for them a
heritage of sorts, and they have watched young people die —
young parents or young aunts or uncles or young cousins or
young children of their own or young friends. So, they call upon
Christ and His early death. Death haunted Christ, they believe.
"Christ must have known long before He died what was coming,"
says Mrs. Williams. She is not speaking out of turn. She is not
really speculating, either. She is saying what she swears by: "I
know the answer; I know that He *did* die young, that He was
crucified. But when I was a child, before I even was told what
happened on the Cross, it was then that I asked my momma

whether He wasn't killed for speaking up so. I told my momma that if Jesus was so brave, He must have been in danger. A lot of people must have been out to hurt Him. 'He who is not with me is against me'; I remember hearing that all the time when I was little. We'd be in church most of the day Sunday, and there wouldn't be a Sunday the minister didn't read those words. Up here you hear them even more. There's also a lot of talk about 'black power' — and our minister says Christ could understand what 'black power' means, because in the Bible Jesus says that you either come around to his side or you get scattered all over the place, and you're without a friend in the world, and then you'll die, that's what.

"Of course, He had a lot of followers for some of the time. But good as He was, there was trouble, because He was trying to help the poor people, the people whose 'load is real heavy,' I think the Book says, and they are people who need relief — they do, we do. The big shots wouldn't let Him get away with being like that. I once asked my daddy why we should try to be like Jesus if he got killed, and He suffered so much in the end. Daddy said I was real smart to ask that, and he didn't know why, but he had some ideas. He said he'd take me to the minister and let him answer me direct, right to my face. So, we went. I asked him, though I was scared to. I must have been maybe six or eight — like that. The minister said Jesus Christ paid the price and died so that we'd all forever after know not to feel sorry for ourselves, and instead of feeling sorry for ourselves we should keep Him up front in our thoughts — because He was a preacher and He was a teacher and He was trying to lead us, and with His death it meant we'll never be as alone as it seems.

"My kids come and ask me all these awful things. I'm afraid of this city, but I'm sure we'll never be able to leave it. What keeps us all from ruin is the Bible and the church we go to. We'll come home from church and my children will tell me they've got to be good, even if they don't want to. Their minds are full of what they heard the minister read from the Bible. The devils are all over, you know. If you're a poor black man, the devils are lying in wait on every street. That's why our children must hear

Christ's words — and what He went through, they go through, I
do believe.

"Wasn't there a time when Jesus said He knew they were going
to kill Him? There was. I remember. His followers cried when He
told them. They probably hoped He was wrong. He kept on
telling them He had to go, He had to — die, I mean. When we
were thinking of leaving Georgia, Mr. Wilson, our minister, told
us to go, to go and be glad we're going. He said, 'Jesus had to go
to Jerusalem. We all have to go to the city. Better to go now than
later. Better to be tested here, right now.' I have a good head on
me for remembering a speech like that. My husband was dead,
and I felt I'd already been tested enough. But I went anyway. I
was afraid they'd come and kill me, too — just shoot me dead.

"A lot of people up here, they come thinking they'd already
seen the worst, and up here it would be the 'triumphal march' —
like the one of Jesus into Jerusalem. But there was suffering
ahead for Him in Jerusalem. And there is suffering ahead for us.
Of course, the rich don't suffer, not like us. The white man, he
has it pretty good. There are poor white folks, though, plenty of
them. My little girl asks me if Jesus was white or black. I tell her
He was neither. How could He be any color? I guess He was
white, though. I never even thought about it; I just figured He
was white. We'd see pictures of Him back in Georgia, and He was
always white. Jesus was a man, a Jew. I never did see a Jew until
I came up here. They own some buildings here. They were
pointed out to me by a neighbor. She said, 'He's a Jew.' I got the
shakes, because I recalled the Jews in the Bible, some of them
were good and some bad. For us they're just more white people,
you might say.

"Now up here it's changing. There's a lot of fighting going on
in our church. The young men and women say He was black.
The minister says we mustn't argue over it. I say let Him be black
and white and every color. He talks like a black man, Jesus does.
His heart has always been with us, you can tell by His words. He
said it all the time that we've got to suffer insults and persecution, and later we'd get that big reward, in Heaven it'll be. If He
talks like a black man that's enough for me. The minister is right:

if we get to arguing and arguing over what color Jesus was we'll be missing the boat. That's what they did a long time ago. They argued over Jesus, and then they killed Him. My son says all we have to do is put on the television set and listen to what the white people say — and then you know what people said about Jesus a long time ago. One white man will say one thing about us, and the next one will say another thing about us, and if you look at the expressions on their faces you can see that they have no use for us, and they'd as soon be rid of us, if they could. I'll think to myself sometimes: what must He think, the good Lord? What must He think about this country we have here, and this city, and the way my people try to do the best they can? The whites don't want any part of us. And they say they're good Christian people — those white folks have the nerve to say they're Christians!"

That last point bothers her a great deal, even as others, white and black, have struggled with the same issue. Who indeed is a good Christian? The men who shot Josephine Williams's husband dead say they are Christians and go to church every Sunday even as she does — and they are most likely Baptists, too, just as she is. Mrs. Clara Allen, quoted at the beginning of this chapter, is also a Christian and a churchgoer, though she has "no great liking for the colored." Mrs. Williams recalls her father's confusion, her mother's confusion, her own confusion; she recalls that their minister "back home" in Georgia also had his moments of doubt, also wondered how people who are full of hate could do it, go to church and pray to Christ all the time. As for the minister Mrs. Williams goes to see in Boston's Roxbury section, he is less puzzled, less surprised, less worried: "I've talked with Mrs. Williams about her husband. It's not as rare as you might believe; many in my church have come here from the South in the last twenty years, and they have had terrible things happen to them down there. But they accepted the pain. They did then. It is only when they come up here that they start to question themselves and wonder how they were able to stand it for so long. That's because in a northern city, poor as the black man may be, he is no longer so completely at the mercy of any white

two-bit bum with a gun — including those sheriffs who are the
'law and order,' you know, of the South. We have our trouble
with the police up here, but no policeman here would dare strut
around the way some of those sheriffs do down there in the part
of Georgia Mrs. Williams comes from. When she asks me about
the church I answer her very directly. I say that Christ was
persecuted by his church, by the rabbis and all the rich and
powerful believers, and eventually they rejoiced when He was
killed. I do not believe He ever expected anything else from any
church, even churches that called themselves Christian. No, He is
betrayed every day. I say that almost every Sunday; I have to,
because it's on the minds of my people.

"We are a religious people. The whites of this country, they are
so mean and violent and prejudiced themselves, and they are so
irreligious themselves, and they are so against God in the way
they act and in their values, that they are only too happy to take
a few angry, shouting militants and think of black people as like
that — noisy and without faith in Christ. But millions of blacks
are God-fearing, so *very* God-fearing! They fill up this church
and others like it all over the country. They pray so hard. Even
up here in the North they do. Have you ever seen your suburban
whites *give* themselves in church — give so much of themselves
to prayer, to singing hymns, to paying attention and listening to
the minister's every word? And my people know their Bible!
They may not know the exact words, but they know the message,
and they can recite and recite the story of Christ's life — His
struggles and His defeats and what He taught and how He was
healed. I ask you: why don't white people know about us? If
they think of us as religious, they consider us superstitious or
uncontrolled in church or childlike. I've read the descriptions;
I've heard them spoken — and from supposed friends of ours.
They would like us to 'grow up,' and be more like them — go to
church an hour on Sunday for the sake of the job, for appearance's sake, and then forget the whole thing. I've had a good
education in theology, but I'm learning all the time about faith;
my teachers are my flock, the people who come here and want to
believe in Him and do believe in Him. Sometimes I wonder how

they do it, keep their faith. But they do. And if they have questions, I can only try to answer them. When Mrs. Williams asked me about 'the bad people,' she calls them, who persist in calling themselves Christians, I told her that it was up to God, and Him alone, to decide who is or is not a Christian, and who will or will not be saved. I was a little impatient with her, and a little stern. I think I was like that because I'm as bothered as she is by such things, and I guess I wanted her to forget it, her question, because it's unanswerable, it's a mystery. Isn't it?

"You know, a woman like Mrs. Williams can't be shrugged off so easily. She thinks about my sermons. She thinks about what I read. I hear her reactions the next week or even the next day when I say something that bothers her or inspires her or worries her. And she's no rare bird. Of course she isn't. I should know! I have to find the time for all these people. They want me to visit with them, and I do. They want to talk about the Bible. Yes, they want to talk about their own troubles, too, but good Christians that they are, they connect their troubles to Christ's.

"There is never an empty seat in this church, or in any other one around here. We bought this church from the Jews. They had a synagogue here; it was a big one, you can see. And over there is a church that used to be a Methodist church for the white people — before the Jews came, I guess. Do you know what the rabbi told me? I invited him to come over and see how we fixed the place up. He's a nice man, and we've become friendly. He said it did his heart good to see how we fill up the place. He said even before the black people started moving in, and his people started moving out, they couldn't ever fill up the synagogue, even on the special holidays. And I have friends, white minister friends, who tell me the same thing. Once in a while I invite them over here. I like to talk with them, and we exchange notes, you might say. They always ask me how I do it, get so many people to attend church. I tell them it has nothing to do with me. They come regardless of me. They come because they are believers. They still follow Christ, for all the disappointments they've had on this earth.

"You ask why. I'll tell you why — at least I'll tell you my

opinion. I believe the average black man can understand Christ's life a lot better than the comfortable white man here in America. The white man who lives in the suburbs, he goes to a beautiful church and he hears some sweetness and light for an hour. He doesn't pay attention to what he reads, if anything, from the Bible, and his minister has learned to be as indirect and inoffensive as can be. Have you ever seen them coming out of those churches? I've watched them sometimes downtown, or on television. They all look as if they've had a nice little time for themselves — before lunch. Do they ever ask who Christ was and why he was hounded to death and what people like them, good and proper and well-off people, thought of Him? Of course not; of course they don't. I'm not really bragging about my people. There are times I wish they could be as indifferent to Christ as a lot of white Christians are! It would mean they have become better-off, people like Mrs. Williams, and in a position to forget about the misery in this world — and that's the one thing Jesus Christ could never put out of His mind. He knew He was headed for trouble. He was a radical. Was He! And they finally got Him! My people know there's only more trouble ahead of them, too, and many of them have had relatives or friends or neighbors killed or badly mistreated. So, they understand. They understand Christ's life because their lives help them do so.

"And in addition, the Christian religion is part of our heritage. We've been going to church for a long, long time, black folks have. The slave masters and their descendants, I'm not sure they ever took Christ seriously. But because we're so 'simple and childlike,' as they've always called us, we've believed Him and worshiped Him and handed down to our children His words and His ideas and His beliefs and the story of His life and His death. I remember when I was about ten or eleven my father told me for about the tenth time the story of the Crucifixion. I really listened to him. He went on and on about the premonition Jesus had that He would be crucified, and the way they all treated him, the big priests in the temple. Then he described the Crucifixion itself to me, how the rabbis and lawyers and politicians and big, important citizens all laughed at Him and treated Him as if He was a thief, a criminal. I said to my dad, 'I understand. I do, Dad.' I can see us, right in my mind, right now. I must have really made an impression on him, because he took me to him and said, 'I see you do, I see you do.' And he looked into my eyes, deep into them. I've never forgotten that moment. I guess my dad and I were saying to each other that we're black, and we *do* understand, starting when we're pretty young we do."

Most of the time when he talks about white people and their inability to comprehend Christ's life he refers to "comfortable whites" or "suburban whites." Upon occasion, however, he slips into "Whitey" and "the white people," and then we have to argue. I will mention mothers like Mrs. Allen, whose everyday struggles are not much different from those Mrs. Williams faces. I will also mention churches I have attended in Appalachia, and in cities like Chicago, Detroit, Dayton and Cincinnati. Frightened and near-starving white people have gone to those cities, I tell him. He listens. And he says nothing. And he goes on talking about the *particular* hardships a poor *and* black man must put up with.

Once, though, we settled things a little. I brought along some tapes I had made, sermons from a mission church not far away from Mrs. Allen's apartment in Chicago. We listened together: "Jesus Christ is the God Who suffered. He is not the God of the rich, the comfortable, the powerful. They killed Him once. They kill Him every day. They ruled the world two thousand years ago. They rule the world now. They were hypocrites then. They are hypocrites now. They were Romans and Jews then. They are Americans and Christians now. They spent their time back then polishing up the lawbooks and making sure they stayed in power. They spent their time back then handing people over to each other, doing each other's dirty work, spying and killing for each other. And today the same thing goes on. The county government people in West Virginia and Kentucky and all the important people in those states who are tied up with them — what do they all do? They do dirty business for each other, and the poor man up in the hollow, he pays for it. He has to grovel for every penny, and often he gets nothing. He comes here to the city and works like a dog doing any work he can find, and he gets slave-labor wages, and the rents are so high and the deductions from his pay — that the labor contractors take out — are so high that he's lucky if he can feed his little children anything. So he's back where he started up in the mountains. And if he'd start protesting, if he'd start marching, if he'd start speaking out, you all know what would be said. They'd call us every bad name in the book, and they'd have us arrested and soon we'd be out of sight, you can be sure, way out of sight. They don't use crosses anymore. They don't crucify 'troublemakers.' They silence you, though — one way or another. And they do it in the name of Jesus Christ, mind you — Who said all His life that the poor man was being unfairly treated and the rich would surely pay for it. But He was no fool, let me tell you. He said they'd never pay until they went up to meet God and found out what He had in store for them. So, you can't expect justice here on this earth, no you can't."

Mrs. Williams's minister certainly agreed with that message. He nodded, and later on as we talked he repeated his fellow minister's remark, that no justice can be expected on this earth. Still, he insisted, justice has to be demanded by those who have a right to it, need it, lack it; and justice *is* done — not always, but sometimes, yes. He was ready to acknowledge a sense of camaraderie with Mrs. Allen and her minister and the thousands like them, but he was by no means ready to surrender a certain uniqueness he feels his people to possess. He finds Christ's life a means of talking about that uniqueness, and indeed, he asserts that his parishioners do so, too: "They don't just talk to me about God as if He were some force up there Who controls everything, some explanation of things. They talk about Jesus Christ, the man who lived a life they find all too familiar. Jesus Christ is their man, you might put it. Well, *you* might *not* put it that way, actually.

"My people, the people who come here, talk to Jesus — talk and talk and talk to Him. 'He's my man,' I'll hear from them. They're not being fresh and insulting. No, not at all. They mean to say that they dig that man, dig Him — and they know all He had to take, and it was a lot. And they find that life, His life, something precious and wonderful. It's not just misery liking company. For a while, believe me, that's what I thought. I used to get so angry at them: they'd come to talk with me, and I could see that all they wanted me to do was repeat some agony Christ had gone through, and then they would smile a little and appear calmed. Once I lost my temper at a woman. She was very much like Mrs. Williams, except that she was born right here in Boston. She'd had a hard life. Her father died of tuberculosis when she was six or seven. During the depression her mother could get no work, and we didn't even have the half-decent welfare system we have now. The mother took to selling herself, and she did it at home. You can imagine what that meant so far as the little girl was concerned — one man after another coming into the house. When the girl grew up she was afraid of men, but she got married and had two children and then she got sick with a bad heart, and her husband was caught stealing and sent off to jail. He said he stole to pay for the doctor's bills. I happen to know him, and I know the doctor, and it was true. But the man was convicted of armed robbery, and he had no money for a good lawyer. That was a while back. We had no government lawyers here, like we do now. I really believe on a first offense he might have been spared prison, especially if he'd been white and had a good lawyer. He denies having a gun. He says the storekeeper reached for *his* gun, and he grabbed it from him, and then the police booked him on armed robbery. He did have a knife, yes.

"I'm not defending the man. How can I? I'm just trying to tell you about a woman who was sick and alone and scared. She came to see me all the time. Do you know what helped her? Each time I would read to her from Matthew or Mark or Luke or John. I'd read: 'He that is without sin among you, let him first cast a stone at her.' I'd read one parable after another, and she'd begin to smile. She'd say He knew, He knew. After a while, I lost patience with her. I told her to stop. I told her she couldn't do that, she couldn't keep listening to Christ's troubles and then smiling at me. Oh, I never should have exploded. It wasn't only what I said, but how I said it. But she was no fool, and she was no child. She stood right up to me. She said that she wasn't enjoying His suffering. She said she felt all alone sometimes, even though she knew there were a lot of miserable people in this world. But somehow what I read to her made a difference. And then do you know what she said? I'll never forget it — and remember, the time is over ten years ago, long before the whole civil rights movement got going. She said, 'Reverend, Jesus must have been coal black, that's what I think.'

"I expected her to smile. I thought she was being sassy. I was ready to explode a second time, and *really* explode. I thought to myself: what a dumb thing to say. We 'reverends,' you know, can be to our flock what the Pharisees were to Jesus. I mean, we can be mean and unkind and uncharitable. We can look down upon our people — not knowing that all the time we are being tested by God just as our flock is. I didn't explode at her. I changed the subject instead. But after she left I couldn't get what she said out of my mind. I'd be walking down the street, and suddenly I'd stop and think about it. I'd look for her in church when I was getting ready to speak. Sometimes I'd see her and I'd want to smile, and sometimes I'd see her and I'd get angry. Finally I went to talk to an old teacher of mine. He taught me how to read the Bible, *really* read it. He knew the Bible, and he could recite it and hypnotize you. I told him what the woman said and how it bothered me. 'Good,' he shouted. 'Don't you see that she has more faith than you or I — or she — will ever realize? She was telling you that God is in her bones and that she is really able to reach for him.'

"I guess I knew that anyway, but I needed to hear my teacher say what he did. I am afraid too many of us ministers spend our lives trying to fit the people in our churches into a certain mold. We want them, even when they are poor and live here in this neighborhood, to be proper and conventional worshipers. We want them to say the right things in Sunday School when they're children and in church later on, or to us when they come see us. But the poor black people up here in the North, a lot of them have little but God to fall back upon! That's the fact a minister has to live with, and he becomes uncomfortable doing it. I really believe that I have much less faith than Mrs. Williams, or that

woman I just mentioned. I'm not saying, mind you, that all poor
people have such faith. I'm just saying that a lot of black people
who come up here have grown up with a deep love of their
church, their minister, their Bible, their hymns, their praying and
celebrating — that's it, celebrating the Lord. They don't read the
Bible like scholars do. They don't stop and study books about the
history of the church. But they are serious believers — sometimes
overserious, I'll admit. You've heard them stand up and shout.
You've seen and heard them participate: speak up, agree, nod
their head, raise their arms, interrupt — they all the time interrupt. I was brought up to expect interruptions, and I interrupted
myself when I was younger, but it's hard being a reverend and
trying to get through a certain service — and always your flock
wants to urge you on or tell you how they're taking what you're
saying or reading."

As for Mrs. Allen, he is convinced that *she* is convinced that
Christ was as white as can be. He is willing to accept her and her
minister's declarations; they, too, find in the Christian service, in
the Bible and in hymns and responsive readings something sustaining beyond words. He is also willing to admit that faith can
be possessive. Maybe each believer wants God to himself or
herself. But if that is so, there is something to worry about: "We
argue and fight over God, just like we argue and fight over skin
color." Not that he doesn't know the history of the Christian
church. Not that he doesn't know how men hunted down one
another in God's name, hunted and betrayed and even killed one
another: "I guess the more passion you put into something, the
more it's yours, and the less you want to share it."

Anyone who wants to analyze the religious faith of a Mrs.
Allen or a Mrs. Williams, its "meaning" to them, had better be
careful indeed of his language, and aware of a little more than
"depth psychology" or the "sociology of religion." Of course those
women find in the church a means of reassurance, a means of self-
expression, a means of dealing with a difficult and often incom-
prehensible world. In church and through the Bible, through
Christ's life especially, they find symbols that make sense of
things, and they also find concrete, practical help which can be

drawn upon every single day. Christ is their teacher, their healer, their adviser, their advocate, their protagonist, their prophet, their lawgiver, their Hero of heroes, their court of last appeal. Christ through His Book and through His ministers offers them hope, purpose, peace, a sense of membership in something larger, in Something. And again, Christ offers a destination, a place to go, a place that will, finally and at last, be *theirs*. They are people who feel deaf, dumb and blind all too often; they feel so not because their senses have failed them, but because they simply cannot exercise those blessed "faculties" (as we doctors call them) to any real effect. They know the wilderness the Bible tells us about. They know it this way, Mrs. Allen's way: "I get up and the sun is out, but I honestly feel it's dark here. I hear noise out in the street but it only hurts my ears. Sometimes I feel as if I'm walking around like in a trance, and I can't pull myself out of it. Once I hit myself against the door. I didn't even see it. My husband says I'm trying to leave this place and go back to West Virginia; he says I'm dreaming, that's all. He's right; I do dream."

In church she also dreams. She reviews her whole life. She recalls being a little girl, then growing up, then leaving her home in Appalachia for the city. And she anticipates the end, too: "I'll go one day, and I hope it'll be back home and not here, but it won't be, I don't think so. You can't feel too sorry for yourself, though. I know I'll never die in a potter's field like He had to — for us. And if it's bad in the city, it's good, too. You can't have everything. We gave up a lot to come here to Chicago, but we feel we made the right move. It's as if we *had* to do it, come here. My minister back home really comforted me before I left. He reminded me that Christ always did what He had to do, even if He knew there was trouble ahead. I laughed and said: 'Reverend, are you telling me that we're all going to be crucified, come the time we get to Chicago?' Well, he laughed and said no. I told him not to worry, for I knew what he was telling me, and it was good advice. My mother used to say the same thing: you mustn't spend too much time trying to see ahead. Do what you have to do. I used to ask her how I'll ever know that, what I have to do. She said God will tell you.

"I never knew how He would until one day my little boy was ailing real bad, and I couldn't scrape up but cornmeal and more cornmeal, and I knew he needed more than that, and we near froze to death in the house. So, I prayed hard. I've never in my life prayed so hard. And I got my answer. I felt myself saying: Clara, it's time to go to the city. Then when my husband came home and he hadn't had any luck at all with his hunting, I said it was time to leave and I was ready, and as soon as possible the better. I said I'd prayed, and God had said yes, we should go right away. My husband said that was fine, because now he knew I wouldn't be going back on myself a few days later. And I never did and I never have. When I'd settled myself with God, I could be firm, and I've been firm ever since we've been up here. I won't say I don't have my dreams. Oh, how I'd like to die in West Virginia! But I know what I have to do. That's one of the lessons the Lord, Jesus Christ, has taught us: you've got to do what you know you have to do."

Call her fatalistic, Mrs. Clara Allen. Call her resigned, or in distress, or sad and depressed, or "psychologically adjusted" to her fate. Say that she resorts to "magical thinking," or has made the best of an exceedingly bad lot by "denying" her fear and doubts, by "rationalizing" what was, in any case, virtually inevitable. Insist that she "identifies" with Christ, "projects" her difficulties on Him — and yes, there are many who would also insist on adding "whoever He or he was or might have been." Point out, in a moment of generosity, how "adaptive" Mrs. Allen's faith is, how useful to her, how handy a "psychological maneuver" it can be to find some authoritative sanction in a world she experiences as vexing, confusing, frustrating. Emphasize how helpful it is to various powers and principalities that the Mrs. Allens of this world are encouraged by their beliefs to sit back and acquiesce, to follow the path of least resistance, to go hungry and suffer in silence, to die without protest. Note how grandiose and unfounded are any comparisons a Mrs. Allen or a Mrs. Williams makes between their arrival in a northern city and Christ's entrance into Jerusalem, or between His dark days like Maundy Thursday and Good Friday and their daily sufferings!

What is left after all those "points" have been made? Should we insist that Mrs. Allen and Mrs. Williams are living heavenly, or impressively noble, or God-sanctioned and exemplary lives? After we add up all the psychological and sociological and political and economic analyses that have been applied to such lives, should we shake our head in outrage, contempt, sadness, pity or bitterness that people can be so ignorant, so deceived, so superstitious, so misled? What are we going to do with them, the poor, the benighted, the illusion-sated, the cleverly indoctrinated men and women of this world who listen and listen and listen and nod and obey and submit and have the gall to *smile* because they feel destined for something big and important and special and rewarding?

In the course of a decade of work I have run through all those questions in my mind, run through a range of "explanations," a range of "attitudes" — a range of "ideological positions," as some would want to describe a distillation of one's confusions. And I have no "solution," no final "answer" for the problems a chapter like this must present to most readers of a book written nearly two thousand years after Christ's birth and published in a rich, mighty, secular America. I want to believe, and I want the reader to believe, that I am not evading either my mind's twentieth-century sensibility or my mind's responsibility to take a stand. I agree with the critics: it *is* easy to become misty and hazy and clouded and silly and make a million "divine" excuses for what is in fact the product of a mean and heartless and unfair social and economic system. One like me can always practice deceit by taking refuge in words like "neutrality" or "science." And yet exactly who am I to deny Mrs. Clara Allen and Mrs. Josephine Williams the full range of their complexity, their humanity, their individuality?

I am trying to say that I believe the two women whose words have dominated this last chapter are utterly themselves, individuals who are mysteriously more than the sum of what all observers or analysts can find and discover and write about and spin theories about. They have their failings: they can be gullible; they can be fatuous; they can be boring. I have more than once tired of hearing them, been annoyed by their remarks, rejected some of the clichés they have learned to believe whole-heartedly or merely mouth unthinkingly. I have wished not only that they might be better educated and more prosperous, but more analytic, more discerning, more circumspect. And would that we *all* were harder and tougher, braver and less deluded! And yet — Mrs. Allen and Mrs. Williams are two proud and tough and by no means defeated human beings. Obscure of birth, familiar with adversity, forlorn and in various (and different) ways persecuted or mistreated, they are denied dozens of rights or opportunities or possibilities; they are filled with conflicts and ambiguities and plagued by historical and psychological ironies that some people must live with rather than ponder or consider "interesting" or try to "resolve." I have attempted to indicate how I grew to respect these two women, and their children and others like them. I have tried to indicate what I gradually learned from them, learned about them, learned about myself, my weaknesses and contrivances and illusions. God knows, maybe I am dwelling on these inconsistencies and contradictions too much, worrying about them too much. But God knows, there is every reason for one like me to worry. How easily we observers can drag the furniture out of the minds and hearts of people, out of their lives, and set down the various pieces before our own greedy eyes and the eyes of others like ourselves, inclined to be well fed but hungry, well informed but lonely. And together we all brag and strut, or more modestly, call names, pin descriptions, ring up our discoveries, our conclusions, our findings. Meanwhile, Mrs. Williams can say, as she did on the last visit I made to her before writing these words: "If we could just sit and *be* with each other. When I was a little girl my mother used to tell us when we'd start fighting and arguing and squabbling, you know — she'd tell us that she didn't want to hear any more, she didn't want to hear us toting up the rights and wrongs and saying who is better and who is worse, and who does this and who does that. She didn't want a lot of explanations, those explanations and more explanations. She'd tell us she wanted us to appreciate each other. She'd say the Bible says there's a time to do all that talking and arguing and there's a time to stop, period — and remember that it's important sometimes to be glad that we're here on this earth. And she'd say we've got to have a better life for ourselves, but we shouldn't fret so much over one thing and the next thing that we forget what's important, really important. My mother believed that there's a lot of evil in the world, but she believed in love, God's love and our own kind — the kind I grew up with, the kind she showed us during all those gray and cloudy days." I believe I want more than anything to say amen to those words.

REFERENCES

CHAPTER II

1. In 1790, the year the first census was taken, 91 percent of the blacks in the United States lived in the South. By 1910, the figure had changed little: 89 percent of the blacks lived in the South. During the First World War the migratory flow northward of southern blacks began — a response to agricultural changes in the South and the need of northern industries for workers. By 1960, 40 percent of America's black population lived in the North and the West, as compared with 11 percent in 1910. Between 1950 and 1960, no less than 1,457,000 blacks left the South, and 88 percent of them went to six states: California, Illinois, Michigan, New York, Ohio, and Pennsylvania. In 1910, 73 percent of the black people in the United States lived in rural areas — on farms or in towns or hamlets with a population of less than twenty-five hundred. (At that time, the rural proportion of the white population was 52 percent.) By 1960, 73 percent of the black people in this country lived in urban areas — an astonishing reversal indeed. (In 1960, 70 percent of the whites lived in urban areas.) Nor is that all; blacks moved not to suburban areas but to the centers of our cities: in 1960, 51 percent of all black people in the United States lived in what Census Bureau analysts call the central city section of "Standard Metropolitan Statistical Areas." A reader intent on "original sources" can turn to U.S. Bureau of the Census, *Historical Statistics of the United States, Colonial Times to 1957* (Washington, D.C.: Government Printing Office, 1960) and update that reference with the Census Bureau's annual *Statistical Abstract of the United States* (Washington, D.C.: Government Printing Office). An excellent article on the subject is Philip Hauser's "Demographic Factors in the Integration of the Negro," *The Negro American*, Talcott Parsons and Kenneth B. Clark, eds. (Boston: Houghton Mifflin, 1966). For broader, more extended analysis and discussion one can turn to *The Changing Population of the United States* by Conrad and Irene Taeuber (New York: Wiley, 1968), and to Stanley Lieberson's *Ethnic Patterns in American Cities* (New York: Free Press of Glencoe, 1963). The impact of the black exodus from the South upon particular cities has been portrayed for New York City by Nathan Glazer and Daniel P. Moynihan in *Beyond the Melting Pot* (Cambridge: Massachusetts Institute of Technology Press and Harvard University Press, 1963), and for Chicago by Otis Dudley Duncan and Beverly Duncan in *The Negro Population of Chicago: A Study of Residential Succession*

(Chicago: University of Chicago Press, 1957). More general descriptive accounts of what our cities have witnessed are to be found in E. Franklin Frazier's *The Negro in the United States*, rev. ed. (New York: Macmillan, 1957); Oscar Handlin's *The Uprooted* (Boston: Atlantic–Little, Brown, 1951), which is about white immigrants; and *The Newcomers: Negroes and Puerto Ricans in a Changing Metropolis*, also by Handlin (Cambridge: Harvard University Press, 1959).

As for Appalachia's people, between 1950 and 1960 more than one million persons left the southern Appalachian region. As with the southern blacks, mountaineers by and large have left subsistence farms (or mining camps) for cities both within and outside their original region. James S. Brown and George A. Hillery title their chapter "The Great Migration, 1940–1960" in *The Southern Appalachian Region: A Survey*, Thomas R. Ford, ed. (Lexington, Kentucky: University of Kentucky Press, 1962). Here is one of their summary comments: "Appalachian people, then, were moving to places where social, cultural, and educational opportunities were better, where higher levels of living could be attained, and where they could take their places in the main streams of American life. The parts of the region with the highest economic and social levels had the greatest holding power. As a result, the Appalachian population was being redistributed at the same time that it was declining. Increasingly, the population has become concentrated in the metropolitan areas in which manufacturing and trade are important, and in the better farming areas." And the authors emphasize something else of great interest and importance: "The Appalachian population is following the national pattern of concentrating its population in metropolitan areas. But the metropolitan areas in which Appalachian migrants are concentrating are primarily outside the region. The region's metropolitan areas are not attracting migrants to the extent other such areas do, and most of the area's cities apparently are contributing to the outflow of migrants." Clearly, sections of America like eastern Kentucky and West Virginia and western North Carolina or Virginia lack cities like Atlanta or New Orleans, to which farm people can go as an alternative to the North. So, as mentioned in the text, it is to Ohio and Illinois and Michigan that mountaineers are drawn — to Cincinnati and Dayton and Chicago and Detroit. Besides this fine article by Brown and Hillery, I would recommend Rupert Vance's "The Sociological Implications of Southern Regionalism," *The Journal of Southern History*, XXVI (February, 1960), and more generally and descriptively, *Uptown: Poor Whites in Chicago*, by Todd Gitlin and Nanci Hollander (New York: Harper and Row, 1970).

2. A relatively brief account of my observations and work in Tunica County, Mississippi, is given in three articles co-authored by Harry Huge: "We Need Help: A Message from Mississippi," *The New Republic*, March 8, 1969; "A Cry from the Delta," *The South Today* (July, 1969), a publication of the Southern Regional Council; and "In Jamie Whitten's Backyard," *New South*, XXIV (Spring, 1969).

3. I first described that work in "Southern Children under Desegregation,"

American Journal of Psychiatry, CXX (October, 1963), and later in *Children of Crisis: A Study of Courage and Fear* (Boston: Atlantic–Little, Brown, 1967).

4. I first described my work in Boston in "Bussing in Boston," *The New Republic*, October 2, 1965. Later I wrote for my colleagues "Northern Children under Desegregation," *Psychiatry*, XXXI (February, 1968). For teachers and school principals I wrote "When Northern Schools Desegregate," *Integrated Education*, IV (February–March, 1966). And I should mention that I tried to describe for children in a fictional way a lot of what I experienced riding on a school bus from a northern ghetto to the less crowded schools of certain urban and suburban communities. See *Dead End School* (Boston: Atlantic–Little, Brown, 1968). I first presented what I had seen of the reactions of white children and parents to Boston's bussing program in "The White Northerner," *Atlantic Monthly*, CCXVII (June, 1966), and also in the psychiatric paper mentioned above. Again, I have tried to describe for children how white boys and girls in the North feel when black children come to their school for the first time in *Saving Face* (Boston: Atlantic–Little, Brown, 1972).

5. I first wrote about my many conversations with that man in "Public Evil and Private Problems: Segregation and Psychiatry," *Yale Review*, LIV (June, 1965), and later in *Children of Crisis: A Study of Courage and Fear* (Boston: Atlantic–Little, Brown, 1967).

6. Again, I mention the article I wrote five years ago, "The White Northerner," *Atlantic Monthly*, CCXVII (June, 1966). I have recently written a more extended description of my work with "working-class" families, and joined the writing to the photographs of Jon Erikson in *The Middle Americans* (Boston: Atlantic–Little, Brown, 1971).

7. In this regard, Miss Freud's book *Normality and Pathology in Childhood* (New York: International Universities Press, 1965) is essential. I have tried to give an indication of the importance of Miss Freud's work to all of us child psychiatrists in "The Achievement of Anna Freud," *The Massachusetts Review*, VII (Spring, 1966). Further references to Miss Freud's work with English children during the Second World War and with the survivors of Nazi concentration camps are to be found in the first and second volumes of *Children of Crisis* and in a book I coauthored with Maria Piers, *The Wages of Neglect* (Chicago: Quadrangle Press, 1969).

8. The use, or rather misuse, of psychiatric and psychoanalytic terminology to label people, and thereby subtly or not so subtly degrade them, is unfortunately still a widespread custom in certain realms of American middle-class life. Words originally meant to clarify the thoughts and feelings and behavior of patients become heavily tinged with pejorative implications, indeed become virtual epithets. Nor is the practice confined to "the lay public" — as one hears just about everyone except psychiatrists described in many clinical conferences and meetings. I would refer the reader to two articles I have written, both responses to concrete experiences in the course of my clinical work and "field work": "A Young Psychiatrist Looks at His Profession," *Atlantic*

Monthly, CCVIII (July, 1961), and "A Fashionable Kind of Slander," *Atlantic Monthly,* CCXXVI (November, 1970).

9. One goes on and on trying to clarify for oneself and for others these sticky matters. I have written about "method" in the two previous volumes of *Children of Crisis.* More "technical" papers of mine which take up the same general issue are "A Matter of Territory," *Journal of Social Issues,* XX (October, 1964), and "Observation or Participation: The Problem of Psychiatric Research in Social Issues," *Journal of Nervous and Mental Diseases,* CXLI (September, 1965).

10. Once again I have to ask the reader to consider what a generation of child analysts has come to know about children *in general* — in contrast, that is, to children who have become "patients," or children from particularly impoverished and persecuted races or "groups" of people. For a broad perspective I would suggest Edith Buxbaum's fine book, *Troubled Children in a Troubled World* (New York: International Universities Press, 1970). Another good book is Helene Deutsch's *Selected Problems of Adolescence* (New York: International Universities Press, 1967). Erik H. Erikson in one way, and Anna Freud in another, have consistently tried to broaden the dimensions of clinical work. Conversely, someone who is doing the kind of work I do must narrow the way he looks at the "fieldwork" he does, so that he keeps mindful of *his* professional emphasis, which concentrates on the "inner life" of the people he describes — in contrast, that is, to the emphasis of a historian or political scientist or anthropologist "working with" the same people or communities. My effort to come to terms with these vexing contrasts is described in *Erik H. Erikson: The Growth of His Work* (Boston: Atlantic–Little, Brown, 1970).

11. As I look back over my thoughts and doubts of the past decade, I realize how all along I have known that many will find thoroughly unsatisfactory any effort on the part of someone like me to write about "others" who are black or extremely poor. Yet one stays with the dilemma and tries to do and say what *seems* right, what *feels* right, what others (such as some of the parents and children described in this book) *say* is right — even as one worries about one's "motives" and limitations and "latent prejudice" and blind spots, and on and on. Here, once more, I cite articles in which I struggled for a point of view — as a white, middle-class professional man who works with poor people, both white and black. I feel I have most successfully done so (argued, perhaps, so as to persuade myself?) when I have written about particular individuals — James Baldwin in "Baldwin's Burdens," *Partisan Review,* XXXI (Summer, 1964); Frantz Fanon in "The Wretched of the Earth," *The New Republic,* September 18, 1965, and "Oppressor and Victim under Colonialism," *African Forum,* II (Summer, 1966); Malcolm X in "What Can We Learn from the Life of Malcolm X?" *Teachers College Record* (May, 1966), a publication of Columbia University; Eldridge Cleaver in "Black Anger," *Atlantic Monthly,* CCXXI (June, 1968); and Stokely Carmichael in "Two Minds about Carmichael," *The New Republic,* November 12, 1966.

12. See the United States Civil Rights Commission, *Report,* following

hearings held in Cleveland, Ohio, April, 1966 (Washington, D.C.: Superintendent of Documents, 1966).

13. See "Serpents and Doves: Non-Violent Youth in the South" in *Youth: Change and Challenge,* Erik H. Erikson, ed. (New York: Basic Books, 1963), and also the articles mentioned above in note 9.

CHAPTER III

1. Since a book like this does not offer a comprehensive bibliography, I can only suggest in connection with this chapter and those to follow some books that have meant a lot to me, caused me to think, sharpened my ideas — or made me want to scream. America's cities deserve the understanding social historians provide — a depth and range of understanding observers like me too often lack, inclined as we are to seize upon what we now find and forget what has been going on for decades, even centuries. And so I recommend, first, Constance Green's fine book *The Rise of Urban America* (New York: Harper and Row, 1965). Another good book by Mrs. Green is *American Cities in the Growth of the Nation* (New York: De Graff, 1957). The "race issue" does not dominate the discussion in either of those books, which of course tells us a good deal. Then, lest the reader forget that our cities have a long tradition of fear and hate, there are books available like the recently republished *The Dangerous Classes of New York* by Charles Loring Brace (Montclair, New Jersey: Patterson Smith, 1967), which first appeared in 1880, and *The Great Riots of New York: 1712–1873* by Joel Headley (New York: Bobbs-Merrill, 1970).

Nor should the social criticism expressed by the children quoted in Chapters III and IV be denied its long-standing tradition. If black youth in a ghetto or Appalachian youth "gone north" mourn a certain lack of "community" they have known "back home," and speak bitterly and sadly about the abrasive and oppressive and stultifying physical and social arrangements our cities require, then others have been echoing such sentiments for a long time — and since they are by and large white, middle-class writers and photographers and professors and architects, perhaps some white or black children who live in Harlem or Chicago's "poor white" ghetto ought to feel less powerless, because just about no one in power has paid much attention to those grown-up and relatively well-off people, however many books they publish. In any event, as the reader thinks about some of the remarks he comes upon in this chapter and those to follow, he or she may want to read Bernard Rudofsky's *Streets for People: A Primer for Americans* (New York: Doubleday, 1969), and in the same vein, Jane Jacobs's earlier work, *The Death and Life of Great American Cities* (New York: Random House, 1961). And before those two fine critics, Henry Van Brunt wrote and wrote about what "buildings" had to do with "society" — with the way people grow up and come to think about one another. Here, I take the liberty of recommending my brother's searching and painstaking effort to show (through his own essays and those of Van Brunt) what our cities might have been like had we been more careful and thoughtful: *Architecture and Society* by William A. Coles (Cambridge: Harvard University Press, 1969).

Finally, I should like to mention *A Way of Seeing*, a lovely, lovely book — a book of Helen Levitt's photographs and James Agee's words, a book that sings of New York City and children and urban life and man's struggle to laugh and reach out and feel a little less lonely during his brief stay on this earth, this crowded and not always kind earth of which our cities are so prominent a part. I look and look again at *A Way of Seeing* (New York: Viking, 1965) and often enough feel its mere seventy-eight pages tell all that a book — this book and dozens of others — can ever tell.

Against this background I will refer to some valuable efforts to describe the black man's fate in America's cities. E. Franklin Frazier's *The Negro in the United States* (New York: Macmillan, 1957) is indispensable, as is his *The Negro Family in the United States* (Chicago: University of Chicago Press, 1966). Needless to say, also indispensable in a discussion of the black man's life in *any* part of the United States is Gunnar Myrdal's *An American Dilemma* (New York: Harper and Row, 1944). Also of great value is *The Negro American*, Talcott Parsons and Kenneth B. Clark, eds. (Boston: Houghton Mifflin, 1966); in particular in that volume, I would mention Lee Rainwater's article "Crucible of Identity: The Negro Lower-Class Family," and St. Clair Drake's essay "The Social and Economic Status of the Negro." Books of recent interest, each with much information about blacks in our cities, are: *Employment, Race and Poverty*, Arthur Ross and Herbert Hill, eds. (New York: Harcourt Brace, 1967), whose subtitle accurately expresses what is to be found — "A Critical Study of the Disadvantaged Status of Negro Workers from 1865 to 1965"; and the companion volumes, *On Understanding Poverty* and *On Fighting Poverty*, edited respectively by Daniel P. Moynihan and James L. Sundquist (New York: Basic Books, 1969).

There is, of course, a growing literature on ghetto life — a literature that is uneven in quality, but certainly responsive to the black man's increasing presence in northern and western cities. Once more I urge, first, the historian's perspective. See *North of Slavery: The Negro in the Free States, 1790–1860* by Leon Litwack (Chicago: University of Chicago Press, 1961); also *A Century of Negro Migration* by Carter G. Woodson (New York: Russell and Russell, 1969), originally published in 1918. And for particular northern cities there is *In Freedom's Birthplace: A Study of the Boston Negroes* by John Daniels (New York: Negro Universities Press, 1968), originally published in 1914; *The Philadelphia Negro: A Social Study* by W. E. B. Du Bois (New York: Schocken, 1970), originally published in 1899; Leo Hirsch, "The Negro and New York, 1783–1865," *The Journal of Negro History*, XVI (October, 1931); and in the same journal, XXXIX (January, 1954), Richard Wade's "The Negro in Cincinnati, 1800–1830." A more recent work is *From Plantation to Ghetto* by August Meier and Elliot Rudwick (New York: Hill and Wang, 1966). Of great significance was the appearance of *Color and Human Nature: Negro Personality Development in a Northern City* by W. Lloyd Warner, Buford Junker, and Walter Adams (Washington, D.C.: American Council on Education, 1941). That volume offers a careful

analysis of the way black youths on Chicago's South Side grow up —
and learn to think and feel in response to a northern city's various im-
peratives. A more recent classic is Elliot Liebow's fine, fine book, *Talley's
Corner: A Study of Negro Street Corner Men* (Boston: Little, Brown,
1966). Before *Talley's Corner*, however, there was *Black Metropolis* by
St. Clair Drake and Horace Cayton, rev. ed. (New York: Harcourt Brace
Jovanovich, 1970), perhaps the most comprehensive look at the blacks
who have gone into our cities in this century. Of importance, too, is
E. Franklin Frazier's *Black Bourgeoisie* (New York: Free Press, 1965), a
book that touches upon the last portraits in this chapter. In *The Wages
of Neglect* (Chicago: Quadrangle Press, 1969), Maria Piers and I have
also tried to write about one way certain ghetto children live and grow up.

I would like to list three recent books by sociologists and anthropolo-
gists that have been of help to me in my medical and psychiatric work
in several ghettos: *Soulside: Inquiries into Ghetto Culture and Community* by Ulf Hannerz (New York: Columbia University Press, 1969);
Life Styles in the Black Ghetto by W. McCord, J. Howard, B. Friedberg,
and E. Harwood (New York: W. W. Norton, 1969); and finally, *Behind
Ghetto Walls* by Lee Rainwater (Chicago: Aldine, 1970). In my own
profession one has had to rely upon *The Mark of Oppression* by Abram
Kardiner and Lionel Ovesey (New York: Norton, 1951). The authors are
psychoanalysts who drew upon blacks from New York City for their
studies — but blacks who were patients, who had reason to seek psychiatric or psychoanalytic help. It is no easy step from clinical practice
and research to social and cultural analysis and criticism — and perhaps
it is an impossible step. I have read and reread *The Mark of Oppression;*
I have learned from it, but also found its emphasis and conclusions one-
sided — because there is to be found even in the most harassed people
(let alone those whose strength eludes psychiatric explanation) substantial evidence of toughness, resilience, originality, resourcefulness.
(Even as I write, this comes across as condescending. Why is the discovery
of something like human "toughness" still so surprising to a psycho-
pathologist? And why is this surprise so important?) Albert Murray has
taken care of every single one of us social scientists, arrogant and self-
centered as we often are, in *The Omni-Americans* (New York: Outer-
bridge and Dienstfrey, 1970). I tried to acknowledge the debt we owe
him in "Human Nature Is Finer," *The New Yorker*, October 17, 1970.

But to continue briefly with a psychiatric emphasis, I would recommend the April, 1970 issue of *The American Journal of Psychiatry* for its
special section of "Inner City Mental Health Services." Especially interesting is "Home Visiting in a Black Urban Ghetto" by John Chappel
and Robert Daniels. Also of interest is *Mental Illness in the Urban
Negro Community* by Seymour Parker and Robert Kleiner (New York:
Free Press, 1966), and *Black Ghetto Family in Therapy* by Sager T.
Brayboy and B. Waxenberg (New York: Grove, 1970). On the psy-
chological (as opposed to the psychiatric) side, one turns to Bertram
Karon's *The Negro Personality* (New York: Springer, 1958); Thomas
Pettigrew's *A Profile of the Negro American* (Princeton, New Jersey:
Van Nostrand, 1964); and Kenneth B. Clark's *Dark Ghetto* (New York:
Harper and Row, 1965). And political scientists and sociologists with a

political cast of mind have given us books like *Negro Leadership in a Southern City* by E. Burgess (Chapel Hill: University of North Carolina Press, 1960); *Politics and the Ghettos*, R. Warren, ed. (New York: Thenton, 1969); and *Ghetto Crisis* by H. Etzkowitz and G. Schaflander (Boston: Little, Brown, 1969).

Yet, after all those references are set down (and dozens more might have been offered here) I find myself thinking of Ralph Ellison's *Invisible Man* (New York: Modern Library, 1963), of Richard Wright's *Native Son* (New York: Harper, 1940), of the Harlem evoked in Langston Hughes's poetry, from *The Weary Blues* (New York: Alfred Knopf, 1926) through *Shakespeare in Harlem* (New York: Alfred Knopf, 1942) to *One Way Ticket* (New York: Alfred Knopf, 1949) and *Montage of a Dream Deferred* (New York: Holt, 1951), of the recent novels John A. Williams has written: *The Man Who Cried I Am* (Boston: Little, Brown, 1967) and *Sons of Darkness, Sons of Light* (Boston: Little, Brown, 1969), and finally of James Baldwin's *Notes of a Native Son* (Boston: Beacon Press, 1957). And I think again of Agee and Levitt in *A Way of Seeing*, and of Bruce Davidson's portfolio of thirty-two photographs included in *The Negro American* (Boston: Houghton Mifflin, 1966) or his more recent *East 100th Street* (Cambridge: Harvard University Press, 1970). Maybe, as Edward Sullivan has so forcefully stressed in "The Relevance of Fiction," *The Virginia Quarterly*, XLVI (Summer, 1970), there is no easy way to an understanding of the complexity of life — all life. Hence, again, we have to call upon novelists, poets, essayists, photographers for those "last words" that, always and refreshingly, tell us: no, there are no last words, no final statements, no theories or generalizations or formulations of conclusions or schemata that quite manage to capture and hold for very long any of us, all of us.

CHAPTER IV

1. Much of what makes for the tension and fear and hate described in this chapter has to do with the arrival of white *workers* or *businessmen* in neighborhoods inhabited by large numbers of *unemployed* men — and so we are compelled to recognize not only a racial problem but a class struggle of sorts. Glazer and Moynihan in *Beyond the Melting Pot* (Cambridge: Massachusetts Institute of Technology Press and Harvard University Press, 1963) make quite clear how difficult it is for blacks in New York to obtain work in various occupations, and Ross and Hill in *Employment, Race and Poverty* (New York: Harcourt Brace, 1967) do the same for the entire nation. See also Gary Becker's *The Economics of Discrimination* (Chicago: University of Chicago Press, 1957). In accounts which range from Oscar Handlin's *The Newcomers* (Cambridge: Harvard University Press, 1959), to James Baldwin's *Notes of a Native Son* (Boston: Beacon, 1955), to *The Autobiography of Malcolm X* (New York: Grove, 1965), the white visitor, whether bent on money, work or pleasure, is always there as part of the scene, someone to be feared, appeased, conned, catered to, and silently or not so silently hated.
2. At least there is *some* substantive work done on the police — as opposed

to other civil servants such as firemen or garbage collectors or welfare workers, who are comparatively less "studied." I realize it may be a mixed blessing, at best, to have a certain breed of observer bearing down on a group of hardworking and embattled men. But a recent book edited by David Bordua makes sense, and shows what of value can be done by sensitive social scientists: *The Police: Six Sociological Essays* (New York: Wiley, 1967). James Q. Wilson's work is also very helpful, very stimulating, very informative. See "Police Morale, Reform and Citizen Respect: The Chicago Case," *The Police* (New York: Wiley, 1967); *Varieties of Police Behavior: The Management of Law and Order in Eight Communities* (Cambridge: Harvard University Press, 1968); and "The Police and the Delinquent in Two Cities," *Becoming Delinquent*, P. G. Garabedian and Don Gibbons, eds. (Chicago: Aldine, 1970). Obviously, there are distinctions in the "makeup" of the various civil service professions — police, firemen, satellite City Hall workers, garbage collectors — but much of what Wilson and other observers (Bordua, Jerome, Skolnick in *The Police*) report about the police applies just as well for all so-called low-level bureaucracies, those which provide various "services" to the people of our urban ghettos — and also provide a continuing source of tension between blacks and whites.

CHAPTER V

1. C. Vann Woodward has shown in *Tom Watson: Agrarian Rebel* (New York: Rinehart, 1938, 1955) how white Southerners were cheated and betrayed by their own fears and hates — while, all the while, the poor of both races suffered and obtained precious little of the money and work they have so desperately needed. A brilliant examination of the southern whites' complicated feelings is to be found in Lillian Smith's *Killers of the Dream* (New York: Norton, 1961). Also of interest is a small and little-known novel by Hodding Carter, Jr., *The Winds of Fear* (New York: Farrar and Rinehart, 1944). I strongly recommend James McBride Dabbs's books, *Who Speaks for the South?* (New York: Funk and Wagnalls, 1964) and *Civil Rights in Recent Southern Fiction* (Atlanta: Southern Regional Council, 1969). And for an honest and suggestive look at the white Southerner of the 1950's, there is Robert Penn Warren's *Segregation* (New York: Random House, 1956).

2. A number of books in recent decades have offered information about so-called white lower-middle-class or working-class people. Oscar Handlin's *The Uprooted* (Boston: Atlantic–Little, Brown, 1951), gives the reader a good historical account of the immigrants who came to northern cities from Europe in the nineteenth and early twentieth centuries. In *Children of the Uprooted* (New York: Braziller, 1966), Professor Handlin brings together essays that throw light on how Americans of the second generation, the children of immigrants, fare in our cities. Again, there is *Beyond the Melting Pot* (Cambridge: Massachusetts Institute of Technology Press and Harvard University Press, 1963) by Glazer and Moynihan, with its account not only of blacks and Puerto Ricans but of the Irish and Italians and Jews of New York City. Of great value is Herbert Gans's description of life among Italian-Americans in Boston, *The Urban Villagers*

(New York: Free Press, 1962), and in a similar tradition is the now-classic *Street Corner Society* by William F. Whyte (Chicago: University of Chicago Press, 1943, 1955). Also of importance are *Workingman's Wife* by L. Rainwater, R. Coleman and G. Handel (New York: Oceana, 1959); and *Blue-Collar World*, A. Shostak and W. Gomberg, eds. (Englewood Cliffs, New Jersey: Prentice-Hall, 1964). An article of real worth is "Characteristics of the Lower-Blue-Collar Class" by A. K. Cohen and H. M. Hodges in *Social Problems*, X (Spring, 1963). Also very helpful is Walter Miller's "White Gangs," *Transaction*, VI (September, 1969). Recent books of interest are Peter Schrag's first-rate study of Boston's school system, *Village School Downtown* (Boston: Beacon Press, 1967), and P. Binzen's *Whitetown, U.S.A.* (New York: Random House, 1970). Perhaps more than any of these books I would recommend one titled *Anti-Negro Thought in America, 1900 to 1930* by I. A. Newby (Baton Rouge: University of Louisiana Press, 1965). The author shows how utterly pervasive that "anti-Negro thought" was — not confined to harassed and insecure workingmen or frightened and hungry night riders in the rural South, but rather very much a part of the nation's cultural and intellectual life, which means a part of its universities, courtrooms, and comfortable neighborhoods. It is so easy for some of us to describe or "understand" the "prejudices" of factory workers or civil servants or white collar workers, but at the same time overlook the sly or merely circumspect or polished snobbery and meanness and hate that many of those "higher up" have constantly demonstrated.

3. Once more I mention Leon Litwack's extraordinary *North of Slavery* (Chicago: University of Chicago Press, 1961). Also of value is Oscar Handlin's *Boston's Immigrants, 1790–1865* (Cambridge: Harvard University Press, 1941). Boston's segregated schools in the nineteenth century occasioned repeated arguments and political or legal struggles. See L. Levy and H. Phillips, "The Roberts Case: Source of the 'Separate but Equal' Doctrine," *The American Historical Review*, LVI (April, 1951). Nor were whites the only ones in Boston (or any other place) to rally around a segregationist position — when it reflected the will of a political majority. Litwack cites "a Negro's defense of segregation," titled "An Address Before the Colored Citizens of Boston in Opposition to the Abolition of Colored Schools." The year was 1850.

4. See "The White Northerner," *Atlantic Monthly*, CCXVII (June, 1966). Also: "Is Prejudice Against Negroes Over-rated?" *Transaction*, IV (October, 1967); "White Pieties and Black Reality," *Saturday Review* (December 16, 1967); "History's Lessons," *Pediatrics*, XLIV (September, 1969); and "Poverty and Health," *American Journal of Psychiatry*, CXXVII (November 1970). See also *The Middle Americans* (Boston: Atlantic–Little, Brown, 1971); and for children, *Saving Face* (Boston: Atlantic–Little, Brown, 1972).

CHAPTER VI

1. A bibliographical essay for this chapter is necessarily briefer than the one which accompanies Chapter III — for the simple reason that

the exodus of Appalachian whites to our midwestern industrial cities (in comparison with the movement of blacks northward from the rural South) has been relatively more recent, less striking and less written about. For one thing, mountaineers are considered by many "us" rather than "them." For another, mountaineers have gone to fewer northern cities and have gone continuously, not in the swift and somewhat desperate and dramatic fashion that characterized the migration from the Black Belt during the First and Second World Wars. A recently published book that does a splendid job of evoking the hopes and worries, the confusions and moral courage, of those mountaineers who have gone to Chicago is *Uptown: Poor Whites in Chicago* by Todd Gitlin and Nanci Hollander (New York: Harper and Row, 1970). Going back in time, one finds of interest *Rural Migration in the United States*, W.P.A. Research Monograph No. 19 (Washington, D.C.: Government Printing Office, 1939); also Gladys Bowles, *Farm Population: Net Migration from the Rural-Farm Population, 1940–1950*, Statistical Bulletin No. 176 of the Department of Agriculture's Agricultural Marketing Service (Washington, D.C.: Government Printing Office, 1956). A number of articles are especially helpful to those readers who want to go beyond the "psychological" emphasis of this book and look into matters of history and social or political struggle. I particularly suggest Rupert Vance's "The Sociological Implications of Southern Regionalism" in *The Journal of Southern History*, XXVI (February, 1960) as a background paper. Then, there is the careful and authoritative essay by James Brown and George Hillery, "The Great Migration, 1940–1960" in *The Southern Appalachian Region* (Lexington, Kentucky: University of Kentucky Press, 1962). Also of value are "The Southern White Laborer Migrates to Michigan" by Erdmann Beynon in *American Sociological Review*, III (June, 1938); "The Urban Status of Rural Migrants" by H. Beers and C. Heflin in *Social Forces*, XXIII (October, 1944); and "Urban Migration and Kinship Ties" by L. Blumberg and R. Bell in *Social Problems*, VI (Spring, 1959). In addition, an informative book is Ronald Needman's *Recent Migration to Chicago* (Chicago: University of Chicago Press, 1958). Other helpful papers are Lewis Killian's "The Adjustment of Southern White Migrants to Northern Urban Norms," *Social Forces*, XXXII (October, 1953); Thompson Omari's "Factors Associated with Urban Adjustment of Rural Southern Migrants," *Social Forces*, XXXV (October, 1956); and a fine paper by George Henderson, "Poor Southern Whites: A Neglected Urban Problem," *Journal of Secondary Education*, XLI (March, 1966). And finally, I would recommend "The Appalachian Child in Chicago Schools" by Ben Huelsman, in *Appalachian Advance* (October, 1968), and "Southern Mountaineers in City Juvenile Courts," also by Huelsman, in *Federal Probation* (December, 1969).

Two good articles for the general public are Hal Bruno's "Chicago's Hillbilly Ghetto," *The Reporter*, June 4, 1964, and Albert Votaw's "The Hillbillies Invade Chicago," *Harper's*, CCXVI (February, 1958). Also, there are a series of good technical papers published in relatively obscure journals, each with Harry K. Schwarzweller as the principal author: H. Schwarzweller and J. Brown, "Education as a Cultural Bridge Between Eastern Kentucky and the Great Society," *Rural Soci-*

ology, XXVII (December, 1962); H. Schwarzweller, "Sociocultural Origins and Migration Patterns of Young Men from Eastern Kentucky," and "Family Ties, Migration, and Transitional Adjustments of Young Men from Eastern Kentucky," Bulletin Nos. 685 and 691, respectively, of the Agricultural Experiment Station of the University of Kentucky (December, 1963, and May, 1964); H. Schwarzweller and J. Brown, "Social Class Origins, Rural-Urban Migration, and Life Chances," *Rural Sociology,* XXXII (March, 1967); and H. Schwarzweller and J. Seggar, "Kinship Involvement: A Factor in the Adjustment of Rural Migrants," *Journal of Marriage and the Family,* XXIX (November, 1967). And last, but not least by any means, out of West Virginia there is John Photiadis's excellent paper, "Changes in the Rural Southern Appalachian Community," No. 7 in a research series of the Office of Research and Development, The Appalachian Center, West Virginia University (Morgantown: West Virginia University Press, 1968).

CHAPTER VII

1. I hope this effort to convey what I hear from black and white children over the years (in contrast to what I heard more briefly in the course of the study described in Chapter VIII) will not come across as a romantic evocation of the wisdom children *always* feel and speak. Children can be as many things as their elders are and teach boys and girls to be: witty or dull, clever or murky, charming or dreary. Yet over and over again I hear children dream about a better, more sensible — and yes, radically different — world; and perhaps they do so simply because they haven't lived long enough to see their hopes and dreams flounder and get declared "utopian" or "unrealistic" or "naïve." In any event I urge that the "architectural fantasies" of these boys and girls of an American city in the late 1960's be compared with the dreams of a French architect in the twenties and thirties and forties. That is to say, I hope Le Corbusier's *Nursery Schools* (New York: Orion Press, 1968) will be consulted by those who may want to see (literally) how "preoccupied" others besides "ghetto children" are with the sun and trees and grass and space — open, inviting, warm, kind space.

CHAPTER VIII

1. The United States is the world's richest, most powerful nation, but its infant mortality rate ranks thirteenth, according to the *United Nations Demographic Yearbook for 1968* (New York: United Nations, 1969). An excellent article on the subject is Frank Falkner's "Infant Mortality," *Children,* XVII (May–June, 1970). The relationship between the child's growth and the medical and nutritional care he or she gets is discussed in Delbert Dayton's "Early Malnutrition and Human Development," *Children,* XVI (November–December, 1969). Nor does Dr. Charles Greene write only about foreign countries in his paper "Medical Care

for Underprivileged Populations," *New England Journal of Medicine,* May 21, 1970.

2. One wonders whether there will ever be an end to the arguments over what "factors" have what share in determining intelligence. Though Gordon Allport's book *Personality* (New York: Holt, 1940) is by no means "contemporary," the author's level-headed, unpolemical and open-minded discussion of the subject is far from "out of date." I recommend Therèse Gouin Décarie's *Intelligence and Affectivity in Early Childhood* (New York: International Universities Press, 1965) as an excellent effort to join together Jean Piaget's landmark investigations and various quite different psychoanalytic studies. Also of value is *Language, Thought and Personality in Infancy and Childhood* by M. M. Lewis (New York: Basic Books, 1963); *Young Children's Thinking* by M. Almy, E. Chittendon, and P. Miller (New York: Teachers College Press, 1966); and *Theories of Child Development* by Alfred Baldwin (New York: Wiley, 1967). The most recent demonstration of social scientists' disagreement over (and wrangling with) the issue of whether "intelligence" is inherited or acquired was incited by Arthur Jensen's now well-known report, which stressed genetic influences in both white and black children. See A. Jensen, "How Much Can We Boost IQ and Scholastic Achievement?" *Harvard Educational Review,* XXXIX (Winter, 1969). See, also, the issue of *Harvard Educational Review,* XXXIX (Spring, 1969) given over to a discussion of Jensen's findings. Still a valuable book is Kenneth Eall's *Intelligence and Cultural Differences* (Chicago: University of Chicago Press, 1951).

3. I have struggled to make sense of those words "culturally deprived" and "disadvantaged" in "Children of the American Ghetto," *Harper's,* CCXXXV (September, 1967). The reader may want to consult Frank Riessman's *The Culturally Deprived Child* (New York: Harper and Row, 1962), and in addition, Helen Rees's *Deprivation and Compensatory Education* (Boston: Houghton Mifflin, 1968). Also of interest (and of real value) is Allison Davis and Robert J. Havighurst, "Social Class and Color Differences in Child Rearing," *American Sociological Review,* XI (December, 1946), and Martin Deutsch, *Minority Groups and Class Status as Related to Social and Personality Factors in Scholastic Achievement,* published originally as a monograph (New York: Society for Applied Anthropology, 1960).

4. One can mention only certain highlights in what has become a genre of sorts — wherein social criticism is mediated through educational criticism. (Needless to say, from the time of Plato to that of Rousseau and Tolstoi, writers and philosophers have speculated about ways of educating children.) Paul Goodman's *Growing Up Absurd* (New York: Random House, 1960) certainly started the recent "movement." Extremely influential have been Edgar Friedenberg's *The Vanishing Adolescent* (Boston: Beacon Press, 1960) and *Coming of Age in America* (New York: Random House, 1965). More recently we have had Jonathan Kozol's *Death at an Early Age* (Boston: Houghton Mifflin, 1967); Herbert Kohl's *Thirty-Six Children* (New York: New American Library, 1967); John Holt's *How Children Fail* (New York: Pitman,

1964) and *How Children Learn* (New York: Pitman, 1967); James Herndon's *The Way It Spozed to Be* (New York: Simon and Schuster, 1968); George Dennison's moving and touching *The Lives of Children* (New York: Random House, 1969); and finally, the exhaustive research reported by Charles Silberman in his book *Crisis in the Classroom: The Re-Making of American Education* (New York: Random House, 1970).

5. See R. Rosenthal and L. Jacobson *Pygmalion in the Classroom* (New York: Holt, Rinehart and Winston, 1968). This book has its "cousins" — books and articles which make the same point in different ways. See J. S. Bruner, *The Process of Education* (Cambridge: Harvard University Press, 1960); and A. H. Passow, ed., *Education in Depressed Areas* (New York: Teachers College Press, 1963). Articles of interest are Robert K. Merton, "The Self-Fulfilling Prophecy," *Antioch Review*, VIII (June, 1948); Elinor Sacks, "Intelligence Scores as a Function of Experimentally Established Social Relationships Between Child and Examiner," *Journal of Abnormal and Social Psychology*, XLVII (April, 1952, Supplement); and B. Bernstein, "Language and Social Class," *British Journal of Sociology*, XI (Winter, 1960). And an excellent bibliography on "fate control" appears in the references at the end of the paper entitled "Generalized Expectancies for Internal versus External Control of Reinforcement" by Julian B. Rotter in *Psychological Monographs: General and Applied*, Vol. LXXX, No. 1 (1966).

6. H. K. Beecher, "Surgery as Placebo," *Journal of the American Medical Association*, July 1, 1961. Of related interest are three other papers by the same author: "The Powerful Placebo," *Journal of the American Medical Association*, December 24, 1955; "Non-Specific Forces Surrounding Disease and the Treatment of Disease," *Journal of the American Medical Association*, February 10, 1962; and "Pain: One Mystery Solved," *Science*, CLI (February, 1966).

7. The Coleman Report, titled "Equality of Educational Opportunity," was published as a 737-page document by the United States Government (Washington, D.C.: Government Printing Office, 1966). A short article of interest by James S. Coleman, "Toward Open Schools," appeared in *The Public Interest*, No. 11 (Fall, 1967). Very helpful and informative is the special issue of the *Harvard Educational Review* titled "Equal Educational Opportunities," XXXVIII (Winter, 1968), which is given over to an analysis and discussion of the Coleman Report.

8. U.S. Commission on Civil Rights, "Racial Isolation in the Public Schools," *Report* (Washington, D.C.: Government Printing Office, 1967).

9. Tolstoi's "second epilogue" to *War and Peace* (New York: Simon and Schuster, 1942) contains an unforgettable and precise discussion of "free will"; and the epilogue itself clearly foreshadows Erik H. Erikson's way of connecting individual lives with broader historical "forces." In *Erik H. Erikson: The Growth of His Work* (Boston: Atlantic–Little, Brown, 1970), I try to indicate how very much Erikson's "psychohistorical approach" has meant to those of us who are clinicians, but also working with particular men, women and children whose lives are making history — whether quietly or dramatically.

10. I have discussed such "methodological" issues in Chapter II of this volume and in various sections of its two predecessors. A valuable book by a cultural anthropologist which documents the child's growing sense of the world — as mediated through his or her sense of racial identity — is Mary Ellen Goodman's *Race Awareness in Young Children* (New York: Collier, 1964). I mention that book in this note because it is important to stress that there are many ways to learn how children think and feel about both themselves and others. See, for example, Catherine Landreth and Barbara Johnson, "Young Children's Responses to a Picture and Inset Test Designed to Reveal Reactions to Persons of Different Skin Color," *Child Development*, XXIV (March, 1953); also my own "Racial Identity in School Children," *Saturday Review*, October 16, 1963.

11. I refer the reader to *Children of Crisis* (Boston: Atlantic–Little, Brown, 1967) and its successor, *Migrants, Sharecroppers, Mountaineers* (1972). I would also mention two articles I wrote for the *Atlantic Monthly:* "In the South These Children Prophesy," CCXI (March, 1963), and "When I Draw the Lord He'll Be a Real Big Man," CCXVII (May, 1966).

12. Yet, of course, children always are quite clear about the circumstances they must face and yield to or try to overcome. One perhaps ought to emphasize that in this regard poor black or white children are no more "intuitive" or "reality-oriented" than other children. See Part V, "Some Clinical Correlations between Parents and Children," in a recent book edited by E. James Anthony and Therese Benedek, *Parenthood: Its Psychology and Psychopathology* (Boston: Little, Brown, 1970). See also Margaret Mead's *Coming of Age in Samoa: A Psychological Study of Primitive Youth for Western Civilization* (New York: Modern Library, 1953). I mention those two books somewhat arbitrarily — to suggest that all over the world, among "primitive" people and in a highly industrial society, among those who are considered "normal" and those who feel themselves to be "troubled," one finds parents and children constantly speaking to one another, letting one another know what that so-called "outside world" urges, requires, encourages, offers, has in store. A fine book that draws upon recollections of "black childhood in white America" by blacks — ranging from slaves in the eighteenth and nineteenth centuries to Richard Wright and Malcolm X in our century — is *Growing Up Black,* Jay David, ed. (New York: Morrow, 1968).

13. A generation of child psychiatrists and child psychoanalysts have described the *problems* of growing children; more recently clinicians have given their attention to children who are not really in "trouble," who have no "symptoms" to speak of, who are essentially "normal." See Anna Freud, *Normality and Pathology in Childhood* (New York: International Universities Press, 1965). A gem of a paper written by Miss Freud is "The Emotional and Social Development of Young Children," *The Writings of Anna Freud, Vol. V: Research at the Hampstead Child-Therapy Clinic and Other Papers* (New York: International Universities Press, 1969). Erik H. Erikson's *Childhood and Society* (New York: Norton, 1950 and 1963) is, of course, utterly important. It is simply not

fair to talk about (write about) children such as the ones whose educational difficulties I am describing in this chapter without reminding oneself and one's readers that however special and painful the experiences a boy or girl of the ghetto comes to know, there are for all children stresses and strains that have to do with growing up, leaving home, going to school — and that no world yet brought into being by man has done away with those stresses and strains, though many "conflict-free" worlds (utopias of this or that kind) have been imagined, written about, suggested as desirable or necessary. All of this is emphatically *not* said to encourage apathy or resignation or "adjustment" to what is or despair over what might be. I simply mean to insist that children, *all* children, have fears and hates and envies and moments (indeed, longer stretches than that) of self-doubt. If it is worse for many of the children who speak in this chapter, at least we can refrain from trying to think about them in such a way that they are cut off, denied the right to share in the more *general* trials and events and challenges suggested by the word "childhood." In *The Image Is You* (Boston: Houghton Mifflin, 1969), I tried to show what black children in a ghetto find interesting and pleasing and joyful about the world — by presenting the pictures they took (the moods they evoke) with a Polaroid camera. And I fear the long essay I wrote to accompany those "documentary photographs" (as "we" are wont to call them) is really inadequate, if not unnecessary. The children's cameras register their moods quite well.

14. This chapter has not, strictly speaking, dwelled upon "school desegregation" in the North, or school integration — though obviously in several cities described that is just what has taken place. There is an abundant literature on the subject, embarrassingly abundant, in view of the limited progress our cities have made in providing black children (or white children from poor families) with halfway decent schools. For instance, Meyer Weinberg has compiled a bibliography of no less than ten thousand "selected entries" (*sic*) in *The Education of the Minority Child* (Chicago: Integrated Education Associates, 1970). For a description of my own work in Boston and elsewhere, I again mention "Northern Children under Desegregation," *Psychiatry*, XXXI (February, 1968). And one can cite reference after reference to describe *today's* educational problems — and forget that no generation in this country's history has lacked similar ones. See Doxey Wilkerson, "The Ghetto School Struggles in Historical Perspective," *Science and Society*, XXXIII (Spring, 1969).

CHAPTER XI

1. The religious sensibilities of migrant workers or mountaineers or sharecroppers do not by any means yield quickly or wholeheartedly to "the urban scene." Quite the contrary — as mentioned, one sees churches all over our northern ghettos, white and black. And in order to comprehend what makes up such a "frame of reference" one has to call upon more than theology or religious history or sociological or psychological analysis

— not that I can say precisely *what* more. Up the hills of Tennessee or Kentucky and into the Delta of Mississippi one feels something in the air, something Millet captures in paintings like *The Sower*, something young southern and mountain poets like George Scarbrough (*Cradly Gift*) and David Verble (*Some Earth Motions*) manage to get across. So, for this note to a chapter on "religion" in our northern cities, I begin with a reference to a fine article by R. B. Weber in *Chelsea*, XXVIII (August, 1970), "Poetry in Tennessee." And from there I move to John Horton's "Time and Cool People" in *Transaction*, IV (April, 1967). Though Mr. Horton is trying to describe the sense of "time," the sense of the future, that urban blacks have, he is also trying to demonstrate what matters to those particular American citizens, what moves them, strikes their fancy, prompts their allegiance, turns them off. In such an article sociological narrative measures up to its true possibilities — and becomes a kind of philosophical essay. Nor do I think it inappropriate to mention at this point J. Glenn Gray's *The Warriors* (New York: Harper and Row, 1959). The author wants to show the intense moral and spiritual struggle that soldiers face as they go off to fight for values and ideals they (sometimes) cherish — even as they go off also to hurt and kill other human beings. War is appealing, is stirring, is awful, is literally murder on a grand scale. And from the battlefield to the ghetto is no long farfetched leap. I constantly hear desperate, hard-praying ghetto mothers or fathers shouting in Pentecostal churches up North words like this: "We have to fight, and maybe we'll lose, but I hope we'll win. You have to do the best you can. You may hurt others, but you'll save your own children, and you'll be a better person for having struggled. Life it's a battle, it's a war. This street, everyone on its is fighting for his side, and you never know who's going to be the winner. And it hurts you, it hurts you, when you see another guy falling, and you know you're going to profit from it — but that's all you can do, I guess." Those who read *The Warriors* and Hannah Arendt's introduction to the book will see why that man's imagery reminds a listener of other moral and philosophical dilemmas.

2. There is a substantial literature on Appalachia's religion, and I have tried to give a sense of that literature in *Migrants, Sharecroppers, Mountaineers*. Earl Brewer's essay, "Religion and the Churches," in *The Southern Appalachian Region* (Lexington, Kentucky: University of Kentucky Press, 1962) should be mentioned in this volume, too — because emigration to Ohio or Illinois does not cause mountaineers to lose their religious ardor. Liston Pope's *Millhands and Preachers* (New Haven: Yale University Press, 1967) also belongs here, as in Volume II of *Children of Crisis*. Of great importance is *Life and Religion in Southern Appalachia* by W. D. Weatherford and Earl Brewer (New York: Friendship Press, 1962).

3. Fifty years ago, Carter G. Woodson described what happened to black people as churchgoers, as passionate and troubled believers, when they went North. See his *The History of the Negro Church* (Washington, D.C.: The Associated Publishers, 1921). See also W. E. B. DuBois, *The Negro Church* (Atlanta: Atlanta University Press, 1903), and E. Franklin

Frazier, *The Negro Church in America* (New York: Schocken, 1963).
Those books (also mentioned in *Migrants, Sharecroppers, Mountaineers*
because they describe the southern as well as northern church life of
blacks) ought to be supplemented by Arthur Fauset's extremely valuable
Black Gods of the Metropolis, Vol. III of Publications of the Philadelphia
Anthropological Society (Philadelphia, 1964).

But black men have been praying *outside* of churches for centuries —
praying with spirituals and work songs, praying through the jazz and
the blues they have wrought out of their suffering. See R. Nathaniel Dett,
Religious Folk-songs of the Negro (Hampton, Virginia: Hampton Institute Press, 1927); also John Lowell, "The Social Implications of the
Negro Spiritual," *Journal of Negro Education*, VIII (October, 1939);
Lydia Parrish, *Slave Songs of the Georgia Sea Islands* (New York: Crea-
tive Age Press, Inc., 1942); and Howard Thurman, *The Negro Spiritual
Speaks of Life and Death* (New York: Harper and Bros., 1947). Of
particular interest are articles such as "Ritual and Stratification in
Chicago Negro Churches," by Vattel Daniel, *American Sociological Re-
view*, VII (June, 1942); "Rock, Church, Rock" by Arna Bontemps,
Anthology of American Negro Literature, Sylvestre C. Watkins, ed. (New
York: Modern Library, 1944); and "The Romance of the Negro Folk
Cry in America" by Willis L. James, *Phylon*, XVI (First Quarter, 1955).

And finally, after all the efforts to analyze the black man's churches,
after all the accounts of what black people have done to make sense of
the world, done with songs and memoirs and superstitions and proverbs
and rhymes and riddles and tales and stories — after all the footnotes
are written (not to mention books) there are the blues and jazz. Ralph
Ellison has made it very clear that the issue is not only one of musical
style but cultural and even religious sophistication — in *Shadow and
Act* (New York: Random House, 1964). And James Baldwin in his
novel *Go Tell It on the Mountain* (New York, Dial, 1963) insists that
the storefront preacher is a wild singer of sorts, a driven musician who
plays as honestly and deviously as many a writer or artist does with the
lives he happens to address rather than portray or paint. So, in this note
to this chapter on "urban religion," I gladly mention David Ritz's article
in *Salmagundi* (Spring, 1970) called "Happy Song: Soul Music in the
Ghetto." And I urge strongly Charles Keil's beautifully done book, *Urban
Blues* (Chicago: University of Chicago Press, 1966). And as in my
previous volume in this series, I mention LeRoi Jones's *Blues People*
(New York: Morrow, 1963), and Paul Oliver's *The Story of the Blues*
(Philadelphia: Chilton, 1969). Finally, there is John Williams's haunting
Night Song (New York: Farrar, Straus, 1961) in which a novelist brings
alive a jazz musician — yes, a preacher of sorts, a minister of a people
whose religious faith is matched only by the threats which that faith
has more than sometimes overcome. Charlie Parker knew what those
"threats" were, knew what awful sadness black men and women have
struggled with, prayed over, screamed about to High Heaven. I cannot
turn words into notes of music, or make theological statements out of
Charlie Parker's version of "Dark Shadows" or "The Street Beat" or

"Lonely Boy Blues" or "New Confessin' the Blues" or "Seventh Avenue" or "What's the Matter Now?" or "Sorta Kinda." But I believe his spirit will continue to be heard on his records — even as the prophets of Israel, in all their mixed despair and hope, still sing to us. So, look at *Bird: The Legend of Charlie Parker* by Robert Reisner (New York: Citadel, 1962). But better, play Bird's music, and maybe for a few minutes escape from words — and from the need to use words as a means of pinning down man's stubbornly elusive "condition."

INDEX

673